SAFETY FIRST

Studies in Industry and Society

PHILIP B. SCRANTON, SERIES EDITOR

Published with the assistance of the Hagley Museum and Library

SAFETY FIRST

Technology, Labor, and Business

in the Building of American Work Safety

1870–1939

MARK ALDRICH

The Johns Hopkins University Press
Baltimore and London

This book has been brought to publication with the generous assistance of the Hagley Museum and Library.

The Johns Hopkins University Press
2715 North Charles Street
Baltimore, Maryland 21218-4319
The Johns Hopkins Press Ltd., London

The following illustrations were reprinted with permission from *National Safety News*, published by the National Safety Council, 1121 Spring Lake Drive, Itasca, IL 60143-3201: "Otto Nobetter" (vol. 5, March 1922); "Savin' Eyes" (vol. 7, May 1923); and "Isn't It About Time" (vol. 12, July 1925).

Early versions of chapters 5 and 6 were previously published in: "Combating the Collision Horror," *Technology and Culture* 34 (January 1993): 49–77, and "Preventing the Needless Peril of the Coal Mine," *Technology and Culture* 36 (July 1995): 483–518 [© by the Society for the History of Technology; all rights reserved]; "Safety First Comes to the Railroads, 1910–1939," *Railroad History* 166 (Spring 1992): 6–33; "Safe and Suitable Boilers: The Railroads, the Interstate Commerce Commission, and Locomotive Safety, 1900–1945," *Railroad History* 171 (Autumn 1994): 23–44.

Library of Congress Cataloging-in-Publication Data will be found at the end of this book.

A catalog record for this book is available from the British Library.

ISBN 0-8018-5405-9

To my family, especially Michele,
and to all those men and women who were killed
while building the American dream

CONTENTS

x

CONTENTS

FIGURES

TABLES

TABLES

PREFACE

In 1907, American coal mines killed about 3,242 men in occupational accidents—probably an all-time high (as was the fatality rate for 1907). The worst coal mine disaster in American history occurred in West Virginia in December of that year, when Monongah mines 6 and 8 blew up, killing 362 men. Railroad accidents killed another 4,534 employees in 1907. It was also a busy time for the steel industry. In 1907 William Hard described how U.S. Steel's South Chicago plant killed forty-six men in the course of a year's work.

None of these accidents happened so very long ago. My father was alive to witness them, and I am therefore but one generation removed from that era—so close in time, I sometimes feel that I can almost reach back and touch it. Yet the world of work safety has been so transformed in the two generations that span my father's lifetime and my own as to be nearly unrecognizable. Most American workers are no longer miners or railroad workers or manufacturing employees or farmers. We are a nation of white-collar employees: salespeople and nurses, engineers, accountants, teachers, and programmers. I am a teacher and an economist. While it would be wrong to suggest that we face no risks in going about our daily work, the dangers we experience are orders of magnitude less than most workers braved only a few generations ago.

Of course, dangerous work still goes on. Mines still blow up occasionally. Logging and lumbering and electric power line work remain risky businesses, and heavy construction continues to kill men in an amazing variety of ways. Hazardous chemicals have also added some new risks to the workplace, and carpal tunnel syndrome seems trivial only to someone who has not experienced it. But on balance, blue-collar jobs too are vastly safer than they used to be. The coal mine fatality rate now is one-tenth its 1907 level. That homicide is at present a leading cause of fatalities on the job is partly a reflection of the extent to which other dangers have receded.

My interest in these matters is partly personal, partly professional. As a child I learned of a great-aunt who worked in the Fall River, Massachusetts, woolen mills as a girl and went deaf at an early age. Years later I became friends with an old West Virginia woman named Minniebelle Smith. She had worked in the North Carolina mills in the 1920s, and she too had become almost completely deaf. Later I learned that weaving rooms in these early mills were so noisy that they seemed to throb. Then, about a decade ago, I did a stint as an economist at the Occupational Safety and Health Administration (OSHA), which was then trying to regulate, among other things, workers' noise exposure. It seemed clear that the workplaces OSHA was trying to improve were already vastly safer and quieter than the ones in which my great-aunt and Minniebelle Smith had labored, yet I discovered that although I was an economic historian, I knew almost nothing about the history of work safety.

This piqued my curiosity, and this book reflects my efforts at self-education. Of course, as I soon learned, historians have in fact dealt with many aspects of the history of work safety, and as the reader will discover, I have borrowed liberally from this literature. But no coherent story exists of work safety as it was in the nineteenth century and as it evolved. This book is an attempt to explain how and why the world of work became less dangerous in the years up to World War II.

It is a tale of economic change, and both these terms deserve emphasis. I have focused on the changing nature of job safety because risks and safety are best understood in a comparative context. This is an economic history because safety is, after all, a matter of working conditions and wages, profits, and costs. I have from time to time employed economic arguments and econometric procedures to illustrate and explain events. Although ideas such as cost-effectiveness, moral hazard, implicit contracts, and opportunity costs have shaped my analysis of the materials, I have avoided economic jargon as much as possible, for such terminology clutters the narrative. For similar reasons, most of the statistical analysis is confined to endnotes or appendices. I try to avoid "data mining" by presenting representative results and by discussing the limitations of the findings. I have also reinforced any statistical findings with other evidence so that very little in this book stands or falls entirely on the basis of a regression coefficient.

But the improvement of work safety involved changes in public policies, in business organization and technology, and in ideas that were only partly economic in origin and rarely susceptible to statistical analysis. The history of work safety is at the intersection of labor history, the history of business, and the history of technology. These branches of inquiry are often pursued separately and rarely made a part of economic history. Whatever the general merits of this division of labor, it will not do for a subject as inherently interdisciplinary as work safety, and so I have tried to tell this part of the story too, and to embed the economic analysis in the real world of politics, business, and labor, where women and men worked and lived.

I am conscious that much has been left out. Economists will not find much on risk premiums, because the data rarely allow their estimation with any precision and because they probably had little to do with changes in work safety. Nor have I usually calculated the cost of various safety programs—a subject of much current interest—for again the data are rarely adequate. While I have tried to see safety from the point of view of ordinary men and women as well as managers, and to talk of failure as well as success, evidence is scarce on employees' views of the safety movement. Hence, much that I say about workers is indirect: it is inferences drawn from behavior or based on what others said about workers. While such evidence needs to be used with care, it can help illuminate the impact of safety on workers' lives. I have largely ignored the development of occupational medicine. The reader will also find little here on agriculture or construction or the service sector, for the sources are thin. For the reverse reason I have chosen to focus on safety, not health. While this distinction is a bit arbitrary, inclusion of health problems would greatly expand an already long work.

Two notes on terminology. First, the safety movement was largely masculine, and in many of the industries where it was active most of the workers were male. That is reflected in my writing: where women were involved I have tried to use gender-free constructions, but miners and steelworkers and others in overwhelmingly masculine occupations are referred to as men. I have also retained terms such as *workmen's compensation* and *manhours*. Second, unless their writing was unclear, I have not corrected the grammar or spelling of individuals quoted, for it seems unnecessary and intrusive.

Many individuals have given time, advice, assistance, and sometimes cash to make this a better work. Robert J. Brugger, my editor at Johns Hopkins University Press, strengthened the manuscript immeasurably by persistently urging me to tighten the writing and emphasize themes. My thanks also go to an anonymous reviewer who provided similar assistance. Mary Yates's editing greatly improved the clarity and readability of the work, while Dr. Alan Leviton of the California Academy of Sciences provided expert computer and photographic assistance.

The Hagley Museum funded my stay there, which allowed me to use their valuable collections, and Smith College supported both travel and many hours of research assistance. Roger Grant, editor of *Railroad History*, and Robert Post, past editor of *Technology and Culture*, not only thought enough of parts of this work to publish them but provided expert criticism as well. Elizabeth Chaney Ferguson kindly lent me her biography of her grandfather, Lucian Chaney. Lisa Immens of the American Society of Safety Engineers responded quickly and helpfully to my request for information. The Library of Congress provided me with a stack pass for several years, without which use of the many nineteenth-century trade periodicals would have been much more difficult. Many staff members at the National Archives helped me through various research collections, but Jim Cassedy's assistance with Bureau of Mines materials was invaluable. The Hagley Museum staff at the Soda House—Michael Nash, Chris Baer, and Marjorie McNinch—were a model of helpfulness, as were Dr. Stuart McGehee and Ms. Eva McGuire of the Eastern Regional Coal Archives. Similarly, the librarians at the Interstate Commerce Commission library—especially Mr. Albert West—and the libraries of the Departments of Labor and Interior provided aid in the use of their collections. I am also grateful to librarians and archivists at Aetna, Carleton College, Catholic University, Harvard's Baker Library, the National Safety Council, the Newberry Library, the Historical Collections and Labor Archives at Penn State, the Pennsylvania State Archives, and Fort Lewis College. At Smith College, Sika Berger, Robin Kinder, Bruce Sajdak, and Pam Skinner, among others, were bloodhounds tracking down obscure research requests.

My wife, Michele Aldrich, who is both an archivist and a historian of science, provided invaluable criticism that sharpened my argument at many points, but probably neither she nor other readers caught all the mistakes, which by long tradition are on my head.

SAFETY FIRST

INTRODUCTION

Thursday, September 15, 1898, was a clear day in Vivian, West Virginia, as Bert Wright recorded in his diary, and by noon the temperature had reached a pleasant seventy-five degrees. Wright was an engineer and general manager of the New Peerless Coal and Coke Company, one of many new mines that were opening up the southern West Virginia coal fields in the 1890s. By the standards of the day, New Peerless was a large and modern mine. Located on the Norfolk and Western Railroad, the company employed about two hundred men. It operated one drift mine in the Pocahontas seam along with about 150 coke ovens. Steam from a seventy-horsepower boiler provided the power that worked the mine. It ran the compressors for the air locomotives that gathered the coal, and it powered the machinery of the tipple. Another forty-horsepower boiler ran a twelve- by five-foot fan that ventilated the mine. Production averaged about fifty thousand tons of coal a year, which was shipped down the Norfolk and Western to the docks at Lambert's Point.

Wright had been at the New Peerless a little over two years. He was a Canadian, born in Quebec in 1863, and like many other engineers of that day, he was mostly self-taught. His engineering education began on a surveying crew on the Canadian Pacific in 1883. From there he went on to other railroad work from Quebec to South Carolina, and in the early 1890s he took a position as engineer and superintendent of the Elk Ridge Coal and Coke, from whence he came to New Peerless.

Wright's diary for the morning of September 15 was taken up with the details of getting the coal out, and he reported them in terse, economical prose. Cars had to be gotten to the miners and coke shipped out; he noted that an inspector was complaining of too much slack (fine coal of little value). In the same matter-of-fact tones Wright went on to record a tragedy. At 2:00 P.M. a miner named T. H. Woods and one of his assistants named Ramsey had been badly burned. Woods was an experienced miner; Wright noted that he had contracted for six rooms and had even been recommended as a suitable mine foreman. The accident occurred when a keg of black powder that Woods was opening with a pickax exploded in his face. Wright listed witnesses to the accident; if the company could prove neglect of duty, Woods could not win a lawsuit. "Otherwise he can," Wright noted.

The next day was also clear, Wright reported, and even warmer. It began on a sour note. There were no empty cars on hand, he complained. Still, it proved to be a better day for getting coal out than he had expected. Ten hoppers were delivered at 8:30 A.M. and fifteen more at 4:30 in the afternoon. Wright briefly noted that Ramsey had died at 3:40 A.M. and Woods at 7:00. "Both are penniless," he wrote. "We furnish coffin and bury Ramsey who has no friends or relatives. Woods we sent to Virginia to avoid keeping widow and children. . . . Accident will cost us $20 if $12 can be collected from County for coffins." [1]

These few routine lines in Bert Wright's diary—probably all the epitaph that Woods and Ramsey got—tell us much about the nineteenth-century world of work and death. Wright was probably saddened by the men's deaths, but he felt no responsibility; after all, Woods had blown himself up with a pick. And while the death of 2 out of 200 workers represents a breathtaking fatality rate of 10 per thousand in a single day, Wright does not seem to have been surprised.

These events at New Peerless and Wright's reactions to them were in no way atypical. Injury and death on the job were routine; similar tragedies were being played out dozens of times each day at other mines, in foundries and steelworks, in laundries and lumber mills, on railroads and construction projects. Most managers, and probably most other Americans, if they thought about these matters at all would have deemed such deaths individual tragedies for which the company bore little if any responsibility.

Through modern eyes the deaths of Woods and Ramsey look very different. What was Bert Wright—a man with no formal training and little mining experience—doing managing such a complex and dangerous business? Why had no one checked Woods's references? What was he doing with a full keg of powder? And how could he have been allowed to open it with a pick when the blast could have ignited gas or dust and blown up the entire mine? Where were the foreman, the safety engineer, and the supervisor? To us, looking back from a century later, it seems clear that the mine management was responsible for these deaths.

This shift in perspective from work accidents as routine matters of individual carelessness to the modern view that accidents reflect management failure is a measure of how much the world of work has changed in the past century. We now surround workers with a host of laws to protect their safety, and we take for granted that companies are responsible for and will take due precautions to ensure the safety of their workers. Sometimes, of course, the legal protections fail and companies are lax. A recent front-page story in the Northampton (Massachusetts) *Daily Hampshire Gazette* read, "Machine Severs City Man's Arm." But the fact that this was headline news, and our shock when we read of such events, underlines how much work safety has improved, for the change in our perception of work accidents reflects an equally dramatic improvement in safety.[2]

Parts of this story are well known. Historians have described the dangers of late-nineteenth-century coal mining, and there are several books that discuss the political economy of mine safety regulation. Metal mine safety has also been reviewed in a number of books and articles. Less has been written on railroad safety, which is surprising, given the volumes that have been penned on American railroads. Still, there is a small literature on train accidents, and some writers have studied the introduction of automatic couplers and air brakes, while broader studies of railroad labor and technology often treat aspects of safety. Everyone has heard of the Safety First movement in manufacturing, although there is no history of the National Safety Council. There are a few studies of state safety commissions. There is also a considerable literature on the origins of state workmen's compensation laws, and there are endless modern econometric investigations of the wage premiums workers may receive in risky jobs.[3]

Although this literature provides glimpses into the history of work safety, it is unsatisfactory. It rarely addresses in any detail why work was, by modern standards, so dangerous, and even the best of it fails to focus on how and why work safety has changed. It is also fragmented, with each writer focusing on one sector of the economy, and often on a brief period of time. It does not add up to a coherent picture of work safety as it had evolved in Bert Wright's day and as it has been transformed during the past century.

In modern writing, work safety is often described as the outcome of engineering design and work practices. Yet in understanding historical change, it is necessary to take a broader perspective, for job safety has been shaped by the process of economic development in two interrelated ways. First, development has changed the kinds of jobs that workers do, and for a very long time it has been shifting employment out of the goods-producing sectors into trade and services, and from blue- to white-collar work. Second, within sectors, engineering designs and work practices evolved as a result of changes in technology, business organization, and labor markets, as shaped by custom and public policy. Both results deserve a bit of elaboration.

By the second half of the nineteenth century, the tide of economic development was transforming the nature of work. Rising incomes and technological changes were moving jobs from farming into mining and, more important, into manufacturing and trade. At first these changes had little effect on the overall safety of work, but by the twentieth century they had gradually reduced the share of employment in dangerous trades, thereby improving the safety of work. Yet at the same time, within important industries work safety was eroding. Large-scale business organizations were spreading throughout mining, manufacturing, railroads, and utilities. In manufacturing, the new technologies were highly automated, capital-intensive processes. In railroads, long trains and heavy equipment became the rule. Even mining, which was less transformed than manufacturing, saw an ever-rising use of explosives and power-operated machinery.

Competitive pressures combined with these new techniques to produce increasingly large firms. The first giants appeared in railroading, well before the Civil War, and in the late nineteenth century they spread to manufacturing, utilities, and trade. Such large companies created unprecedented problems of control. Beginning with the railroads, companies created increasingly complex organizational structures to fix responsibilities and define lines of authority. Functional specialization appeared with line and staff departments such as sales, finance, and production, all reporting to a central office, and some companies organized along divisional lines as well.

Because the new techniques were capital-intensive, large firms all faced the need to transform high fixed cost into low unit cost. This led to a wholesale drive to expand output, and it clashed head-on with the old craft traditions of workers' control. The craftsman, be he miner or blacksmith or woodworker, marched to his own drum. He set his own standards for quality, worked at his own pace, and looked out for his own safety. By the early years of the twentieth century the independent craftsman was in full retreat. Employers were increasingly trying to control production-level activities, and their efforts to implement the various forms of scientific and systematic management were all devoted to enhancing productivity and lowering costs. Although advocates of these schemes also claimed that they would promote workplace harmony, employers' interests in shop-floor activities usually stopped with productivity. Bert Wright's responsibility was to get the coal out, not to look after the safety of careless workers.[4]

The new machines and processes and their dangers were not the product of "disembodied historical forces." Instead, the new technology reflected the efforts of individuals and businesses to increase production and cut costs under conditions in which work injuries were of little economic consequence. For during these years judges crafted a common law of employers' liability that encouraged economic development by placing most of the burden of work injuries on the injured employee. Bert Wright thought the deaths of Woods and Ramsey would cost the company about $20, and such bargains no doubt blunted the interest of the New Peerless managers in work safety. This combination of modern methods and employer indifference to accidents was a recipe for risk.[5]

The net effect of these developments was to generate some jobs that by modern standards were astonishingly lethal. Today the most dangerous work is timbering and logging, which reports a fatality rate of 129 per hundred thousand workers but which employs only a tiny fraction of the labor force. A century ago, in 1890, railroad workers constituted about 4 percent of the labor force and ran risks that averaged 3.14 per *thousand*, or two and a half times the risk of the most dangerous of modern jobs. Subgroups of railroad workers such as trainmen experienced even higher death rates, perhaps 9 or 10 per thousand or more. The 290,000 men in coal mining constituted another 1.5 percent of the labor force who ran similar risks. In heavy construction and utilities, at cement kilns and Bessemer furnaces, at sawmills and powder mills and laundries, only a century ago large numbers of men and women in the dangerous trades routinely ran job risks that we can barely comprehend.[6]

As these figures suggest, there has been a breathtaking improvement in work safety from Bert Wright's day to our own. Employment has continued to shift into relatively safe jobs, and so a smaller proportion of the labor force works on the railroad or mines coal or makes steel than did so a century ago. Even the dangerous trades have become much less risky. This too has been the result of changes in business organization, technology, and labor markets, as shaped by custom and public policy.

For all but a privileged few workers, the nineteenth-century labor market resembled the model depicted in economists' introductory texts. Wages and employment were set by supply and demand. The shop floor was the "empire of the foreman." His primary job was to get out the goods, and working conditions, promotion, safety, and hiring and firing were all at his discretion. For workers this was a world of danger and uncertainty, while for employers it resulted in high labor turnover, poor morale, and occasional upheavals in the form of mass strikes. Both groups struggled to find an alternative. Increasingly, Progressive managers and in some cases labor unions tried to modify the old employment relationship, and the foreman's empire began to shrink.

Companies reshaped production processes to provide more regular employment; they created personnel departments to reduce the foreman's arbitrary power and to regularize hiring and firing and promotion. And in the twentieth century they began to see work safety as a matter to be addressed by systematic management.[7]

Employers' interest in work safety was sharply influenced by public prodding. Three styles of public policy generated the safety movement. The regulatory approach effectively began with steamboat inspection in the 1830s and was reflected in the various state bureaus created to regulate the safety of railroads, mines, and factories and, on the federal level, in the Interstate Commerce Commission. A second approach relied on voluntarism; it provided information or publicized bad practice, thereby encouraging companies to improve safety by reducing its costs or raising its benefits. Early efforts to improve railroad safety employed publicity as well as regulation. In the twentieth century, Progressive reformers not only wielded the regulatory stick with renewed enthusiasm, they also investigated and publicized work accidents, thereby threatening companies with even stricter rules. Progressivism also yielded the Bureau of Mines, which was intended to undertake scientific investigations that would discover safer mining practices and speed their introduction. The third approach was to raise the cost of accidents, and here reformers scrapped the old system of employers' liability in favor of workmen's compensation. This complex of external pressures on the large corporation initiated the modern safety movement. It was one of the most enduring and important, if neglected, results of Progressivism.

The safety movement soon developed its own institutions and ideology. A safety market evolved that helped develop and spread information on the new, less dangerous, production technologies. The impact of these developments was greatest at large, highly visible companies that were implementing the managerial revolution. The new compensation laws affected them most directly, and many came to value the good public relations and other political benefits that resulted from better safety. Such companies also developed safety departments. Nestled within the administrative structure, these were staff organizations, often run by engineers, who saw better safety as both a professional duty and the justification for their corporate position. They therefore represented a continuing institutional force for accident reduction within the large firm. The result was that at some businesses, work safety became a management responsibility. In contrast, smaller, less visible companies and sectors of the economy such as coal mining, where modern management techniques were slow to take root, exhibited far less safety-consciousness than did the corporate giants.

Safety work was therefore part of a much broader process in which corporate leaders were establishing management controls over the large firm. But if safety came to be dominated by managers and professionals, initially workers and foremen played an important role, for early safety work was reactive—a response to existing hazards—and who knew danger better than the men and women who experienced it? By the 1930s employee involvement in work safety was becoming less important, however, for safety was becoming increasingly proactive—a matter of factory layout, machine design, hazard assessment, and job evaluation, all of which were the duties of engineers and other managers.[8]

Thus, to workers the improvement in job safety had two faces. Men and women were far less likely than in years past to be injured on the job, but they also had far less freedom to determine their own work practices. It was not that safety was a necessary part of managerial control over work—had that been true, the safety movement would not have been so clearly a result of the policy changes discussed above—but rather the reverse. Only with managerial control over the workplace could safety be improved. By long tradition, Woods and Ramsey had been left free from any supervision save the requirement that they get out the coal, and they paid with their lives. So part of the price of better safety was paid in the loss of workers' control.[9]

On the eve of World War II a significant number of large companies had transformed job safety from the conditions that had existed only two generations earlier. Injury or death on the job with the resulting loss of earnings had been one of the great terrors of nineteenth-century work. In large factories, on most railroads and at most utilities and metal mines, at some coal mines and construction sites, danger no longer stared a worker in the face in quite the same way. Serious work accidents had become rare enough to be shocking, and neither managers nor workers accepted death on the job with the matter-of-fact resignation that had characterized Bert Wright's day.

Such dramatic events beg for explanations. Why had late-nineteenth-century mines and railroads and manufacturing establishments become so dangerous? Were American firms more or less dangerous than their European counterparts? How important has the shift in employment into relatively safe jobs been in improving work safety? What public policies proved most effective in encouraging improvements in work safety during the twentieth century? What brought about changes in management attitudes from Bert Wright's day to our own? What companies and industries were most successful, and what strategies proved most effective? How did workers respond to these new rules and conditions? Together these matters are the subject of this book.

Remains of a Cleveland and Toledo locomotive after its boiler blew in 1862. Faulty gauges, poor workmanship, and bad judgment all played parts in these disasters. *(Scientific American)*

CHAPTER ONE

PERILOUS BUSINESS

The Beginnings of Railroad Work Safety
1850–1900

Even in the forms of sudden death on the rail, nature seems to take
a grim delight in an infinitude of surprises.
CHARLES FRANCIS ADAMS, MASSACHUSETTS RAILROAD COMMISSION, 1879

A sense of self-interest on the part of the railroad companies is undoubtedly the most
effectual safeguard toward securing the ends of safety and convenience.
JOSEPH NIMMO, U.S. DIVISION OF INTERNAL COMMERCE, 1876

The slaughter of railroad employees began almost as soon as the first lines were built. In the 1850s the New York State Railroad Commission routinely published casualty lists, and gradually the picture of railroad risks began to emerge. By the 1880s American railroads had become far more dangerous than those in Europe, and a diverse band of railroad men, state commissioners, and reformers began a campaign for safety couplers and air brakes that culminated in the federal Safety Appliance Act of 1893. Writing in 1899, before the act was fully operational, the editor of *Engineering News* had already concluded that the accident record for that year "fully vindicates the wisdom of the . . . law of 1893." [1]

Between 1890 and 1909, fatalities to trainmen from coupling cars and those due to falls from cars and striking overhead obstructions fell sharply (figs. 1.1 and 1.2). To reformers these results suggested the need to extend federal regulation, for deaths from other causes hardly declined at all (table A1.1). Yet these same data supported another lesson as well. Even if federal legislation was successful, and that is less clear than reformers imagined, its impact was extremely limited. Perhaps instead of pressing for more safety regulation, the critics needed to discover a way to harness the interest of railroad managers to the cause of safety. This split has characterized the safety movement throughout its history.

FIGURE 1.1. Coupling Fatalities and Injuries per Thousand Trainmen,
Three-Year Moving Averages, 1890–1909

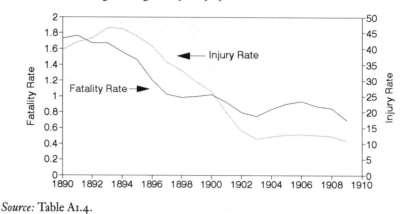

Source: Table A1.4.

FIGURE 1.2. Braking Fatalities and Injuries per Thousand Trainmen,
Three-Year Moving Averages, 1890–1909

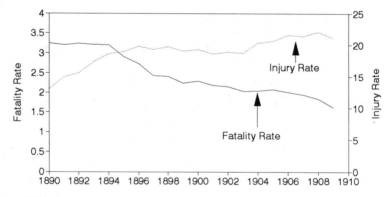

Source: Table A1.4.

The Risks of Railroading

As that acute observer of American railroads, Charles Francis Adams,
noted, death came to nineteenth-century railroad men in a remarkable
variety of ways. The first recorded steam railroad fatality in the United
States occurred on the South Carolina Railroad, on June 17, 1831. Ap-
propriately enough, the victim was an employee, a black fireman on the
locomotive *Best Friend of Charleston*. He was no doubt a slave, and his
name has been forgotten. According to a company report published in
the *American Railroad Journal*, the hissing valve so irritated the man that,
not having been trained to the contrary, he "ventured on the expedient
of confining it by pressing the weight of his body on the level-gage."

The resulting explosion "blew poor Sambo sky high." The engineer and two other men were also injured.[2]

The explosion of the *Best Friend* illustrated that the new steam railroad technology was by no means benign, and that safety, like every other aspect of railroading, had to be learned by a painful process of trial and error. The lesson was soon reinforced: in 1834 a boiler on the Baltimore and Ohio (B&O) exploded, and eight years later a blast on the Harlem Railroad killed the engineer and the fireman. But bursting boilers, however spectacular, were a minor hazard compared with the risks from train wrecks.

Although early trains moved very slowly—usually no faster than ten to fifteen miles per hour—both the rolling stock and the permanent way were extraordinarily flimsy. A New York commission of 1853 reported a host of sloppy construction practices and complained that "many serious accidents arise from the practice . . . of opening roads for public travel before the work upon them is completed." Six years later, Connecticut's railroad commissioners evaluated the New Haven, New London, and Stonington, finding "many of the rails too much crushed and worn to be longer depended on." The line also needed "a large number of new ties." On the New Haven and New York it found that "many of the rails are nearly off the chairs," and that "the track at some points needs adjusting." Such conditions, along with many other equipment and roadbed defects, made derailment a common event.[3]

Early bridges were usually wooden trusses—iron began to be used about the time of the Civil War—and their builders commonly possessed little understanding of either materials strength or the need for strain calculations. The coroner's jury investigating the Ashtabula (Ohio) bridge that collapsed on the Lake Shore in 1876, killing about eighty people, concluded that the bridge went down under a normal load as a result of "defects and errors made in designing[,] constructing and erecting it." Ashtabula spurred major improvements in bridge design and operation. The Erie developed standard, performance-oriented bridge specifications, and all the major roads improved their inspection procedures. But train weight was increasing too, and after three bridge failures during 1883–84, New York's railroad commissioners began a thorough investigation of all railroad bridges in the state. It found many for which no competent strain analysis had ever been done. About 25 percent needed to be upgraded, and 5 percent needed to be completely rebuilt.[4]

Early trains also ran a considerable risk of head-on collisions because none of them had decent brakes, they hired too few brakemen, and all were single-track lines with trains controlled by timetables and train

Bridge disasters were common on nineteenth-century American railroads. This pileup occurred on the Cumberland and Pennsylvania Railroad, probably in the 1860s. *(Courtesy Baltimore and Ohio Railroad Museum)*

In the early and mid-nineteenth century, single-track lines, primitive signaling devices, and human error could lead to gruesome head-on collisions. This one occurred at Camp Hill, Pennsylvania, in 1856, killing sixty-six passengers and trainmen. The regular passenger train failed to stop at a siding so that excursion cars could safely pass. *(Library of Congress)*

orders. In theory, meeting places were arranged at which the inferior train moved to a siding to let the superior train pass. In practice, this did not always happen. Train orders could be misread, and sometimes crews simply ran trains without regard to the rules, following only "smoke orders"—running until you saw the smoke of an oncoming engine and then looking for a siding.[5]

The primitive system of train scheduling and signaling was also a recipe for trouble, and as traffic grew and increasing train weight made stopping more difficult, collisions became common. One old-time employee of the Nashville and Chattanooga recalled that in the 1850s that line experienced about two such wrecks a day. One of the most famous collisions was the one that occurred at Camp Hill Station, Pennsylvania, on July 17, 1856, when a train failed to take a siding as required. Adams described the events as a "holocaust," in which "five cars in all were burned and sixty six persons perished." Traffic growth led to more closely spaced trains too, and stationmasters were not always up to the challenge. Adams remarked that occasionally when a train passed through a station it was met by the stationmaster who held up several fingers to indicate the number of minutes since the previous train had passed. As a result of such practices, rear-end collisions also became increasingly common.[6]

Adding to these dangers were the differing conditions and operating practices that characterized each road. In 1880 the U.S. commissioner of railroads noted that there was no signal that carried the same meaning on all the railroads in the country. Thus, four short blasts of the whistle meant "recall the flagman" on the B&O, "note the flag on the engine" on the Allegheny Valley, "call for a switchman" on the Central of New Jersey, and "call for fuel" on the Cumberland Valley. Such rampant creativity in signaling, combined with many other differences in rules and physical conditions—such as clearances—meant that safety experience was firm-specific. Yet nineteenth-century railroad workers were notoriously mobile because of the boom-and-bust character of the work, the expansion of railroading into the West, and the seasonality of maintenance. A Bureau of Labor survey of sixty major carriers in 1889 compared the actual number of men employed during the year with the theoretical number necessary for a 313-day work year. For all workers combined, 212 workers were employed for each 100 jobs. Some men seemed to move aimlessly from job to job and were called "boomers." Charles Brown was one; he worked as a brakeman, switchman, and fireman for thirteen years on thirteen different roads.[7]

The combination of firm-specific safety conditions and high labor turnover often led to disaster. As Kentucky's railroad commissioners observed, "There are so many variations in the [signal] systems in use that they are constantly leading to accidents. An employee leaving one road and going to another finds it hard to forget what he had been practicing for years." And Charles Brown remarked on the very different dangers he found in the New York Central Manhattan yards compared with those on the Union Pacific, in Green River, Wyoming. "They had more ways of killing a man . . . than any other yards I ever switched cars in," he claimed.[8]

Public interest in train wrecks was usually in proportion to the number of passengers slaughtered. Newspaper headlines routinely referred to "horrors" and "dreadful accidents." Descriptions, often complete with pictures, reported the results in delicious detail. The New York *Herald Tribune* of the 1870s is typical: "Upon the ice near the wreck a body was found with the entrails torn out and the head and legs crushed. . . . The dead, with four exceptions, were burned so as to be unrecognizable from the features and there are but three that could possibly be identified from the shreds of clothing adhering to the roasted flesh."[9]

Train accidents killed far more employees than they ever did passengers, but most were "minor," resulting in the death of only a workman or two. Thus, on May 31, 1859, when the Canal Railroad's 10:45 A.M. accommodation train out of Northampton, Massachusetts, ran into two cows and threw brakeman Charles Simmons from the train, killing him, it was hardly news at all. Even such a railroad man as Charles Francis Adams never bothered to report that the engineer of the excursion train was also killed in the Camp Hill wreck.[10]

In addition to the prospect of being killed in a train wreck, many other dangers threatened the life of a railroad man. In July 1872 the Norwich and Worcester reported that H. G. Grover "was riding a freight car and in attempting to leave it for the purpose of turning the switch, slipped and the whole of the car passed over him, [killing him instantly]." Unprotected frogs (track crossings) were like traps set to catch yardmen. In October 1873 Edward Herenden "caught his foot in a frog and was unable to extricate it in season to save himself," the Norwich and Worcester informed the Connecticut Railroad Commission.[11]

But far and away the worst risks to trainmen derived from the need to couple cars and ride their tops to operate hand brakes. Together these caused almost half of all fatalities to trainmen, and state reports reveal that they had been the leading causes of death since at least the early 1850s. One old-timer remembered that before the Civil War at least two men had been killed and two more injured by hitting one bridge while riding freights on the Nashville and Chattanooga. In New York during 1851–52, 28 percent of all fatalities resulted from falls from trains.

The experience of the Erie Railroad supplies details: "October 7, 1851. George Dresher, brakeman, when near Delaware, fell from the top of a car and was run over; both of his legs being mangled and then amputated, and his death afterward occurring." [12]

In 1890 there were nearly 750,000 railroad workers, and they constituted about 4 percent of the entire labor force. By modern standards they ran a truly extraordinary level of risk, experiencing a fatality rate that averaged 3.14 per thousand workers from 1889 to 1892, which was roughly equal to the risks of bituminous coal mining (tables A1.1 and A2.1). But the death rate for trainmen was about 9 per thousand, which made even the early years of anthracite mining, when fatalities averaged 5 per thousand, seem positively safe by comparison. Moreover, not all trainmen experienced the same dangers. The death rate for brakemen on mixed freights for 1908–10 (table 1.1) was 11.41 per thousand, and this was after the Safety Appliance Act. Fatality rates for all trainmen had been 63 percent higher in 1889–91 than in 1908–10; if this proportion held for freight brakemen, their fatality rate would have been 17.4 (1.63 × 11.41) per thousand during the first period. Moreover, men who were injured and then died within twenty-four hours were not reported as fatalities under Interstate Commerce Commission (ICC) rules, and they amounted to at least 10 percent of reported fatalities. Thus, the true death rate for these brakemen may have been about 19.3 per thousand. These dangers were annual risks, and over the years the odds cumulated. For example, if the annual risk to trainmen was 9 per thousand, during a twenty-year period about 17 out of a hundred would die on the job, and in thirty years the chance increased to 24 out of a hundred. [13]

Moreover, risks probably increased in the late nineteenth century in part because of the growth in traffic density, and in train size and speed. Freight car interchange also became increasingly common, thereby increasing the diversity (and risk) of the conditions that men experienced. E. M. Reed, superintendent on the Hartford and New Haven, explained how unfamiliar equipment caused the death of brakeman Robert Barnes, who struck a bridge on July 26, 1872: "The bridge is about 18 feet in height over the rails and there is ample room for the tallest man standing on any ordinary freight car, but Mr. Barnes . . . was standing on a very high hay car" owned by another line, the Boston and Albany. [14]

As railroading spread to the South and West, the new lines were staffed by men from older, eastern roads, and this geographic expansion may have compounded the risks of such job hopping. Charles B. George began railroading in 1847 on an ancestor of the Boston and Maine and worked his way west on five different carriers, finally winding up on the Chicago and Milwaukee in 1855. George thought his experience was

TABLE 1.1. Fatality and Permanent Injury Rates per Thousand Railroad Workers by Occupation and Activity, 1908–1910

	Engineer		Fireman		Conductor		Brakeman	
	Fatality	Injury	Fatality	Injury	Fatality	Injury	Fatality	Injury
Passenger	5.55	1.28	4.10	1.35	1.54	0.53	2.73	1.37
Freight	4.15	1.29	4.72	2.24	4.65	1.68	10.70	6.11
Yard	1.66	1.43	1.90	1.22	4.37	2.32	8.60	4.72
Mixed	4.15	0.69	4.42	1.77	7.62	3.05	11.41	3.92

Source: Senate Commission on Employers' Liability and Workmen's Compensation, *Report*, vol. 1, 62d Cong., 2d sess., 1912, S.D. 338.

typical: "It would be impossible to name even a fraction of those who left the [eastern] roads . . . to take positions on lines tributary to Chicago," he claimed. Between 1873 and 1909, Henry Clay French worked as a messenger boy, telegrapher, conductor, brakeman, and switchman for twenty-one different railroads before he finally settled down for a two-decade stay with the Union Pacific. The spread of railroads increased the variability of physical conditions and rules, which must have reduced the value of the easterners' safety experience.[15]

The first national figures on the risks of railroading are from the Census of 1880, while ICC reports begin only in 1889. Comparison of the fatality rate for 1880 with those of the early 1890s suggests that railroading was becoming more dangerous, but this is rather scanty evidence, given the volatility of fatality rates and the likelihood of underreporting. A number of state railroad commissions provide enough data to compute railroad worker fatality rates from the late 1860s on, however. A regression analysis (see note) for the period 1868 through 1893 with dummy variables to control for states yields a weakly positive trend. By contrast, the trend in passenger fatalities per billion passenger-miles is strongly negative.[16]

Both these results may well reflect the nature of the sample. States with commissions that collected injury data were more likely to try to reduce injuries than were other states, and their interest in safety grew over time. Thus, national data on passenger safety (not shown) show no trend from 1880 to 1889, while safety clearly improved in the states that gathered statistics. The weak upward trend in worker fatality rates in the states that were most concerned with safety therefore reinforces the national data, which suggest worsening safety for railroad workers in the late nineteenth century.

Comparative Risks of British and American Railroading

In the early 1870s the *Railroad Gazette* began to publish statistics of American railroad casualties along with reports of railroad accidents in Great Britain derived from that country's Board of Trade, and the differences were striking. In 1889 the fatality rate for railroad employees in the United States stood at 2.8 per thousand, which was nearly 50 percent higher than the British figure for the same year. Worse, as critics unfailingly reminded the railroads, the British accomplished that safety record in spite of having a traffic density nearly four times higher than that in the United States.[17]

Every year the statistics told the same story, finally moving the *Gazette* to exclaim, "It is discouraging to have those Britishers continue their march toward perfection year after year." As the *Gazette* was quick to point out, however, the dangers of the American roads were not simply the result of managers' callous indifference to safety. They were the by-product of an "American system" of railroading that was fundamentally different from British practice.[18]

American and British carriers differed in both product and practice. In 1890, British railroads logged more passenger- than freight-train-miles, while in the United States, conditions were reversed. From the beginning, great distances and low population density ensured that in America freight traffic predominated. By 1890, freight train mileage exceeded passenger mileage by about 50 percent.

American and British construction had also begun to diverge well before the Civil War. *The Permanent Way and Coal-Burning Boilers of European Railways*, by Zerah Colburn and Alexander Holley, vividly contrasted British and American railroad engineering of the 1850s. Colburn and Holley observed that British railroads were capitalized at about $196,000 per mile, which was about four times the American figure. Some of this difference, they admitted, resulted from higher land costs and legal fees in Britain. But not all of it. The authors excoriated the American railroads for their practice of constructing the permanent way in such flimsy fashion as to belie its name. They found that grades were milder and alignment "quite superior" in Great Britain. In addition, British lines, with less than nine thousand miles of road, contained seventy miles of tunnels, while bridges in the United Kingdom were mostly of masonry. By comparison, American roads went literally to great lengths to avoid tunnels—in 1855 there were but 11.5 miles of tunnel in 26,000 miles of track—and built their bridges out of wood.[19]

Colburn and Holley thought that most of these departures from

European practice made little economic sense, and they denounced American construction techniques. Earthwork was narrow, steeply sloped, and poorly drained. American rails were laid directly on crossties and were so thin that they deflected from train weight, thereby wearing out the ties and placing every train on a permanent uphill grade. Colburn and Holley claimed that a more expensively constructed roadbed such as was found in Britain would yield a handsome return in reduced operating expenses. Their contention was probably mostly wrong, for it was widely ignored.

Gradually both British and American engineers began to realize that each country's railroads were a reflection of its economic and political landscape. An analysis of English and American railroading by Edward Bates Dorsey, read to the American Society of Civil Engineers in 1885, created a considerable stir. Parts of it were reprinted on both sides of the Atlantic, and while some of its conclusions were sharply criticized, the description of construction techniques was not. Dorsey summarized the comparative capital-intensity of British construction methods, saying that construction "is generally much superior, stronger, more substantial and a great deal more costly on the English roads than on ours. . . . Our system of rushing the road through and completing it at leisure times, is not practiced there." He thought that this result stemmed partly from the political constraints under which British engineers operated, with each road having to be approved by Parliament and the Board of Trade, and he contrasted this situation with that of American engineers, who had been "free to invent and adopt the best system."[20]

Other engineers emphasized economic circumstances. American construction techniques, it was noted, economized on scarce engineering talent. The British engineer Robert Gordon stressed the importance of traffic density in explaining the differences between British and American construction practice. Gordon argued that the sparseness of traffic on American roads necessitated their "economical construction," and he cited Arthur Mellen Wellington for support. Wellington was a respected civil engineer and editor of the influential *Engineering News*. His monumental *Economic Theory of the Location of Railways*, first published in 1877, was the Bible of railroad construction economics. In it Wellington developed the formulas showing conditions under which investments to reduce distance, curvature, and grades were economical, and he stressed in all cases that the key was the likely level of traffic on the road.[21]

Gordon also drew liberally on Dorsey's work, and on conversations with other American engineers. He quoted D. J. Whittemore of the Chicago, Burlington, and Quincy, who said that his line had been built cheaply and was improved only "as the demands of remunerative business warrant." Whittemore made the point another way, observing that under present traffic conditions, if the Pennsylvania could save a mile of distance at a cost of £100,000, "it would be [good] policy now to do so; yet if in its inception this had been attempted, bankruptcy would have followed." As Gordon described the American approach, "Economy of construction of American railroads consisted in the small outlay in first cost of grading alignment and heavy works, and in the gradual adaptation of the roads to the traffic requirements." Gordon went on to explain that such engineering practices were a rational response to American conditions: "The general problem an American engineer sets before himself is — not which is the best possible constructed line . . . — but of all possible lines . . . which . . . will give a minimum of interest of first cost and a minimum of cost of operation of the traffic likely to be developed."[22]

Thus, the reason English engineers built bridges out of masonry while their American counterparts employed wooden Howe trusses was the comparative cost of skilled labor and wood in each country. Similarly, American trunk lines made relatively "free use of steep grades and sharp curves," and embankments in England were flatter. Double-tracking was common in England and nearly unheard-of in America. (Even as late as 1890, only about 6 percent of American roads were double-tracked, whereas in Britain the figure was about 63 percent.) "Level crossings were everywhere . . . [and] fencing was often dispensed with." Gordon noted one important way in which Colburn and Holley's advice had been followed: "Economy was to be sought for elsewhere than in either rolling stock or . . . rails and sleepers." By the 1880s American roads had abandoned the thin rails that had so irked Colburn and Holley. With wood comparatively cheap, they still used lighter rail than did British lines but employed more crossties per mile. American carriers also continued to lay rail directly on the ties, which rapidly wore them out but economized on expensive rail chairs.[23]

In fact, by the 1880s not only rails and ties but also rolling stock and traffic practices had been adapted to American conditions. Sharp curves and poor grading on American roads made the rigid eight- to nine-foot wheelbase of British cars unworkable, while high speeds over American lines were out of the question. Americans responded to their poorly built permanent way by developing the bogie truck, which, because it was flexible, would "work well on rough roads with sharp curves that . . . [British cars] could not run on." Gordon went so far as to claim that the "essential differences between American and English practice originate in the universal use by the former of the bogie truck." The bogie allowed the development of larger equipment, and Gordon, who was used to the eight- to ten-ton British freight cars, remarked with awe on the twenty- to thirty-ton monsters he had seen in the United States. American locomotives were also early users of equalizing bars to distribute weight evenly over the drivers—an obvious advantage where the roadbed was "elastic."[24]

In addition to employing larger cars, American roads avoided the need for double-tracking by running freights that were longer and heavier than their British counterparts and were pulled by a single locomotive. That locomotive was likely to be made of thinner iron and to carry higher steam pressure than a British engine, and to be "overfired" —effectively trading away coal and safety, which were cheap, to save capital and labor, which were not. In Britain, trains were shorter and ran more frequently and at higher speeds. As *Engineering News* noted, "The comparative shortness of hauls makes this [small cars and short trains] far less objectionable economically than it would be in this country."[25]

The British practice of running frequent trains at high speed led to the early adoption of the block-signal system of train spacing and the interlocking of switches and signals. Interlocking prevented a signal from showing a switch to be closed when it was in fact open, while the block-signal system controlled train spacing by dividing the track up into a series of blocks, each of which was controlled by a signal. No train could enter a block as long as the signal showed that it was occupied. Under the manual block system that was used in Britain, the signals were controlled by station men, and information on train location was relayed up and down the line by telegraph operators. According to the *Railroad Gazette*, almost 80 percent of British road had been block-signaled before the Board of Trade required it on all lines in the 1880s. By contrast, the low speeds and thin traffic that characterized American railroading—along with the high wages of skilled telegraphers, to be noted below—also slowed the adoption of the block system and interlocking in the United States. The earliest American data (1906) reveal that only 22 percent of all road was block-signaled.[26]

By the 1880s a consensus had emerged among engineers on both sides of the Atlantic that most differences between British and American railroading, far from being irrational as Colburn and Holley had suspected, in fact resulted from disparate capital and labor costs and traffic density, and from the regulatory climate. These differences held profound consequences for safety. This can be illustrated with the aid of figure 1.3, in which a given amount of transportation output (curve Q_0) can be produced with various levels of accidents and workers, with other inputs unchanged. Given these possibilities and the cost of accidents

FIGURE 1.3. Technological Change and the Accident Rate

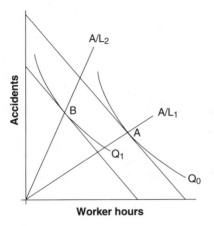

and labor, firms choose a cost-minimizing accident rate, at point A on A/L_1. The point to note is that improvements in technology can shift the curve inward and change its shape. As has been stressed, American technology evolved in ways that economized on capital and labor. But these methods often raised risks. That is, they shifted production possibilities to Q_1, leading employers to choose the cost-minimizing point B on A/L_2. Since the ratio of accidents to workers is higher on A/L_2 than on A/L_1, the accident rate rises.

Charles Francis Adams spoke for most knowledgeable observers when he claimed that the relative dearth of bridge accidents and derailments in Britain reflected the generally more substantial construction of permanent way in that country. Head-on collisions were virtually unknown on British railroads because single-track lines were similarly rare, while the widespread use of block signals resulted in many fewer rear-end collisions than in the United States. Widespread fencing, the absence of road-rail crossings at grade, and the almost complete interlocking of rail crossings with switches were all capital investments that further reduced British casualty rates. Together these differences probably account for much of the disparity between passenger accident rates in Britain and the United States.[27]

But even if no American railroad employee had been killed in derailments or collisions, worker risks in America would still have exceeded those in Britain by a wide margin. American carriers were far more freight-intensive than British lines, and freights were more dangerous than passenger work. Moreover, American freight equipment was much more deadly to work with than its British counterpart. The small size of British trains and cars required much less braking power than the longer

A brakeman making a link-and-pin coupling, probably in the 1870s. The need to stand between cars that were coming together and guide link into slot made a brakeman's work extraordinarily dangerous. *(Courtesy Association of American Railroads)*

and heavier American trains required. Hence, trains in Victorian Britain were controlled by brakes on the locomotive and a "braking" car. Although freight cars had brakes, these could be operated only from the ground and were used exclusively for moving cars around yards. During this period American freights, of course, required individual brakes operated from the top of cars in order to stop the train. In Britain, where there was no such need to ride the top of freights, the life of a brakeman was much less hazardous.[28]

The smaller cars and trains in Britain also put much less strain on couplers than American rolling stock did. Hence, well into the twentieth century, British cars were coupled with three-link chains draped to a hook. These couplers could be connected while the train was stationary, and the connection could usually be made by a man using a pole and standing outside the buffer blocks. The slack that three-link couplers generated was manageable with small British cars and short trains, and British freight cars also carried spring-loaded buffers to absorb the shock of starting and stopping. Because British cars had been standardized by the 1850s, these buffers were in the same place on each car. In the United States, three-link couplers had been abandoned well before the Civil War in favor of the stronger link and pin, which required a man to go between moving cars to couple it. American buffer blocks, instead of being standardized and spring-loaded as in Britain, were simply wooden beams placed wherever a company fancied them. Brakemen called them man-killers, and they must have worsened the risks from freight car interchange. In Britain, by contrast, if a shunter (as the British termed yardmen) did have to go between the cars, the buffers were more likely to protect him than kill him.[29]

These differences in brake and coupling technology translated directly into enormous differences in worker safety. As can be seen from table 1.2, in 1889–90, before large-scale use of automatic couplers, the mortality rate of American trainmen from coupling was about 84 percent higher (1.73/0.94) than that of British "guards, brakemen and shunters." Even more striking, mortality from the three sources most closely related to the peculiarities of American coupling and braking technology exceeded the mortality of British railroad workers from all causes by about 17 percent in 1889–90.

Differences in the labor market also led British roads to employ more skilled-labor-intensive methods of production. In 1894 the *Railroad Gazette* pointed out that British lines routinely employed nineteen men to the mile, compared with five in the United States. (British companies employed not only more men per mile of road, which might be expected

TABLE 1.2. The Comparative Safety of British and American Railroad Workers, 1889 and 1895

	1889	1895
British trainmen[a]		
All causes	4.26	3.22
Coupling	0.94	0.83
American trainmen		
All causes	8.52	6.45
Coupling	1.73[c]	1.20
Braking[b]	3.25[c]	2.44

Source: British data are from H. Raynar Wilson, *The Safety of British Railways* (London: P. S. King, 1909), chap. 18. U.S. data are from the present volume's table A1.4.

Note: Death rates are per thousand employees.

[a] Guards, brakemen, and shunters.

[b] Deaths from falls from cars and striking overhead obstructions.

[c] Data are for 1890.

given their higher traffic density, but also more men per passenger-mile or ton-mile of freight transported.) As the *Gazette* noted, these additional workers were telegraphers, station men, and others in low-risk occupations. The addition of so many workers in such comparatively safe jobs naturally gave British roads injury rates that were lower than those in America.[30]

But skilled workers reduced accident rates in a more positive fashion than by just avoiding death. Charles Francis Adams noted that the manual block system required trained telegraph operators, and he thought that its adoption in Britain reflected the comparative cheapness of skilled labor as well as the heavier traffic prevalent there. When manual block signals were used in the United States, American lines provided their operators less training than was customary abroad. Writing in 1890, one railroad official explained that "as soon as a boy gets so he can send a message he is given a position [as telegraph operator] at some small station." Seventeen years later the Block Signal and Train Control Board also pointed out how much better trained and supervised British signalmen were than their American counterparts, some of whom were farm boys with but three months of experience or students on summer vacation.[31]

Contemporaries believed that the comparatively tight labor market and high turnover in the United States also reduced the safety of American railroads. "To a foreigner, and a Britisher in particular, there seems to be a lower value placed on human life in America," wrote British engineer H. Raynar Wilson in 1906. On railroads this resulted from the lack of discipline: "Americans have naturally no respect for their superiors," Wilson claimed, and he blamed this cultural deficiency on "the state of the labor market [which] gives British companies a large field from which to draw." As a result, British employers could be choosy in whom they hired and promoted. Workers who refused to follow orders or were careless could be removed and would not be hired by other lines. And since the British employees were less likely to quit, new men were more thoroughly trained. Wilson contrasted this situation with the lack of discipline on American roads, which resulted from the scarcity of labor, concluding that "there are more mishaps due to failures to obey orders or neglect to carry out instructions than to any other cause."[32]

British railroads were therefore much safer than American lines in large measure because of the economics of their construction and operation. The substantial roadbeds of double-tracked and block-signaled line traversed by light equipment and run by a well-disciplined, stable labor force translated into injury rates that lines constructed and operated under the American system of railroading simply could not match.

But, as Dorsey stressed, public policy, as manifested in the Board of Trade, also shaped British practices. Wilson observed to *Engineering News* that the control exercised by the Board of Trade "furnishes one of the secrets of the immunity from railway accidents in Great Britain." Most American railroad men opposed any government institution with the powers of the Board of Trade. They urged patience, for the same market forces that had adapted railroading to American conditions would also result in safety improvements as rapidly as was "practicable." But their critics waited impatiently for results and eyed the Board of Trade with ever-increasing envy.[33]

Improving Railroad Safety

The passage of the federal Safety Appliance Act of 1893, which mandated the use of air brakes, automatic couplers, and handholds on freight cars, was the most visible consequence of decades of efforts to improve railroad safety. But many other technological changes also shaped carriers' accident rates. Some worsened risks, as depicted in figure 1.3, but others, either by design or by happenstance, improved safety. After a series of disastrous wrecks in the early 1840s, the Boston and Albany introduced new operating procedures specifying more clearly the duties of road masters and clarifying lines of authority. And in 1851 when the Erie began to use the telegraph to speed up train movements, it surely improved safety as well. Collectively these and many other changes in technology and business organization helped offset the increased dangers arising from larger, faster, and more frequent trains.

Although many of these safety improvements were introduced voluntarily by the railroads, some were given a nudge by the states. New Hampshire invented the first railroad commission in 1844, and by 1891 thirty-four states had some form of commission. State regulation shaped railroad safety in two interrelated ways. The first approach relied on voluntarism. Most commissions investigated and reported accidents, and many contemporaries believed that these were the major ingredients necessary to improve railroad safety. Once the facts were known, an informed public opinion would pressure the railroads to improve their procedures.[34]

The most outspoken champion of this voluntary approach was Charles Francis Adams, chairman of the Massachusetts commission. In 1871 a disastrous rear-end collision on the Eastern Railroad at Revere, Massachusetts, killed twenty-nine people. The Eastern was a single-track line operated without air brakes or a telegraph; it also lacked a siding at the Revere station, and the stationmaster was inexperienced.

The wreck touched off an explosion of public outrage that Adams skillfully used to cajole the state's carriers into adopting improved operating rules and equipment. His campaign was assisted by the blizzard of liability claims that descended on the Eastern, costing it a half-million dollars and no doubt disposing all the carriers to look more favorably on ways to reduce passenger accidents. The result, as one historian has written, "constituted a safety revolution in Massachusetts [railroads]." As Adams put matters, "the world advances through the lessons of bitter experience," and when he wrote *Railroad Accidents* in 1879, he expressed the hope that it would pressure the carriers to adopt air brakes and block signals.[35]

Adams's approach was most effective when backed by public opinion and liability suits. Hence, it was best suited to prevent disasters that involved passengers and worked poorly when only employee safety was at stake. New York's commissioners also believed that "accidents are expensive, particularly if they cannot be hushed up." But after recommending safety railings on freight cars, they ruefully noted that "the railroads have utterly ignored the suggestion."[36]

A number of states also developed a considerable body of law specifying that carriers adopt various safety devices and procedures. Most such efforts dealt with passenger safety and probably contributed to the decline in passenger fatality rates noted above. But states also legislated protection for workers, including the use of automatic freight car couplers. In their 1871 report the Massachusetts commissioners observed, "Of the accidents to employees, six occurred in coupling cars and the board . . . hope[s] that this source of accidents may soon be removed by the invention of some satisfactory self-acting coupler, suitable for freight cars." The lack of such a coupler did not deter several states, including Massachusetts, from requiring one, however. Their actions both speeded the development of the new technology and stiffened railroad opposition to federal safety legislation.[37]

The Railroads Develop Safety Appliances

Both the automatic coupler and the air brake were first developed for use on passenger cars. More than most inventions, the air brake was the work of one man: George Westinghouse. While traveling by train one day in 1866, Westinghouse was delayed by a wreck ahead. Irritation was apparently the mother of invention, and within a year he had developed the rudimentary ideas for the air brake and filed an intention to patent. By the late 1870s air brakes had become standard equipment on most passenger trains. The early air brakes were unsuitable for freights, which were longer and heavier than passenger trains, but Westinghouse continued to improve his product, and in 1881 he began commercial manufacture of freight train air brakes. By September 1887 Westinghouse had developed a "quick-acting" air brake that could stop long trains quickly and without dangerous shocks to the rear cars.[38]

The development of a satisfactory freight car coupler took longer than the air brake had taken. Until the 1870s both passenger and freight cars were connected by the link-and-pin coupler. The link and pin was not only dangerous to couple; it also resulted in considerable slack between cars. As a result, trains started or stopped with a crash that often damaged cars, merchandise, or passengers. And in a wreck, cars coupled by link and pin often "telescoped." That is, the rear cars crashed through those in front, with horrifying results.[39]

The coupler that ultimately won the hearts and minds of railroad men was developed by Eli Janney, in cooperation with the Pennsylvania Railroad. By 1873 Janney had developed a workable passenger car coupler that is the ancestor of the modern railroad coupler. It was a close coupler and did away with slack. Since slack was especially undesirable when air brakes were employed, Janney's coupler and Westinghouse's brake were complementary inventions. Janney soon persuaded the Pennsylvania to try his coupler, and in 1880, at the behest of its president, J. Edgar Thompson, who urged him to do something about freight car coupling accidents, Janney strengthened his device so that it could be used in freight service. In 1888 the Pennsylvania began to equip new freight

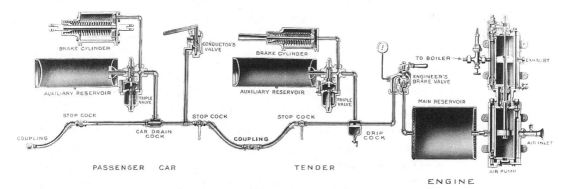

Engineering drawing of the Westinghouse air brake, 1872. When a trainman opened a valve, reducing pressure in the line, air pressure from the auxiliary reservoir applied the brakes. Such technology reduced the need for brakemen to ride freight cars and apply hand brakes, but the new devices also encouraged railroads to assemble unusually long trains, thereby increasing other risks. (*Courtesy Association of American Railroads*)

equipment with Janney couplers, and in 1890 it started to equip all cars.[40]

Janney was not the only inventor of what purported to be an automatic coupler, and by the early 1880s dozens of couplers that promised to work automatically were on the market. The Master Car Builders (MCB) had been formed in 1867 to find common solutions to the railroads' technical problems, and that association was now forced to choose among a large number of more or less worthy candidates. The large number of couplers, plus the pressure to adopt one of them, caused two very different kinds of problems. The MCB might make the wrong choice, thereby saddling the industry with the wrong coupler. Or, if it failed to act, one or two major lines might adopt the wrong coupler, and because of the economics of freight car interchange, the entire industry would standardize on it—the sort of event that was later to yield typewriter keyboards beginning with QWERTY. As the *Railroad Gazette* summarized matters, the coupler situation was "in a fog."[41]

But the alternative danger of inconsistent couplers was just as real. In 1882, Connecticut became the first state to require automatic couplers. Massachusetts and New York followed in 1884, then Michigan in 1885, Iowa in 1890, and Ohio in 1893. Yet no single coupler was on all the state lists. Clearly the MCB needed to make haste. Finally the car builders realized that they should not try to find the One Best Coupler but should rather settle on a *type*. The Janney type, which could be used with air brakes, was the only acceptable candidate. With this insight events moved rapidly, and in 1888 an MCB coupler was agreed on.

Because passenger cars were rarely interchanged, any passenger carrier that adopted safety appliances got their full benefit. But such was not the case for freight equipment. The railroads' adoption of air brakes and automatic couplers was hindered by the widespread interchange of freight cars, which meant that a line that lost cars could not capture all the benefits of its investment. In addition, if cars without air brakes were carried on an air-braked train, they had to be placed at the end, which complicated work in the classification yards. The experience of the Chicago, Burlington, and Quincy (CB&Q) in the mid-1880s, as it wrestled with the question of whether or not to install air brakes, reveals the importance of freight car interchange. Although operating men were enthusiastic about the air brake, the CB&Q's vice president, T. J. Potter, was skeptical. He worried about maintenance costs. In addition, "The other thing which is not clearly shown is how should we get the benefit of the air brake if other roads did not adopt it? When we have a heavy business we carry as many cars of other railroads as we do of our own East of the Missouri River." The Santa Fe and the Central Pacific were installing air brakes, and Potter concluded that the Burlington should wait for the results of their experience. And wait is exactly what the Burlington did. Finally in 1890 the company began a systematic policy of equipping its largest cars.[42]

The experience of the CB&Q was probably typical. The Westinghouse Company remarked that an "important influence against its [the air brake's] consideration was the interchanging of freight cars." Potential customers agreed. The New Haven claimed that it handled about 90 percent foreign freight cars and explained that "few of these are equipped with power brakes [so] we have decided to await more general equipment before supplying power brakes to our own freight cars." The roads that pioneered in the introduction of air brakes were those that exchanged relatively little equipment. In addition, all were western lines, which found hand brakes costly to use because of the relatively high wages paid to brakemen in the West, and also because hand brakes on the steep western grades tended to lock and cause flat wheels. Westinghouse claimed that there were approximately ninety-two thousand sets of air brakes on freight cars in 1889, and about 64 percent of them were on just four major Western systems: the Union Pacific, the Northern Pacific, the Southern Pacific, and the Santa Fe.[43]

Freight car interchange was also the "chief obstacle" to the use of automatic couplers, wrote Arthur Wellington in 1887. "No real benefit would be derived from such a coupler until it had come into almost universal use," he explained, "whereas the first practicable passenger car coupler was adopted by a few roads almost immediately . . . each gaining the full benefits of their own expenditure." Problems of workability also impeded the spread of automatic couplers. Many lines that bought in the 1880s found the new equipment expensive and unreliable. The Chicago, Milwaukee, and St. Paul responded to a survey by the Wisconsin Board of Railroad Commissioners, claiming that the MCB coupler wore out rapidly and often broke apart. The Milwaukee, Lake Shore, and Western also said that it had tried an automatic coupler that had not proved very satisfactory.[44]

Most contemporaries believed that the modest cost of killing brakemen also retarded the spread of both forms of safety appliance. Westinghouse thought that the "incentives which have led to the application of brakes have been in the main pecuniary and not to any extent humanitarian." The decisive factor was their "value in operating railroads more economically," he pointed out, while employee safety was merely an added bonus. Most other writers agreed. The *Railroad Gazette* bluntly observed that "it is economy to provide against accidents to passengers. If the much more numerous accidents to the employees could be made equally costly to the companies, there is good reason to believe that much more pains would be taken." The Kentucky Railroad Commissioners asked rhetorically, "Is the general understanding correct that car coupling receives slight attention from the companies because it costs nothing to get another brakeman when one is disabled or killed, whilst patent couplers are expensive?"[45]

The cost to the railroads of worker injuries could have been reflected in poorer-quality or more transient help, or in wage risk premiums, or in court-mandated compensation costs. Contemporaries were skeptical of wage premiums. "According to the generally accepted theory of political economists," wrote an analyst for New Jersey's Bureau of Labor in 1888, "men are paid in proportion to the risks they run. . . . As a matter of fact nothing of the kind occurs." Yet there is some evidence that railroads were forced to compensate employees for risk by paying higher wages. Job dangers may also have raised turnover and reduced labor quality. Charles Brown claimed that the Union Pacific's Green River (Wyoming) yards were so dangerous that boomers would stay only long enough to make a stake. And in 1901, after the introduction of automatic couplers, an ICC inspector reported that "since this work has become so much less hazardous, a more steady and better class of men are gradually coming into it." But for either risk premiums or labor quality to have created safety incentives, they would have had to be company-specific, and railroad managers would have had to know about them and be willing to act on them.[46]

Yet in the enormous literature on safety appliances, neither risk premiums nor the effects of risk on labor quality are ever seriously discussed. Neither the records of the Burlington nor any of the public or private writings by officials of the Westinghouse corporation mention them. Nor does any of the debate in the railroad journals even mention their existence. In an 1889 article typical of the genre, Arthur Wellington of *Engineering News* explained the many benefits that would accrue to railroads from installing automatic couplers, but he never mentioned better labor quality or reduced risk premiums.[47]

Most nineteenth-century writers focused not on wage premiums but rather on the failure of the legal system to make injuries costly enough to induce railroads to protect workers. By contrast, improved safety for passengers not only attracted business; it reduced expensive lawsuits, as the Eastern Railroad discovered the hard way. The Kentucky Railroad Commissioners, quoted above, concluded that "if the distinction between employees and others in the matter of negligence were done away with, a few verdicts from juries would have a tendency to bring about a change in the list of accidents from this cause [coupling]."[48]

The common law governing accidents to employees during the nineteenth century was shaped by judges who wished to encourage economic development. Beginning in the 1840s they developed a body of rules that reduced the risks and costs of enterprise by making it extremely difficult for injured workers or their dependents to win judgments against their employers. In 1842, Massachusetts Chief Justice Lemuel Shaw ruled in *Farwell v. Boston and Worcester Railroad* that the company was not liable for the injury to an engineer caused by negligence of a "fellow servant"—a switchman who had failed to throw the switch. In effect, Shaw ruled that workers had freely contracted to assume the normal risks of the job. Hence, an injured man was owed no more than his wages. Later cases broadened this defense and added some others. Only when an employer was "negligent" was an injured employee likely to win a suit, and even here courts often found employers guiltless if the injured was also guilty of contributory negligence. Employers were required only to exercise due care; they might be obligated to warn of dangerous conditions, but not to remedy them.[49]

The common law changes, and gradually courts chipped away at many of these defenses. In addition, some states passed statutes forbidding their use or limiting their scope. Moreover, sympathetic juries could sometimes be found, and so railroad claim agents preferred to settle injury claims out of court. Some carriers responded to the threat of such costs by requiring prospective employees to sign forms in which they agreed to assume the risks of employment. They also established relief funds that were largely employee-financed. Workers were required to join and were forced to waive their right to sue as a condition of membership. The first of these was begun by the B&O in 1880. According to an ICC survey of eighty-three large carriers in 1896, twelve had such a relief system, and all twelve required employees to waive the right to sue. Such systems must have sharply reduced carriers' accident costs and safety incentives.[50]

That work accidents were cheap is confirmed by both case study and statistical evidence. Histories of the Illinois Central and the CB&Q show that fatalities settled out of court usually cost less than $300. Charles Brown, who worked as a trainman for many carriers before he was injured, recalled that his father had been killed in a wreck on the Monon in December 1889. His widow received no more than back wages. A statistical analysis (see note) of worker accidents and injury costs on Ohio railroads for 1873–88 also demonstrates the modest cost of employee accidents. Each additional nonfatal injury cost about $38, while another fatality added only about $43 to costs. By contrast, in 1884, Ohio railroads killed 1,693 horses, mules, cattle, sheep, and hogs at an average cost of $79.59 each.[51]

That the spread of safety appliances was retarded by freight car inter-change, by problems of coupler quality, and by the cheapness of brake-men has led modern historians to conclude that their diffusion was com-paratively slow. One writer claims that "neither air brakes nor couplers were greeted with much enthusiasm," while another terms the intro-duction of air brakes "comparatively sluggish." In fact, both air brakes and automatic couplers were adopted quite rapidly in comparison with other new railroad technologies such as steel rails and diesel locomo-tives. The first steel rails were installed in 1862, and by 1880 "almost 30 percent" of track was made of steel. Thus, use of steel rails grew at an average (uncompounded) rate of 1.6 percent per year. Between 1925 and 1950 the proportion of diesels grew about 1.2 percent per year. Figure 1.4 shows the diffusion of safety appliances from 1889 on. If we date the introduction of the Janney coupler in 1880 and the air brake in 1881, their use grew at a rate of about 1.6 percent per year to 1893— the last year in which application can be termed voluntary. This was too slow for the critics, however, and so they turned to legislatures to in-crease the pressure.[52]

The campaign for laws requiring automatic couplers originated with the state railroad commissions. While the specter of inconsistent coup-ler laws haunted the MCB, in fact the legislation seems to have had little impact, because of the limited power of states over interstate commerce. The New York commission spoke for the other states with coupler laws,

FIGURE 1.4. Diffusion of Automatic Couplers and Air Brakes, Three-Year Moving Averages, 1889–1910

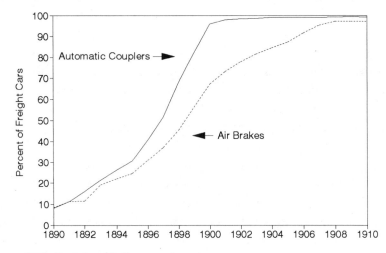

Source: ICC, Statistics of Railways, various years.

noting that its power was limited by the fact that "a large portion [of cars used in New York] is the property of corporations without the state." Because of such limitations, the most that states could do would be to force railroads to use automatic couplers on their in-state cars. Since most state commissioners thought that nonuniform couplers were more dangerous than the link and pin, they may have been reluctant to enforce the law even where they could. In the meantime, development of the MCB coupler had rendered all state laws—and their couplers— obsolete. The failure of state legislation turned reformers' eyes toward Washington. At the same time, the prospect of repeating on a national scale the debacle of mandating obsolete equipment hardened the carriers' opposition to federal legislation.[53]

The campaign for federal railroad safety legislation dates from at least the 1870s. One bill, introduced in 1877 by James Garfield, had been drafted by Charles Francis Adams and would have applied voluntarism on the national level, for it set up a board of railroad commissioners to investigate accidents. The *Railroad Gazette* endorsed the approach, believing that the board would function like the British Board of Trade, which had "greatly hastened the introduction of well-tested and approved appliances in Great Britain." Garfield's bill died, and another, introduced in 1879, would have allowed a government board to require specific safety appliances. This the *Gazette* termed "one of the least wise projects for legislation that has ever been proposed." The editors preferred instead making the carriers liable for their damages, for under such circumstances "no one else can have such an interest as they in securing safety." This view of matters squelched federal control until the 1890s and helped shape the carriers' response to the Safety Appliance Act of 1893.[54]

The coalition that finally achieved federal legislation was led by Lorenzo S. Coffin. Coffin had been on the Iowa Railroad Commission and had seen firsthand the effects of the old link-and-pin coupler. He was a devout man for whom social reform was a Christian duty, and he advocated the adoption of safety appliances with a religious fervor. Writing in 1903 of his accomplishments, he said simply, "It was God behind the movement. . . . I was used by Him." Coffin's years on the Iowa commission had honed his political skills. Like the doctor who sugarcoats his pills, Coffin tried to craft a bill that the railroads could swallow. The cause of safety appliances could not have found a better advocate.[55]

Coffin galvanized the railroad unions to become active in the drive for national legislation. Most of the states that had attempted to legislate automatic couplers came to support a federal law. The ICC also publicized the issues and coordinated the activity of those who favored legislation. In 1890 it published national statistics revealing the extent of coupling accidents. Senator Henry Cabot Lodge took the measure of the data in a popular article entitled "A Perilous Business and the Remedy."[56]

By the late 1880s the railroad journals were gradually shifting their views on federal safety appliance legislation. Under Arthur Wellington, *Engineering News* was the first to favor a federal law. In December 1887 Wellington threw his support behind Coffin in an editorial entitled "Needed Railroad Legislation." By 1890 even the *Railroad Gazette* had reluctantly concluded that "legislation is inevitable." From then on, it shifted focus to "the principles which must lie at the bottom of such legislation if it is to be effective."[57]

The railroads themselves have usually been portrayed as unalterably opposed to safety legislation. In fact, a few lines favored national legislation, and the opposition of other lines depended very much on just what sort of law was being discussed. Much of the railroads' opposition seems to have resulted primarily from the fear that a federal law would mandate specific couplers, as had states' regulations. Charles Francis Adams, now president of the Union Pacific, intoned that "all statutory legislation on this subject is unwise and impolitic." He thought that it would lead to an equipment monopoly, and that private enterprise, spurred by the fear of damage suits, would provide an adequate remedy. Theodore Ely, general superintendent of motive power of the Pennsylvania, bluntly claimed that "the results [of state laws regarding safety appliances] have, as a rule, been disastrous." E. B. Wall, also from the Pennsylvania, thought that the wrong coupler could "retard the benefits to be gained in economies of operation."[58]

When Congress first seriously addressed the issue of safety appliances in 1890, the railroads' worst fears seemed about to come true. Although one bill, written by Coffin and submitted by Senator William B. Allison of Iowa, would have left the choice of safety appliances up the carriers, another introduced by Senator Shelby M. Cullum proposed a national commission to make the decision. Safety appliance legislation went nowhere in 1890, and Congress returned to the matter in 1892. Although a few lines favored legislation, the views of H. S. Haines, who spoke for the American Railway Association (ARA), were more typical. Pointing out that ARA carriers already had nearly two hundred thousand cars equipped with automatic couplers, he pleaded, "In the interests of humanity, all that you are called on to require if you are called on to require anything, is that the man shall not be required to go between the cars to couple them in the ordinary performance of his duties. . . . If you are going to do anything, you have got to legalize what we have done. You must do that if anything." Coffin echoed Haines and claimed that the ARA was not opposed to the right kind of legislation at all: "If you will read Colonel Haines talk . . . you will see between the lines all the way through this thought, 'Gentlemen I wish you would pass a law so that we can be reinforced.' The railroads oppose legislation, but there is little opposition to legislation of this kind now."[59]

Coffin understood that the carriers were much less opposed to a bill that would simply require some form of automatic coupler than to one that specified the technology to be employed. The bill that was passed and signed into law on March 2, 1893, was written by Coffin, and it dropped the hated commission. Among other provisions, the bill required all freight cars to couple and uncouple without the need for anyone to go between cars. The locomotive and a "sufficient number" of cars were to be equipped with air brakes so that the engineer could control the train. Both provisions were to go into effect January 1, 1898.

The editors of *Engineering News* concluded that by promoting uniformity, the law was "designed to benefit the railways." They also expected that legislation would greatly hasten the diffusion of safety appliances. Without it, they thought, twelve to twenty years would have been necessary for the use of automatic couplers to become widespread. These high hopes were quickly dashed: six years later the *News* excoriated the carriers for a policy of "delay and obstruction." A modern historian has also claimed that "faced with the Safety Act the industry settled in for a period of resistance." There is, of course, an obvious contradiction in these positions: if the carriers dragged their feet, how do we know that the law speeded up the diffusion of safety appliances?[60]

It certainly seems as if the carriers had little intention of hurrying into compliance (fig. 1.4). As it became clear that many lines would not meet the January 1898 deadline for equipping cars with automatic couplers, the railroads petitioned for a five-year extension. The ICC held hearings on the issue at which the carriers that were not going to comply again leaned heavily on their financial woes. Even the *Railroad Gazette* could not entirely swallow this argument, pointing out that the Southern Pacific, which had paid no dividends, had managed to equip 69 percent of its cars with automatic couplers, whereas the Chicago and Alton, with only 38 percent of its cars equipped, was paying 8 percent.[61]

The Alton, however, was unrepentant. Its representative at the hearings delivered a seventeen-page plea for the "rights of the shareholders," which he termed as sacred as the wages of employees, noting also that over half the company's stockholders were women and children. But the commissioners were less swayed by the burden the act placed on women and children than by the fact that the carriers in compliance favored an extension for their wayward brethren. These lines unanimously argued that to penalize the noncomplying roads would also hurt those that had complied with the act, because of the interchange of traffic. Failure to grant the extension would cause a "general car famine . . . that would be a public calamity," *Engineering News* concluded.[62]

It also helped that the railroads' most powerful opponents had apparently agreed to an extension before the hearings even began. Coffin led the opposition, and his political skills were as sharp as ever. He began with a hard line, saying that the commission should consider nothing but safety. Gradually, however, Coffin let himself be talked into a grudging compromise. "Mr. Coffin: In consultation with the chiefs of these brotherhoods, we had concluded that we would consent to an extension, perhaps—tentatively but nothing more—to an extension of one year, and still gentlemen I hesitate even to consent to that." What is remarkable about this farce is that nearly a year earlier, in January 1897, Coffin had written the ICC that an extension of one year would be acceptable to him, and that in fact he would settle for two. A two-year extension to January 1, 1900, was granted. Probably all of the important parties to the hearing knew its outcome before it began. By arguing publicly for no extension at all, Coffin allowed the ICC to satisfy everyone while seeming to favor no one.[63]

In December 1899 the railroads requested yet another extension. This time the lines claimed that the extreme demand for freight cars made it impossible for them to comply, and they virtually dared the ICC to do anything about it. They received a seven-month extension until August 1, 1900. This was too much for the brotherhoods. The editor of *Railroad Trainman* observed that the only thing automatic about the coupler law had been "the automatic request on the part of the companies for more time."[64]

Since modern historians and contemporaries alike have been unsure as to how much the Safety Appliance Act actually accomplished, I have tried to answer this question by estimating the impact of regulation on the proportion of railroad rolling stock equipped with air brakes and automatic couplers. I assume that this proportion can best be described by a logistic function of time (T). Regulation (Reg) is a dummy variable that is 1 from 1893 to 1901 and 0 before and after, and (Reg$*T$) measures the effects of the new law. Fitting such an equation to data for ten regions of the country from 1890 through 1909 for both brakes and automatic couplers (table A1.6) reveals no evidence that the Safety Appliance Act speeded up the diffusion of either air brakes or automatic couplers.[65]

Both advocates and opponents of the Safety Appliance Act assumed that automatic couplers would reduce injuries only after they had largely replaced the link and pin. It was universally assumed that joining an MCB coupler to a link and pin was more dangerous than joining two link-and-pin couplers. Moreover, as *Engineering News* pointed out, the high risks assumed to exist in joining link-and-pin with automatic couplers were especially serious because the proportion of such couplings would rise for a time as the proportion of automatic couplers increased.[66]

The effectiveness of safety appliances also depended on how well they were maintained. The ICC routinely complained that the carriers failed to maintain the new equipment, while *Engineering News* charged the carriers with a policy of delay. Yet the *News* also maintained that the investment in brakes and couplers "returns good interest to the railways," while the ICC also crowed that the carriers themselves admitted the benefits of safety appliances.[67]

The economics of freight car interchange provide an explanation of how air brakes could be both profitable and yet not maintained. Testifying to Congress in 1902, Edwin Moseley stressed that the agreed-upon fee of 25 cents to maintain brakes on foreign cars was too low. Such a fee encouraged each line to try to pass on to connecting carriers both its own and foreign cars in need of maintenance. In a sort of Gresham's law of railroading, bad brakes drove out good. Moseley noted that the fee was being raised to 40 cents per brake, and he expected that this would solve some of the problems. It did. Writing in 1902, ICC inspector R. R. Cullinane noted that since "the price was raised to a reasonable rate for cleaning [air brake triple valves], they have had much more attention paid to them."[68]

But incentives were only part of the maintenance problem. Even in the late 1890s the new equipment often worked poorly, and it proved a headache to keep in good repair. In 1902 Albert Sullivan of the Illinois Central claimed that air brakes were as difficult to maintain as a locomotive. ICC inspectors complained that there were too few air plants and instruction cars, and that the carriers had inadequately trained their repairers or had trained the wrong personnel. At about the same time, the *Railroad Car Journal* contained numerous complaints about coupler wear and breakage. There were also a bewildering variety of MCB-type couplers: in 1899 the ICC listed ninety-nine different makes plus a large number of "unclassified," which made keeping an inventory of spare parts a nightmare. In 1900 G. W. West, superintendent of motive power for the New York, Ontario, and Western, observed that "the great variety of [coupler] patterns makes repairs expensive," and he claimed that many carriers failed to stock parts for couplers not in general use. ICC inspector George Martin bluntly asserted that the "rail-roads make no effort to keep repair parts for the many couplers in use." Other inspectors complained that parts from couplers that were not in fact interchangeable were often combined. As late as 1899 some writers to *Locomotive Engineering* even wanted to scrap the MCB coupler entirely, a position the editor termed "madness." [69]

Matters slowly improved. By 1905, when the carriers agreed not to accept foreign cars with defective appliances, and as wear gauges and cast-steel couplers came into general use, the problem of coupler wear and breakage finally began to assume manageable proportions. Air brake problems also declined. Technical men formed an air brake association and developed and publicized standards for maintenance, while the railroads equipped their yards with air plants to test brakes, purchased instruction cars, established proper maintenance schedules, trained engineers and mechanics, hired brake inspectors, and employed defect cards to keep track of inoperative equipment.[70]

To construct a statistical test of the impact of the new equipment, the analysis in figure 1.3 can be employed to make accident rates depend on various measures of output, safety appliances, and other variables. The accident rates are injuries or fatalities to all employees from coupling cars or from falls and overhead obstructions. (The effect of safety appliances on risks from collisions is postponed until chapter 5.) The results are presented in tables A1.7 and A1.8.

This analysis suggests that merely equipping freight cars with automatic couplers had little impact on fatality rates, although it may have reduced injury rates. (The data also suggest that the increasing use of automatic couplers raised injury rates for a time, as *Engineering News* postulated, but the effect on fatalities is much weaker.) Such results are consistent with contemporaries' views. As emphasized above, it was not simply the introduction of automatic couplers that accounted for the safety gains, but rather the gradual learning that resulted in improvements in design and maintenance and method of use. These and other improvements increased the productivity of safety equipment and are captured by the trend.[71]

Similarly, fatalities due to the need to brake trains declined not simply because of the increasing use of air brakes, but rather because of qualitative changes that improved their efficiency. In addition, air brakes had virtually no effect on injuries, perhaps because they increased train speeds and encouraged the growth of larger trains, which worsened the risks from close clearances. In addition, the increasing use of long trains caused a relative growth in the number of yardmen, who had higher injury rates than road freight brakemen. And the new equipment carried its own dangers; trainmen were required to go between cars to make or break the air brake connection, and the operation of hand brakes was made more risky by the use of air.[72]

Conclusion

The nineteenth-century American system of railroading was a response to thin traffic, the scarcity of capital and labor, and the comparative cheapness of natural resources and accidents. As a result, American carriers were primarily freight haulers. They were staffed by employees who often possessed little firm-specific experience. American trains were also larger and heavier than those in Britain. They were more difficult to couple and brake; they ran over comparatively flimsy, single-tracked lines that crossed each other at grade; and they eschewed fencing and block signals. As a result, American carriers became far more dangerous to workers than European carriers were. These dangers led to two distinct policy responses. One effort tried to interest railroad managers in voluntarily reducing accidents by chipping away at their liability defenses and employing public opinion to press for greater safety. This approach contributed to steadily decreasing risks for passengers, but it failed to improve employee safety fast enough to satisfy reformers. As a result, the second approach—that of mandating safety equipment—was adopted in the Safety Appliance Act of 1893. In 1901, with the act fully in force less than a year, the ICC pronounced it a great success, noting rather smugly that "the policy of the Congress . . . is amply vindicated in what may be called 'business considerations' and without any regard to the question of safety of life and limb."[73]

Yet the results of the Safety Appliance Act were far more complex than the ICC and many others have claimed. There is little evidence that the diffusion of safety appliances on freight equipment was laggard or that it speeded up after passage of the law. Nor was safety equipment a Great Innovation that dramatically reduced the dangers of railroading, for its full impact was realized only after a number of minor improvements and complementary changes in standards and techniques of maintenance and in employee training, work practices, and supervision. Without this sort of learning by using, safety appliances would have had much less impact. In addition, as both Charles Francis Adams and the *Railroad Gazette* editors understood, safety required managerial commitment. The new law did nothing to stimulate a broader interest in work safety on the part of railroad managers, and so other dangers remained as great as ever.

Two morals could be drawn from this tale. One was that technology and regulation were of limited value without the active interest of railroad management in work safety. This was the essence of the Safety First movement that swept through railroading after 1910, but it was not the lesson chosen by the railroads' critics. They saw the Safety Appliance Act as a dose of bad-tasting medicine forced down the railroads' throat for their own good by stern old Dr. Congress. By opposing the law, the roads also lost both moral and business authority, for if they fought legislation that benefited them, perhaps the critics understood railroading better than the carriers themselves. And since the prescription of couplers and brakes had proved so effective, why not increase the dose? As the twentieth century opened, a storm of proposed work-safety legislation rained down upon a railroad management still as indifferent to work safety as ever. Discussion of these developments will be postponed until chapter 5; the next three chapters shift the focus to the dangers of nineteenth-century American mining and manufacturing and to the nascent safety movement.

CHAPTER TWO

NEEDLESS PERILS

Toward the Regulation of Coal Mine Safety
1870–1910

In the murky chamber of the coal mine where God's sunlight can never come,
mephitic and inflammable airs abound.
ANDREW ROY, OHIO MINE INSPECTOR, 1874

There are a few of us alive yet. Oh, God for one more breath. Ellen, remember me
as long as you live. Good-bye darling.
HENRY BEACH, WHO DIED TRAPPED BY A MINE EXPLOSION,
COAL CREEK, TENNESSEE, 1902

It is . . . misleading to presume that operators will . . . make their mines safe
because it "pays" to do it.
W. E. JONES, WYOMING MINE INSPECTOR, 1911

December 1907 was the worst month of the worst year for mine disasters in American history. One blast, at Monongah, West Virginia, extinguished the lives of 362 men. A total of 703 men died in coal mine explosions that December, and the toll for the entire year came to 919 in eighteen major disasters. Like train wrecks, mine fires and explosions made the news. The *New York Times* announced Monongah with the front-page headline "350 Men Entombed in Mine Explosion," while *Harper's* wrote of the "Needless Peril of the Coal Mine." These perils may have been needless, but they were by no means new. In 1869 a mine fire in Avondale, Pennsylvania, claimed 110 lives. It led directly to the first state safety legislation in Pennsylvania and Ohio, and the trail of tragedy from Avondale to Monongah was directly responsible for the founding of the United States Bureau of Mines in 1910.[1]

Disasters were by no means the worst risks a coal miner faced. From 1906 to 1910—the worst half-decade for gas and dust explosions in American history—explosions accounted for only about one-quarter of

FIGURE 2.1. Coal Mine Fatality Rates per Thousand Workers, Great Britain and the United States, Three-Year Moving Averages, 1870–1939

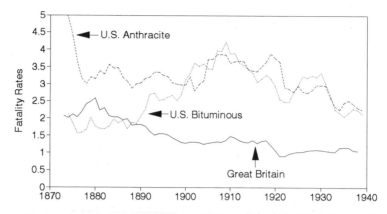

Source: Table A2.1; H.M. Chief Inspector of Mines, *General Report and Statistics,* various years.

miners' mortality. As was typical, falls of roof and coal were roughly twice as lethal. Together these and other dangers put coal mining among the most dangerous of American industries. Moreover, as figure 2.1 reveals, safety in bituminous mining deteriorated sharply after the 1880s. Even adjusted for changes in manhours (table A2.1), the fatality rate in 1910 was about *twice* as high as it had been a generation earlier. In anthracite, after some early gains, risks also rose, although much more mildly. By 1900 about 430,000 men—some 1.8 percent of the labor force—mined coal in the United States. Their death rate surpassed that for coal miners in every other modern nation by a wide margin, and the gap was increasing as safety abroad was steadily improving. Why American coal mining became so dangerous is the topic of this chapter.

"The Needless Peril of the Coal Mine"

To understand why American coal mining was so dangerous requires some grasp of both mining methods, which were determined by the operators, and day-to-day mining practice, over which both mineworkers and operators had some say. American mining methods were shaped by geology and economics. From the 1880s on, bituminous coal was mined not only from the great Appalachian fields but also in the Middle West, the Rocky Mountains, and even Washington State. While these beds varied considerably in quality and geologic characteristics, they also had important common features. Compared with Europe, all the major fields in the United States had vast quantities of coal near the surface, and many beds were horizontal or gently dipping and unfaulted.

As late as the mid-1920s the average depth of underground bituminous shaft mines was only about 260 feet (table 2.1). Thick seams were common: the Mammoth seam was fifty feet deep in places, and the great Pittsburgh beds averaged seven feet. In the 1920s seams in Wyoming averaged 101 inches and those in Washington, 62 inches.[2]

A DANGEROUS CRAFT

A mine might be opened by sinking a shaft, but with so much coal near the surface, outcrops were common, and many operators preferred the lower costs and quicker returns of opening a drift or slope mine into an outcropping. Once the mine was opened, it could be worked by either room-and-pillar or longwall methods. Longwall mining relied on the use of large quantities of mine waste for roof support, which made it poorly adapted for working the thick coal seams at shallow depths that characterized American conditions. In the usual version of longwall mining (fig. 2.2), work proceeded outward from the shaft to the edge of the property. Because of the large amount of "dead work" (excavation of dirt and rock) required, longwall mining was profligate of labor, but it used little timber to control the roof and recovered about 90 percent of the coal in a seam. It was also highly effective in preventing subsidence of the surface—an important consideration where land was valuable.[3]

In Europe, labor and capital were cheap and timber expensive compared with American conditions, while coal seams were thin and deep (table 2.1) and costly to mine. In the 1890s, for example, American coal prices averaged about $1 per ton, while in Britain they were nearer $4. American wages were also much higher than those abroad, although

TABLE 2.1. Physical Conditions of British and American Bituminous Mines, ca. 1925

	British	American
Average depth in feet	1,023	262
Percentage of output from large mines	67	49
Average thickness of beds in inches	50	63
Percentage of output machine cut	18	70
Pounds of explosives per ton of coal	0.12	0.44
Percentage of workers below ground	82	86
Output per man-day in tons	0.89	4.07

Source: Data are from F. G. Tryon and Margaret Schoenfield, "Comparison of Physical Conditions in British and American Mines," *Coal and Coal Trade Journal* 57 (Sept. 1, 1926): 934; (Sept. 8, 1926): 965–67; (Oct. 7, 1926): 1087–89; and (Nov. 4, 1926): 1202–6.

FIGURE 2.2. Longwall Mining Using the Advancing System

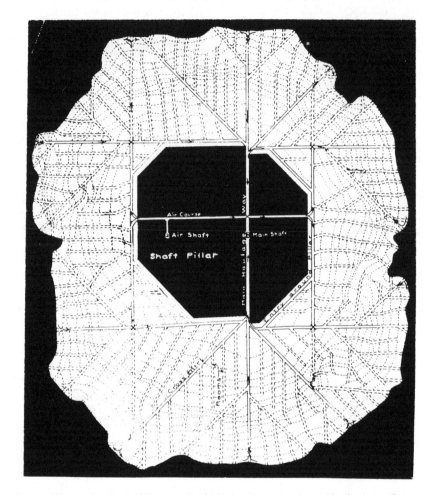

Source: Illinois Geological Survey, Coal Mining Investigations, "Preliminary Report on Organization and Method of Investigations," *Bulletin* 1 (Urbana, 1913).

national differences in statistics make direct comparisons difficult. American miners' daily earnings (gross of powder and other expenses) were on the order of $1.50 to $2 in 1886, while weekly net earnings of piecework miners in Britain ranged from $5 to $6. In continental countries earnings were even lower than in Britain.

While both geology and economics induced European collieries to employ longwall techniques, the same forces made longwall methods unattractive to American operators. With labor and capital more expensive and coal cheaper than in Europe, most operators preferred room-and-pillar methods, which yielded quicker returns and higher labor productivity but used prodigious quantities of timber for roof control.

FIGURE 2.3. Room-and-Pillar Mining Using the Block System

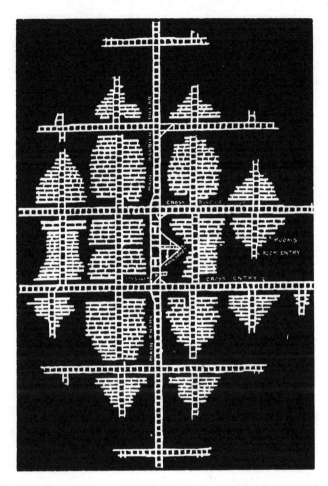

Source: Illinois Geological Survey, Coal Mining Investigations, "Preliminary Report on Organization and Method of Investigations," *Bulletin* 1 (Urbana, 1913).

Room-and-pillar mining also recovered less coal: a survey in the early 1920s put the recovery rate to date at about 65 percent.[4]

Room-and-pillar methods first drove main entries into the coal; then side headings were driven off the main entries, and panels of rooms separated by coal pillars were driven off the side entries (fig. 2.3). Track was laid down the main and side entries into each room, and the rooms were worked from the outside in. Overall roof support was accomplished with coal pillars, while timber props supported the open work. As a result, relatively little dead work was involved, but usually at least some surface subsidence occurred. Sometimes, after the mine had been worked to the edge of the property or as a panel was worked out, the

Necessary though hardly sufficient protection against roof falls, posts in a coal mine seldom went up as close to the cutting face as this worker appears to be setting them. *(Courtesy Eastern Regional Coal Archives, Bluefield, WV)*

pillars were removed (the shaded area in fig. 2.3) and the roof allowed to cave. When a room or a panel was abandoned, the work moved into the mine. As one mining engineer put it, "A mine grows. It is distinctly a thing of growth. . . . No work is ever done in exactly the same place or exactly the same way. The work is always slowly advancing."[5]

Mine work involved a number of distinct occupations of varying degrees of danger (table 2.2). In 1909 only about 4 percent of all mineworkers were salaried officials or proprietors, and there was little functional specialization. Although a large mine might employ a corps of engineers and a few other staff officials, many did not, and small operators were unlikely to do so. The highest operating official at the mine was the superintendent, although he exercised little day-to-day supervision. Below the superintendent there were usually separate foremen for surface and underground work. About 90 percent of bituminous mine-workers were employed below ground, and only 1.4 percent of them were supervisors. Within the mine, the foreman was supreme. Assisted by a handful of subordinates, he was responsible for hiring and firing the men, setting piece rates, mining the coal, coordinating the transportation, maintaining ventilation, ensuring safety, and opening up new work. About 14 percent of underground men were service workers, of whom the largest group was the transportation men. The remaining 84 percent of underground men were miners or miner's laborers.[6]

A "practical miner," as an experienced man was termed, was—in his own eyes and those of his employer—a skilled and independent craftsman. Terminology made this clear. Tipple workers, haulage workers, and other service men were paid by the hour and termed "company men" or "day men." Although the miner was an employee subject to company rules, custom gave him the status of an independent contractor. As if to emphasize his independence, he was called a "contract man" and was paid by the ton, not the hour. In anthracite mines the tonnage rate was even linked to the price of coal by a sliding scale, further emphasizing the miner's independence. As befit an independent contractor, he also supplied his own tools and sometimes hired a boy or laborer to help him who was not even listed as a company employee.

Far in the workings, the miner probably would not see a supervi-

TABLE 2.2. Occupational Fatality Rates, Illinois Coal Mining, 1910–1914

	Workers	Fatalities	Fatality Rate
Cagers	3,428	13	3.79
Drivers	23,276	120	5.16
Laborers	20,302	64	3.15
Loaders	71,279	38	0.54
Machine men	16,023	56	3.50
Miners	174,280	365	2.09
Shot-firers	2,504	30	11.98
Timbermen	6,270	23	2.67
Trackmen	6,674	9	1.35
Trappers	6,038	13	2.15
Not classified	36,483	76	2.08
Total	366,557	807	2.20

Source: Data are from Illinois Bureau of Labor Statistics, Annual Coal Report (Springfield, 1910–14).

Note: The fatality rate is per thousand employees.

sor more than once a day. Supervision was rare because it was expensive in the vast labyrinth of underground workings and yielded little payoff when the miner was paid by the ton. Such conditions underlay the miner's status as an independent contractor, or what the economist Carter Goodrich called "the miner's freedom." Miners rarely worked to the tune of a company whistle. "He comes to work when he pleases and he goes out when he pleases. We are not able to control him," one operator told the Bituminous Coal Commission in the 1920s. Miners not only came and went when they pleased, they labored very largely as they pleased. Timbering, track laying in rooms, drilling, undercutting, and blasting coal were only loosely supervised by the company. Custom even gave miners property rights to their rooms. In the 1920s Goodrich told of a miner who was injured and stayed out for three weeks without notifying the boss, who still held his place for him. Such independence attracted men who did not work well in harness: when asked why he had returned from factory work, a black miner told Goodrich that in the mines "they don't *bother* you none." A writer in *Industrial Management* advised readers not to hire ex-miners, because the work had unfitted them for factory discipline. Mining conditions extended this freedom at least in part to the company men too, for as Goodrich noted, you can't boss men you can't see.[7]

The ambiguity over whether miners were employees or independent operators carried over into matters of safety, and the men's wide freedom to determine work practices often led to tragedy. It also blurred responsibility, and because danger usually resulted from a combination of work practices and working conditions, it allowed operators to blame accidents on the "careless" behavior of the men. Mineworkers, on the other hand, tended to see the chances they took as their own business and blamed all other dangers on the operators. Thus, each group saw safety as the responsibility of the other. Andrew Roy, Ohio's first mine inspector and himself an ex-miner, not surprisingly emphasized the importance of the managers in providing a safe workplace: "No other class of workmen are so dependent upon employers as miners. The engineer, machinery, ropes, ladders, etc. . . . are furnished by the employer; the passageways of the mine . . . , the props . . . and the ventilation . . . are beyond his [the miner's] control, subject only to the will of the operator. . . . In the murky chamber of the coal mine where God's sunlight can never come, mephitic and inflammable airs abound."[8]

Many managers simply lacked the skill to run safe mines. In the 1870s Roy sarcastically noted that some non-gassy mines were run "by men who cannot tell why air, when heated, flies upward." Before state law required testing and certification, anyone could run a mine. But while certification of mine officials had become common by the twentieth century, competence was by no means assured. In 1912 a Colorado operator claimed that "not over five percent" of his brethren were "in any way familiar with the [state mining] statute."[9]

Operators' lack of skill resulted in part from the shared belief that the miner was responsible for his own safety, and in part from the low cost of accidents in the days before workmen's compensation. Colorado reported the coroner's verdict on each fatality, and in 1897—a typical year—there was not a single case in which a jury blamed the operator. In 1917, when a Huerfano County (Colorado) jury actually indicted a boss, the editors of the United Mine Workers *Journal* were so astounded that they reported it as news, claiming that this was the first such occurrence in fifteen years. Other states were little better. In 1909 one writer referred to an explosion in the Lick Branch (West Virginia) mine, observing that "the coroner's verdicts are, as usual, farcical." Such verdicts made recovery of damages difficult. Just before World War I, fatalities cost Virginia producer Stonega Coke and Coal about $356 each in liability payments. As a result, operators often seemed as concerned with the safety of their mules as with the men, or so workers sometimes claimed. The economics were reflected in a song common in the Alabama mining camps about 1900: "Kill a mule, buy another. Kill a nigger, hire another."[10]

Mine dangers were sometimes reflected in the labor market in ways that generated other costs to employers, however. Some inspectors observed that shot-firers received extra compensation for their especially dangerous job (table 2.2). And Andrew Roy observed that "a majority of . . . [miners] would be found ready at any time to work in the most dangerous places . . . for an advance of a few cents per ton." Occasionally men might respond to danger by quitting. Perry Gilpin explained, "I quit mining because I got hurt every time I turned around." Charlie Crawford recalled why he left mining: "I never did get used to it. I was always scared of the mines from the time I started. I was as scared the last as I was in there the first day." Dave Tuffs was so frightened that he began to have nightmares: "I got so I couldn't sleep at night. I could dream of slate falling all night. I'd heard so much of it and I'd missed it just by minutes of slate that thick falling as far from here over to the railroad. [It would] completely cover everything. I just got to putting that together with the trouble I was having with my lungs and I just quit working in the mines."[11]

Yet if some men left the mines because they were too dangerous, most did not. In 1937 Aubrey Rose explained to the Bureau of Mines that while he intended to quit, most of his fellow miners seemed ignorant of the risks. And other work was often scarce. Asked why he became a miner, Charlie Campbell spoke for many who went into the mines: "Well at that time that was about all they was to work at here," he said. Campbell also explained how he coped with the dangers. Asked if he wasn't afraid of the machines, he explained, "Well no, I wasn't afraid of them. You're not scared of nothing that you're raised up with." In all events, there is little evidence that wage premiums or labor shortages induced operators to improve mine safety.[12]

Nor did most accidents generate important property losses to employers. Haulage accidents or falls of roof and coal, which collectively might account for 60–70 percent of all deaths, were likely to cost the operator little in the way of destroyed property or lost output. The only kinds of accidents that were expensive enough to interest operators were explosions and fires. Explosions often destroyed capital equipment and sometimes wrecked the entire mine, stopping production for a considerable period. And mines that blew up often enough had trouble attracting workers. Charlie Campbell explained that while he had been scared his first day in the mines, "I got so I wasn't afraid of nothing." But even he drew the line at working in gassy mines. "I never did work with the gas in the mines," he recalled. "I was always too scared of it." For such reasons, operators showed more interest in preventing explosions than other forms of danger. In the 1830s the pits of the Mid-Lothian Coal Company (of Virginia) got such a bad reputation for blowing up that the company advertised that it had hired an experienced English foreman and "had not spared any labor and expense deemed necessary to secure the absolute safety and comfort of the hands in their mines." In 1910 Colorado's inspector noted that "mine disasters drove hundreds of men from the camps."[13]

Mine inspectors often testified to the role of market forces in encouraging efforts to prevent explosions. In 1876 a Pennsylvania inspector noted that "in collieries where . . . gas is evolved, with but few exceptions the ventilation is passably good. Then again, in collieries which do not generate . . . gas, with few exceptions the ventilation is very far from being up to the requirements of the law." At about the same time, Andrew Roy also noted that gassy mines were usually well ventilated and run by superior men, a result he attributed to the expense of explosions.[14]

Except for such disasters, however, mine dangers excited little interest from operators. With the boss indifferent or incompetent, or both, the layout and operation of the mine could make it a risky place to work, and danger began the moment a man entered the mine. In shaft mines, hoists sometimes broke, as happened on August 10, 1870, at the

Heins and Glassmire colliery of Middleport, Pennsylvania. The drum had no brake, and so the cage, which contained twelve men, plummeted down the three-hundred-foot shaft and broke through the sump cover into the water below, trapping and drowning nine of the men. Shafts were also rarely guarded, and inspectors routinely reported deaths such as that of Stantanty Patalone, who was found on April 25, 1883, at the bottom of the no. 2 shaft of the Nanticoke (Pennsylvania) mine. Apparently he fell off the cage.[15]

Haulage work was especially dangerous ("drivers" in table 2.2). Entries and rooms were usually barely wide enough for mine cars, and men who walked near the trips could be caught by a train, as happened to Frederick Klein, who was crushed to death between a car and a pillar on May 25, 1900. Because track was typically put down in slapdash fashion, derailments also took their toll. Well into the twentieth century, few mine cars had brakes; drivers were supposed to control the cars with the help of the mule, and by using wooden wheel blocks. But couplings were rarely inspected and sometimes broke, and the use of chain harnesses rather than rigid steel shafts made it hard for the mule to control the trip. Even in the 1940s the old link-and-pin coupling was still common. Where beds were pitched or faulted, haulage ways had steep grades, and loaded mine cars sometimes got away, with lethal results. Even the mules were dangerous. As late as 1929 one mine recorded its first fatality in twenty-three years when a mule kicked its driver in the head. "It seems rather hard luck to have a mule be instrumental in spoiling one's record," a Bureau of Mines engineer observed. No doubt the driver would have agreed.[16]

Far and away the worst risks resulted from falls of roof and coal. If the operator left insufficient coal in the pillars, the mine might begin to squeeze—that is, collapse—making it a potential deathtrap. The results of unskilled development—nonparallel entries, pillars of varying sizes—also placed dangerous stresses on the roof. As late as the 1920s the Coal Commission described the "lack of system in planning operations" that led to roof falls, creeps, and squeezes.[17]

But most deaths from roof falls occurred at the workface, often after the miner had been repeatedly warned of the dangers. Pennsylvania inspector Robert Mauchline reported the death of John Curran as follows: "[Curran] was fatally injured by a fall of top coal. The assistant boss . . . notified . . . [him] to either prop up or blast down the dangerous top coal. Curran replied that *he knew how to act* and shortly after fired a shot. . . . The top coal . . . fell." [18]

While inspectors often railed at such "suicidal" behavior, they understood that the system of mining was at fault. Tonnage rates put a premium on chance-taking. "When men learn to value their lives more than the price of a wagon of coal, the mine will lose its death record," one inspector observed. In short, the piece-rate system, unlike an hourly wage, induced miners to trade safety for income. The ex-miner John Brophy described the choice: "An experienced miner would often work calmly under conditions that would terrify a novice. This was . . . because he had to work steadily . . . to get out a good day's production."[19]

Brophy's observation also highlighted the importance of experience in avoiding injury, and firm-specific expertise was as important in mining as it was on railroads, for each mine was different. Labor turnover in mining was also high, and here too the cost of on-the-job learning about danger could be death. In 1923, officials at Stonega Coke and Coal reported that a miner who was killed by a roof fall had twenty-five years of experience. But he had been at work only three months in their Exeter mine, and they laid his death to "lack of training in roof of this character." Other conditions also differed from mine to mine and field to field. Some were gassy while others were not, and some dusts were more explosive than others. As one operator rhetorically asked the West Virginia Mining Commission of 1907, "Does a man who works in a mine that is free from gas learn the conditions that exist in a gaseous mine?" Compounding matters was the constant evolution of the mine itself, for if a new area brought gas or a poorer roof, even mine-specific experience might become a dangerous guide. In 1935, West Virginia's chief inspector claimed that half that state's injuries resulted from "men working in new places under unfamiliar conditions."[20]

While the trade-off between safety and income encouraged miners to take chances, the economics and ethos of mine supervision gave the miner freedom to make his own trade-offs. The foreman could tell John Curran to set a prop, but he could not stay to see that the order was obeyed or to advise when another was needed. Wyoming's mine inspectors blamed roof falls on the absence of supervision, claiming that the companies needed a roof inspector for every thirty miners. These economic circumstances were reinforced by the miner's status as a contract man. Foremen treated miners not as subordinates to be ordered around but as equals whose judgment deserved the respect that befitted an independent contractor. "With regard to this class of [experienced] miners, the bosses are rather too much inclined to comply with their wishes regarding the need of propping or pulling down loose rock or coal," a Pennsylvania inspector noted.[21]

Miners who thought they were being accorded insufficient respect sometimes reacted with prickly independence: when told to set a post, John Curran curtly noted that he "knew how to act." Another ob-

Miners often took chances with roof control. Failure to set posts properly allowed this large piece of slate to fall in early January 1917, killing a miner in the Superior Coal Mine, Gillispie, Illinois. *(National Archives)*

server commented that "all through West Virginia the average English-speaking miner will give you a 'cussing out' if you say too much to him about setting up a post, etc." The New Mexico inspector reported that when he pointed out dangers, "the miner replies saying that if he . . . is willing to take the risk, he does not see how it is anybody else's business." [22]

Blasting down coal was one of the most difficult and dangerous parts of mine work, even for skilled and experienced men. Yet most operators left the men largely free to blast as they wished, and as a result, many blew themselves up. Misfires were common, and consequently many miners died inspecting a shot they thought had missed. Miners also regularly opened twenty-five-pound metal powder kegs with a pick, and sometimes this caused a spark. The combination of open-flame lamps and black powder could also lead to disaster. In 1883 "John Greenage, a miner, had his lamp on his head while filling a cartridge with powder, and he set his hat on fire. The full keg of powder was on his lap . . . a cartridge in his left hand, and while trying to extinguish his burning hat with the other hand, [he] caused a spark to fly into the powder and explode it. . . . He died the following day." Blasting also weakened the roof and blew out timbers. The bigger and more frequent the charges, the worse the risks. [23]

Most mines gave off at least some methane, which is explosive in concentrations exceeding 5 percent and which can help propagate a dust explosion in even smaller quantities. These dangers were magnified because the role played by coal dust was only poorly understood. In the 1880s a few experts began to warn that dust might explode, but among practical men this long remained a minority opinion. Nor was there any clear understanding of how to prevent such blasts. A few operators attempted to water or remove the dust, but such procedures were rarely successful.

Gas could be detected with a flame safety lamp, which could be used for illumination as well. Gas was indicated by an elongated flame with a blue cap. The test was subtle, and it required good vision. A British report indicated that many experienced men could not use it to detect even dangerous levels of gas. A Pennsylvania inspector concurred, claiming that the lamp would not detect 3 percent methane—which left little margin for error. Gassy mines were sometimes operated with closed—that is, safety—lights, but it is by no means clear that such lamps saved more lives than they took. They allowed the operation of mines that would otherwise have been too dangerous to work. In addition, state laws often required safety lamps only in gassy *parts* of mines, and miners sometimes wandered into gas with an open light. In addition, as one witness explained to the commission investigating the Mammoth mine explosion in 1891, "the mines are daily and hourly changing." Mammoth had been free of gas four or five hours before it exploded. Safety lamps also altered both operators' and miners' behavior, providing a false sense of security. Some operators simply substituted safety lamps for ventilation, and the men often took chances too. One inspector reported seeing a man deliberately suck the flame through the gauze to light his pipe, and he noted that safety lamps were routinely disassembled in the mine for such purposes. And the lamps were themselves not entirely safe. Sometimes they became defective or broke, with lethal results.[24]

Blasting was also a prolific source of explosions. If a shot was not stemmed, or stemmed with coal dust, or overcharged, or not undercut, or drilled too deep, or at an improper angle, it might blow out, sending a sheet of flame into the room that might ignite gas. Sometimes the dust went too, killing everyone in the mine. Such blasts added an element to mine risks not present in most other kinds of work. In railroading, a worker's safety depended primarily on his employer and on his own actions and those of a few other employees. But in mining, risks depended on the behavior of everyone else, and the system that left operators only loosely responsible for safety while giving the men wide freedom to labor as they pleased was a formula for disaster. One man might stray into an abandoned area full of gas, or leave open a single doorway, which could lead to a gas accumulation to be set off by smoking, or an open-flame lamp, or blasting, or an electric spark, thereby blowing up the entire mine.

DETERIORATING SAFETY

In the United States, coal has been mined since colonial times. There are reports of Virginia "cole pitts" in 1720, but these early ventures were shallow, unmechanized, and probably relatively safe. The first recorded gas explosion occurred around 1810, but its toll is unknown. Although there are no statistics for these early years, it seems likely that by 1869, when Pennsylvania passed the first law governing safety in anthracite mines, risks had been increasing for some time.[25]

For the 1870s and early 1880s, fatality rates in bituminous mines reflect conditions in Pennsylvania, Ohio, and Illinois, and these states accounted for 59 percent of total employment as late as 1889. Thereafter the industry spread south and west. For the years 1903–13, the Bureau of Mines calculated that the nationwide fatality rate was 1.97 per million manhours. But for West Virginia it was 2.59, for Wyoming 2.86, for Alabama 2.89, for Colorado 4.01, and for New Mexico 7.20.[26]

These dreadful records resulted in part from lax mining laws. But mining methods and natural conditions also played a role. The dusts of most Rocky Mountain coals were extremely explosive, a condition made worse by the dry climate. In Utah, coal was mined from seams that were sometimes thirty feet thick. Timbering and roof control were therefore difficult, while thick seams ensured that coal was left on the floor and roof, which increased dust. Grades were often steep (10–12 percent), and because heavy production encouraged use of large mine cars, haulage accidents were common. Other western states also had adverse conditions. One engineer attributed Washington's high fatality rate to "steep pitches, faults, igneous intrusions, highly explosive coal dust, extremely friable coals . . . very gassy coal beds, rugged topographical conditions, inherently bad roof and floors, thick beds and heavy cover." In addition, as on the railroads, the shift in economic activity to new areas, if it increased the variability of work conditions, may have reduced the value of prior experience.[27]

It is possible to calculate a measure of the impact of interstate shifts in employment between 1882, when the fatality data are entirely from Pennsylvania, Ohio, and Illinois, and 1910, which was roughly the peak for fatality rates. The procedure is to compare the actual increase in rates with the increase that would have occurred if the employment distribution had remained as it was in 1882. Table 2.3 reveals the impact of employment changes when they are weighted by 1910 fatality rates.

TABLE 2.3. The Impact of Interstate Shifts in Employment on Fatality
Rates, Bituminous Coal Mining, 1882 and 1910

	Employment Distribution	
	1882	*1910*
Fatality rates in 1882 [a]	0.836	—
Fatality rates in 1910 [a]	1.552 [b]	2.113

Source: Data for 1882 are from table A2.1. Data for 1910 are from W. W. Adams, "Coal
Mine Fatalities in the United States, 1939," BM *Bulletin* 444 (Washington, D.C.,
1940), table 68.

[a] Per million manhours.

[b] The rate for 1910, using the 1882 employment distribution, is the average fatality rate
in Pennsylvania, Illinois, and Ohio for 1910.

Actual rates rose about 150 percent [(2.113 −0.836)/0.836], while rates
within the original coal-mining states increased about 85 percent [(1.552
−0.836)/0.836]. Thus, interstate shifts in mining "account for" about
43 percent [(150 −85)/150] of the observed rise in fatality rates over this
period.[28]

In anthracite mining, uneven productivity growth also contributed
to the increase in fatality rates. During the late nineteenth century the
productivity of outside workers rose sharply because of the increasing
size of breakers, the substitution of shaking screens for hand methods
in removing impurities, and similar improvements. These increases in
scale and mechanization increased mine risks in two ways. First, the dangers of outside work rose (table 2.4). And second, as the productivity of
above-ground workers rose, their share of employment declined. Since
these remained the least risky jobs, this too raised the average level of
risk, and in fact it accounted for about 62 percent of the entire increase
in fatality rates over these years.[29]

Many contemporaries blamed rising fatality rates largely on a deterioration of worker quality brought about by the influx of new immigrants who were unskilled and unable to speak or understand English.
In 1892, Pennsylvania inspector James Blick called attention to the number of new immigrants, claiming that "these men do not understand our
language, . . . know nothing whatever about underground work, and are
utterly incompetent to protect themselves." The dangers resulting from
lack of skill and experience have been noted, but lack of English could
also be fatal. In 1883 Thomas Maley was a recent Polish immigrant who
neither spoke nor understood English. On September 5 he was working
as a loader when miners in an adjoining room fired a shot on the separating pillar. They gave the usual warning, but he did not understand it

TABLE 2.4. Anthracite Mining Fatality Rates and Employment Shares,
Inside and Outside Workers, 1881–1910

| | Inside Workers | | Outside Workers | | All Workers, |
	Fatality Rate	Percent	Fatality Rate	Percent	Fatality Rate
Average, 1881–90	4.44	62.2	1.20	37.8	3.22
Average, 1891–1900	4.21	63.5	1.22	36.5	3.12
Average, 1901–10	4.27	69.3	1.75	30.7	3.49

Source: Data are from Pennsylvania Department of Mines, *Annual Report, Bituminous, 1918* (Harrisburg, 1919), table 19.

Note: The fatality rate is per thousand employees.

TABLE 2.5. Fatality Rates by Ethnic Group, Inside and Outside Workers,
West Virginia Coal Mining, 1911–1915

| | English-Speaking | | Non-English-Speaking | | All | |
	300-Day Workers	Fatality Rate	300-Day Workers	Fatality Rate	300-Day Workers	Fatality Rate
Inside	131,188	7.73	87,383	9.17	217,571	8.30
Outside	38,183	2.54	9,323	4.50	65,897	2.92
Total	169,391	6.56	96,906	8.71	266,077	7.34

Source: Rates are derived from West Virginia Department of Mines, *Annual Report* (Charleston, 1911–15).

Note: Rates are per thousand 300-day workers, computed as (employment times days worked) divided by 300 for each county for the five-year period. English-speaking workers are those categorized as American, Negro, English, Scotch, Irish, and Welsh; the non-English-speaking include all other groups, including workers of unknown ethnicity.

and was killed. In 1908 Colorado's inspector claimed that roof falls were most prevalent "in those districts where miners foreign to the English speaking countries were employed."[30]

Yet one cannot infer that new immigrants worsened risks from a simple comparison of their fatality rates with other groups, because more of the newcomers could have worked in relatively dangerous jobs. As a partial control, West Virginia figures can be employed to calculate separate fatality rates for inside and outside workers by ethnic group. Table 2.5 presents such information for the years 1911–15. As can be seen, the non-English-speaking group of workers was disproportionately employed in the high-risk, below-ground occupations in which they had a higher fatality rate. Yet if all inside and outside men had had the rates of the English-speaking workers, West Virginia's death rate would have fallen from 7.34 to 6.56 per thousand 300-day workers, or by about 11 percent. These findings suggest that the influx of new, non-English-speaking immigrants was not the major force driving the rise in fatality rates.[31]

Both the mining press and inspectors also blamed the rising fatality rate after 1880 on the spread of mechanization. That is, they claimed that some forms of technological change in mining were "risk increasing," just as they were on railroads (recall fig. 1.3). On the surface, tipples grew in size, horsepower increased, coal handling was mechanized, and electricity was introduced. Below ground, trolley haulage entered the mines, and electric drills and coal-cutting machines substituted for older ways. In 1895 the editor of *Colliery Engineer* claimed that "in the past eight years the . . . increased use of machinery has increased the dangers [of mining]." Four years later, Pennsylvania's chief mine inspector bluntly stated that "the use of electricity in any form in coal mines is a menace to life, limb, and property."[32]

In fact, the new technology reduced some risks while increasing others. Electric coal-cutting machines were probably less dangerous than blasting without undercutting the coal ("shooting off the solid"), but they were more dangerous than pick-mining had been. The cutters were themselves lethal, while use of machines also made roof support near the coal face difficult, and so made roof falls more likely. In addition, most equipment was poorly grounded and insulated. The cables that attached undercutting machines to the overhead wires routinely frayed or broke and were spliced in the mine in slapdash fashion. One report written in the late 1920s described a mine in which there were an average of 1.7 splices per cable per week. The consequences were predictable. One victim of such practices was Andy Martinocki, who on May 27, 1907, touched the worn cable of a cutting machine in an Ohio mine and was killed.[33]

Mechanization of haulage also added to mine risks. The early efforts to use steam- or gasoline-powered trolleys had been so dangerous that they were abandoned, and so electricity predominated. Many mines ran 500- or 600-volt DC trolley wires unshielded a few feet above the haulage way. This relatively high voltage was preferred because it economized on cable, if not on miners. Or mules: one writer thought it was "amusing to see the care the mules take to avoid coming in contact with that line of copper running along the sides of the entries." Miners took similar pains but were not always successful. The Black Diamond mine in Belmont, Ohio, ran a 500-volt cable about four feet above the rail. The cable could have been shielded with boards or old fire hose, but

Using a machine to cut coal, dangerous enough, was made worse by the wearing of carbide lamps that could set off coal gas. *(Courtesy Eastern Regional Coal Archives, Bluefield, WV)*

that would have been expensive. On June 21, 1906, Joseph Verba probably brushed against it, but his death had no witnesses.[34]

Haulage accidents were second only to roof falls as a cause of fatalities, and they rose sharply in the 1890s. As mining productivity increased, more coal had to be transported, and as mines grew in size, distances increased, thereby increasing the exposure of men who walked to work. Mine cars grew in weight from two to as much as ten tons each, and electric locomotives increased speeds from two to ten miles per hour. When such methods were employed in haulage ways that had been designed for mules, they reduced clearances, increased derailments, and brought to mining all of the dangers of working in a railroad tunnel.[35]

A simple comparison of fatality rates by cause suggests the importance of mechanization in raising mine risks. Accidents from underground haulage and electric shock reflect the impact of mechanization on mining risks. From the early 1890s—the first years for which appropriate data are available—to the 1910-14 period, these causes account for about 44 percent of the increase in the fatality rate.

As mines grew in size and depth and increased their use of machinery, explosion risks increased from 0.3 per thousand workers in 1870–90 to 0.65 per thousand in the half-decade between 1910 and 1914. A Pennsylvania anthracite inspector writing in 1879 explained that "mining is conducted on a different scale to what it was a dozen years ago, the mines being much . . . more dangerous being so much deeper and more extensive." Deeper mines were warmer, which raised the temperature of air entering the mine. This increased the air's ability to absorb water, thereby drying out the workings and raising the risks of explosions (and also roof falls).[36]

Deeper mines with more working faces and abandoned areas were also increasingly likely to contain gas. A statistical analysis (see note) based on a study of Illinois mines in 1915 reveals that the volume of gas rose disproportionately with depth, and a doubling of both depth and mine size increased the volume of gas by 250 percent, thereby perhaps swamping the ventilation system. In 1900 West Virginia's chief inspector noted ominously that "within the past five years a number of mines in this State have become gaseous."[37]

Mechanization increased explosion risks because sparking electrical equipment multiplied sources of ignition. Early pick machines also generated far more dust than did the process of undercutting coal by hand, while the use of trolley haulage stirred up dust and disrupted ventilation. Larger mines with more miners also required more air, which necessitated an increase in its velocity. This stirred up dust and deposited it on the walls and roof, where it was most dangerous. In addition, more miners meant more potential sources of ignition, as was illustrated by the explosion at Rolling Mill mine in Pennsylvania, which blew up in 1902, killing 112 men. *One man* had taken an open light into a gassy area. Such tragedies were more likely to occur in large mines, and when large mines exploded, many men died. As West Virginia inspector James W. Paul put it, "The most incompetent and unskilled miner establishes the safety within a mine."[38]

The increasing tendency of miners to use large amounts of powder and to shoot off the solid also dramatically raised the odds that someone would explode the mine. Solid shooting used much more powder than blasting did when the coal had been undercut, and it also produced relatively more slack (fine coal), which was traditionally of little or no value, although the miners found it easier to shovel than lump coal. But in spite of the waste it created, solid shooting raised both miners' productivity and — unless they were penalized for slack — their incomes. Writing in 1904, the Ohio inspector George Harrison claimed that "any miner of middle age can well remember . . . when blasting coal off the solid was almost unknown." During the 1880s, however, the demand for fine coal increased as it began to be used for coking and as boiler fuel. Companies with access to such markets were less inclined to discourage solid shooting, while competition for miners made even those operators who opposed the practice reluctant to ban it. As a result, solid shooting became increasingly common, and by 1911, the first year for which reliable data exist, a majority of coal was mined in this manner in Arkansas, Oklahoma, and Kansas. In 1907 Harrison claimed that in solid shooting, "from 6 to 18 pounds of blasting powder are used in one charge . . . trap doors are wrenched off their hinges; stoppings and brattices blown out; props . . . swept out of place; loaded and empty cars are often turned over; iron and wooden track rails are twisted and broken to pieces." An Arkansas geologist reported that coal had been blown forty feet after a solid shot. Since the use of shot-firers had become universal, he reported, miners used larger shots. Such blasts were themselves dangerous, and they weakened the roof and blew out props. Solid shooting thus contributed to the rise in fatality rates from roof falls—which jumped from about 1.3 per thousand workers in 1890-95 to 1.8 per thousand in 1910-14. These large blasts would also set off mine explosions that might not have been ignited by more modest sources of ignition.[39]

In Arkansas, Illinois, Kansas, and Oklahoma, the operators tried to discourage solid shooting by screening the coal and refusing to pay for what passed through the mesh. The miners responded by inducing legislatures to require payment for "mine-run" rather than just lump coal. In 1897 both Illinois and Kansas passed mine-run laws, and Arkansas and Oklahoma followed in 1905 and 1908. Payment for mine-run coal gave an added boost to solid shooting with heavy shots because it created the incentive to blast as much coal as possible, irrespective of its quality. As one Arkansas miner put it, "I always find an auger when I start looking for a pick." When asked how he would pick down a chunk of coal, he said, "With two feet of powder." The Kansas inspector reported that some miners mixed black powder with dynamite—an especially dangerous practice, for the dynamite would blow the more slowly burning powder out into the room. Others would drill a single hole six to eight feet deep and load it with up to sixteen sticks of dynamite. The blast often blew out every prop in the room.[40]

In 1897, Illinois passed a mine-run law, and the miners promptly increased the share of coal shot off the solid from 50 percent in that year to 56 percent by 1905. Powder use per ton of coal also grew sharply as miners drilled fewer but larger-diameter holes. Normal practice required shots to be fired one at a time and to contain perhaps 2.5 pounds of powder. In 1904 the explosion of the Peabody mine in Sherman, Illinois, resulted from three simultaneous blown-out shots, each one of which was estimated to contain nine pounds of powder. Not surprisingly, fatalities from powder explosions in Illinois jumped, from eleven in 1897 to eighty-eight in 1905.[41]

In that year the miners persuaded the legislature to require the operators to employ shot-firers—with results similar to those that obtained in Arkansas. "So terrific have been some of the explosions in our coal mines, that, had they occurred when the usual complement of men was at work, not a single life would have been spared," the Illinois inspector reported in 1908. As George Harrison put it, the law transferred danger "from the men who are responsible for it to the innocent shot-firer who is induced to accept that position because of the small extra wages." Finally some operators that paid for mine-run coal realized that the solution was to require the shot-firer to charge the hole. As ex-miner Monroe Quillen recalled, "I'd be going to shoot four sticks of powder in a hole to make it real loose so I could shovel it, he'd shoot a stick and a half and crack it. Then I got to take a pick and get it all out in blocks . . . but they paid me the same per ton, block or slack. I'd rather load slack coal than block any day, it's much easier to shovel."[42]

While some operators undertook serious efforts to reduce explosion risks, not all companies did so. A Wyoming inspector warned against presuming that "operators will provide all the essentials to make their mines . . . safe because it 'pays' to do so," and he concluded that many were "blind to their own interests." Such blindness was understandable. It was easy to underestimate the risk of explosions, for they been increasing only gradually and remained rare events. And if the risks seemed remote, the costs of prevention did not, for an effective program would have required not only tighter supervision to reduce the miner's freedom but also better ventilation and control over all sources of ignition. Thus, even the best operators compromised. Inspectors often tried to "educate" operators to the benefits of safety precautions. In 1874 Andrew Roy claimed that "it is in the interest of the operators to ventilate," and other inspectors made similar claims. But often only an explosion could awaken management concern. Colorado's inspector noted that after a blast in the Sunshine mine killed sixteen men in 1897, the company introduced low-flame explosives, hired shot-firers, and began to blast only when the men were out of the mine, none of which procedures were required by the state's mine law.[43]

BRITISH AND AMERICAN MINE SAFETY

The first available data on anthracite mine safety in the United States in the 1870s show fatalities per worker to be vastly higher than in Great Britain (fig. 2.1). Bituminous mining was somewhat safer in America than in Britain in the early 1880s, but the situation rapidly reversed, with fatality rates rising sharply in this country while falling steadily in Great Britain. Every other important European coal-mining country also exhibited sharply lower mine risks than the United States. Just as the slaughter on American railroads excited awe among Europeans, so by the twentieth century had the dangers of American coal production become the talk of the world mining community. In 1908 the English *Colliery Guardian* sarcastically observed, "There is one record to which our transatlantic cousins may lay claim without fear of emulation; for in the matter of safeguarding its workmen, the United States enjoys the unenviable reputation of being the most backward of the civilized nations."[44]

Most contemporaries believed that higher American productivity was the cause of higher fatality rates. The *Colliery Guardian* told its British audience that the "boom in cheap [American] coal has been secured partly by the sacrifice of safe conditions in mining." In 1905 the American *Mines and Minerals* claimed that one reason for the higher risks in this country was that "intensity of production is greater here than [in] Europe. By this we mean that fewer men are employed for the same tonnage in this country." Both the higher productivity and the risks of American coal mining resulted in part from the geologic and economic circumstances that led to an American system of coal mining that differed sharply from European mining methods. As Ohio inspector Thomas Morrison explained to the Mine Inspectors' Institute in 1910, "The fact is, our system of mining is at fault." "In foreign countries," he pointed out, "mines are worked on what is known as the 'long-wall' system."[45]

Initially British mines had been shallow, and room-and-pillar (called pillar-and-stall) techniques were widely employed there too. But by the 1850s, as mines grew deeper and seams thinner, longwall mining was becoming increasingly widespread, as was documented by several parliamentary committees that investigated mine accidents. In the 1850s a select committee reported that "*long wall* working, which in some districts has been extensively used . . . is gradually making its way into all parts of the country." British mining experts were impressed with the safety of longwall methods, but the committee probably revealed the main reason for the spread of those methods when it noted that "for obtaining the greatest quantity of coal, the longwall system is preferable to any other." Thirty years later, in 1881, a royal commission investigating accidents heard similar testimony. Mine manager John Nixon told the commission that during the past fifteen years he had helped spread longwall techniques to South Wales. By the 1890s, while American mines continued to be developed using room-and-pillar techniques, most British miners probably labored in mines that used longwall methods.[46]

These contrasts in mining techniques led to sharp differences in worker safety. The fatality rate in British mines fell steadily in part because of the shift to longwall methods. Longwall mining concentrated underground workers along a relatively few coal faces, thereby reducing the costs of supervision. In addition, since proper mining required that the faces be advanced in coordinated manner, the payoff to supervision was considerable. Not surprisingly, therefore, British mines had a much higher ratio of supervisors to workers than was customary in the United States. Probably this is why one inspector told a royal commission on accidents in mines in 1881 that longwall methods improved discipline. Pennsylvania mine inspector Thomas Mather observed that British mines typically employed three fire bosses (gas inspectors) for every section of sixty-six men. "I would like to see the mine in Pennsylvania or any other state that would hire three fire-bosses for 66 men," he commented. Mather thought that the main reason for the comparative safety of British mines was the "close personal supervision of the mine at the face by inside officials . . . as they (the English) have a man on the ground looking out for trouble. That is the secret of their success."[47]

Longwall methods also resulted in less open work than room-and-pillar mining. Hence, as a parliamentary commission of the 1850s explained, they reduced roof falls and improved ventilation. Experience confirmed this judgment, as testimony to the royal commission of 1881 revealed. Inspector Thomas Evans testified that the relative safety of his district was due to the use of longwall techniques, while inspector T. E. Wales claimed that longwall mining had reduced gas accumulation in old workings, and that this was the principal reason for the decline in explosion fatalities. Longwall working also generated less coal dust than room-and-pillar methods, because there were no pillars to crumble. In addition, British coal seams were thin; in the United States thick seams led to coal roofs and floors, which also resulted in more coal dust.[48]

Inspector William Alexander told the commission that longwall mining was "much safer as regards falls." A miner, William Wight, who had some experience working with longwall methods, concurred with this judgment. And since longwall mining used roof pressure to bring down the coal, it required little blasting. Alfred Hewlett, who managed an eighty-five-hundred-man colliery, stressed that longwall mining needed "much less powder," while manager Richard Bedlington concluded that "the longwall has abolished powder as much as you can well do so." In 1894 the Pennsylvania inspector H. McDonald noted that the fatality rate from roof falls was higher in the United States than in Britain because coal was more likely to be blasted down here. In addition, as *Black*

Diamond pointed out, blasting the thick coal seams in this country required large quantities of powder.[49]

In 1909 yet another royal commission concluded that "the longwall system of working . . . has come more and more into use in all the coal fields of the United Kingdom, and where the conditions allow of its being followed there is no doubt that its adoption is characterized by less accidents from falls of ground." The main reasons, the commission thought, were that in longwall mining there was no pillar removal, roof was exposed for a much shorter period of time, and as a result timber stood for a shorter period. Other writers noted that the height of coal seams in the United States made roof support more difficult.[50]

British and American mines differed in other important ways too, and by the twentieth century, as table 2.1 makes clear, the contrasts had become striking. English operators employed relatively more men above ground than their American counterparts employed. If the same share of American as British mineworkers had labored above ground, American fatality rates would have been reduced about 4 percent. British mines were also far deeper and older than those in this country, and probably as a result productivity stagnated in Britain while it rose in the United states. British haulage techniques were also comparatively safe. Because older mines tended to have smaller shafts, British mine cars were petite in comparison with those in the United States, holding sometimes less than half a ton of coal. Haulage was usually done by endless rope and was much slower than in American mines. In addition, because a longwall mine was basically a circle, it required less haulage for a given tonnage than the room-and-pillar method required. Roof pressure also sometimes caused cutting machines to bind, which, along with the relatively low wages of British miners, slowed the spread of machine-cutting in Britain.[51]

These ideas can be illustrated by again referring to figure 1.3. In terms of the diagram, British mining evolved from point B on Q_1 to A on Q_0, and both risk and productivity declined. (Recall that both curves represent the same amount of output produced with different methods.) American production methods, by contrast, were going in the opposite direction at about the same time. As critics observed, American mines combined more favorable natural conditions with a higher fatality rate.

Comparing the safety of longwall and room-and-pillar mines in this country yields some insight into the contribution of mining methods to the differences between British and American mine safety. Illinois contained the largest concentration of longwall mines; about 8 percent of that state's coal was won by this method. It was also the only state that collected information on mining methods that allows comparison of their relative safety. Such a comparison, since it is within one state, is unaffected by differences in regulations, and less influenced than many interstate comparisons by extreme differences in geology. It is as close to a controlled experiment as the data permit.

During the period 1908–14, Illinois longwall mines had a fatality rate of 1.19 per thousand workers, compared with 2.31 for that state's room-and-pillar mines. And since longwall mines worked more days, the disparity in rates per 300-day worker is even more striking: 1.77 for longwall and 3.78 for room-and-pillar mines. In Britain over the same period the fatality rate per worker averaged about 1.36.[52]

While this analysis suggests that differences in mining methods account for much of the disparity in risks between British and American mining, Britain's mine safety legislation was also an important cause of its declining fatality rate. The first British safety regulations were contained in an act of 1850 that set up a staff of four inspectors and required operators to report fatalities. The law was strengthened in 1855 and again in 1860. These acts included general regulations governing ventilation, the lining of shafts, the maintenance of cages, and the use of safety lamps in gassy mines. They also required each operator to establish his own safety rules, which required approval by the inspector.

In 1887 two important modifications were incorporated into mining law. The owner, agent, or manager of the mine was made responsible for violations of the mining acts unless he could prove that he had taken "all reasonable means . . . to prevent . . . non-compliance." Under this new provision, top managers were routinely prosecuted and convicted. Although fines were modest—ranging from £2 to £10 for superintendents and owners—typically 80–90 percent of prosecutions were successful, and the law may have forced operators to take a more direct interest in the safety activities of subordinate officials. In addition, the act required systematic timbering and specified that the distance between props was not to exceed six feet. There is clear evidence that this rule had the desired effect. The death rate per thousand from roof falls had been falling slowly since 1873, no doubt as a result of the gradual extension of longwall mining. After passage of the new rules, the fatality rate plummeted from about 1.1 per thousand in the late 1880s to about 0.75 in the mid-1890s.[53]

In 1896 a law gave the secretary of state the power to prevent the use of any explosive in any mine, and the next year rules were promulgated that required the use of shot-firers and allowed only low-flame explosives to be used in gassy mines. In 1911 a major revision of the law prohibited the use of electricity in gassy mines and otherwise carefully governed its use. One result was that trolley haulage—which in the United States was becoming an increasingly important source of electrocutions, explosions, and haulage accidents—was effectively banned in Britain. Thus, by 1911 British regulations governed the major risks of mining. Certified bosses were required, and they and their superiors were held accountable for obeying the law and for setting out and following their own codes of rules. Ventilation, haulage, explosives, safety lamps, timbering, and electricity were all strictly regulated.[54]

Development of State Regulation, 1869–1910

As American coal mines developed in the mid-nineteenth century, they depended for much of their labor upon British immigrant miners. These men brought both their mining skills and their experience with successful safety regulation, and American laws therefore bore the imprint of British experience, although in highly imperfect fashion. The operators, of course, typically opposed regulation, and since mine safety was rarely a matter of public concern, they were usually able to stave off the miners' demands unless a major catastrophe generated sufficient public outcry to tip the balance in favor of state controls. This "regulation by outrage" was similar to the voluntarism Charles Francis Adams applied to the railroads, and it had similar defects, for both approaches relied on disaster. On railroads it was most effective in preventing wrecks that killed passengers, and in mining it emphasized prevention of fires and explosions, leaving most other dangers largely unregulated.

While safety regulation reflected an operator-miner battle in which the public occasionally intervened, operators invariably participated in drafting mine laws to prevent anything too radical, and some voluntarily went beyond the law. Miners, on the other hand, tended to support regulations that imposed safety requirements on the operators such as ventilation, the number of entries, and certification of managers and fire bosses. But they often opposed regulations governing blasting or the use of electric cap lamps, or other rules that might cut their incomes or reduce their freedom.

PENNSYLVANIA INNOVATES

On April 12, 1869, Pennsylvania became the first state to regulate mine safety. The miners, aided from time to time by the mining press, had been petitioning the legislature for a safety code since the 1850s, but all such efforts had been throttled by operator opposition. The law of 1869 applied only to anthracite mines in Schuylkill County. It established state mine inspection, required an "adequate amount of venti-lation," and mandated that ventilating furnaces should be constructed to "prevent ignition of coal." A fire boss was required, and he and the mine boss were generally charged with the safety of the mine. There were also a number of other general safety requirements. The empha-sis on ventilation and the concern with gas reflected the British laws of 1850 and 1855 as well as recent American experience, for as mines had become deeper, gas explosions had become more common.[55]

On September 6, 1869, a bit less than five months after the new law was passed, the Avondale mine shaft caught fire from the sparks of its ventilating furnace. Since it was a single-shaft opening, most of those inside were trapped. In all, 110 died. Avondale was located in Luzerne County, and so it was not subject to the 1869 law, which might have pre-vented the tragedy had its provisions been applicable and enforced. A second opening would also have saved the men. In 1870, with the press in an uproar and miners' petitions pouring in, the legislature strength-ened the safety code to require, among other things, double entries. Avondale thus began a long tradition in which tragedy led to the en-actment or tightening of mine safety regulations. In 1877, after years of petitions and investigations, regulation was extended to bituminous mines by an act modeled on the earlier anthracite legislation. It too was repeatedly strengthened to require certified bosses, better ventilation, and safety lamps.[56]

IMITATION IN REGULATION

In 1872, Illinois became the second state to pass a coal mine safety law. In its emphasis on ventilation and the prevention of disaster, the new law resembled that of Pennsylvania, but in a departure from that state's practice it failed to provide for mine inspection. Not until 1885—after a flood at the Diamond mine drowned sixty-nine miners—was state in-spection on the Pennsylvania model established. In Ohio the Avondale disaster immediately led to pressure for mine safety legislation, and as in Pennsylvania, local unions led the fight. Andrew Roy introduced a mine safety bill in 1871. In 1872, Ohio experienced its first major mine disaster when an explosion killed ten men, and in 1874 the governor signed a mine safety act and appointed Roy the first inspector.[57]

As elsewhere, the primary concern in Ohio was with ventilation. In his first annual report, Roy claimed that "the chief complaint of the miners was bad air. . . . They speak of it [the law] as the ventilation act." Roy later observed that "the miners care little for other needed reforms in mining in comparison with ventilation." In fact, he noted, they re-ferred to him as the "air inspector."[58]

As coal mining spread south and west in the 1880s, so did state regulatory efforts, but in most cases they were pale reflections of Pennsylvania's statutes. West Virginia's first mine law was passed in 1883, but certification of mine bosses was not required. As a result, when the Red Ash mine blew up in 1900, killing forty-nine men, the foreman had not known how much ventilation was required. Not until 1907 did West Virginia's law include such basic provisions as the requirement that gassy mines be operated with safety lamps.[59]

Colorado's first mining law of 1883 was routinely described by early inspectors as "very incomplete" and "wholly inadequate," for it governed little more than ventilation. Years later the state's chief inspector observed laconically that the state "didn't have any law before [1913]." A series of explosions in 1910 led to reform. The new law of 1913 was the product of a committee dominated by large operators such as Colorado Fuel and Iron, and it largely codified their practices. Wyoming's mine law came in 1886, right after a blast at a Union Pacific mine killed thirteen men. Utah passed a mine law after statehood in 1896. Its provisions governing explosions were strengthened after an explosion at the Winter Quarters mine in 1900 killed two hundred men, or about 16 percent of the state's miners.[60]

ASSESSING STATE SAFETY REGULATION

By the early 1890s, as table 2.6 reveals, every important coal-mining state had a safety code. Typically their primary focus was the prevention of explosions. Most governed ventilation and the number of openings, while some also regulated aspects of blasting and required certified mine managers and testing for gas. Most contemporaries believed that the laws were at least mildly beneficial. In 1890 *Colliery Engineer* attributed the "wonderful improvement" in the safety of Pennsylvania's anthracite mines to the legislation of 1869 and 1870. That state's bituminous mine law had "produced equally beneficial results," the editor asserted. In 1895 Kentucky's inspector also claimed that improvements in ventilation had been "chiefly wrought through the operations of the mining law."[61]

As noted above, market forces were also encouraging operators to prevent explosions, and some went beyond the law. Colorado's inspector noted that "Colorado Fuel and Iron ranks first in making improvements not compulsory or demanded by the law." Other inspectors also reported mines that voluntarily improved ventilation and made other attempts to prevent explosions. But whatever the gains wrought by state laws and market forces, they were unable to stem the sharp rise in fatality rates after 1880. Inspectors often claimed that the problem was

TABLE 2.6. Mine Safety Legislation, American States and Great Britain, 1913

	Date of Enactment[a]	Number of Inspectors	Number per Inspector	
			Mines	Miners
Alabama	1891	7	32	4,079
Arkansas	1889	1	53	4,652
Colorado	1883	5	34	2,398
Illinois	1872	12	44	6,827
Indiana	1879	6	39	4,844
Iowa	1873	3	68	6,867
Kansas	1883	6	25	3,224
Kentucky	1884	6	55	4,926
Maryland	1876	1	67	5,645
Missouri	1881	3	69	5,115
Montana	1889	1	43	3,630
New Mexico	1891	1	36	4,329
Ohio	1874	13	51	1,018
Oklahoma	1891	4	24	2,516
Pennsylvania				
Anthracite	1869	25	11	8,130
Bituminous	1877	30	50	6,621
Tennessee	1881	3	45	5,961
Texas	1907	1	27	5,101
Utah	1891	2	30	2,079
Virginia	1912	1	60	9,162
Washington	1883	2	27	2,887
West Virginia	1883	13	61	5,975
Wyoming	1886	2	31	4,166
Great Britain	1850	36	90	29,055

Source: State data are derived from Albert Fay, "Coal Mine Fatalities in the United States, 1870-1914," BM *Bulletin* 115 (Washington, D.C., 1916). British data are from Royal Commission on Safety in Coal Mines, *Appendices* (London, 1938), 3.

[a] Date the law was passed by legislature.

inadequate resources, but in fact resources were not the major problem. Pennsylvania's James Roderick was among the most dedicated and aggressive of state mine inspectors. Yet he was skeptical that additional manpower would greatly improve safety. "For all practical purposes, the number [of inspectors] is entirely sufficient," Roderick announced, and he pointed out that Pennsylvania had more inspectors per inside employee than any country in Europe.[62]

Table 2.6 reinforces Roderick's conclusion. The ratio of mines and miners to inspectors for each state and for Great Britain in (about) 1913 demonstrates that by British standards, most states had an adequate number of inspectors. Data on inspections per mine from the few states for which such data are available also show similarity to British practice. Statistical analysis (see note) also supports Roderick's contention. The decline in the ratio of inspectors to mines from a peak in 1884 to a trough in 1904 probably raised risks about 10 percent.[63]

The great failing of state inspection resulted from the legislation, which was incomplete, poorly written, and hard to enforce. In Britain, where mining laws were a national matter, operator influence was diluted, and regulations governed the main hazards of mining. American state law, by contrast, bore the strong imprint of operator influence. The product of disaster, it focused mostly on the prevention of explosions and failed to address other important risks of mining. By all accounts, Pennsylvania had the best mine laws and inspectors in the country. Yet it had no means to prevent roof falls, even though they were the leading cause of fatalities. Similarly, trolley haulage was all but unregulated, and there was not even the semblance of an electrical code until 1911. Even explosion risks were inadequately addressed, for no state law regulated all the sources of ignition.[64]

Poor drafting also undercut the provisions of some laws. Neither operators nor miners liked safety lamps, which yielded little light and therefore reduced productivity. Accordingly, Pennsylvania's law required their use only in gassy parts of mines. It also prohibited use of electricity where safety lamps were employed, which sharply increased the costs of employing safety lamps, thereby discouraging their use. One inspection committee reported that "if we enforce the discontinuance of electrical machinery, they will discontinue the use of safety lamps . . . [which] would leave reasonable grounds for the discontinuance of permissible explosives and . . . shotfirers." The committee concluded that "to comply with the letter of the law . . . would, in our opinion, render the mines much less safe than they are at present."[65]

Most state laws necessarily contained broadly written provisions that allowed inspectors some discretion. This discretion meant that the laws might be stretched, but it contributed to enforcement difficulties. Again, Pennsylvania's efforts to prevent explosions supplies examples. The law required coal to be "properly undercut," which in 1904 James Roderick interpreted to mean that solid shooting must be banned. He was met with a "storm of censure and criticism." In 1909 Roderick attempted another broad reading of the law, urging inspectors to forbid the use of black powder in gassy and dusty mines "if *in your opinion* . . . [its use] is a menace to life." This too yielded a storm of protest. The miners opposed the use of low-flame explosives because they were more expensive than black powder and yielded less lump coal. The men struck, and Roderick backed down.[66]

Administrative procedures added to these problems of enforcement. In 1906 one West Virginia inspector complained of the delays he faced in trying to get an injunction requiring a mine to improve ventilation. He also noted that "a coal company in this region is able to bring [an] unlimited number of witnesses, who are willing to testify anything, against the state." In most states fines for violations were trivial—Kansas provided no penalty for violating the provision against solid shooting—and in contrast to the situation in Britain, top managers were largely immune from prosecution. Trying to put the best face on matters, West Virginia's chief inspector, James W. Paul, announced what could well have been the motto of every inspector in the country: "The law is not wholly ignored in any part of the state."[67]

Twentieth-Century Disasters

The culmination of these events came in 1907. Even before December it had been a bad year: two hundred men had been killed in ten major explosions. But as matters turned out, this was merely a tune-up. Pennsylvania inspector Henry Louttit had been worried about the Naomi mine, which was in Fayette City, just south of Pittsburgh. It was known to be gassy and to be worked with open lights and bare electric wires, even on the return air current. In November 1906 he had received a letter from Francis Feehan, president of United Mine Workers District 5, forwarding a miners' complaint that the mine needed better ventilation and that there was a "constant danger of serious explosion." Louttit wrote the foreman and visited the mine himself and found that it was indeed gassy and poorly ventilated. He visited the mine in February, May, and August 1907 and repeatedly warned about its ventilation. On November 18 Louttit again wrote the foreman, calling his attention especially to ventilation and urging that he keep the mine in "legal condition" at all times. The foreman replied the same day, informing Louttit that "the law is being complied with." On the evening of December 1, at about 7:45 P.M., Naomi exploded. Someone had left a door open, causing a gas accumulation. The normal workforce in Naomi was about 350 men. Fortunately, December 1 was a Sunday and the evening force included only thirty-four men, every one of whom, however, was killed.[68]

The aftermath at Monongah, West Virginia, where on December 6, 1907, the worst coal-gas and dust explosion in American history killed 362 men. *(National Archives)*

Five days later the employees in Monongah (West Virginia) mines no. 6 and 8 were not so lucky. The mines had been connected—which saved the expense of second openings but effectively doubled the number of men at risk. Three hundred and sixty-two men died there. Ventilation at the face was poor, and the mine was dusty and gassy, but open lights were used, and the men did their own blasting with black powder. A little more than two weeks later the next tragedy struck, at the Yolande (Alabama) mine no. 1. The mine had not been inspected for gas, and a miner's open lamp touched off a blast that killed fifty-seven men.[69]

Next to go was Pittsburgh Coal's Darr mine in Jacob's Creek, Pennsylvania. Inspector John Bell visited Darr in May 1906. It was dry and very dusty, and he immediately wrote both the foreman and the superintendent, warning them to use safety lamps, for he had also found gas in "dangerous quantities." Superintendent Archibald Black replied, assuring Bell that the mining laws would be carried out. In February 1907 and again in June the inspector wrote Black, warning him of poor conditions and receiving the same soothing response that all would soon be well. In September he again urged Black to "take steps at once to have the ventilation increased." "I will take this matter up," Black cooed. On December 19 a blown-out shot or open light touched off the gas and dust, killing all but one of the 240 men at work. The last day of the year was marked by three blown-out shots that ignited the dust in the Bernal mine in Carthage, New Mexico, and killed eleven more men.[70]

A few observers had seen these disasters coming. *Colliery Engineer* had been warning of the dangers of coal dust for a decade. Pennsylvania chief inspector James Roderick also had a premonition of disaster. Writing to Ohio inspector James T. Beard on December 7, 1907, before Darr exploded, Roderick said, "I have been in dread for months about the conditions of the mines in the western part of this State and have made every consistent effort to remedy matters, but have met a stumbling block each time in that the law does not give me the right to interfere." Nor were European observers surprised by this latest evidence of American recklessness. *Colliery Guardian* summarized conditions at Monongah, observing that "it would be difficult to find a combination of circumstances more favorable to an explosion."[71]

But the coal operators appeared genuinely thunderstruck. A. B. Fleming, the operator of Monongah, seemed in shock when he testified to the House Committee on Mines and Mining in March 1908. Monongah had been one of their safest and best mines, Fleming said, and he had no idea why it blew. "Another such explosion as we have had would kill us all," he testified. A writer in the *Engineering and Mining Journal* claimed that "there is not one experienced operator in this field who would heretofore have believed that a disaster of such magnitude [as Monongah] could have occurred in the Fairmont district."[72]

Federal interest in coal mine disasters had begun, in a small way, in 1904. Under the guidance of Joseph A. Holmes, the Technologic Branch of the United States Geological Survey started to investigate mine explosions. This produced a timely report in 1907 in which Holmes stressed the need for a better understanding of the causes of explosions. He thought that conditions would continue to worsen "unless information obtained through comprehensive and impartial investigations may serve . . . as an intelligent basis both for legislative enactments and for agreements among persons associated with mining operations."[73]

Western metal miners had been campaigning for a federal department or bureau of mines for years. The disasters of 1907 led the coal operators and the United Mine Workers to join the fight, and after much bickering a bill was finally passed in 1910. The bureau had no power of inspection or supervision. Instead, it reflected the tradition that explosions resulted from operator ignorance. Its purposes were "to conduct scientific investigations especially with a view to preventing the loss of life and waste of resources which now characterize and bring discredit upon American mining." A sum of $500,000 was appropriated, of which $200,000 was to be used to investigate the causes of explosions.[74]

Conclusion

Throughout the late nineteenth century, British mine safety steadily improved as operators shifted to longwall techniques and safety regulations were tightened. American mine safety, by contrast, deteriorated sharply. At the turn of the century the English *Colliery Guardian* concluded that American mining methods revealed a "general disregard for life that would never be tolerated here." As on the railroads, the worsening of mining risks resulted from the evolution of a peculiarly American system of production. Changes in technology resulted in larger, deeper, more mechanized mines, while changes in the market for coal and coal mine labor shifted employment to the more dangerous regions of the South and West. Miners' skills also deteriorated, while the market raised the premium on solid shooting. These developments led to an erosion of safety that swamped state regulatory efforts. American mine laws focused largely on disaster prevention, but they were poorly written, weakly enforced, and inherently unable to stimulate managerial commitment to safety.[75]

The miner's traditional freedom blunted operator interest in safety, and this tradition was reinforced by liability rules that made most accidents cheap. Market forces did encourage some efforts to prevent explosions, but even these were weak. The causes of such disasters were only imperfectly understood, and a truly effective program of prevention would have been expensive and would have required a level of managerial control over blasting and other aspects of work that would have been little short of revolutionary. The Bureau of Mines was established to discover and disseminate information on the causes of mine dangers, and its efforts are detailed in chapter 6.

CHAPTER THREE

MANUFACTURING DANGERS

The Development of the Work Safety Movement
1880–1925

Among the many objects to which a wise and free people find it necessary to direct their
attention, that of providing for their safety seems to be the first.
JOHN JAY, THE FEDERALIST PAPERS, 1787

Safety, in order to be successful, must be a business and not a charity.
NATIONAL ASSOCIATION OF MANUFACTURERS, 1917

We lead the world by miles in accident prevention. We lead the world
by leagues in accident occurrence.
ROYAL MEEKER, PENNSYLVANIA DEPARTMENT OF LABOR AND INDUSTRIES, 1923

Frederick Hoffman, a statistician working for the Bureau of Labor
Statistics (BLS), estimated that there were perhaps twenty-five thousand workplace fatalities in America in 1908—a figure he advanced
as little better than a guess, for no comprehensive, accurate statistics
existed. Crystal Eastman and other writers put flesh on these statistical bones. In *Work Accidents and the Law* Eastman recounted the fate of
Adam Rogalas, a Russian immigrant. He had been employed at a grain
elevator in Pittsburgh when, on October 17, 1906, the floor above his
workplace gave way and he was crushed. Rogalas left a wife and four
children. The company offered to settle with his wife for $400, but she
refused and brought suit for $20,000. Six months later she lost the case
and received nothing. The journalist William Hard described the fate
of John Zolnowski, who was nearly burned to death and was left permanently disabled while cleaning an open-hearth furnace. He too recovered nothing because, a court ruled, he had voluntarily assumed the
risk of his job. "Steel is War," Hard wrote; "machines . . . make business
one long war." "Is the public concerned?" he wondered. "If it says it is,
then it is." [1]

Hard and Eastman were describing the results of a workplace made extraordinarily dangerous by nineteenth-century industrialization. But even as they wrote, that world was passing away, for a quiet revolution in work safety was already beginning. Why early industrialization proved so dangerous and what institutional and attitudinal changes underlay the new work-safety movement during the twentieth century are the topics of this chapter.

The Machine Age and the Industrial Worker

In the first half of the nineteenth century, Americans developed an industrial technology sufficiently distinct that Europeans described it as an American system of manufacturing. Like the American systems of railroading and mining described earlier, it evolved in part as a response to conditions of labor and capital scarcity and resource abundance. In manufacturing, its defining characteristics were the extensive use of highly specialized powered machinery and the production of goods with interchangeable parts. In industry after industry, the new technology of water- and then steam-powered machines increasingly displaced older, more labor-intensive methods, enormously increasing the scale of production. The average size of plants rose sharply, and in some industries giants appeared. Iron, for example, had once been produced on small plantations and worked in blacksmith shops. By 1900 the largest plants in that industry employed between eight thousand and ten thousand workers.[2]

Some who reflected on such matters thought that these changes had worsened the safety of work, for by the twentieth century, as fragmentary data attest, manufacturing dangers had risen to extraordinary levels. At DuPont the fatality rate hovered around 3.7 per million man-hours (table A3.3), while the Pennsylvania Railroad shops recorded a rate of serious injuries of nearly 9 per thousand *per month*. "Previous to the introduction of machinery into modern industry," wrote the New York State Compensation Commission in 1910, "industrial accidents were relatively few and unimportant." In the same year David Van Schaack, a safety engineer for Aetna and soon to be president of the National Safety Council, agreed that there had been an "increasing danger to life and limb involved in the pursuit of industrial occupations." A decade later a safety engineer for the Travelers Insurance Company made roughly the same point. "In every industry the substitution of mechanical devices for manual methods has introduced corresponding elements of danger," he claimed. Some businessmen agreed. In 1913 Leslie Robertson of Ford Motor Company told the National Association of

Reenactment of an injury that occurred in the 1920s at the Pennsylvania Railroad shops, Philadelphia. *(Courtesy Hagley Museum and Library)*

Manufacturers (NAM), "It is a far cry from the . . . old hand drill . . . to the present day machinery of a large industrial plant, but the element of injury has been ever present in an increasing ratio as modern development and methods have been utilized."[3]

These dangers were the outcome of technological change under a system of employers' liability that made work accidents cheap enough to ignore. Factories operated under the same legal protection provided to nineteenth-century railroads and mine operators whose employees were injured or killed on the job, and they were largely shielded from damage claims by the evolving system of employers' liability law. Crystal Eastman surveyed the compensation paid to dependents of 235 married men killed in work accidents and found that 53 percent received only the funeral expenses and others not even that. Even where the dependent received something, the amount was usually pitifully small, and most settlements or awards were accompanied by long delays. As a result, the development of production methods focused on economizing labor or capital, or on expanding output, largely without reference to worker safety. To take but one example, the universal milling machine evolved in response to the need for expanded production during the Civil War, and its gears and point of operation were rarely guarded. Other new machines and processes had similar origins, moving Ohio's factory inspector to complain that "the inventors of machinery do not seem to look beyond the perfection of production and the important matter of safety to life and limb has been entirely ignored."[4]

Not only had industry become more dangerous; American industry was preeminent in the world in the "maiming and mangling and killing of those who attempt to earn their bread in the sweat of their faces," or so former commissioner of labor Charles P. Neill told the National Safety Council in 1913. About the same time, businessman John Calder also admitted that "in this matter [of accident prevention], the United States has lagged considerably behind Great Britain, Germany and France." In 1920 another former commissioner of labor, Royal Meeker, claimed that American producers still led the world in injuries. There is only modest statistical support for these claims, for data problems make international comparisons difficult. Iron and steel work was riskier in this country than in Germany (see below). In addition, fragmentary American figures (table A3.4) yield manufacturing fatality rates well above 0.20 per thousand workers in the years before World War I. In British manufacturing over about the same period, rates ranged between 0.16 and 0.21 per thousand, and in France risks were similar.[5]

A CATALOG OF INDUSTRIAL RISK

First there was the power itself. In the 1830s the steam engine had begun to replace water and animals and human muscle as a source of industrial power. High-pressure engines were profligate of wood but much cheaper to build than those with low-pressure boilers. With fuel cheap and interest rates high, Americans adopted the high-pressure engine, while in Europe, with the circumstances reversed, the low-pressure engine predominated. Almost immediately boilers started blowing up, and those with high pressure were especially lethal. A Treasury report of 1838 listed four explosions of stationary boilers to date with ten dead. As use of steam spread, so did explosions. Since many boilers were located in small rural establishments, the blast usually claimed only a few lives. But larger establishments in urban areas were a different story. The "Hague Street Disaster" in New York City killed sixty-seven workers in 1850; in 1867 a boiler explosion in Philadelphia killed twenty-eight. That same year marked the foundation of the Hartford Steam Boiler Inspection and Insurance Company, a firm devoted entirely to matters of boiler safety.[6]

Early boiler explosions resulted in part from the fact that neither the properties of iron nor those of high-pressure steam were widely understood. As late as 1882 the Hartford Steam Boiler Company announced yet another theory of boiler explosions, sarcastically noting that "the periodical 'explosion idiot' has again put in an appearance." In addition, some boilers were simply poorly made, and poor maintenance and operation remained common. The Hartford Company complained that boiler tenders, especially at small firms, were often inexperienced. Farmers who used steam-powered threshers after the Civil War were often ignorant of the most basic safety procedures, and boiler explosions soon began to mark the harvest season. Gilbert Lathrop told of being hired in 1880 at age sixteen as a boiler attendant by his uncle— "who knew as little about a steam boiler as I did." Lathrop later recalled one time when he had added water to a near-empty boiler: "When the cold water hit those red hot plates, steam began blowing from . . . every seam . . . and the boiler visibly swelled. But that was all." He concluded that "God was watching out for me that day." But God did not always come to the rescue. When the boilers exploded in the Philadelphia dye works of Gaffney and Nolan on June 1, 1881, killing three people and injuring six, the Hartford Company described the engineer as "wholly inexperienced . . . entirely ignorant . . . [and] intemperate."[7]

Many employers also encouraged overfiring as an alternative to purchasing a larger boiler, in effect trading away safety to save capital. The Hartford estimated that between 1883 and 1907, exploding boilers killed over seven thousand individuals; by contrast, boilers killed about seven hundred people in Britain and four hundred in Germany over the same period. The company thought that this disparity was not simply due to the number of boilers involved or to better reporting in this country but in fact represented an "indictment against the United States."[8]

Power distribution throughout the mill was even more dangerous than its generation, although usually less spectacular in its effects. Louis Ernst, a sixteen-year-old boy working in an Ohio mill on October 1, 1888, was caught by the steam engine crosshead and thrown with such force that he was killed. From the engine, power flowed first to a flywheel and then throughout the mill via a maze of shafts, gears, counter-shafts, pulleys, and belts, each with its own dangers. Flywheels could burst, with lethal results, and larger, faster flywheels were disproportionately deadly. Aetna Insurance Company reported one nine-ton flywheel, twenty feet in diameter, that ran out of control, killing two men and injuring ten while demolishing its powerhouse and the next-door armory and damaging several railroad cars, an icehouse, and a hotel. When the first safety department was created at Joliet Steel in 1892, its first official act was to order an inspection of all flywheels.[9]

Belts and pulleys were usually designed without a margin of safety, and slippage or breakage were both routine and dangerous. The shafting, turning at hundreds of revolutions per minute, could catch clothing, throwing the individual with enough force to kill. Andrew Jubreed, who worked for Carnegie Steel, was one such unfortunate. On April 19, 1907, he was caught in a shaft—around which there was no guard—and killed. Early shafting was made of wood, and the pulley was simply a built-up section of the shaft. Such an improvisation would often throw its belt, which would then wrap around the shaft, either breaking the belt or firing the countershaft across the mill. Protruding set screws made collar shafts especially deadly. On August 21, 1906, Walter Calhoun was working above some elevated shafting, painting the ironwork for Carnegie Steel. His coat was caught on a set screw, wrapping him around the spinning shaft and killing him. It is no wonder that in 1913 *Textile World* listed the Allen recessed set screw as an important safety invention.[10]

Pulleys, belts, and gears transmitted power to the machines, and any one of them could catch an unwary worker. To start a machine, a worker shifted the belt from the idler to the drive pulley; if the operation was done without the aid of a belt shifter, he risked being caught. Fred Colvin, editor of *American Machinist*, described what usually happened when a beginner tried to put on a belt with a quarter-turn in it: "As soon as he got it on (remember that the shaft pulley was always in motion), off it would fly immediately and wrap itself around the machinist and his lathe." Although this may sound comic, Ohio's factory inspector reported that on August 27, 1888, Michael Schlarth had tried to throw off a belt and was caught between it and the pulley and instantly killed.[11]

In the 1850s British investigators touring American industries remarked with awe on the extent of mechanization, and they described in some detail the machinery they saw. Safety features were never mentioned. Thirty years later the 1880 Census depicted a host of new machines that were transforming metal- and woodworking. None had guards either on their gears or at the point of operation. Such machinery was dangerous even at rest, for vibration would sometimes cause a belt to shift spontaneously from the idle pulley into drive. William Hard recounted the fate of Sarah Knisley, who worked in a hardware factory surrounded by unguarded cogwheels. One day she caught her hand and was drawn into the gears. Her entire left arm had to be amputated. A court awarded her no compensation because, of course, she had known of the risk.[12]

Large metal planes that slid back and forth on a fixed bed acted like a giant pair of scissors on anyone caught between the bed and the plane. A worker who bent down at the wrong time, perhaps to retrieve an object dropped into the bed, would lose a hand or an arm. Punch presses had to be hand-fed, and if the operator failed to remove a hand before activating the press—the result of a moment's lapse of concentration—the machine would shear off a finger, or two, or sometimes most of the hand. To make matters worse, when parts wore, some presses would spontaneously repeat. Buick factory no. 12 lopped off thirty fingers in the first six months of 1919. Other companies had even worse records. At the peak of wartime production in 1917, eight workers lost fingers in a single day at one metal-stamping plant.[13]

Woodworking machines were even more dangerous, for they operated at higher speeds, and were no more likely to be guarded. In 1892 Minnesota's factory inspector complained that the ripsaw had been around fifty years and had killed and maimed thousands of workers before anything was done to guard it. And where guards existed, their use seems to have been rare. Surface planers (joiners) developed an especially evil reputation. The head was square, not round, thereby ensuring that an injury would remove several fingers or a hand rather than just a piece of flesh. In June 1888 an Ohio woodworker, Frederick Freer, aged twenty-two, lost all of the fingers of his left hand to a joiner. The next year that state's factory inspector called the joiner "the most dangerous piece of work-working machinery in existence," while Maine's inspector claimed that it had "maimed more men for life than all other machinery in woodworking establishments combined." George Orris of the Carpenters Union recounted the story of a wood shaper that tossed its knife fifty feet, cutting the throat of a workman. Orris also told the story of one woodworkers' local where the president would say, when a motion was on the floor, "All those in favor make it known by holding up your stumps."[14]

With machinery, as with flywheels, scale mattered. Small grinding wheels presented little danger. Yet large high-speed grinding wheels, if they cracked, could explode, killing or maiming anyone in the immediate vicinity. Similarly, small power saws were dangerous mainly to the fingers. More powerful saws could kick back the wood with sufficient force to kill. An early treatise on woodworking machinery claimed that American saws were more likely to kick back than their European counterparts because of the long rip fences on American machines. One writer described the workings of a sawmill edger as follows: "Not only does it frequently kill its operator, but no one in the vicinity is safe when it starts to throw or kick back a piece of board." Moses Gaskill was running a resaw in an Ohio mill in October 1888 when it rammed a stick through his neck at the base of his skull, killing him. In logging, safety deteriorated as steam-powered highline skidders introduced early in the twentieth century to snake out timber proved more dangerous than older methods. One safety man reported that his shop foreman had vowed to kill on sight the man who invented the steam skidder.[15]

In meat packing, mechanization led to the use of machines that even sounded dangerous. There were guillotines. Hashers lived up to their name, having "probably been the cause of more amputations than any single item." Company safety experts thought that the "head splitter" was much more dangerous than the old hand cleaver. In steam laundries the mangle also earned its title: in 1894 Maine's factory inspector reported that eleven women in the state had lost fingers in one year. In the words of one historian, "Mechanization had transformed paper making from a relatively safe craft to a relatively dangerous industry." In 1922 one writer claimed that the finishing room in a paper mill "contains a more diversified assortment of finger crushers, arm removers, and bone breakers than any [other] place of its size in any large industry in the world." In both paper and rubber mills the giant calender rolls could catch a man in the bite. Ernest Beck of U.S. Rubber was told that in the days before safeguarding, men working alone had gone completely through the rolls with no one the wiser until remnants of them and their clothing were found in the pan below.[16]

Even in textiles, which had long been mechanized, power use accelerated, as did the number of machines per worker. When faster looms threw a shuttle, they threw it harder and farther—sometimes as far as thirty feet. In addition, American mills packed in more looms than European mills, thereby leading to more thrown shuttles. Clearances and aisles also shrank, which lessened a worker's chances of escaping the machines. One of them caught fourteen-year-old Carmelia Teoli, who was scalped by the gears of a spinning frame at American Woolen in July 1909. She received no compensation, although the company paid her medical bill. In Massachusetts, textiles led all other industries in the proportion of injuries due to machinery.[17]

While construction techniques remained largely unmechanized, steam shovels and derricks brought new dangers to excavation work.

But more important was the growth of large-scale projects. Tunnel and caisson work could give a worker the bends, and a representative of the rock drillers and compressed-air workers told the New York State Commission on Employers' Liability that 250 out of the nearly 700 members of his local would get the bends in a "good" year for tunnel work. One of the men, he reported, "is bent over . . . nearly at right angles . . . and he can never get over that." The previous year, which the union representative termed "a very slack time," had seen seven men killed on the job out of about four hundred at work, the implied annual fatality rate being 17.5 per thousand workers. Other construction unions told the commission similar stories. In five years, 130 of 2,500 members of a structural-iron workers' union were killed on the job, an annual fatality rate of 10.4 per thousand. The rate for excavators was even higher: 18.1 per thousand (in five years workplace fatalities claimed 632 out of about 7,000 members), and the steam fitters announced that while their membership had risen 200 percent over the previous decade, their injuries had increased 500 percent.[18]

The rapid electrification of urban areas that began in the 1880s created new jobs, many of which were extraordinarily risky. Worst of all were the dangers to outside electrical workers who put up poles and transformers and strung wires. Steadily rising voltage made their lives increasingly dangerous, and every month *Electrical Worker* carried a long list of casualties. In September 1900, Local 21 in Philadelphia reported three deaths in the previous three months; Local 34 of Cleveland listed one death from electrocution and one from a fall; Local 20 of New York listed two killed by electrocution. In 1907, Local 20 was able to obtain a risk premium of 25 cents per day. Those workers earned the money: in 1908 another New York City local had sixteen out of eighty members killed on the job.[19]

Of course, not all new techniques worsened workers' risks. Steam shovels and derricks might bring new dangers to construction, but they may also have reduced the need for men to work in dangerous trenches and excavations. In woodworking, the shift from up-and-down to circular saws in the early nineteenth century greatly worsened the risks from kickback, but the subsequent introduction of bandsaws again reduced dangers. Freight elevators accounted for many deaths, but whether they were more or less dangerous than stairs is not clear. Moreover, data from the early part of the twentieth century invariably reveal that no more than half of all injuries stemmed from the use of machinery. However, many of those that resulted from falls and spills and burns were probably a result of the new techniques and increasing scale of modern production. And power and machines accounted for a disproportionate share

A young textile worker demonstrates how another boy lost his arm on the job. *(Author's collection)*

of the most serious accidents. In textiles, three-fourths of severe accidents stemmed from the use of machines, and other machine-intensive industries yielded similar results.[20]

Work practices as well as technology shaped the safety of work. In the nineteenth-century factory, most managers above the level of foreman had concerned themselves rather little with the details of the factory floor. This was the domain of the foreman; he hired and fired at will, and labor turnover was high, especially among the unskilled. Craftsmen were the aristocrats of labor. They handed down trades from father to son and in some cases supervised their own helpers. Dangerous practices were sometimes part of the craftsman's code; they were traditional, and they reflected his manliness. Factory inspectors complained that workers often refused to use safety devices simply because they were new. Foremen, who were themselves the product of such traditional methods of instruction, provided some training and supervision for machine tenders and unskilled workers. But neither safety instruction nor rules seem to have been common. Each employee was expected to look out for himself, and individual workers decided such important details as what clothing to wear, where to stand when dressing a drive belt, or how to feed a saw.

By the 1890s, as production methods became more capital-intensive, employers became increasingly concerned with "soldiering," and they reached down to control the shop floor. The period saw widespread experimentation with piece rates and bonus plans, culminating in Frederick Winslow Taylor's system of scientific management. The aim of all such schemes was to increase production, and work safety remained largely an individual responsibility, outside the employer's purview. Yet because production involved coordination between workers, it became all but impossible for any single employee to look out for himself. Dangerous work was an inevitable outcome. In an increasingly mechanized and interdependent workplace, with high labor turnover and many hazards that were plant-specific, and with the boss pressing for higher output, risks abounded.[21]

Repairmen, for example, were often injured by having an operator start up the machine they were attempting to fix, and electrical workers were killed when someone would activate a line on which they were working. Workers also took chances, and they were rewarded for it if they lived. One safety expert claimed that piece rates led textile workers to the dangerous practice of cleaning moving equipment. A representative of the building trades also asserted that piece rates increased accidents. The superintendent of a cement plant reported that a pusher, who was paid by the barrel, removed the screen from a screw conveyer to speed up the job. He fell in and was killed.[22]

Few nineteenth-century manufacturing industries were more completely transformed by new techniques than iron and steel, and by the time Hard and Eastman were writing, few were more dangerous. In 1907, the first year for which any statistics are available, the American industry had a death rate of 0.7 per million manhours. By contrast, the German steel industry had a death rate of about 0.2 per million manhours at about the same time. The source of the American statistics—Lucian Chaney of the BLS—probably knew more about safety in iron and steel than anyone else in the country, and he thought that the headlong drive to increase output had increased accident rates in the years before 1907. Other writers also believed that the new techniques used to expand production had worsened workers' risks.[23]

The scene after a blast-furnace mishap at Cambria Steel, Johnstown, Pennsylvania, 1914. Making work at blast furnaces extremely risky were the multiple hazards of hot metal, asphyxiation, and (here) explosion. *(Courtesy Hagley Museum and Library)*

Four developments eroded the safety of steel work. First, blast furnaces grew rapidly in scale. In 1880 a large furnace might have been 75 feet high and 20 feet in diameter at the bosh (the largest part); by 1900, furnaces 110 feet tall and 22 feet in diameter were common. Because furnaces were top-loaded, the higher they grew, the worse were the risks to workers from falls or falling materials. Higher blast rates were also introduced. This "hard driving" of large furnaces led to spectacular increases in output, but it also brought unprecedented dangers. Should the material in the furnace hang up and then slip, an explosion might blow the top off the furnace, killing or injuring the top fillers and possibly the men below as well. "I remember the time when the operation of the blast furnace was not a hazardous occupation and likewise I have seen it become a very hazardous operation," commented J. H. Ayres of National Tube in 1915.[24]

In one especially deadly accident, "a slip caused the dust catcher to burst, and the escaping gas formed a sheet of flame which fatally burned five men and injured four others." Increasing furnace size led to more violent slips, while the shift to fine-textured Mesabi ores increased their frequency. In addition, higher pressures and temperatures increased the risk of breakout—a rupture of the furnace wall. In a "typical" breakout, "without warning iron came through the jacket into the ditch, which had only about six inches of water in it, where it caused an explosion. One man was killed and another seriously injured." One engineer summarized the results of these newer furnaces: "It was found that design and capacity had . . . gone beyond the limit of control [leading to] slips of undreamed of violence, . . . [while] bosh failures became features of practice, and . . . breakouts were not infrequent." In 1910, blast furnaces had a fatality rate one-third higher than the iron and steel industry average.[25]

The substitution of Bessemer steel for puddled wrought iron as the industry's main product also worsened worker risks. Puddling was a hot, dirty, highly skilled job, and it required enormous strength. But it was not very dangerous. In 1910 the Labor Department study showed no fatalities out of a total of about thirteen hundred workers in puddling plants. Bessemer-steel production, by contrast, was every bit as dangerous as it looked, the worst risks being from explosions and spills of hot metal. As J. H. Ayres told the National Safety Council in 1916, "The adoption of the Bessemer process was accompanied by great sacrifice of life and limb." In 1910 its fatality rate was the highest of any department in the industry.[26]

A third factor contributing to higher risk was that steel fabrication became increasingly mechanized after 1880, and the new machinery brought new dangers. Mechanized rolling yielded fewer minor accidents than the older hand-rolling process, but it yielded more severe accidents. In 1910 the death rate in mechanical rolling was precisely twice that in hand-rolling. Finally, as in anthracite mining, technological change raised risks by reducing the share of safe jobs. The Labor Department divided workers into "productive" occupations, which were directly connected with steelmaking and were relatively dangerous, and such "nonproductive" and comparatively safe jobs as mechanics, the yard force, and the electrical department. The introduction of mechanical materials handling and of machinery that needed fewer repairs reduced the proportion of nonproductive workers in one plant from about 50 percent in 1905 to 30 percent in 1910, thereby raising the average injury rate.[27]

These risks were unique to steel work. But steelmaking also exposed employees to most of the other dangers that had become common to large-scale factory production. The increase in plant scale meant that hundreds of unguarded walkways high above the factory floor could produce fatal falls. Arthur H. Young, who went on to a distinguished career as a safety expert and who virtually founded the field of industrial personnel relations, began work at age thirteen in 1896, at the Joliet works of Illinois Steel. On his first day he was required to climb a ladder to oil a spinning shaft high above the factory floor. "I still have distinctly a feeling of horror," he recalled many years later. "There was absolutely no thought given to safety."[28]

In addition, cranes could drop materials, or the craneman or repairman could fall, or the crane might run over a worker. Boilers, flywheels, shafts, gears, belts, and pulleys, as well as presses, grinding wheels, and other metalworking machines, were abundant and unguarded. Steel mills even had carpentry shops with their own peculiar risks from saws, planers, and joiners. Finally, a steel mill was also a railroad yard; the South Chicago works of Illinois Steel had about 130 miles of track that presented all of the dangers associated with railroading of that era plus one more: because the steel yards were not engaged in interstate commerce, the old link-and-pin coupler was still used.[29]

Steelworkers' risks, like those of other workers, depended on work practices as well as technology. The ability of skilled craftsmen to control the "stint"—the speed and amount of work—declined in the late nineteenth century, and employers increasingly controlled work processes. Gang foremen, called "pushers," drove the men to get the maximum of work from them, and safety suffered as a result. And here too each man's safety also depended on the actions of other workers, yet no one assumed ultimate responsibility. William Hard recounted the story of four men who were killed when molten iron came through the side of a blast furnace. It seems that when the firebrick had fallen out, someone patched the hole with fire clay, which wore out rapidly.[30]

Not all changes in work practices or technology worsened steelworkers' risks. The introduction of skip hoists to load blast furnaces, although they increased the dangers from mechanical sources, probably improved safety on balance by eliminating the need for top fillers, who had run a prodigious risk from asphyxiation. But the net impact of all these changes almost certainly reduced safety. A statistical analysis (see note), based on departmental data for the steel industry in 1910 indicates that after controlling for department and the presence of a safety organization, larger plants had sharply higher injury frequency rates. Given the growth in plant size, these large plants must have been comparatively new, and if so, the industry's injury rate must have been rising.[31]

In 1883 the New Jersey Bureau of Labor solicited the views of working people on the conditions of their lives. Many urged the need for compulsory education; others worried about their co-workers' addiction to drink. They complained about poverty, the power of capital, and their long hours of work. Some worried that they would be displaced by machinery or convict labor. Many of the workers whom the survey quoted came from dangerous and unhealthy trades. There were carpenters and iron miners, iron molders and machinists, glassworkers and hatters. Yet except for the cigar makers, who complained about tobacco dust, no one commented on the unhealthful or dangerous nature of the work.[32]

Other state surveys yielded similar results. Nor did workers very often strike to improve work safety. In a series of reports on strikes and lockouts, the U.S. commissioner of labor reported the causes of strikes by industry and year from 1881 through 1900. Even in the most dangerous industries, safety was almost never the dominant motive for a strike. In the building trades the report listed a total of nearly forty-two thousand strikes, which it attributed to more than 250 causes over this period. One was against the violation of city regulations, and another was for better safety. In coal and coke it reported 14,575 strikes attributed to more than three hundred causes. More than nine thousand directly involved wages, and many more were indirectly over matters of compensation. There were six strikes for better ventilation, one against using an unsafe mining machine, one to enforce a state rule governing timbering, and one to get a new safety catch on an elevator cage. There were also five opposing the introduction of a new safety lamp and one to allow smoking in the mine during lunch. Other industries suggest even fewer safety-motivated strikes.[33]

Of course, safety may have been part of the motivation for strikes over hours of work, for many believed that fatigued workers were more likely to have accidents, and perhaps it lay behind disputes over other working conditions. No doubt there were also unreported strikes and other labor disturbances stemming from the dangers of work. For example, when a mine fire at Cherry, Illinois, killed 259 miners in 1909, a near riot ensued. But the detail with which the commissioner of labor reported motives and the routine listing of multiple motives suggest that work safety cannot have been a major source of labor unrest.[34]

The lack of worker militancy over safety and health reflected the realities of working-class life. "That poor people are used to trouble is a commonplace," Crystal Eastman observed. Death and injury and illness on the job were matters of fact, just as was the death of a child from typhoid fever or a husband from tuberculosis or a wife from puerperal fever. Some workers responded to the dangers of the job with a kind of bravado, and Eastman thought that railroaders usually affected a "laughing, soldier spirit." But in most cases Eastman observed that workers and their families spoke of work injuries and other misfortunes in a "matter of course" way. So they spoke, and so they behaved. Work accidents were to be endured, and when safety came to the workplace, it came from the top down, not the bottom up.[35]

STIRRINGS AT U.S. STEEL

Some employers have always been concerned with on-the-job safety, but systematic and widespread company-directed safety work is a very modern invention. As a large manufacturer of gunpowder, DuPont demonstrated an understandable interest in the prevention of explosions, and in 1811 the company issued what may have been the earliest set of corporate safety rules. In spite of these efforts, however, it experienced recurring disasters throughout the nineteenth century. H. C. Frick Coal and Coke seems to have stressed safety in the 1890s, while Illinois Steel had some kind of safety program as early as 1892. But none of these organizations had any wider influence.[36]

The modern Safety First movement was born at United States Steel in 1906. In May of that year, chairman of the board Elbert H. Gary first met with the casualty managers of the operating companies to discuss safety. He probably got the idea from a safety program run by Robert J. Young, a casualty manager at the South Chicago works of Illinois Steel, a company subsidiary. Two years later, in March 1908, Gary again met with all the operating company casualty managers. He told them, "We should like to take a prominent part . . . in every movement that is practical to protect employees . . . and any requisition which is made for the expenditure of money to install equipment to protect our people will be honored." This meeting resulted in the formation of the Committee on Safety of United States Steel. That same month Young set up the first safety committee, composed of workmen at the blast furnaces of Illinois Steel's South Chicago works. Two years later, on May 1, 1910, U.S. Steel introduced its voluntary accident relief plan.[37]

Company spokesmen always described U.S. Steel's motivation as humanitarian, but humanitarianism as Gary saw it was in the company's best interest. As the world's largest corporation, with half of industry capacity, U.S. Steel had been subject to almost continuous public attack since it was formed, and in May 1906—the same month Gary first met with his casualty managers—the *Chicago Tribune* published a scathing indictment of the hospital at the South Chicago plant. The next year William Hard again applied the heat, publishing "Making Steel and Killing Men" and "The Law of the Killed and the Wounded" in *Everybody's* magazine. Ironically, like the *Tribune* Hard also criticized the South Chicago works of Illinois Steel, which was probably the only plant in the industry that had any safety program at all at that time.[38]

These criticisms underlined U.S. Steel's need for favorable publicity. Years later L. H. Burnett, vice president of Carnegie Steel, explained that the company's motives had been humanitarian, but in a revealing phrase he observed that other justifications "might not have received the hearty support of the press." Improved safety also supported other goals that Gary cherished. The proper treatment of employees, he told a meeting of the iron and steel manufacturers in 1911, would diminish the attractiveness of "the ideas of the anarchist or the socialist." And in 1913 he reminded the presidents of his subsidiaries of the need for good relations with their employees and to this end urged that they "never hesitate to request appropriations for expenditure of money . . . to prevent accidents." To stockholders Gary stressed that management had a duty not only to them but also to the public and to the company's workers. Safe and healthful working conditions were, he stressed, both "right" and "of advantage to employers."[39]

Soon an unexpected bonus appeared. Although Gary clearly believed that improved safety was in U.S. Steel's self-interest, neither he nor anyone else expected it to turn a profit. In fact, the company almost immediately discovered that it could do well by doing good. In 1912 Raynal Bolling, the company's assistant general solicitor, told the American Iron and Steel Institute that U.S. Steel was spending about $750,000 a year in accident prevention. The resultant reduction in injuries, he calculated, saved over $1.4 million a year in injury payments that the company would have made "in common decency." While this "profit" was the saving of a self-inflicted cost, it cannot have escaped either Bolling or his audience that the rapid expansion of workmen's compensation was transforming safety work from self-interested humanitarianism into a truly profitable activity.[40]

U.S. Steel's every move was news, and its safety campaign led to a bonanza of highly favorable publicity that the company never missed a chance to encourage. Between 1909 and 1914 a spate of articles praising U.S. Steel's efforts—some by company men such as Bolling and David Beyer of American Steel and Wire—appeared in such widely read periodicals as *Survey*, *Scientific American*, *Literary Digest*, and *Engineering Magazine*. Several National Safety Council round-table discussions were also largely devoted to the topic of U.S. Steel's techniques. Bolling, John Dickson, Robert Young, and Gary himself detailed the company's safety activities to the American Iron and Steel Institute. U.S. Steel never ceased to claim that safety paid, both because it led to improved labor relations and because the reduction in costs "far exceeded the amount spent in reducing accidents." U.S. Steel was the dominant corporation of its day, and its well-publicized activities shaped the approach to accident prevention taken by many other companies when the revolution wrought by workmen's compensation moved them to begin safety work. The National Association of Manufacturers summarized the company's importance in 1916: U.S. Steel "has been used as a model by many other corporations entering into safety work. To this corporation must be given the credit of doing more to further the cause of safety than any other one source, as the willingness to advise and co-operate with others has given the movement much valuable assistance."[41]

The Public Says It Is Concerned

By the early twentieth century almost no one could be found who would defend employers' liability as it then existed, but there was a spectrum of opinion on whether it should be modified or scrapped and what to replace it with. England had severely limited employers' use of the fellow-servant defense in 1880, and in 1884 Germany had implemented a no-fault workmen's compensation system that England also adopted in 1897. Some of these changes were publicized in a report by the U.S. commissioner of labor in 1893. Beginning with a bill introduced into the New York legislature in 1898, the compensation of work accidents gradually became a public issue, and in the years 1903–6, Massachusetts, Connecticut, and Illinois appointed commissions to study the problem. This rising interest was reflected in the number of articles on employers' liability listed in the *Reader's Guide to Periodical Literature*, which increased from nine during the years 1900–1904 to sixty-three during the next five years. The movement received a substantial push in 1908 when, at the urging of President Theodore Roosevelt, Congress enacted a compensation act for federal workers. Thereafter events moved rapidly: between 1909 and 1911, several more ineffective laws were passed. Of greater long-run importance, another twenty states set up commissions to investigate employers' liability and workmen's compensation.[42]

PREVENTIVE AND CERTAIN COMPENSATION

The commissions documented in impressive detail just how poorly employers' liability worked, and they essentially replicated Eastman's findings. In 1909 the New York State Employers' Liability Commission castigated the uncertainty, waste, delay, penuriousness, and contentiousness of the existing system. It also dismissed the idea that wages reflected trade risks, simply observing, "That theory does not work out." Other state commissions produced similar findings. The Illinois commission gathered data on the cases of 614 workers who had been killed on the job. It found that almost one-third of them (204) received no compensation at all. Of the remainder, 24 had successfully sued in court, receiving an average of $1,364 each, while 281 had accepted an out-of-court settlement that averaged $1,144. There were 111 suits still pending, and the commission found that the average court case took about three years to settle. Thus, the average award or settlement (including those who got nothing) was $696. Of course, not all of this went to workers' families, for legal fees had to be paid from court settlements.[43]

Led by the American Federation of Labor (AFL), virtually all labor groups initially favored retaining employers' liability, but with laws that sharply curtailed company defenses, and some district assemblies never abandoned this position. But by 1909 Samuel Gompers had changed his mind. Several studies of the responsibility for accidents had been undertaken to determine what fraction of all injuries might be compensated under modified liability. The largest study covered forty-six thousand injuries under the German system and was publicized by the BLS. It suggested that at most 27 percent of all accidents might be compensable. Such figures helped convert Gompers to the cause of workmen's compensation. He was also impressed, he told the New York commission, with the interest in accident prevention he had seen among employers on a recent visit to Germany.[44]

Most Progressive reformers had also concluded that employers' liability needed to be entirely scrapped in favor of workmen's compensation. Like Gompers, they believed that such laws would reduce the death toll. William Hard put this argument bluntly. In 1907 he had described a steelworker who was killed when a slag pot, which was being lifted by the flange because its handle was broken, had tipped, pouring boiling metal on the man. "Just suppose the company had to pay . . . $20,000 every time a ladelman was killed," Hard argued. "Do you think that any slag-pot would ever be raised by its flange? That is the real question. And the answer is, No."[45]

Most important of all, many employers also disliked the existing system. Both the National Association of Manufacturers and the National Metal Trades Association supported compensation, and so did many regional employers' associations. In part this was because they viewed compensation as inevitable, and they wanted to be sure that nothing too radical was passed. There were also more positive reasons for business support. Employers complained loudly of the inefficiency of the liability system, for little of what they paid in premiums actually went to injured workers. The New York commission discovered that benefits received by workers accounted for less than 36 cents of every premium dollar, and other states produced similar results. The remainder went to cover administrative costs or fees to "ambulance chasing, shyster lawyers," as employers termed them. The NAM's 1911 guidelines for workmen's compensation legislation required that at least 75 cents, "and preferably 90 cents," of every premium dollar be paid out as benefits.[46]

Businessmen also stressed that workmen's compensation would stimulate accident prevention. George Gillette, the business representative on the Minnesota commission, favored a law partly for this reason. Ferdinand Schwedtman, head of the NAM's Committee on Industrial Indemnity Insurance and Accident Prevention and author of its report *Accident Prevention and Relief*, told a gathering of insurance executives in 1912, "Our creed places greatest importance on accident prevention. Not the cheapest law or system but the law or system which most encourages prevention of accidents is to our minds the best." Nor was this simply the opinion of the leadership. Magnus Alexander of General Electric—who was a member of the Massachusetts Workmen's Compensation Commission and also of the NAM—was greeted with applause when he told that association that workmen's compensation must be "preventive, punitive, educative and certain."[47]

Of greatest importance to business executives was that employers' liability poisoned relations with their workers and led, in the language of the day, to class warfare. The NAM officially described employers' liability as "antagonistic to harmonious relations between employers and wage-workers." The system had been a "fruitful source of worry, dissatisfaction and friction," a representative of the laundries told the National Safety Council in 1912. Such concerns led some large companies to drop liability insurance entirely. "Our policy is to settle for accidents practically without regard for legal liability," Hinsdill Parsons, a lawyer for General Electric, told the New York Employers' Liability Commission. This was not charity. General Electric's policy allowed it to use compensation as a disciplinary measure. Since few cases went to court, this policy also reduced costs and "resulted in a great deal better satisfaction to the employees." Yet such a remedy was beyond the reach of smaller companies. While a large company might choose to self-insure, handling its injury cases according to its own lights as to what was desirable, those with fewer resources had to purchase liability insurance with results that Crystal Eastman perceptively described:

The injured workman loses . . . to begin with, his chance of appealing for compensation on other than legal grounds. For . . . the insurance company contracts only to assume the employer's legal liability not to underwrite his moral responsibilities or carry out the promptings of his sympathy. In the second place, if . . . the workman commences a suit, he must fight the insurance company[,] . . . in all likelihood . . . a more formidable antagonist than his employer.[48]

Employers who supported workmen's compensation did so in spite of overwhelming evidence that it would increase their costs. The insurance expert Miles Dawson testified to the New York commission that "compared with the present," workmen's compensation would increase costs "two and a quarter or two and a half times." Business organizations were also well aware that studies of accident responsibility predicted that even under a more liberal system of employers' liability, only a fraction of all workers would collect. Moreover, by 1911, the year the first effective workmen's compensation act was passed, the railroads had two years of experience under the 1908 Federal Employers' Liability Act, which sharply curtailed the carriers' defenses. This law did indeed raise costs, but a 1912 study of railroad experience under that system showed that payments for death still averaged less than was contemplated by any of the workmen's compensation laws.[49]

Experience quickly revealed that compensation would prove expensive. A BLS study published in 1910 compared costs in New York under the employers' liability system with costs under its new workmen's compensation act. For virtually every category of risk, costs were sharply higher under the new system. The NAM study, also published in 1910, reviewed the experience of Germany and New York, bluntly concluding that "the cost in dollars and cents of an equitable compensation scheme, as expressed in insurance rates, is much higher than our present employers' liability method." The owner of the Avery Manufacturing Company told the first meeting of the National Safety Council that the 1911 Illinois workmen's compensation law had boosted his rates from 40 cents to $3.35 per $100 of payroll; we were, he remarked, "dazed." Other early compensation laws yielded similar results. Massachusetts's 1912 act increased rates for the boot and shoe industry from 15 cents to 80 cents per $100, and other industries also experienced dramatic rate increases. Michigan's law was also passed in 1912; its new rates were between three and five and one-half times what they had been under employers' liability. Thus, those employers who actively supported workmen's compensation could not have imagined that it would turn out to lower their costs. George Gillette, who led the Minnesota Employers'

Association campaign for workmen's compensation, feared that such a law might triple members' costs. These worries led him to advocate a system with modest benefits partly supported by employee contributions, but he continued to support compensation despite its expense.[50]

By 1911, with the AFL, many academics, and major business groups supporting some kind of workmen's compensation law, events began to move quickly. In that year Washington became the first state to pass an effective law. By 1920 forty-two states plus Alaska, Hawaii, and the District of Columbia had passed workmen's compensation acts, and in 1940 every state but Mississippi had some form of law. The encouragement of safety had been a major goal of all the groups supporting compensation legislation; this aim was clearly stated in the Massachusetts, Indiana, and California laws, and it was implicit in most of the others. The most important aspects of the laws from the perspective of accident prevention were the proportion of workers who were covered and the costs that were imposed on employers.[51]

Almost all state laws initially excluded the self-employed, farm workers, and domestics, while some states only covered employees in certain "hazardous" activities. In 1940 twenty-five state laws still excluded "small" employers. This was a significant exception in some sectors of the economy, such as retail trade and construction, where many employees worked in firms that escaped coverage, but few manufacturing workers were excluded by the small-firm exemption. Census figures for 1921 show that half of all manufacturing plants employed an average of 3.2 or fewer employees, which would have exempted them in fourteen states at that time. Yet these plants accounted for only about 3 percent of manufacturing workers. Hence, for manufacturing, coverage was roughly equivalent to the proportion of employees in states with compensation laws. For workers in all sectors combined, coverage gradually increased, a development due not only to the extension of state laws but also to the decline in self-employment and the inclusion of previously excluded occupations.

Workmen's compensation generated safety incentives because of the accident costs it imposed on employers, and these in turn depended on the benefits paid injured workers. Initially benefits were extremely modest. This was due to the need for employer support, and also to the fact that it was thought that more adequate payments would promote malingering. Thus, most states provided no compensation for injuries resulting in less than one (sometimes two) weeks of disability. In most states, however, workers suffering injuries that lasted the requisite length of time would then receive compensation from the date of occurrence. Compensation was usually from half to two-thirds of lost wages, with

TABLE 3.1. Workmen's Compensation Death Benefits, Selected Years, 1915–1940

	1915	1920	1930	1940
Massachusetts	$2,590	$3,076	$3,469	$3,683
Deflated[a]	2,590	1,559	2,109	2,691
New York	3,241	4,451	6,260	5,598
Deflated	3,241	2,255	3,806	4,254
Pennsylvania	3,128	3,564	4,072	4,130
Deflated	2,908	1,806	2,474	2,975
Wisconsin	1,753	2,343	4,256	4,822
Deflated	1,753	1,187	2,588	3,490
All states maximum	3,829	4,396	5,585	5,935
Deflated	3,829	2,227	3,396	4,295

Source: Data are from New York State Department of Labor, "Thirty Years of Accidents and Workmen's Compensation," *Industrial Bulletin* 44 (Jan.–Feb. 1945): 47–53; Massachusetts Industrial Accident Board, *Annual Report* (Boston, various years); Pennsylvania Department of Labor and Industry, "Biennium Report," in *Special Bulletin* 47 (Harrisburg, 1939); Wisconsin Industrial Commission, *Wisconsin Labor Statistics* and *Workmen's Compensation* (Madison, various years); and Arthur Reede, *Adequacy of Workmen's Compensation* (Cambridge: Harvard Univ. Press, 1947), table 10.

Note: The New York data are for fiscal years through 1920 and calendar years thereafter; the Massachusetts data end in 1939; the Pennsylvania data begin in 1916 and end in 1938. Data for individual states are average settlements for death claims; figures for all states are the legal maximum payment.

[a] Deflated using the consumer price index in *Historical Statistics of the United States,* series E-135, 1915 = 100.

both a maximum and a minimum weekly wage. For permanent injuries, states usually limited compensation to some maximum period. In the 1920s, for example, payments for total disability usually ran for no more than three hundred to five hundred weeks. Compensation for death depended on the number of survivors, but it too was limited, usually to no more than $3,000–5,000.

Benefits were gradually made more generous in most states. While there is no single measure of benefits, payments for death yield a large enough number of cases to be reliable and are unaffected by differing degrees of severity. Hence, they probably provide a good measure of the overall trend in payments. Arthur Reede calculated the average of maximum payments for death in all states from 1915 to 1940. These data, in along with figures on actual payments for several states, are presented in table 3.1. Clearly, World War I inflation severely eroded workmen's real compensation benefits—and therefore the real injury costs that they imposed on employers. The fall in prices immediately after the war and again in the early 1930s, plus rising payments, gradually improved matters. But on the eve of World War II real benefits in most states were probably only modestly higher than they had been a quarter-century earlier, and they remained far below workers' lost wages.

Reede also demonstrated that the more serious the injury, the lower the proportion of lost wages compensated. Hence, an employee who broke an arm and lost two weeks of work was more fully compensated than one who lost an arm or who was killed. Together these findings suggest that because employers paid only a small part of the costs of accidents, safety incentives were too weak; and that compensation was more effective at encouraging prevention of minor injuries than at preventing fatalities or permanent disabilities.

Benefits payments (plus an expense loading) translated into premium rates paid by companies. Whether these premiums encouraged safety depended on their size and on how sensitive they were to individual firms' risks, and states immediately found that applying average rates to all firms in a certain risk category could have perverse results. In such a situation, workmen's compensation could generate even less incentive for accident prevention than had the old system of employers' liability, for a firm's premium would be independent of its injury rate. As Harvey Kelly of Washington State told the International Association of Industrial Accident Boards and Commissions in 1920, "The careful employer, who cuts his accident cost to the minimum through safeguarding and safety educational work found his efforts nullified by the careless employer. . . . Both paid the same rate for insurance."[52]

The way out of this bind was some form of individual merit rating. Ohio pioneered with experience rating in 1911. Under this scheme a firm's premium depended upon its past injury record—meaning that companies with poorer records paid higher rates. Large companies that could self-insure were, of course, entirely experience-rated. Companies that purchased insurance, if they were above a certain size—in the 1920s some states put the cutoff at about $175 of premium at the average rate for the risk class—had their premium partly determined by their success in accident prevention. While only about one-fourth of all employers were experience-rated during the late 1930s, they included about three-fourths of all insured payroll. But the incentive such rating provided depended on the weight given the company's own experience, and this increased with company size.

A typical rating scheme in the 1920s worked as follows. The company's actual rate, x, was determined thus:

$$x = P_m + z(P_c - P_m) \text{ and } z = P_m N/(P_m N + K)$$

where P_m is the manual premium, or average rate for the risk class, P_c the premium indicated by the company's own experience, N the company payroll, and K a constant determined by judgment. The experience modifier z rises with payroll. For large companies it approaches unity, and as it does, the firm's premium approaches P_c—the rate indicated by its own experience. For small firms z might be quite low, and since compensation benefits and premiums were themselves low, the safety incentives were often minuscule. The experience of a machine shop insured through the Standard Accident Insurance Company illustrates the point. It cut accidents from ten in 1918 to one in 1921 and compensation costs from $105 to $3. But its premium fell only $37.

A second form of merit rating, pioneered by Pennsylvania in 1916, was schedule rating. This approach gave discounts to companies that followed state safety codes, guarded machines, installed first-aid stations, or made other safety improvements recommended by their insurance carriers. An insurance representative claimed that manufacturers responded much more quickly to the argument "If you guard that machine you are going to get a reduction in your rate" than to the state inspector. Schedule rating reflected the theory that injuries could best be prevented by addressing specific hazards. Although in 1940 thirteen states still integrated workmen's compensation and safety standards in this manner, the trend was away from schedule rating because of the difficulty in measuring the effects of specific safety improvements, and because by then, thinking emphasized the need for more general management interest in safety. The theory of injury prevention is discussed in more detail below, while the effects of schedule rating in mining are reviewed in chapter 6.[53]

REINFORCING SELF-INTEREST

While much of the support for workmen's compensation stemmed from the belief that it would motivate employers to improve workplace safety, many reformers wished to reinforce self-interest with legal requirements. This was not a new idea. State regulation and inspection of steam boilers had begun in New York in 1867, and in 1877 Massachusetts became the first state to pass legislation governing factory safety. The law called for suitable fire exits and for safeguards for moving machinery and power transmission. Ohio, Pennsylvania, Indiana, and other states followed with legislation governing such matters as construction practices, machine guards, ventilation, and requirements for exits.

These early efforts seem to have had only modest effects. Minnesota's first law was utterly toothless. Although the inspector claimed that he had been able to persuade some companies to guard machines, in 1893 guarding was made compulsory. But there were never enough inspectors, and the laws—like those for mine inspection—were often poorly written. In 1903 Iowa's inspector complained that only 187 of his 503 recommendations had been complied with. He recommended that his force of inspectors be increased to three so he could better inspect the state's nearly fifteen thousand shops and factories. At about the same time, Indiana had four inspectors to cover eighteen thousand workplaces, Minnesota had five for eleven thousand, and other states were similarly understaffed.[54]

Representatives of the building trades complained bitterly to the New York Commission on Employers' Liability that construction safety laws were virtually worthless. The law required planking immediately below the top floor on steel buildings over three stories, but the Department of Labor could inspect only if it received a complaint. The chief inspector informed the commission that there had been few complaints in the previous two years, although "I have seen situations repeatedly requiring attention." He also noted that prosecution of violations was rarely successful, a result he attributed to the fact that juries were composed of "all manufacturers, as a rule." In addition, it proved virtually impossible to write laws that were specific enough to be enforceable and yet flexible enough to fit a broad range of industrial conditions, while technical change often made laws obsolete shortly after they were written. For example, on high construction work, nets or scaffolds might make planking unnecessary.[55]

Such difficulties led to the formation of regulatory commissions, which, it was hoped, would bring both expertise and flexibility to the task of regulating workplace safety. In 1911, Wisconsin established the first industrial commission; it was empowered to hold hearings and to make and enforce its own safety regulations as well as those passed by the legislature. By 1923 seventeen states with about 57 percent of all manufacturing wage earners had adopted the Wisconsin idea.[56]

Most states that lacked commissions also had far fewer safety regulations. In 1923, North and South Carolina had no legislation at all, while Florida and Georgia regulated only the employment of women and children. In other states the most common laws required building exits, mandated an electrical code, or covered mines only. Only two states without a commission covered machine tools or punch presses; one state without a commission regulated cranes; none controlled use of compressed air.[57]

Even in supposedly progressive states with commissions, enforcement of safety regulations seems not to have been very strict. Perhaps because many commission members came from business, they favored persuading employers to comply rather than bludgeoning them to do so. C. W. Price of the Wisconsin Industrial Commission—and an alumni of International Harvester—explained his state's approach: "The one word which the deputies keep uppermost in mind is CO-OPERATION." Penalties were a last resort, and in Massachusetts during the 1920s inspectors often issued only two or three citations a year. California could order a company to "show cause" why an unsafe machine should not be ordered out of use. An employer who failed to show cause could have the machine tagged, thereby making its use illegal. In 1927, a typical year, only 308 orders and 87 tags were issued. Wisconsin tried to encourage compliance with its safety regulations by increasing the workmen's compensation payment where an injury resulted from the violation of a safety provision. The payment was to go to the worker directly from the company—not from the insurer. During the mid-1920s these payments amounted to about $82 per injury, which added about 15 percent to the average claim cost of these accidents.[58]

For many employers the threat of citations may have been more important than the severity of the penalty, for they did not think of themselves as lawbreakers and tried to comply. By 1919 it was the policy of the Joseph Bancroft and Sons textile-finishing mills that all new machines should be ordered with guards that conformed to state laws. And when a DuPont operating officer balked at expenditure for safety equipment, Louis DeBlois, the company safety engineer, informed him that the law required it. Since DuPont experts had served on the state boards that helped draft such laws, it would be embarrassing for the company to violate them, DeBlois pointed out.[59]

The proliferation of state safety regulations and the development of schedule rating for workmen's compensation increased the need for standardization. Private efforts to standardize safety equipment dated from 1913-14 and were designed to ensure quality and reduce costs. In 1913 the NAM's *American Industries* promised to advertise safety devices "only if we are convinced of the merit of the advertised proposition." More important were the efforts of insurance companies and the Conference Board on Safety and Sanitation—a group composed of the NAM and trade associations representing the metal trades, founders, and electrical equipment producers. Carl Hansen's *Universal Safety Standards* (1913) was an effort by workmen's compensation carriers to develop consensus standards. In 1914 the Conference Board also began to standardize safety devices to which it gave its trademark NASO, for National Affiliated Safety Organizations, and which it sold at cost.[60]

While private efforts helped standardize equipment, they could do nothing to standardize state safety codes which, if inconsistent, might torpedo the private actions. Inconsistent state regulations not only made little sense, they hampered efforts of equipment producers to design and sell safer products, while insurance inspectors needed standard guidelines to recommend. By 1917 David Beyer had become chief safety engineer for Liberty Mutual, where he became an expert on textile industry safety. He had concluded that standards would "help a great deal" as different state codes were giving machinery manufacturers great difficulty. A representative of Norton Abrasives agreed, claiming that "the machine tool builders want to . . . [install safeguards] but they cannot by reason of the laws of the various states." Norton had in fact produced a guard for a grinding wheel, and then found that it did not conform with all of the state laws. World War I also demonstrated the virtues of standardization, and in 1918 the five major engineering societies combined to form the American Engineering Standards Committee. A year later, at the urging of the National Safety Council, the National Bureau of Standards sponsored two conferences on standardizing safety codes. Overall guidance in the matter of code development was then given to a committee of the American Engineering Standards Committee. It promptly delegated the development of specific codes to sectional committees composed of manufacturers and users of equipment as well as employees, regulatory authorities, and members of interested engineering societies. By 1928 forty codes had been issued or were being developed governing such subjects as grinding wheels, machine tools, construction work, paper mills, and power transmission.[61]

These codes received wide publicity from engineering societies and the National Safety Council, and the Bureau of Labor Statistics issued them as bulletins. The National Bureau of Casualty and Surety Underwriters, an umbrella group for the workmen's compensation insurers, also urged its members to follow the codes. In addition, the International Association of Industrial Accident Boards and Commissions, which had been formed in 1913 to include state and federal agencies concerned with industrial safety, exhorted its members to follow the codes as closely as possible. This was not as simple as had been expected. The codes were voluntary, and companies could pick and choose among their provisions. But when Pennsylvania tried to adopt the power-press code as a regulation in 1924, industry representatives complained so loudly at public hearings that the code had to be thoroughly revised. By 1926 it was more acceptable and was adopted in its entirety by Pennsylvania, Maryland, and New Jersey and in part by a number of other states.[62]

Gradual and partial adoption seems to have been the fate of most of the codes. Where they were adopted and enforced, there is little doubt that they reduced injuries. They also improved safety in states in which they were not adopted. The standardization of safety-equipment requirements encouraged the use of such equipment by improving quality and reducing costs for all potential buyers. For example, the grinding-wheel code became the Bible of the industry, and by the mid-1920s producers routinely guarded wheels. The rubber code proposed by New Jersey in 1923 roused Firestone and other large producers to action. Working closely with machinery producers, they developed new and low-cost devices to stop the big calender rolls. These devices were widely employed even in states without codes, and the industry supported efforts to develop a national code based on the New Jersey model.[63]

Inventing the Safety Movement

While the original interest in safety at U.S. Steel and a few other large companies owed little or nothing to workmen's compensation, the same cannot be said of most other companies. By the early 1920s about 57 percent of all manufacturing employees were in states with safety commissions, while about 93 percent of employees in manufacturing were in states with workmen's compensation acts. Fatalities that had only recently cost companies a few hundred dollars at most now fetched $1,000–3,000 (table 3.1). Loss of an arm or a leg cost $1,500–1,600, while hands and feet cost $1,200–1,300 and an eye about $1,000. As supporters of workmen's compensation had hoped, this legal jab in the bottom line aroused companies' interest in accident prevention as never before. "Since the Workman's Compensation Acts of the past two years more real safety work has been done in the United States than in any ten years preceding," C. W. Crownhart of the Wisconsin Industrial Commission told the National Safety Council in 1912.[64]

Business executives admitted the truth of this claim. Magnus Alexander of General Electric had been active in support of the Massachusetts compensation law. He informed the National Safety Council that, "barring a few notable exceptions, employers . . . did not get very busy on . . . accident prevention and safeguarding until they were forced by legislation." A representative of the Washington State lumber producers claimed that "little had been done prior to the passage of our industrial laws." Since then, he noted, "greater thought and time has been given to safe-guarding." L. B. Robertson of Ford admitted to the National Safety Council that his company had not begun safety work until the Michigan law was passed. Robertson had a dry sense of humor. The "awakening consciousness on safety came at about the same time as compensation laws," he observed.[65]

INSTITUTIONS IN THE SAFETY MARKET

Making a commitment to reduce accidents was one thing; doing it was another matter. Companies that began safety work needed equipment—machine guards, safety glasses and shoes, safety posters, movies, and pamphlets. These new requirements led to the development of markets for safety equipment as suppliers gradually responded to employers' demands. But what employers needed most was information. Workmen's compensation presented employers with a novel problem: production processes had to be modified to produce goods with fewer accidents, and companies had only the foggiest idea how to do it. The resulting frustration was revealed by one steelman who fumed to a safety consultant, "What you want to do is enclose this plant in a glass case and operate it from the outside." The demand for information was supplied by the U.S. Bureau of Labor Statistics and state regulatory agencies and by a host of private institutions created especially for the task.[66]

The first requisite was to develop a measure of risk, for just as the wheat market needs to agree on what constitutes a bushel, so safety work requires an accepted measure of risk. The most important work of the Bureau of Labor Statistics in the field of injury prevention was its creation and collection of reasonably accurate statistics. One looks largely in vain through reports of nineteenth-century state labor or railroad commissions for evidence on injury rates. Most states that collected any information at all simply listed the number of casualties without even defining very precisely what constituted an injury. Occasionally—but rarely—it was recognized that to be meaningful, such data had to be expressed relative to some exposed population, but even the Interstate Commerce Commission seldom presented its injury statistics in this manner.

On its own initiative, the bureau had decided to investigate safety as part of the 1910 study of labor conditions in the steel industry that had been requested by Congress, its purpose being "to demonstrate the need for workmen's compensation." It broke new ground by defining a disabling injury as one resulting in at least one lost workday, and it advanced American practice by introducing the method pioneered by the German Insurance Commission of expressing injury frequency rates in terms of hours of exposure. This and subsequent studies of the iron and steel and machine-building industries gave wide publicity to the bureau's methods of constructing injury statistics and to the effectiveness of safety work in these industries.[67]

The bureau's method of calculating frequency rates was so obviously an improvement that it was widely adopted. Progressive businesses were coming to view accurate injury statistics as a necessary tool of systematic management, for only with comparative and historical data could one judge the success of a safety program. For example, the Mansfield Sheet and Tin Plate Company reorganized its safety program in 1925 when statistics revealed it to be in the bottom half of the industry. And when broken down by cause and nature of injury, statistics were the building blocks on which a rational approach to accident prevention could be constructed. Power transmission injuries, for example, suggested the need to guard belts and shafts, while eye injuries might reveal the need for safety glasses. And since injuries were obviously an evil, in the Progressive vision statistics had moral force as well as scientific value. In 1916 the commissioner of labor statistics, Royal Meeker, asserted that the bureau's accident statistics had "aroused the conscience of the responsible officials in the steel plants." As a result, he claimed, "the industry has set to work . . . to reduce the number of accidents." Other writers stressed that statistics were the only way small producers could be convinced of dangers.[68]

The National Safety Council was an early convert to the bureau's methods. The bureau's Royal Meeker was the first chair of the council's Committee on Accident Statistics and helped ensure its adoption of the bureau's definitions in 1914. Most large companies also employed them, as did most trade associations that assembled accident data. A few companies, especially coal mines, persisted in expressing injuries per unit of output, as productivity growth allowed them to claim progress in accident prevention, but the bureau fought this heresy, and it gradually died out. Later, when the bureau discovered that frequency rates could be used to mislead as well as inform, it began to calculate severity rates. But as these were designed to be ammunition in the war over injury causation, they will be discussed in the next section of this chapter. By the late 1920s safety experts also began to distinguish between the causes of accidents and injuries. A fall, for example, might be the cause of an injury, but the "real" cause of the accident that led to this injury might be a slippery floor. During the 1930s the bureau helped to develop more sophisticated cause classifications that were then gradually adopted.[69]

The bureau was more successful in creating than in collecting injury statistics, for it had no power to compel reporting. Commissioner of Labor Statistics Ethelbert Stewart organized the International Association of Industrial Accident Boards and Commissions to coordinate state safety activities. But neither he nor subsequent commissioners met with much success in their efforts to achieve uniform state statistics. Inconsistent definitions and the absence of information on exposure made most such data inadequate. Voluntary reports from the iron and steel producers provided nationwide information on the progress of safety in that industry from 1907 on, and gradually other industries agreed to cooperate. Drawing on such sources, the bureau began publishing the first nationwide estimates of manufacturing injury rates in 1926.

While few states gathered useful injury statistics, some of the state workmen's compensation commissions or industrial boards began accident prevention activities that went far beyond the simple promulgation and enforcement of laws. In part this was simply a response to employer demands for information, and in part it was an effort to encourage companies to accept the new legal framework and to go beyond it. In 1912 the newly formed Massachusetts Industrial Accident Board began work with a burst of energy. It published safety booklets, filled its annual reports with pictures of properly protected machines (and gruesome photographs of workers who had been maimed by unprotected equipment), advised employers on accident causation and the importance of safety organizations, and encouraged the insurance companies to do the same. It also established a Massachusetts Museum of Safety and circulated stories of successful accident prevention. After safety work was given to the State Board of Labor and Industries in 1916, such activities petered out and safety orders became more prominent—although prosecutions for violation remained rare.[70]

California also stressed the educational aspects of safety work in *California Safety News*, which began publication in 1917 and contained safety advice, success stories, and articles by executives testifying that accident prevention paid. Under the guidance of its chairman, Will French, the commission launched an aggressive safety campaign among oilfield workers during 1921. Wisconsin's Industrial Board also conducted a campaign to sell safety to employers. In 1912 it hired C. W. Price away from International Harvester's safety program. Price toured the state for the board, selling safety as a patent medicine that would reinvigorate company profits. In 1919 the board began publication of the *Wisconsin Safety Review*, a journal much like the California publication begun two years earlier. The board also used movies, buttons, and a traveling exhibit in its campaign. New York instituted annual industrial safety congresses in 1916, and in the 1920s it began safety contests. Ohio began industrial safety congresses in the 1920s. New Jersey, Pennsylvania, and other states also held safety contests from time to time.[71]

State activities were supplemented, and in the 1920s overshadowed, by private institutions. The most important of them was the National Safety Council. The council was the child of the Association of Iron and Steel Electrical Engineers. The association's leadership in industrial safety was an outgrowth of its professional work. Its membership was, of course, drawn in considerable measure from U.S. Steel, and Judge Gary's efforts had no doubt concentrated the attention of that company's engineers on safety matters. But the membership may have been peculiarly receptive to safety problems anyway. In 1910 the application of electricity to steel production was still a new and rapidly evolving field—the association itself had been formed only in 1906—and the safe design and standardization of electrical equipment were therefore live issues. As late as 1921, for example, some engineers still believed that 600 volts "can be taken across the fingers." S. C. Coey, an electrical engineer at Youngstown Steel, claimed that "it was largely from a growing realization of the electrical hazards . . . that the safety first movement really had its inception." [72]

Walter Greenwood, an electrical engineer at U.S. Steel, recalled in 1928 that by 1912, safety matters had come to dominate the association's business to such an extent that it was decided to form another association devoted to such matters. The chairman of the safety committee, Lew Palmer—a recent Princeton graduate in electrical engineering, now employed by Jones and Laughlin Steel—had the idea to open the new association to other groups interested in safety, and he went on a "missionary tour of industrial concerns and government bureaus." In September 1912 a cooperative safety congress was held in Milwaukee under the auspices of the association. In fact, it was the first meeting of the National Safety Council. [73]

The council's beginnings were modest enough—a handful of representatives from manufacturers, railroads, insurance companies, and government agencies turned up for the 1912 meetings—but the idea had deep appeal. In 1913 the council had forty members, but by 1914 its membership had grown to about eight hundred, and those interested primarily in workplace safety had divided into industrial groupings such as iron and steel, paper, mining, railroads, and others. In 1920 the council boasted 4,104 members representing over 6 million employees. It was a "co-operative, non-profit, universal . . . clearing house as to safeguards and methods," as its early publications proclaimed. Safety, by implication, was too important to be left to the dictates of profitability. While this seems a strange idea for an organization supported by the largest corporations of the day, it reflected a tension that characterized the safety movement from the beginning. [74]

Nearly everyone acknowledged that it was workmen's compensation that had awakened the interest of corporate management in safety, but most of the individuals who comprised the safety movement were not motivated by costs or profits. Many of those who attended the first safety meetings such as Lew Palmer and David Beyer were engineers. Others such as Robert Young, who had been a casualty manager at Illinois Steel, were middle-level company executives. All went on to devote their careers to safety work. For the engineers, safety became a professional duty, and all safety officials were attracted by its humanitarianism. To these men, and relatively few women, the nonprofit and cooperative aspects of the council stood for more than the usual trade association functions. The watchword Safety First, which was probably originated by Young, reflected this view; safety was a moral duty and should take precedence over production. It was an end, not simply one more means to increase profits. This vision of safety as an independent corporate goal was articulated by Louis DeBlois, who was among the most influential members of the newly emerging safety movement and was elected president of the National Safety Council in 1923. DeBlois had graduated from Harvard in 1899 with an engineering degree. Thereafter he went to DuPont, where he organized and directed that company's safety work until 1927. DuPont, he believed, had a "moral obligation to provide a safe workplace."[75]

Business leaders, on the other hand, while they acknowledged the need to cooperate and share information, saw safety mostly as a matter of economics, not morals or welfare. Melville Mix, head of the Dodge Manufacturing Company and as concerned with worker safety as any businessman of his era, articulated this view. In 1914 he told the NAM that "Safety First is not a philanthropic movement on the part of the employer, . . . [it] is an investment." Or, as Commissioner of Labor Statistics Ethelbert Stewart put the matter somewhat later, "Interest [in safety] generally has the image of a human on one side and the image of an eagle [on a gold coin] on the other." Safety experts did not always like this reality, but they accepted it. In his presidential address to the National Safety Council in 1918, the engineer David Van Schaack told his colleagues, "Our work . . . while essentially humanitarian in nature, must be conducted on business principles if it is to be appealing, effective, and enduring." Thus, safety was to be an economic entrée that came with a side order of humanitarianism. The result was a certain creative tension in the movement. Safety experts developed the organizations and information without which little safety work would have been profitable, and the need to justify their work in economic terms led them to campaign tirelessly to persuade their employers that safety really was good business.[76]

The National Safety Council was most valuable for the service it provided as an information clearinghouse. The early annual meetings

provided wide-ranging discussions of safety technology and methods—
especially those of U.S. Steel subsidiaries—and they also included trade
shows at which prospective buyers could inspect the latest offerings of
safety equipment manufacturers. These were matters of vital importance because safety work was so poorly understood. The safety inspector for the National Metal Trades Association told the council in 1912,
"We find every-where a lack of knowledge more than a lack of interest." A representative of the Bancroft textile mills came away from the
sixth meeting of the council overflowing with new ideas. He reported
that the consensus was that safety work was a "paying proposition," and
he described the details of safety programs at similar-sized companies.
Another member concluded that the exhibits alone had justified his attendance at the meeting, while still another claimed, "I came here . . .
for the sole purpose of learning something about punch press work." [77]

The council also established a Safe Practices Committee that issued
pamphlets on ladders, scaffolds, and other devices, while a Bureau of
Information provided a blizzard of bulletins, posters, movies, speakers,
and up-to-date information on changing state regulations. For a time
the council also seems to have acted as an employment bureau for safety
engineers, and in 1934, when the Civil Works Administration desper-
ately needed safety advice, the council furnished it with experts on both
the national and state levels. In 1919 it began publishing *National Safety
News*, which provided information on effective safety techniques and
was designed to interest foremen and workers as well as experts. Its
Committee on Accident Statistics worked closely with the BLS to standardize injury data, and the council also set up a Committee on Safety
Equipment Standards in 1913. It was absorbed in 1919 by an engineering
section of the council whose members, as engineers, allowed it to work
"as equal in professional attainments and dignity to the great national
engineering societies." [78]

Similar though less comprehensive functions were provided by some
trade associations and professional societies. In 1910 the NAM organized a Committee on Accident Prevention, and in 1911 it introduced a
section on "Prevention of Industrial Accidents" as a regular feature in
its journal. In 1913 it included a regular monthly supplement on safety
appliances. The NAM also provided a safety engineering service that
would inspect plants at $10 a day for members and $15 for nonmembers.
The National Metal Trades Association also undertook plant inspections. The Portland Cement Association organized a bureau of accident
prevention, which began publication of its *Accident Prevention Bulletin* in
1914. Under the energetic leadership of Henry Reninger of the Lehigh
Portland Cement Company, the bureau also regularly staged safety

contests among members and was probably the most active and effective of all the trade associations involved in safety work. The National Electric Light Association formed an Accident Prevention Committee in 1913, and three years later it began to publish a safety supplement in its journal. The National Founders' Association, Millers' National Association, American Gas Association, Lumbermen's National Association, Tanners' Council, and Sheet Metal Ware Association also became more or less active in safety work before World War I, while the American Petroleum Institute started an accident prevention campaign in the 1920s.[79]

Business and trade journals such as *Engineering Magazine*, *Textile World*, *Paper Trade*, *American Machinist*, and others also began to publish safety information, and a demand for textbooks sprang up that David Beyer, Louis DeBlois, and other writers quickly supplied. Engineering societies such as the Illuminating Engineers and the American Society of Mechanical Engineers also devoted more attention to safety problems. A sign of the times was that the journal *Insurance Engineering* changed its name to *Safety Engineering* in 1913, and in 1919 it became the journal of the American Society of Safety Engineers, which had been formed in 1911.[80]

Workmen's compensation also interested insurance companies in accident prevention as employers' liability never had, and a number of companies were formed specifically to insure and reduce workmen's compensation risks. Under the system of liability, since few accidents were compensated, prevention was a poor investment and money was better spent fighting claims. Compensation reversed these incentives: since few cases were contested, prevention paid off. Because insurance companies served many clients, they could develop a specialized expertise in their engineering and inspection services that few employers could match. Not only did they attend trade and safety meetings such as those of the National Safety Council; they also had far more experience with accident prevention than most of their clients and were far better positioned to evaluate policies.

Specialization was carried to an extreme in the "trade mutuals" such as Lumberman's Mutual, which was formed specifically to underwrite compensation risks and which covered only lumber and woodworking establishments. It focused specifically on woodworking machine accidents and campaigned to have its clients introduce equipment with automatic feed. Hardware Mutual was another specialized product of the compensation laws. The laundry operators set up their own Employers' Indemnity Exchange, while the Integrity Mutual Company began as an insurer of flour mills. Such companies had antecedents in the earlier fire mutuals: Hardware and Integrity Mutual were both spin-offs from fire insurance companies with similar names, and their stress on accident prevention reflected the earlier successes in fire prevention.[81]

In 1913, the first year of the Massachusetts compensation law, Aetna Life Insurance Company informed the Massachusetts Industrial Commission that "the company has increased the efficiency of its inspection service to a considerable degree." Aetna reported that it had made about 36,000 inspections and 108,000 recommendations for improvement, of which 58,000 were accepted. The Massachusetts Employees' Insurance Association claimed in 1915 that it was continuing the safety campaign it began with the introduction of workmen's compensation. Georgia's compensation law of 1921 brought the Maryland Casualty Company to that state. Just before the law went into effect, the company shipped eleven safety engineers to the state who inspected every plant they were allowed into. Other companies also reported stepped-up accident prevention work. Most insurance inspections were probably not very detailed: in 1915 the Travelers had a force of 220 inspectors who performed nearly 235,000 inspections, or about three and a half a day. But large and dangerous projects got real scrutiny. Travelers claimed that when it accepted coverage of one large construction project, it began by going over the plan and specifications and then kept an inspector on the job every day.[82]

Insurers developed a safety package for their clients. After an inspection they would provide a list of hazards that required remedy, many of which would qualify for schedule discounts. They also offered expertise in establishing a safety organization and supplied the company with posters and safe-practice pamphlets. Lumberman's Mutual provided clients with "L-M-C" standards of safety. Contractor's Mutual provided each inspector with a book to show clients; it listed machinery guards together with their price and the name and address of the manufacturer. The Travelers published booklets such as "Accident Prevention in Paper Mills," and in 1912 it started *Travelers Standard*, a journal devoted to safety engineering. On average, from 1923 through 1939, insurance carriers spent about 2.8 percent of their earned premiums, or about $4.8 million a year, on such safety-related activities.[83]

Most carriers also devoted resources to improving medical treatment. In 1913, Liberty Mutual set up a system of clinics, as did Maryland Casualty Company, while Travelers developed a Surgical Division. Michigan Mutual, which had been formed specifically to provide compensation coverage, built a forty-bed hospital and also placed surgeons in some large plants, while Integrity Mutual developed an industrial surgery in

Chicago. Such clinics once again reflected the gains from specialization. Very few cities or towns had either the facilities or the experience to handle industrial casualties, and as a result, local care was often poor. Permanently disabled workers were expensive, and so company clinics sometimes spent far more on their patients than the few hundred dollars most state compensation laws allowed for medical claims. The result was "shorter periods of disability and fewer permanent injuries."[84]

Florence Lincoln benefited from such care. Both her arms had been burned and crushed in a flatwork ironer, and the right had been amputated immediately. The left arm, which had not healed properly, was scheduled to be removed when Integrity Mutual took over and brought her to its Chicago surgery. She regained full use of her left arm and was fitted with an artificial limb, thereby becoming only partially disabled and saving company money. The representative of one company explained that it had spent $3,000 to rehabilitate a total-disability case because the compensation would have amounted to $8,000.[85]

Insurance companies were also well placed to undertake safety research. Michigan Mutual insured many metalworking shops and saw so many punch-press accidents and guards that it developed its own. Similar experiences with accidents from the stitching of flour bags led Integrity Mutual to develop and require use of a stitcher guard. When a Travelers client reported problems with worker exposure to benzene, which was being used as a solvent, the insurance company's researchers developed a substitute. Travelers engineers also patented guards for such dangerous machines as the platen printing press and the leather-embossing press that, in the spirit of Safety First, they allowed to be used royalty-free.[86]

Insurers claimed that their safety work got results. *Travelers Standard* presented graphs demonstrating sharp declines in injury rates for companies that adopted its safety recommendations. The Slater cotton mills began safety work after Liberty Mutual's inspection revealed Slater to be one of the more dangerous mills in Massachusetts. Liberty also showed Bancroft how to compute its injury rate and sent representatives to employee safety meetings. Bancroft responded to an early report of a Liberty inspector by deciding to "guard all places on the report shown to be dangerous." A representative of Lumberman's Mutual described the plants in his industry before workman's compensation as "just as naked as a new-born babe from the safeguards," and Hart Palmer of St. Paul and Tacoma Lumber agreed, noting that "inspections made by insurance companies proved to be the initial step to better safety methods." He also stressed the value of Aetna's pamphlet "Woodworking Safeguards."[87]

These groups were the major institutions in the emerging private safety market, and they provided a variety of services to their customers, the private employers. Collectively they developed, certified, and supplied safety equipment, staged contests, inspected members' plants, improved medical care, and collected and disseminated injury statistics. Perhaps of most importance, they provided a forum in which ideas on injury prevention were debated and disseminated.

THE CAUSE AND PREVENTION OF INJURIES

The nineteenth-century employer's view of injuries was admirably summarized in several injury reports from the Lancaster textile mills in Clinton, Massachusetts, to the American Mutual Liability Insurance Company. In April 1896 Eliza Dervieu, an employee of many years, injured her foot stepping on a nail that protruded from a board on the floor near her machine. The report described the cause as the "injured's own carelessness," as she had know that the nail was there. In the same mill on July 21 of that year, a sixty-year-old worker, J. L. Wyman, was overcome by heat while in the boiler room. Again the injury report attributed the accident to "the man's own carelessness as he knew the danger of his occupation." And when an unguarded gear injured fifteen-year-old John Gibbons, this too was said to be the result of his own carelessness.[88]

That the vast majority of injuries were either due to "trade risks" or the result of "careless" worker behavior was an article of faith among most nineteenth-century business people. In either case, injuries were neither the fault of nor preventable by employers, or so most of them thought. Such explanations were valuable as long as employers' liability held sway. Company claim departments had been fighting organizations; that trade risks were "assumed" was one of their weapons. The assertion of worker carelessness, which implied absence of fault on the part of the employer or at least contributory negligence by the worker, was another. Once workmen's compensation required employers to pay for all accidents, the idea that trade risks were inevitable, having lost its economic value, gradually disappeared. B. F. Affleck, president of the Universal Portland Cement Company, enunciated the new view to the National Safety Council in 1924: "We will probably find means to avoid many accidents which we now class as unavoidable," he predicted. Later, Louis DeBlois argued that the existence of plants that ran for long periods with no accidents implied that there was no such thing as an "unpreventable accident." By the 1930s Herbert W. Heinrich of the Travelers was claiming that 98 percent of all accidents were preventable, while DuPont's safety department thought that all accidents could be avoided.[89]

Carelessness also lost its value at law. It had always been a better label than an explanation, and writers such as Crystal Eastman—who had no economic motive for glossing over the causes of accidents— had pointed out that what was called careless behavior was often more properly attributed to youth or inexperience. William Hard had perceptively observed that workers might be less reckless if their bosses had an economic interest in discouraging rather than encouraging such behavior. As Lucian Chaney pointed out, laws that required compensation of all injuries shifted the focus of employers from carelessness as a legal defense to its cause and prevention. Modern methods of accident prevention could not have arisen, Chaney thought, as long as the old system of liability held sway. Yet like the grin on the Cheshire cat, carelessness lingered on long after workmen's compensation had destroyed its legal value. In 1917 Arthur Young of Illinois Steel told the readers of *Industrial Management* that the installation of "every safety device" could prevent only about 25 percent of all injuries, for there still remains "the naturally careless workman." Four years later, in 1921, Fred Lange of the Ohio Industrial Commission delivered a similar message to the same audience. "One of the principal sources of accidents is the worker himself," he claimed. "Carelessness, thoughtlessness and lack of knowledge all conspire to cause him injury."[90]

This view hung on for a number of reasons, one of which was simply habit. And because injuries are often the outcome of a sequence of complicated and rare events, understanding them took time. The old view was also partly correct: worker carelessness did indeed cause some injuries. Blaming injuries on careless worker behavior also seemed to justify a particular approach to safety work. If most injuries resulted from unsafe acts, then it seemed plausible that the proper solution was to modify worker behavior through selection, education, training, and enforcement of rules, all of which were, happily enough, cheaper than reengineering the workplace. "The posting of reasonable rules and reasonable enforcement," a representative of the paper industry told the National Safety Council in 1915, "will do more to prevent accidents than most any other form of safeguarding."[91]

The need for education and training was reinforced by the discovery that newly hired workers were much more likely to be injured than those with more experience. This relationship had been demonstrated in the BLS study of the steel industry released in 1913. In 1917 J. S. Herbert of Cambria Steel claimed that Cambria's accident rate among employees with less than thirty days' experience was twelve times the company average, and other employers reported similar, though less dramatic, findings. The solution, clearly enough, was to target the new workers for an extra dose of education. Carelessness also traded for moral coin, even if it no longer mattered at law. The notion that injuries were due to careless workers salved the employer's conscience, absolving him of blame and allowing him to see accident prevention in paternalistic terms—as a gift, not as an obligation to prevent something for which he was at fault. No doubt the doctrine that workers were careless also meshed nicely with some employers' social Darwinian views and ethnic prejudices.[92]

Gradually most safety experts ceased describing accidents as a result of careless employee behavior. For one thing, it irritated the very workers they were trying to coax into safer habits. And serious accident investigations—themselves the fruits of workmen's compensation —often suggested that even if a worker had been careless, the real problem was inadequate training, or improper work practices or job design. This put a rather different perspective on matters. Employers had been increasingly trying to control just these aspects of workplace behavior in order to step up the pace of production. It thus appeared that management—not the injured worker—was responsible for behavior that led to accidents.

The alternative to the view of safety that stressed worker behavior was that serious accidents had physical causes. Safety therefore required "engineering revision." This view also shifted the focus from worker carelessness to managerial failure, and it was articulated most clearly by Lucian Chaney. Chaney had come to the U.S. Department of Labor in 1908 from Carleton College, where he had taught mathematics, biology, and geology since 1882. Science and religion coexisted easily in Chaney's breast. The son of deeply religious parents (his father was a minister), he viewed injury prevention as the application of science and mathematics to achieve Christian goals. "This congress is distinctly a phase of applied Christianity," he told the first meeting of the National Safety Council. Chaney's faith in the progress of science and its applications far exceeded his faith in the malleability of worker behavior. "If the reduction in serious accidents is to be dependent principally upon the perfecting of human nature, such elimination must remain an iridescent dream," he asserted. By contrast, Chaney claimed, engineering revision could "result in the entire elimination of fatalities."[93]

Chaney first used the term *engineering revision* in 1917, but it had been implicit in his study of safety in iron and steel released in 1913. It implied, he emphasized, not simply machine guarding, but "the widest possible application of engineering skill to the safety of industrial plants."

Chaney stressed that machine and building design and location and lighting were all aspects of safety that required the engineer's skills. He dismissed as myopic the claims made by business representatives that because machine guarding could prevent only 20–30 percent of all injuries, worker carelessness must account for the rest; Chaney thought that many other kinds of injuries could also be prevented by physical changes in the workplace. Moreover, the dramatic reductions in injury frequency brought about largely by educational campaigns were misleading, for the injuries prevented were minor. Most serious injuries could be prevented only by engineering revision, Chaney believed. To support this position he developed a measure of injury severity. It assigned lost workdays to accidents resulting in death and permanent injuries, and calculated the severity rate as the number of lost workdays relative to the number of manhours. After some modifications the index was widely adopted.

Using this index and his data from the iron and steel industry, Chaney built the case for engineering. "A notable decline in [injury] frequency might be accompanied by . . . rising severity," he stressed. Yet "without exception . . . a conspicuous decline in severity could be correlated with engineering improvements." As further evidence, Chaney reported that the assessment of safety committees concurred with his findings. They found that engineering changes could have prevented only 7 percent of 1,642 injuries reviewed, but 57 percent of all deaths and major mutilations. Chaney concluded that frequency rates were a useful index of minor injuries, and he admitted the importance of experience, education, and other "human factors" in reducing such injuries. But severity rates reflected death and major injury, and could be diminished only by reengineering the workplace.[94]

Although Chaney was the most prominent spokesman for this position, it was meat and drink to the newly emerging profession of safety engineering. By the twentieth century, engineers had become self-conscious professionals and were increasingly inclined to see themselves as society's problem solvers. Safety had always been important in such aspects of the profession's work as bridge and boiler design, but it had not figured prominently in machine and plant construction. This was a short step to take, however. *Efficiency* was a good word in the engineer's lexicon, while *waste* was a bad one, and it was easy to see accidents as a form of waste. John Calder, an engineer and general manager of Remington Typewriter, claimed that "the principles of safeguarding the workers should be as much a part of the education of the engineer as should those of efficiency in other directions." W. P. Barba emphasized to the American Society of Mechanical Engineers (ASME) the "waste

... of productive power" that injuries represented. The Hoover Commission report of 1921 also stressed the waste represented by industrial injuries, which the commission claimed amounted to over $1 billion in 1919. A growing group of individuals trained as electrical or mechanical engineers began to devote more and more of their time to the prevention of such waste, and to call themselves safety engineers.[95]

The American Society of Safety Engineers was formed in 1911, and its original name—the United Association of Casualty Inspectors—reveals its origins in insurance engineering. Like most other emerging professional societies, it suffered from growing pains. The first difficulty was to establish that safety engineering both was an important function and contained a distinct body of engineering wisdom. David Beyer was an early member who helped define the profession. In 1901 he joined the engineering department at American Steel and Wire—a U.S. Steel subsidiary—and when the company began safety work in 1908, he became its chief safety engineer. Thereafter he devoted full time to safety and in 1912 became vice president and chief safety engineer for Liberty Mutual, where he remained until he died in 1937.[96]

Beyer tried to link safety work to the traditional professional concerns of engineers. "It is the primary duty of the engineer to eliminate needless expense and waste," he told the ASME in 1915. Preventable accidents were "one of the most appalling wastes in industry," he thought. Beyer also heartily endorsed Chaney's view that engineering revision was the core of effective safety work. Like Chaney, he pointed out that while machine accidents were only a fraction of the total, they were apt to be severe. Moreover, other kinds of accidents could also be prevented by mechanical means. Falls, falling objects, electric shocks, explosions, and corrosive substances were all risks that engineers could reduce. There was, he thought, "a real danger of underestimating such guards."[97]

Along with other safety engineers, Beyer emphasized the primacy of engineering revision over educational campaigns designed to prevent "carelessness." The difficulty with this position was summarized by Chaney in one word: cost. Safety engineers had to persuade businesses that their high-priced approach to accident prevention made sense, but the problem of balancing safety and expense raised sensitive ethical issues. In 1914 a committee on ethics of the mechanical engineers delicately urged that a "reasonable degree of safety" be provided, and one engineer acknowledged that "we have constantly to bear in mind what is desirable and what is feasible having in regard the matter of expense." While most engineers realized that safety must be "practical," as Van Schaack had stressed, their position was made more difficult by the bias against prevention of serious injuries built into the workmen's compensation laws. In the 1920s the need to justify expensive safety programs led to several attempts to link safety to productive efficiency and to claims that accidents had important hidden costs beyond those of workmen's compensation (see chap. 4).[98]

Safety engineers were also beset from another direction and were forced to defend their emerging profession from brother engineers who charged that safety work was not "real engineering." This professional defensiveness appeared about the time of World War I, just as safety engineering was emerging as a separate field. Louis DeBlois, as a Harvard graduate and head of DuPont's safety program, was no doubt unaccustomed to feelings of inferiority. In 1918 he addressed the ASME, asserting that "safety engineering is not child's play." DeBlois thought he sensed a certain apathy toward safety among his fellow engineers. It was "not a matter for 'practical men,' not a passing fad, but real work for real engineers." It was, he concluded rather defensively, "true engineering."[99]

The main trade journal *Safety Engineering* published numerous articles in a similar vein defining and defending the new profession. Chester Rausch emphasized that safety engineering was a profession, but he too was worried that because it dealt with people as well as with things, the profession was not receiving its due. Rausch recognized that safety work might well involve worker education and similar activities. But he defined safety engineers as individuals who, by dint of their technical training and experience, understood and directed the laws of nature to reduce accidents. This was "equivalent to other engineering efforts," he asserted. Other writers also emphasized that real safeguarding was not simply covering a danger spot, it was "using all your ingenuity to devise some sort of improvement that will make . . . an accident impossible."[100]

Gradually safety engineering established itself as a separate profession. The American Society for Safety Engineers adopted a constitution and bylaws in 1916 and an emblem in 1918: a Norman shield on a green background. Although World War I nearly led to the its demise in 1918, the society's membership rose from 188 in 1919 to 341 in 1921 and to 1,028 in 1930. A lobbying arm and educational qualifications were established; in the early 1920s a member was required to have an engineering degree or practical experience. Professional licensing remained a dream, however. In 1925 the society merged with the engineering arm of the National Safety Council, and it did not reemerge as a separate organization until after World War II. These attempts to professionalize safety engineering did more than simply boost the status and salary of the membership. Professionalization also enhanced the importance of safety work within the corporation. As a later society brochure explained, "The better your education, the greater your experience, the higher your organizational position, the better results you can expect from your program." As such claims suggest, status problems remained. As late as 1946 one writer referred to safety engineers as "illegitimate and the black sheep of the engineering profession."[101]

Safety engineers were successful in infiltrating their ideas into the engineering curriculum. By 1925 the University of Pittsburgh, Penn State, Ohio State, and Carnegie Institute of Technology were all incorporating safety into courses on machine and factory design. In 1931 another survey added Columbia, Michigan, the University of Tulsa, the Colorado School of Mines, and the University of Louisville as schools doing work of "special interest." What they taught, besides safety techniques, was a professional ethic that J. M. Woltz summarized in a talk before the Society of Industrial Engineers. Injuries that stemmed from physical causes Woltz described as "failures on the part of the engineer."[102]

Conclusion

In the latter half of the nineteenth century, new and larger sources of power and machinery, along with a series of developments in labor management, transformed the conditions under which industrial workers labored. In a legal climate that made work accidents cheap, safety was eroded by the growth of factory size and by the spread of mechanization and employer control over the pace of work. While similar developments characterized European nations, fragmentary evidence suggests that American industry, like American mines and railroads, may have been especially lethal. In the twentieth century a rather strange alliance of reformers, unionists, and business executives responded to the increasing dangers of work with compensation and tightened state safety laws. These in turn gave birth to the modern safety movement.

The movement developed a network of public and private institutions that both encouraged safety activities on the part of firms and provided them with the information and the goods and services necessary for this work. Although economic incentives created and propelled the safety movement, it soon developed individuals and organizations that advanced their own safety agenda. Men and women came to devote their lives to the cause, and while they had to justify their work in economic terms, they saw safety as more than a matter of profit and loss. For safety engineers, engineering revision became a matter of professional standing, and they precipitated the first serious inquiries into the cause and prevention of workplace injuries. The conclusion that injuries resulted from professional or managerial failure rather than from workers' carelessness represented a stunning reversal of earlier belief, but its full implications became clear only when companies tried to prevent injuries. How manufacturing companies, railroads, and coal and metal mines went about the business of safety—and with what results—are the subjects of the next three chapters.

MANUFAC-
TURING
DANGERS

CHAPTER FOUR

A MANAGEMENT RESPONSIBILITY

The Business of Manufacturing Safety
1906–1939

Out of this nettle, danger, we pluck this flower, safety.
HOTSPUR, *HENRY IV, PART I*

*A very few establishments are doing an enormous amount of safety work and
making an enormous amount of noise about it. The great majority of plants [are]
doing . . . nothing and saying nothing about it.*
ETHELBERT STEWART, U.S. COMMISSIONER OF LABOR STATISTICS, 1927

Work safety in manufacturing improved sharply during the first four
decades of the twentieth century as a result of changes in labor markets,
in technology, and in business organization. The central feature of the
period was the integration of safety work into the management structure and ideology of the largest firms. In 1908, with the exception of a
handful of large companies, organized safety work was entirely absent
from American manufacturing. In that year U.S. Steel pioneered in developing a safety program that was widely emulated by other large companies. DuPont both followed and improved on the U.S. Steel model.
By the mid-1920s, DuPont managers were articulating what had been
implicit from the first: work safety was a management responsibility. In
1929 an Illinois survey of 325 manufacturing plants found that nearly
three-fourths of those with more than five hundred employees had a
safety organization. In the mid-1930s a national survey found that about
half of all manufacturing plants had a safety director.[1]

The safety work undertaken by these companies had both a "soft"
and a "hard" side. The soft side emphasized the need for worker cooperation and employed slogans, pep rallies, and contests toward this
end. The hard side downplayed worker cooperation and stressed the
need for management control over all aspects of work. In the beginning
the soft vision predominated (although the need for discipline was never

ignored), but as companies began to stress that safety was a managerial responsibility, its harder side emerged. By the beginning of World War II such safety work, along with important changes in technology and labor markets, had led to dramatic declines in injury rates throughout most of manufacturing.

The Beginnings of Company Safety Work, 1906–1925

Early safety work almost invariably included three components. The first was organizational. A safety department was created, usually under the supervision of an engineer, and safety committees were then set up that typically included both workers and representatives of all levels of management. The second and third components of the program were education and engineering revision. After a hazard survey, the safety department recommended safeguards and began worker education to redesign both the workplace and the worker.

REDESIGNING WORK AND WORKERS: THE U.S. STEEL MODEL

The first modern safety organization was developed at the South Chicago works of Illinois Steel by Robert J. Young, during the period 1906–8. Young, who was manager of the plant's department of safety and relief, organized committees of workers who were paid for their time and whose job it was to inspect the plant and make recommendations to the manager on improvements in conditions and practices. The committee head was given authority to send men to the foremen to be disciplined, if need be, and to "stop the operation of the mill" if there was something wrong with the machinery that might lead to an accident. There were also department committees, made up of foremen (and sometimes including workmen), which investigated accidents. Finally, there was a plant committee that included "important officials" whose job it was to make inspections, investigate accidents, and decide on safety suggestions coming from below.[2]

U.S. Steel added several layers when it adopted this structure. Each subsidiary corporation had its own committee, the functions and membership of which were similar to the plant committee. The buck ultimately stopped at the Central Safety Committee, which included a representative of U.S. Steel and of five (later seven) subsidiaries. The central committee also performed inspections; on the basis of its findings and of suggestions coming from below, it made recommendations to the subsidiaries. It thus served partly as a clearinghouse ensuring that improvements developed in one plant would be implemented throughout the corporation. In 1910 the central committee claimed to have inspected seventy-eight plants and to have accepted 92 percent of the fifty-two hundred recommendations it had received. By 1912, 4,678 workmen had served on safety committees.[3]

U.S. Steel's prestige and the wide publicity given this program — one insurance company even published it as a booklet — ensured that it would be studied carefully by other companies. A number of employers were skeptical of workingmen's committees. One industrial engineer thought that safety work should be done by the safety engineer and that workers should work. "It is purely a matter of efficiency," he announced to his colleagues. There were also questions about the desirability of letting workers investigate accidents that might "reveal some fault on the part of the foremen or some mistakes on the part of the company," and about whether the workers should be allowed to choose their own safety committee members. In 1913 C. W. Price of the Wisconsin Industrial Commission asked a round-table discussion of the National Safety Council (NSC) about the desirability of appointing a workers' committee in a "new" (i.e., unguarded) plant. Might it not be better, he wondered, to "wait until after the 'high spots' had been covered — the more flagrant conditions?"[4]

Walter Greenwood of Carnegie Steel, a U.S. Steel subsidiary, did not seem to think this was a problem. Arthur H. Young, who had been a roll hand at the Joliet works, was then supervisor of labor and safety at Illinois Steel, and at the start of his career as an industrial relations counsel. Young explained that putting workers on the committees "proves to the men that the management is vitally interested in them." It also provided them with limited power to shape the new rules under which they would work, a point Young chose not to emphasize. His company also intended to allow workers to pick their own representatives. Illinois Steel also had committees of workmen and foremen investigate accidents and were satisfied with the result. C. M. Brading of Wisconsin Steel, an International Harvester subsidiary, told the council, "We are thoroughly satisfied with the . . . workmen's committees." Such claims must have been convincing, for many companies that undertook safety work followed the U.S. Steel model and organized safety committees that included workers.[5]

The committees included the foreign-born and sometimes black as well as native white workers. "We have not found it difficult to get the foreign community to comprehend the safety movement," Robert J. Young of Illinois Steel told the National Safety Council in 1913. According to Arthur Young, the yard department safety committee of the South Chicago plant contained two foreigners, neither of whom knew English and one of whom was illiterate in his own language. Both were

THE ROAD TO HAPPINESS

Across the stream of ignorance, over the bridge of education, avoiding the path of carelessness and the byway of indifference, leads The Road to Happiness.

If you know this road, and have been traveling it, appoint yourself a guide — to show your less fortunate brother The Road to Happiness this coming year.

Late in 1913 U.S. Steel beckoned workers across the stream of ignorance, over the bridge of education, and onto the Safety First road to happiness. *(Author's collection)*

"good men and make practical suggestions," he reported. Moreover, by serving they could secure "the broadening influence of other more advanced and better educated men." At Commonwealth Steel in the 1920s, black men made up the safety committees of the chippers, chainmen, and laborers. The company encouraged them to develop their own rules for safe work practices, and they sent delegates to the integrated plant-wide safety committee.[6]

Female workers were usually relegated to inferior positions within the safety movement. In 1920 Nellie Schwartz of the New York State Bureau of Labor complained that "it is difficult to find any safety committees in shops where only women are employed, and . . . where men and women are both employed, it is the men who carry on the safety campaign." Apparent exceptions were International Harvester and American Woolen Mill, which included women on their safety committees. Another textile mill that included women on its safety committees did not allow them to conduct inspections because of their supposed lack of mechanical sense, however.[7]

Including workers on the safety committees yielded a number of benefits to companies. One of their most important functions was, as Price put it, "to convince . . . [workers] of the sincerity . . . of the safety movement." Because many safety men stressed the importance of worker behavior in causing accidents, they felt that employee cooperation was vital. Frank McKee of Fairbanks-Morse said that his company had adopted the Illinois Steel structure; he emphasized that in "accident prevention work, the more co-operation that can be secured from the employee the better the results will be." The committees also gave workers a collective voice in creating new safety rules and put peer pressure on the recalcitrant, both of which helped secure cooperation.[8]

Inclusion of workers also acknowledged the realities of the early-twentieth-century workplace: employees often had wide discretion on how they performed their tasks and usually knew more about a plant's dangers than their supervisors did. The committees allowed employers to tap this knowledge. Robert Young was probably the first to discover this. "Conferences with foremen and workmen will point out things that it would take a man a long time to discover through observation," he admitted. The safety engineer at Winchester beseeched his foremen and workers to point out hidden hazards that "we could not locate even with the most careful investigation." "The workman is the best source of suggestions for safeguarding the plant," acknowledged W. E. Worth, superintendent of the Chicago Tunnel Company. J. J. Heelan, a safety engineer for Aetna, urged his colleagues to "endeavor to bring out any inherent ability which may exist among the workmen." M. H. Fellmer of the W. H. Markham Company went even farther. "Just try forming such a committee from the workmen and turn them loose to . . . look for conditions they would change if they owned the plant," he suggested. He predicted that they would "show you many a condition that needs material improvement" and that "if properly taken in hand will result in a material increase in efficiency."[9]

The need to enlist employees' cooperation if safety work was to be successful reinforced the importance of engineering revision. Although many safety men persisted in claiming that worker behavior was responsible for 70–80 percent of all injuries—a conclusion that drove Lucian Chaney to develop severity rates and to stress that engineering revision was more than just machine guarding—instinctively many safety experts understood that efforts to encourage safer work habits depended upon making the plant safe. Nineteenth-century manufacturing work had involved an implicit contract: both workers and managers understood that work would be dangerous and that it was up to the worker to look out for himself. Workmen's compensation increased employers' safety incentives, but not those of employees. Thus, when companies tried to change the contract by instituting safety work, they often encountered apathetic, hostile, or suspicious workers. For a firm to begin accident prevention by stressing changes in work practices would have convinced employees that this was just one more version of the speed-up. Since workers could withhold their cooperation, a "gift" in the form of some money spent to improve work conditions was necessary to induce them to trust the company's good faith sufficiently to return the favor.[10]

Robert Young explained the U.S. Steel view to readers of *Iron Age:* "What folly it would be to try to enforce rules or train the workmen into thinking of their own and others' safety if we did not show our desire to prevent accidents by doing all in our power to make working conditions as safe as possible." The editor of the Portland Cement Association's *Accident Prevention Bulletin* claimed that two-thirds of all injuries could be prevented only by education. Yet he understood that safeguarding was vital because it provided "tangible proof of a company's interest," without which, he emphasized, educational programs would be doomed. Arthur Young also observed dryly that "suggestions made by recommendations must not be forgotten as this disheartens the men." One safety committee started out making recommendations, but the company vetoed those that cost any money. "We think this is all bluff," the committee members explained to a Liberty Mutual inspector when he asked why they seemed so apathetic.[11]

U.S. Steel practiced what the Youngs preached. The company claimed that from 1910 to 1914 it spent about $500,000 a year on accident prevention. Robert Young, David Beyer, and other company publicists described the changes that U.S. Steel made. The construction of viaducts allowed employees to cross the rail yards safely, and railings were installed on high walkways throughout the mills. The company made cranes safer by constructing footwalks for repairers and operators, and by enclosing gears so that when they broke, men working below would no longer be endangered. Crane hooks were modified to prevent the possible loss of a finger by the man hooking the load and also to prevent the load from dropping. Close clearances around railroads were blocked. Power transmission gears, belts, and shafts were guarded. The beds of metal lathes were enclosed, and thousands of other machines were guarded. Because steel companies were among the leaders in safety, many of these guards had to be invented from scratch. However, purchasing departments soon began to give preference to properly guarded machinery, and they even went so far as to inscribe this fact across the

Most industrial safety began with protection from moving parts. *Top:* Wheels to this charging machine for an open-hearth furnace have been fitted with metal cow-catcher-like devices. *Bottom:* Belt guards protected limbs from mangling and improved labor productivity. *(Courtesy Hagley Museum and Library; author's collection)*

top of their stationery. Given the volume of business involved, this must have provided a sharp spur to safety innovation among machine producers.[12]

Armco, Bethlehem, Commonwealth, Inland, Jones and Laughlin, Lukens, Midvale, Youngstown, and other steel producers followed U.S. Steel's lead. Lucian Chaney pointed out that hot-metal breakouts, which had been the leading cause of severe injuries in blast furnaces in 1910, had virtually disappeared by 1919. The reason was that the furnaces had been rebuilt and strengthened. Chaney also noted that the risk of asphyxiation had been diminished by raising the gas pipes and improving the valves. These and other measures precipitated a revolution in the safety of steel work in about a generation (table A3.1). In 1907 about 250 out of every 1,000 men who worked a full (3,000-hour) year were injured [(80.8 × 3)/1,000]; by 1939 U.S. Steel had cut this number to about 3.[13]

These procedures were replicated at hundreds of other firms. From 1910 through 1912, Kodak undertook an intensive campaign to guard machines and made a movie of the results that it showed to employees and rented to the National Association of Manufacturers. Between 1912 and 1914, John Deere spent about $50,000 to guard its plants in Moline, Illinois, thereby reducing its compensation premium by one-third. From 1911 to 1917, nearly every meeting of the safety committee of the Joseph Bancroft and Sons textile mills recorded some new safeguard installed as a result of prodding by a company safety man or an insurance company inspection. In 1920 the company began to review all purchases of new machines for safety features. The Amoskeag textile mills installed locks on picking machines so that they could not be opened while the beaters were in motion. Belt shifters were also installed on carding machines, which had long been a prolific source of injury. Burroughs thoroughly guarded its machinery in 1913 and promptly cut its workmen's compensation costs from 36 cents to 9 cents per $100 of payroll.[14]

Henry Ford, who never did anything in moderation, went whole hog into safeguarding. "Production without safety," Ford pronounced, "is inefficient." As a result, "machines . . . were redesigned; equipment thrown out; buildings were remodeled; processes were changed." When Ford engineers designed safety features for machines, they also sent along blueprints to the equipment makers urging their incorporation. At DuPont, engineers drew up blueprints for proper machine design and placement. That firm also followed U.S. Steel's practice of giving preference in the purchase of new machines to those with proper safety features. In 1921 a writer for *National Safety News* remarked on the extent to which engineering revision rather than simply "after thought machine guarding" had come to characterize DuPont's work. The metalworking firm A. O. Smith began its safety work in 1913. Its central safety committee "at once set out to guard machines . . . and the entire plant was equipped with safety devices as quickly as possible." [15]

The purchase and installation of safety equipment rarely resulted from any sophisticated calculation of costs and monetary benefits. Costs and worker risks did matter; most large companies made sure that insurance savings more than paid for their safety expenditures. And probably one reason for the lack of safety enthusiasm at textile companies was the costs implied by their high machine-to-worker ratio. In 1931, when Liberty Mutual suggested additional safeguards to the Bancroft mills, the company rejected the advice because "neither the premium saving nor the hazard involved would justify making the required changes." The lack of any very precise information about risks ensured that specific safety decisions were invariably based on rules of thumb. After a review of plant hazards, when a suggestion was made by a workers' committee, if it was not too expensive and funds were not tight, and if the danger seemed real—perhaps because it had caused a recent accident—the responsible official would make the change. J. D. James of New Jersey Zinc even claimed that his company sometimes followed the suggestions of workers' committees "whether in our judgment a guard is advisable or not." But sometimes matters also worked out the other way: "The question will come up 'How much will it cost to put a guard rail on this particular platform?' The engineer will estimate . . . $5,000. . . . Then someone will . . . say 'when did you have an accident [there] . . . ?' 'I cannot remember one in five or six years' [the foreman will say]. Then they will say 'Oh we will just let that go.' " [16]

A manufacturer of papermaking machinery said that while safeguards of calender rolls had been termed impossible, "I do not consider any problem impossible . . . if an industry is willing to pay the cost." Calender guards cost $750, and "I have not felt the paper mill industry was interested to that extent." Sometimes interest could be stimulated by an injury investigation that revealed the benefits of a guard in a particularly graphic way. A representative of Studebaker told the National Safety Council that officials at his company had always believed that the square sheer was impossible to guard at the point of operation until the horror of two amputations in the same year drove them to find a way. [17]

Such activities created a market for safety devices. Large users such as Ford and U.S. Steel initiated designs that they publicized and shared with other machinery users, and they also demanded that suppliers incorporate safety features into new equipment. Institutions such as the National Safety Council, insurance companies, state regulators, and trade journals publicized the new equipment, and producers gradually responded, offering the products for sale to all users. Occasionally the process was reversed: United Shoe, the monopoly producer of shoe machinery, pioneered in the safe design of equipment because its policy of leasing ensured that it bore the full cost of any accidents its products caused. More typical was the experience of the machine tool producer Fairbanks-Morse. As early as 1913 the company reported that some buyers—perhaps including U.S. Steel—were now giving preference to guarded equipment. A company representative thought that "machine tool makers are waking up more and more to the fact that . . . safeguards is one of the selling points of the machine."[18]

A representative of the laundry industry thought that insurance savings had led to demands that equipment manufacturers invent added safeguards. When the meat-packing firm of Wilson and Company finally figured out how to guard the head splitter, the New York Industrial Commission promptly widened the market by requiring its use in all plants in the state. By 1917 one manufacturer of woodworking machines was reportedly unwilling to sell equipment without guards, because it, rather than the user, got the blame for accidents. By the end of World War I, textile equipment producers such as Saco-Lowell, Crompton and Knowles, and Whitin Machine Works were installing guards on their looms; they also put locks on pickers, drawing frames, and other machines so that they could not be started unless the guards were in place. Surety Safety Equipment Company representatives regularly attended woodworking sessions of the National Safety Council in the 1920s and gave demonstrations of their machine guards to potential customers. In 1920 David Beyer claimed, with some overstatement, that "most of the standard machinery manufacturers have designed guards for their equipment."[19]

But even the most devoted advocates of engineering revision admitted that the safety movement could never reach its full potential without employee cooperation. Many dangers simply could not be guarded. In addition, development of effective guards required much learning, and some early ones were highly imperfect. Such guards increased dangers by leading workers to take chances under the illusion that they were safe. Lone Star Cement recounted the experience of one of its cement pullers who stepped through the wire mesh covering a screw conveyer and had his leg severed at the thigh. Burroughs discovered that a hand-tripping device for punch presses failed when the spring wore, "causing quite a number of accidents." Robert Young described such devices as traps to catch workers. These considerations led engineers to insist that guards needed to be foolproof and to concur with their employers on the importance of having employees learn to work safely.[20]

This stress on worker education with its implicit assumption that behavior was malleable sharply distinguished the early American safety movement from its European counterpart. Frederick Ritzmann, chief of the Safety Section of the International Labor Office (ILO), pointed out that the European safety movement had begun with strict requirements for machine guarding, which focused employers' interests on complying with the law instead of preventing injuries. In the United States, on the other hand, the ineffectiveness of early state legislation combined with the spread of workmen's compensation encouraged businesses to see safety in business terms, not legal terms, and to seek out cost-effective means to prevent injuries. Thus, while American companies attempted to enlist the active collaboration of employees in safety work with a variety of educational campaigns, European businesses concentrated almost exclusively on safeguarding. Not until the mid 1920s did European employers begin to emulate American techniques.[21]

When safety officials talked about educating the workers to work safely, they meant many things. Initially the problem was simply to convince workers that management was acting in good faith, and an important reason for having workers perform inspections and injury investigations was to demonstrate to employees that not all injuries could be prevented by safeguards. The second and far more important step in the process was to prevent "carelessness." As safety committees undertook hazard and injury investigations, they began to compile rules of safe and unsafe practices. As early as 1904, Illinois Steel developed a rule book of safe practices, and both foremen and workers were expected to learn it and were examined on it. Because investigations revealed that a disproportionate number of injuries were suffered by green help, companies began to devote special efforts to inculcating safe habits in their new workers. This placed a new responsibility on the foreman. Illinois Steel seems to have pioneered in this as in so many other areas. Foremen were required to instruct new workers in safety, and they presented new employees with the rule book on which they were later examined; if the worker did not know English, an interpreter was to "talk safety" to him. If he could not write, he was given an oral examination by the interpreter.[22]

Almost everything could be done more or less safely, and company rules began to cover an increasing number of activities. J. R. Davis of U.S. Gypsum explained that in quarry work many serious hazards could not be guarded—the use of gantry cranes to hoist rock from mine to mill being one of them. In response, the company studied the process and drew up rules for safe practice. In woodworking, new rules required saws to be kept sharp, for dull blades were more likely to cause accidents. There were safe ways to pile materials, safe places to stand while dressing drive belts, safe methods of placing ladders and of climbing down them, safe methods of lifting, safe ways to sharpen a knife, safe ways to attach a lifting hook, open a fire door, feed a saw, tighten a nut, rig a gangway, lift a load, and move a cart.[23]

There were also safe ways to dress. In many industries the new practices required that workers wear protective clothing such as safety shoes, leggings, special gloves, and safety glasses. Such requirements gradually generated suppliers of these new devices. Safety shoes originated about 1903; steel-toe shoes were first marketed in 1925. The first "hard-boiled hats," as they were then called, were introduced into mining in 1919. Safety glasses date from 1903; they were used at U.S. Steel as early as 1907. They were described to the National Safety Council in 1912, and in 1913 Julius King Optical was advertising them to the readers of *American Industries*. By 1916, exhibitors at the NSC meeting were offering goggles, respirators, safety shoes, and other personal protective equipment.[24]

The new equipment was often unpopular with workers, as it was sometimes ill fitting and unfashionable. Goggles were hot, and they regularly fogged up. The early safety shoes fit so poorly and looked so bad that workers at Lukens Steel—who called them "canalboats"—refused to wear them, and the company dared not force the issue. These difficulties were gradually overcome. In the 1920s manufacturers began to advertise more stylish safety shoes and better-fitting safety glasses, and some companies let employees choose their own styles of protective equipment. Such tactics helped Lukens overcome workers' initial aversion to safety shoes. Publicizing the fact that a two-ton weight had fallen on the foot of an early convert without hurting him may also have helped. A representative of Champion Paper admitted that the best way out of the "goggle problem" was to eliminate the need to wear them, which no doubt cheered the engineers in his audience. But where that could not be done, Champion required goggles and if need be would fire those who repeatedly failed to wear them. By the mid-1930s a survey of eighty-eight large and medium-sized metalworking firms revealed that nearly all required at least some employees to wear safety glasses, while about half required some use of safety shoes.[25]

The new dress codes had a dramatic effect. Between 1918 and 1932 General Electric reduced eye accidents from about 24 per thousand employees annually to less than 1 per thousand. In 1920 twelve eyes were lost in Buick factory no. 12; by 1922 the toll had been reduced to one.

In 1925 the safety director at Pullman was finally able to persuade management to mandate safety glasses for all employees. As a result, he claimed, eye injuries disappeared, and by 1929 the new rule had prevented ninety-four cases of blindness. Similar procedures helped the company reduce the overall injury rate by two-thirds, from 9.9 to 3.3 per million manhours between 1927 and 1939. In 1928 the National Society for the Prevention of Blindness and the National Safety Council surveyed 538 establishments with about 578,000 employees to discover the effect of safety glasses in saving eyesight. Companies were asked the number of workers whose lenses had been shattered or splattered with hot metal or injurious chemicals. The total, for 1926 and 1927 combined, was 7,411 employees, or 1.3 percent of exposed workers. About 2,700 of these workers had both lenses destroyed. These results cannot be generalized, for the survey was not a random sample. But in the mid-1930s the national health survey discovered that 19 percent of all single-eye blindness was occupationally related; presumably it had been higher in earlier years.[26]

Although some Progressives thought women needed special protection from workplace dangers, most safety workers saw no need to provide an additional margin of safety for their female employees. But women's fashions did present special safety problems, as the textile industry had long known and as other industries discovered when they placed women in novel jobs during World War I. Jewelry was undesirable, and Armour forbade it. Women's long, loose-fitting skirts were also dangerous in a shop full of moving machinery, especially where they sat to operate machines that had moving parts under the table. Peter O'Shea of Greenfield Tap and Die recommended the installation of skirt guards, while other writers favored shorter skirts or bloomers. By 1918 a number of clothing suppliers had responded to these new demands: the Sweet-Orr Corporation, which made men's work clothing, now proudly advertised its "Sweet-Orr Womanalls." Because such clothing was so unattractive, and correspondingly unpopular, the women's division of the Massachusetts Safety Council staged a style show in the early 1920s to encourage more fashionable designs.[27]

Long hair also placed its wearer at risk around moving machinery. When beards had been in fashion, men were not exempt from these dangers. Fred Colvin described the fate of one bewhiskered nineteenth-century machinist whom he termed "luckier than some other operators I knew." "Zeke was literally in up to his ears. His . . . frame was wrapped solidly around the lathe. About 8 inches . . . of his . . . beard was inextricably bound up in the gears. . . . He had become part of his machine." By the twentieth century few men wore beards, but a woman who operated

®31635

Women workers assembling artillery shell fuses in a World War I munitions plant. Safety caps and bloomers reduced the danger that hair or clothing might be caught in gears and belts. A better solution, safety engineers argued, was to guard the belts—here visible in typical profusion. *(Library of Congress)*

a drill press faced not only the usual risks from transmission machinery and gears but also the possibility of being scalped should her hair be caught by the spindle. As a result, companies began to require that women workers wear caps.[28]

Unfashionable, often devastating to a hairdo, and hot in the summer, the caps were decidedly unpopular. Hair nets were usually substituted in hot weather when the women rebelled and refused to wear caps, as happened at Bancroft in 1917, but even hair nets were unpopular, according to a representative of General Electric. In spite of worker antipathy, caps and hair nets continued to be required in many plants long after machine guards, direct electric drive, and the new shorter hair styles of the 1920s had made them obsolete—a testimony, no doubt, to inertia and to male dominance of the safety movement. Nor, until World War II, does much effort seem to have been expended to make the caps attractive, and other modifications of women's fashion were also slow in coming. Safety shoes for women were first produced in 1929, but high heels were a continuing menace that led to a disproportionate number of falls among women workers. The first women's safety shoe with a protective toe was introduced by Lehigh Shoe in 1942. Similarly, hard hats for women and the Saf-T-Bra did not make their appearance until World War II.[29]

Workers sometimes resisted the new methods. Some employees, who apparently preferred income to safety, feared that the new procedures would reduce their pay. As noted, piece rates provided the incentive for textile workers to clean moving equipment. Machine guards were sometimes badly designed, and C. L. York of General Electric claimed that the reluctance of workers at his company to operate machines with safety devices resulted from their fear that the guards would slow production, for they too were on piece rates. To induce them to try the devices, General Electric offered to guarantee their average rate of pay. And Bancroft and Lukens Steel were not the only companies in which employees resisted the use of protective equipment that they found unpleasant or unfashionable. In meat packing, metal-mesh gloves were uncomfortable, and a women butcher at Wilson also claimed that they dulled her knife. The safety expert sarcastically observed that the "flesh and bone of her own left hand would not dull the knife quite as much."[30]

The new rules and equipment also represented a loss of workers' control over their work lives. "We found a great deal of contempt for our efforts on the part of the men," the superintendent of a Kimberly-Clark mill explained. The problem, he thought, was that "the old-timers disliked being told how to do a job without being hurt. Their idea was that someone had to get hurt, occasionally." In addition, danger was manly. When William Sellers and Company first made protective leggings available, the molders refused to wear them until one was seriously burned. The need to convince the men that using safety equipment was not a sign of weakness doubtless explains how the original "hard-boiled hats" got their name. That term had long been used to describe an especially manly worker; hence, the wearer of a hat with that name could not be accused of being effeminate. Other protective equipment was also potentially suspect. When one packing house first installed knife guards, the employees promptly ground them off. The plant superintendent explained that "old notions are difficult to supplant." He recalled that after his first cut, the foremen had told him, "You need only ninety-nine more cuts to be a butcher." In 1938 president Charles Hook of Armco also recalled that in the past "the fellow who wasn't willing to risk his safety was looked on in modern terms as a sissy." The safety movement, with its host of company-imposed rules and equipment, challenged these old notions and reduced workers' freedom to follow traditional methods of work.[31]

To show employees how to work safely and to persuade them to adopt these new methods and equipment, safety experts borrowed the tools of the ad man. By 1918 F. E. Morris of Armco had concluded that "to me it looks like a selling proposition all the way through." Five years later R. T. Solensten, bulletin editor of the National Safety Council, informed the faithful that "the right kind of advertising will put on the map any product that has merit, . . . and what advertising will do for the commercial product it will do for safety." He should have known, for the safety bulletin board with its bulletins and posters became a primary vehicle for spreading the gospel. Just how different this approach was from European practice is revealed by the ILO's observation that in 1925 there were not one hundred safety posters in the entire United Kingdom, whereas the National Safety Council—which was by no means the only source—was producing them at the rate of thirty-six a month. The object of posters and bulletin boards, according to Solensten, was to stimulate thought, create goodwill, and instruct.[32]

Some appealed to workers' family affection or showed the monetary costs of injuries. A few treated accidents as dumb or used cartoons featuring the blundering characters Willie Everlearn and Otto Nobetter, who invariably chose the most dangerous way of doing a job, to make the same point with humor. Yet such techniques had to be used carefully. Harping on "carelessness" or ridiculing individuals rather than practices was likely to alienate, not motivate, workers. Posters sometimes depicted the right and wrong way to perform a specific act, and some of DuPont's creations cast the instruction as a contest to see how many unsafe situations and acts could be discovered. Companies with many foreign workers published their posters and bulletins in several languages. Some posters displayed the benefits of safety glasses, and a few gruesome creations depicted the consequences of accidents. Most companies also tried to include local material on their bulletin boards. Bad tools or broken goggles were a favorite. One writer suggested combining a pair of broken goggles and two glass eyes with the caption, "Which would you rather wear?"[33]

Companies sometimes enlisted community pressure to encourage workers to adopt safer work habits. In 1912, Illinois Steel gave a banquet to ministers and priests in the Joliet region, showed them slides of the company's work, and asked them to talk to the men and their families. The company also invited the workers' children to a movie. There the youngsters were informed that if their fathers were not wearing a safety button, it meant that they did not know the safety rules and were likely to get hurt. The children, it was hoped, would question relatives without a button, thereby encouraging them to learn the rules. The company also got its rules published in foreign-language newspapers. Somewhat

National Safety Council poster of the 1920s showing "Otto Nobetter" living up to his name. *(Courtesy National Safety Council)*

The National Safety Council promoted the wearing of safety glasses. This laborer testified that they had saved his eyesight. *(Courtesy National Safety Council)*

later, G. A. Orth of American Car and Foundry explained that his company tried to reach its black workers through neighborhood ministers. "We have them thoroughly saturated with the idea that it is almost sinful to become injured," he bragged.[34]

Ethnic stereotypes were also marshaled to reinforce safety work. C. L. Harrison of Harrison Lumber thought that the "negro is like a child," but he concluded that "once hurt, he will avoid the chance of similar injury." White workers, he thought, were more "bull headed" and therefore less likely to learn from experience. F. E. Morris of Armco told a joke about a "man of color" who had been killed on the job. According to other black workers, an autopsy revealed that "that thair culled fella's head hadn't nevah been used." The implication was that black workers too could learn to work safely.[35]

In at least one instance the employer's racial stereotyping seems to have redounded to the benefit of black employees. Like other southern sawmills, the Murray Corporation organized safety committees among both its black and white workers. In the mill that employed whites it did relatively little safeguarding, because it considered those employees "reasonably intelligent and susceptible of education." But in a mill run with workers who were described as "colored, uneducated, [and] unintelligent," the company decided that the machines needed to be "so thoroughly guarded that no hazard is apparent."[36]

Safety supervisors also used movies to deliver their message. In 1920 DuPont bought a two-reel movie *Why* from U.S. Steel, which it screened in all plants to workers and executives alike. In 1925 the Bancroft mills showed a film rented from the National Safety Council that entitled the company to a workmen's compensation credit. Plant magazines were also created, or enlisted, to serve the cause. These publications ran the gamut from three- or four-page ventures to slick, commercial-quality efforts published by very large companies. The *Staley Journal* (of A. E. Staley Manufacturing) began in 1917 with four pages edited by the safety director and evolved into a forty-four-page general-purpose plant organ by 1922, but it continued to publish safety suggestions and articles by the plant physician. Marathon Paper put out a *Safety Bulletin* beginning in 1914 that reported on contests and safety progress in both English and Polish. The Milwaukee Western Fuel Company *Transfer* began as a safety bulletin in 1914. Atlantic Refining put out the *Atlantic Seal*, which ran to thirty-six thousand copies, and published safety cartoons, limericks, and plant news.[37]

But to sell safety to the workers, no technique was more widely used than the safety contest. Again U.S. Steel pioneered, for Robert Young believed that competition was "absolutely essential." By the 1920s the contests had become widespread, and they took many forms. Large multiple-plant companies such as DuPont and U.S. Steel regularly held interdepartmental or interplant contests. Sometimes the contest was simply to see if a past record could be bettered; DuPont, for example, often staged no-accident weeks or months. In 1923 the company also began to offer a president's prize to plants that ran for a specified period without injuries. In 1927 the program was revamped—there were too many winners—and a general manager's prize, a president's prize, and a board of directors' prize were established. DuPont also began its poster competitions in 1927, and in 1935 it instituted a contest to see which plant could discover and remedy the most unsafe practices and conditions.[38]

Under the sponsorship of their trade journal, *The Paper Industry*, Champion, Nekoosa-Edwards, Kimberly-Clark, Marathon, and other big paper companies staged industrywide or sometimes regional competitions beginning in 1924. The next year sponsorship was taken over by the Paper and Pulp Section of the National Safety Council, and other sections of the council began similar contests. The Portland Cement Association regularly made June a "no-accident month," and it also staged industrywide contests to see which plant could achieve the lowest accident frequency rate. Both industries also collected injury statistics for a large number of their members that revealed significant safety gains (table A3.2).[39]

The contests generated a number of benefits for the firms that staged them. Companies hoped that they would improve morale, but their most direct effect was to produce a sharp drop in injury rates—a result that suggests the existence of considerable inefficiency during non-contest periods. Employers believed that the intense concentration on safety generated by the contests would encourage voluntary acceptance of the new methods and carry over to long-term gains in safer, and more productive, work practices. Seen in this way the contests were like intensive behavior-modification sessions. The Portland Cement Association's June contests usually cost competing plants less than $50, and at first they resulted in sharp declines in that month's injury rate. Over time their impact diminished as the annual injury rate declined, which suggests that the contests may indeed have had the long-term results employers desired.

The prize in such contests was sometimes a token monetary reward. Safety officials believed that the motivation to work safely was out of all proportion to the money involved. One worker explained why: no one wanted to be the person who prevented everyone else from getting the cash. In addition, while the new rules might come from above, a successful contest was something the employees had done and could

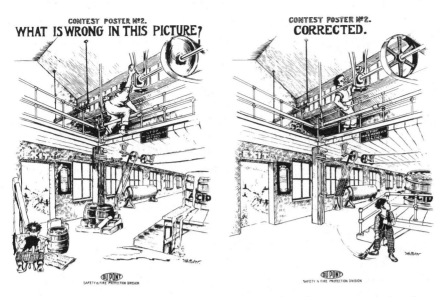

In the 1920s a series of posters at DuPont invited workers to test their safety awareness. The "wrong" image illustrated sixteen violations of workplace safety. They included a blocked exit; a worker succumbing to distraction; boards stacked against wall; unguarded belts and pulleys; unguarded gears; a blocked emergency shower; spilling acid; an attempt to oil operating machinery; climbing over a rail; and a fire extinguisher with a broken hose. *(Courtesy Hagley Museum and Library)*

take pride in. Thus, like workers' committees, safety contests provided workers a limited say in the safety movement. One firm noticed that when its workers won a $5 prize, they often kept the bill. Sometimes the prize was not cash but rather a trophy or a safety memento that went to each worker. The winning plant in the Portland Cement Association contests got to keep a $1,500 trophy—"7,000 pounds of carved and polished concrete"—until the next contest.[40]

Such efforts in persuasion were also reinforced by harsher methods. In most companies a worker who refused to follow the safety rules got a "heart-to-heart" talk from the foreman; repeated failures resulted in suspension or dismissal, even of valued employees. In 1924, the Bancroft mills finally removed an elevator operator who persisted in unsafe practices. Since bonuses and safety campaigns were substitutes for discipline, the companies that were most attracted to them were those where supervision was most difficult. With accidents expensive and supervision nearly impossible, bonuses were widespread on street and interurban railways. A 1923 survey revealed that thirteen of eighty-three such companies paid bonuses for accident prevention, and a second survey done in 1926 found that the number had risen to thirty-one. Cement producers and quarries—and, as will be seen, steam railways and mines—were also addicted to safety contests, and all were industries where employees often worked unsupervised. Yet even where supervision was not difficult the contests were widespread, probably because most employers agreed with Armco's F. E. Morris, who advised, "Put on the soft pedal when you talk of discipline. Don't make safety enemies."[41]

Companies also improved medical procedures. Workmen's compensation laws probably did more than any other single event to induce employers to provide medical examinations and first aid for their employees. An early convert, Avery Manufacturing engaged two physicians, equipped an up-to-date dispensary, and gave all workers a physical examination immediately after the Illinois Workmen's Compensation Act became effective on May 1, 1912. G. L. Avery explained why: "We did not propose to pay workmen for injuries received prior to May 1st or received after May 1st if received in places *other* than while in *our* employment." Avery also noted the company's improved first aid: a doctor could be available within twenty minutes rather than the hour and a half it had formerly taken.[42]

Other companies that improved their medical care stressed that early treatment kept down compensation costs. Prior to these changes, companies had ignored minor injuries, leaving them to be treated by the workers as best they could. In the packing houses a cut, even one that reached the bone, was treated with a spit of tobacco juice. Fred Colvin had been a lathe operator in the 1880s. When the lathe ripped open a finger, revealing the tendons, a fellow worker applied a bandage dosed with shellac. When Colvin got an eighth-inch metal sliver embedded in his cornea, the same helpful fellow dug it out with a jackknife, apparently with no lasting ill effects to Colvin. Not all applications of folk medicine had such happy results, however, and a favorite theme of the safety literature was the neglected scratch that led to blood poisoning and an expensive amputation. In 1926 DuPont's safety organization publicized the case of a worker who failed to wear safety glasses as required and got a bit of lime in his eye. Instead of going to the first-aid station he let it go, ultimately losing his eye and costing the company about $4,600 in compensation payments and fines.[43]

Employers also found out that medical examinations could help them reduce injury costs in other ways. It was discovered that large numbers of workers needed glasses, and Armco reported a crane accident that might not have happened had the operator worn glasses. Bad vision was usually correctable, but individuals with heart conditions, hernias, and breathing difficulties posed more serious problems. Companies tried to place such people in jobs that would not exacerbate the condition. Since the criteria for job placement reflected the prevailing medical wisdom of the day, the result may not always have been successful. DuPont's physician believed that blond workers were "more likely to develop skin disease when working with acids," and he tried to place them accordingly. Similarly, a doctor at Carter Oil stressed that the "thin and wiry types" were suited only for manual labor.[44]

Some applicants were simply turned away—surely a result not intended by the framers of workmen's compensation legislation. Company physicians and employment representatives swore that such cases were rare, however. "Our object is not to bar people who are subject to accidents from our industry, but to . . . place them . . . wisely," claimed Mary Baker, the employment secretary at Kimberly-Clark, and in 1935 a representative of National Cash Register claimed that in thirty-five years his company's rejection rate had averaged only 0.5 percent. In 1930 a Conference Board survey revealed that over half of all establishments with more than five hundred employees gave preemployment physical examinations, and periodic reexaminations had also become widespread.[45]

DUPONT AND THE CREED OF MANAGEMENT RESPONSIBILITY

Safety departments were necessarily staff, not line, organizations. This was not always clear, especially in the early years of the movement, and some companies such as Inland Steel and DuPont initially made the safety director responsible for accident reduction. Even with a commitment to safety on the part of top managers, the results of such divided responsibility were invariably unsatisfactory because they failed to provide line managers with the proper incentives. A representative of the safety committee of the National Electric Light Association explained that his industry's accident record compared unfavorably with that of steel and railroading because safety remained a staff function at the electric companies. By the early 1920s a consensus had emerged that while the safety organization should establish the program, results were the responsibility of operating personnel.[46]

This required that the safety department have sufficient power within the company to make its standards stick. One writer emphasized that the safety department needed "a place in the high councils" of the firm, while another noted that if anyone could veto a safety regulation, "then that plant has no need for a safety engineer." Thus, considerations of both status and effectiveness lay behind safety workers' claims that their department should report directly to top management. Yet whatever the department's corporate position, the safety engineer could only reduce accidents "by demanding results from his organization . . . [from] superintendents and foremen to the men themselves," as David Beyer pointed out in 1921. Thus, the engineer was a manager whose success depended on his ability to enlist the rest of the corporation in his war on accidents.[47]

The need to motivate operating officials in safety had been apparent from the start; how to go about it was less clear. The second meeting of the National Safety Council included a round-table discussion on the topic "How to Reach the Foreman." Judging by the number of times this subject came up in subsequent meetings, it must have continued be a problem. As Robert Young explained, "The superintendent's attitude and the foremen's attitude toward . . . [safety] will be reflected by the workmen." Enlisting the foremen required what Arthur Young termed both "molasses" and "vinegar." Companies tried to persuade foremen to support safety by including them in the same propaganda blitz that was aimed at employees. Some companies also distributed special safety literature to the foremen. The Milwaukee Western Fuel Company carried this approach to an extreme, distributing various bulletins of the Wisconsin Industrial Commission, subscribing to *Safety Engineering*, and purchasing accident prevention supplements to *American Industries* and *Scientific American*. Companies also put foremen on the safety committees and involved them in the design of safety regulations.[48]

Just as companies paid foremen bonuses for exceeding production quotas, so some began to offer them bonuses for good accident records. Steel producers paid safety bonuses that could run as high as $200 per year, and that were independent of the severity of the injury—the foremen getting the same reward for preventing a scratch as a broken neck. Lucian Chaney argued that such an incentive system would encourage foremen to concentrate on reducing minor injuries and to ignore more serious injuries that were more difficult to prevent. Chaney assembled injury data from iron and steel plants both with and without bonus systems for the period 1912–17. But an analysis of his data (see note) reveals no significant impact of the bonus on either injury frequency or severity, suggesting that the effect of the bonus may have been swamped by production incentives.[49]

At some companies the molasses was supplemented by a liberal dose of vinegar. "We hold . . . [the interest of the foremen in safety] by having meetings occasionally, but the superintendent is on their trail all the time," explained T. H. McKenney, a superintendent at Illinois Steel. In fact, McKenney noted, this policy was applied not just to the foremen but to the entire operating management of the plant: "At a meeting, the general superintendents . . . were asked for their cooperation . . . to get the undivided attention of foremen . . . to bring about a reduction in accidents; in fact they were told that a reduction must be brought about—that the superintendents would be held responsible; the superintendents would hold the general foremen responsible and the general foremen the sub-foremen." Consolidated Water Power and Paper made the department head "absolutely responsible for safety." Foremen who violated safety rules or who required their workers to do so were sometimes fired. Youngstown Sheet and Tube made this clear in its safety rule book. The section of rules for superintendents and foremen began with a blunt warning: "The general management of this company HOLDS EACH SUPERINTENDENT RESPONSIBLE FOR ALL ACCIDENTS." Companies with successful safety programs, such as Illinois Steel, usually informed their foremen that promotion would depend on their safety record as well as on their ability to produce.[50]

Safety men realized that line officers would be responsive to safety only if top management was firmly behind the program. C. W. Price, who had spent five years touring Wisconsin for that state's industrial commission trying to cajole employers into adopting safety programs, explained his conclusions to the National Safety Council in 1917: "The first [indispensable feature of a safety program] is to convince the general manager—the man who holds the pocketbook. In every case where I have succeeded in getting the general manager to go with me . . . things have happened." A safety man from American Steel and Wire concurred, claiming that his company's success had been due to "the determination on the part of our executives to produce safety first—then produce steel." This determination was no doubt enhanced by the unwavering support of top management, including, of course, Elbert H. Gary. Similarly, at Kimberly-Clark Paper, accident prevention was enthusiastically supported by several vice presidents, one of whom was named Kimberly.[51]

The key role of management was articulated most clearly by Louis DeBlois, director of safety at DuPont, in a paper entitled "Supervision as a Factor in Accident Prevention" that was presented to the National Safety Council in 1919. Responding to a paper by Lucian Chaney on the importance of engineering, DeBlois pointed out that both engineering and worker behavior required management supervision. Moreover, he emphasized that instead of being a " 'side show' endorsed by top management," safety must be part of the business of production. The top manager should state to all the line officers that "we are responsible for results." While some companies had followed this approach, at least in part, no one had articulated so clearly the need for organizational responsibility from top to bottom. Arthur Young, who only two years earlier had attributed most accidents to carelessness, was struck by De-Blois's argument, saying, "I see my error and I think we can't too quickly get away from . . . [placing responsibility on the employees] and instead hold the owners of the businesses responsible." Later Young described DeBlois's paper as the origin of the idea that "safety was an integral part of normal operating procedure." One reason DeBlois's talk was so well received was that the audience knew he was describing the DuPont approach, and that company had already gained a reputation for effective safety work. "Never have I met the sustained perfection in safety organization that exists" at DuPont, said Arthur Young.[52]

As Alfred Chandler has emphasized, DuPont pioneered in developing modern techniques to manage large, multiunit enterprises. DuPont also led the way in incorporating safety as a management objective. While the company had long been interested in the prevention of explosions, its work remained extraordinarily dangerous—far exceeding the risks of even most mining and railroad jobs (table A3.3). A more general concern with worker safety dated from about 1911, when separate safety committees were organized for the black-powder and high-explosive operating divisions. Officials familiarized themselves with U.S. Steel's methods and then made a thorough inspection of the various plants that chronicled a long list of dangerous conditions "plenty of [which] are serious." Early safety work consisted largely of efforts to improve these conditions, and top management was involved from the start; Lammot DuPont, who was a member of the black-powder safety committee, was not only on the board of directors but was also director of the black-powder division. Pierre and Irénée DuPont and many other top officials were also intimately involved with the day-to-day activities of these committees. Their degree of involvement, and the care with which they husbanded the company's resources, is captured by the response to De-Blois's request that the company join the National Safety Council in 1913. He was forced to clear the matter with Irénée DuPont, then assistant to the general manager. DuPont thought the $75 dues might not be warranted, and he proposed that DeBlois obtain a personal membership instead. He did.[53]

Despite the interest of top management in safety matters, the company initially made the error of placing the responsibility for safety largely on the safety department rather than on the operating personnel. Hence, early results were not deemed satisfactory. In 1917 the approach to safety was reorganized and, as one vice president later put it, "management took over the responsibility." This responsibility was made clear to the operating personnel by the continued, detailed involvement of top executives in safety. What had changed was accountability: in 1919 when DeBlois spoke to the National Safety Council it was a company axiom that all injuries ultimately reflected a failure of the operating managers.[54]

As company president in the 1920s, Irénée DuPont retained his interest in the details of safety work, but he seems to have loosened up the purse strings slightly. In 1921, when DeBlois sent him a requisition to spend $500 to join the Delaware Safety Council, he approved it—although only after checking with DeBlois's boss. The company calculated injury frequency and severity rates by plants, and these statistics were routinely sent to the president, who commented on them. A high rate for the engineering department in 1925 prompted this question to DeBlois: "Can you tell me whether there is anything that can be done to improve this?" Irénée DuPont also requested studies of accident costs and the savings from prevention work. Such attention to detail reflected good management; the company privately noted that accident prevention paid well, with an average return on investment of 60 percent per year.[55]

By the early 1920s World War I and a series of mergers had turned DuPont into a giant multiple-product firm. Yet the company's safety organization does not seem to have faltered. Although DuPont had dozens of plants by this time, the manager who won a companywide safety contest still received a letter of commendation signed by the president. While the newly acquired properties invariably had injury rates much higher than DuPont's, one safety man noted the dramatic effect on them of applying DuPont's methods: "The next year they reduced their accidents to a ridiculously low amount. There was no change in equipment, there was simply the reinforcement from the management down, of an intensive drive to cut out accidents."[56]

Top management's interest in safety reflected more than the simple fact that accident prevention was good business; it also stemmed from a deeper sense of responsibility. Having read somewhere that liver difficulties that were often blamed on alcohol sometimes resulted from the copper in the liquor, Irénée DuPont wrote to ask if copper exposure might be a problem in the bronze-powder plant. "I . . . would like to be assured that the company is taking every precaution to prevent loss of health by its employees," he said.[57]

This involvement continued after Lammot DuPont became president, and it must have been a powerful incentive to operating officials—especially when combined with the view that injuries were their responsibility. The company routinely described injuries that appeared to be due to worker negligence as "the result of lack of sufficient instruction and proper supervision." One result of this stance was that the idea of "trade risk" virtually disappeared: "Practically all accidents are avoidable in one way or another," Irénée DuPont instructed DeBlois. "We will never be satisfied until all manufacturing operations are conducted without accident," another top official told operating managers. In a letter to "All General Managers and Presidents," written in 1933, Lammot DuPont told them that "accidents can be prevented by strong effort on the part of supervisory forces." He urged his audience to bring the "full realization of management's responsibility for accidents" to their operating officials. DeBlois and other safety men at DuPont gave wide publicity to the company's safety work. Its remarkable effectiveness was also reported from time to time, reinforcing the hope of safety men that other companies would also come to see safety as a management responsibility.[58]

New Developments in Company Safety Work, 1920-1939

Although the idea that safety was integral to good management had become an axiom at DuPont and some other large companies as early as World War I, it spread only gradually in the 1920s. Safety experts encouraged this view by trying to show that *safety* was synonymous with *efficiency* and by demonstrating that injuries were more costly than had been suspected. As the idea of managerial responsibility became more widely accepted, it gradually changed the nature of safety work. At first much safety work had been reactive, and committees of workers had been used to discover and change conditions and practices that had long been unsafe. While companies still used "evangelistic" techniques to motivate safe work habits, this approach no longer dominated the safety movement. Instead, the "hard side" of safety grew in importance as the movement became proactive. Personnel officers, engineers, purchasing agents, and other professional managers selected and trained workers, analyzed hazards as well as accidents, and designed jobs, machines, and factories to control conditions, behavior, and injuries.

SELLING SAFETY TO THE BIG BOSS

By the early 1920s, safety directors were anxiously looking for new ways to interest the "big boss" in safety work and, not coincidentally, to strengthen the position of safety engineers in the corporate hierarchy. With safety work less than a decade old and with the safety department a staff organization, safety workers were vulnerable, especially in recessions or if safety progress seemed slight. Even Louis DeBlois at DuPont was not immune from feelings of marginality. In early 1924 he wrote president Irénée DuPont, complaining that his salary was less than that of comparable individuals at U.S. Steel, International Harvester, Ford, and similar firms. The problem was not money—DeBlois had turned down jobs that offered more—it was professional status and his position in the corporate hierarchy. After a long review of his credentials and the benefits that had accrued from safety gains, DeBlois concluded that his low pay must reflect a system of job rating that classified him as filling "a minor executive position." He soon left DuPont.[59]

War and postwar developments heightened these tensions at all large companies. Inflation had dulled the edge of workmen's compensation, making it difficult to justify the extensive programs that safety officers desired, while the postwar crash had led some companies to shuck safety work or—almost as bad, as safety engineers saw it—to give it to the welfare department. In addition, injury rates were probably increased by the business cycle upswing in the early 1920s, which called into question the efficacy of previous efforts. Leonard Hatch of the New York State Department of Labor claimed that the manufacturing death rate in his state was higher in 1925 than it had been in 1913. Insurance companies also sounded the alarm as the rise in injuries, the fall in wages after World War I, and the increasing liberalization of compensation laws produced a sharp upswing in claims relative to premiums. The need to find new ways to interest management in safety work was becoming pressing.[60]

To justify their efforts, safety workers argued that safety yielded many benefits in addition to the reduction in compensation payments. In his letter to Irénée DuPont, DeBlois had pointed out the humanitarianism of safety work and claimed that it improved morale and reduced labor turnover. Equally important, safety work provided a common ground that helped bring labor and management together, perhaps forestalling unionization. Advocates of better safety also noted that accidents often damaged machines and products as well as workers. One engineer observed that he had more success in getting equipment guarded by pointing out the damage that could be done to the machine from a nut carelessly dropped into the gears than by stressing workers' risks. Safety also required increased attention to details that would coincidentally increase productivity, or so its advocates asserted. The problem with such claims was that they were hard to document and therefore easy to ignore. Charles Hook of Armco—never one for excessive delicacy—bluntly described the difficulty: "You know what an arm or a leg is going to cost you, but a lot of our managers fail to realize that efficiency is held to a very low standard because of . . . accidents." In the mid-1920s two efforts were made to justify safety work and safety workers by quantifying some of these broader costs of accidents.[61]

One approach was clearly articulated in a 1925 editorial in *Management and Administration* by L. A. Alford, who had been a member of the Hoover Commission on waste in industry. Echoing Louis DeBlois, Alford stressed that progress depended upon safety becoming an executive responsibility. The way to stimulate executive interest, he thought, was to demonstrate the "correlation between safety and production." This claim had some merit. There were innumerable instances of safety-induced technological progress in which making work safer raised productivity. Sometimes a safety device made the machine more efficient. American Steel and Wire developed a wire stop that was designed to prevent the employee from becoming entangled in a snare, an accident that was usually fatal. The new stop, it found out, reduced wire breakage. Similarly, Carnegie Steel eliminated the accidents that befell cleanup men in unloading coal from barges by redesigning the crane bucket so that no cleanup men were needed. Even better, crane operators who no longer had to look out for cleanup men could work faster. The roundheaded joiner was first produced in 1904 by Yates Manufacturing for a German buyer. Not only was it safer than the old square head, but it also held more blades, thereby improving the quality of the work.[62]

Safer machines also encouraged operators to work faster. The introduction of saw guards, it was reported, increased output. But the most dramatic example in which safety raised worker output occurred with the redesign of punch presses. August Kaems was a safety engineer for the Wisconsin Industrial Commission who had become obsessed with punch press injuries. After much experimentation he concluded that the way to prevent presses from removing fingers was not to install guards but to redesign the press so that the worker never had to put a hand under the ram. He placed one press on an incline—thereby allowing it to be fed from a slide—and installed a kick-out. The results were so startling that Kaems paid his own way to the NSC meetings in 1919 in order to report on them. Not only had his design largely eliminated injuries, but output rose, he claimed, from six thousand pieces a day to thirteen thousand. Kaems reported other instances of output being raised by even more startling amounts, and he noted that one businessman whom he had converted to this approach reported output increases of 15–100 percent with no injuries when presses were modified. Kaems's findings were given wide publicity: *American Machinist* reprinted one of his papers, and an engineer for Liberty Mutual sitting in Kaems's audience introduced the new techniques to his customers and later reported similar results.[63]

These examples supported the longstanding creed of the safety engineer that injuries were a symptom of inefficiency. The electrical engineer Walter Greenwood thought this could be generalized: "Nothing has been done yet toward making electrical equipment more efficient that did not result in making it more safe, and nothing has been done to make it more safe that did not result in higher productive efficiency."[64]

In the mid-1920s the National Bureau of Casualty and Surety Underwriters, which had become alarmed by the rise in compensation costs, undertook to support this claim. Its general manager, Albert Whitney, commissioned the American Engineering Standards Committee to do the investigation, and in 1928 its findings were published in *Safety and Production*. Whitney wrote the introduction, in which he artlessly revealed that the goal had been to "show that safety and production go together." The ultimate purpose of the demonstration was to "interest executives in the subject." The book was therefore an effort in persuasion, not an assessment of evidence. The study surveyed nearly fourteen thousand companies with almost 2.5 million employees, and while the findings are of interest for what they reveal about the ability of some industries to improve safety, the sample was anything but random. As a result, the statistics yield only a "cursory, disparate and untrustworthy view of American industry," as a friendly reviewer concluded. The writers claimed to find "a high degree of correlation between industrial safety and industrial productivity," suggesting that a company might do well by doing good. But even they must have had nagging doubts about this claim, for they also reaffirmed the initial idea of Safety First as an ultimate moral duty: "Industrial executives have as much responsibility to initiate accident prevention as to initiate improvement in productivity," they asserted.[65]

A more influential effort to convince managers of the broader benefits of safety was the work of Herbert W. Heinrich, a safety engineer for Travelers. Born in 1886, Heinrich was trained as a machinist and seems to have learned his engineering in correspondence school and in the navy during World War I. In 1926 he published "The Incidental Costs of Accidents to the Employer." Basing his study on ten thousand cases in Travelers' files, he estimated that on average an accident cost four times more than its workmen's compensation costs. These additional costs included the wages paid to the injured employee and to others who stopped work because of the accident, overhead expenses, the time lost by the foremen and superintendents, the spoilage of materials, broken tools, and lost orders. Heinrich's "rule of four" was the answer to a safety expert's prayer; by quantifying what had been vaguely asserted for years, the rule justified their efforts and helped solidify their corporate position. Accordingly, Heinrich's study was reprinted at least nine times during 1927 and 1928. It quickly became an article of faith among safety workers and was supported by several independent studies.[66]

As Heinrich noted, the logic of his analysis suggested that even uncompensated injuries were costly. On the basis of further studies of seventy-five thousand injuries, he claimed that 98 percent were preventable by management, and of these, 88 percent were due to unsafe acts and 10 percent to unsafe conditions—the 88:10:2 ratio, as it came to be called. He further argued that for each injury resulting in a lost workday there were about twenty-nine more minor injuries and three hundred accidents that by pure luck caused no injury at all. Accidents and injuries were like falling dominoes, Heinrich claimed, with the injury being the last domino in the line. Remove any single domino from the sequence, and the injury would be prevented. Heinrich also argued that serious accidents were atypical; their prevention would not necessarily eliminate other more minor but sometimes equally expensive accidents. Thus, the safety movement needed to focus on accident prevention, not injury prevention, he thought, and to do so required a better analysis of causes than was currently available. Heinrich gave as an example a mill worker who slipped on a wet floor and broke a kneecap. While the proximate cause of the injury was a fall, the ultimate cause was a slippery floor. Moreover, slipping accidents might have been occurring for years without a serious injury. This analysis was largely responsible for the development of an improved American Standards Association code for classifying accident causes that was finally published in 1937. Although the new classification proved cumbersome, parts of it were being applied before World War II.[67]

Heinrich's analysis was widely cited and enormously influential. His 1931 book *Industrial Accident Prevention* went through numerous editions, was translated into several languages, and remained a standard text in the field until the 1980s. His ideas were embodied in easily remembered ratios—4:1, 88:10:2, 300:29:1—and they offered something to nearly everyone interested in occupational safety. Heinrich's emphasis on separating the cause of the accident (the hazard) from the cause of the injury encouraged more sophisticated injury investigations. In the 1930s, companies such as DuPont began detailed hazard assessments, and by the 1970s, fault-tree analysis was being employed to quantify the relation between hazards and injuries. In spite of Heinrich's protestations that even injuries due to unsafe acts might have engineering solutions, his 88:10:2 ratio seemed to comfort executives who wished to concentrate on training instead of engineering. Yet his emphasis on management responsibility and the 4:1 ratio of hidden costs appealed to safety engineers who were trying to interest top managers in more ambitious safety programs.[68]

Heinrich's work helped to justify the position and activities of safety departments at the large firm, but the need to interest the big boss in safety was greatest at the little firm. In the early years of the safety movement, experts saw no reason why small, single-plant firms should not be as active in safety work as their larger competitors. By the 1920s, however, it was becoming clear that safety work was largely confined to large plants. In 1921, out of 6,343 "risks" covered by Massachusetts workmen's compensation insurance, 43 percent had an annual payroll of $5,000 or less, and 96 percent of this group were without a safety organization. In contrast, only one-quarter of those with more than $100,000 of payroll were without a safety organization. The Illinois survey undertaken in 1929 yielded broadly similar conclusions: while 75 percent of plants with five hundred or more workers had safety organizations, only 20 percent of all plants with fifty or fewer workers undertook organized safety work.[69]

Such results both frustrated and alarmed safety experts. They responded with efforts to design organizations for small plants. Safety publications featured numerous articles on this subject as well as others emphasizing the need for safety work by the small employer and a few success stories. Yet they never succeeded in converting more than a fraction of small firms to the cause of work safety. In 1925, establishments reporting injuries to the National Safety Council averaged 673 employees, yet the average manufacturing establishment contained fewer than 45 wage earners that year. "The small plant is taking little or no interest in accident prevention," Ethelbert Stewart concluded in 1927. Statistics seemed to bear him out. Surveys undertaken by the council and by state commissions indicated that, then as now, small plants had higher injury rates than large plants.[70]

The failure of small employers to join the safety movement reflected both the workings of the safety market and the companies' internal structure. In 1927, 40 percent of all establishments had an average of 2.7 employees, according to the Census of Manufactures, thereby exempting many of them from workmen's compensation. Slightly larger firms were not experience-rated—thereby making their premiums independent of their safety work—and only the very largest companies were entirely experience-rated. Insurers were also unlikely to devote much inspection time to small establishments, because their premiums did not justify the expense, Stewart pointed out.[71]

Small establishments were also less specialized than their larger counterparts. Employees performed a broader range of tasks and were therefore less experienced with the safety requirements of a given activity. Maintenance work was also likely to be unspecialized. In small woodworking shops, as one writer pointed out, saws were always dull because there were no full-time sharpeners. Because production runs were short, machinery too was unspecialized. Such equipment was more difficult to guard because it required a different setup for each task.[72]

Most important of all, small establishments could not afford a safety department. Because safety was often a somewhat marginal staff function at large companies, the department had a constant need to justify itself to cost-conscious managers, and the best justification was constant progress in injury reduction. Not surprisingly, therefore, the safety literature was full of exhortations to managers that no letup in safety work was possible and ever-greater efforts were needed. Louis DeBlois caught this institutional role of the safety department at DuPont when he urged plant managers to attend the NSC meetings. "Two or three days at the Congress would save them four or five days of aggregate 'nagging' by the Safety Division," he advised. Small establishments, without a safety department, had no organizational nag whose survival depended on improvements in safety.[73]

Without a professional safety advocate at his ear, the manager of a small establishment was likely to underestimate risks, safety experts thought. Because small plants had few employees, and because injuries were rare events, they could be a poor guide to hazards. Consider a hypothetical plant in 1926, with ten employees, each of whom worked a forty-five-hour week for fifty-two weeks. It would accumulate 23,400 annual hours of exposure. If the plant were so dangerous that one person would be killed per million hours—which was over six times the manufacturing average for that year—it could expect one fatality every forty-three years. In such a shop severe injuries would be rare and the possibility of learning from them correspondingly small. Safety committees would lose interest in their work. A safety expert trying to preach accident prevention to such an employer was likely to be met with the response, "We haven't had anybody hurt badly in years. Go across the street to that big plant with 430 workers; they kill somebody every couple of years." The big plant, of course, would be about half as dangerous as the small one.[74]

Even among large companies, by no means all the big bosses pursued effective safety work. A 1925 insurance company survey of textile companies claimed that "slightly less than 45 percent of the industry is giving safety a thought." As noted, this abysmal showing may have resulted in part from the high ratio of machines to workers in textiles, which made safeguarding expensive. But another difficulty lay in the incompatibility of a safety department with the mills' managerial structure. G. W. Cook of Travelers pointed out that textile mills lacked functionally specialized departments. A safety department was therefore foreign to their entire method of management. At other companies, where management was apathetic or failed to improve conditions, safety work was either nonexistent or simply a show.[75]

To combat such failings, management journals relentlessly stressed managerial responsibility, and gradually a sprinkling of general managers, vice presidents, and presidents began to attend NSC meetings during the 1920s. Membership in the council increased about 130 percent during that decade. *National Safety News* carried articles such as "By-products of Accident Prevention" by the president of West Penn Power. A vice president at RCA thought the word *accident* was misleading; he suggested that *colax* might be a better term, as it suggested that company laxity had been the cause. In 1930 the *News* published "Management's Responsibility Is Clearcut," by W. V. DeCamp, general man-

TABLE 4.1. Safety Work in Manufacturing, by Industry, 1935–1939

	Percentage of Workers to Whom Service Is Available			
	Safety Director		Shop Committees	Accident Records
	Full-Time	Part-Time		
Chemicals and allied products	36.7	35.9	65.6	95.3
Cigars and tobacco	4.9	22.8	44.9	93.4
Stone, clay, and glass	24.0	21.1	43.0	92.6
Clothing	0.7	6.9	19.3	89.1
Food products	9.4	21.7	32.6	89.1
Iron and steel	44.8	24.5	65.3	96.9
Metals (except iron and steel)	19.8	37.3	54.7	95.3
Leather	5.9	22.8	35.8	96.7
Lumber and furniture	7.2	20.6	35.1	90.2
Paper and printing	16.6	21.8	49.0	94.1
Textiles	12.3	25.9	52.2	97.4
Miscellaneous manufacturing	37.9	35.9	63.3	94.9
All manufacturing[a]	24.6	24.2	52.2	94.4

Source: Data are from U.S. Public Health Service, "A Preliminary Survey of the Industrial Hygiene Problem in the United States," *Bulletin* 259 (Washington, D.C., 1941), tables 4, 9, and 11.

[a] Each industry is weighted by its share of employment in 1929.

ager of United Verde Copper. From a safety expert's point of view, De-Camp was the very model of a modern general manager. "Management is solely responsible for safety in your organization," he told readers.[76]

Several surveys provide glimpses of the extent of organized safety work toward the end of the interwar period. The best of these was part of a 1936–39 Public Health Service survey of industrial hygiene. The survey sampled about 1.4 million gainful workers in manufacturing (12 percent of the total) in fifteen states, and it was reasonably representative of both industries and firm sizes. It provides an accurate although limited picture of the extent of safety work for this period, and some of its findings are presented in table 4.1.

Clearly, by the mid-1930s the keeping of accident records—an outcome of workmen's compensation laws—was all but universal, but organized safety work was not. About half of all workers were employed in plants that had either a full- or a part-time safety director. Most of these safety organizations were in the larger plants. Only 2.2 percent of employees in plants with fewer than one hundred workers, versus 33 percent of employees in larger plants, had a full-time safety director.

SAFETY IN THE DEPRESSION

The efforts of safety experts to institutionalize accident prevention paid dividends as the economy slid into depression after 1929. Although the National Safety Council saw its membership drop and its budget decline, there seems not to have been a wholesale abandonment of safety work among larger companies. The depression may also have given safety a boost because it probably increased the rate at which older, more dangerous plants were scrapped. Some firms such as California and Hawaiian Sugar Refining even stepped up their safety work in the early 1930s in an attempt to cut costs. To encourage such activities, safety periodicals continued to publish titles such as "Our Safety Department Earns a Profit." Still, efforts were pared back. The Bureau of Labor Statistics claimed that in some establishments "safety activities were curtailed greatly." This was especially the case among smaller plants, where safety work had been marginal at best. Minnesota's compensation act was elective, and that state reported that from 1917 to 1930, only 7,301 employers had chosen not to be covered, while an additional 9,093 companies dropped out between 1930 and 1937. Colorado reported a similar experience, and when Pennsylvania liberalized its compensation act in 1937, it met with a wave of rejections.[77]

The experience of twenty years of private safety work was also marshaled by New Deal programs, and they in turn helped spread safety work in the private sector. The Civil Works Administration borrowed the National Safety Council's engineer, Sidney Williams, who became its director of safety. With the blessing of Harry Hopkins, Williams promptly telegrammed state administrators informing them that safety was an executive responsibility and suggesting the name of a safety engineer who might be borrowed from a cooperating private company. The usual program of safeguarding, first-aid training, and education was undertaken.[78]

The Public Works Administration (PWA), Works Progress Administration (WPA), and National Recovery Administration (NRA) also helped themselves to safety expertise that had been two decades in the making. At the behest of the National Safety Council, all PWA contracts included a standard clause requiring the contractor to meet applicable American Standards Association codes. The WPA also included a safety organization, and under an executive order of 1935, work followed safety procedures and codes. In early 1934 the Department of Labor also established a committee to develop health and safety standards to be included in NRA codes. Codes submitted after March of that year were required to meet a host of safety standards that included machine guarding, worker training, physical examination, and injury reporting.[79]

These procedures prevented many injuries. Relying on the experience of private construction companies and noting that most of the newly hired workers knew little about construction, insurers had predicted that the CWA would experience injury rates of 100 per million manhours; the actual rate was 40. The rate for WPA projects in 1935 was 22, which was less than that of construction companies reporting to the National Safety Council. In addition, while some of these programs were short-lived, they all helped spread safety to the private sector. Machinery producers who hoped to see their products used on CWA, PWA, or WPA construction were forced to conform to safety codes. The public works exposed millions of employees to organized safety work, many of them probably for the first time, and may also have encouraged safety work among at least some private contractors.[80]

THE HARD SIDE OF SAFETY WORK

As safety became a managerial responsibility in the 1920s, it came to rely more on the skills of safety engineers, personnel directors, and other technically trained individuals, while the role of workers and foremen was correspondingly reduced. Attempts to motivate employees through bonuses and contests did not die out, but they were no longer at the heart of the safety movement. Instead emphasis shifted to engineering evaluation of hazards, to job evaluation, and to instruction in safe work techniques. In his 1926 text Louis DeBlois suggested that new ideas were now most likely to come from safety engineers. "Probably it [the safety committee] has no logically permanent place," DeBlois concluded. Later he wrote with obvious satisfaction that "one no longer hears the foreman called 'the key man.'" The change was reflected in a shift in terminology. Initially safety workers had focused on the need for employee education. Rules and discipline had always been involved, but they had often been derived from safety committees that included employees and foremen, and the education amounted to little more than exhortation to follow these rules. By the 1930s, rules had become more formal and detailed; at Ford there were forty-three safety rules for crane operators governing all manner of work practices. Safety experts now talked of training rather than education, and they meant instruction in the rules and work practices that company engineers had designed. One writer summarized the new approach as "control of environment and control of behavior."[81]

One result of the new approach was an increasingly thorough investigation of injuries and hazards. Initially investigators reared under the old system of employers' liability found it difficult to shed the view that automatically blamed the workman. In 1935 Robert Shaw of the Murray Corporation acknowledged that early investigations attributed far too many accidents to worker carelessness. As the writings of DeBlois and Heinrich began to influence thinking about safety, investigations became more impartial and correspondingly more valuable. A 1933 editorial in *National Safety News* echoed the sentiments of an increasing number of safety workers. "'Carelessness' is a feeble alibi," the editor announced. "Its presence in any accident report should be sufficient to start an investigation."[82]

As early as 1912, Youngstown Sheet and Tube had developed a thoroughly bureaucratized accident-reporting system that employed twenty-two separate forms. Twenty years later it subjected "serious" injuries to preliminary, intermediate, and formal investigation, the last of which included the plant superintendent. Witnesses were interviewed, the work practice was studied, and a formal written report was made recommending changes to avoid future injuries. The report, in turn, was made available to employees and was shared with other plants through a safety exchange. Similarly thorough procedures were followed at General Electric, DuPont, Western Electric, and other large companies. By the late 1930s, Armco and U.S. Leather investigated all accidents.[83]

Accidents were not the only way to learn about dangers, and engineers began to undertake systematic hazard assessments instead of leaving such tasks to workmen's committees. Job analysis was used to bring out risks just as it was being employed to enhance output. Van Hunter, safety supervisor at International Harvester, noted that the medical, engineering, and safety departments all cooperated in a companywide hazard survey. He argued that each job must "be thoroughly studied for its accident possibilities." A textile company reported that after studying spinning, it gave the job of cleaning the machines to a special crew that worked after hours. Job analysis was also used to fit the worker to the task—for example, women were not placed on jobs that required heavy lifting—and it reflected the new emphasis on training, instead of exhorting, employees to perform their jobs the safe way. A representative of the National Metal Trades Association emphasized the need "to instruct workmen properly in the control of tools or processes." W. F. McClellan of Armour contrasted what he called the "up-to-date" foreman who provided the employee with safety instruction with the old-style foreman who had simply turned a new employee loose. In 1931 a writer in *Factory and Industrial Management* caught the new mood: "Training—Not Band-Playing—Makes Safe Plants" was the title of his article.[84]

Requiring the foreman to instruct employees in safe work practices and holding him responsible for injuries led companies to initiate safety training for foremen too. C. H. Murray of Armco thought that training workers in safe work habits was one of the keys to his company's accident prevention program, but he felt that training supervisors was even more important. Many companies were already training foremen in production and personnel management, and safety was added to the list of topics. One writer concluded in 1929 that the "hard boiled foreman is as out of date as the horse and buggy."[85]

The "mental causes" of accidents, in Boyd Fisher's phrase, also began to interest employers during the 1920s. Researchers discovered that some workers seemed to be "accident-prone," and much effort was expended to find a psychological basis for this apparent statistical fact. Most of the academic research was done in Britain, but the findings were routinely reported and discussed at meetings of the National Safety Council and in the pages of *National Safety News*.[86]

American employers were interested in the finding that some workers were accident-prone, but most remained skeptical of its psychological basis and of the value of mental testing either to select employees or to target their safety training. Safety men stressed that workers might be accident-prone because they were in high-risk jobs, or because their supervision was poor, or—as the efficiency experts claimed—because they were unsuited to the job. Harold Miner, director of safety at DuPont in the late 1930s, claimed that a study of the company's multiple-accident employees had invariably discovered work conditions to be the real cause. The Bancroft mills termed workers with two or more accidents "accident-prone." But they were not counseled; they were transferred or fired. General Electric tried to solve the problem of its accident repeaters by changing work methods or apparatus, or by transferring the employee. Carl Auel of Westinghouse stressed the role of proper worker training and placement and concluded that "the term 'accident prone' carries a stigma altogether too sweeping in its implications . . . [and should] be allowed to drop into oblivion."[87]

THE MACHINE AND THE WORKER

Experience with safety work also led to more complete engineering revision of both machines and plants. Initially most companies had simply confined themselves to guarding the obvious danger spots and requesting that machinery makers do likewise. Even such minimal efforts were by no means universal. In 1931 a producer of paper machinery reported that "several years ago" none of his customers had ever requested safeguards. But, he reported, "conditions have changed since then." As late as 1935 a representative of the meat packers claimed that guillotines typically came from the manufacturer unguarded. Betty Piontkowsky, who ran a machine in the lard refinery at Armour in 1935, recalled that the job still needed sharp eyes, "else I could get a hand mashed easy." At about the same time, one steelworker described a crane that was finally guarded only after it had killed a man. Some machines simply could not be made safe; one user claimed that textile print machines defied guarding. Existing factories were equally difficult—and expensive—to make safe. F. A. Wiley, an engineer at Wisconsin Steel, observed that old plants "built previous to the days of the rigid demands for safety" were only made to conform with new safety requirements "in a mild way."[88]

The solution, as Lucian Chaney had seen, was redesign of both factories and equipment. By the time of World War I, U.S. Steel, DuPont, and other large firms that built new plants had begun to design the recommendations of their safety engineers into new construction. A new automobile plant of 1920 had "safety . . . built into the bricks, concrete, and steel." In 1922 the recently completed Anheuser Busch plant in St. Louis was "as nearly 'fool proof' as safety engineering can make it." Skylights, sawtooth roofs, and white paint ensured proper illumination of workplaces, while automated bottle labeling reduced worker exposure to the risk of exploding bottles. The Lever Brothers plant in Hammond, Indiana, that opened for operation in 1930 was described as "made to order for the safety man." In 1910 the largest plants in the steel industry had been the least safe; in 1929, they were the least dangerous (see note). This turnaround may have reflected the greater prevalence of safety work at larger plants; it surely reflected the engineering revision that Wiley had noted. In a new Jones and Laughlin strip mill built in the 1930s, "the safety factor was considered in all details." One detail was the design of clearance between crane stops and building supports, which added $40,000 to construction costs, but "because of the additional measure of safety, it is considered money well spent."[89]

Machinery also began to come through with safety features designed in. In metalworking, increasing specialization had led to the separation of die designers from users, resulting in the construction of dies without regard for their safety. Company safety departments bridged this gap, and by the 1930s design engineers were treating safety as a professional responsibility. The need for a guard was a sign of poor design. Giant metal-stamping dies used by the automobile industry weighed up to twenty tons and were difficult and dangerous to move; by the 1930s designers had begun to build them with chain slots for ease of movement.[90]

From the very beginning, U.S. Steel, Ford, and some other companies had insisted that machinery makers include safety features in their products. The practice spread as an increasing number of companies had the safety department inspect specifications for new equipment and as safety men convinced purchasing agents that safety was part of their responsibility too. New textile print machines were constructed "so as to eliminate . . . [the] hazard." Paper mill equipment was also made safer; calender stacks now included reversing mechanisms so that when the paper jammed, the machine could be cleared mechanically rather than by hand. Fourdrinier machines, which were nearly completely automatic in operation, were designed for simpler and safer maintenance. The big rubber producers insisted to General Electric and other machinery producers that new motors conform to safety codes for safety stopping even when installed in states with no code.[91]

An NSC survey undertaken in the early 1930s found that new laundry equipment was vastly safer, although "much old type machinery is still in use . . . [and] continues to take its grisly toll." The improvements were due to safety codes in important states that were intended to protect women workers from injury. Shoe machinery too was well guarded because the monopoly supplier, United Shoe Machinery, insisted on it. Some milling machines now came through with power control levers that pulled outward so that an accidental bump would disengage, not engage, them. One maker of grinding wheels had built in an automatic shutoff that would activate when the wheel wore to a predetermined size. Many new punch presses required two-handed operation. Most manufacturers now routinely guarded gears and sprockets. Yet the redesign of machinery for safety was uneven. Users complained that "none of the companies . . . have safeguarded their machines 100 percent," and in some cases the producer offered the equipment both with and without safety features.[92]

Safer machines and factories resulted both from conscious efforts of safety organizations and from improvements in technology that were in good part independent of the safety movement. In 1932 G. M. Briggs, a safety expert for the National Safety Council, concluded that "most of the progress [in machine safety] made thus far has been accomplished in the effort to improve production and lower costs, and in very few cases have machines been redesigned solely . . . to reduce the hazard." In short, technological change decreased accidents more than labor, thereby reducing risks. Far and away the most important such improvement was the electrification of factories for both power and illumination. Electricity brought risks of its own, of course. It seems amazing that as late as the 1920s some engineers still considered 600 volts or less to be harmless, and in mining, the introduction of electricity did raise net risks (see chap. 6).[93]

Yet safety engineers were unanimous in their opinion that, on balance, electricity improved factory safety. Briggs singled out the application of individual electric motors to machinery that swept through manufacturing after 1910. Unit electric drive utilizing centrally purchased power reduced injuries in several ways. It led to a scrapping of the maze of boilers, flywheels, shafts, gears, pulleys, and belts that had been a significant source of injuries. In addition, individual electric-drive machines would not start spontaneously, as did the old belt-driven machines, and since electric motors needed no flywheel, they could be equipped with solenoids for instantaneous stopping. Electricity, in turn, allowed a revolution in factory design. Without overhead shafting, cranes could be used for materials handling, and natural lighting could be employed. Machines could also be laid out in the most efficient sequence, reducing accidents from materials handling.[94]

Improvements in electric lighting also contributed to safety gains. Travelers engineer R. E. Simpson studied ninety-one thousand injuries that occurred in 1910, and claimed that nearly 24 percent were either directly or indirectly due to poor lighting. Simpson's claim was welcome news to safety and illuminating engineers, to the utilities, and to General Electric and other producers of lighting equipment, and it was widely cited. Improvements in technology and declining electricity prices led to dramatically lower lighting costs in the early years of the twentieth century; one engineer claimed that he could buy sixteen times more illumination per dollar in 1928 than in 1912. In addition, the national electric lighting code recommended sharp increases in factory illumination. Better lighting was also aggressively marketed by the National Electric Light Association in an industrial lighting sales campaign in the mid-1920s. The association claimed that the 1925–26 campaign persuaded over eighteen thousand factories to upgrade their lighting. Surveys of the steel industry in 1911 and 1923 revealed sharp increases in light intensity in most processes.[95]

By 1920 Simpson was claiming that because of improvements in illumination, only 15 percent of injuries were related to poor lighting. Other studies of companies that increased illumination also sometimes claimed that injuries declined, although none ever documented such claims in detail. Progress continued throughout the 1930s. Steel cold-rolling departments rarely had illumination in excess of 5 foot-candles in the 1920s. In the late 1930s the cold-rolling department of the Jones and Laughlin mill noted above had nearly 11 foot-candles of illumination, and other departments were similarly well lit.[96]

Many other improvements in technology contributed to safety gains in manufacturing during the first four decades of the twentieth century. Machine shops reduced eye hazards by substituting welding for high-powered chisels and by using machine welders, while rubber producers substituted less hazardous substances for ammonia. Everywhere companies were mechanizing materials handling with cranes, conveyers, and small powered lifts and trucks. Most safety engineers realized that the impact of this new equipment was conditional on how it was employed. "The mere installation of . . . [conveyers and traveling cranes] will not prevent accidents, for the operating conditions must be studied and safe practices and rules developed," one writer instructed the readers of *Factory and Industrial Management*. If unguarded and used without proper work practices, such equipment could lead to injuries more severe than those the older hand methods had caused. But because the new machines reduced the need to handle materials and eliminated the difficult and dangerous practice of coordinating teams of men to lift heavy items, their proper employment would result in "a noticeable decrease in the number of accidents."[97]

Changes in machine lubrication yielded clear-cut safety improvements. In the nineteenth century the oiling of machinery and power transmission apparatus had been dangerous work, exposing the oiler to moving parts and sometimes requiring him to climb high above the factory floor. And if bearings were lubricated sufficiently to operate for any length of time, the oil poured out, leading to floors that were constantly slippery and thereby worsening the risks of everyone else in the factory. Improved oils, the use of grease and roller bearings, automatic or power lubrication systems, and, of course, electrification all became increasingly common in the twentieth century. Gradually the old-time oiler and the messy, slippery floors that accompanied him disappeared from factory work.[98]

Safety Trends, 1907–1939

The net effect of these influences on the course of worker safety is difficult to determine because of the paucity of information on injury rates. Before the mid-1920s adequate industry data exist only for steel, cement, and paper and pulp producers. These figures (tables A3.1 and A3.2) reveal that at least some sectors of the economy were improving safety, but they are of questionable representativeness. A somewhat more comprehensive picture for the pre-1926 period can be pieced together from state data. Only a few states collected information that allows calculation of fatality rates for manufacturing workers (table A3.4). These data are hardly precise. They are sensitive to random fluctuations, while reporting differences between states imply that they cannot be compared. But they can be used to spot trends, and taken together they suggest that for manufacturing as a whole, there were probably only very modest improvements, if any, in safety up to the late 1920s. In 1926 both the Bureau of Labor Statistics and the National Safety Council began to publish injury statistics for a large group of plants. Once again the data are neither entirely adequate nor strictly comparable, but they are a great improvement and almost certainly good enough to reflect trends.[99]

The monthly separation rate in manufacturing fell from about 10.1 per 100 workers in 1910–18 to about 4.9 in the 1920s, or by about 52 percent. Statistical analysis (see note) suggests that if new hires followed the same trend, such a decline reduced frequency rates by around 27 percent over this period. From 1926 through the late 1930s and into World War II, turnover rose, however, thereby increasing injury rates. Declines in hours worked may also have contributed to the reduction in injury rates. Average hours worked fell about 12 percent between 1909 and 1926, which the analysis suggests would have reduced frequency rates about 11 percent. From 1926 to 1939 the workweek fell about 16 percent, implying a 15 percent fall in injury frequency. Controlling for these labor market influences, injury rates fell 3.7 percent per year between 1926 and 1945. With important changes in the labor market controlled, the trend in injury frequency must reflect changes in technology and the spread of organized safety work. Over the twenty-year period these forces reduced injury rates about 50 percent.[100]

The effect of safety work is also suggested by the relationship be-

TABLE 4.2. Injury Rates of National Safety Council Members, by Length of Membership, 1929

Period of Affiliation	Number of Establishments	Injury Index	Severity Index
1913–17	696	0.855	0.951
1918–21	397	0.937	0.914
1922–25	645	1.083	0.985
1926–29	601	1.235	1.185

Source: Data are from R. L. Forney, "How Much Has the Council Helped?" *NSN* 22 (Dec. 1930): 23–24.

Note: Injuries are per million manhours; severity is lost workdays per thousand manhours. For each period and industry, the affiliating firm's injury or severity rate is expressed relative to the 1929 rate for all firms in that industry. The results are weighted and aggregated using 1929 shares of manhours.

tween injury frequency and the length of time a plant had been a member of the National Safety Council, for it is plausible that the decision to join the council marked the beginning of serious safety work. In 1929 the council computed indices of its members' injury rates by length of membership, controlling for industry. The results (table 4.2) show that in 1929, firms that had affiliated with the council in 1913–17 had injury frequency rates only 69 percent (0.855/1.235) as high as those that joined after 1925. While such findings could simply reflect that larger, safer firms joined earlier, they hold up even when similar-sized establishments are compared. Analysis of members of the Portland Cement Association yields similar results.

These insights can be reinforced and supplemented by an analysis of manufacturing injury statistics by state and industry collected by the Bureau of Labor Statistics for 1925 and 1927. These data, when matched to Census state-industry characteristics and to workmen's compensation data, reveal the importance of changes in the factory system and in public policy in shaping the safety of work. Horsepower per manufacturing production worker rose from a bit over 1 in 1869 to about 4.7 in 1927. Statistical analysis (table A3.5) reveals that each unit increase in horsepower per worker raised injury rates as much as 3 percent, which supports the argument that increased mechanization worsened workers' risks. In the twentieth century a number of forces helped counter the impact of increasing mechanization. Compensation for injury rose in real terms from (at most) a few dollars to two-thirds of weekly wages in many states. The analysis suggests that $1,000 of higher compensation cost reduced injuries about 4 percent. In addition, controlling for horsepower, larger establishments had sharply lower injury rates, a result consistent with the earlier finding that larger steel plants had lower frequency rates.

Probably large plants were safer because they were more likely to be experience-rated and to have a safety organization, and because they were newer and used safer plant layout and machine technology. It seems likely, therefore, that after about 1910, when such changes became important, the increase in establishment size served to reduce injury rates. The significance of the state control variables may capture differences in safety regulations. Finally, the number of salaried employees also grew relative to wage earners, rising about 70 percent between 1899 and 1939. This increased supervision seems to have sharply reduced injuries—just as safety experts claimed it would.

Conclusion

On the eve of World War II, factory work was, for many employees, significantly safer than it had been four decades earlier. Changes in public policy, in labor markets, and in technology and business organization combined to produce this result. While the reduction in hours worked may have improved safety, the decline in labor turnover clearly did so—both directly and because it raised the payoff to company safety work. Electrification and improvements in factory and machine design also made a partly independent contribution of work safety. But the dominant feature of the period was the spread of organized safety work among the larger establishments.

In 1900 no manufacturing company had a modern safety organization. Safety training, the design of safe work practices, and the guarding of dangerous machinery were all but nonexistent. Although managers were attempting to control the pace of production, their concern did not extend to its safety. The worker was still held responsible for his own fate, and most business executives, if they thought about such matters at all, would have viewed the killing and maiming of workers as a regrettable but inevitable result of combining careless employees with modern production methods. Yet men and women increasingly labored under conditions over which they had less and less control.

After 1910 the spread of compensation legislation encouraged large firms to establish safety departments. These were staffed with engineers for whom better safety was a professional and organizational imperative. Linked through a newly created institutional network, the organized safety movement campaigned to adapt management attitudes and behavior to the new realities of work. The success of this endeavor came to be reflected in the creed of systematic management that injuries were neither inevitable nor the fault of employees. Safety equipment, training, and job design were all management responsibilities, and even injuries that stemmed from workers' errors reflected imperfect supervision. These changes were often imposed from above, and they disrupted traditions, burdened workers with new procedures and equipment, and reduced their ability to shape their own work lives. As a result, the road to better safety was marked by minor rebellions against work rules and machine guards and hard hats as employees learned to accept the new regime. The Portland Cement Association safety trophy described the changes somewhat differently, informing its recipients that "Safety Follows Wisdom."

167

A
MANAGEMENT
RESPONSI-
BILITY

CHAPTER FIVE

COMBATING COLLISIONS AND OTHER HORRORS

Railroad Safety
1900–1939

The relative *and not the intrinsic value of train control must be considered. . . .*
As a relative *life saver it isn't worth the money it costs.*
A. H. RUDD, PENNSYLVANIA RAILROAD, 1926

Your ties are rotten,
your tracks are worse,
and yet you holler
"Safety First."
UNKNOWN RAILROAD POET, CA. 1915

The beginning of the twentieth century found railroad safety still dominated by issues left over from an earlier era. New dangers soon appeared, however, and accident rates soared. Public clamor matched railway casualties and led to laws to improve statistics and investigate accidents in 1901 and 1910. By 1903, with broad public support, the Interstate Commerce Commission was cautiously advocating more safety equipment— in this case, block signals to prevent collisions. The commission also pressed for a limitation on trainmen's hours of service in order to reduce collisions. Many of the railroad unions also supported such a law, and the brotherhoods campaigned for an employers' liability law and for a host of other safety regulations as well. The ICC played a subordinate role in most of these legislative ventures, preferring to focus on the problem of collisions. Gradually the commission concluded that railroad management was so lax that block signals would not do the trick, and in 1922 it turned to automatic train control.

These proposals and other schemes ranging from laws to mandate spark arresters to proposals for a collision prevention contest rained down upon the carriers, which remained as indifferent to worker safety as ever. And while the railroads had been partly discredited by their opposition to the Safety Appliance Act, they managed to fend off some of the more expensive of their opponents' ideas. Yet the threat of such legislation and the rise in injury costs finally interested railroad managers in work safety, and increasingly after 1910 they adopted the same sorts of safety organizations that were spreading throughout manufacturing. Combined with improvements in railroad technology and the gradual shift of the industry from expansion to contraction, Safety First yielded dramatic reductions in worker casualty rates. Even the ICC was impressed, and by 1928 it tacitly admitted that automatic train control had been an expensive error. Under a still watchful eye, it allowed the carriers to choose their own safety priorities.

Combating the Collision Horror, Round I

In 1898, as the nation emerged from the worst depression in its history, railroad casualties took off, with collisions leading the pack. At their peak in 1907, worker casualty rates from collisions were more than double, and passenger rates more than triple, their 1896 level (figs. 5.1 and 5.2). And since both passenger-miles traveled and the number of workers employed rose over this period, the actual numbers killed and wounded rose even more dramatically: in 1897, "only" 53 passengers and 164 workers died in railroad collisions; in 1907, 214 passengers and 572 workers lost their lives from this cause. "The collision horror," the ICC lamented in its annual report for that year, "remains a crying evil."[1]

RAILWAY MASSACRES

The crying evil made wonderful copy, however, and the popular press enjoyed few things more than a good railroad wreck. A spate of articles on "the railroad accident problem" had appeared in 1891–92, but interest waned as casualties fell in the middle 1890s. The soaring accident rate after 1897 was a journalistic godsend, and the number of articles with titles such as "Railway Massacres" echoed the rise in casualties. Just two stories on railroad accidents are listed in the *Readers' Guide to Periodical Literature* in 1901; there were thirteen in 1903, nineteen in 1906, and thirty-nine at the peak of the carnage in 1907.[2]

Some writers had a legislative agenda. Many suggested an extension of the Safety Appliance Act of 1893 to cover block signaling or other devices. John J. Esch, congressman from Wisconsin and future ICC commissioner, stressed the beneficial effects of safety appliances and called for a program requiring block signals, steel cars, limitations on hours of service, additional inspectors, and training requirements for employees. Carl Vrooman, writing in *McClure's* in 1907, reminded readers of the

FIGURE 5.1. Collision Injury and Fatality Rates per Billion Passenger-Miles, Three-Year Moving Averages, 1889–1939

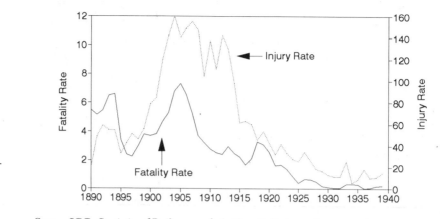

Source: ICC, *Statistics of Railways* and *Accident Bulletin*, various years.

FIGURE 5.2. Collision Injury and Fatality Rates per Thousand Railroad Employees, Three-Year Moving Averages, 1889–1939

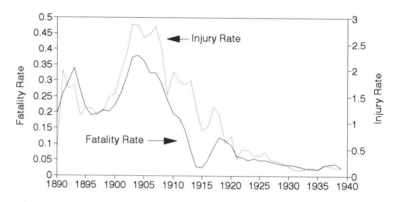

Source: ICC, *Statistics of Railways* and *Accident Bulletin*, various years.

decline in accidents due to the automatic-coupler law. He also pointed out the powers of the British Board of Trade and called for "vigorous legislative action" to require block signals and automatic train stops.[3]

Although it routinely decried the extremely misleading comparisons of British and American accident rates often drawn by popular writers, the railroad press also became alarmed. In 1901 *Engineering News* called for a law giving the ICC power to investigate accidents. In 1903 it cautiously urged the introduction of automatic train stops, and in 1906 it again called for investigation of accidents. In 1909 it advocated giving the ICC control over all forms of railroad safety. *Railway Age* stressed the impact of increased traffic density, arguing that on a single-track railroad the chance of head-on and rear-end collisions rose with the number of trains per day (N) as $(N/2)^2 + N - 2$ ($N > 1$). For example, with one train each way per day ($N = 2$), one head-on and no rear-end collisions are possible. With two trains each way per day ($N = 4$), there are four possible head-on and two possible rear-end collisions. According to the *Age*, this relationship suggested the need for more "scientific and accurate forms of traffic regulation."[4]

The *Age* also repeated the claim of British observers that tight labor markets eroded discipline, although it admitted that the problem was exacerbated by the practice of punishing men who, by obeying the rules, caused trains to be late. The journal urged the use of automatic signals that would diminish accidents by "reducing the human agency in signaling to a minimum." The editors also encouraged the carriers to develop a device that could apply the brake "in spite of the engineman." The *Railroad Gazette* came to similar conclusions and placed ultimate responsibility for accidents on the general manager, whose duty it was to enforce discipline. The editors admitted that they had "preached this doctrine [of better discipline] since time immemorial." The problem was that "no one has discovered any way by which to make the railroad companies carry it out." The editors therefore called for an extension of the act of 1893 to include mandatory block signaling. Such a law, they noted in a later editorial, would "bring the laggard into line," as had occurred with automatic couplers.[5]

The ICC also became increasingly alarmed as the collision toll mounted. Beginning in 1902 it published brief descriptions of train accidents, calling attention to those that it claimed resulted from the long hours of trainmen, absence of block signals, inexperience of employees, and lack of automatic train stops. In 1902–3 it drafted a model bill mandating the use of block signals under its supervision that Representative Esch introduced in Congress every year from then on. It also urged legislation limiting trainmen's hours of service.[6]

HOURS OF SERVICE, TRAIN CREWS, AND TRAIN LENGTH

Limiting the hours of trainmen had been a goal of the railroad brotherhoods since the 1890s, but the urgency of the problem increased sharply in the early years of the twentieth century as economics pushed the carriers in the direction of longer, heavier trains pulled by ever-larger locomotives. By about 1905 articulated compound "Mallets" weighing 160 tons and with a tractive effort of 65,000 pounds had been introduced. These monsters could pull more cars with more freight per train crew, but they also made trainmen's lives miserable. Until

171

COMBATING COLLISIONS AND OTHER HORRORS

the automatic stoker was introduced, firemen on the new locomotives might have to shovel five thousand pounds of coal an hour. In addition, such long freights were only capable of very slow speeds, and they often crawled along at no more than eight miles per hour. One fireman on the Santa Fe described the new regime as follows: "[We] are worked like brutes, not like men. Single engines pull 75 or 80 cars in one train, and any company requiring a fireman to shovel coal for a train like this is guilty of brutality in the worst form. It keeps men out on the road until they are sleepy and worn out and wholly unfit for labor."[7]

Senator Robert La Follette and Congressmen Esch heard the men's plea, and in 1906 they introduced bills setting a limit of sixteen hours per day for trainmen. Both the Engineers and the Trainmen passed resolutions endorsing hours limitation, but probably because the law would reduce the incomes of workers who were paid by the hour, or who received overtime for long runs, the brotherhoods' support for the bill was mixed. The railroad press mildly supported the law, and the *Railroad Gazette* claimed that most companies thought it inevitable. Still, the carriers fought vigorously. H. U. Mudge, vice president of the Rock Island, challenged the premise that shorter hours would improve safety. He pointed out that the bill would raise the number of men hired and observed that "railway officials would prefer to trust their own lives and those of passengers entrusted to their care to an engineer or conductor of long service and good habits for a longer period than 16 hours than with the transient men who will be picked up to move the traffic in times of heavy movement no matter how few hours such men may work."[8]

The strongest support for limiting trainmen's hours came from the ICC. Edwin Moseley testified to Congress in favor of such limitations, as did W. P. Borland, chief of the commission's Bureau of Safety. The Accident Reports Act of 1901 had required carriers to provide details of their injuries under oath, and Moseley read a list of accidents and casualties that he claimed had resulted from long hours of service. He also reminded the committee of the lessons of the Safety Appliance Act of 1893. The companies had unanimously opposed that bill too, yet now they were "very glad it was enacted." Lest anyone miss the point, he concluded that hours limitation was "in the interests of the railroad[s] as much as . . . in the interests of the employees and of the public." Borland asserted a public interest in the matter: "These rules [private agreements between companies and men over hours of service] are concerned merely with the interests of the men and do not affect the interests of the public at all."[9]

The impact of the sixteen-hour law on train scheduling seems to have been modest. A survey by the *Railroad Gazette* immediately after the law went into effect showed that a number of carriers shortened their divisions and hired extra crews, but many reported that no important change was found necessary. Perhaps the carriers simply increased train speed, in effect trading fuel for labor. If so, whatever effect the law may have had on improved safety would have been in part offset by the rise in train speed that it induced.[10]

A second part of the law, which limited telegraph operators and train dispatchers to nine hours a day, was introduced by Representative A. P. Murphy, himself an "old-time telegrapher." The companies claimed that the nine-hour law would cause a serious disruption in their manual block signal systems. Manual block signals required telegraph operators, and most companies staffed offices with two men working twelve-hour shifts. The nine-hour limitation would increase costs both because of the need for an extra man and also, according to C. R. Gray of the Frisco line, because it would drive up wages. *Railway Age* thought it might result in the closing of one-third of all telegraph offices and concluded that it would "bring about in one year what it would have taken ten years to accomplish in bringing the telephone into use in railway work."[11]

In the face of thirty thousand union-inspired telegrams, Congress chose to ignore the railroads' dire predictions. The Hours of Service Law was passed on March 4, 1907, and went into effect on March 4, 1908. As expected, the law resulted in the closing of "an exceedingly large number of small telegraph offices all over the country." Between 1908 and 1909, while total railroad employment rose about 4.6 percent, employment of telegraphers fell 1.6 percent. Some lines such as the Illinois Central and the Burlington abandoned their manual block signal systems and returned to the older, and more dangerous, time-interval method of scheduling. Others hired a third telegrapher who was "notably deficient in experience." Still other carriers substituted the telephone for the telegraph or turned to the automatic block system. "Congress has done all it could to prevent the extension of manual blocking," concluded a disgruntled signal engineer on the Burlington.[12]

At about the same time, the railroad brotherhoods launched a campaign both in the state legislatures and on the national level to enact full-crew (the carriers termed them excess-crew) and train-limit laws. A typical full-crew law would have required a sixth person—an extra brakeman—on freights of over twenty-five cars. Train-limit legislation usually set a maximum of fifty or seventy cars per train. Although the brotherhoods claimed that these laws would enhance safety, the connection seemed much less clear than with legislation limiting trainmen's hours, and their main purpose was probably to hamper long freight trains and reduce the trainmen's workload. This at least was the view of the carriers, and they claimed persuasively that such laws would be likely to worsen safety and drive up costs. Such arguments sidetracked federal legislation, but a number of states proved more receptive to the brotherhoods' position. By 1914 only Arizona had a train-limit law, but twenty-one other states had some form of crew requirement. Although many such laws were toothless, in the aggregate they cost about $6 million per year, the carriers claimed.[13]

PRAISEWORTHY METHODS OF SIGNALING

Separating trains by a space interval maintained by some sort of signal is inherently the best way to prevent collisions. The road is divided into blocks, and the entrance to each block is governed by a signal, which may be either manually or automatically controlled. The manual block system was developed in Britain in the 1840s and was in nearly universal use by the 1880s. It was first introduced into the United States in 1863, on the Central Railroad of New Jersey between Philadelphia and Trenton, by Ashbel Welch, the company's president and chief engineer, right after a disastrous rear-end collision. In the simplest form of the manual block system, the entrance signal is controlled by a telegrapher. When the block is occupied, he sets the signal to red; when the train leaves his block, a telegrapher at the entrance to the next block sends him a message and he sets his own signal to clear.

The automatic block controlled by a track circuit was a labor-saving American invention developed by the engineer William Robinson. His invention was first installed in 1870 on the Philadelphia and Erie. Robinson's device divided the road into blocks of track that were insulated at each end and that had a battery connected to both rails. A relay magnet is also connected to the track, and the current from the battery closes the relay, which in turn keeps a secondary circuit closed to hold a semaphore signal in a clear position. Since the signal can show clear only when the circuit is closed, the system is fail-safe, as any loss of power shifts the signal to stop. Thus, a short circuit due to a train entering the block, to a loss of battery power, or to a broken rail automatically activates a danger signal.[14]

Initially neither the manual nor the automatic block system spread rapidly in the United States. Manual blocking was more expensive in the States than in Britain because of the high cost of telegraphers in this country, and the thin traffic on most American lines reduced the payoff to any signal system. Railroad critics almost unanimously urged an extension of block signals, although there was increasing interest in both cab signals and a relatively untried device that would automatically stop trains that ran signals. On June 30, 1906, Congress finally responded to

This Long Island Railroad locomotive plowed into the rear of a freight on July 10, 1909. Railroad safety advocates hoped that block signals—or, better, automatic train control—would prevent such disasters. *(Library of Congress)*

years of prodding by the ICC and others and passed a joint resolution authorizing the commission to investigate and report on block signals and automatic train controls.

A 1907 ICC study described in some detail various forms of block signal systems. It also gathered the first hard evidence on the extent of their use on American railroads. To no one's surprise, the study called for mandatory extension of the block system under ICC supervision—a policy the commission had been advocating since 1903—concluding that "it is undeniable that collisions on our railroads could be reduced to an exceedingly small number by the efficient management of block signals." The automatic train stop was relegated to a minor role because it "would prevent that last small percentage of such accidents as are due to the engineman falling dead at his post, and other like causes." The study acknowledged, however, that little was known of either automatic train controls or cab signals, and it called upon Congress to authorize an investigation and tests at government expense of these and "such [other] safety devices as appear to be meritorious." Congress promptly appropriated $50,000 for the task, and the Block Signal and Train Control Board was born.[15]

Between 1908 and 1912 the board published four annual reports and a final report. In conjunction with the ICC's 1907 study and its annual reports, these documents depict the evolution in official thinking on the causes of collisions that led the ICC to abandon its earlier campaign for block signals and to embrace instead what seemed to be the perfect technological fix: the automatic train stop.

In its first report the board rather skeptically noted the "European idea that with proper indication the engineman can be relied upon." The board also reviewed British railroad practice and remarked enviously on the better training and supervision of signalmen to be found there. The second report, issued in 1909, called for government supervision of the manual block system, which the board hoped would establish those "praiseworthy methods of signaling . . . which are in vogue in Great Britain." Sounding like an editorial out of the *Railroad Gazette*, the board concluded that "there is probably no one factor so important to the safety of railroad operations . . . as the promotion of good discipline."[16]

One longtime goal of the reformers was finally realized in 1910. With little opposition from the carriers, Congress amended the Accident Reports Act of 1901 to allow ICC investigation of train accidents. In the tradition of Charles Francis Adams, it was hoped that the dissemination of information and the glare of publicity would improve safety. But accident investigation had another effect. By allowing the commission to determine the causes of collisions, the amendment supplied the statistical ammunition for the ICC's emerging campaign for automatic train control.

By 1911, in its third report, the board was beginning to conclude that urging better management and discipline on the railroads was a hopeless task, for in an inspection of train dispatching and signaling systems it uncovered a truly frightening number of slapdash practices. It found mistakes in train orders, and hand signals given from telegraph towers in violation of company rules. On one carrier it observed trains routinely crossing each other's tracks without a stop. It discovered one telegrapher who was eighteen years old and had but three months' experience. Another carrier employed boys on school vacation as telephone operators. Chastened by such findings, the board echoed the conclusions of British observers: "The American is not reared with the discipline which becomes a part of the man and governs his actions mechanically. . . . The automatic stop, therefore, while it might be unnecessary under different social conditions, may be expected to add to safety under conditions which do exist . . . until we shall come to achieve discipline of the right sort."[17]

In its fourth report the board sharply criticized the carriers for their laxity in developing the automatic train stop, and in its final report it returned to the problems of management. These were "largely due to causes which have their roots in the conditions of society in America." Deep-seated problems require drastic measures, and a majority of the board called for automatic train control and for comprehensive supervision of all aspects of railroad safety "similar in character to that now administered through the British Board of Trade." [18]

The ICC's own annual reports echoed this increasing distrust of railroad management. While the commission had advocated an extension of the block system since 1903, it gradually came to focus instead on those collisions that resulted from a failure of trainmen to obey the signal. In 1911 it strongly urged the carriers to experiment with train control devices. In 1912 the ICC emphasized for the first time that the block system "by no means insures immunity from collisions," noting the many accidents that resulted from "dereliction of duty" on the part of employees, and it again urged development of a scheme to "neutralize the effects of human error." In 1913 it returned to this theme and also requested broad powers to investigate safety conditions and to require carriers to implement its recommendations. In 1917 it began to publish lists of collisions that it had investigated and stressed the number of them preventable only by automatic train control.[19]

Thus, the ICC increasingly came to focus on those few, but often spectacular, collisions that resulted from the failure of trainmen to obey block signals. This restricted vision led the commission to conclude that railroad management was so lax that the value of the block system would be nullified unless Congress could be persuaded to place it under ICC supervision. What was needed, therefore, was a foolproof technological device such as an automatic train stop that could reduce collisions even in the absence of management commitment. Ironically, by the time the ICC had concluded that railroad management was hopeless, matters were already beginning to improve. Collision casualty rates peaked between 1907 and 1912; thereafter they dropped sharply (figs. 5.1 and 5.2; table A1.5).

THE DECLINE OF THE COLLISION HORROR

Why collision casualties rose so sharply after 1897 and why they subsequently fell so sharply are questions at least partly amenable to statistical analysis (table A1.9). These findings suggest that traffic density, which rose about 5 percent between 1897 and 1907, increased the casualty rate about 12 percent. The diffusion of air brakes was far more important. Between 1897 and 1907 the share of equipment so equipped rose 246 percent, which sharply increased employee collision casual-

Collisions killed far more trainmen than passengers. In November 1916 a runaway freight sideswiped another train, causing a wreck that killed seven Pennsylvania Railroad workers. *(Courtesy Hagley Museum and Library)*

ties. Air brakes led to break-in-twos, and they encouraged faster speeds. Perhaps they also inclined engineers to ignore caution signals under the misapprehension that the train was under control.

From 1906 to 1939, employee casualty rates from collisions fell precipitously. As the railroads claimed, train-limit laws reduced safety because longer trains diminished collision rates. So did block signals. In 1906 only about forty-eight thousand miles of track, or 22 percent of the total, were block-signaled. Thereafter the figures rose sharply, reaching 38 percent by 1915, 44 percent by 1929, and 59 percent on the eve of World War II. This rapid diffusion was a response to the rise in collisions after 1897 and to the carriers' fears of regulation, and clearly it went a long way toward solving the problem. In addition, the slowing of employment growth and the decline in traffic density also made employees' lives safer.[20]

The Hours of Service Act made only a minor contribution to the decline in collision casualties. The ICC gathered data on all collisions and derailments that occurred during the period July 1901–September 1906 in which the train crew had been on duty more than fifteen hours. These figures include casualties to employees and others, most of whom were passengers. They amounted to 2.9 percent of all deaths and 0.7

percent of all injuries to passengers and workers between 1901 and 1906. According to the ICC, by 1912 the law virtually ended accidents due to long hours. Thus, had the Hours of Service Act been operative during the years 1901–6, it could have reduced casualties by these amounts at most.[21]

Although Congress held hearings on block signals and a host of other safety appliances during 1913–14, nothing came of them. Aroused by the scent of regulation, the carriers finally mobilized effectively. Speaking through the Special Committee on Relations of Railway Operation to Legislation, they conducted surveys that demonstrated progress in installing various safety appliances. Moreover, the decline in collision rates after 1907 muted public outcry and reduced the demand for legislation. Congressman Esch was only temporarily diverted, however. The increase in traffic density and employment in 1917 and 1918 led to another spurt of collisions, confirming his suspicions that the improvement in railroad safety had been ephemeral. Seeing his moment, Esch pounced. With the memory of these recent events still fresh, he was able to include section 26 in the Transportation Act of 1920, which gave the ICC broad authority to require block signals or "other safety devices."

"The Danger of Serious Derailment Is Ever Present"

Most of the public outcry over train wrecks and most legislative proposals were aimed at what the ICC called the collision horror. But derailments also rose sharply after 1897, peaking in about 1912. Thereafter they declined, but more slowly than did collisions. Gradually the ICC became alarmed; in 1911 it called attention to derailments, and in 1912 it warned that on many railroads "the danger of serious derailment is ever present." By 1915 the commission remarked with some surprise that derailments now outnumbered collisions.[22]

Table 5.1 contains data on the causes of derailments. They reveal that roadbed and equipment rather than employee negligence accounted for most derailments. Broken rails caused more serious wrecks than did other forms of roadbed failure such as soft track or bad ties. Rail failure accounted for 18 percent of all roadbed-related accidents, but it caused 29 percent of all fatalities and 34 percent of all injuries due to roadbed failures. This is not surprising; broken rails often caused wrecks while trains were traveling at high speeds. By contrast, soft track or bad ties caused far less serious accidents because such conditions were well known and trains usually crept over the worst parts of the roadbed.

The carriers responded to the rise in derailments with numerous improvements in roadbed and equipment. Real maintenance expenditures

TABLE 5.1. The Causes of Derailments, 1902–1915

	Number of Accidents	Fatalities	Injuries	Cost of Damage and Cleanup
Defective roadway	18,018	696	21,421	$14,113,813
Broken rail	3,345	205	7,341	3,967,188
Bad ties and soft track	3,046	62	2,742	1,985,025
Other[a]	11,627	429	11,338	8,161,600
Defective equipment	40,872	641	11,055	32,786,374
Employee negligence[b]	4,728	460	5,310	3,424,544

Source: Data are from ICC Accident Bulletin 56 (1915): 38–41.

Note: The casualties include all persons.

[a] Spread rail, sun kink, irregular track, and miscellaneous.
[b] For 1904–15, as earlier years are unavailable.

on roadbed and structures per mile of track rose nearly 40 percent between the 1890s and the 1920s. Technological improvements also contributed to the decline in derailments as the carriers introduced anti-rail-creep devices and tie plates, substituted steel for cast-iron wheels, and introduced the steel-side-frame truck, stronger couplers, improved air brakes, and more. The upsurge in broken rails also sparked a major research effort by the carriers and the steel companies that lasted thirty years. Because broken rails caused the worst derailments and led to the most intense remedial efforts by the carriers, they are the focus of this section.

In the early years of the twentieth century, rail failures rose steadily, causing increasing concern among the carriers. By 1904 the Pennsylvania was pressuring its suppliers to improve quality and was complaining about the "large number of broken rails" it had received from Cambria Steel. The American Railway Association also became alarmed and in 1906 established a Committee on Standard Rail and Wheel Sections to meet with manufacturers and develop better rails. In 1907 the matter suddenly achieved greater visibility. A New York State Railroad Commission investigation found that from January through March of that year nearly three thousand rails had failed in that state—nearly triple the number of three years earlier. Nationwide there were three hundred accidents from broken rails in 1907, up from a mere seventy-eight in 1902. The result was an explosion in both the popular and the technical press and yet another threat of tighter regulation. In response the ARA turned the matter over to the American Railway Engineering Association (AREA), where a testing facility was established in 1910 that was jointly funded by the ARA and the steel producers.[23]

The railroads and most impartial observers attributed the sharp increase in rail failures to poor manufacturing techniques that resulted in piped (hollowed-out) ingots or left too much slag in the top. Some writers blamed the poor quality control on the greed of the steel trust. *Scientific American* referred at times to a "ring of steel producers" and the "one colossal concern which can furnish [rails]." In the seller's market that prevailed after 1900, the companies rolled rails too quickly, critics claimed, before the chemical reactions had had time to proceed, and producers also reduced the amount of discard from the top of each ingot from nearly one-quarter to perhaps one-tenth, thereby allowing too much slag in the rail. In addition, with the exhaustion of low-phosphorous ores, Bessemer steel was becoming increasingly brittle. The Baltimore and Ohio reported that out of one shipment of ten thousand tons of rails, 22 percent were found to contain defects in their first year of use.[24]

The steel companies responded to this assault by turning the economic argument around and charging that the problem resulted from a headlong increase in axle loads and train speeds, and from the penny-pinching of carriers who specified rails that were too light and contained too much carbon (which made them durable but brittle). They also noted that flat wheels or poorly counterbalanced locomotives running over bad roadbed could break the best of rails. The problem, as they saw it, was that the carriers did not want to spend the money needed for proper maintenance or rail quality.[25]

Under pressure from the carriers, manufacturers gradually improved their techniques. Beginning in 1902 the AREA sharply tightened recommended testing requirements, and six years later the ARA adopted new specifications governing rail sections. A few large carriers such as the Pennsylvania and the New York Central also carried on parallel research; the Pennsylvania experimented with manufacturing techniques, while the Central tested titanium rails. In 1908 the AREA began to collect rail failure statistics, which it published annually, and the data were separated out by production method (Bessemer versus open hearth) and individual mill. By 1915, five-year failure rates were available for 1908, 1909, and 1910. They revealed that Bessemer rails failed between 12 percent and 88 percent more often than open-hearth rails, and they also showed enormous mill-to-mill variations in failure rates for the same type of rail. In response, the AREA began to inspect and report individual mill practice. Together the shift to open-hearth steel and the publicity given to bad practice began to improve rail quality.[26]

Railroad technical men also acknowledged that fast, heavy trains were part of the problem. Part of the solution lay in redesign of the rail section and in a shift to heavier rails. When the Pittsburgh and Lake Erie introduced the new 2-8-2 Mikado locomotive with 75,000-pound wheel loads, it experienced a spurt of rail failures that declined only with the shift from the 100- to the 115-pound rail. Average rail weight rose from 77 pounds per yard in 1912 to 82 pounds in 1920 and to 91 pounds in 1930. No doubt some of the decline in failure rates stemmed from this source. Other developments such as improvements in locomotive design that reduced rail stress for a given weight and speed also contributed to the decline in the number of derailments.[27]

While the railroads were coping with some of the causes of broken rails, new dangers were arising, however. Internal transverse fissures were first detected in 1911 in a broken rail on the Lehigh Valley that had caused a derailment at Manchester, New York, killing twenty-nine people and injuring sixty-three. Thereafter the number of rails discovered to have such fissures increased sharply, a problem due—the ICC claimed rather ominously—to the "cold rolling" of the rail by heavy wheel loads. Would train weight be prescribed, railroad men must have wondered, if the ICC finally got the power over safety that critics wanted? Predictably, the carriers blamed this problem too on poor-quality steel and bad manufacturing techniques.[28]

Transverse fissures proved to be a far more difficult problem than other causes of rail failure. They were especially dangerous because unlike many other defects, they usually could not be detected until the

FIGURE 5.3. Five-Year Rail Failure Rates per Hundred Miles of Track, 1908–1940

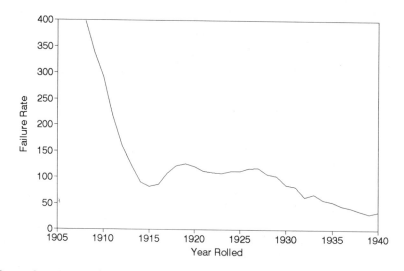

Source: American Railway Engineering Association Proceedings, various years.

rail failed. Finally in 1926, after a number of early detection techniques proved unsatisfactory, E. A. Sperry proposed a novel method that so impressed the railroads that they funded its development. In late 1928 the carriers pronounced his detector car a success, and it was in virtually continuous use from 1929 on.[29]

Discovery of the causes of such failures also proved troublesome. Under the watchful eye of the ICC, the carriers, along with the steel industry and the Bureau of Standards, funded dozens of research projects over nearly two decades. The breakthrough came in 1928, but it resulted from British, not American, efforts. Following up on earlier American research that linked transverse fissures to tiny shatter cracks in the steel, the British engineer C. Peter Sandberg demonstrated that the cracks could be prevented by controlling the rate at which rails cooled. In 1931, American steel manufacturers and the carriers began a joint research project into transverse fissures under the direction of H. F. Moore at the University of Illinois. Moore provided careful laboratory support for Sandberg's findings. Manufacturers responded, and the introduction of controlled-cool rails in the mid-1930s virtually did away with transverse fissures.[30]

Together these research efforts gradually reduced all forms of rail failure (fig. 5.3) and staved off further regulation. With the improvements in roadbed and equipment noted above, the reduction in rail failures resulted in a dramatic decline in casualties from derailments. About ninety-six fatalities a year had resulted from defective roadbed and equipment between 1902 and 1915; by 1929 the number had fallen to fifty-two even though train weight, speed, employment, and passenger-miles in that year all exceeded the average of the former period.

Ash Pans, Boilers, and Safety Appliances

The safety of locomotives and rolling stock was not an issue that sold magazines, and perhaps because of the relatively low political visibility of the issue, the ICC played only a minor part in supporting related legislation. But locomotive safety was of immediate interest to the brotherhoods. With the public indifferent and the ICC largely uninvolved, matters boiled down to a contest between labor and capital.

It is easy to romanticize steam locomotives, but to the men who worked them, locomotives were dirty, noisy, and dangerous. One of their special risks was the need to empty the ash pan. This was the job of the fireman, and on many locomotives it required crawling underneath to empty the pan. What could happen to a man in such a spot was vividly described when Congress held hearings on an ash-pan bill in 1907:

Brother Belaire crawled under the engine to hoe out the ash pan; the head brakeman came along, pulled the pin behind the engine and called the engineman to go ahead; the engineer, forgetting that his fireman was under the engine, made an attempt to pull out; then the fireman made an attempt to crawl from under but got no farther than his two hands on the rail, and although the engine only moved about five feet it was enough to cut his hands off. . . . John Kenny . . . while cleaning ash pan on S.P. engine No. 640, at Woodville, Texas, was scalded to death [on] account of [the] blowpipe blowing out of [the] boiler.

Not very many men were hurt this way. ICC data for 1907 indicate that 14 were killed and 119 injured while cleaning ash pans under the locomotive. The implied fatality rate for trainmen was 0.04 per thousand. By contrast, the fatality rate from coupling cars in 1907 was twenty times greater (table A1.4). While the dangers from ash pans were not great, they must have been hard to accept, because they seemed so unnecessary. H. R. Fuller, representing the Locomotive Engineers, the Firemen, and the Trainmen at the congressional hearings, presented evidence from the Baldwin Locomotive Company that about 40 percent of all new engines came equipped so that they could be cleaned from the outside and that these cost no more to purchase. As always, the railroads opposed legislation, but their arguments went unheard. The Ashpan Law passed Congress on May 30, 1908, and went into effect on January 1, 1910.[31]

In 1910 Congress gave the ICC power to designate the location of safety appliances on freight cars and to require their maintenance, and in 1911 the dangers of locomotives again led to legislation. In 1831, at the very dawn of American railroading, the *Best Friend of Charleston* had blown up, killing the fireman, because he had tied down the safety valve. Explosions of this type, due to excessive boiler pressure, were quite rare. Most disasters were the result of low water, which weakened the boiler, causing it to fail under normal operating pressures. Alfred Bruce, a modern historian of locomotives, described the consequences: "When the water level falls below the top of the firebox crown sheet the latter immediately becomes overheated, at the same time losing much of its tensile strength. . . . [This] causes the crown sheet first to pocket downward between the staybolts, and then to pull off the ends of the staybolts, eventually rupturing with disastrous results." As Bruce also noted, because the explosion was at the back of the locomotive and was directed downward, it often blew the boiler hundreds of yards ahead without even derailing what was left of the engine. The first glimpse of just how many trainmen met their end in this manner was provided by

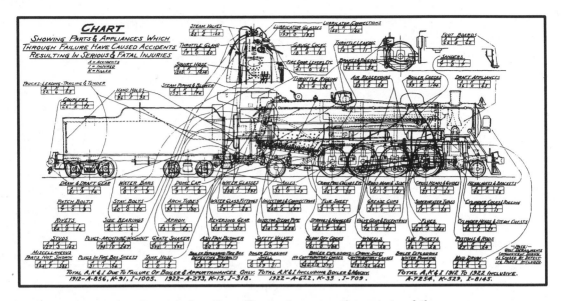

Interstate Commerce Commission chart illustrating steam locomotive failures that resulted in the injury or death of railroad workmen between 1912 and 1922. (*Author's collection*)

the ICC. Boiler explosions killed 265 employees and injured 3,536 between 1905 and 1909. Most of the killed and injured were trainmen, and their annual death rate from boiler explosions was about 0.19 per thousand—about one-fourth of the death rate from coupling cars.[32]

In 1904 the Brotherhood of Locomotive Engineers adopted a resolution endorsing federal regulation of locomotive safety, and in 1909 the first bills were introduced into Congress. The Firemen and Enginemen and the Brotherhood of Locomotive Engineers led the fight. "Brother A. A. Row is exerting every effort for the passage of this bill," the editor of the *Locomotive Firemen and Enginemen's Magazine* informed his readers, and he urged the membership to write letters of support. The ICC never publicly endorsed the idea, nor did it testify for the bills.[33]

As initially drafted, these bills required that locomotives be equipped with specific types of safety equipment and that the boiler be "well made." Each boiler was to be examined by a government inspector every three months. The result was an explosion that blew railroad management all the way to Washington. The Special Committee on Relations of Railway Operation to Legislation was apparently formed in response to these bills. Speaking through it, the railroads violently objected to both their principle and their content.

The companies cited a survey by the special committee that attributed 98 percent of all explosions to low water, which it blamed on the engineers. Charles Paulding of the New York Central also objected to the implication of the legislation, blandly assuring the committee that "if we thought that one life could be saved by government inspection or that an injury to one man could be obviated by an inspection by the government, we would not be here." This was too much for the bill's sponsor, Senator Elmer Burkett of Nebraska, who snapped, "You used the same arguments against safety appliances." The carriers also had more specific objections to the original bills. They complained that the bills would result in inspections by both the government and the companies, thereby adding to expensive downtime. They also disliked the writing of specific devices into law, as it might freeze technology, while the requirement that boilers be "well made" would involve the government in boiler design.[34]

The railroads' howls of anguish were echoed in the railroad press, and the *Railway Age* even went so far as to term the bills "vindictive." In the face of such a storm, the advocates of federal inspection trimmed their sails. The amended version of locomotive inspection dropped the specific safety devices and no longer required direct government inspection. Instead, the carriers were required to file inspection rules with the ICC and were to perform their own inspections under government supervision. Since this bill followed almost precisely the legislative guidelines that the special committee had formulated, the carriers acquiesced, and it passed easily on February 17, 1911, and became law on July 1 of the same year.[35]

By 1914 the carriers were claiming that compliance with the new rules was costing them $4.5 million annually. But locomotive accidents also fell about 45 percent per locomotive-mile from 1912 through 1915, which the ICC immediately attributed to the beneficial consequences of its supervision. Yet after 1915 the improvement stopped for about a decade. The stabilization resulted from a number of causes. Broadening the act in 1916 made inspections more difficult and so reduced their number, as did the increasing complexity of locomotives, while World War I resulted in an increase in locomotive use and the transfer of inspectors to other work. By the early 1920s the ICC's Bureau of Locomotive Inspection was worrying about the rise in locomotive accidents and excoriating the carriers for the "general deteriorated condition of [their] motive power."[36]

In 1924 Congress authorized additional inspectors. Partly as a result, accidents and fatalities again began to decline. On the eve of World War II, locomotive accident rates had fallen 75 percent and fatality rates 72 percent from their 1912 levels. Once again the ICC took full credit for these developments. In 1929 it asserted that the value of added inspections was "strikingly illustrated in the reduction in . . . accidents." But the improvement in locomotive safety reflected more than just federal regulation. Down to the early 1920s, both fatalities and accidents resulting from boiler explosions due solely to low water declined more sharply than those related to defects. Thus, the gains in locomotive safety during these years may have resulted as much from the carriers' newfound interest in Safety First as from federal regulation.[37]

The decline in locomotive accidents after 1924 also reflected changes in the nature of railroading. The mid-1920s saw the end of a century of expansion as automobiles and trucks began to cut into the carriers' markets. This period was also marked by sharp improvements in locomotive efficiency and reliability. The combined effect was to reduce the carriers' demand for locomotives and to render the older motive power uneconomical. As a result, the number of locomotives in service began to decline after 1924; by 1930 there were 9,297 fewer engines in service than there had been six years earlier. The proportion of defective locomotives, which showed no downward trend until 1924, fell sharply thereafter. Thus, the stock of locomotives began to grow both newer and safer from about 1924 on. Trainmen decried the loss of jobs that resulted from the increasing use of trucks and automobiles, but the jobs that remained grew somewhat less risky.[38]

TABLE 5.2. Potential Safety Gains from Locomotive and Rolling Stock Legislation, 1908–1910

	Year	Fatalities		Injuries	
		Number	Rate	Number	Rate
Ash pans	1907	14	0.04	119	0.37
Boiler inspection	1905–9	265	0.19	3,536	12.49
Defective handholds, etc.	1908	17	0.06	882	3.24
Total			0.29		16.10
Total as percentage of average rate, 1908–10			5.10		13.84

Source: Ash-pan data are from U.S. House Committee on Interstate and Foreign Commerce, *Hearings on H.R. 19795, Ash Pan Bill* (Washington, D.C., 1908), 4. Boiler inspection data are from U.S. Senate Committee on Interstate and Foreign Commerce, *Hearings on S236 and S6702 to Promote the Safety of Employees and Travelers upon Railroads by Compelling Common Carriers by Railroad to Equip Their Locomotives with Safe and Suitable Boilers and Appurtenances Thereto*, 61st Cong., 2d sess., Mar. 22, 1910, S.D. 446. Handholds data are from *Congressional Record*, 61st Cong., 2d sess., Dec. 15, 1909, 45:159.

Note: Rates are per thousand trainmen.

Table 5.2 contains estimates of the risks to trainmen from ash pans, defective locomotives, and defective freight car safety appliances for the years immediately prior to 1910. These numbers represent what the maximum potential impact of legislation would have been if it had been completely effective. While the data are rough, they suggest that these laws could have resulted in at most a 5 percent drop in trainmen's fatality rates. Nor, as noted, did the Hours of Service legislation make a major contribution to improved railroad safety. Such data point to a conclusion with which many railroad critics might have agreed: it was virtually impossible to force the railroads to improve safety by piecemeal legislation. This view had led the ICC and members of the railroad press to advocate broad government control over railroad safety. They never got their wish, but just as Charles Francis Adams had used the threat of regulation to encourage nineteenth-century Massachusetts railroads to improve safety, so the prospect of ever-stricter government controls finally pushed the carriers to embrace organized safety work. Along with the myriad improvements in signaling, rail quality, and other equipment, Safety First finally began to reduce the slaughter of railroad workers.

Safety First Comes to Railroading

The acknowledged father of Safety First in railroading was Ralph C. Richards, longtime general claim agent of the Chicago and North Western Railroad. Richards had joined the North Western in 1870 as an errand boy, and in 1882 at the age of twenty-seven he became general claim agent. As late as 1910 the North Western killed 107 men and injured nearly 9,000 in the course of a year's business. Richards's job made him intimately familiar with these statistics, and he was appalled by the carnage. In 1905 he prepared a series of articles on railway accidents for the *Railroad Gazette*, which were published in book form by the Association of Railway Claim Agents in 1906. In that year he tried unsuccessfully to interest the management of the North Western in a safety campaign. Four years later the company changed its policy, and in May 1910 Richards established the first railroad safety organization.[39]

SPREADING THE SAFETY GOSPEL

In 1912, just two years after Richards inaugurated the safety movement on the North Western, the ICC noted in its annual report that "great possibilities . . . lie in the so-called safety committees which have been organized on many roads." That same year the Central Safety

Committee of the North Western claimed that forty-seven other roads with 152,000 miles of track, or about 40 percent of the U.S. total, had adopted its Safety First organization. Surely this ranks as one of the most rapid mass conversions in history, and the questions arise why it occurred when it did and why it came so rapidly.[40]

Part of the answer is that rising injury costs finally began to attract management's attention. States such as Iowa, Alabama, and Massachusetts had passed employers' liability laws that chipped away at the carriers' legal defenses, and in 1898 the Erdman Act made it illegal to require membership in a relief system as a condition of employment and voided contracts that made benefits conditional upon waiving one's right to sue. Even worse, from the carriers' perspective, in 1908 Congress changed the employers' liability law that governed workers in interstate commerce. The new law effectively abolished the fellow-servant and assumption-of-risk defenses that had shielded employers from liability. In addition, the brotherhoods had begun to use their high casualty rates as a lever to pry wage increases from the carriers during arbitration hearings, while the spread of workman's compensation for casualties to intrastate employees also threatened to increase carriers' injury costs.[41]

The effect of changing liability rules is depicted in table 5.3. Clearly the carriers' relief systems paid more in the 1890s than the Ohio railroads had paid a decade earlier. And if the relief systems' payments were typical of those received by other workers during the 1890s, average compensation payments rose sharply between that time and 1908–10. Workers with temporary injuries in the latter period received over six times the average compensation for all injuries during the former period. Such events must have led most railroads to expect a future of rising injury claims. If so, they would have been correct: between 1910 and 1932 the average real cost of major injuries rose about 70 percent, and the cost of worker casualties began to intrude into corporate decision making.[42]

On the North Western, Richards reported that accidents increased "alarmingly" between 1909 and 1910, and management asked him to implement his ideas. The Pennsylvania publicly acknowledged that escalating casualty rates were the motive behind its venture into organized safety in 1910. Its worker injury costs again exploded after 1917, nearly doubling by 1924 and leading it to undertake a massive safety campaign beginning in that year. The electric urban and interurban railroads also instituted safety work in response to sharply rising claims. Charles Hill, safety agent for the New York Central, explained that until new report-

TABLE 5.3. Compensation for Injuries and Fatalities under Employers' Liability Laws, 1880–1932

	1880	1894–1895	1908–1910	1932
Minor injury	$—	$ —	$ 73	$ 57
Major injury	—	—	1,673	2,844
All nonfatal	36	16	130	—
Fatal	40	686	1,222	2,768
All	40	44[a]	203	224

Source: Data for 1880 are coefficients from the equations in chapter 1, n. 51; they are marginal and the other figures average costs. The figures for 1894–95 are from railway relief departments and from Emory Johnson, "Railway Relief Departments," BLS *Bulletin* 8 (Jan. 1897): 39–57. The 1908–10 data and those for 1932 are both in U.S. Federal Coordinator of Transportation, *Cost of Railroad Employee Accidents, 1932,* 74th Cong., 1st sess., 1935, S.D. 68, table 20.

Note: The data for 1880, 1894–95, and 1932 were converted into 1908–10 prices using the price index in *Historical Statistics of the United States,* series E-135.

[a] Since the proportion of injuries and fatalities for 1894–95 was unavailable, this was computed using the 1908–10 proportions.

ing requirements were required under the Accident Reports Act of 1901, the company had been unaware of just how rapidly casualties were increasing. The discovery, he said, shocked the Central into instituting a safety program. Additional evidence that injury costs were in the minds of managers who instituted safety programs is the near universality with which claim agents were members of safety committees.[43]

Richards's ideas were adopted not only because carriers were becoming increasingly concerned with accident costs but also because the safety movement provided the carriers with a shield to fend off increasingly expensive and intrusive government regulations. While some of the proposed bills, such as the ash-pan law, were relatively innocuous, the carriers saw others, such as the train-limit and full-crew bills and the original locomotive inspection bills, as serious threats. But even locomotive inspection was trivial compared with bills that would have regulated railway clearances or given the ICC powers similar to those of the British Board of Trade.

In 1909 W. L. Park of the Union Pacific warned the Western Railroad Club that safety had to be improved "unless railroad men are willing to let the politicians take from their hands the reins and govern the railroads." Three years later, in May 1912, F. C. Rice of the Burlington made the same point to the annual meeting of the ARA. He reminded the members of all the laws to regulate railway safety that had been passed

or were pending and concluded that unless the carriers voluntarily reduced accidents, regulation would "extend its control to all details of
operation." He noted that some carriers had organized safety committees and urged individual railroads and the ARA itself to "enter with
increased enthusiasm and energy on a campaign for the reduction of
accidents." Unless they did so, he concluded, "I entertain grave fears as
to the results."[44]

Rice's warning that the carriers were in danger of losing control over
their operations was hardly far-fetched, and his audience knew it. Moreover, the railroads' aggregate safety image depended on the actions of
each carrier, and so some form of "safety cartel" was required that could
pressure individual railroads and jointly reduce accidents. Hence, the
ARA adopted a resolution to investigate safety matters. A year later the
Executive Committee presented to the membership the report of a subcommittee on transportation composed of Ralph Richards and safety
agents of other major carriers. The report outlined the North Western's
safety organization and urged its adoption by all railroads.[45]

A MANAGEMENT RESPONSIBILITY

Like managers everywhere, nineteenth-century railroad executives
had blamed accidents on the lack of discipline, which was in turn the
fault of unions, or the men themselves, or virtually anybody, it seemed,
except management. A poet writing in *Railroad Trainman* gave the employees' response in "Blame It on the Engineer":

> A lurch that flings the rushing train,
>   A roaring shock that rips and rends,
> The Groan of death the shriek of pain,
>   And—Holy Holy Dividends.
> The Engineer—poor chap he's killed
>   That makes the explanation clear
> A trusted servant tried and skilled
>   We'll blame it on the engineer.

Management's urge to "blame it on the engineer" had been powerfully
reinforced by self-interest. It was generally acknowledged that rules
were designed to be paraded in liability court, not to be obeyed. *Railway
Age* claimed that "any engineman who fails to make his schedule time
habitually . . . is likely to be discharged." In 1906 the *Railroad Gazette*
noted a court case in which an employee was hit by a train after the
foreman had claimed he would be the lookout for the worker. The court
ruled that the foreman could not assume that right for the railroad. The
Gazette observed that "this decision was, of course, a warning to the

company to avoid any official assumption of responsibility," and went on to point out that the new employers' liability law had recently made such doctrine obsolete.[46]

Richards and other railroad safety men endlessly preached the need for official assumption of responsibility. Richards routinely called for improved supervision. An accident, he noted, "is a notice to the division officials . . . that there may be something wrong in the method of doing the work." This position was increasingly voiced by the railroad press. In an open letter to its readers entitled "What Are We Going to Do about Railroad Accidents?" the *Railroad Gazette* stated bluntly that "the General Manager is responsible and has the power to stop most of the loss of 1,000 lives in collisions and derailments." Old attitudes die hard, however, and several general managers responded by complaining that the brotherhoods had destroyed discipline. D. L. Cease, editor of *Railroad Trainman*, promptly wrote the *Gazette* and asked for examples. None was forthcoming.[47]

Many railroad managers were receptive to the safety message just then, because reducing accidents not only cut costs, it also generated favorable publicity at a time when the carriers badly needed it. Safety men such as Charles Dow of the New York Central were often chosen to present the company position in opposition to full-crew or train-limit legislation. Work safety also appealed to the carriers as an area in which capital and labor shared a harmony of interest during a period when labor relations were becoming increasingly fractious. "The whole idea of our safety movement is co-operation with the men," Richards claimed. To W. T. Tyler, general manager of the St. Louis and San Francisco, the safety movement was a place "where both labor and capital can meet on common ground." Thus, while the railroads were becoming increasingly hierarchical and bureaucratic, the safety meetings themselves were often modestly democratic. As Richards described the North Western, "The men do not attend [safety meetings] as brakemen or enginemen or division superintendents but as committee-men, and every man is on an equality."[48]

Railroad safety officials also tried to appeal to top managers in other ways. They acknowledged that improvements should be made "so far as practicable," and Richards never tired of preaching that it was the "little accidents," the ones that killed or injured only one person at a time, that did most of the damage. And little causes often had cheap cures: at the North Western, he pointed out, "our [machine] guards are all homemade and do not cost much." While benefits included a reduction in claims, safety officers invariably talked the broader language of efficiency. The two, in fact, came to be virtually synonymous. Safety, it was alleged, reduced absenteeism and labor turnover, and it allowed the carriers to attract a better class of men. As the head of safety on the Pennsylvania summarized matters, "Preventable accidents are a form of inefficiency."[49]

While Richards stressed that accidents represented a failure of management and were "not inevitable," he thought that their proximate cause was usually man failure. Speaking on the "Conservation of Men" to North Western employees, he pleaded, "If you want to change conditions you can do so tomorrow; if you don't want to change it will never be done, because you people and no one else can do it." Richards's emphasis on supervision, and his belief that most accidents involved man failure that only the men could correct, led him to create a safety organization remarkably like that employed by U.S. Steel—apparently a case of simultaneous invention. Rather than making safety the duty of some staff engineer with no operating responsibility, the North Western structure involved the men, and it included operating officers from top to bottom. As in manufacturing, railroad officials discovered that this structure worked better than safety organizations that excluded the men or placed primary responsibility on the safety officer. But the North Western's structure required strong leadership. As C. I. Leiper, a general manager of the Pennsylvania's central region, told a safety meeting, "The thing of prime importance from the General Manager's standpoint is to recognize his own responsibility and in turn re-emphasize the responsibility of general and division officers, their assistants and supervisory forces."[50]

Workers also needed to be convinced, and W. L. Park, now general superintendent of the Southern Pacific, advised his colleagues that actions spoke louder than words: "Do not neglect those things which are beyond the control of the men; otherwise they will accuse you of insincerity." At the 1915 meeting of the National Safety Council, Walter Greenwood, representing a railroad subsidiary of U.S. Steel, responded sharply to a series of papers blaming accidents on worker carelessness. To tell a brakeman not to kick a coupler when there was no safer way was simply hypocrisy, he warned, and would bring the whole movement into contempt.[51]

It did. As explained by a master such as Ralph Richards, accidents were a shared responsibility. Richards scolded the men for taking chances and urged them to see that their fate was, in considerable measure, in their own hands. Yet he never implied that the blame for accidents was all theirs. The North Western, he admitted, "is just as much to blame as you are." One of his first acts was to have the North Western's Central Safety Committee tour all the divisions and correct the unsafe conditions they found. But on some carriers Safety First quickly became little more than a public relations campaign to blame accidents on workers. As a result, while some of the brotherhoods had at first praised Safety First, their enthusiasm quickly waned.[52]

In 1913 one contributor to the *Locomotive Engineer's Journal* claimed that his experience on a safety committee "has thoroughly convinced me that railroad officials mean just what they say." But by 1920, in an editorial entitled "Safety Last," the journal was claiming that there was "very little to the whole movement but the pretense." No one was more enthusiastic over Safety First at the outset—and no one became more critical—than D. L. Cease, longtime editor of *Railroad Trainman*.[53]

Cease was hardly a management toady. He had thrown down the gauntlet to the *Railroad Gazette* demanding evidence that the brotherhoods were causing the lack of railroad discipline, and *Railroad Trainman* was full of articles in a similar vein. But he wholeheartedly embraced the early safety movement and urged his readers to trust in management's good faith: "The time has come when employees cannot afford to regard every innovation from the employer with suspicion. We must take him at his face value until we learn he does not mean what he says . . . so, when one of the great railway systems tells its men that it is interested in their safety . . . it is proper to believe the statement and join the effort toward carrying out its work." *Railroad Trainman* sounded this theme time and again in 1912 and 1913, urging its readers to give the safety movement the benefit of the doubt and denying that safety rules were simply a way to avoid employers' liability. Cease also publicized various companies' safety efforts, even going so far as to reprint Richards's "Conservation of Men." But by 1914 he was having a change of heart, and in 1915 he bitterly denounced Safety First as a sham, terming it "simply another method of throwing dust over the accident record." Although he admitted that a few roads were sincere, he concluded that on most of them Safety First had simply taken the place of the old nineteenth-century safety rules, which were intended to protect the employer from liability, not the workman from danger.[54]

In spite of the brotherhoods' disillusionment, railroad safety quickly became institutionalized. The ARA endorsement must have given it a powerful boost, and in 1912 what was to become the Steam Railroad Section of the National Safety Council held its first meeting. Thereafter its membership mushroomed, and by 1917 eighty-seven roads with 139,000 miles of line, or about 35 percent of the U.S. total, were members. World War I gave the railroad safety movement another push. In February 1918 the U.S. Railroad Administration Transportation Division, under the leadership of C. R. Gray, lately of the Union Pacific and a longtime Safety First enthusiast, organized a Safety Section. It sent a questionnaire to all Class I railroad safety organizations, discovering that "there was no uniform or well defined method in vogue, and with the exception of a limited number of roads, safety work was supervised by no particular officer. . . . On some railroads, after a trial, safety work was subordinated to something 'more important'. This created in the mind of the employees . . . the thought that the effort was not sincere." The survey also confirmed that safety organizations involving the men were much more successful than those that were entirely management-run. As a result, in May 1918 each Class I railroad was required to organize safety committees modeled on the North Western structure described above, and each was strongly urged to join the National Safety Council. These committees received the enthusiastic backing of the brotherhoods. Cease explained why he was once again a safety enthusiast: "It differs from the former plan in that it will be applied practically and not used to cover up railroad practice." By 1919 a safety campaign was in full swing.[55]

The most important effects of federal control were the structure it put in place and the experience it provided. In 1920, as the carriers faced the transition to private control, they determined to keep up the good work. This time, led by Isaiah Hale, chief safety officer of the Santa Fe, they tried to enlist the active cooperation of the brotherhoods. Hale made several unsuccessful efforts to convince union presidents of the carriers' sincerity. Finally, on September 25, 1920, he called a meeting in Chicago of his counterparts on twenty-four major railroads and union leadership including the editors of the major railroad labor journals.

Cease editorialized that the meeting was "one of the most practical he ever attended." The safety officers managed to convince him that they really did have the backing of top management. He responded, as did the editors of the journals representing the Conductors, the Firemen and Enginemen, and the Switchmen, by urging his readers to "lend their full support to the work" and by setting up a Safety First section of the journal. The carriers kept their end of the deal; in July 1921 the ARA took over the Safety Section from the U.S. Railroad Administration.[56]

IMPLEMENTING SAFETY FIRST

Railroads that developed successful safety programs all adopted procedures similar to those being employed by safety-conscious manufacturing companies. As in manufacturing, the first requisite was that the company spend some money to improve working conditions, thereby purchasing the employees' trust. To this end the carriers guarded machines, discarded poor-quality tools, widened clearances, policed the yards, and fixed or modified broken or dangerous equipment. Such improvements increased safety directly, while the willingness of the company to spend money demonstrated to suspicious workers that it was acting in good faith. The trainmen's response was overwhelmingly positive. Writing to *Railroad Trainman* in 1922, a Burlington employee who was a member of its safety committee observed, "I suppose that no one was more skeptical than I was when told that such a movement was to be inaugurated on the Burlington Railroad. I was elected as one of the Chicago Division Safety Committee. . . . Whenever it was shown that . . . an unsafe condition existed, it was promptly corrected. Obstructions . . . have all been removed. The yards have been cleaned up [and] overhead structures protected." By contrast, a company that launched a safety campaign without cleaning up its house (and yards) engendered cynicism rather than cooperation. Rather than preaching safety, "would it not be better to eliminate some of these dangers," the *Locomotive Engineer's Journal* asked. Similarly, a Chesapeake and Ohio (C&O) employee snapped that "this railway could inspire more confidence in the employee by showing him that it places life and limb above the dollar." A worker on the B&O also reacted angrily to a poster urging him not to go between cars to adjust couplers. The cause, he noted, was not force of habit but defective appliances.[57]

Still, as one safety officer put it, "no safety appliance is safe in the hands of an unsafe man." Thus, after improving conditions, the next requisite was to improve and enforce the code of rules governing the proper way to work. Hundreds of seemingly minor rules governing practices that had once been at the discretion of the employee or foreman were for the first time written down and enforced. On the Burlington, yardmen were prohibited from working with engines that had ice or snow on the footboard "no matter how long it takes." On the Boston and Maine (B&M), couplings were not to be adjusted while the train was moving, and in yard work, instead of having a man run ahead to flip a switch while the train was moving, the train was stopped first. On the North Western, men were prohibited from getting on the footboard of a moving engine from the front. On the Union Pacific, trainmen were required to face forward and were instructed in the proper manner of riding and getting off of cars and of handling brake clubs. The Pennsylvania required that track jacks be used only on the outside of the rail; it required goggles to be used in certain specific activities; it prohibited workers from using spike mauls as sledge hammers. These new and newly enforced rules took the control of work practices away from foremen and employees. It was the price they paid for a safer workplace.[58]

Specifying the "proper way" was one thing; reorienting a company's culture to bring it about was another, involving, as Cease put it, teaching "an old dog new tricks." The difficulties existed on both the management and the employee level. Nineteenth-century safety rules were made to be broken, and companies experienced considerable difficulty in persuading foremen and other subordinate officials to change these old ways. One trainman on the Big Four complained that "the principles of Safety First will never become fixed until subordinate officials are advised specifically that safety must be given the right of way over time." An employee on the Lake Shore thought the company's safety program was "a mighty good thing," but he noted that "some of the minor officials are not as sincere in this matter as they should be." One trainman on the B&M observed a trainmaster bawl out a conductor who, for safety reasons, did not get his freight over the road quickly enough.[59]

F. W. Mitchell, director of personnel on the New Haven, advised that "every foreman should realize that he bears the same relation to safety as he does to production." Most carriers tried to inculcate this new view of foremanship using the usual carrots and sticks. Many paid foremen bonuses for good safety records, and every year major railroads sent large numbers of their foremen, trainmasters, master mechanics, and others to the national safety meetings. They also began to penalize officials who turned in poor accident records. Large carriers such as the Pennsylvania, which kept accident statistics by region, division, and department, used the same comparative techniques employed by DuPont and other multiple-plant manufacturing companies. In the company's view, "the Division with the worst accident records should render as good performance as the Division with the best records." The Union Pacific was famous for its meticulous investigation of even the most minor accidents. When such an investigation revealed that an employee had been required to violate a safety rule, the officer who had issued the order was dismissed.[60]

Such procedures produced dramatic results. In the years immediately prior to the spread of Safety First, both the Block Signal Board and the ICC had repeatedly lambasted the railroads for sloppy operating practices. So rapidly did events change, however, that by 1914 the commission remarked with some surprise that "improvement is to be noted in the matter of inspection and supervision of train service employees . . . largely due to the work of safety committees." The Chicago Great Western demonstrated just how successful accident prevention could be when the careers of midlevel managers depended on it. The company began its safety work in 1912. In 1914 it reported a total of 1,020 casualties, and by 1927 the number had fallen to 81. Management attributed this success to the policy of "making safety work a regular part of operations and safety records an index of an officer's efficiency."[61]

Enforcing safety rules at the expense of getting traffic over the road made a powerful impression on the men. "I could name many corrections of unsafe conditions," said a Burlington trainman, "but the one that appealed to me most was the positive ironclad instruction that men should not go between cars for any reason while cars are in motion." Not all rules were so popular, and where safety meant extra work, the men sometimes ignored the new methods. One B&M employee had to warn twenty-three men in one month—some of them more than once—against the "asinine habit" of kicking drawbars. He concluded that "the employee himself is the greatest obstacle to the perfect fulfillment of . . . the Safety First movement."[62]

D. L. Cease had denounced the railways when they tried to blame all accidents on workers. But in a speech to the National Safety Council in 1922 he too acknowledged that some men seemed indifferent to their own lives and those of others. He noted that after so many years of fighting the companies for everything they got, many employees were naturally suspicious when better safety was offered them, seemingly free of charge. But Cease also thought that risk taking was deeply ingrained. The time was, he noted, when a man was not considered a good railroader unless he had been "car bit." To change such attitudes would take a generation, he thought.[63]

The trainmen's union did its part to reshape employee behavior. President William G. Lee told the National Safety Council in 1919, "I have endeavored in every honorable way to encourage those for whom I speak to assist in the Safety First Movement," and individual lodges incorporated safety discussions into their proceedings. H. R. Lake, a superintendent on the Santa Fe, frankly admitted that his efforts to interest the men in safety had gone nowhere until he enlisted the active support of the locals. *Railroad Trainman* kept up a steady beat of materials urging the men to support the carriers' safety efforts. By 1922 it reported some early fruits of its campaign: the decline in injuries had allowed insurance benefits to be raised without any increase in premiums.[64]

Cease also underestimated the carriers' ingenuity. Improving safety required tighter enforcement of rules. As a result, beginning with the North Western in 1906, the carriers instituted surprise "efficiency" tests to see whether trainmen, station men, maintenance-of-way employees, and others were following company rules. Such tests seem to have spread rapidly to many of the other large carriers such as the Santa Fe, the Rock Island, and the Illinois Central. The Pennsylvania instituted a discipline committee in January 1911 to go over the records of enginemen, and that company's employee representation plan also improved discipline.[65]

Personnel management procedures were also improved. The spread of railroad pension plans and their likely impact on labor turnover has already been noted, and in 1917 Thomas H. Carrow of the Pennsylvania reported that "normal" turnover was only 30 percent per year—far less than in the nineteenth century. Still, one-third of all injuries were suffered by employees with less than six months' experience, Carrow reported. In the 1920s, efforts were made to reduce turnover still further by reducing the seasonality of maintenance employment. With employment stable and turnover low, companies could be much more picky about whom they hired and could spend more time with each man in safety training. By the 1930s about one hundred large carriers administered preemployment physicals to all employees, and sixty roads reexamined older workers. On the Pennsylvania in the 1920s a sign was hung in the employment office stating bluntly, "WE DO NOT WANT careless men in our employ." New shopmen were given physical examinations to ensure proper job placement. They were then given safety instructions, personal protective equipment, and "more than ordinary supervision and attention the first weeks at least." On the Union Pacific new trainmen were given examinations on where they would find close clearances rather than being left, as in the old days, to discover them through "personal contact." On both the Pennsylvania and the Union Pacific, men who repeatedly violated safety rules were fired.[66]

The railroads' ability to select and supervise maintenance-of-way personnel was also enhanced by changes in the work process in the 1920s and 1930s. Spurred on by fears of labor shortages, the carriers transformed maintenance work by introducing a host of gasoline- and electric-powered machinery. Contemporaries claimed that the new cranes and power-operated wrenches, adzes, jacks, spike drivers, and tampers were all less dangerous than hand techniques. The new equipment also led the carriers to reorganize work into smaller gangs of specialized and trained machine operators that could be more closely supervised. The combination of safer machinery, better training, and improved supervision dramatically improved the safety of track work.[67]

But even more than in manufacturing, the essence of Safety First in railroading was unceasing worker education. Companies that cleaned up unsafe conditions, and improved and enforced their rules, still had to motivate workers. This was especially important for the railroads because supervision was usually far more difficult than in manufactur-

This National Safety Council poster from the 1920s placed worker education at the center of railroad safety efforts. *(Courtesy National Safety Council)*

ing companies. Charles G. Dow, safety agent of the New York Central, stated the problem clearly: "Railroad officials cannot observe the actions of all employees, nor any considerable part of them, at all times and it is therefore important that the employees themselves become imbued with the safety spirit." As Cease had observed, the culture of work on nineteenth-century railroads awarded status to the employee who had been "car bit." Reorienting such values to fit twentieth-century corporate needs required twentieth-century techniques. Once again, it was a job for the ad man. "In selling the safety idea," H. G. Hassler of the Pennsylvania told the ARA Safety Section in 1926, "advertising was one of our chief factors." Publicity, poetry, pep talks, buttons, banners, movies, and safety contests were the arsenal of the safety agent in the war on accidents.[68]

In the 1920s, safety contests spread through the carriers like a religious revival. A survey of 101 railroads undertaken in 1930 found that 53 regularly used safety contests, while another 25 simply circulated accident statistics. Each year the National Safety Council gave an award to the carrier with the lowest casualty rate; companies often staged accident reduction campaigns to try to win it, or the Harriman Safety Medal, or companywide trophies. And in 1924 the ARA Safety Section set as a goal a 35 percent reduction in casualties by 1930.[69]

This campaign had all of the ballyhoo of a giant camp meeting. At the height of the campaign in 1927, the ARA distributed over a million pieces of safety literature to its 128 members. The Pennsylvania, which by the early 1920s had become alarmed at the rising compensation costs resulting from its mediocre safety record, threw itself into the campaign. In 1927 it invented the Elisha Lee Safety Banner, named after a company vice president. Costing a modest $24.75, the gold version went to the division with the lowest casualty rate, while the division with the largest percentage reduction got a silver banner. In 1928 the payoff was raised, and a President's Safety Trophy was awarded. One motto used in the Pennsylvania car shops was:

Unless your Body is Composed of the Following Ingredients
Do not Disregard Safety Measures
Head—Concrete
Brains—Mush
Flesh—Rhinoceros Hide
Skin—Asbestos

The Pennsylvania also employed other techniques to improve safety. In 1928 superintendent of safety Thomas Carrow tightened safety requirements, which considerably improved supervision and, he claimed, shaved two points off the accident record.[70]

In the late 1920s the ICC began to worry that safety contests would encourage injury underreporting, for the contests were "represented to the employees to be like a baseball game in which avoidance of cases . . . is the basis for scoring hits." That underreporting existed is incontestable. In 1940 the commission investigated the injury files of six carriers and found significant underreporting on three of them. On the Chicago, Milwaukee, and St. Paul it even discovered one iron man who had his thumb crushed and amputated, but who never lost a day of work. But such underreporting probably did not account for a significant share of the observed decline in injury rates. In 1936 the commission began to collect data on both reportable injuries (those resulting in more than three lost workdays) and injuries not exceeding three lost workdays. The years 1936–39 showed no trend in the ratio of these two. Also, if underreporting was significant, carriers with relatively low reportable injury rates should have had relatively high nonreportable injury rates. Yet in fact the data yield a positive relationship between nonreportable and reportable injuries (see appendix 1).[71]

W. N. Doak was national legislative representative of the Trainmen in 1930. Doak saw the world through trainmen's eyes, and he was not noted for throwing bouquets at the carriers. But Doak's job made him thoroughly familiar with railroad safety, and even he was impressed. Surveying the gains in safety after 1923, Doak penned a trainman's epitaph for Ralph Richards. "These figures speak well for the work of the safety committees," he said.[72]

Combating the Collision Horror, Round II

On the morning of January 12, 1919, New York Central train no. 17, the Wolverine, left Rochester for Buffalo, traveling west on track 1 of four main tracks, all of which were protected with automatic block signals. When it arrived at signal station 37, an interlocking plant that controlled crossovers between the tracks, the train stopped; there engineman Gibbons informed the tower man that his locomotive was not steaming properly, and he asked for an engine. Train no. 11, under the command of engineman Friedley, had also left Rochester for Buffalo on track 1, just thirteen minutes behind the Wolverine. At 3:42 A.M., near South Byron, New York, it collided at about fifty miles per hour with the rear end of train no. 17. Twenty-two people were killed and seventy-one injured.

The signal controlling entry into the block that train no. 17 occupied (the rear home signal) was approximately thirty-four hundred feet east of train no. 17; a warning signal (the distant signal) for that block was nearly five thousand feet east of the home signal. Engineman Gibbons had also whistled his flagman back to protect his train. How could train no. 11 have run both a distant and a home signal and ignored the flagman's warnings? Friedley had been without rest (but not on duty) for eighteen hours, and he probably fell asleep. In addition, it was a cold night, and the flagman had probably not gone back as far as he said.

The wreck of the Wolverine at South Byron symbolized the railroad accident problem as the ICC had come to define it by 1919. That human error could result in such collisions revealed a fatal flaw in the block system, the commission concluded. This perception led the ICC to abandon its longstanding commitment to expanding the use of block signals in favor of automatic train control, which it thought would be a foolproof technological substitute for better management and discipline. W. P. Borland, chief of safety for the ICC, wrote the report on the wreck of train no. 17. "The automatic train-control system is the only . . . remedy which has been advanced to meet the conditions producing such accidents," he concluded. Two years after Borland penned his report, in January 1922, the ICC ordered the forty-nine largest railroads to begin installation of automatic train controls.[73]

THE DEVELOPMENT OF TRAIN CONTROL

Automatic train control refers to devices that either automatically stop or govern the speed of a train. The prevalence of collisions on nineteenth-century railroads led to early interest in such devices, and one was first patented in 1867. It could sound the whistle and shut off steam. By the 1890s the Fitchburg Railroad, the Boston, Revere Beach, and Lynn, and some other lines were experimenting with automatic stops that involved a movable mechanical trip beside the rails and a train contact that controlled the brake application. A block signal that showed red would raise the trip so that any train running the signal would automatically be stopped. The first such device to be permanently installed was on the Boston Elevated in 1901, and automatic train control is now all but universal on modern rapid-transit systems.[74]

Beginning with the ICC *Report on Block Signals* in 1907, public agencies increasingly took the lead in encouraging the development of train control. The ICC report publicized interest in this issue, and over its four-year life the Block Signal and Train Control Board reviewed and evaluated large numbers of train control plans. After the board expired in 1912, the ICC took over this function. It was in turn briefly superseded by the U.S. Railroad Administration's Committee on Automatic Train Control in 1919. By this time dozens of devices involving several distinct approaches to train control had evolved. The committee reviewed and categorized the devices. A simplified version of its categorization is presented below:

Character of Control	Class of Device	Type of Device
Intermittent	Contact	Mechanical
Intermittent	Contact	Electrical
Intermittent	Noncontact	Induction
Continuous	Noncontact	Induction

The most typical device employed an electrical contact or inductor. A train passing over such a roadside device would receive a signal indicating the status of the track ahead; if it was occupied, the brakes would automatically be applied and the train stopped. Since a train stop could prevent a collision only if the brakes were applied at full braking distance before an occupied block, trains could not pass an approach ("caution") signal without being stopped, so line capacity would be sharply reduced unless the system was equipped with a "forestaller." This device would allow the engineman to acknowledge the restrictive signal and trip an override, thereby retaining control of the brakes. The forestaller was to become a bone of contention between the carriers and the ICC.[75]

The automatic train stop was but one of the fruits of the electro-mechanical revolution that transformed railroading during these years, and to the carriers it was by no means the juiciest. Simple train stops did nothing to increase track capacity, and if a forestaller was not used, they would reduce it. Their only benefit was to enhance the safety of the block system. Yet efficiency checks and other Safety First programs were already improving the performance of the block system at a fraction of the cost of automatic stops. Far better safety investments were available to the carriers. For example, the interlocking of switches and signals could reduce costs and increase track capacity (e.g., by eliminating the need to stop before a crossover) as well as prevent accidents. Car retarders ended the need to use hand brakes, and therefore to ride cars, in classification yards, thereby cutting labor costs and virtually eliminating accidents. Automatic block signals could be substituted for the manual variety, and as wages rose this became an increasingly attractive option. The experience of the Seaboard shows why. In the mid-1920s it replaced manual with automatic block signals on about 252 miles of track, with a saving in costs that yielded about an 18 percent return on investment.[76]

The railroads therefore faced no lack of safety investments that were more attractive than automatic train control. Moreover, they must have realized that if they were to develop a workable train control device, they would face enormous pressure to install it. Hence, after some initial enthusiasm, they did as little as possible to advance the state of the art. Installations by the individual carriers also reflected this foot-dragging approach. In 1913 the Chicago and Eastern Illinois installed a train stop on 107 miles of road. That carrier was followed by the C&O, which installed a similar device on twenty-one miles of road in 1916, and the Rock Island, which installed a stop on twenty-two miles of road in 1919. And that was all. All the devices were intermittent electrical-contact stops that could be forestalled. By 1921 the *Railway Review* had concluded that the carriers had no intention of developing train control.[77]

ELIMINATING "THIS FACTOR OF HUMAN JUDGMENT"

This tepid response also failed to satisfy the ICC. Section 26 of the Transportation Act of 1920 empowered the ICC to require block signals or "other safety devices." Given the commission's focus on collisions that the block system would not prevent, this meant train control. In

January 1922 the ICC issued a tentative order requiring forty-nine carriers to install automatic train control without forestalling devices on at least one passenger division by January 1, 1925.

Long an advocate of compulsory block signals, *Railway Age* initially favored the order, terming it a "wise step." The editors soon had a change of heart, however. The commission claimed that the roads it chose were "selected with regard to the measure of the risk of accident in connection with traffic conditions thereon." But as the *Age* demonstrated, this was nonsense. The commission provided no evidence of risk, nor did it have information on traffic conditions on sections of road, and it gave the carriers considerable choice on where the installation would be made. In fact, the carriers chosen were all those with gross earnings of at least $25 million. Many had little or no signaling. For some time the *Age* had urged the development of cab signals, which were used in Europe and were much cheaper. By April 1922 the *Age*'s editors had thoroughly soured on train control, asking rhetorically, "What could be more absurd than the grandiose idealism of spreading a costly experiment over ten thousand miles of track and five thousand locomotives under forty-nine different and variously qualified experimenters and bosses with no effective co-ordination?"[78]

Hearings began in March 1922, with the carriers claiming that train control was still experimental. They also urged the commission to investigate whether there might not be better safety investments—such as block signaling—and they asked to be allowed to use the forestaller if train control was required. The commission's response was contained in its final order, issued that June. It had narrowed its focus from railroad safety to the prevention of collisions that resulted from running block signals. And it saw the solution wholly in technological terms: "train control devices . . . to protect against human failure." Such a view precluded use of a forestaller, and the commission reiterated that "this factor of human judgment is the factor which an automatic train stop is designed to eliminate." To the carriers' argument that block signaling was a more cost-effective alternative, the commission responded irrelevantly that "the danger is ever present that the engineman may fail to . . . obey the signal."[79]

The commission had expected that the carriers would install the sort of simple electrical-contact train stop already employed by several roads. Indeed, it used these carriers to support its claim that train control was no longer experimental. In a masterstroke of illogic it then found these installations illegal, for all employed a forestaller. The unintended effect of this decision was to tilt the economics of train control away from the simple automatic stop, for such a device, if it could not be forestalled, reduced track capacity. In addition, most companies felt that the electrical-contact ramp was inherently not very satisfactory and would soon be superseded by more complex devices. Accordingly, a number of carriers began to develop continuous inductive control devices. The Pennsylvania had been planning to experiment with continuous speed control even before the commission's order. It began installation in February 1922 on a part of the line not covered by the commission's order. Unlike most carriers, it made the installation without wayside signals, but since the manufacturer offered them at small cost, the Pennsylvania installed cab signals that revealed to the engineer the condition of the track ahead.[80]

Because many carriers experimented with relatively untried and complex methods of train control, progress was slow, and the ICC responded with a second order on January 14, 1924, almost a year before the first installations were due to be completed. The second order placed additional requirements on the carriers named in the first order and included forty-five additional railroads as well—all those with gross revenues in excess of $1 million. Supported by *Railway Age*, the carriers petitioned to extend the time for the first order and to cancel the second.[81]

This represented the high tide of the commission's efforts to devise a foolproof anticollision device. At the hearing, the carriers continued to claim that train control would provide less safety for the money than many alternative investments. Just how narrow the commission's thinking had become on this matter was revealed by commissioner Johnston Campbell's response to the railroads' argument that grade crossings represented a more serious safety hazard. "The law does not give us the right to trade off train control for grade crossing elimination," he (incorrectly) claimed. Commissioner Clyde Aicheson faced this difficult choice squarely: he urged the carriers to reduce both kinds of accidents. The railroads also pointed out that there had *never* been an accident due to the forestaller on the voluntary installations of train stops that included that device.

And A. H. Rudd, chief signal engineer of the Pennsylvania, drove a freight-train-sized hole in the ICC's compilation of collisions that it alleged could have been prevented by train control. He pointed out that many collisions that the ICC claimed would have been prevented by train control had occurred at low speeds; even with train control and no forestaller, trains that stopped and then continued could still collide. The foolproof device, it seemed, was not foolproof at all.

The railroads won a partial victory. The second order remained in force for the larger carriers. But with commissioners John Esch, Frederick Cox, and Charles McChord dissenting vigorously, the ICC allowed use of a forestaller. It also stayed the order applying to the smaller lines. The changed composition of the commission partly accounts for this shift in its stance. Commissioner Frank McManamy in a concurring opinion agreed with the carriers that train control was a poor safety investment and seemed disposed to an even more substantial retreat than had been ordered.[82]

The modified second order was more acceptable to the carriers, and progress was rapid. A number of roads that had been experimenting with speed control shifted to the simpler stop and forestaller. The Pennsylvania turned from continuous speed control to the simpler continuous stop and forestaller with cab signals on its two required divisions. Other carriers were allowed to scrap train control, at least in part. The Kansas City Southern was entirely exempted because the "risk of accident is slight," while the Missouri Pacific got the commission's second order indefinitely postponed in return for its installation of 391 miles of block signals. So much for commissioner Campbell's claim that the law did not allow the ICC to trade off train control.[83]

In July 1927 the ICC announced a general investigation of the status of train control. The prior two hearings had been the result of "show cause" investigations in which the burden of proof was on the railroads to explain why an ICC order to extend train control should be rescinded. This time, over the vigorous objection of hard-liners such as Esch, the hearing was to be on the more open-ended issue of whether or not additional train control installation should be required. Moreover, the railroads had a more favorable audience. Train control had become the responsibility of the three commissioners comprising ICC Division One. Of the three, Joseph Eastman was a longtime supporter of train control, while commissioner McManamy had made his reservations plain in 1924. This gave the decision to the third commissioner, the newly appointed Richard Taylor, who had been general manager of the Mobile and Ohio.

More had changed by 1927 than the makeup of the ICC. The railroads no longer claimed that train control was experimental, and several carriers were voluntarily installing it on substantial portions of their lines. Safety First also returned dividends at the hearings, as it helped persuade the commission that the carriers were taking responsibility for improving safety. Along with declines in passenger traffic and improvements in signaling, it had helped reduce passenger fatalities from collisions to the vanishing point. Only six passengers were killed in railroad collisions in 1927.[84]

As the collision evil receded, other safety issues assumed greater importance. The old argument that grade crossing protection should be a higher priority than train control now received more serious consideration. In June 1928 commissioners McManamy and Taylor, with Eastman dissenting, concluded that this was not the time for more train control. Thereafter the commission staged a graceful retreat. As early as 1929 W. P. Borland, chief of the commission's Bureau of Safety, admitted to the annual meeting of the ARA Signal Section, "I do not hesitate to say that there have been many things done in the past that should not have been done." But, he blithely announced to the men whose money he had helped squander, the whole episode "is all water over the dam."[85]

With the sharp deterioration in traffic and finances after 1930, the carriers looked to cut expenses in any way they could. One avenue was to substitute cab signals for train control. By 1934, of the forty-four carriers originally affected by train control, twenty-one had received permission to scrap some or all of the system, or to convert it to cab signals.[86]

While the early experiments with train control were largely the outcome of private decisions by inventors and railroads, the initiative shifted to the public sector after 1906. In part this was because public pressures to install such unprofitable safety devices discouraged the carriers from experimenting with them. Automatic train control was thus the one major railroad safety device whose invention and development were largely the result of government prodding. Its rapid development was an important achievement, but the ICC's orders constituted a far larger experiment than was necessary to improve the technology. And perhaps because train control was poorly designed to reduce collision rates, it does not seem to have done so. Statistical analysis (see note) suggests that train control had little impact on a carrier's collision rate.[87]

Automatic train control evolved as a technological remedy for what critics of railroad safety believed was a deep-seated defect in the character of American railroad managers. Two implications flowed from this analysis. First, because the defect seemed to stem from American character, a foolproof technical solution was needed. The result was an effort to improve safety that bypassed railroad management. Second, because the focus was on a particular kind of accident, the issue of whether there were better uses for the money was ruled out of bounds. The commission never acknowledged safety alternatives to train control, but they dominated the thinking of railroad men. *Railway Age* thought there were "better uses for the money," and A. H. Rudd bluntly summarized the issue: "The *relative* and not the intrinsic value of train control must be considered, and I am here to tell you that in my opinion, as a *relative* life saver, it isn't worth the money it costs."[88]

Think Back to the Link-and-Pin Days

Railroad safety became a public issue again in the 1930s as the brotherhoods backed state and federal full-crew and train-limit bills as well as legislation to require improved maintenance. Such bills were largely make-work projects, however, for railroad safety improved continuously throughout the 1920s and 1930s. *Railway Age* charged that anyone who believed such legislation would improve safety was "dishonest or too ignorant to have any opinion on the subject." By 1939 the employee fatality rate had declined 84 percent from its 1891 high, while the injury rate had declined 82 percent from its peak in 1916. Various revisions to the official data (tables A1.1–A1.3) change these conclusions only in detail.[89]

Henry Clay French retired from the Union Pacific in 1930. His career as a railroad man had begun on the Hannibal and St. Joseph, in 1873, and he marveled at the great changes in safety that had occurred since the link-and-pin days. These were mostly due to the "enforcement of Safety First," he thought. *Railway Age* agreed; in 1935 it hotly defended the railroads against claims that their improved safety records had been forced on them by federal and state legislation. Such gains were an achievement of private enterprise, the journal claimed. In fact, better safety arose out of three interrelated set of forces. Railroad labor and product markets evolved from a period of headlong growth through relative stability to steep decline. During the same period new technologies were making railroading increasingly safe. Finally, companies modified their management structures to ensure much more detailed control over railroad work and safety.[90]

Statistical analysis (table A1.10) supports these contentions. Declines in employment growth and traffic density can take some of the credit for railroad safety gains, while reductions in exposure—a result of the long-term fall in hours worked as well as of depression-induced work sharing—also reduced worker accident rates. Air brakes improved some forms of worker safety but worsened others, and their statistical insignificance here reflects that fact. In addition, as demonstrated, safety gains from either brakes or couplers probably depended more on their qualitative improvements than on the number of them in use. Controlling for these influences, fatality rates trended down by 2 percent and injury rates by more than 4 percent per year. These gains stemmed in part from the diffusion of Safety First work and from unmeasured technological improvements. Sometimes, as with block signals and better rails, the improvements were made in response to deteriorating safety records, but sometimes better safety was simply a by-product, as was the case with improved track maintenance techniques, more reliable locomotives, and car retarders.[91]

In a sense, then, *Railway Age* was entirely correct. Few of the improvements in railroad technology or operating techniques can be directly traced to government legislation, and the safety gains from most of this legislation were modest indeed. What the *Age* failed to acknowledge, however, was that the spread of Safety First owed something to the requirements of the U.S. Railroad Administration, to the rise in injury costs, and especially to the threat of expensive and intrusive regulation. These changes in the political and economic environment finally worked, as Charles Francis Adams had thought they would, to interest railroad managers in work safety.

Conclusion

As in manufacturing, the railroad safety movement developed its own internal momentum, and some managers came to see *safety* as synonymous with *efficiency*, while accidents symbolized all that was wrong with the old, lax, nineteenth-century style of railroading. In the old days railroading had been romantic, and it had allowed workers wide latitude in how they performed their day-to-day activities, while "today's railroadman is graded by how safe his work is," as Henry French observed. As elsewhere, the men did not always like the new rules and sometimes ignored them—which is why the carriers unleashed their safety campaigns—but most of them probably agreed with the trainman on the Lake Shore who thought that the results were "a mighty good thing."[92]

CHAPTER SIX

LESS BLOOD ON THE COAL, MORE DESPAIR IN THE HOMES OF THE MINERS

Safety in the Coal Fields
1910–1940

When the man at the face learns to carry out instinctively the directions given in the rules formulated for his benefit the accident-rate will not exceed one-fourth of the present one.
HOWARD EAVENSON, U.S. COAL AND COKE, 1915

Accidents that occur in their district or in their mines are a reflection on . . .
[the mine officials] even though the victim should commit suicide.
EDWARD O'TOOLE, U.S. COAL AND COKE, 1911

On January 10, 1940, three decades after the Bureau of Mines had been formed, Pond Creek mine no. 1, in Bartley, West Virginia, exploded, extinguishing the lives of ninety-one miners. It was followed by five other explosions that year; the toll came to 276 lives. The explosion fatality rate in bituminous mining in 1940 was 0.57 per million manhours— higher than it had been in 1910, the year the bureau was created. In fact, 1940 was an unusually bad year. There had been more progress than these statistics suggest, and explosions were the one area in which coal mine safety improved (fig. 6.1). Despite state and federal efforts and the Safety First movement, the underground fatality rate from all other causes combined was virtually the same as it had been in 1910. While manufacturing, railroading, and metal mining (see below) sharply reduced accident rates before World War II, coal mining remained the stepchild of the safety movement.

The Bureau of Mines and the Movement for Mine Safety

When the Bureau of Mines was formed in 1910, its mandate was to increase and diffuse the scientific understanding of mine dangers. This approach reflected operators' shock at the disasters of 1907 as well as widespread ignorance among even technical men on how to avoid them,

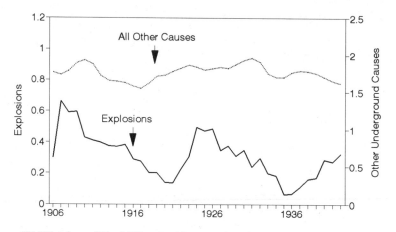

FIGURE 6.1. Coal Mine Fatality Rates per Million Manhours, Explosions and Other Underground Causes, Three-Year Moving Averages, 1906–1939

Source: W. W. Adams, "Coal Mine Accidents in the United States, 1942," BM *Bulletin* 462 (Washington, D.C., 1944), table 70.

and it continued the traditional focus of public policy on disaster prevention. Joseph A. Holmes, who became the bureau's first director, had stressed the value of "impartial investigations," and Herbert M. Wilson, a bureau engineer, expounded a similar vision to the Coal Mining Institute of America shortly after the bureau was founded. "That the Bureau will have no authority to enforce the adoption of its recommendations is not a matter of concern," Wilson explained. It was even a virtue: "Such authority would jeopardize its chief purpose—the making of impartial investigations." In the Progressive vision, once ignorance was banished, good results were sure to follow, and Wilson concluded with a summary of the Progressive credo: "The largest influence [of the bureau] can only be through the acquisition and publication of impartial data which should appeal to . . . the industry and to an intelligent public opinion."[1]

Wilson's vision of the bureau's role sounds like Charles Francis Adams's recipe for railroad safety, but there were important differences. Adams had tried to educate the public as well as the carriers, and his efforts in persuasion were backed by a credible threat of regulation. Wilson, by contrast, overestimated the appeal of the bureau's "impartial data" to the operators, for sometimes safety technologies were not cost-effective, and sometimes companies were blind to self-interest. Thus, the diffusion of new technology proved more complex than Wilson had imagined.

Nor could the bureau rely on the hammer of public opinion, as Wilson assumed, for mine safety was far less visible than railroad accidents.

In addition, the bureau's credibility as a scientific institution required that it be able to visit actual working mines, which could be done only with the operators' permission. The need to keep in the companies' good graces therefore prevented the bureau from simply publishing scientific findings, for impartial data could sometimes be damning criticism, and the operators well understood the danger of stirring up public opinion. In 1927 a bureau press release that seemed to compare coal mine safety unfavorably with that in metal mines aroused the wrath of Harry Gandy, secretary of the National Coal Association, who promptly sent the bureau's new director, Scott Turner, a thinly veiled threat. Such work, Gandy warned ominously, "retards the bureau's usefulness." Lest Turner miss the point, Gandy reminded him that the bureau needed the operators' cooperation.[2]

Dan Harrington was the operators' most vocal critic at the bureau. He was a 1900 graduate of the Colorado School of Mines and had worked as a mining engineer and superintendent before coming to the bureau in 1910. In 1924 he became chief of health and safety. "It is unfortunate," Harrington remarked, "that the public is not given the information which we have concerning the conditions in mines which are bound [to cause explosions]." After reviewing explosions at three Utah operators in 1930, another bureau engineer was less diplomatic. "Every damn one of them should be indicted for involuntary manslaughter," he growled. But nothing could be publicized without the consent of the operators. Francis Feehan came to the bureau from the United Mine

In 1911 the industry paper *Coal Age* warned mine operators that explosions could dislodge the rock of public opinion and cause an avalanche of costly mine safety laws. (*Author's collection*)

Workers (UMW), and he retained a miner's view of matters. The bureau's policy of silence, he argued, "has in effect afforded protection to the criminal carelessness [of the operators]." In 1940, when Secretary of the Interior Harold Ickes finally ordered the bureau to release its reports of explosions, the UMW *Journal* reported it with the headline "Secrecy of Bureau of Mines Broken at Last."[3]

The shift from employers' liability to workmen's compensation provided an economic prop for the bureau's efforts. Like other employers, many coal operators favored this change. In 1910 the American Mining Congress went on record in support of compensation legislation, and in 1911 the editor of *Coal Age* advocated compensation over "liability acts that carry financial ruin wherever applied." Stonega Coke and Coal supported Virginia's shift to compensation and even lobbied the legislature for the bill.[4]

Bureau personnel were also enthusiastic about workmen's compensation, for they hoped that schedule rating could be employed to induce operators to comply with its recommendations. George Rice had come to the bureau from the U.S. Geological Survey (USGS), which he had joined in 1908. Rice was an 1887 graduate of the Columbia School of Mines and had already finished one career as a mining engineer and supervisor. Later he recounted the genesis of his interest in mine safety. He had been superintendent of an Illinois mine that exploded, killing five men. "This incident so deeply impressed me that I especially studied the prevention of explosions," he explained. In 1915, when Rice learned that the Associated (insurance) Companies were forming a mine inspection department, he urged the bureau's director, Van Manning, to support the idea. If the insurance companies would incorporate bureau recommendations into their ratings, "I have a vision . . . that there would be an enormous leverage . . . for improvements in mining," Rice explained.[5]

Rice's vision soon became a reality, for insurance companies began to offer credits that encouraged the spread of a whole host of safe practices. But schedule rating proved no more effective at fostering safety in mining than elsewhere, for it encouraged a focus on safety techniques rather than on the achievement of fewer accidents. Dan Harrington put his finger on the problem: "Success in safety in mining cannot be attained by stressing any one point, but . . . [rather] constant attention must be given to all accident causes." By the mid-1930s only Utah and Pennsylvania still employed schedule rating.[6]

Experience rating was another matter. As Herbert Wilson, who had left the bureau for the Associated Companies, put it, "Experience rating . . . has been useful in producing a better moral hazard, that is, a more

214

SAFETY
FIRST

lively interest by the management in safety matters." But in mining as elsewhere, the formulas used to calculate experience rating blunted its impact except for the largest operators. The bureau's engineer C. A. Herbert noted the result of such incentives in Indiana: "There is a flat rate for all companies. In other words, a mine with a good experience pays exactly the same rate as a mine with a bad accident experience and there is really little incentive . . . to reduce accidents." Herbert pointed out that there were "several companies who have discontinued their insurance and are now carrying their own and the greater interest these companies are now taking in accident prevention work is quite noticeable." Some employers admitted the problem. As a representative of the Southern Appalachian Coal Operators Association put it, "I am carrying insurance and injuries . . . cost me nothing.[7]

For all of their limitations, the compensation laws and the bureau's activities were the main forces propelling improvements in mine safety in the years after 1910. Together they helped bring about a sharp reduction in explosion fatalities after 1930, and they encouraged a broader concern with safety at a relatively few large mines. Their failings were revealed by the many mines where safety work remained unknown or ineffectual, and by disasters such as the Pond Creek explosion in 1940.

The Campaign against Mine Explosions, 1910–1939

The Bureau of Mines employed three main techniques to prevent mine explosions. The first line of attack was to prevent the occurrence of explosive mixtures of gas and dust. To this end its scientists and engineers studied the circumstances under which dust was explosive and designed procedures to neutralize the danger. A parallel strategy was adopted to reduce the sources of ignition. This required development, testing, and certification of equipment and explosives. The third effort was to improve mine rescue and first-aid equipment and techniques. The bureau also campaigned to have the operators introduce these new and safer mining methods.

SCIENCE AND THE CAUSE OF MINE EXPLOSIONS

On September 3, 1803, the English Wallsend colliery blew up. According to a report published at that time, "The workings were very dry and dusty, and the survivors . . . were burnt by . . . ignited dust." It was the first recorded observation that coal dust might be explosive. From time to time other writers also suggested that coal dust might explode. In an 1845 report commissioned by Parliament on an explosion in the Haswell colliery, Michael Faraday and Sir Charles Lyell observed that "it is not to be supposed that firedamp was the only fuel; the coal dust . . . would instantly take fire."[8]

At the time, such views were in a distinct minority. But gradually, as a result of numerous investigations of explosions, the possibility that coal dust could explode became increasingly accepted among experts, if not operators. After 1900 a worldwide upsurge in mine explosions encouraged increased interest in the problem. In France an explosion at Courrières in 1906 claimed the lives of eleven hundred miners and led in 1907 to the creation of an experimental station at Liévin to study the cause and prevention of mine explosions. In Britain the Mining Association established a similar research facility at the Altofts colliery in 1906. In 1911 the facility was moved to Eskmeals and taken over by the government.[9]

In 1908 the technologic branch of the USGS sent a team led by Joseph A. Holmes and chief mining engineer George Rice to tour European testing facilities. Upon their return, the survey established a testing laboratory at Pittsburgh, Pennsylvania, that included a gallery for conducting coal dust explosions under Rice's direction. In 1910 the technologic branch was transferred to the Bureau of Mines, and that same year the bureau began its own experimental mine at Bruceton, Pennsylvania, that would allow testing under more realistic conditions than could be obtained in a gallery. In the fall of 1911 the bureau began experiments on the explosibility of coal dust. The purpose of the coal dust investigations was not simply to prove that dust was explosive. They were intended to discover both the conditions that led to dust explosions and the methods of prevention. Most important, the experiments were a graphic way to convince skeptical operators, state inspectors, and miners of the dangers of coal dust. Thus, the decision to experiment in a mine rather than a gallery reflected the need to persuade practical men that dust would explode under operating conditions.[10]

In 1911 the bureau decided to hold a national first-aid meet in Pittsburgh. The program was to include a coal dust explosion as well as rescue and first-aid contests. The guest list was extensive, including President William Howard Taft, members of the administration and Congress, and representatives of the mining industry. The event was held on October 30 and 31, 1911, and on the second day the party journeyed by train to Bruceton, just south of Pittsburgh, to view what proved to be an extremely realistic explosion.

At 6:15, against a darkening, rainy sky, the blast was set off. Rice described the results: "At the main entry the flames rose above the forest trees to a height variously estimated from 200 to 500 feet. . . . A limb of a tree was set on fire 154 feet from the mouth of the mine. . . . The explosion was heard at Monongahela city, 12 miles to the South. . . . A mine car . . . weighing about 2000 pounds was thrown over the top of . . . [a] coal car and landed 184 feet away." Privately Holmes termed the demonstration an educational triumph: "The effect of the explosion (after dark) . . . was so much more impressive than it possibly could have been during the day time. . . . No amount of writing or talking could have been so forceful in teaching this great lesson [that coal dust will explode]." Bureau chemist Clarence Hall had a more down-to-earth assessment: he suggested that the demonstration be repeated each time the House Appropriations Committee was in session. Educational though the lesson may have been, it required extensive reinforcement. As late as 1927 Dan Harrington reported that "a number of mining men" in Alabama did not believe that coal dust alone would explode. In an effort to convince the doubters, the bureau staged public coal dust explosions from time to time.[11]

From 1911 through the 1930s the bureau conducted hundreds of coal dust experiments, paralleling similar work in England and on the Continent. At the experimental gallery at Altofts, on July 18, 1908, William Garforth demonstrated that a zone of rock dust could stop an explosion. The bureau followed Garforth in measuring the explosibility of coal dust by the proportion of inert material required to prevent propagation of an explosion. Explosibility depended on the ratio of volatile matter to total combustible matter, which included both volatile matter and fixed carbon, or $V/(V + FC)$. The bureau also found that the presence of gas greatly increased the explosibility of dust. These relationships are presented in figure 6.2. The area on and above a curve is the region of nonexplosibility, but all points below it are explosive.[12]

The bureau's findings demonstrated that virtually all American bituminous coal dust, if sufficiently fine and mixed with gas, was highly explosive. In 1915 Rice presented these findings to the British Institution of Mining Engineers. His talk produced consternation in his audience. British experiments had found that the presence of gas had little effect on the explosibility of coal dust, and that explosibility rose linearly with the proportion of volatile materials. There was no immediate explanation for these inconsistencies.[13]

The need to resolve these differences spurred the development of formal British-American cooperation, which began in 1924. As each country tested dusts from the other, it gradually became clear that their divergent results stemmed from differences in experimental design, which in turn reflected the mining methods and laws in each country. Explosibility depended upon the physical configuration of the

FIGURE 6.2. Explosibility of Coal Dust

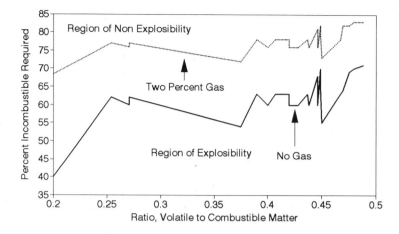

Source: George Rice and H. P. Greenwald, "Explosibility Factors Indicated by Experimental Mine Investigations, 1911–1929," BM *Technical Paper* 464 (Washington, D.C., 1929).

testing apparatus, and the Bureau of Mines—whose need to persuade practical men was greatest—employed a mine. In Britain, where researchers' findings had a greater chance of becoming law, a gallery was employed. But the most important cause was that the British employed about twenty ounces of black powder as a source of ignition. Reflecting the much larger charges of explosive used in American mines, the bureau employed a four-pound shot.[14]

The coal dust experiments were the most important safety-related scientific investigations conducted by the bureau, but it also certified and improved the safety of mine equipment and explosives. Bureau certification worked like a Good Housekeeping Seal of Approval. Users could be sure that bureau-approved materials were safe and effective if used as intended. The bureau also received a large number of requests to certify worthless and often dangerous devices. One of them was the Carbon Monoxide Gas Converter. The inventor cheerfully admitted that "it is theoretically impossible to convert monoxide or hydrogen sulfide to oxygen"; but, he claimed, "practically it is not." Needless to say, he failed to obtain bureau endorsement. By reducing the amount of such worthless "safety" equipment, bureau activities encouraged the spread of the real thing.[15]

Some of the most valuable of the bureau's work was its tests of the newer safety explosives that had been designed to replace black blasting powder. Research established that whether an explosive would touch off a potentially explosive mix of gas and dust depended on both the type of explosive and the conditions under which it was used. The important characteristics of an explosive are the duration and temperature of its flame. Just as quickly touching the tip of a match need not burn your finger, so even a hot-flame explosive will not cause ignition if it burns quickly enough. What came to be called "permissible" explosives are somewhat cooler than dynamite and have a flame duration much less than that of black powder. When used as intended, they would not ignite gas or dust. But to be safe, the maximum charge could not be exceeded, and they had to be stemmed (packed) with clay, not coal dust, and fired with an approved electric detonator.

In the United States the first "safety powder," sold under the trade name Masurite, was introduced in 1902 in the mines around Johnstown, Pennsylvania, as a result of the Rolling Mill disaster of that year, which killed 112 men. In 1904 an explosion at the Harwick mine that extinguished another 179 lives further spread its use. In early 1909 the USGS published the first list of "permissible explosives." Under the Bureau of Mines, testing continued, and many of the early safety powders were found to be anything but safe. The list of permissibles evolved as new explosives were added and old ones withdrawn; by 1917, 153 explosives were listed as permissible.[16]

The bureau also set standards for permissible flame safety lamps and electric cap lamps and for electrical mining machinery, and it helped improve mine rescue apparatus. A bureau chemist also invented the Burrell gas detector to replace the old safety lamp. It was easier to read, was much more accurate, and would not blow up the mine as the old safety lamp sometimes did. Ironically, Pennsylvania's mine law, which required safety lamps to test for gas, effectively banned the Burrell detector as late as 1928.[17]

Portable electric lamps appeared in British mines as early as 1889. In the United States the first such lamps were used in anthracite mines of the Philadelphia and Reading Coal and Iron Company in 1908. Government interest began with the USGS and continued under the bureau. In 1913 the bureau issued safety specifications to guide manufacturers in producing permissible electric lamps. The payoff was rapid. In Pennsylvania, authorities initially refused to allow use of electric lamps where safety lamps were required, but by 1913 they had reinterpreted the law to admit the new equipment. Colorado's new mine law of 1913 allowed only bureau-certified electric lamps in gassy mines.[18]

Scientists for the bureau also tested and improved rescue equipment. Initially most of these, such as the Draeger model, came from Germany. The inability of the Draeger to vary the amount of oxygen was dangerous, for mine rescue might be so physically taxing that a wearer could

A Bureau of Mines rescue team at the Benwood (West Virginia) disaster of April 1924. One hundred nineteen workers died in the mine. *(National Archives)*

suffocate—as happened to two rescue workers in the 1913 explosion at the Phelps Dodge Stag Cañon mine in Dawson, New Mexico. Bureau physicist W. E. Gibbs and mining engineer James W. Paul developed respirators that varied the flow of oxygen to meet user demand and improved on the regenerative process. Bureau engineer G. S. McCaa also invented a small self-rescuer for miners to carry that could filter out carbon monoxide for about thirty minutes. It received bureau approval in 1924. The bureau also tested all forms of electrical mining machinery and classified spark-proof apparatus as permissible.[19]

SPREADING THE TECHNOLOGY OF SAFETY

The Bureau of Mines did far more than simply discover and certify safer mining technology. It also developed an arsenal of techniques to encourage operators to adopt the new methods. One of its first efforts was to encourage the spread of mine rescue equipment and techniques. As usual, there was a European precedent to follow. The first mine rescue station in Britain was established in 1902, and by 1910 there was a central rescue station in every coal field. The beginnings of formal mine rescue work in America date from 1907, when Anaconda Copper purchased four sets of Draeger breathing apparatus. The first use of breathing apparatus in a mine disaster was by USGS personnel at Monongah (West Virginia) in 1907, and in 1909 their rescue of men who had been trapped for a week by the Cherry (Illinois) mine fire provided much favorable publicity.[20]

Federal activity was expanded rapidly under the bureau. Its scientists were impressed by the work of British physiologist J. S. Haldane—which showed that many deaths from explosions resulted from asphyxiation rather than from the blast itself—and in September 1910 the bureau established two permanent rescue stations in addition to the four it had inherited from the USGS. The bureau also bought and outfitted seven Pullman cars for rescue work and training. Pictures of bureau cars and their teams of men emerging from a mine, sometimes bringing an injured miner to safety, quickly became regular newspaper features. Rescue work also proved an inspiration to poets of the heroic school:

> When the damp explodes in a distant room,
>   Or the roof of an entry falls,
> Sealing the men in a living tomb
>   With thick and soundless walls;
> When the women crowd at the open shaft
>   And wail as the women do,
> It's then that we call for the nerve and craft
>   Of the Boys of the Rescue Crew!
> They take the smoke
>   As a sort of joke;
> They dare the fire damp too;
>   For it's all their trade,
> And they're not afraid,
>   The Boys of the Rescue Crew![21]

Mine first aid began in Great Britain in the 1880s with the St. Johns Ambulance service. Its American origins date from 1899, when Dr. Matthew J. Shields organized a team at the Delaware and Hudson anthracite colliery. The men took up collections and bought their own equipment. As Shields laconically observed, "The company was appealed to but gave no encouragement." Shields's work received wide publicity and soon spread to the other large anthracite producers. Shields went on to organize first-aid work at several other large companies including Tennessee Coal, Iron, and Railroad. First-aid competitions quickly became common. In September 1910 Holmes addressed a first-aid meet of the Philadelphia and Reading Coal Company, and with the Reading's assistance he added first aid to the bureau's rescue training.[22]

The bureau saw its role as a way to prime the pump of private (or state) demand for rescue and first aid. Some states and private operators did indeed develop their own rescue capabilities, which they sometimes offered to other mines in times of need. By 1937 a survey revealed that there were three hundred private rescue stations nationwide with about twenty-three hundred sets of breathing apparatus.[23]

The expansion of private first aid and rescue capability increased the demand for bureau training. The bureau also encouraged demand by sponsoring first-aid competitions, and in 1915 it held the second of what came to be annual nationwide mine rescue and first-aid competitions. At their peak in 1920, ninety-three teams from twenty states competed. Thereafter the steam went out of the idea. Finally the bureau concluded that the meets had outlived their usefulness, and it canceled the contests in 1931. As one engineer sourly noted, they had become a fruitful source of ill-will, for the losers all hated the bureau.[24]

While the first-aid and mine rescue teams were usually segregated by race, black miners were just as likely to be trained as their white counterparts. C. A. Sine, safety engineer at Stonega Coke and Coal, gave the reason. "First aid has the same value wherever practiced," he observed. Stonega held "colored" first-aid contests and publicized its work to the "Interracial League," probably as an effort to attract black workers. The bureau's policy with respect to race was passive: when one engineer asked about training black miners, he was told, "Be guided entirely by the wishes of the company's management." Companies often sent separate white and black teams to the first-aid competitions. Although the prizes for both white and black winning teams were typically identical, the winning white team somehow always outscored the best black team by a point or two.[25]

These programs were popular with companies because the bureau supplied teachers and the men trained on their own time, making the training nearly free to operators. (Some metal mines did pay their men for safety training, but high labor turnover reduced their incentives to do so.) Moreover, the companies earned a return on this investment by the miners and the bureau in the form of reduced injury costs or a schedule-rating discount. The bureau's D. J. Parker observed that "when it becomes obligatory by state law for them to take out compensation insurance . . . companies are eager for bureau first aid training."[26]

First-aid work motivated by the prospect of an insurance discount may not have been all that effective. Pennsylvania inspector Alexander McCanch claimed that the "Pittsburgh and Westmoreland Coal Company's station is only nominal, being a mere subterfuge to secure favorable compensation rating." Another Pennsylvania inspector, John Pratt, observed that the "rate of insurance [discount] is 21 cents and that for roof falls is much less so everyone goes after first aid." Pratt also observed that companies that self-insured "work along a quite different line in regard to safety. Very little attention is given to first aid. . . . They are using many more safeguards to protect the lives of workmen."[27]

By 1937 the bureau had provided some form of first-aid or rescue training to over nine hundred thousand men. Despite the inefficiencies noted by the Pennsylvania inspectors, the training saved many lives. The bureau claimed that from 1908 to 1917, 142 men were rescued from mine disasters by bureau personnel while 924 men were rescued by others, most of whom must have had bureau training. The bureau also routinely received reports in which its graduates provided lifesaving first aid. Given the underreporting of such instances, the bureau claimed that "it is conservatively estimated" that two hundred lives a year were saved by first aid.[28]

First-aid and rescue training proved easier to sell than permissible equipment and rock-dusting—probably because the price was right. The bureau's training cost the miners nothing, and it paid off to the operators. Safety equipment, by contrast, was burdensome or expensive, and operators balked at using it. In the late 1920s a Pennsylvania inspector tried to get Westmoreland Mining to make all its equipment permissible (i.e., explosion-proof). The company dug in it heels, claiming that this would cost $1,450 per machine, or $25,000 for mining machines alone. "I am inclined to take a very broad view of the situation," Secretary of Mines W. H. Glasgow concluded. Permissible equipment also required a level of maintenance that few mines could muster. In the early 1930s a bureau survey of electrical equipment discovered an astounding array of shoddy maintenance practices that destroyed the safety of permissible machines. "One of the outstanding impressions gained," the authors concluded, "is that many defects . . . are attributable either to lack of understanding . . . or else to downright neglect or indifference." By 1939 only about 40 percent of all mining machines in use were permissible, and probably many of those were poorly maintained.[29]

The bureau's efforts to spread the use of permissible explosives met with unalloyed hostility from many of the miners. In 1912, when the secretary of the interior tried to require permissible explosives in mines on public lands in Wyoming, there was a strike at the Owl Creek Coal Company. A similar order in 1914 for Oklahoma Indian lands also produced several strikes. The miners' apparent ingratitude was not altogether irrational. The men were rarely consulted when permissible explosives were introduced, and their use was part of a broader move— supported by the bureau, and by some states and companies—to take control of blasting out of the hands of the individual miner. By the early

FIGURE 6.3. Diffusion of Safety Equipment, Bituminous Coal Mining, 1900–1940

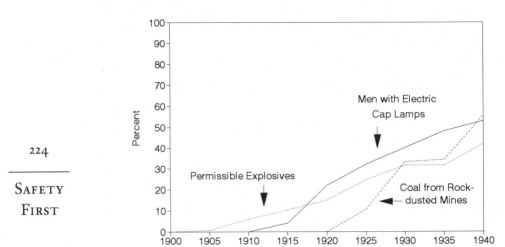

Source: H. B. Humphrey, "Historical Summary of Coal Mine Explosions in the United States," BM *Bulletin* 586 (Washington, D.C., 1960).

1920s Colorado, Kansas, Oklahoma, Pennsylvania, and several other important coal-mining states required use of shot-firers in some mines, and by the late 1930s a few states even required electric blasting from the surface when no men were in the mine.[30]

In addition, permissibles gave off poison gases. They were also more powerful than black powder and more expensive—even when used in the correct quantity, but especially if miners underestimated their punch and used too much. And since they were faster acting than black powder, they shattered the coal, thereby yielding less lump and cutting the miners' incomes where coal was screened. In 1910, at a joint conference between union miners and operators in the Pennsylvania, Ohio, and Indiana fields, the union proposed that mines employing permissibles either shift to a mine-run method of payment or raise the rate they paid for lump coal. The companies, of course, refused. Thus, labor disputes combined with technical problems to retard the spread of permissibles. On the eve of World War II only about 45 percent of all explosives used in coal mines met bureau standards (fig. 6.3).[31]

Nor did the shift to permissibles always yield safety gains, for their use encouraged operators to skimp on other forms of safety—an outcome the bureau had not bargained on. In 1916 an Alabama inspector noted that one of the mines in his district introduced permissibles and promptly dismissed all of its fire bosses. And in 1920, when permissible explosives set off an explosion in the Phelps Dodge Stag Cañon mines, killing five men, a bureau investigation concluded that more than the limit charge had been used, and that the shot had been poorly tamped. Privately Dan Harrington described the disaster as an excellent example of the dangers of half-baked safety procedures.[32]

In the history of mine explosions there had been no greater killer than the miner's open-flame light. One might suppose, then, that both miners and operators would have leaped at the chance to replace it with the much safer electric cap lamp. Yet the use of that device also spread at a stately pace (fig. 6.3). Here again the problem was that while the new lamps were less likely to cause an explosion than other forms of illumination, they had other drawbacks. Early cap lamps required a battery pack that weighed about five pounds and sometimes leaked electrolyte onto its wearer. Neither trait endeared the lamp to the miners. They also gave out very little light—a bit over 1 candlepower, or roughly one-fifth that of carbide lamps. Thus, while electric lamps lowered explosion risks, their poor light increased the risk of other accidents and cut into labor productivity and miners' incomes. Not until the 1920s did electric lamps provide enough light to compete effectively with carbide. Thereafter they improved rapidly, until by 1934 a three-cell version yielded about 66 candlepower.[33]

The burdens of these early electric lamps were mostly shouldered by the men who used them. To operators they usually promised few costs and the possibility of fewer explosions. In addition, in the early 1920s many insurers began offering schedule discounts to mines that used closed lights. Since the men usually paid for their own lights, the happy result was another example of operator profits on miner investments, or so the operators hoped. But attempts to require electric cap lights sometimes precipitated a labor dispute. In 1918 Van Manning, soon to be the bureau's director, reported a strike at the Old Ben (Illinois) mine. The miners "demanded that open lamps be used," he noted. Never having had to wear a lamp for eight hours, he found this position "not understandable."[34]

Opposition to the new lamps reflected more than just their cost and inconvenience. In 1919 Colorado's inspector noted that "there is a tendency on the part of the mine officials to allow employees [with electric cap lamps] to work in places where the gaseous condition is such that they could not work in otherwise." Sometimes the men responded by claiming that if a mine was too dangerous for open lights, they deserved a wage increase. In 1923 the bureau noted one contract between the UMW and Virginia operators that called for a wage premium in mines with closed lights, and the bureau began to worry that such agreements could sabotage its efforts to spread safer techniques.[35]

Nor were operators always enthusiastic about electric lamps when they had to bear some of the costs. In Pennsylvania some operators joined their men in opposing the new lights because the mine law required them to test for gas or use other forms of permissible equipment in closed-light mines. Other states also retarded the spread of electric cap lamps by requiring permissible machinery when they were employed. In 1934 the bureau reported that such lights were not used in many West Virginia mines because their introduction would be a tacit admission that the mine was gassy and would therefore result in an order to employ only permissible electrical machinery.[36]

In Oklahoma, efforts to introduce electric cap lamps involved the bureau in a three-way shootout among the miners, the operators, and the state inspector. In early 1923, Rock Island mine no. 12 attempted to require electric cap lamps. The shot-firers struck, requesting a wage increase. Later in the year, when a mine inspector ordered closed lights in Rock Island no. 10, the men petitioned in complaint. They were backed —to the bureau's consternation—by the chief mine inspector, Edward Boyle, who refused to allow the mines to be worked with electric lights. Boyle was elected, and like all good Progressives, the bureau's engineers had a low opinion of elected officials in jobs requiring expertise. At one point Rice claimed that Boyle was in the pay of the open-light interests and contemptuously termed him a "politician and a bootlegger."[37]

But as events were to reveal, Boyle was playing a high-stakes game, dangling the promise of electric lights to induce operators to make other safety improvements. The miners' motivation was no less complex. In a broadside probably written in March 1924, entitled "A Synopsis of Reasons Why the Closed Lamp Is Opposed by the Rank and File of Miners Employed in Mine No. 10," the miners presented their grievances. They complained that the new lights were cumbersome and gave little light. They also stressed the poor ventilation in the mine and the use of nonpermissible explosives, and claimed that if the law were obeyed, closed lights would be unnecessary. The synopsis closed with a revealing plea: "The rank and file has never been given the opportunity of presenting arguments against the closed lamp." In sum, the lamps were burdensome and placed the onus of safety on the men, not the operators, and the men had been allowed no voice in determining their own work practices.[38]

At about the same time, Tom Bost, president of UMW Local 7, which the Rock Island had locked out, sent a similar missive to the bureau, complaining that the men had not been consulted in the switch to electric lamps. Director H. Foster Bain responded, urging the men to wear the lights. Bost replied, and he too complained over the men's loss of control over their work lives. "It seems that you have entirely missed the point of our letter," he lectured Bain. "We feel that before wishing upon us the burden of wearing a safety lamp, we should be given some consideration and should have been given the opportunity of working in cooperation [with the bureau and the state]." At this point, partly at the behest of the bureau, which had urged John L. Lewis to intervene, the national UMW announced that open lamps were a grievance for which compensation should be adjusted, and in May 1924 it ordered the locals back to work—with electric lamps.[39]

Everyone had reckoned without Boyle, however, who promptly issued an order forbidding the lamps. The Rock Island then counterattacked, applying for an injunction setting aside Boyle's order. The company also heaved another bomb into Boyle's tent, publicly claiming that he had failed to secure a bond and therefore was not legally chief inspector. Boyle was not so easily defeated. He posted bond and, since the injunction was for the Eastern District of Oklahoma, promptly moved to the Western District and mounted a counterattack. He wrote Bain claiming that the bureau was interfering in state affairs. Boyle also sent a draft of a new mining law requiring operators to employ permissible mining equipment—which was impossible for the bureau to oppose and was guaranteed to stick in the operators' craw. The next round went to the bureau and the operators; in July an appropriate district court was found to issue an order enjoining Boyle's prohibition of electric cap lights. The victory, though no doubt delicious, was short-lived. Boyle appealed, and the state supreme court upheld him in November.[40]

That Boyle was not simply sailing with the political wind is also revealed by his behavior during a second run-in he had with the bureau. In the spring of 1926 the Superior Smokeless Coal Company in Tahona, Oklahoma—also a union mine—closed for thirty days to clean the mine and install rock-dust barriers. The mine also employed permissible explosives. By these actions the company hoped not only to reduce explosion risks but also to demonstrate good faith to the men and to Boyle before asking to switch to closed lights. The miners were convinced and promptly printed up a handbill:

Tribute to Our Company
SUPERIOR SMOKELESS COAL & MINING COMPANY

To make us safe they have sprinkled dust
In Entries Air Courses, Rooms of Each of Us;
And When Ready—an Enclosed Lamp—will furnish tomorrow,
That cannot light the gas, to fill our Homes with Sorrow.

LESS BLOOD ON THE COAL

We appreciate their efforts towards safety, whatever they do,
And celebrate our Happiness Giving a Free Big Barbecue,

At Tahona Okla.

A union Mine where all combine,
Their efforts to produce
Clean Coal for use,
That will demand
The Best Price of the Land.
High Prices means high wages.[41]

Boyle was unmoved. Again he refused to allow closed lights unless permissible mining equipment was used. On September 2, 1926, an explosion in the Tahona mine killed sixteen men. A bureau investigation reported that the mine was "very gassy and [the] ventilation by no means effective." It also described a number of other changes that would be required "if this mine is to be made even reasonably safe" but concluded that open lights had set off the gas. However noble Boyle's motives, his actions contributed to the death of sixteen men.[42]

Oklahoma's experience, with local variations, was replicated in several other states. Attempts to introduce electric cap lights in Indiana mines had resulted in sporadic strikes and protests since at least 1916, some of which stemmed from the increased risk that resulted from use of the new equipment. The president of Princeton Coal Company reported with refreshing candor that the local union went on strike on April 8, 1924, when "our boss ordered these men to put on the lamps and load coal out of an exceptionally gaseous place." Yet open-light mines sometimes took the same chances. On February 20, 1925, an open light caused a blast that killed fifty-two men in the City mine in Sullivan, Indiana. The operators favored a bill requiring closed lights, but even *after* the City mine disaster, it was opposed by the Sullivan local of the UMW and by the state inspectors. The miners petitioned the legislature, explaining their stance. Closed lights, they claimed, "would only be the beginning of other, more dangerous evils, including . . . carelessness in our air systems . . . and other disregard for old and abandoned workings where dangerous and noxious gases are liable to gather." [43]

The bureau had been waiting for just such an occasion and promptly issued a press release urging use of electric lamps. The next maneuver was to appeal to the national UMW. The bureau's W. D. Ryan, himself a former union man, met privately with former secretary of labor W. B. Wilson—who had once been a miner and whose brother had been killed in a mine—in the hope that Wilson could influence the union. But, as Ryan discovered to his shock, Wilson opposed the lamps. By mid-1926 just 5 percent of Indiana miners worked with electric lights. A little over a decade later another Indiana mine blew up, killing two miners and injuring three others. C. A. Herbert of the bureau reported that this mine had used permissible explosives and rock-dusting, and that the explosion was due to open lights or a trolley. Herbert reported that "the company would like to furnish electric cap lamps" but was prevented from doing so because "any employees belonging to the UMW . . . are fined $25 if caught wearing an electric cap lamp."[44]

In Illinois, use spread more rapidly: by 1926 about 24 percent of underground men had electric lights. But here again the new technology got caught in a complex political crossfire. In Illinois the UMW was riddled with factionalism, and in 1929 a dissident group got a bill introduced in the legislature to ban electric cap lamps—"bug lights," as the men contemptuously termed them, because they gave about as much light as a lightning bug in a bottle. Local UMW officials did little to oppose the bill, but the Illinois operators led by Joseph Zook appealed to both the bureau director, Scott Turner, and Commerce Secretary R. P. Lamont to intervene. Zook's plea fell upon receptive ears: for a state to outlaw equipment the bureau had certified as safe would be a major setback. Lamont wired the governor, and Turner dispatched the bureau's biggest gun, George Rice, who met with the governor and the speaker of the house. The Illinois Senate passed the bill, but the House rejected it.[45]

Guerrilla warfare continued throughout the year, and although the dissidents lost the war, they won their point. Dan Harrington, who was no friend of union labor, agreed that "the miners are in part justified in their statement that some of the mines using the closed lights have defective ventilation." The companies even admitted the point. In a telling letter to his fellow operators that somehow became public, Zook revealed their motives. Had the bill become law, he argued, "sooner or later a disastrous explosion would [have] occur[ed]." The result would be "in all probability [that] the legislature would be called upon to pass reactionary legislation requiring all mines in the state to . . . rockdust, install flame-proof motors and make other very expensive changes." Thus, the threat of regulation, which induced safety work in steel and on the railroads, led the Illinois operators to throw the burden upon the men.[46]

These experiences pointed out a problem with the new safety technology that the bureau had failed to appreciate. Without managerial commitment, safer equipment might simply induce offsetting behavior. Yet explosions had multiple causes, and introducing electric lights or permissible explosives might do little good if they led the operators to skimp on ventilation, dismiss fire bosses, or ignore sparking machinery.

The most important of the bureau's efforts to prevent mine explosions was its campaign to encourage the use of rock-dusting, which was a straightforward result of its coal dust experiments. While efforts to reduce sources of ignition could always be undone by a single match, rock-dusting appeared foolproof, for in a properly rock-dusted mine, the coal dust would not explode. Accordingly, the bureau promoted it far more aggressively than any other safety program. Its efforts went far beyond the simple publication of impartial data that Wilson had described and represented a form of aggressive public entrepreneurship designed to create a market for rock-dusting.

On November 8, 1911, the Victor American mine no. 3 in Delagua, Colorado, exploded, killing seventy-nine men. The next year, at the urging of George Rice, superintendent W. J. Murray made Victor American the first American producer to introduce rock-dusting. That same year the Bureau of Mines first recommended rock-dusting, and an article also appeared in *Coal Age* advocating its use. In 1915 the Pittsburgh Coal Company began hand application of rock dust, and in 1917 Old Ben Coal, in a replay of the experience of Victor American, introduced rock-dust barriers after one of its Illinois mines blew up, killing eighteen people.[47]

The bureau tried to encourage the spread of rock-dusting with publicity and by stimulating the development of mechanical distributors. It built and advertised its own rock-duster, and in 1916 it sent a form letter to machinery producers enclosing a blueprint and offering constructive criticism to any producer who would develop a machine. The letter and specifications were also published in *Coal Age* at about the same time. But the industry responded to these various efforts with a yawn. Rock-dusting was expensive, costing perhaps a penny per ton of coal, and companies preferred safety measures whose costs fell largely on the miners. In 1923 fewer than a dozen mines employed rock-dusting, and those often did it in slipshod fashion. In that year the bureau began to plan a large-scale publicity campaign to sell rock-dusting to skeptical operators.[48]

At about the same time, disaster came to the rescue. Old Ben had exploded again in 1921, but the damage was limited by dust barriers—a fact the bureau made widely known. Then, on February 8, 1923, the Phelps Dodge Stag Cañon mine no. 1 blew up, killing 120 men. It was the worst disaster in a decade, and it shook all the Rocky Mountain producers into a consideration of dusting. The key to widespread use, as Dan Harrington stressed, was "to make it as low in cost as possible." As a result, the bureau again tried to encourage mechanization, sending a form letter to equipment manufacturers in December 1923. This time it had more success. By the late 1920s there were several rock-dusters on the market. Nor did the bureau ignore the supply of rock dust. It developed standards for fineness and the allowable proportion of free silica, notified quarries of the potential market, and published a bulletin of maps and lists of sources. For a time bureau engineers even contemplated trying to get a free supply of limestone from state penitentiaries.[49]

In 1924, disaster again lent a helping hand. Utah had some of the most explosive coal dust in the country, and mining methods that left coal in the roof ensured that little inert material mixed with the dust. On March 8, Castle Gate mine no. 2 in Castle Gate (Utah) exploded, killing 172 men. Two months later, luck finally ran out for the Benwood (West Virginia) mine. It was known to be gassy but had been worked using open lights and black powder for sixty years without an explosion. One hundred and nineteen men died there.[50]

Castle Gate was the catalyst the bureau had been waiting for. As Harrington put it, "We now have an opportunity to accomplish something really worthwhile by making a good stiff fight." Castle Gate also coincided with a speaking tour by British scientist Richard V. Wheeler from the mine experiment station at Eskmeals. Britain had required rock-dusting in 1920, and Wheeler's enthusiastic endorsement of rock-dusting in practice impressed the American operators. Rice later sarcastically observed that the bureau had finally decided that word of mouth was a more effective means of communication than publications because "our mining people did not read."[51]

The rock-dusting campaign also picked up important support from a variety of other quarters. In 1924 John B. Andrews, editor of the *American Labor Legislation Review*, began to focus on mine explosions. Each issue of the *Review* contained news of the latest disaster, items about mines using rock-dusting, and articles by bureau personnel, other experts, and mine managers, all favoring rock-dusting. Recognizing valuable publicity, the bureau covertly supported Andrews's work, funneling him information on mine explosions, state laws, and the costs and progress of rock-dusting. All the trade journals and the mining societies also joined the campaign, printing a barrage of favorable editorials and articles by engineers and operators with experience in rock-dusting. By late 1924 R. Dawson Hall, editor of *Coal Age*, had concluded that "we have rockdusted our paper so thoroughly lately that all its explosive quality has been destroyed."[52]

All the publicity was intended to pressure as well as inform the operators, and as early as 1911 *Coal Age* had warned that explosions might lead to stricter mine laws. Yet the publicity's main effect was probably informational, for there is no evidence that the spread of rock-dusting was a coordinated response to regulatory threats.

Changes in state laws also gave the rock-dusting campaign a gentle nudge. By 1939 eleven states had laws that required rock-dusting, although their effects were largely nullified because they allowed companies to substitute watering instead. Market incentives were more important, for operators understood that explosions could be extremely expensive. The bill for Castle Gate came to $1 million, according to Harrington. In addition, by July 1924 sixteen important coal-mining states, including Pennsylvania, Illinois, Iowa, Kansas, Utah, New Mexico, Colorado, Oklahoma, and Alabama, were giving schedule-rating credit for rock-dusting of 10–20 cents per $100 of payroll. This not only lowered costs, it also converted the benefits of rock-dusting from an unlikely future payoff to an immediate annual saving. Ten years later Rice claimed that rock-dusting had been rarely used until schedule rating gave it substantial credit. President Eugene McAuliffe of Union Pacific Coal agreed: "I think the compensation premium should be given credit for rockdusting," he concluded.[53]

While no more than a handful of mines had rock-dusted in 1923, a bureau survey showed that by 1925 the number had increased to 177. By 1927 about 6.5 percent of all bituminous mines were rock-dusting, but they were the larger operators and employed one-fifth of all underground employees. Use spread slowly thereafter, reaching its prewar peak in 1937 when 8.5 percent of all mines employing 43 percent of all miners protected the men with rock dust (fig. 6.3).[54]

Rock-dusting would prevent major disasters if properly done, but as the bureau gradually realized, it was no panacea. Just as the use of closed lights could cause an explosions if the practice encouraged poorer ventilation, so a bad job of rock-dusting might be worse than none at all if it led to the relaxation of other measures. Bureau engineer G. S. McCaa reviewed the results of one explosion in a rock-dusted mine and remarked that "there appears to be a false sense of security on the part of the rockdusting crews . . . and the men take liberties with ventilation and open-type equipment." Moreover, few companies dusted to bureau specifications. "I have yet to see a thoroughly rockdusted mine," one engineer reported to Harrington in 1928. Eugene McAuliffe told of a Wyoming operator who bought five hundred pounds of limestone, stored it in sacks outside the mine, and was reported in journals as operating a rock-dusted mine. As late as 1942 a bureau survey showed that only 24 of 332 rock-dusted mines met its standards.[55]

In spite of these difficulties, the explosion fatality rate finally began to fall after 1930 (fig. 6.1). The timing of the decline—which lagged the spread of electric cap lamps and permissible explosives but coincided with the large-scale use of rock-dusting—is instructive. It suggests that use of safer lamps and explosives had little impact—either because of offsetting behavior or because they needed to be used jointly to prevent ignitions—but that rock-dusting was effective, even when not done to the bureau's standards. The bureau admitted as much, and by the mid-1930s it was claiming that rock-dusting saved two hundred lives a year. A statistical analysis (see note) suggests that while this claim may have been inflated, by the late 1930s rock-dusting had sharply reduced the explosion fatality rate.[56]

Safety First Comes to Coal, 1910–1930

A few mine operators had begun safety work before compensation laws were passed. As noted, the Pennsylvania anthracite producers began first-aid training around 1905, and in 1912 the Delaware, Lackawanna, and Western even developed an illustrated book on the prevention of mine accidents that it published in Polish, Lithuanian, Italian, and Russian as well as English. These and a few others were the exceptions, however. Except for their efforts to prevent explosions, most operators showed little interest in improving safety under the regime of employers' liability.[57]

"SAFETY—THE FIRST CONSIDERATION"

In coal as elsewhere, the impact of workmen's compensation was greatest on the large producers, and gradually many of them responded to these new incentives by setting up a safety department. Like railroads and manufacturing companies, coal operators discovered that successful safety work needed to be a line responsibility. Phelps Dodge learned the lesson the hard way. The company began safety work in 1913 but found that operating personnel left matters up to the safety inspectors. In 1925, chastened by the Stag Cañon disaster, it instituted a new system modeled on that of U.S. Steel in which the general manager chaired the safety committee.[58]

Successful safety work followed the usual formula of first improving the physical condition of the mine. As Thomas Fear, general manager of Consolidation Coal, put it, the company must first "purchase the safe working places." E. H. Shriver, superintendent of Armco's Nellis (West Virginia) mine also thought that the first requisite was to put the property in top physical condition. He then listed four essentials for safety work: financial management must spend money; operating management must support the program; foremen must be held responsible for discipline; and employees must cooperate.[59]

Some of the earliest and most effective safety work was begun at U.S. Coal and Coke, a U.S. Steel subsidiary with mines in Gary, West Virginia. It was following parent-company policy, for its safety organization was identical to that of U.S. Steel. The company motto was "Safety—The First Consideration," and it was the direct responsibility of the top operating official. General superintendent Edward O'Toole chaired a companywide safety committee that oversaw all aspects of the program. The company also hired its own corps of mine inspectors, and it appointed workmen's committees that inspected each mine and reported directly to the general superintendent.

U.S. Coal and Coke opened its Gary mines around 1902, and safety was designed in from the beginning, although the entire program was not implemented until about 1910. O'Toole was an engineer, and his approach stressed engineering; the company even went so far as to develop blueprints for its baseball team's bats. One of its superintendents, J. R. Booth, explained the importance of engineering. He emphasized the need for a large fan and unobstructed ventilation, and he noted that his mines had straight haulage ways with mild curves and good track. They were wide enough for a man to pass a coal trip but as an extra precaution had regular refuge stations. There were also separate manways free of trolley wires and other hazards. Booth also stressed the role of proper mine layout in reducing the costs of supervision: "If we can lay out a mine so . . . [that the assistant foreman] has less distance to travel . . . he will have more time to devote to each man."[60]

Most mines were not so well designed. In 1902 Kentucky's inspector had blamed roof falls on "faulty methods of mining" and went on to catalog a whole list that included mining out wide spaces, nonparallel courses, and thin pillars. No doubt many of the mines he indicted were still killing men in the 1920s. As late as 1937 the consequences of poor layout in a Colorado mine were graphically revealed in a Bureau of Mines report by W. H. Forbes. A piece of roof fifteen feet wide by seventy feet long fell, killing two men. Forbes explained the cause: there was "no uniform system of room width and depth, size of pillars or method of pillar extraction." As usual, Dan Harrington was more blunt: "A rotten system of mining," he scribbled on the report.[61]

At U.S. Coal and Coke, mine layout reinforced personnel management—both because it demonstrated management's good faith and also because it facilitated monitoring. By 1909 the Gary mines had a book of safety rules printed in seven languages that set out requirements for

U.S. Coal and Coke, a U.S. Steel subsidiary, stressed engineering controls for safety. It shielded trolley wires in the mine shaft and designed its own cars with brakes. *(Courtesy Eastern Regional Coal Archives, Bluefield, WV)*

both bosses and men. Minimum air velocity was prescribed both at the entry and at the last breakthrough in each room. All coal was to be undercut, and dust was removed prior to blasting, which was done by subforemen who were required to use permissible explosives in a bureau-approved manner. There were rules for track laying and clearance and for the installation of electrical equipment. Trolley wires were guarded wherever men might touch them. Perhaps most important, systematic minimum timbering regulations were drawn up and followed for each mine. These rules were subject to modification in light of experience. All injuries were investigated, and written reports were filed on the changes that would have to be made to avoid similar accidents in the future.

The object of all these rules was to stifle the miner's freedom, or as company engineer Howard Eavenson tactfully phrased it, to "reach the man who is actually doing the work at the working face with the superior knowledge of the higher officials." Safety was therefore part of a systematic effort to extend management control. U.S. Coal and Coke tried to induce voluntary acceptance of safe mining techniques, and in cooperation with the bureau it made a movie to "show the miners exactly how the work should be done with safety and efficiency." But the rules were also strictly enforced through a system of close supervision. A subforemen had no more than twenty-five to thirty-five men to supervise, and eighteen was the goal. Since workings were relatively concentrated, he could visit the work face every three hours. When he gave an order, he was required to remain until it was carried out. In 1910 the company began to grade foremen and subforemen on the safety of their sections and assigned demerits based on the number of unsafe conditions or injuries for which each was responsible. At the end of the month subforemen with fewer than ten demerits received a $5 bonus, while foremen got $10. For subforemen and foremen who worked for six months without a demerit, the bonuses became $15 and $25 respectively.[62]

Some other mines followed similar procedures and established enviable safety records over long periods. In 1912 one bureau engineer who visited the Frick mines—also subsidiaries of U.S. Steel—reported, "I was particularly impressed . . . with the tremendous effort toward greater safety." In the late 1920s the fatality rate in Frick's Pennsylvania mines averaged about 25 percent below the state average. Tennessee Coal, Iron, and Railroad was yet another U.S. Steel subsidiary. It had an average fatality rate of 0.64 per million manhours from 1920 to 1929, less than one-third of the national average. The bureau described a Utah mine of Columbia Steel (a U.S. Steel subsidiary) as "very nearly a model mine." A bureau safety inspection of one of Wisconsin Steel's mines in 1936 revealed that it too followed the safety standards set by the parent corporation. It had reduced the fatality rate from 1.6 per million manhours in the 1916–20 period to half that level in 1931–35. Ford Collieries, a subsidiary of Michigan Alkali, also maintained a successful safety program similar to that of U.S. Coal and Coke. From 1920 to

1931 Ford's fatality rate averaged 0.19 per million manhours, about one-tenth of the national average.[63]

The Union Pacific mines in Wyoming began safety work in 1911 when a Bureau of Mines team trained some of the men in first aid. The UP mines were unionized, and members of the safety committees were chosen by the union locals and inspected the mines along with the safety engineer. Little came of these early efforts, for the company was unable to persuade the workers of its good faith, and the union eventually stopped electing men to the committees. In 1923, with the advent of Eugene McAuliffe as president, work was expanded. McAuliffe had been reared a Canadian. He began work as a fireman and then progressed to fuel officer for several railroads, and in 1908 he founded the International Railway Fuel Association. It was a short step from saving coal to saving lives. Between 1923 and 1932 the company spent over $1 million, or about 4 cents per ton of coal, on safety. In 1925 a "Code of Standards" was published governing clearance, installation of track, guarding of machinery, electrical installation, and requirements for systematic timbering. It was followed in 1929 by a "Code of Rules and Regulations for the Government of Employees," which was enforced by close supervision.[64]

In the summer of 1931 the company introduced an annual raffle of two automobiles, the participants being only those workers who had passed the year without a lost-time accident, and in 1933 it required all men to undergo an eye examination and to wear safety glasses that the company furnished. Hard hats and safety shoes came in 1934, and all employees were required to take first-aid training. In the late 1930s hiring was transferred from foremen to the superintendent, and new men were provided special training on how to mine according to company rules. Between 1923 and 1939 the fatality rate fell from 2.25 to 1.19 per million manhours, while the injury rate declined from 64 to 16.[65]

The parallel between mine safety programs and those in manufacturing was often self-conscious, for many thought that the key to mine safety and prosperity was to adopt the systematic-management techniques being employed elsewhere. An article on Armco stressed that the company had introduced job training, time clocks, and other "factory methods" in an effort to improve safety and reduce turnover and absenteeism at its Nellis mine. Thus, the miner's freedom—like that of the railroad employee and the factory worker—was under attack by the new management controls at those companies that were trying to improve safety.[66]

The men responded to the new safety rules in a number of ways.

Frank Fugate recalled that the company safety inspector would hand out demerits to the men whose rooms were improperly timbered, and that after so many demerits a man would be fired, but he liked the results: "So after that, it was a great help, that was," he recalled. Fugate's enthusiasm may have been exceptional, for most operators discovered that enforcement was a major problem. New safety procedures occasionally led to strikes, but sometimes men simply quit. In 1917 a Pennsylvania inspector reported that the entire labor force left one mine that had tried to ban solid shooting. The safety engineer at Stonega Coke and Coal claimed that state regulations requiring use of large-diameter timber for roof props reduced miners' incomes and led them to quit.[67]

The most widespread response of both the men and the foremen was simply to ignore an unpopular regulation. Virtually all operators that implemented a safety program responded by tightening discipline, usually by increasing supervision. Instead of winking at safety violations, companies now developed standard, measured punishments. Consolidation Coal employed peer pressure to encourage employee acceptance of its regulations. A "sheriff, police and safety court" composed entirely of employees "tried" and punished workers who were caught violating rules.[68]

Most operators viewed discipline as a last resort, for voluntary compliance was inherently preferable and monitoring was expensive in room-and-pillar mining. Accordingly, bonuses were widely employed to motivate careful work among both low-level managers and workmen. As on railroads, the difficulties of supervision made such schemes especially attractive. Union Collieries combined the bonus with peer pressure; it divided employees into work groups, with the winner getting a substantial sum—roughly $24—every three months. A worker whose injury disqualified his group sometimes received a more serious injury from his teammates. Companies also employed the usual array of banners, slogans, contests, and safety bulletin boards. In the late 1930s Carrs Fork Coal even sent a letter home "TO THE WOMEN FOLK OF OUR MEN" claiming that "A GOOD WOMAN IS THE STRONGEST POWER IN THE WORLD AND WE WANT IT USED TO PREVENT ACCIDENTS." In it the company superintendent noted that "my MOTHER always knelt and prayed with FATHER and me before we left for the mines," and he urged the wives to "give them a BE CAREFUL with your daily GOOD BYE."[69]

The bureau aided and abetted these encouraging developments in a variety of ways. It issued a steady stream of publications stressing the benefits of safety and the need for management commitment, and in 1923 it began a safety inspection service. Operators were free to ignore these recommendations, and hence the bureau rarely suggested very expensive changes. But some companies made good use of its expertise. In 1932 the bureau inspected Union Collieries for the third time in three years and found that twenty-two of its previous recommendations had been enacted. "We appreciate this," Scott Turner wrote the company.[70]

In 1930 the bureau also developed a five-day safety training program for mine management. And to encourage safer work habits among the men, it established the Holmes Safety Association in 1922 to set up chapters at mines. These groups promoted safety through first-aid training, contests, and talks, sometimes by bureau personnel, but the idea does not seem to have caught on; by 1933 only 338 had been formed. In 1924 the magazine *Explosives Engineer* approached the bureau with the idea of a national mine safety competition. Contests began in 1925, with the winner receiving a "Sentinels of Safety" trophy. Yet here again the idea does not seem to have been very popular. In the late 1930s only about seventy of the more than six thousand bituminous mines routinely entered the contests.[71]

The bureau also worked behind the scenes, poking and prodding the states to improve the quality of their work. In the mid-1920s, when Alabama's new chief inspector began a campaign to reduce roof-fall accidents through systematic timbering, bureau engineers were full of praise. In 1931 Dan Harrington tried to fire up Utah's flagging safety movement with an information circular that bared that state's sins and detailed the policies needed for redemption. This stirred up O. F. McShane, head of Utah's industrial commission. He circularized his inspectors, noting the bureau's report and informing them that "inspections should be made more frequently." He also wrote the operators urging them to follow the bureau's circular.[72]

Most bureau engineers thought that states were the weak link in mine safety, with out-of-date laws and inspection services riddled with ingrates, incompetents, and political hacks. In a letter to John B. Andrews, Harrington claimed that one state chief inspector had never been in a mine before he assumed office. "The really competent mine inspectors are by far in the minority," he concluded. George Rice's assessment was even more scathing. The inspection force in Illinois was "generally poor," as were most of the inspectors in West Virginia. Warming to his theme, Rice announced that Oklahoma had a "wretched election system" and Alabama a "weak inspection force," while the inspector in Colorado was described as "obstinate and dogmatic." In fact, Rice concluded, "Pennsylvania is the only state which has some high class inspectors."[73]

But even the best was none too good. After the chief inspector of mines, James Roderick, died in 1917, the most striking characteristic of

Pennsylvania's inspection service was its lack of direction. In 1928 a representative of the Anthracite Operators Conference wrote Secretary of Mines Glasgow asking him for suggestions on how to prevent accidents. Glasgow had no suggestions to offer. In 1929, at the department's behest, the state modified its anthracite law to require hard hats for shaft workers. Yet in a passage that revealed just how limited his thinking had become, Glasgow informed the editor of *Coal Age* that "no effort was made to obtain legislation requiring the use of safety helmets in the bituminous mines as the accident records do not indicate the need of such action."[74]

Yet if state safety work left much to be desired, except in its efforts to prevent explosions, the bureau's work was also unfocused and half-hearted. Initially the bureau had shown some interest in preventing fatalities from roof falls, which accounted for about half of all deaths, and in 1912 it wrote to state inspectors, soliciting suggestions on how such deaths might be reduced. Patrick Grady of West Virginia spoke for the majority when he stressed the need for improved supervision and the use of systematic timbering. Grady even sent along a blueprint of the timbering methods used by U.S. Coal and Coke. Yet nothing came of this early effort, and the agency mostly ignored roof falls until 1925, when George Rice proposed a study of their causes to the bureau's Mine Safety Board. The proposal was rejected, Rice claimed, because the board did not know how to study them.[75]

In 1927 the bureau did begin such a study after a congressional appropriation had directed it to do so, but nothing came of it, and the bureau never launched the sort of large-scale campaign to encourage more systematic timbering that it had employed to speed the introduction of rock-dusting. Perhaps, as Rice had suggested, the problem was that roof falls did not seem amenable to laboratory analysis or did not present any obvious technological challenges. Yet an alternative technology— roof bolting—was already in scattered use in a few metal mines. The bureau does not seem to have learned about this approach until it was described in the mining literature in 1943, and did not begin to study it until 1948.[76]

"WE ARE GOING BACKWARDS"

By 1930, coal mine accidents showed no improvement. Part of the problem was that some of the same forces that had driven up fatality rates in the nineteenth century were still at work. Bituminous mines were increasing in size and depth, while mining continued to move into newer, higher-risk states. Mechanization also continued apace, and the increasing use of electrical mining equipment tended to reduce labor more than it did accidents, thereby raising the fatality rate (table A2.4). In addition, World War I had produced a burst of bad mining practice as the inordinate demand for coal led companies to skim the cream by mining wide rooms and leaving small pillars. This reduced the fatality rate in the short term, and so roof falls declined during the war. But it made subsequent mining exceedingly hazardous, as is reflected in the ballooning of roof-fall accidents in the 1920s.[77]

Many mines also began to extract pillars—a highly dangerous task. When E. S. Pennington was crushed by a huge piece of slate while drawing pillars at a Stonega mine, company safety engineer C. A. Sine warned that "the mines of this company are being developed on the plan to draw pillars and unless . . . a better system of timbering [is instituted] then we may expect an increase in accidents." The lack of safety progress in anthracite mining in the twentieth century also stemmed in part from the worsening dangers in the industry. As the mines became increasingly worked out, pillar extraction and work in caved ground became more common, and both were highly hazardous.[78]

Moreover, at many companies top management long remained indifferent to safety. M. A. Hanna began a safety campaign in 1927 only because "our record was so bad we were working on a [workmen's compensation experience] penalty." E. L. Berger, general manager of Bell and Zoller, reported that when the fatality rate in one of the company's mines reached an incredible 9 per million manhours in 1929, he finally realized that "we were wrong in our general attitude toward safety." Only then did the company begin systematic efforts to remove hazards and redesign equipment. In 1927, under UMW pressure, Washington State modified its mine law to require operators to set up safety committees, but their response was apathetic. "Our safety educational laws are not receiving the attention . . . they deserve," the state's inspector lamented.[79]

Sometimes the problem was an inability to motivate lower-level personnel. At Stonega Coke and Coal a Bureau of Mines engineer reported, "The company has been sincere, but whether that attitude has been shared by the minor officials and men is doubtful." Similarly, Charlie Campbell recalled working in one mine where the foreman would warn whenever the inspector was due to come around so that the men could "have everything up to date."[80]

Hudson Coal was a large anthracite producer and typical of the companies that implemented halfhearted safety programs. In 1899 the company had not been interested enough in safety to support Matthew Shields's first-aid work, but by the early 1920s it had a safety department and a code of safety rules. Yet as general manager Cadwallader Evans later noted, "The safety program we had been carrying on was one more on paper than in our hearts and minds." In the late 1920s, stung by the company's rising fatality rate, Evans determined to get results. These efforts continued throughout the 1930s, but progress was glacial, probably because the company's penny-pinching failed to motivate either midlevel managers or workers. In 1939 bureau engineer Simon Ash toured one of Hudson's collieries. "The things that impressed me most," Ash wrote, "are practices which were in effect years ago and it is quite evident that progress in safety has not advanced to the degree it has in other mining regions."[81]

Dan Harrington thought that the costs of accidents were simply too low to justify adequate safety precautions. He reacted thus to the news that there had been five men electrocuted in Alabama mines in the first ten months of 1930: "If the first one had cost $50,000, the second, third, fourth, and fifth probably would not have occurred." Harrington's point, that major increases in the cost of accidents were required, was probably correct. The accident rate was not very responsive to increases in workmen's compensation costs (table A2.4). This result reflected the high cost of accident reduction, which bureau engineers put at 5–10 cents per ton of coal, or as much as 30 percent of net profits. In addition, compensation costs had little impact at the many mines in which the near absence of experience rating blunted their consequences.[82]

The state of the coal market also retarded the spread of safety work during the 1920s and 1930s. The cause, some writers have suggested, was an excessively competitive market structure that ground down profits and prevented safety investments. But the problem was not structural, it was historical. It was too much capacity—the result of declining demand—not too much competition that reduced profits, as the experience of the anthracite producers makes clear. By 1902 a dozen large producers had come to dominate that industry, successfully colluding on prices. But cartelization does not seem to have led to any burst of safety-consciousness.[83]

Thus, industry structure had little to do with poor mine safety, but the profit squeeze that stemmed from excess capacity after World War I did impede safety work by reducing available funds and leading companies to postpone needed work. Stonega virtually closed its safety department during the sharp depression in 1921, and Dan Harrington claimed that the explosions at Dawson (New Mexico) in 1923 and Castle Gate (Utah) in 1924 resulted in part from the fact that, under the press of retrenchment, the operators had neglected watering. State inspectors acknowledged these problems. In 1928 Pennsylvania's secretary of mines,

W. H. Glasgow, admitted that "this department has in the past been very reasonable and I fear entirely too lenient in the matter of accepting 'poor business conditions' as a reason for a reduced standard of safety."[84]

Operators were especially reluctant to make mine-specific safety investments that would not be profitable in any mine with a short life expectancy, and as the industry contracted after 1920 this must have included a large fraction of the smaller mines. The bureau discovered this fact of life when it made safety suggestions to Robert Gage Coal in 1928. It had recommended larger crosscuts, a new air shaft, shelter holes, sprinklers, and similar items that could have had no salvage value. A company official thanked the bureau and said they would follow the advice "as far as we consider practical." But he went on to remark that "of course you will understand the mines are old and some of them will not last very much longer."[85]

More than just costs and benefits impeded mine safety. In mining as elsewhere, the logic of successful safety work led companies to accept the responsibility for accidents, to try to control the work process, and to motivate employees to work safely. These ideas were novel in manufacturing, but they were revolutionary in mining, where custom still ruled and the miners were called contractors. Most managers found it difficult to grasp the idea that they were responsible for the men's safety. In 1928, when most manufacturing trade publications were preaching managerial responsibility for accidents, the editor of the American Mining Congress *Journal* was outraged by Herbert W. Heinrich's claim that 88 percent of mine accidents resulted from supervisory failure. "Blame should be on him who violates orders," the editor sputtered. And when Pennsylvania's secretary of mines hectored one company for its poor safety record, its vice president reacted petulantly: "It seems to us, Mr. Secretary, that you are placing the whole burden of safety upon the coal operator."[86]

Whether motivated by economics or custom, the disinclination of many coal operators to accept this burden was reflected in the weakness of the various coal mine safety organizations. The 1922 meetings of the National Safety Council's Mining Section were attended by representatives of only five coal companies and a handful of owners of captive mines. In 1929 Francis Feehan remarked on "the small representation at this meeting of the coal men." Nor was there any more interest in safety at the industry's major trade group. The National Coal Association had no safety committee before 1928. Instead, it contented itself with peppy assessments such as that delivered by secretary Harry Gandy to the National Safety Council in 1927. In a talk entitled "Keeping Everlastingly at It," Gandy compared fatalities per ton in the United States with those in Europe, and the comparison made the American industry look like a paragon of safety-consciousness.[87]

The day after Gandy spoke, Eugene McAuliffe also addressed the council, and he delivered a withering assessment of coal's safety record. McAuliffe scornfully referred to Gandy's "cheerful figures" and presented instead comparative fatality rates per worker. He concluded that the bituminous coal industry was "lagging" because "the men who speak for the industry decline to ally themselves with the progressive methods now employed by other similar industries." McAuliffe also charged that the Bureau of Mines had "failed of growth" in recent years because of the "barrage of criticism" it had received from the industry, and he bluntly concluded, "We are going backwards."[88]

McAuliffe's broadside seems to have shaken the operators' complacency, but change came slowly. When West Virginia's chief mine inspector, Robert Lambie, addressed the National Coal Association in 1930, he remarked that "it is not so encouraging to see so many men leave the room." C. F. Richardson, president of West Kentucky Coal, also thought that there were "too many empty chairs with too important a subject to be given so little attention by our members." Finally, in 1931 the association's safety committee launched a nationwide safety drive in concert with the Bureau of Mines. The chairman was Milton Fies of Alabama's Debardleben Coal. Fies immediately distanced himself from Gandy's optimistic figures. "The argument has been advanced, that because of our better record based on production there is 'less blood on the coal produced in this country than in foreign countries,'" Fies observed, "but I would state with all possible emphasis that there is more despair in the homes of the miners."[89]

Organized Safety Work in Metal Mines, 1910–1939

In the late nineteenth century, metal mine fatality rates seem to have been stable, although the statistical evidence is fragmentary. In 1911 the Bureau of Mines began collecting data on metal mine fatalities, adjusted for days worked (tables A2.5 and A2.6), and these can be used to derive rates per million manhours. Such figures for iron and copper mining, along with bituminous coal, are shown in figure 6.4, and the contrast could not be more striking. As can be seen, at the time the bureau was formed all three branches of mining were about equally dangerous. Yet while coal mine safety improved little over the next three decades, the fatality rates in metal mining fell sharply.

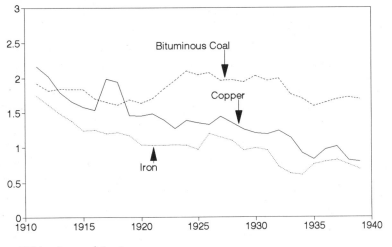

FIGURE 6.4. Metal and Coal Mine Fatality Rates per Million Manhours, Three-Year Moving Averages, 1911-1939

Source: Tables A2.1 and A2.6.

TECHNOLOGY, ORGANIZATION, AND SAFETY

Metal mining had more in common with anthracite than with bituminous coal mining. By the twentieth century most underground copper and iron mines were deep—sometimes as deep as three thousand feet. Mining was usually undertaken on a number of levels that were accessed from a shaft. While the actual mining methods the men employed to win the ore had little in common with the room-and-pillar techniques used in coal, the risks were surprisingly similar. Men usually entered and left the mine riding open cages up and down the shaft. As in anthracite and the few deep bituminous mines, this generated a host of dangers. The cage could move at a thousand feet per minute, and the early ones had neither sides nor safety catches. The rope might break, or a man might fall from the cage. Or the engineer might overwind and dump the men back down the shaft. In the mine itself, poorly guarded abandoned shafts were a constant source of risks.

Mining the ore was a matter of drilling, blasting, loading, and hauling. Some drills were powered by compressed air, and the compressor occasionally exploded; electric drills carried a risk of shock. Dynamite also took its toll, as did haulage accidents. Metal mines were not subject to gas or dust explosions, but fire was a constant menace. In 1917 a fire at one of the North Butte Mining Company shafts killed 161 men. As in coal, however, roof falls were the most serious single hazard. Above ground, most metal mines operated crushing mills and smelters, and machinery accidents were therefore common.

The improvement in metal mine safety after 1910 resulted in part from changes in mining methods and technology that were largely independent of the safety movement. In copper mining, operators introduced cable-drawn scrapers to move the ore, an innovation that both raised productivity and reduced the need for men to labor under bad roof. Of far greater importance was the shift from underground to surface mining. Open-pit mining of copper, iron, gold, and silver grew rapidly during these years. Initially such mining had been done by hand methods, which made it very safe but not very attractive to the operators because productivity was low. The rapid introduction of giant railroad shovels and, later, electrically powered caterpillar-driven shovels as well as other forms of machinery increased the dangers of open-pit mining, although it still remained far safer than subsurface work. But mechanization also reduced the relative cost of strip mining and therefore shifted employment to the surface.[90]

This tendency of technological change to shift the composition of employment toward surface workers at open-pit mines was offset in part by increases in the productivity of surface workers at underground mines due to improvements in crushing and concentrating facilities. In iron mining the share of surface employment at underground mines fell from about 30 percent in 1914-16 to 27 percent on the eve of World War II. As in anthracite mining, such changes raised the average fatality rate at underground mines because they reduced the share of relatively safe jobs.

These employment shifts—the rising proportion of open-pit miners and the falling share of surface workers at underground mines—roughly canceled each other in iron mining. About 59 percent of all manshifts were worked underground in the years 1914-16, the first period for which the data are available, and in 1937-39 the share was still 57 percent. But in gold mining the proportion of employment underground declined from 75 percent to 64 percent over the same period, and in copper the share of below-ground employment fell from nearly 70 percent to 58 percent. The fatality rate per thousand 300-day workers in copper mining declined about 44 percent; had employment not shifted to the safer jobs, it would still have fallen about 37 percent. Thus, technological changes that shifted workers into safer jobs accounted for roughly 15 percent $[(44 - 37)/44]$ of the safety improvement in copper mining and virtually none of the safety improvement in iron ore extraction. Most of the gains occurred, therefore, because work underground, and at the crushing and concentrating plants and the strip pits, became safer. This in turn was the outcome of organized safety work.

ORGANIZING THE METAL MINES FOR SAFETY

By the twentieth century the mining of iron ore and copper was increasingly the province of large firms. In copper the number of mines declined from 226 in 1919 to only 51 in 1939 while average mine size doubled. Three companies—Anaconda, Kennecott, and Phelps Dodge —dominated the industry. Their combined share of ore production rose from about 40 percent of the industry total in 1911 to nearly 75 percent in 1939. Iron ore was nearly as tightly controlled. Between 1909 and 1919 the number of mines fell from 407 to 177 that were run by 100 operating companies. In fact, production was much more concentrated than these figures indicate. The Temporary National Economic Committee released figures showing that in 1937 one firm—Oliver Iron Mining Company—controlled 42 percent of total production. Oliver, along with Pickands, Mather, Cleveland-Cliffs, and M. A. Hanna, accounted for 77 percent of all shipments. By contrast, soft coal was mined in 1939 from over fifty-eight hundred mines operated by over five thousand companies, and the largest firm controlled no more than 5 percent of total production.[91]

The significance of this concentration of control over metal mining was not that large firms with market power were invariably much safer than their smaller counterparts. Had that been true, anthracite mining would have been a model of safety. Rather, the importance of high concentration in metal mining was that it required effective safety work on the part of only a handful of organizations to bring about an important improvement in the safety of the industry. Safety gains at Oliver or Phelps Dodge could significantly reduce the injury rate in iron or copper mining, while similar work by a bituminous producer such as Union Pacific Coal or Ford Collieries could not. Size may not have caused these companies to undertake safety work, but it magnified the consequences.

As usual, rising injury costs were the spur that goaded the large metal mines to begin organized safety work. Both the iron and the copper mines in the Lake Superior region seem to have faced escalating injury costs even before the passage of workmen's compensation laws. After 1900, Michigan's copper producers faced a rising tide of liability suits, while the Bureau of Mines reported that Minnesota was also a hotbed of contingency-fee lawyers. In 1911, Wisconsin passed its workmen's compensation law. Michigan and Minnesota followed in 1912 and 1913. The prospect of rising costs led Oliver Mining, a U.S. Steel subsidiary, to set up the region's first safety organization in 1910. Cleveland-Cliffs followed in 1911 and the other large iron mines shortly thereafter. Michigan's copper companies also rushed to embrace the new Safety First movement soon after compensation became law.[92]

Arizona's workmen's compensation law took effect in 1912, and Phelps Dodge, with most of its copper mines in that state, started safety work in 1913. New Jersey Zinc first organized safety committees in 1913, two years after that state introduced compensation. Anaconda's safety organization began in 1914, the year before Montana's compensation law went into effect.[93]

These companies pursued the same strategies to reduce accidents that were being adopted at U.S. Coal and Coke, Union Pacific, and a few other large coal producers. Oliver employed the U.S. Steel safety organization, which included both the heads of operating divisions and workmen. Cleveland-Cliffs had an almost identical organization. New Jersey Zinc also had workmen's committees, as did Phelps Dodge after 1925. Anaconda's bureau of safety included the president, general manager, and managers of each operating department. Safety inspectors were employed who reported unsafe conditions directly to the bureau, while mine superintendents were required to report to the bureau how they had resolved the problem. Most other large producers also developed structures that placed ultimate responsibility on the operating personnel.

In metals as in coal, successful safety work began with investments in mine layout and machinery. The Bureau of Mines reported that one large Lake Superior iron-mining company—probably Oliver—spent $138,000 on safety devices in 1911. Cleveland-Cliffs also invested a considerable sum in safety. Between 1914 and 1920, Anaconda charged about $550,000 to improvements in the safety of its Butte (Montana) operations, and this figure did not count many safety investments charged to other accounts.

But the centerpiece of all the programs was the development and enforcement of safer mining practices. Accident investigation and analysis provided feedback to safety work, which gradually evolved into a set of formal rules and operating practices that governed all facets of the work. In 1912, Cleveland-Cliffs had rule books in three languages with an introduction by the company president. Accidents were recorded using a system borrowed from Illinois Steel. Anaconda began safety work by first developing an accurate set of accident statistics that recorded the number, cause, and treatment of each injury. By the early 1920s it had a book containing 152 separate safety rules. Both Oliver and Phelps Dodge investigated all accidents and modified their rules on the basis of experience. Another large iron producer used its central safety office to spread safety insights discovered in one mine to its other properties. In 1917 the safety manual at Pickands, Mather contained 186 rules. Yet as safety habits became institutionalized, the need for rules declined. By 1937 the Pickands, Mather manual had shrunk to fifty-six rules. According to a company inspector, "Many of the earlier rules covered employer behavior which by this time was taken to be a matter of course and a routine part of operation."[94]

Work at Phelps Dodge in the 1930s also reveals how thoroughly safety had been integrated into work routines. "As far as possible, all work is standardized," the Bureau of Mines reported of the company's Morenci mine. All blueprints for work were checked for safety, and work practices were governed by a "Text Book on Safe Methods of Mining." All blasting was to be done electrically. Standard timbering methods were set out for each area of the mine, and timber itself was cut above ground to standard sizes. All jobs required men to wear hard hats, and safety shoes and goggles were mandatory for certain tasks. Similarly, the bureau reported that at the company's Old Dominion mine, "timbering in blasting, haulage and development has been standardized throughout the mine so that if a man is transferred he will have identical working conditions as far as possible."[95]

These new operating practices were supported by a new system of personnel management. By the early 1930s hiring at Phelps Dodge was the province of an employment agent. New men were first given a physical. They then received a thirty-seven-page book of safety regulations, some safety instruction, and finally a test on the rules. A perfect score on the safety test was required before beginning work. Each man was also provided with a hard hat, safety shoes, goggles, safety belt, respirator, and other necessary equipment and was required to take a first-aid course and to pass an examination on it. When a new man began work, he was instructed on work practices by the shift boss and given a special "probation" time card that required him to work under the supervision of an experienced man until the shift boss certified that he was able to work independently. Nor were the foremen neglected in this process. From time to time the company required them to attend training conferences that stressed both safety and efficiency.[96]

As usual, the men did not always appreciate this assault on traditional practices, for companies encouraged compliance by tightening discipline. A supervisor at the Quincy copper mine explained that the men were making "great complaint because our discipline had become so rigid." Incentives were also employed. New Jersey Zinc introduced bonuses for shift bosses in 1913, and in the late 1920s the foreman's bonus for safety work was universal among Arizona copper mines. Anaconda also published each injury with the name of the foreman attached in its company magazine, the *Anode*, while Phelps Dodge graded each foreman's workplace and posted the results in a conspicuous place. Calumet and Hecla developed poster contests like those employed at DuPont to see who could spot the most unsafe practices. Phelps Dodge awarded certificates to men who went for long periods without accidents, and prizes and dinners to all workers when a mine went ninety consecutive days without a lost-time injury. A companywide safety trophy went annually to the division with the best record.[97]

These procedures were not different in any important way from those pursued at safety-conscious coal mines. But the bituminous operators practicing effective safety work employed only a small fraction of the industry's employees, whereas safety-conscious metal mines dominated their industries. Phelps Dodge came late to effective safety work. But from 1924 to 1930 it cut the fatality rate from 2.7 to 1.5 per thousand 300-day workers while its lost-time injury rate declined from 339 to 12. And Phelps Dodge employed about one-fifth of all copper miners.[98]

No New Deal for Coal Safety, 1930–1939

In the 1920s the declining demand for coal had impeded safety work, and in the 1930s, as the market collapsed, the problem worsened. In 1932, under the onslaught of depression, Consolidation Coal virtually ceased its safety work, and Alabama's state inspectorate also nearly closed up shop. That same year a representative of Vesta Coal informed the Bureau of Mines that "the general condition of business, for the past three years, has, in large measure, prevented expenditures that we would have otherwise made in the interest of accident prevention." Safety work also seems to have been relaxed at Stonega Coke and Coal. Later in the decade bureau engineers who visited one insolvent mine that had exploded noted that the company "has attempted to keep operating without spending the money necessary to keep the mine in a reasonably safe operating condition."[99]

Yet if depression hindered safety work in some mines, there were crosscurrents as well. Rising injury costs in the early 1930s led Knox Consolidated Mines to inaugurate a new safety program in July 1933 that led to a sharp drop in injury rates. The 1930s also finally witnessed the widespread use in coal mines of personal protective equipment—a cheap, effective means of improving safety that had long been common practice in many manufacturing companies, quarries, and metal mines.[100]

Personal protective equipment invariably resulted in sharp reductions in compensation costs, because of either schedule-rating discounts or reduced claims for companies that self-insured. In either case, where employees bought their own gear, the result was one more example of operator profits on worker investments. In 1928, when Phelps Dodge introduced safety shoes at its Stag Cañon coal mines, the rate of foot-related injuries plunged by two-thirds. In 1936 a writer in the American Mining Congress *Journal* described the payoff to safety shoes: "Toes are not a vital necessity to a man, but he has many of them which may be paid for in compensation." The going rate in Illinois, he noted, was $125 per toe, except for the big toe, which went for $400.[101]

Madeira Hill was a large anthracite producer that began to introduce hard hats in 1929; by 1932 it had cut the compensation cost of head injuries from about $8,000 a year to nearly zero. Union Pacific Coal finally began to require safety glasses in 1933. The company was remarkable in that it paid for both safety glasses and an eye examination, the initial cost coming to about $6,100. Yet the annual saving due to fewer eye injures amounted to about $2,000. As American Optical blithely informed operators in its advertisement for safety glasses, "You can't sell coal at a profit if you buy eyes on the side."[102]

The slow spread of such a profitable investment was the residue of nineteenth-century ideas that the miner was an independent contractor and largely responsible for his own safety. As a result, when companies did introduce the equipment, they nearly always made its use voluntary and required workers to buy their own. For their part, the men often resisted the new equipment. Not only were the early hard hats heavy and ill-fitting, the dusty, humid mine atmosphere often made vision difficult for anyone wearing safety goggles. As ideas about accident responsibility evolved, and as companies searched for inexpensive ways to improve safety, more and more mines began to require protective equipment. Still, change came slowly. In 1933, Pennsylvania gave workmen's compensation schedule discounts to companies that equipped all their employees with protective equipment. Yet as late as 1939, a survey of 512 small and medium-sized mines found that only 181 qualified for the hard-hat discount, 118 for shoes, and 72 for goggles.[103]

LABOR AND CAPITAL

It was an enduring article of faith among the United Mine Workers that a nonunion mine was an unsafe mine. In fact, the attitude of the UMW toward work safety was complex and sometimes contradictory. At the highest level the union and its predecessors had almost always been a strong voice for stricter state and federal legislation, and these

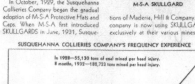
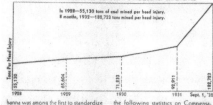
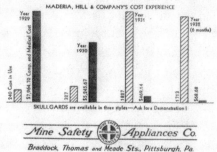

Mine operators found hard hats profitable, especially when miners bought them, as recommended in this advertisement from the early 1930s. A Navaho Indian miner displays modern, safety-minded headgear. *(National Archives)*

efforts continued throughout the 1920s and 1930s. A Bureau of Mines engineer termed the 1927 Washington State law that required companies to institute safety committees "a result of the union's efforts," and Eugene McAuliffe admitted that Wyoming's rock-dusting law was the product of UMW lobbying, as the operators had "moved heaven and earth" to prevent it. In 1938 the UMW's national convention called upon President Franklin Delano Roosevelt to convene a conference on mine safety. It was held in April but produced little but bickering. The union continued to campaign for federal inspection of coal mines, which it finally achieved in 1941.[104]

Yet safety was rarely an important topic at conventions, and it received little space or editorial comment in the UMW *Journal*. Contracts usually included a boilerplate clause stating that the operator could make and enforce reasonable safety rules; otherwise they rarely discussed the matter. This was a strategy that appealed to both sides. Most companies distrusted their locals and were loath to allow them much say in safety matters. Dan Harrington claimed that when he had been a mine superintendent "there was never a single case or instance where I secured the slightest cooperation from the union . . . in trying to put over anything of a safety nature . . . [unless] there was something in the proposal which would give the union . . . an increase in pay." The unions, for their part, were reluctant to bargain—and perhaps give up income for safety—when they suspected that most safety work benefited the company anyway because it reduced compensation costs. In 1933, section 8 of the Bituminous Coal Code contained a clause stating that "employers and employees shall cooperate in maintaining safe conditions of operation." With only modest exaggeration Francis Feehan, a former president of UMW District 5, told the National Safety Council that it was the first contract that ever mentioned safety.[105]

After 1934, as the UMW swept through the industry, some operators claimed that New Deal unionism would imperil mine safety. These worries were not entirely fantastic. The first response of many miners upon joining the union was to toss their hard hats into the air—as far as possible. Others miners burned them. Yet if the union made such actions possible, it also provided the men a collective voice that ultimately induced them to accept company safety rules. At the 1934 meeting of the National Safety Council some coal companies remarked with evident surprise that the UMW was cooperating with their safety work.[106]

Union locals and district leaders often played an important role in law enforcement, and they sometimes pressured both operators and men to improve conditions. As early as 1914, when the Arkansas state inspector had tried to shut a mine that had only one opening, the men complained bitterly until local union leaders "roasted" them for it. In late 1933 the Souden mine of Valley Camp Coal signed an agreement with UMW District 5, and the men promptly discarded their hard hats. But the agreement included a clause stating that "prior practice and custom not in conflict with this agreement may be continued," and there was provision to use an umpire to settle disputes. Both the company and the union requested Feehan to settle this one. In February 1934 Feehan ruled that the men must wear the hats. This had been a foregone conclusion, as the UMW representatives must have known when they agreed to Feehan as an umpire. Union leaders intended to air the men's grievance, but they also intended that the men should wear hard hats.[107]

Feehan's finding set an important precedent, for similar disputes were erupting throughout the coal regions. In March 1934 the Crescent mine local of Pittsburgh Coal voted to do away with hard hats and safety glasses. The dispute went before a board of arbitration in which members of the district and the local—including Joseph Yablonski, who later died a martyr to the cause of union democracy—hashed out the matter with representatives of the company and the Coal Control Association. The men's complaint was that the goggles obscured their vision and made wedging down slate more dangerous. And the hats were miserably uncomfortable: "A lot of men will tell you that they would rather have 2 or 3 stitches in their heads than wear hard hats," Yablonski claimed, and he asserted that the company's real motive in introducing hard hats was to get a compensation credit. The decision was a compromise: safety equipment was retained for most operations, but goggles were no longer required in slate work, and the company and the local were directed to select a committee to try to improve the comfort of the hats. Finally, in 1935, the basic Appalachian Agreement between the union and operators specified that the operator was allowed to require safety hats, shoes, and goggles.[108]

The spread of unionization also indirectly affected mine safety by raising wages and encouraging the spread of strip mining and the mechanization of underground work. Use of electrical undercutting machinery and trolley haulage continued to spread, and locomotives and mine cars grew steadily in size. Although mechanization reduced some risks, Dan Harrington believed that each new machine increased the potential hazards of mining. He bluntly stated that "the coal mining people in the United States . . . have it in their power to make mechanized mining much safer than the older more primitive 'manual' mining." But he stressed that this was far from inevitable, and when new machines were combined with old management methods, they worsened risks. By 1929 Harrington was claiming that one-third of the deaths from roof falls happened because of poor timbering that resulted from the need to move mining machines, or because timbers had been knocked out by trolleys. Harrington also stressed "the recklessness with which electrical equipment was introduced into the mines," and privately he argued that electricity should be banned in gassy and dusty mines.[109]

Beginning in the 1920s the word *mechanization* took on a new meaning as coal men began to use it exclusively to refer to mechanical loading that employed conveyers, electric scrapers, and pit car loaders. Mechanical loading steadily grew in importance, and by 1939 one-third of all coal was loaded by machine. The result was a transformation of mine work. Mechanical loaders handled prodigious amounts of coal, but to be efficient they had to be fully utilized. This finally spelled the demise of the old room-and-pillar system of mining and with it the miner's famous freedom from direct supervision. In the late 1920s and 1930s the need to minimize machine downtime led the industry to develop various forms of "concentrated mining" that focused the work in smaller areas. The inevitable result, or so enthusiasts for the new technology claimed, would be improved safety, for supervision would now be easier. An editorial in the American Mining Congress *Journal* explained that "in mechanized mining, the men work in groups where they are subject to constant supervision so that effective safety practices . . . [can be enforced]."[110]

Some coal men also stressed that mechanical loading would finally bring "factory methods" to the coal industry. Because machine downtime was expensive, mechanical loading would require systematic safety work, its advocates claimed: "To improve performance of machines time study engineers are constantly at work. Out of their studies, together with the studies of safety engineers, come standard practices for loading machine operation, timbering cutting, track laying drilling, shooting, etc. These standard practices eliminate . . . hazards." Like other forms of underground mechanization, mechanical loading also encouraged the shift of mine employment toward relatively safer jobs on the surface. With operations speeded up, the miners could no longer pick out impurities underground, and companies increasingly built above-ground mechanical washeries. As a result, the surface share of manhours at underground mines rose from 12 percent in 1920 to 14 percent in 1939 and to 16 percent by 1944.[111]

None of the safety claims for mechanized loading impressed Dan Harrington. While concentrated mining reduced the costs of safety supervision, it worsened many risks. Harrington pointed out that mechanical loading brought additional electrical hazards to the mine, and that it increased the dangers of explosion simply because it speeded up operations. This made ventilation more difficult and liberated more gas. The higher productivity of mechanical loading increased the incentive for companies to blast with men in the mine, and in 1931 one of Utah's mine inspectors noted that companies were drifting away from outside shooting. Confirmation of these risks came in 1938. A shot-firer at the Duvin mine in Providence, Kentucky, set off an entire box of permissibles, killing twenty-eight men, when he inadvertently touched an ignition wire to a trolley cable. Nor was this an isolated example: the number of disasters ignited by electricity rose steadily from six during the period 1901–9 to ninety-five during 1931–39. And the machinery itself was dangerous: one conveyer in Castle Gate mine no. 2 killed three men in a year. The new machines were also noisy, which made it harder to hear the roof "work," and they made close timbering at the work face difficult. Fatalities from roof falls rose with the introduction of mechanical loading in West Virginia until cross-timbering was required. Mechanization also led to more and faster haulage with bigger cars and locomotives, possibly in the same narrow haulage ways and over the same old rickety tracks.[112]

The statistical evidence on the impact of these new mine technologies is mixed. Illinois data seem to show that mechanical loading had no significant impact on fatality rates. This may simply reflect conditions unique to Illinois, however, for other estimates based on Census data (table A2.4) suggest that although energy was a slightly better substitute for accidents than for labor, overall technological change reduced labor hours more than it did fatalities, thereby raising the death rate.[113]

A DECIDEDLY UNIMPRESSIVE RECORD

In 1937 Dan Harrington delivered a blast to the American Mining Congress in which he recited the coal industry's failures: many programs lacked "the active personal interest of the 'men higher up.'" Perhaps recalling the behavior of Joseph Zook and the Illinois operators, Harrington charged that the companies often began safety campaigns "by throwing essentially the entire change in procedure on the workers with very little if any expenditure of effort, time or money by the company." Three years later he concluded that "real progress in preventing fatalities has been made in the past 25 or 30 years only in explosions and accidents due to use of explosives."[114]

Harrington's assessment was essentially accurate: while the death rate from other causes hardly changed during the interwar years, the explosion fatality rate fell to an all-time low in the late 1930s, with 1939 marred by only one major disaster. Public concern with mine safety had always turned on disaster. As a result, the Neeley-Keller bill to require federal inspection of coal mines that had been submitted to Congress in April 1939 was going nowhere. But it was about to get an unexpected boost.

Pond Creek mine no. 1 in Bartley, West Virginia, was in many safety matters a model mine. It needed to be, for it was one of the most gassy mines in the country. A bureau sample measured 1.5 percent gas on the return air, implying the need for better ventilation. The coal itself was only moderately explosive [$V/(V + FC) = 0.18$], but combined with the gas this implied that at least 63 percent rock dust was required to render the dust nonexplosive. It was rock-dusted on the haulage ways and at the workface but not in trackless areas. The mine was operated entirely with permissible mining equipment, and used electric cap lamps and permissible explosives in a bureau-approved manner. But it blew up. At about 2:30 P.M. on January 10, 1940, while the operating officials were holding a safety meeting, the spark from a spliced mining cable set off a blast that rolled through the east side of the mine, killing 91 of the 138 men at work.[115]

A little over two months later, on March 26, Hanna Mining Company's Willow Grove mine no. 10 in Neffs (Ohio) exploded, killing another seventy-two men. The mine was virtually free of rock dust, although the bureau termed its coal dust "highly explosive" [$V/(V + FC) = 0.44$]. It was officially non-gassy, but one bureau air sample found 2.46 percent methane. Like Pond Creek, it needed better ventilation. The men wore electric cap lamps, but the mining machinery was nonpermissible, and trolley haulage was on the return air. The source of ignition was a black-powder shot that had been stemmed with coal dust. Before the year was out four other mines exploded, bringing the toll to 276 killed. It was the worst year for explosions since 1924.[116]

These disasters blew the Neeley-Keller bill out of Congress. In spite of nearly unanimous opposition by state inspectors and the operators, federal mine inspection became law in 1941, and a decade later another disaster at Centralia, Illinois, finally led to federal regulation.

Conclusion

The informal arrangement by which the Bureau of Mines was to disseminate scientific and technical wisdom to the operators was not quite the failure that the disasters of 1940 seemed to imply, for Pond Creek and Willow Grove were exceptional in a way that Monongah and Darr had not been. The larger failure was, as Harrington had noted, the lack of progress in other areas of mine safety. Part of the problem stemmed from the continued transformation of coal mining, as more machinery and power were employed in deeper, gassier mines. But much of the blame for poor mine safety lay with the "men higher up." Although some managers were able to improve safety even as their mines grew deeper and more mechanized, the gospel of systematic-management control of work safety simply never spread beyond a few large operators.

Such lethargy reflected the tradition that safety was the miner's responsibility. It also resulted from the fact that coal mine safety lacked the institutional support of a strong trade association that had proved so effective on railroads and in some sectors of manufacturing. Nor did public policy provide a powerful spur to reduce most kinds of accidents. Companies discovered that comprehensive safety programs were expensive while most accidents were not. Explosion risks declined because workmen's compensation incentives were reinforced by the threat of property damage, and because the Bureau of Mines concentrated its efforts on these dangers. Ironically, given the powerful role of disaster in leading to stricter mine laws, if the bureau and the operators had been a little more successful in preventing explosions, federal regulation might have been postponed indefinitely.

CHAPTER SEVEN

CONCLUSION

Economic Change and Work Safety
1870–1939

The desire of food is limited in every man by the narrow capacity of the human stomach;
but the desire of the conveniencies and ornaments of building, dress, equippage
and household furniture seems to have no limit.

The division of labor is limited by the extent of the market.
ADAM SMITH, *WEALTH OF NATIONS*, 1776

The coal industry . . . does not measure its saving of people in terms of fatal accidents [per
manhour] but in terms of the total human effort in . . . mining a million tons of coal. In the
U.S. we produce coal with the least loss of life of . . . any country in the world.
T. T. READ, BUREAU OF MINES, 1925

Previous chapters have traced the evolution of workplace safety in mining, manufacturing, and railroading down to World War II. Under the
sway of weak employers' liability laws, changes in technology, business
organization, and labor markets resulted in work that by the twentieth
century had become remarkably dangerous. After about 1910 these same
forces, now shaped by tighter liability and compensation laws, sharply
reduced the dangers of work in manufacturing and railroading and in
metal mining, if not coal mines. But for all workers in the economy,
changes in safety cannot be discovered by simply looking at the evolution of risk in each sector. The overall level of safety depends as well
on the distribution of workers among occupations and industries, and
it would be possible for each industry and occupation to show safety
gains and yet—if employment were to shift to high-risk activities—for
the overall injury rate to rise. This chapter discusses the impact of these
economywide changes in economic structure and again relates them to
the forces driving economic development. The last section of the chapter then draws some broad conclusions on the evolution of work safety
in America.

Economic Structure and Worker Safety

Post–Civil War economic development led to sharp changes, both in the industrial composition of employment and in the structure of occupations. Most Americans were once farmers; now most of us are white-collar workers. My great-grandfather was a farmer, then a factory worker, then an entrepreneur; my father was a factory worker, a storekeeper, and a car salesman; I am a teacher and writer. These changes can be understood, at least to a first approximation, in simple supply-and-demand terms. Suppose figure 7.1A represents the supply and demand for a product. Demand depends on population, income, the good's price, the price and availability of substitutes and complements, and individuals' tastes, while supply depends on costs of production and is assumed to be continuously expandable at the current price. The level of employment in this industry and its job composition depend on the level of output, on production technology, and on the relative costs of various grades of labor and other inputs.

Three aspects of economic development can cause output and/or employment to change. Income growth will cause output and employment in this industry to shrink relative to the rest of the economy if product demand grows more slowly than income (curve D' in fig. 7.1B). If demand grows more rapidly than income (D'' in fig. 7.1B), the reverse will occur. The development of new or better substitute products elsewhere, or a decline in their relative price, could also reduce the relative growth of output and employment in this industry. Finally, technological improvements within the industry's production processes that lower costs can shift the supply schedule down (fig. 7.1C). Output will then increase more (D_2) or less (D_1), depending upon the responsiveness of sales to price. The industry's share of employment could grow or shrink, depending upon how much output is increased and how much the improved technology saves labor per unit of output.[1]

The effects on overall risk of such employment shifts among industries can be estimated as follows. In any year the economywide injury rate is an average of the rates in each industry, with individual industry rates weighted by their shares in total manhours. Changes in the overall injury rate may therefore reflect changes in the distribution of work as well as intra-industry changes in risk. The effect of shifts in employment patterns can be isolated if industry-specific injury rates are arbitrarily held constant. When two periods are being considered, if either beginning- or end-period injury rates are employed, the change in the economywide injury rate will reflect only shifts in employment patterns. Unfortunately, injury rate data are not available for an early

FIGURE 7.1. Effects of Income and Productivity Changes on Industry Output

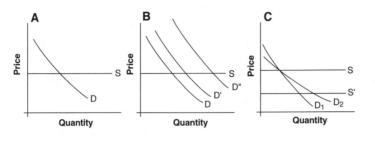

enough period to make full use of this approach. Hence, in the following, end-period injury rate data will be employed to investigate the impact on work safety of changes in the distribution of employment.

Obviously, industries can be defined more or less broadly, and so this approach can be employed to investigate the effect of changing employment patterns among manufacturing and other broad industrial groupings as well as shifts among individual manufacturing industries. Occupational changes can also be analyzed, and in fact, as was shown above, in both the steel industry and anthracite coal mining, late-nineteenth-century changes in the occupational mix probably worsened risks. By contrast, in the twentieth century the shift in employment from underground to surface work in both coal and metal mining improved safety.

SECTORAL SHIFTS IN EMPLOYMENT AND THE ECONOMYWIDE INJURY RATE, 1869–1948

At the broadest level, the economy can be divided into sectors or industry groups such as agriculture, construction, manufacturing, services, and so on. Table A3.6 presents sectoral shares of manhours from 1869 through 1937 and—since that latter date may unduly reflect the influence of the Depression—for 1948 also. As can be seen, the dominant changes were the decline of farming, from over 41 percent to less than 15 percent of total manhours, and the rise of employment in government, trade, and manufacturing. Mining first grew—its share of employment peaked around 1920—and then declined slightly. But for the expansion of petroleum and gas extraction it would have fallen even more sharply, as all the more traditional forms of mining were in full retreat after World War I. Finance, insurance, and real estate grew modestly, as did communications and public utilities.

The net impact of these employment shifts from 1869 to 1948, weighted by injury and fatality rates circa 1939, is presented in the bottom two rows of the table. These data represent what injury (death) rates would have been had 1939 risks obtained for each year. That is, injuries would have been about 31 percent higher in 1948 (14.27/10.93) and fatalities about 12 percent higher (0.182/0.162) had the 1869 pattern of employment obtained. A note of caution is in order, however, for somewhat different conclusions might result if injury rate data for 1869 or even 1899 were used. That is because manufacturing risks almost certainly declined more than risks in most sectors, at least after the mid-1920s, while agriculture may have become increasingly dangerous as it mechanized. If so, then use of end-period injury data will overstate the improvement in safety resulting from employment shifts. Still, while these results are anything but precise, they are surely accurate enough to support one important conclusion: economywide fatality rates began to decline in the early twentieth century, and injury rates somewhat later, as the tide of economic development shifted employment into relatively safer channels.

Changes in both demand and supply account for the important sectoral shifts that improved work safety over these years. Obviously, the dominant feature was the movement out of agriculture into less risky kinds of work such as trade and manufacturing. Typically, purchases of farm products are not very responsive to changes in income. As Adam Smith explained, and as innumerable budget studies have demonstrated, most of us obey what has come to be termed Engel's law—we reduce the share of our expenditure devoted to food as our income increases—and we purchase relatively more manufactured goods and services. Thus, nineteenth-century surveys typically revealed that urban households spent 40–50 percent of their income on food; by the 1960s this share had declined to about 25 percent. Such behavior ensured that demand for farm products grew more slowly than national income.[2]

In addition, while farm labor productivity grew slowly during the nineteenth century, it took off in the 1920s as a result of increasing mechanization and crop hybridization. Since demand for most agricultural products is not very price-sensitive, the fall in manhours per unit of output was not offset by increases in purchases, and so total manhours and employment fell even though technological change reduced costs and prices. The combined result of rising labor productivity and the slow growth of sales relative to income was that the share of agriculture in employment and manhours declined steadily while total farm employment and manhours peaked in the early 1920s and then began a long slide. In some cases the decline in farm work may have been a result of rising productivity and wages elsewhere. The (mostly post–World War II) decline in employment in cotton production may have been in considerable measure a response to the increasing attractiveness of manufacturing jobs. If so, cotton mechanization was largely a result of its diminishing labor supply.[3]

As noted above, the importance of this shift was probably magnified if, as seems likely, agriculture became increasingly dangerous as it mechanized. There are only a few glimpses of how machinery may have affected risks. The introduction of portable steam boilers to power threshers and other machinery after the Civil War added the risk of explosion to the others that farmers faced. But all forms of machinery, such as threshers, also took their toll. Floyd Clymer's father was a doctor in a small Colorado town early in the twentieth century. Clymer recalled that "at times it seemed to me that his largest practice came from the owners of threshing machines and the accidents they caused. . . . Many a trip I made with Dad to find a thresherman injured because his clothing had become caught in the belts or pulleys." Kansas data reveal that during the 1930s, about 30 percent of all farming deaths in that state resulted from use of machinery, and about 10 percent resulted from tractors alone.[4]

Still, if economic development had simply shifted workers out of farming and into construction or mining, it would have raised the overall dangers of work. But that, of course, did not happen. Instead it was trade, manufacturing, and a host of other comparatively safe activities that experienced relative growth. Trade employment grew as income rose because the increasing specialization in production required increasing exchange of commodities, and probably also because slow productivity growth in that sector led it to absorb manhours. The growth of manufacturing employment reflects the other side of Engel's law: rising incomes lead individuals to devote a larger share of their earnings to items other than food. In addition, the development and rapid cheapening of entirely new goods—processed food, ready-made clothing, sewing machines, refrigerators, radios, automobiles, and many others— also probably contributed to the relative growth of manufacturing. But manufacturing's share of employment increased less rapidly than its share of output because of wage-induced substitution of materials and capital for labor together with labor-saving technological changes.[5]

Because mining was so dangerous, the modest decline in its share of manhours merits some attention. As will be seen, stagnating demand for output—the result of increases in efficiency and the rise of substitutes—contributed to this decline. Probably technological improvements in mining did also. Demand for most minerals such as bituminous coal, copper, and iron is derived from the demand for the final products of which they usually comprise a small part. This fact implies that demand would be insensitive to price changes unless good substitutes for the mineral exist. Of course, if improvements in technology are relatively labor saving—as appendix 2 suggests was the case for coal—they are especially likely to reduce employment.

Copper production, employment, and productivity grew steadily until about World War I. Although output fluctuated wildly thereafter, it exhibited little growth in spite of the rapid increase in use of electrical equipment and the building boom of the 1920s. This retardation of demand growth reflected production efficiencies in copper use, along with the increasing substitution of scrap for new copper. In addition, exports declined as new sources of supply were discovered outside the United States. Productivity, however, continued to skyrocket after the war. Although a host of more or less important improvements contributed to the productivity gains, the "most important event in the history of copper mining" was the industry's shift to open-cut and block-caving methods of mining after about 1910. With output stagnant and productivity increasing rapidly, employment stopped growing, and in the 1920s it fell sharply.[6]

Iron mining exhibited an almost identical pattern. While output had grown rapidly during the nineteenth century, a slowing of the growth of the steel industry and declining ore use per ton of steel—a result of the shift to scrap induced by increased use of open-hearth steelmaking—resulted in stagnating production after about 1910. As in copper, productivity in iron mining grew sharply. After 1892, with the opening of the Mesabi range, iron mining became increasingly concentrated in large open-pit mines where labor productivity was more than double that in underground production. Moreover, as in copper, the relative advantage of open-cut mining increased in the 1920s and 1930s. Although these gains resulted partly from a host of minor improvements in drilling and blasting, the introduction and improvements in power-shovel loading were the most important source of productivity gains. Early shovels were steam-driven. They ran on railroad tracks, were nonrevolving, required a crew of as many as twelve men, took a bite of perhaps three cubic yards, and loaded about two thousand tons in a ten-hour day. By the 1930s, shovels were electric-powered, ran on caterpillar treads, had eight-yard buckets and three-man crews, and loaded one thousand tons an hour.[7]

As discussed earlier, the large-scale introduction of open-pit mining for copper and iron directly improved mine safety because it was much less dangerous than underground mining. But open-pit mining and other techniques that enhanced labor productivity reduced injuries in a less direct way also. Because they increased labor productivity so greatly, and because the demand for ore was probably not very price-sensitive, open-pit mining reduced the demand for labor. Miners' sons were forced to find work elsewhere. This was often a painful process, especially in the 1930s, and many were no doubt unemployed for long periods. But when they found work, it was likely to be less dangerous than that of their fathers.

The decline of both anthracite and bituminous coal mining also began in the 1920s. Until about 1923, output, employment, productivity, and manhours all grew steadily. Thereafter, output began a long slide, and with productivity growing modestly, employment and manhours declined. The major cause of declining manhours in coal was the fall in demand for the product, which resulted from efficiency gains in its use and interfuel competition with oil. Anthracite, which was largely used for home heating, steadily lost markets to oil throughout the 1920s. The decline in demand for bituminous coal was more complex. Again, the spread of substitute products played a role. Hydroelectricity, natural gas, and oil pushed coal out of a few markets, while the increasing use of gasoline-powered trucks and automobiles had a more indirect effect by reducing demand for railroad services.[8]

But improved efficiency in energy use was of far greater importance in curtailing markets for bituminous coal. F. G. Tryon of the Bureau of Mines thought that this was a lagged response to high prices. "The demand for coal is like a lump of tar in cold weather," he claimed. "It yields very little to sudden pressure, but if the pressure is long continued will flow out of shape and perhaps never return to its original position." Seen this way, the decline in energy use was a fortuitous by-product of war. This is unlikely, for the runup in energy prices during World War I was exceedingly brief. After 1920, coal prices sagged, yet conservation continued. A more plausible explanation links the rise in energy efficiency to improvements in the technology of the largest users that were largely independent of prices.[9]

Railroads had been the largest single user of bituminous coal, and they continued to account for 30 percent of all consumption as late as 1923. But coal use per ton-mile fell sharply between 1916 and 1930, by about 30 percent, and then much more slowly until 1939. Energy productivity in passenger haulage also increased sharply. These gains were not the result of shifts to diesel or electric power. They resulted instead from a host of improvements in motive power, operating practices, track, and signaling that were motivated by attempts to increase capacity, not save fuel. The shift to longer trains, for example, saved labor and—by reducing the need for double-tracking—capital as well as fuel. Locomotive size was constrained by clearances, and the use of higher steam pressures, superheaters, feedwater heaters, and other modifications represented efforts to raise power within such constraints. Fuel saving was simply a by-product of these improvements. As noted earlier, improvements in the reliability and efficiency of locomotives reduced their risks to trainmen; in a more indirect manner these improvements also reduced coal mine fatalities because they moved men out of the mines.

Similarly, technological progress at electric utilities, in the form of larger boilers, higher steam pressures, and better recovery of waste heat, cut coal use per kilowatt-hour in half between 1919 and 1930. The impact of such gains was magnified because centrally generated power increasingly ousted steam engines and locally generated power from the market. In steel production, coal use per ton of pig fell about 20 percent in the interwar years, while the shift from beehive to by-product coke production reduced coal use another 20 percent as a result of greater efficiency in the use of by-products. Cement production was another major user of coal that sharply reduced its consumption per ton and began to substitute natural gas for coal during these years.[10]

Labor-saving technological change in mining probably contributed to the reduction in coal manhours. In anthracite, output per manhour rose at about 1.5 percent per year over the entire period 1890-1938. It increased about 2.1 percent per year in the two decades after 1919 because of increased mechanization, and such gains contributed markedly to the decline in employment. In bituminous coal over the entire period, mechanization was even more important, for productivity increased 1.9 percent per year, although it grew more slowly, about 1.6 percent per year, after 1919. As T. T. Read of the Bureau of Mines claimed, even though coal mining was not especially successful in reducing injury rates per manhour, the industry's ability to increase productivity decreased the nationwide injury rate because it shifted manhours and men out of coal and into other work.[11]

EMPLOYMENT SHIFTS IN MANUFACTURING AND WORKER SAFETY, 1899–1948

Chapters 2 and 3 described the rise of the safety movement in manufacturing and presented data showing that after the mid-1920s, manufacturing work became increasingly less dangerous. While there is no doubt that safety work contributed to these gains, so did shifts in the industrial composition of manufacturing. Table A3.7 presents manhour shares of major manufacturing industries from 1899 to 1948. In addition, injury and severity rates—the latter because fatality rates are unavailable—for 1939 are also presented.

These industry shares for each year, when weighted by 1939 injury or severity rates, reveal what the manufacturing injury rate would have been with that year's employment distribution. For example, if the employment distribution had remained as it was in 1899, the manufacturing injury rate would have been about 21 percent higher than it was in 1948 [(18.2 − 15.1)/15.1], while the severity rate would have been increased by 31 percent [(2.04 − 1.56)/1.56]. As is evident, virtually all of the improvement in safety occurred from 1899 to 1929. This gain resulted from the growing share of employment in such relatively safe industries as electrical machinery, chemicals, transportation equipment, rubber, and nonelectrical machinery—all of which had come to be more or less dominated by large, safety-conscious firms. The safety improvement also reflects the decline in the most dangerous industry of all: logging and lumbering. This industry remained the province of the small firm. With an injury rate nearly as high as construction and a severity rate of about 6—four times the manufacturing average—lumbering and logging was, as one writer has put it with only modest hyperbole, "more deadly than war." The sharp decline in its share of employment therefore had a major impact on the average safety of manufacturing.[12]

The relative eclipse of lumbering reflected the decline of America's wooden age. A study conducted in the 1930s summarized matters thus: "The decline in the demand for lumber was the principal factor responsible for the decline in employment." Steel and concrete increasingly came to be the materials of choice. Ironically, at the very time that William Hard and others were excoriating the steel industry for its dangers, the gradual transformation of the economy from wood to metal was improving the safety of manufacturing work. This shift was partly a result of price and quality changes: during the nineteenth century the relative price of steel declined sharply, and between 1890 and 1929 wholesale metal prices exhibited almost no change. Steel quality and metalworking technology also improved. By contrast, in spite of continual improvements in logging and lumber techniques, depletion in timber supplies resulted in a nearly 150 percent increase in inflation-adjusted lumber prices between 1870 and 1929.[13]

In the face of these changes in price and quality, wood use retreated. Railroads and mines began timber preservation programs. Barbed wire replaced wooden fences, while wooden sidewalks gave way to concrete and brick. Boxes and barrels came to be made of cardboard and steel rather than wood, and steel largely drove wood out of the production of ships, railroad cars, and automobiles. In addition, some major timber users such as railroads, mines, and agriculture themselves declined or at least began to grow more slowly. Urbanization also played a major role in the decline of wood, because multiple-family urban dwellings used less wood per family than had their rural counterparts.[14]

At the same time that lumbering's share of employment was falling, the share of employment in such increasingly safe industries as machinery and transportation equipment was expanding. Here the main force was probably income-responsiveness. The demand for new electric consumer durables such as washing machines, refrigerators, radios, vacuum cleaners, and so on grew disproportionately as individual incomes rose, and modern studies suggest that the demand for automobiles is income-responsive as well. Thus, the long-term rise in incomes and the other complex changes that led to a shift in employment from lumbering to the production of machinery and automobiles made Americans' work lives safer. Of course, one result has been that more of us now become highway statistics.[15]

OCCUPATIONAL SHIFTS, 1869–1940

The economywide injury rate changed not only because the industrial composition of the labor force evolved but also because of changes in the occupational mix. In part these amount to the same thing—farming is both an industry and an occupation—but the overlap is by no means complete. The occupational structure also evolved and became increasingly specialized within industrial groupings. Occupational changes were partly a reflection of improvements in science and technology that created entirely new occupations and diminished the significance of others (typist and chemical engineer on the one hand, hostler on the other). They were also simply an outcome of an expanding economy, for as Adam Smith instructed, the division of labor is limited by the extent of the market. More specifically, development changed the nature of both firms and their employment, for with larger markets, economies of scale (ignored in fig. 7.1) yielded larger companies—which typically had increasingly specialized employment patterns—and it yielded specialized firms as well. As a result, the occupational mix has changed dramatically during the past century.

Since reported injury and fatality rates for industries usually include all occupations, job changes account for some of the observed changes in industry injury rates (as was pointed out in the discussion of mining in chaps. 2 and 6). Still, it is instructive to view such employment shifts for the economy as a whole. The distribution of nonfarm employment—assumed here to reflect the distribution of manhours—among broad occupational groups for all workers and for women is presented in table A3.8. The estimated injury and fatality rates for each occupational class for 1940 are also presented.

For all workers the central change was clearly the shift from service to manual and especially clerical and sales work. These broad shifts in the patterns of work reflect deep-seated changes in the structure of the economy. The decline in the share of service jobs and the growth of manual occupations between 1870 and 1900 resulted primarily from an increase in the relative productivity—and therefore wages—of goods production as the increasing payoff to manual labor reduced the attractiveness, and therefore the supply, of domestic labor. In addition, the service sector itself evolved as commercial laundries and bakeries developed substitutes for live-in cooks and maids.[16]

Of greater importance, especially in the twentieth century, was the rise in professional, technical, and managerial jobs and the growth of clerical and sales occupations. The rapid increase in sales occupations reflected the growth in specialization and trade discussed above, while the increase in clerical work and professional, technical, and managerial occupations reflected in part the growth of very large firms. In addition, new technologies such as the typewriter and various duplicating machines raised the productivity and lowered the cost of office work, which could have increased the demand for office workers.[17]

Chapter 1 described the efforts of the Boston and Albany Railroad to cope with the unprecedented safety and related problems of running a large railroad by instituting managerial innovations. As other carriers followed this lead, their activities created large numbers of middle managers—trainmasters, superintendents of motive power and maintenance of way, freight claim agents, general claim agents, and so on—and they created telegraphers, bookkeepers, clerks, and similar office workers whose job it was to record and speed the flow of information needed to run the organization. The share of managerial occupations rose from about one-quarter of all railroad employment in 1890 to almost one-third in 1900. None of these jobs, needless to say, was likely to be as dangerous as running a train.

In the late nineteenth century, as large firms evolved in manufacturing and distribution, this sort of specialization was replicated on a grand scale. Here too size required the creation of administrative hierarchies that included not only operating managers but also numerous staff positions in law, accounting, finance, and elsewhere, while some companies such as Singer, John Deere, and International Harvester set up their own sales departments. In addition, each office required the usual host of lower-level employees to move all the paper that was being created. These changes in occupations were reinforced by improvements that raised the payoff to specialized scientific and technical education. In 1875 the Pennsylvania Railroad hired chemist Charles B. Dudley and set up the first corporate testing laboratory. Other railroads followed this lead, and steel companies, electrical equipment manufacturers, and other large firms also began to hire chemists, mechanical and electrical engineers, and a host of similar professionals.[18]

At the same time that individual companies were creating administrative structures staffed by salaried white-collar workers, other firms providing specialized business services also expanded rapidly. These included, for example, investment bankers, consulting engineers, and insurance companies such as Hartford Steam Boiler. Together these changes account for much of the growth in low-risk managerial and white-collar work, and as a result, the ratio of salaried employees to wage earners in manufacturing grew steadily, from about 8 percent in 1899 to 13 percent in 1939.[19]

In fact, occupational shifts had partly offsetting effects on worker safety. Service work was reasonably safe compared with manual labor, and so the relative growth in the number of craftsmen, operatives, and laborers raised average injury rates up to about 1900. Clerical and sales jobs, by contrast, were even safer than service occupations, and so the net impact of occupational changes for all workers was quite modest during the nineteenth century. After 1900, however, the growth of clerical and sales and of professional, technical, and managerial work predominated, thereby modestly reducing injury rates.

Table A3.8 also presents estimates of the effects of employment shifts on work safety for women workers, assuming provisionally that men and women in the same occupation had the same injury rate. Because women were overrepresented in the relatively safe service jobs in each period, their average injury rate was sharply lower than that of the labor force as a whole. As can be seen, the movement of women from services into manual labor may have raised their injury rates modestly and their fatality rates sharply during the late nineteenth century. In addition, the evolution of women's service work from domestic to commercial (e.g., laundries) probably raised their risks, and so the initial increase depicted in the table probably overstates the effect of occupational shifts. After 1900, however, the more rapid movement of women than men into white-collar work reduced their injury and fatality rates even more sharply.

In fact, use of average occupational injury rates for all workers probably overstates the rate for women, because they were also concentrated in relatively safe suboccupations. Between 1916 and 1930, Pennsylvania collected employment separately by sex for both wage and salary workers in manufacturing, and it collected injury data for manufacturing by sex (but not by type of job). Statistical analysis of these data (see note) indicates that even when controlling for the distribution of men and women between wage and salaried work, women had relatively low injury rates, probably because they held the safer jobs when doing wage labor. In fact, in this sample, their injury rate was about 85 percent less than that of men. Occupational and industrial segregation, it seems, did not entirely lack compensations.[20]

The Evolution of Job Safety

As the above analysis makes clear, economic development has resulted in the long-term evolution of employment from farming and mining to manufacturing and trade, from wood- to metalworking, and from manual labor to white-collar work. Such shifts probably improved work safety for much of the twentieth century. Of course, there have been crosscurrents. Mining employment rose in the late nineteenth century, and after 1920 the shift from railroads to trucking worsened risks. But gradually, what might be called the invisible hand of economic development has been increasing the safety of work. Of course, job safety also depends on intra-industry and occupational changes, and here, as has been shown in previous chapters, change was more complex. In some areas the dangers of work clearly rose after the Civil War. In the twentieth century, however, the invisible hand of economic development has been reinforced by the more visible effects of the work safety movement.

THE CHANGING SAFETY OF THE AMERICAN SYSTEM OF PRODUCTION

By World War II, concern with work safety had become institutionalized in many large firms. As economic activity picked up in 1940 and 1941, and as hiring and labor turnover increased, so did work injuries in many sectors of the economy. After Pearl Harbor, all-out mobilization enormously increased the pressure. Not only did the number of new hires skyrocket, but the workweek was also extended, and the military depleted the supply of experienced workers, including key supervisors. But the safety movement was also mobilized, and the striking conclusion that emerges from these years is the modest impact that war had on work safety. Although the railroads experienced an enormous traffic boom that caused their injury rate to jump sharply, the fatality rate increased by only about one-quarter. Similar events characterized copper mining, while in iron mining, fatality rates remained virtually unchanged.

At Union Pacific Coal the fatality rates fell steadily throughout the war, although labor turnover doubled to about 200 percent per year, and for the industry as a whole the fatality rate declined mildly—in part because technological change continued to shift employment to the surface. In manufacturing, although the rate for temporary injuries climbed, the frequency of death and permanent injuries declined steadily after 1941.[21]

When war began, private safety organizations, working in large measure through the National Safety Council, helped staff and support the various federal agencies concerned with work safety. The council supported safety work in ship construction by the Maritime Commission, and the National Committee for the Conservation of Manpower in War Industries also drew on the council's expertise to help stimulate companies' interest in work safety. As discussed above, manufacturing fatality rates in 1944 were half what they had been in 1926, controlling for labor turnover. Between 1941 and 1945 there were 13,600 men and women killed on the job and 171,100 permanently injured. But for the impact of organized safety work, there might have been twice this many.[22]

That injury and fatality rates rose so little in spite of the enormous pressures generated by the wartime labor market reveals the extent to which work safety had become institutionalized in a little over three decades. Only a generation earlier, the parents of the wartime workers had entered workplaces that nineteenth-century economic development had made extraordinary dangerous, and many American industries had become far more risky than their European counterparts. Both the dangers of the late-nineteenth-century American workplace and the safety revolution that occurred during the first half of the twentieth century reflected the interplay of technology, labor markets, business organization, and public policy.

The growing dangers of work in industrializing America resulted from the post–Civil War spread of what contemporaries and modern historians have termed the American system of production. Although historians have focused on the uniquely American characteristics of manufacturing, there was also an American system of railroading and mining. What made these production methods distinctively American was their adaptation to the American conditions of labor and capital scarcity and resource abundance. While most writers have stressed the mechanization, the drive for interchangeable parts, and the high productivity that resulted, it is clear that high risk was also integral to these production methods.[23]

From before the Civil War until well into the twentieth century, American and British railroads evolved along sharply divergent paths. The distinctive characteristics of American carriers—their emphasis on freight and their flimsy construction, single tracking, long trains, heavy equipment, link-and-pin couplers, and lack of block signals—were all adaptations to the low population density, thin traffic, great distances, and capital and labor scarcity that characterized this country. These same characteristics increased the dangers of American railroading. Combined with a geographically expanding market for railroad labor, high labor turnover, and minimal firm-specific experience, they resulted in worker risks that far exceeded those on British carriers.

The dangers of work were rising in other sectors of the economy as well. In coal mining, fatality rates rose steadily after 1880, and by 1900 the dangers of American mining far exceeded those in any other advanced nation. These high risks resulted in part from the fact that abundant coal supplies and high labor costs in the United States made room-and-pillar mining techniques economical, while in Europe natural resource conditions dictated the use of longwall methods, which economized on lives as well as coal. In addition, the risks of American mining rose because of the influx of unskilled, non-English-speaking labor, and because of the increase in mine size and depth and the growing use of explosives and power machinery.

In iron and steel, the growing scale of production and the shift to Bessemer steel, as well as other changes in technology and labor organization, eroded the safety of work. Elsewhere in manufacturing, factory size and the use of power also increased. Use of specialized machinery grew rapidly, and employers gained increasing power over production. Indirect evidence and the claims of contemporaries suggest that these forces may have eroded work safety throughout manufacturing and that American factories may have been more dangerous than their European counterparts.

If safety deteriorated in important sectors of the economy, this was the outcome of two related aspects of early technological change. First, the new production methods were usually introduced either to expand output or cut costs, or both, and largely without reference to their impact on work safety. For example, increases in blast furnace size raised output and lowered costs—and worsened worker risks. Although employers were sometimes forced to pay a wage premium to compensate employees for risky work, or to accept poorer-quality help or higher labor turnover—any of which might have encouraged safety concerns—there is very little evidence that companies were able to discern and respond to these accident costs in the fog of factors that governed labor markets. In addition, the courts were fashioning employers' liability laws that placed much of the responsibility for safety on the worker.

Under such conditions, managers usually behaved as if the impact of new techniques on the cost of work accidents could be ignored. So milling machines were introduced without guards, blast furnaces grew in size, and saw fences were developed without reference to kickback. In laundries, power irons speeded up operations, although they sometimes quite literally mangled the women who worked them. Electrical mining machinery reduced costs even though it was installed with almost total disregard for safety.

Second, when new techniques were introduced, their risks were sometimes recognized, and then sometimes modified, only through a process of "learning by using." Early airplanes had one decisive advantage—speed—but they were remarkably risky. Their development resulted from much experimentation, which was also extremely dangerous. Gradually these risks came to be understood and reduced, but for a very long time air flight remained a highly dangerous business. Something like this may have characterized the introduction of much nineteenth-century technology. Thus, high-pressure steam boilers were developed and widely used at a time when neither the properties of steam nor those of iron were well understood, and the process of learning about design, operation, and maintenance was marked by many explosions and many casualties.[24]

Learning about risk may also have been retarded by the modest size of most early businesses, for injuries were rare even in highly hazardous situations. As the scale of production increased, dangers became clearer. The publication of injury data by states also helped reveal risks, for even the hazards of the link-and-pin coupler were not fully recognized until states began to report them, and probably the same was true for mangles and joiners and all the other new machines that were transforming the worker's world.

Hence, the late-nineteenth-century workplace became increasingly risky because employers had little incentive to learn about and reduce risks, and because learning was both difficult and time-consuming. Efforts to humanize this new industrial order began early, and again much learning and trial and error was required. Early railroads instituted management innovations in an effort to reduce the risks of collisions, and state railroad commissions were making modest efforts to protect workers well before the Civil War. While automatic couplers and air brakes were the most important of early railroad safety equipment, their diffusion was far more complex than has been appreciated. There is no evidence that the carriers were unusually slow in adopting these safety appliances, and their diffusion was probably not appreciably speeded up by the Safety Appliance Act of 1893. Nor are either couplers or air brakes usefully seen as a Schumpeterian Great Innovation that immediately and dramatically improved safety. Instead, literary and statistical evidence suggests that air brakes worsened some risks—to the great surprise of their advocates. And as with other new technologies, the full effectiveness of both air brakes and automatic couplers was felt only after a long learning period that involved modifications in the technologies and in training, maintenance, and a host of rules governing everything from work practices to freight car interchange.

Elsewhere after the Civil War, a few states began to inspect and regulate mines and factories and to publish statistics. But in the twentieth century it was the increasing political threats to large corporations, along with the spread of compensation legislation, that finally stimulated employer interest in job safety. While the historical evidence that compensation laws helped generate the modern safety movement is clear-cut, most econometric analysis (including that presented in appendix 3) finds little or no impact of workmen's compensation laws on safety. Such disparate findings underline the need to supplement statistical studies with historical analysis. There are several reasons for this apparent conflict. First, the econometric literature compares interstate differences in programs, whereas the historical evidence pertains to the substitution of compensation for employers' liability. Second, compensation had its greatest effect on large companies. These were increasingly becoming multiple-plant operations, and they did not tailor their safety programs to the cut of individual state laws. DuPont, for example, did not have more lax standards for plants in Delaware than for those in Pennsylvania, even though the former state provided lower compensation benefits for fatalities. Finally, compensation induced modifications in machine and factory design that affected all users in all states.[25]

The old fault-based regime of employers' liability had compensated few injuries. Hence, it reduced managers' interest in learning about safety and encouraged the view that accidents were the fault of employees. In contrast, workmen's compensation, or the new employers' liability law on railroads, shifted more of the cost of accidents to employers, thereby raising the payoff to company safety work. As a result, employers now tried to learn how to prevent accidents, and safety workers began to stress that injuries were the fault of managers, not workers.

While workmen's compensation acts helped bring forth the modern safety movement, the effectiveness of safety work resulted from its institutionalization within the management structure of large firms. In the early twentieth century the largest coal mines and steel mills were the most dangerous, but by the 1930s matters had reversed. Larger, newer mines and factories were now usually safer, for many large companies had formed safety departments and hired safety professionals, many of whom were engineers. These men and a very few women were the backbone of the safety movement. For them, safety was a profession, not simply a means to achieve lower costs. But the need to justify their existence led company safety departments to lobby for continued reductions in accidents. To bolster their case, safety workers spoke the language of business and stressed that accident reduction achieved far more than simply a saving in compensation costs. Safety paid because it resulted in higher productivity, better worker morale, lower turnover, and a better public image. In economic terms, safety was one of the sources of "efficiency jobs"—that is, combinations of pay and job characteristics that were better than the market required.[26]

While the initial impulse toward safer production came from managers, the success of company safety work required worker commitment as well. Yet compensation legislation contained no incentives for workers to change their customs, and many were suspicious of new programs that they understood were designed to save employers money. As a result, companies had to bargain for worker commitment, and so early safety work had a "soft" side. In part this was because it was reactive—that is, it was a response to existing dangers, and workers were the best source of information about job hazards. As David Montgomery has put it, the "manager's brains" were still "under the workman's cap." Companies responded with safety committees that provided workers a limited collective voice in the redesign of work, and they experimented with a number of other strategies designed to encourage worker enthusiasm for safety.[27]

The need to demonstrate good faith ensured that successful safety work almost invariably began with a company "gift" that included highly visible machine guarding and other potentially expensive modifications to plant and equipment. In Europe, where laws on machine guarding were relatively strict, this remained the focus of safety work. American employers, by contrast, thought of machine safety as partly a way to induce stubborn employees to adopt safer work habits, and early American safety work emphasized worker committees, educational campaigns, and prizes and bonuses for safe work. These were an alternative to supervision and discipline and were especially prevalent at firms where supervision was difficult or expensive.

Safety work also induced technological change. Within companies, safety gains resulted from continuous learning that led to innovations in equipment and work practices. Often the new techniques were not merely safer but were superior along other dimensions as well. The roundheaded joiner was less lethal than the older square-headed model and yielded better-quality work as well. Guards on metal-stamping machines speeded up production as workers discovered that they no longer needed to trade income for safety. When steel companies redesigned crane buckets to eliminate the need for coal handlers, they discovered that cranemen with no need to worry about the safety of other workers could also work faster. As a result of such activities, serious safety programs tended to generate continued reductions in accidents long after they were set up. In addition, safety programs both directed and speeded up the learning process when new technologies were employed. For example, in the 1920s, when materials handling was automated in manufacturing and new machinery was employed on railroad maintenance of way, risks were reduced rather than increased.

While early safety work had been reactive and "soft" and had emphasized the role of workers, by the 1930s safety engineers and other professionals had seized the throttle. This was the "hard" side of the movement, for safety work now became more proactive, and it involved worker selection and training, job evaluation, and hazard assessment, as well as what Lucian Chaney had meant by "engineering revision," including factory layout and machine and process design. Hazards might now be discovered and controlled before they killed someone, but the role of the worker was now to follow orders.[28]

These developments were part of a broader process in which corporate managers were modifying organizational structures to control the large firm. Alfred Chandler has documented managers' efforts to control the flow of production and sales, while other writers have stressed that modern management extended to the details of production and labor relations as well. Companies began to take command of the shop floor, and they created bureaucracies to deal with personnel management. Historians have disagreed on how to weigh the effects of these changes on workers' lives. Some have stressed the loss of workers' control, while others have emphasized that employees gained fairer, more predictable jobs as a result. The safety movement was part of this process: work safety came at a price, and part of the bill was that workers lost control over work practices that had once been theirs to define.[29]

Workers' responses to these changes were as varied as the safety movement itself. Henry Clay French noted approvingly that railroaders were now graded on how safe they were, and a trainman on the Lake Shore termed the safety movement "a mighty good thing." The miner Frank Fugate thought the introduction of safety work was "a great help." At companies where workers were convinced that the employer was serious about accident reduction, workmen's committees and safety campaigns usually generated enthusiastic responses, for they involved workers in a serious way in shaping their own work. But where the safety program existed on paper only, it engendered cynicism, not enthusiasm. The union locals at Union Pacific Coal abandoned the company's early safety committees because they thought the program was a sham, and another company safety committee described a program that refused to spend money to clean up conditions as "all bluff." D. L. Cease characterized many early railroad safety programs as "a way of throwing dust over the accident record."[30]

In serious safety programs, new rules and personal protective equipment were often unpopular, especially when imposed from above. They were an assault on traditional, sometimes masculine, ways, and they were sometimes unpleasant and expensive. The result was a host of minor rebellions: women refused to wear caps, foundrymen refused to wear leggings, miners walked out when blasting was regulated, or they burned their hard hats. On the eve of World War II, as unions became established, they sometimes provided workers a collective voice that eased them into the new ways of work, but personal protective equipment remains unpopular to this day.

The safety movement also led to institutional innovations outside the firm that resulted in what I have dubbed the safety market. Equipment suppliers sprang up, and trade associations in paper production, metalworking, and many other areas began to support and publicize safety work. Sometimes, as with the Portland Cement Association, effective trade association work seems to have been an important catalyst that helped achieve sharp safety gains. Similar activities were begun by insurance companies and by some states. Safety engineers developed their own journals and professional society, and they worked to modify the agenda of other engineering societies and to incorporate safety into the college engineering curriculum. Of all such innovations, the most important was the establishment of the National Safety Council, which linked together other participants in the safety market. These groups developed safer production techniques and disseminated their findings through meetings, publications, voluntary safety standards, and state codes. Such actions reduced the cost and difficulty that firms experienced in learning about safety, thereby hastening its spread.

At some companies and in some industries the safety movement contributed to sharp reductions in worker injury and fatality rates. Safety First took hold on steam railroads around 1912. Its impact was reinforced by a host of safer technologies, and by pronounced changes in the railroad labor market as turnover declined and companies instituted new personnel policies. The combined result was a roughly 80 percent decline in the fatality rate between 1891 and 1939. At about the same time, safety work also blossomed at the handful of large firms that dominated metal mining. Along with some technological changes that reduced risks—such as the shift to strip mining—safety work sharply reduced dangers here too. Large utilities and even a few construction companies also began to reduce injuries. In manufacturing, large companies in such industries as steel, cement, metalworking, chemicals, paper, and food processing undertook increasingly effective safety work. Along with the decline in labor turnover after World War I, and the introduction of such new technologies as mechanized materials handling and electrification, safety work began to reduce manufacturing injury rates from the mid-1920s on.

Yet the spread of organized safety work was highly uneven. Many safety programs, even at large operators, were ineffective. Sometimes top management was indifferent, but often it was ineffective. The literature is full of managerial hand-wringing over the difficulties of reducing accidents. Probably this resulted from a failure to "buy" worker commitment and from incentives for midlevel managers that continued to emphasize production over safety. Yet if safety was unevenly pursued at large companies, at small firms the problems were usually worse. While the higher risks at such companies resulted in part from the comparative absence of safety incentives under workmen's compensation, these dangers also reflected small firms' lack of specialization. Small producers lacked safety departments. And since smaller firms had fewer manhours of experience, accidents were a poorer guide to hazards than at larger companies. Small companies also used more general-purpose tools that were harder to guard, or older equipment that lacked modern safety features.[31]

Nor did coal mine safety improve very much in the interwar years. The ongoing shift of mining to western states raised risks, as did the continuous increase in mine depth and size. In addition, electric-powered machinery—which was reducing risks in manufacturing as it replaced shafting and belting—probably worsened the dangers of coal mining, where it substituted for the pick and the mule. The difference was partly a matter of costs; for example, the mine environment was much more difficult to control, while factory electrification did not usually need to be made spark-free. In addition, mine electrification usually occurred in the absence of strong safety organizations.

Some large coal mines did develop effective safety programs that required careful use of the new electrical machinery, and that cut work accidents sharply, but these were the exception. Systematic safety was expensive in mining, for it required costly changes in equipment and layout as well as close supervision, and in small mines workmen's compensation provided little incentive to improve safety records. In addition, coal was also a tradition-bound industry, and long after such ideas had disappeared from manufacturing, managers continued to think of miners as independent contractors largely responsible for their own safety. Although here as elsewhere, safety workers labored to cultivate the creed of management responsibility, in such poor soil it mostly failed to take root.

THE POLITICAL ECONOMY OF WORKER SAFETY

In 1943 Max Kossoris of the Bureau of Labor Statistics told the National Safety Council, "You have by no means licked your problem. Your efforts must be increased." Kossoris was referring to the war-induced rise in some injury rates, and also to the fact that safety work had failed to permeate all sectors of the economy. Still, work was far less risky than it had been a generation earlier, in part because of the efforts of the men and women whom Kossoris challenged. But if the safety movement was in large measure an outcome of changes in corporate management, work safety had always been shaped by public policy, and Kossoris was by no means the first public servant to urge safety workers to increase their efforts.[32]

Even as nineteenth-century American economic development was worsening risks, under the pressure of unions and middle-class reformers states and the federal government were also developing innovative policies to ameliorate the dangers of work. Three different policy styles emerged: regulation, voluntarism, and use of economic incentives. The impact of these policies depended upon the economic context in which they were employed, and on the particular policy mix, for these approaches were not nearly as distinct as such a listing suggests. For example, compensation laws used schedule rating to provide an economic incentive for specific safety actions, and the Bureau of Mines, although devoted to the voluntaristic approach, campaigned to improve state laws and to get its recommendations adopted in schedule ratings. State railroad, labor, and mining commissions were all examples of the regulatory approach, as was the Interstate Commerce Commission. Yet each group at one time or another publicized accidents, sometimes hectored companies, described safety devices, publicly praised firms with above-average records, and campaigned for better laws.

Both Charles Francis Adams and the *Railroad Gazette* thought that voluntarism could be far more effective than regulation. While this claim may be exaggerated, the ability to legislate safety nearly always proved more difficult than reformers imagined it would be. Regulatory agencies sometimes focused too narrowly on dramatic, politically sensitive risks while ignoring less visible but more serious dangers. And perhaps because regulators usually had no way to encourage managerial interest in safety, they were often enamored with the idea that safety could be improved by a specific technological fix. Both points are illustrated by the experience of the ICC with automatic train control.

Paradoxically, then, the threat of regulation could be more effective than regulation itself. Even the Safety Appliance Act of 1893 had an indirect as well as a direct effect on railroad safety. To reformers and to the ICC it became the Great Example that justified further safety legislation such as automatic train control and laws regulating hours of service, boiler inspection, train length, clearance, and crew size. The laws that were passed had little effect, but the railroad safety movement was a coordinated response to the threat posed by such expensive, intrusive laws. Its effectiveness helped persuade the ICC to abandon its high-cost, low-payoff experiment with automatic train control. U.S. Steel's early commitment to work safety was also intended to buy better public relations. Probably that consideration also figured in the calculations of other steel producers after 1913, when the Bureau of Labor Statistics published its study of safety conditions in the industry. These companies faced political threats that were clearly credible and that were reinforced by compensation laws or, in the case of railroads, by stricter employers' liability that raised the cost of injuries.[33]

But voluntarism also had limitations, as the efforts of the Bureau of Mines reveal. The bureau was premised on the notion that business-government cooperation—as opposed to government coercion—was the best way to hew the rough edges off private enterprise. The bureau's scientific work yielded important improvements in the technology of mine safety. Yet it focused far too narrowly on the politically popular and scientifically interesting problem of preventing mine explosions. The bureau's efforts also demonstrate that voluntarism was likely to be most effective when backed by economic incentives or the threat of regulation, for its attempts to spread safety technology were retarded by its inability to publicize bad practice and by the weakness of compensation incentives.[34]

Voluntarism was most effective when applied to large firms with strong trade associations. Such companies often had both the need for favorable publicity and an institutionalized safety-consciousness, while experience rating ensured them an economic payoff from accident prevention. Trade associations provided both information and peer pressure, for each company's safety work generated external political benefits: every firm in an industry gained when one of them reduced injuries. An industry with relatively few firms and a strong trade association could form a safety cartel—as in railroads, steel, or metal mining—and significantly reduce injuries in a whole sector of the economy.[35]

Such conclusions provide an interesting perspective on deeply held American beliefs that competition and small business are the foundations of economic virtue. In the Progressive demonology, no businesses stood more condemned than the railroads and U.S. Steel. U.S. Steel was the largest firm of its day and the center of a more or less formal steel cartel. And as a bastion of antiunion sentiment, it was the symbol to critics of all that had gone sour with the American capitalism. Yet U.S. Steel was also the center of the safety movement that included such giant railroads as the Pennsylvania and the Union Pacific, the dominant firms in metal mining including Phelps Dodge and Anaconda, and such manufacturing "trusts" as DuPont, International Harvester, General Electric, and Kodak. Like the steel corporation, many of these firms developed an enduring commitment to work safety, and their factories and mines led the way in reducing accidents. Had the antitrusters been more successful in their efforts to dissolve these giants, work safety would probably have suffered.[36]

The history of occupational safety also provides a cautionary tale for anyone wishing to make easy generalizations about the relationship between economic development and worker safety. Conservative publicists are fond of discussing economic progress, and some writers have claimed that richer is safer. It does seem that twentieth-century structural changes in the economy have gradually shifted workers out of the dangerous trades. Yet nineteenth-century economic development also increased worker risks in some individual sectors of the economy. And in the twentieth century, when riches have yielded safer work, the gains have resulted not only from the normal workings of the market but also from the visible hands of private managers influenced by public policies.

If the claim that richer is safer needs to be qualified, the alternative vision that "nature knows best" is even less accurate. As the twentieth century comes to an end, many Americans seem obsessed with the dangers of new technologies. But the shift of employment to man-made work sites in manufacturing, services, and trade, and away from hard-to-control "natural" work sites in mining, logging, and farming, combined with the invention of the safety movement, has made our work lives far less dangerous than those of men and women who labored only three generations ago.[37]

Steam Railroad Injury
and Fatality Rates
1880–1939

This appendix contains two sorts of materials. The first are tables that contain Interstate Commerce Commission data on injuries and fatalities, along with a discussion of the limitations of these data, and tables that present injuries and fatalities on a manhour basis or that correct for undercounting. The second are tables containing the analyses referred to in chapters 1 and 5.

Railroad Accident Data

The ICC first requested accident data in companies' annual reports to it in fiscal 1888 (July to July), and the information was presented in *Statistics of Railways* from that date until 1909. Beginning in 1890 these data were also broken down by region of the country. The commission presented its accident data in a variety of ways: sometimes the figures included employees who were off duty as well as those at work, sometimes not. Similarly, casualties to switching and terminal roads were not always treated consistently. Since the only data that extend into the nineteenth century include accidents to (most) off-duty employees, I have employed them. These off-duty personnel consisted mostly of men who were traveling to and from work, and in the 1920s they amounted to 3–5 percent of reported fatalities, so their inclusion makes little difference. These data cover fatalities on all carriers except for the years 1908–10, which exclude switching and terminal roads.

The ICC's employment statistics exclude switching and terminal roads from 1908 on. I have added Harold Barger's estimates of employment on switching and terminal roads from 1921 on and have used the 1921 ratio to interpolate for 1911–20 — but not for 1908–10 — to make them comparable with the injury data. These employment and fatality figures, for 1889 through 1939, are contained in columns 1 and 2 of table A1.1. The revised employment data are also used to construct the injury and fatality rates for all workers by cause in table A1.5. The injury and fatality rates for trainmen are based on unrevised ICC data.[1]

Until 1901 all injury data were reported to the ICC in the carriers' annual reports and appeared in *Statistics of Railways*. The Accident Reports Act of 1901

TABLE A1.1. Railroad Employee Injury and Fatality Rates, All Employees and Trainmen, 1880–1939

| | Per Thousand Employees | | | | Per Million Manhours, All Employees | |
| | All Employees | | Trainmen | | | |
	Fatality Rate	Injury Rate	Fatality Rate	Injury Rate	Fatality Rate	Injury Rate
1880	2.20	8.60	—	—	—	—
1889	2.67	27.10	8.52	81.70	0.91	9.20
1890	3.27	29.90	9.52	85.91	1.04	9.48
1891	3.39	33.34	9.57	96.30	1.07	10.55
1892	3.11	34.43	8.88	91.00	0.97	10.76
1893	3.12	36.30	8.72	105.08	1.03	12.01
1894	2.34	30.03	8.26	105.18	0.73	9.44
1895	2.31	32.78	6.45	93.50	0.75	10.67
1896	2.25	36.24	6.59	97.84	0.75	12.12
1897	2.06	33.62	6.05	85.47	0.67	10.94
1898	2.24	36.30	6.68	91.65	0.74	11.96
1899	2.38	37.67	6.46	92.98	0.77	12.14
1900	2.21	38.94	7.30	91.90	0.72	12.65
1901	2.50	38.41	7.35	79.96	0.79	12.18
1902	2.49	42.49	7.42	95.26	0.80	13.58
1903	2.75	46.06	8.09	100.37	0.98	16.26
1904	2.80	51.75	8.96	124.13	0.91	16.75
1905	2.43	48.36	8.10	121.53	0.82	16.28
1906	2.58	50.43	9.20	129.34	0.82	16.04
1907	2.71	52.42	7.98	128.24	0.92	17.77
1908	2.37	57.44	6.78	131.80	0.75	18.09
1909	1.74	49.90	4.87	105.58	0.57	16.28
1910	1.99	56.31	5.41	111.11	0.68	19.13
1911	2.09	72.98	5.16	124.26	0.69	24.09
1912	2.04	80.25	4.81	124.45	0.67	26.35
1913	1.98	91.28	4.63	142.86	0.67	30.87
1914	1.84	93.39	4.63	142.86	0.62	31.64
1915	1.34	86.20	3.15	125.00	0.44	28.62
1916	1.53	91.29	4.14	146.81	0.51	30.54
1917	1.73	94.29	4.30	137.80	0.58	31.60
1918	1.75	79.72	4.39	119.04	0.59	27.02
1919	1.05	64.63	3.02	99.44	0.42	25.77
1920	1.20	69.56	3.60	122.11	0.47	27.06
1921	0.82	59.26	2.15	86.47	0.36	25.71
1922	0.94	66.44	2.27	94.53	0.39	27.63

| | Per Thousand Employees | | | | Per Million Manhours, All Employees | |
| | All Employees | | Trainmen | | | |
	Fatality Rate	Injury Rate	Fatality Rate	Injury Rate	Fatality Rate	Injury Rate
1923	1.03	77.94	2.61	102.92	0.42	31.43
1924	0.83	67.63	1.99	88.49	0.34	28.02
1925	0.87	64.59	2.14	87.67	0.36	26.80
1926	0.89	59.40	2.08	89.99	0.37	24.55
1927	0.86	48.05	1.98	75.89	0.34	19.15
1928	0.76	40.50	1.61	67.38	0.32	16.91
1929	0.81	34.65	1.88	60.80	0.34	14.38
1930	0.62	22.82	1.49	41.49	0.27	9.85
1931	0.51	17.55	1.20	33.87	0.23	7.97
1932	0.53	16.26	1.31	31.19	0.25	7.76
1933	0.52	15.48	1.26	27.14	0.25	7.41
1934	0.52	16.26	1.21	27.19	0.24	7.53
1935	0.57	15.90	1.29	27.03	0.26	7.28
1936	0.64	19.87	1.53	32.77	0.28	8.67
1937	0.60	20.38	1.44	31.78	0.26	8.88
1938	0.51	16.60	1.21	25.96	0.23	7.35
1939	0.51	16.57	1.13	26.98	0.22	7.21

Source: The 1880 data are from *Tenth Census of the United States, 1880: Transportation.* For 1889 on, see text. Total employment figures are from the ICC and are presented in *Historical Statistics of the United States,* series Q-398. Trainmen's employment is from the ICC *Statistics of Railways* and *Accident Bulletin,* various years. Fatalities and injuries for all workers and trainmen are also from these sources. Manhours for 1921 on are from the ICC *Accident Bulletin.* Prior to 1921, manhour data were estimated. For details, see text.

Note: Total employment figures have been modified by the addition of switching and terminal employment from 1911 on. Trainmen include enginemen, firemen, brakemen, and conductors; their employment figures are unmodified.

established a dual system of reports. Companies continued to report injuries and fatalities in *Statistics of Railways,* but the act required that the carriers file, under oath, separate reports that the commission published in its *Accident Bulletin*s. However, these included only "all collisions, derailments or other accidents resulting in injury . . . arising from the operation of such railroad." This act had two contradictory effects. By requiring reports under oath it probably increased reporting, as, for example, the ICC's longtime secretary and safety expert Edward Moseley believed. But because it only covered accidents that stemmed from the "operation" of the railroad, workers on wharves and docks and in the railroad shops were excluded. From 1902 through 1909 there were therefore two parallel sets of accident data, and these do not always agree either in the details or in the total.[2]

The Accident Reports Act of 1910 scrapped this dual system of reporting. Thereafter all reportable accidents were contained in the *Accident Bulletins*. The result was a major increase in reported accidents to employees, which jumped from about 96,000 in (fiscal) 1910 to 126,000 in 1911. After 1910 there were no major changes in the statistics until 1922, when injury and fatality rates per million manhours were first reported. Also in the 1920s, as noted above, the major carriers instituted widespread safety contests, which the commission worried led to underreporting, and it claimed that the decline in injuries "considerably exaggerates the improvement that has taken place."[3]

There are many other difficulties with the official figures. For example, suicides were included prior to 1927 but not after that date. A more serious problem is that the commission defined reportable injuries as those resulting in more than three lost workdays, thus making then not comparable to other injury data in which all lost-workday injuries are included. Reportable fatalities were those occurring within twenty-four hours of the injury. Yet the Bureau of Labor Statistics data on injuries and fatalities in manufacturing had—at least in theory—no statute of limitations on such revisions, and coal mining tended to include as fatalities men who died a much longer time after the injury. Hence, the ICC's definitions understate the relative risk of railroading.[4]

Thus, the published accident statistics are inaccurate, inconsistent, and not comparable to other data that include all injuries or are published on a man-hour basis. The latter problem is the easiest to rectify. The commission began to publish information on manhours in 1921, but these covered only Class I—including Class I switching and terminal—railways, and manhour estimates for groups of workers such as trainmen are unavailable. For earlier years, total employee manhours, on which columns 5 and 6 of table A1.1 are based, are derived from John Kendrick.[5]

Four other corrections can easily be made to the basic data in table A1.1. The effects of the two accident reporting acts can be modeled econometrically. Table A1.10 provides estimates of the effects of changed reporting requirements. The table is simply unclear as to the possible impact that changed legal requirements may have had on reported fatalities, and so no changes are made to the reported rates. However, equation 4 indicates that reported injury rates increased 27.9 percent $[(\exp 0.248) - 1]$ in 1911. The injury rates in table A1.2 are thus increased by this amount prior to that date.[6]

As noted above, the ICC thought that safety contests led the carriers to keep men on the job or bring them back to work early, thereby reducing reportable injuries and perhaps inflating those resulting in three or fewer lost workdays. An investigation undertaken in 1939 showed clear evidence of underreporting on several carriers. The equation below was estimated for 112 Class I carriers for 1936 and shows that in fact companies with few reportable injuries (R) also had few unreportable injuries (NR). Underreporting could still have existed, but it may have been less than the commission thought.[7]

$$\ln(NR) = 0.605 + 0.468[\ln(R)]$$
$$(2.81) \quad (4.44)$$
$$R^2 = 0.14; N = 112$$

This equation can also be used to estimate nonreportable injuries per million manhours before 1936. If it does reflect some degree of underreporting among those carriers with low reportable injuries, then it will most overpredict nonreportables when reportables are low. Since reportable injuries were higher in earlier years, the effect should understate the downward trend in injury rates over time. The exponential version of this equation, $NR = 1.832R^{.468}$, was used to estimate nonreportables that were added to the estimated reportables in column 2 of table A1.2, and the results are presented in column 3 of that table.

The next change is to include subsequent fatalities (those injuries in which the workman died more than twenty-four hours after being hurt). The ICC required the reporting of subsequent fatalities in train and train-service accidents beginning in 1920, and found that they averaged around 11.89 percent of reported fatalities from 1920 to 1930 and rose sharply to nearly 20 percent of reported fatalities in the 1930s. Although the sources of this upward trend are unclear, it may reflect improvements in medical care that resulted from carrier Safety First programs. I have assumed that these proportions also hold for non-train accidents and have therefore employed them to modify the fatality rates in table A1.1. For the years prior to 1920, rates are increased an average of 11.89 percent, and for 1920 on, the actual annual percentage undercount is added. The results are presented in table A1.3.

These revised estimates change in degree, although not in kind, our understanding of the safety of railroad work. The addition of subsequent fatalities increases death rates per worker during the late nineteenth century by 12 percent and from the 1920s on by 15–17 percent, thereby making the carriers' safety performance during these years somewhat less impressive.

Using the corrected fatality figures, and expressing the results on a manhour rather than a worker basis, yields two important results. First, the actual improvement in safety was somewhat milder than the official figures suggest. An equation of the form $\ln(Y) = a + Bt$, fitted to official figures on fatalities per thousand employees (table A1.1, col. 1), yields a decline of 4.3 percent per year from 1889 to 1939. By contrast, similar analysis indicates that corrected fatalities per manhour (table A1.3, col. 2) fell only 3.31 percent per year. Second, use of rates on a manhour rather than a worker basis sharply reduces the relative risk of railroading compared with mining. In 1906, the first year it reported such data, the Bureau of Mines reported a bituminous coal mine fatality rate of 1.84 per million manhours. Even with the inclusion of subsequent

TABLE A1.2. The Impact of Underreporting and Nonreportable Injuries on Injury Rates per Thousand Employees and per Million Manhours, 1889–1939

	Per Thousand Employees, Underreporting	Per Million Manhours	
		Underreporting	Nonreportable
1889	34.66	11.77	17.58
1890	38.24	12.12	18.01
1891	42.64	13.50	19.69
1892	44.04	13.77	20.02
1893	46.43	15.35	21.93
1894	38.41	12.07	17.95
1895	41.92	13.64	19.87
1896	46.35	15.50	22.11
1897	43.00	14.00	20.30
1898	46.43	15.30	21.87
1899	48.18	15.53	22.14
1900	49.17	16.17	22.91
1901	49.13	15.58	22.21
1902	54.35	17.37	24.34
1903	58.91	20.79	28.38
1904	66.19	21.42	29.11
1905	61.85	20.82	28.40
1906	64.50	20.52	28.05
1907	67.04	22.72	30.63
1908	73.47	23.13	31.10
1909	63.83	20.82	28.41
1910	72.02	24.47	32.65
1911	72.98	24.09	32.22
1912	80.25	26.36	34.83
1913	91.28	30.87	40.00
1914	93.39	31.64	40.86
1915	86.20	28.62	37.42
1916	91.28	30.54	39.62
1917	94.29	31.60	40.82
1918	79.72	27.02	35.59
1919	64.63	25.77	34.15
1920	69.56	27.06	35.63
1921	59.26	25.71	34.09
1922	66.44	27.63	36.29
1923	77.94	31.43	40.63
1924	67.63	28.02	36.73

	Per Thousand Employees, Underreporting	Per Million Manhours	
		Underreporting	Nonreportable
1925	64.59	26.80	35.34
1926	59.40	24.55	32.74
1927	48.05	19.15	26.45
1928	40.50	16.91	23.79
1929	34.65	14.38	20.75
1930	22.82	9.85	15.20
1931	17.55	7.97	12.81
1932	16.26	7.76	12.54
1933	15.48	7.41	12.09
1934	16.26	7.53	12.25
1935	15.90	7.28	11.92
1936	19.87	8.67	13.70
1937	20.38	8.88	13.96
1938	16.60	7.35	12.01
1939	16.57	7.21	11.83

Source: Columns 1 and 2 are from columns 2 and 6 of table A1.1, with the years prior to 1911 multiplied by 1.279. Column 3 adds to column 2 estimates of nonreportable injuries computed using the formula described in the text.

TABLE A1.3. The Impact of Subsequent Fatalities on Fatality Rates, 1889–1939

Year	Per Thousand Workers	Per Million Manhours	Year	Per Thousand Workers	Per Million Manhours
1889	2.99	1.01	1903	3.07	1.08
1890	3.66	1.16	1904	3.14	1.01
1891	3.80	1.20	1905	2.72	0.92
1892	3.48	1.09	1906	2.89	0.92
1893	3.49	1.15	1907	3.03	1.03
1894	2.62	0.82	1908	2.65	0.84
1895	2.56	0.84	1909	1.94	0.63
1896	2.52	0.84	1910	2.23	0.76
1897	2.30	0.75	1911	2.33	0.77
1898	2.50	0.83	1912	2.29	0.75
1899	2.67	0.86	1913	2.21	0.75
1900	2.47	0.80	1914	2.06	0.70
1901	2.79	0.89	1915	1.50	0.50
1902	2.79	0.89	1916	1.71	0.57

TABLE A1.3. Continued

Year	Per Thousand Workers	Per Million Manhours	Year	Per Thousand Workers	Per Million Manhours
1917	1.94	0.65	1929	0.91	0.38
1918	1.95	0.66	1930	0.69	0.30
1919	1.18	0.47	1931	0.58	0.26
1920	1.33	0.52	1932	0.61	0.29
1921	0.96	0.42	1933	0.61	0.29
1922	1.05	0.44	1934	0.61	0.28
1923	1.16	0.46	1935	0.68	0.31
1924	0.94	0.39	1936	0.75	0.33
1925	0.96	0.40	1937	0.70	0.31
1926	0.99	0.41	1938	0.61	0.27
1927	0.94	0.37	1939	0.60	0.26
1928	0.85	0.35			

Source: Data are from table A1.1, with subsequent fatalities added using procedures described in the text.

fatalities, the comparable rate for railroading (0.92) was only half as high. But on a per-worker basis the railroad fatality rate was 85 percent of that in coal [(2.89/3.38) × 100] that year.

According to the official figures on injuries per worker, work safety deteriorated in spectacular fashion from 1889 to World War I, with injury rates almost tripling during these years. Given that fatality rates declined over this period, such an increase is hard to believe, and it probably reflects increasingly accurate reporting, even before the Accident Reports Act of 1910 ballooned the data. The revisions contained in column 1 of table A1.2 reduce this increase by nearly one-third, but the upward trend may well still be at least in part an artifact of better reporting.

Although inclusion of underreported injuries prior to 1911 reduces the apparent deterioration of safety in the early years, when estimated nonreportable injuries are included and the data are expressed per manhour, the result is a substantial diminution in the rate at which safety improved over the entire period. Uncorrected injuries per million manhours (table A1.1, col. 6) decline at 11.1 percent per year, while the corrected figures (table A1.2, col. 3), improve at 8.8 percent per year.

Aside from slightly tarnishing the railroads' record, these figures have two other implications. First, they increase railroad productivity gains when safety deteriorated and decrease them when safety improved, where productivity is defined inclusively to mean both transportation services and work safety. Second, they imply that attempts to infer worker risk premiums from the official injury and fatality data may be substantially in error, and—because risks are undercounted—the wage premium will be overstated.

TABLE A1.4. Injury and Fatality Rates per Thousand Trainmen, by Cause, 1890–1909

	Coupling		Braking[a]	
	Fatality Rate	Injury Rate	Fatality Rate	Injury Rate
1890	1.73	39.61	3.25	12.99
1891	1.80	44.68	3.15	16.83
1892	1.49	45.88	3.31	17.09
1893	1.73	48.73	3.19	18.82
1894	1.45	44.47	3.11	20.52
1895	1.20	38.53	2.44	17.99
1896	0.96	39.64	2.64	20.99
1897	0.91	29.10	2.23	18.79
1898	1.07	30.99	2.35	19.41
1899	1.01	28.26	2.10	19.02
1900	0.98	19.89	2.40	19.52
1901	0.78	11.37	2.03	17.24
1902	0.62	10.96	1.99	19.87
1903	0.83	11.92	2.06	19.11
1904	1.06	13.81	2.06	22.05
1905	0.81	12.50	2.09	20.68
1906	0.93	12.57	1.88	21.91
1907	0.86	12.78	1.85	21.76
1908	0.73	11.65	1.78	22.69
1909	0.50	8.23	1.24	18.88

Source: Data are from the ICC *Statistics of Railways* and *Accident Bulletin*, various years.
[a] Fatalities and injuries due to falls from cars and striking overhead obstructions.

TABLE A1.5. Injury and Fatality Rates per Thousand Railroad Employees, by Cause, 1889–1939

	Coupling		Braking[a]		Collisions	
	Fatality Rate	Injury Rate	Fatality Rate	Injury Rate	Fatality Rate	Injury Rate
1889	0.406	9.15	0.755	3.12	0.237	1.04
1890	0.493	10.47	0.811	3.38	0.155	0.51
1891	0.506	12.23	0.811	4.34	0.386	1.98
1892	0.460	12.57	0.842	4.44	0.348	1.65
1893	0.495	12.80	0.820	5.42	0.283	1.71
1894	0.322	9.28	0.627	4.27	0.186	1.15
1895	0.371	10.36	0.642	4.63	0.171	1.28

TABLE A1.5. Continued

	Coupling		Braking[a]		Collisions	
	Fatality Rate	Injury Rate	Fatality Rate	Injury Rate	Fatality Rate	Injury Rate
1896	0.277	10.23	0.647	5.12	0.215	1.27
1897	0.260	7.63	0.547	4.86	0.199	1.15
1898	0.317	7.99	0.599	4.86	0.206	1.22
1899	0.280	7.28	0.543	4.73	0.201	1.47
1900	0.277	5.14	0.575	4.78	0.259	1.55
1901	0.185	2.58	0.485	4.04	0.325	1.95
1902	0.140	2.41	0.483	5.03	0.357	2.32
1903	0.214	2.70	0.493	4.47	0.437	2.87
1904	0.237	3.10	0.493	4.90	0.345	2.85
1905	0.166	2.56	0.393	4.50	0.303	2.62
1906	0.196	2.55	0.418	4.74	0.326	2.68
1907	0.184	2.60	0.408	4.67	0.342	2.83
1908	0.155	2.35	0.403	4.88	0.209	2.43
1909	0.103	1.58	0.267	3.85	0.168	1.54
1910	0.121	1.76	—	—	0.209	1.95
1911	0.121	1.72	—	—	0.172	1.78
1912	0.108	1.82	—	—	0.050	1.72
1913	0.103	1.79	—	—	0.018	1.80
1914	0.097	1.52	—	—	0.013	1.28
1915	0.056	1.25	—	—	0.047	0.85
1916	0.077	1.25	—	—	0.096	0.93
1917	0.090	1.35	—	—	0.127	1.30
1918	0.084	1.19	—	—	0.140	1.15
1919	0.053	0.98	—	—	0.067	0.63
1920	0.071	1.14	—	—	0.085	0.74
1921	0.045	0.87	—	—	0.031	0.32
1922	0.047	0.86	—	—	0.059	0.51
1923	0.052	1.00	—	—	0.057	0.48
1924	0.038	0.86	—	—	0.046	0.38
1925	0.035	0.83	—	—	0.045	0.38
1926	0.034	0.84	—	—	0.055	0.44
1927	0.026	0.73	—	—	0.035	0.30
1928	0.021	0.66	—	—	0.029	0.28
1929	0.034	0.55	—	—	0.043	0.24
1930	0.020	0.39	—	—	0.031	0.17
1931	0.009	0.30	—	—	0.025	0.12
1932	0.018	0.28	—	—	0.028	0.11

	Coupling		Braking[a]		Collisions	
	Fatality Rate	Injury Rate	Fatality Rate	Injury Rate	Fatality Rate	Injury Rate
1933	0.010	0.24	—	—	0.015	0.13
1934	0.016	0.24	—	—	0.028	0.12
1935	0.015	0.25	—	—	0.015	0.13
1936	0.021	0.28	—	—	0.051	0.20
1937	0.018	0.32	—	—	0.040	0.19
1938	0.006	0.24	—	—	0.022	0.14
1939	0.011	0.27	—	—	0.016	0.15

Source: Injuries and fatalities by cause are from the ICC *Statistics of Railways* and *Accident Bulletin*, various years. Employment data are the same as those for all workers in table A1.1.

[a] Fatalities and injuries due to falls from cars and striking overhead obstructions.

Statistical Analysis of Railroad Safety

TABLE A1.6. The Impact of Regulation on Purchases of Safety Equipment, 1890–1909

Independent Variables	Air Brakes	Automatic Couplers
Trend	0.163	0.453
	(3.76)	(3.21)
Trend*	0.0005	−0.050
Reg	(0.12)	(4.04)
Trend*	0.00004	−0.00007
Density	(4.32)	(2.81)
Trend*	0.00003	0.0001
Profcar	(1.07)	(1.87)
R^2	0.63	0.15
D.W.	1.33	1.35
N	160	160

Note: The dependent variable is $\ln[P/(1 - P)]$, where P is the proportion of freight cars equipped with safety equipment. Reg is a dummy that is 1 for 1893 to 1901 and 0 otherwise. Density is train-miles per mile of track. Profcar is net income per freight car. Figures in parentheses are *t*-ratios. Both equations contain ten regional dummies. They are estimated employing a Cochran-Orcutt correction and are freight-car-weighted using a TSP routine.

TABLE A1.7. Determinants of Injury and Fatality Rates from Coupling
Railroad Cars, 1891-1909

Independent Variables	Fatality Rate		Injury Rate	
	(1)	(2)	(3)	(4)
Coupler	0.953	−0.022	3.57	−0.838
	(1.23)	(0.10)	(4.76)	(3.07)
Coupler²	−0.874	—	−3.66	—
	(1.31)		(5.98)	
Density	0.0003	0.0003	0.0005	0.0006
	(2.13)	(2.09)	(4.86)	(5.01)
Train weight	0.001	0.0005	0.002	0.001
	(0.95)	(0.44)	(1.88)	(0.79)
Employment change	−0.1423	−0.094	−0.292	−0.231
	(0.43)	(0.28)	(1.84)	(1.40)
Report '01	0.132	−0.052	0.129	0.053
	(1.09)	(0.49)	(1.67)	(0.64)
Trend	0.085	−0.076	0.095	−0.102
	(3.87)	(3.63)	(5.27)	(4.77)
R^2	0.54	0.54	0.72	0.61
D.W.	1.88	1.87	1.89	1.88
N	180	180	180	180

Note: The dependent variable is the natural log of the coupling fatality or injury rate.
Employment change is the change in employment divided by lagged employment.
Coupler is the proportion of freight cars equipped with automatic couplers. Density
is train-miles per mile of track. Train weight is tons per train. Report '01 is a dummy
variable that is 0 for years up to 1901 and 1 thereafter. Figures in parentheses are
t-ratios. All equations also contain ten regional dummies. They are estimated using
the Cochran-Orcutt correction and are employment-weighted using a TSP routine.

TABLE A1.8. Determinants of Injury and Fatality Rates from Braking
Trains, 1891-1909

Independent Variables	Fatality Rate		Injury Rate	
	(1)	(2)	(3)	(4)
Air brake	0.541	0.012	−0.244	−0.484
	(1.45)	(0.06)	(0.35)	(1.32)
Brake²	−0.694	—	−0.933	—
	(1.69)		(1.23)	
Density	0.0002	0.0002	0.00 3	0.0003
	(2.49)	(1.92)	(2.79)	(2.52)

TABLE A1.8. Continued

Independent Variables	Fatality Rate		Injury Rate	
	(1)	(2)	(3)	(4)
Train weight	0.541	0.002	0.0001	0.0002
	(1.45)	(2.59)	(0.13)	(0.16)
Employment change	−0.187	−0.110	0.477	−0.448
	(1.08)	(0.64)	(3.09)	(2.92)
Report '01	0.135	0.090	0.195	0.175
	(1.99)	(1.45)	(2.58)	(2.37)
Trend	−0.068	−0.078	0.030	0.009
	(4.53)	(5.77)	(1.09)	(0.44)
R^2	0.66	0.66	0.26	0.27
D.W.	1.88	1.85	2.12	2.10
N	180	180	180	180

Note: The dependent variable is the natural log of the fatality or injury rate (the sum of injuries or fatalities from falls plus overhead obstructions, per thousand employees). Air brake is the proportion of freight cars equipped with air brakes. For definitions of other variables, see table A1.7. Figures in parentheses are *t*-ratios. All equations also contain ten regional dummies. They are estimated using the Cochran-Orcutt correction and are employment-weighted using a TSP routine.

TABLE A1.9. Determinants of Railroad Employee Collision Casualties, 1890–1939

Independent Variables	1890–1909	1906–1939
Air brake[a]	1.76	—
	(4.08)	
Train weight	0.004	0.0007
	(2.67)	(1.04)
Train length[b]	—	−0.053
		(3.50)
Density	0.0007	0.0006
	(4.68)	(3.87)
Telegraph operators	−0.043	—
	(2.95)	
Employment change	−0.233	0.785
	(1.02)	(2.33)
Exposure[c]	—	0.0006
		(3.45)
Block signals[d]	—	−3.11
		(1.49)

Independent Variables	1890–1909	1906–1939
Report '01	0.451	—
	(4.13)	
Report '10	—	0.034
		(0.16)
Trend	−0.114	−0.002
	(4.21)	(0.18)
R^2	0.42	0.98
D.W.	1.81	1.97
N	170	34

Note: The dependent variable is the natural log of the employee collision casualty (fatality plus injury) rate per thousand workers. Train length is cars per train. Exposure is manhours per worker. Telegraph operators are per mile of track. Block signals is the proportion of main track with block signals. Report '10 is a dummy variable that is 0 up to 1910 and 1 thereafter. For definitions of other variables, see table A1.7. Figures in parentheses are *t*-ratios. Equations for the period 1890–1909 contain ten regional dummies. They are estimated using a Cochran-Orcutt correction and are employment-weighted using a TSP routine. The second-period equations contain a constant term and are estimated using the Cochran-Orcutt technique.

[a] Air brakes are excluded from the second set of equations, as 95 percent of all equipment was air-braked by 1906.
[b] Train length is unavailable before 1900.
[c] Regional exposure data are unavailable.
[d] Block signals are unavailable before 1906.

TABLE A1.10. Determinants of Railroad Injury and Fatality Rates, 1889–1939

Independent Variables	Fatality Rate		Injury Rate	
	(1)	(2)	(3)	(4)
Exposure	0.0006	0.0006	0.0002	0.0002
	(5.11)	(5.90)	(1.87)	(1.84)
Employment change	0.494	0.695	0.163	0.183
	(2.69)	(4.10)	(1.13)	(1.12)
Density	0.0002	0.0002	0.0004	0.0004
	(2.75)	(2.54)	(4.93)	(4.35)
Air brakes	−0.136	0.987	1.37	1.43
	(0.26)	(1.87)	(1.21)	(1.22)
Automatic couplers 0.079	−0.655	−1.10	−1.14	
	(0.24)	(1.92)	(1.52)	(1.53)

TABLE A1.10. Continued

Independent Variables	Fatality Rate		Injury Rate	
	(1)	(2)	(3)	(4)
Fela '08	—	−0.294	—	0.028
		(3.57)		(0.27)
Report '01	0.193	0.095	0.037	0.033
	(1.86)	(0.99)	(0.37)	(0.34)
Report '10	−0.030	0.093	0.246	0.248
	(0.43)	(1.39)	(2.69)	(2.67)
Trend	−0.021	−0.024	0.044	−0.044
	(3.65)	(4.92)	(3.00)	(2.97)
R^2	0.97	0.98	0.63	0.62
D.W.	1.94	1.98	1.21	1.20
N	49	49	49	49

Note: The dependent variable is the natural log of the fatality or injury rate per thousand workers. Fela '08 is the federal employers liability law passed in 1908. For definitions of other variables, see table A1.7. Figures in parentheses are *t*-ratios. All equations also contain a constant term. They were fitted using a Cochran-Orcutt correction.

Coal and Metal Mine Injury
and Fatality Rates
1870–1939

This appendix presents the basic available data on mining fatality and injury rates that underlie the text and figures in chapters 2 and 6. It describes both the sources of these figures and the calculations that were undertaken. The appendix also contains a statistical analysis referred to in chapter 6 regarding the impact of workmen's compensation and technical change on mine safety.

Coal-Mining Statistics

Pennsylvania's act to regulate its anthracite mines in 1870 required the reporting of deaths. This began the systematic collection of information on coal mine fatalities. As regulation spread, so also did the gathering of fatality records. Before 1889 all mine employment data derive from these state regulatory efforts. From then on the U.S. Geological Survey began to collect consistent information on mine employment nationwide. Beginning around 1910, the Bureau of Mines became a central collection agency to which states reported fatalities, and it attempted to systematize record collection. The bureau also drew together much of the earlier state data.

The figures in table A2.1 on fatality rates per thousand workers and per thousand 300-day workers were compiled by the Bureau of Mines from these state data. The records on fatalities and employment for anthracite are virtually complete for the entire period, for the data come entirely from Pennsylvania. For bituminous coal the early records are much more spotty. Before 1910 they are based on states with inspection and reporting requirements, but they reflect about 90 percent of the industry after 1889. Fatality rates per million manhours beginning in 1906 for bituminous mining and 1911 for anthracite mining are also bureau estimates. For the years prior to those dates I estimated the manhour fatality rates.[1]

The data become increasingly complete and reliable as we move nearer the present. The information on fatalities gathered before World War I is inconsistent and probably incomplete—even for inspection states. Sometimes men who died during the initial opening of a shaft were not counted. On the other hand, some suicides and fatalities among visitors were probably included.[2] Nor did states employ a consistent time period in accounting for fatalities subsequent to injuries. In 1914, as part of an effort to systematize data collection, the bureau surveyed state methods for classifying fatalities and found a blizzard of confusing and inconsistent practices. One West Virginia inspector counted only men who died within nine days of an injury. Some states set the period at a month, while others chose a year and a day. Some had no time limit at all. There were even internal inconsistencies: apparently every Pennsylvania inspector got to choose his own time period.[3] In addition, some states reported on a fiscal-year and some on a calendar-year basis, but the bureau claimed that it was able to convert all such figures to the calendar year. In 1916 the bureau called a conference of state mine inspectors and other interested parties to develop consistent record keeping. This bore fruit; by the end of World War I, standard reporting forms and a statute of limitations of one year for fatalities had been adopted. Such standardization no doubt improved the quality of the data, but it also probably led to a spurious increase in measured fatalities.[4] The 1916 conference also developed standard forms for the reporting of all lost-workday injuries, but nothing immediate came of these efforts. During the 1920s mines accounting for about 2 percent of total employment began to collect and report such information to the bureau as part of the National Safety Competition. Nationwide estimates are not available until 1930, however.

The bureau defined mining employment to include workers in and around the mines but excluding office workers and coke-oven employees. The exclusion of office workers imparts an upward bias to the data and makes them not comparable to either railroad or manufacturing injury data, but the error is likely to be small, for wage earners typically accounted for 93–96 percent of mine employees, and some salaried employees (such as foremen) were included in the bureau data.

The pre-1889 employment information collected by the states contains some coke-oven workers and is otherwise subject to error. Beginning in 1906 for bituminous mines and 1911 for anthracite mines, the bureau presented figures on annual hours worked. Until the 1930s these data are calculated, not based on actual payroll observations. They are the product of employment times days worked times hours per day. The bureau measured days worked by the number of days the tipple was in operation (tipple time), while daily hours were also based on the time the mine was reported to be open (daily hours open).[5] However, some men may have been in the mines even when the tipple was not at work, thus biasing down reported exposures. In 1931 the bureau began to collect data from a few mines on actual payroll hours worked. It found that use of tipple time underestimated annual hours worked by about 10 percent in these mines, thus overstating fatality rates by the same amount.[6]

By the late 1930s most of the information on hours worked seems to have come from payrolls, although the bureau never supplied exact figures. By itself the shift from tipple time to payroll hours would have resulted in a spurious drop in measured fatality rates. However, the miner's famous freedom implied

TABLE A2.1. Coal-Mining Fatality Rates, 1870–1939

	Bituminous Mining			Anthracite Mining		
	Per Thousand Workers	Per Thousand 300-Day Workers	Per Million Manhours	Per Thousand Workers	Per Thousand 300-Day Workers	Per Million Manhours
1870	—	—	—	5.93	—	3.06
1871	—	—	—	5.60	—	2.89
1872	—	—	—	4.98	—	2.57
1873	—	—	—	5.46	—	2.81
1874	2.11	—	—	4.33	—	2.23
1875	1.60	—	—	3.37	—	1.74
1876	1.00	—	—	3.22	—	1.66
1877	2.17	—	—	2.90	—	1.50
1878	1.86	—	—	2.92	—	1.51
1879	2.02	—	—	3.81	—	1.96
1880	1.43	—	0.66	2.75	—	1.42
1881	1.67	—	0.78	3.59	4.87	1.71
1882	1.95	—	0.84	3.54	4.87	1.71
1883	1.68	—	1.19	3.58	4.56	1.60
1884	2.26	—	1.19	3.28	5.12	1.80
1885	1.68	—	0.84	3.58	5.26	1.85
1886	1.85	—	0.95	2.70	4.13	1.46
1887	1.55	—	0.74	2.95	4.25	1.49
1888	2.23	—	1.06	2.98	4.10	1.44
1889	1.77	—	0.87	3.11	4.81	1.69
1890	2.15	2.85	1.00	3.00	4.50	1.58
1891	2.86	3.85	1.35	3.39	5.01	1.76
1892	3.05	4.17	1.46	3.24	4.91	1.72
1893	2.26	3.32	1.17	3.42	5.21	1.83
1894	2.26	3.96	1.36	3.38	5.34	1.87
1895	3.09	4.78	1.68	2.95	4.51	1.56
1896	2.51	3.92	1.35	3.36	5.79	2.03
1897	2.38	3.64	1.28	2.82	5.64	1.98
1898	2.64	3.75	1.42	2.82	5.57	1.97
1899	3.05	3.91	1.48	3.30	5.72	2.01
1900	3.74	4.79	1.82	2.85	5.15	1.81
1901	3.16	4.21	1.60	3.53	5.40	1.90
1902	3.93	5.13	1.94	2.03	5.25	1.84
1903	3.47	4.63	1.76	3.44	5.01	1.86
1904	3.35	4.98	1.93	3.82	5.73	2.12

TABLE A2.1. Continued

	Bituminous Mining			Anthracite Mining		
	Per Thousand Workers	Per Thousand 300-Day Workers	Per Million Manhours	Per Thousand Workers	Per Thousand 300-Day Workers	Per Million Manhours
1905	3.53	5.02	1.95	3.89	5.43	2.01
1906	3.38	4.76	1.84	3.43	5.28	1.96
1907	4.99	6.40	2.47	4.23	5.77	2.14
1908	3.50	5.44	2.11	3.89	5.84	2.17
1909	4.15	5.58	2.15	3.40	4.78	—
1910	4.00	5.53	2.11	3.55	4.65	1.72
1911	3.53	5.02	1.92	4.02	4.90	1.81
1912	3.31	4.46	1.71	3.45	4.48	1.66
1913	3.79	4.90	1.90	3.52	4.10	1.52
1914	3.19	4.90	1.89	3.31	4.05	1.50
1915	3.02	4.47	1.72	3.32	4.33	1.60
1916	2.98	3.38	1.50	3.47	4.11	1.66
1917	3.50	4.33	1.72	3.77	3.98	1.66
1918	3.30	3.97	1.62	3.75	3.83	1.60
1919	2.71	4.16	1.72	4.11	4.64	1.93
1920	2.78	3.79	1.57	3.38	3.74	1.56
1921	2.18	4.38	1.82	3.43	3.80	1.58
1922	2.45	5.16	2.14	1.91	3.81	1.58
1923	2.77	4.65	1.92	3.23	4.62	1.61
1924	3.08	5.39	2.23	3.10	3.39	1.41
1925	3.12	4.79	1.98	2.50	4.12	1.71
1926	3.48	4.86	2.00	2.74	3.37	1.40
1927	2.93	4.60	1.90	2.96	3.94	1.64
1928	3.31	4.90	2.02	2.78	3.85	1.60
1929	3.39	4.63	1.91	3.18	4.24	1.77
1930	3.28	5.26	2.16	2.94	4.22	1.76
1931	2.40	4.42	1.81	2.75	4.43	1.84
1932	2.36	4.85	2.00	2.05	3.83	1.59
1933	1.99	3.58	1.48	2.21	3.58	1.49
1934	2.09	3.52	1.62	2.47	3.61	1.50
1935	2.09	3.53	1.67	2.66	4.26	1.78
1936	2.28	3.46	1.64	2.39	3.73	1.56
1937	2.44	3.74	1.77	2.17	3.44	1.58
1938	1.98	3.68	1.74	2.34	4.08	1.94
1939	1.95	3.29	1.56	2.24	3.61	1.71

TABLE A2.1. Continued

Source: For fatality rates per worker and per 300-day worker, see W. W. Adams, "Coal Mine Fatalities in the United States, 1939," BM *Bulletin* 444 (Washington, D.C., 1940), table 83.

Fatality rates per manhour for bituminous mining from 1906 on are from Adams, "Coal Mine Fatalities," table 68; prior to 1906, rates are calculations by the author based on table A2.2.

Fatality rates per manhour for anthracite mining prior to 1906 are calculated from data in table A2.2; for 1906-13, see Albert Fay, "Coal Mine Fatalities in the United States, 1870-1914," BM *Bulletin* 115 (Washington, D.C., 1916), table 41; for 1914-26, W. W. Adams, "Coal Mine Fatalities in the United States, 1927," BM *Bulletin* 293 (Washington, D.C., 1929), table 38; for 1927-29, "Coal Mine Accidents in the United States, 1930," BM *Bulletin* 335 (Washington, D.C., 1933), table 43; for 1930-39, "Coal Mine Accidents in the United States, 1940," BM *Bulletin* 448 (Washington, D.C., 1942), table 75.

TABLE A2.2. Derivation of Coal-Mining Fatality Rates per Million Manhours, 1870-1905

	Anthracite Mines			*Bituminous Mines*			
	Employment	*Thousands of Manhours*	*Fatalities*	*Employment*	*Days Worked*	*Hours per Day*	*Fatalities*
1870	35,600	69,057	211	—	—	—	—
1871	37,488	72,719	210	—	—	—	—
1872	44,745	86,796	223	—	—	—	—
1873	48,199	93,496	263	—	—	—	—
1874	53,402	103,589	231	—	—	—	—
1875	69,966	135,720	236	—	—	—	—
1876	70,474	136,744	227	—	—	—	—
1877	66,842	129,660	194	—	—	—	—
1878	63,964	124,077	187	—	—	—	—
1879	68,847	133,549	262	—	—	—	—
1880	73,373	142,329	202	50,363	227	9.5	72
1881	76,031	159,627	273	40,097	227	9.5	67
1882	82,200	170,236	291	80,683	245	9.5	157
1883	91,421	201,492	323	70,817	273	9.5	219
1884	101,073	184,357	332	91,296	200	9.5	206
1885	100,324	184,357	359	112,854	212	9.5	190
1886	103,044	191,868	278	116,665	206	9.5	216
1887	106,517	210,478	314	122,260	221	9.5	190
1888	122,218	253,113	364	163,299	221	9.5	364
1889	123,676	227,935	385	159,522	214	9.5	283
1890	126,000	239,400	378	165,217	226	9.5	355

	Anthracite Mines			Bituminous Mines			
	Employ-ment	Thousands of Manhours	Fatalities	Employ-ment	Days Worked	Hours per Day	Fatalities
1891	126,356	243,666	428	184,327	223	9.5	528
1892	129,050	242,744	418	188,090	219	9.5	573
1893	132,944	248,805	455	222,147	204	9.5	503
1894	131,603	237,548	445	227,039	171	9.5	503
1895	142,917	266,114	421	233,307	194	9.5	721
1896	148,991	246,278	501	231,486	192	9.5	582
1897	149,884	213,589	432	238,701	196	9.5	567
1898	145,504	210,112	411	246,337	211	8.8	651
1899	139,608	229,444	461	255,999	234	8.8	780
1900	144,206	221,411	411	288,242	234	8.8	1,078
1901	145,309	270,570	513	335,498	225	8.8	1,061
1902	148,141	163,248	300	362,076	230	8.8	1,424
1903	150,483	278,991	518	406,098	225	8.7	1,408
1904	155,861	280,548	595	417,512	202	8.6	1,400
1905	165,406	320,058	644	449,962	211	8.6	1,588

Source: Employment, days worked, and fatalities are all from Fay, "Coal Mine Fatalities in the United States." For manhours and hours per day, see text.

that use of daily hours open probably overstated actual daily hours worked, thereby biasing fatality rates downward. As mining became more systematized in the 1930s, actual daily hours probably converged with daily hours open. Thus, the calculation of annual hours using tipple time and daily hours worked contained offsetting—though not necessarily canceling—biases.

It should be clear that these data are far from precise. Writing in 1950, Dan Harrington observed that "it has been difficult—in fact almost impossible—to obtain man-hour statistics that are anything like reliable . . . and this condition continues to exist." Harrington went on to observe that when "the relatively much more nearly accurate data of the recent past as to accidents . . . per million manhours of exposure are compared with the estimated or calculated hours of exposure 10, 20 or 30 years ago the results are so undependable as to be almost fantastic."[7]

Rushing in where even the bureau feared to tread, I have extended backwards to 1870 for anthracite mining and to 1880 for the bituminous sector the series on fatality rates per million manhours using variants of the bureau's methods. The procedures are as follows. For anthracite mining, the employment and fatality data (table A2.2) are from the Bureau of Mines. Estimates of manhours for 1880, and for 1890 on, are from a Works Projects Administration (WPA) study of productivity in the mining industries.[8] These are essentially derived from Census estimates of employment times days worked times an assumed 9.5 hours per day. I calculated manhours for 1870–79 as the product of each year's employment times the ratio of manhours to employment for 1880. For 1881–89, manhours are the days worked times employment (both taken from the Bureau of Mines) times an assumed 9.5 hours per day.

For bituminous mining, employment and fatality data are for inspection states only and are taken from Bureau of Mines work. Manhours are again a product of employment, days worked, and daily hours. Although WPA sources estimated manhours, they are for the entire industry and cannot be matched to inspection states. I therefore adopted an alternative procedure. Nationwide estimates of days worked and hours per day for 1880 and 1890 on are from WPA sources.[9] I assumed these to be representative of inspection states. For days worked, 1881–89, I took the average of Ohio and Illinois, since Pennsylvania data are not available. Daily hours are assumed to be 9.5, which is what the WPA report estimated for both 1880 and 1890.

Factor Substitution, Technological Change, and Coal Mine Safety

The arguments in chapter 6 that accident rates were unresponsive to workmen's compensation payments and that technological change was risk-increasing are based on a version of a translog cost function, fitted to Census data for coal-mining states from 1919 through 1939. Data allow the estimation of four share equations for fatalities, labor, energy, and supervision, which take the following form:

$$S_1 = A_1 + B_{11} \ln Pf + B_{12} \ln Pl + B_{13} \ln Pe + B_{14} \ln Ps + B_{15} \ln T$$
$$S_2 = A_2 + B_{21} \ln Pf + B_{22} \ln Pl + B_{23} \ln Pe + B_{24} \ln Ps + B_{25} \ln T$$
$$S_3 = A_3 + B_{31} \ln Pf + B_{32} \ln Pl + B_{33} \ln Pe + B_{34} \ln Ps + B_{35} \ln T$$
$$S_4 = A_4 + B_{41} \ln Pf + B_{42} \ln Pl + B_{43} \ln Pe + B_{44} \ln Ps + B_{45} \ln T$$

where $S_1, S_2, S_3,$ and S_4 are, respectively, the shares of fatalities, labor, energy, and salaries in total costs.[10] $Pf, Pl, Pe, Ps,$ and T are the maximum workmen's compensation cost, average annual earnings of full-time nonsalaried workers, the price of purchased power, average salaries, and a trend.[11] The A and B terms are coefficients to be estimated.

These equations are constrained to be homogeneous and symmetric ($B_{ij}=B_{ji}$). This allows derivation of the parameters of the fourth equation from the first three and so only they are estimated. The results are presented in table A2.3.

The B_{i5} coefficients represent the bias in technological change; a negative sign implies that it economized on that factor, while a positive sign implies that it was factor-using. The other B_{ij} coefficients can be used to estimate elasticities of substitution according to the formula $E_{ij} = (B_{ij}/S_i * S_j) + 1$, with results presented in table A2.4.[12]

These data yield two tentative findings. First, since B_{25} exceeds B_{15} in absolute value, technological change reduced labor more than it did fatalities,

TABLE A2.3. Factor Share Equations, Bituminous Coal Mining, 1919–1939

Parameter	Coefficient	T-Statistic
A_1	−0.0378	2.57
B_{11}	0.0056	3.65
B_{12}	−0.0061	2.57
B_{13}	0.0003	0.32
B_{15}	−0.0002	0.37
A_2	0.9368	29.79
B_{22}	0.0196	1.65
B_{23}	0.0020	0.43
B_{25}	−0.0080	2.61
A_3	0.0336	2.04
B_{33}	−0.0027	0.89
B_{35}	0.0063	3.36

Note: For interpretation, see text.

TABLE A2.4. Elasticities of Substitution, Bituminous Coal Mining, 1919–1939

Fatalities/labor	0.277	Labor/energy	1.040
Fatalities/energy	1.510	Labor/supervision	0.545
Fatalities/supervision	7.091	Supervision/energy	−2.03

Source: Estimated from data in table A2.3 employing the formula $E_{ij} = (Bij/S_i * S_j) + 1$.

thereby raising the fatality rate. Second, the elasticity of substitution between fatalities and labor is low ($E_{fl} = 0.277$); only a very large rise in workmen's compensation compared with wages would have induced a significant decline in the fatality rate.[13]

Metal-Mining Statistics

Fatality and injury rate data for mining other than coal are all but nonexistent prior to 1911. Some states collected information on both fatalities and employment in metal mining, and for the period 1894–1908 these were assembled by Frederick Hoffman to compute fatality rates per worker. I have reproduced these figures plus estimates of days worked to compute the fatality rates per worker and per 300-day worker prior to 1911 in table A2.5. Hoffman's figures are almost certainly underestimates, both because they probably include some employees—but not fatalities—at ore-dressing plants, but also because there are no data from places such as Arizona where mining was largely unregulated and therefore probably relatively dangerous.[14]

TABLE A2.5. Metal and Nonmetallic Mining Fatality Rates, 1894–1939

	Per Thousand 300-Day Workers						Per Thousand Workers, Total
	Copper	Gold, Silver	Iron	Lead, Zinc	Non-metallic	Total	
1894	—	—	—	—	—	3.83	3.39
1895	—	—	—	—	—	—	4.79
1896	—	—	—	—	—	4.29	
1897	—	—	—	—	—	—	3.82
1898	—	—	—	—	—	—	3.59
1899	—	—	—	—	—	—	2.87
1900	—	—	—	—	—	—	3.18
1901	—	—	—	—	—	—	3.47
1902	—	—	—	—	—	2.70	2.74
1903	—	—	—	—	—	—	2.40
1904	—	—	—	—	—	—	2.76
1905	—	—	—	—	—	—	3.41
1906	—	—	—	—	—	—	2.98
1907	—	—	—	—	—	—	2.83
1908	—	—	—	—	—	—	2.37
1909	—	—	—	—	—	—	—
1910	—	—	—	—	—	—	—
1911	5.18	4.28	4.64	4.03	2.01	4.45	4.19
1912	4.53	4.32	3.90	4.28	1.66	4.10	3.91
1913	4.08	3.83	3.29	3.90	3.02	3.72	3.57
1914	3.85	4.06	3.78	4.32	3.73	3.92	3.54
1915	3.72	4.79	2.88	5.37	2.43	3.89	3.61
1916	3.64	4.05	3.41	3.14	3.00	3.62	3.41
1917	5.88	4.03	3.54	4.09	2.48	4.44	4.25
1918	3.45	4.27	3.45	3.58	1.67	3.57	3.54
1919	3.54	4.41	3.09	4.13	1.65	3.47	3.22
1920	3.43	4.20	2.34	3.27	2.89	3.16	3.11
1921	3.70	3.29	3.04	2.58	1.98	3.09	2.45
1922	3.00	5.35	3.00	2.64	2.39	3.54	3.25
1923	3.11	3.93	2.38	2.73	2.67	3.01	2.98
1924	3.55	4.99	2.95	2.76	1.94	3.51	3.39
1925	2.94	3.83	2.54	3.32	1.71	2.99	2.93
1926	3.45	3.27	4.23	3.05	2.62	3.47	3.36
1927	3.46	3.91	2.45	2.64	2.19	3.10	2.94
1928	3.03	2.60	2.16	1.62	2.13	2.50	2.40
1929	3.03	3.66	2.98	2.08	2.29	3.03	2.95
1930	2.76	4.49	2.68	1.63	0.75	2.92	2.63

TABLE A2.5. Continued

| | Per Thousand 300-Day Workers | | | | | | Per Thousand Workers, Total |
	Copper	Gold, Silver	Iron	Lead, Zinc	Non-metallic	Total	
1931	3.01	2.88	1.91	2.56	1.63	2.53	1.95
1932	3.01	3.66	1.18	3.95	1.56	2.89	2.01
1933	2.49	2.20	1.82	0.85	1.39	2.45	1.67
1934	1.96	1.33	1.59	0.91	1.23	2.36	1.74
1935	2.05	2.86	2.15	2.26	1.01	2.42	1.78
1936	2.60	2.70	2.01	3.33	0.45	2.37	3.20
1937	2.26	2.60	1.73	1.47	1.52	2.20	1.97
1938	1.66	1.27	1.69	3.38	0.80	1.99	1.51
1939	2.17	2.08	1.55	2.88	1.37	1.99	1.54

Source: Fatality rates per worker for 1893–1908 are for metal mining only and are taken from Frederick Hoffman, "Fatal Accidents in American Metal Mines," *EMJ* 89 (Mar. 5, 1910): 510-12. For the procedures employed to compute rates per 300-day worker for this period, see text. The data from 1911 on are from W. W. Adams, "Metal and Nonmetal Mine Accidents in the United States, 1942," BM *Bulletin* 461 (Washington, D.C., 1944), table 35.

Beginning in 1911 the bureau collected data from companies on lost-workday injuries, fatalities, employment, and days worked from metal and nonmetallic mines, which it used to compute the fatality rates per 300-day worker that are presented in table A2.5. The bureau never discussed in detail the reliability of these data, but it did point out that the rise in reported injury rates was probably an artifact of better reporting, which was itself the result of workmen's compensation laws.[15]

The fatality and injury rates per million manhours for copper and iron mining from 1931 on in table A2.6 are bureau data, and they derive from payroll figures. The figures for 1911-30 are my estimates. They employ the bureau data on fatalities and injuries. The bureau presented data on employment but not manhours in copper mining from 1911 on. Identical employment data, along with estimates of manhours, are contained in a WPA study of copper mining, and these are the figures employed.[16] For iron mining a somewhat different procedure was necessary. The bureau presented figures on employment and manshifts, but not manhours. Manhours along with average hours per day are available in a WPA study on iron mining, but the employment data do not precisely match the bureau's figures.[17] Hence, for iron mining, manhours were computed as the product of the bureau's figures on man-days times average hours per day. For 1911-14 I employed the 1915 estimate of daily hours.

307

MINING

TABLE A2.6. Copper- and Iron-Mining Injury and Fatality Rates per Million Manhours, 1911–1939

	Copper		Iron	
	Fatality Rate	*Injury Rate*	*Fatality Rate*	*Injury Rate*
1911	2.16	93.12	1.74	94.50
1912	1.89	107.67	1.48	116.14
1913	1.70	96.17	1.23	65.44
1914	1.61	130.08	1.42	79.75
1915	1.55	133.99	1.08	74.56
1916	1.52	133.16	1.26	88.95
1917	2.45	130.56	1.26	80.69
1918	1.44	134.22	1.13	74.12
1919	1.48	129.00	1.13	72.64
1920	1.43	134.67	0.85	72.64
1921	1.54	132.31	1.11	77.25
1922	1.25	133.66	1.13	66.46
1923	1.30	145.45	0.87	55.03
1924	1.48	144.80	1.09	51.42
1925	1.22	146.10	0.95	59.71
1926	1.44	120.12	1.57	49.60
1927	1.44	109.01	0.92	38.42
1928	1.26	92.08	0.81	36.75
1929	1.26	93.26	1.15	34.68
1930	1.15	55.50	1.00	30.49
1931	1.24	62.90	0.72	19.78
1932	1.24	46.16	0.44	16.59
1933	1.04	54.49	0.72	19.90
1934	0.81	45.43	0.66	20.12
1935	0.85	65.76	0.89	17.83
1936	1.09	80.77	0.84	25.02
1937	0.94	94.99	0.72	30.12
1938	0.69	60.58	0.70	15.99
1939	0.90	58.93	0.64	16.87

Source: For 1911–30, see explanation in text. For 1931 on, rates are from Adams, "Metal and Nonmetal Mine Accidents in the United States, 1942," table 37.

Manufacturing and Economywide
Injury and Fatality Rates
1870–1939

This appendix contains three sorts of information. First, there are data on injury and fatality rates for important companies and industries. Second, there are state fatality rate data and statistical estimates of the determinants of injury frequency by state and injury for 1925 and 1927. Finally, there are tables that estimate the effects of long-period changes in industrial or occupational composition of the labor force.

Company and Industry Injury Rates

Beginning around World War I, there is an immense amount of fragmentary information on company and industry injury rates. Most of it is for short periods, however, or is otherwise unsatisfactory, and so I have made little use of it. The steel industry voluntarily provided its data to the Bureau of Labor Statistics, but the information covered most of the industry. In 1923 the Census listed 470,000 workers employed in blast furnaces, steel works, and rolling mills, while the sample reporting to the BLS included 434,000 300-day workers. Hence, the figures must be representative. U.S. Steel never made its injury rates public, preferring instead to present the information in the form of percentage declines from some earlier period. However, Lucian Chaney inadvertently identified them, and I have linked his data to later BLS materials to trace out U.S. Steel's safety record.

The DuPont data are from various unpublished sources in that company's papers at the Hagley library. The cement and paper industry data, like those from the steel industry, derive from voluntary collections. For cement, the data for 1919 represent 67 out of 123 establishments listed in the Census for that year; by 1927, 146 of the 161 plants in the industry reported. It seems likely, therefore, that these figures provide a trustworthy picture of safety progress in that industry.

The information on the paper and pulp industry is less complete. In 1921 only 26 out of an industry total of 738 establishments provided information, but they employed 31,000 of the industry's 115,000 employees, which implies, of

TABLE A3.1. Steel Industry Injury, Fatality, and Severity Rates, 1907–1939

| | United States Steel | Steel Industry | | |
	Injury Rate	Fatality Rate	Injury Rate	Severity Rate
1907	—	0.7	80.8	7.2
1908	—	—	—	—
1909	—	—	—	—
1910	—	0.5	74.7	5.2
1911	—	0.3	51.5	3.5
1912	—	0.4	62.2	4.2
1913	60.3	0.4	59.6	4.3
1914	43.5	0.3	50.0	3.2
1915	41.5	0.2	40.0	2.7
1916	44.5	0.3	43.0	3.5
1917	34.5	0.4	47.7	4.0
1918	28.8	0.4	39.4	3.6
1919	26.1	0.4	41.6	3.6
1920	22.9	0.2	38.3	3.7
1921	13.2	0.2	30.8	2.5
1922	13.0	0.2	33.0	2.7
1923	12.7	0.2	33.2	2.7
1924	10.2	0.3	30.8	3.0
1925	8.2	0.2	28.3	2.5
1926	6.8	0.2	20.9	2.3
1927	5.3	0.2	18.8	2.2
1928	—	0.2	20.6	2.4
1929	—	0.2	20.0	2.0
1930	7.7	0.2	17.8	2.3
1931	7.8	0.2	17.5	2.3
1932	8.1	0.2	16.8	2.1
1933	9.1	0.2	19.5	2.3
1934	8.1	0.2	19.7	2.5
1935	6.3	0.2	14.9	2.2
1936	7.2	0.2	15.8	2.1
1937	6.8	0.2	15.4	2.2
1938	5.7	0.1	10.0	1.9
1939	4.4	0.1	9.7	1.8

Source: For U.S. Steel, see Lucian Chaney, "The Statistical Factor in the Accident Experience of the Iron and Steel Industry," Industrial Accident Prevention Conference Proceedings, in BLS Bulletin 428 (Washington, D.C., 1926): 35–40; "Statistics of Industrial Accidents in the United States to the End of 1927," BLS Bulletin 490 (Washington, D.C., 1929); "Injury Experience in the Iron and Steel Industry," MLR

TABLE A3.1. Continued

43 (Dec. 1936): 1370-84; and "Injury Experience in the Iron and Steel Industry, 1938 and 1939," *MLR* 51 (Aug. 1940): 322-33. For the industry as a whole, see BLS *Bulletin* 490 and various issues of *MLR*.

Note: Rates for fatalities and all injuries are per million manhours. Severity rates are lost workdays per thousand manhours.

TABLE A3.2. Injury, Fatality, and Severity Rates for Cement and Paper and Pulp Producers, 1909-1939

	Portland Cement			Paper and Pulp	
	Fatality Rate	Injury Rate	Severity Rate	Injury Rate	Severity Rate
1909	—	97	—	—	—
1910	—	67	—	—	—
1911	—	77	—	—	—
1912	—	—	—	—	—
1913	—	—	—	—	—
1914	—	—	—	—	—
1915	—	—	—	—	—
1916	—	—	—	—	—
1917	—	—	—	—	—
1918	—	—	—	—	—
1919	1.7	43.5	9.9	—	—
1920	0.9	43.9	10.6	46.3	2.6
1921	0.7	42.5	8.0	41.7	2.8
1922	0.8	40.9	6.5	47.8	2.4
1923	0.6	41.6	5.4	43.5	2.7
1924	0.7	35.3	5.9	41.6	2.1
1925	0.6	26.1	5.0	38.4	2.2
1926	0.5	22.8	4.0	32.0	2.0
1927	0.3	14.6	3.0	30.3	2.0
1928	0.4	10.6	3.8	24.7	2.2
1929	0.5	9.6	4.2	28.4	1.8
1930	0.3	6.3	2.5	23.7	1.9
1931	0.5	5.6	3.3	20.6	—
1932	0.2	4.7	1.8	17.8	1.9
1933	0.2	4.8	2.4	19.5	1.7
1934	0.5	7.1	4.3	19.1	2.0
1935	0.3	6.9	3.0	17.1	1.9
1936	0.4	7.6	3.8	17.7	1.6
1937	0.4	5.2	3.1	18.5	2.0

TABLE A3.2. Continued

	Portland Cement			Paper and Pulp	
	Fatality Rate	Injury Rate	Severity Rate	Injury Rate	Severity Rate
1938	0.3	4.6	2.4	15.3	1.2
1939	0.1	4.3	2.0	15.2	1.7

Source: For cement, the data for 1909–11 are estimates from J. R. Curtis, "Analysis of Accidents in the Cement Industry," NSC *Proceedings* 26 (1937): 250–52; other figures are from Portland Cement Association *Accident Prevention Bulletin*, various issues. Paper and pulp data are from *National Safety News and Accident Facts*, various issues.

Note: Rates for fatalities and all injuries are per million manhours. Severity rates are lost workdays per thousand manhours.

TABLE A3.3. DuPont Company Injury, Fatality, and Severity Rates, 1903–1937

	Injury Rate	Fatality Rate	Severity Rate
1903	—	3.78	—
1904	—	3.82	—
1905	—	3.08	—
1906	—	3.19	—
1907	—	5.21	—
1908	—	3.05	—
1909	—	1.72	—
1910	—	2.07	—
1911	—	1.08	—
1912	43.15	0.68	9.26
1913	37.54	1.58	10.70
1914	29.66	0.57	4.52
1915	17.30	0.57	4.09
1916	31.20	1.11	8.03
1917	23.50	0.40	3.53
1918	19.20	0.46	4.08
1919	20.33	0.44	4.07
1920	15.08	0.64	4.90
1921	14.71	0.38	3.80
1922	10.60	0.51	5.05
1923	11.08	0.35	3.86
1924	8.50	0.55	4.17
1925	12.80	0.52	4.17
1926	10.30	0.42	3.27
1927	3.40	0.28	2.32

	Injury Rate	Fatality Rate	Severity Rate
1928	4.92	0.22	2.14
1929	4.75	0.18	1.87
1930	4.04	0.12	1.72
1931	2.23	0.08	0.83
1932	2.29	0.24	2.11
1933	2.90	0.13	1.61
1934	3.03	0.23	2.24
1935	2.10	0.07	0.99
1936	2.02	0.07	0.86
1937	1.85	0.09	0.82

Source: Data are from "Comments on Personal Injury Statistics, Twelve Months Ending December 25, 1924" and "Personal Injury Statistics, Twelve Months Ending December 21, 1937," Administrative Papers, boxes 68 and 71, accession 1662, DP.

Note: Rates for fatalities and all injuries are per million manhours. Severity rates are lost workdays per thousand manhours.

course, that they were much larger than was typical. The data become increasingly representative, however; by 1925, 99 (of 763) plants reported, and they employed 42,000 of the industry's 124,000 workers. In any year the reporting plants probably had lower-than-average accident rates. For this reason, and because the sample becomes increasingly representative, it probably understates the true decline in injury frequency and severity.

State Injury and Fatality Rates

TABLE A3.4. Fatality Rates per Thousand Manufacturing Workers, Selected States, 1911–1939

	California	Maryland	Massachusetts	New York	Pennsylvania
1911	—	—	0.18	—	—
1912	—	—	—	—	—
1913	—	—	—	—	—
1914	0.68	0.36	—	0.26	—
1915	—	—	0.23	—	—
1916	—	—	0.20	—	0.73
1917	—	—	0.23	—	0.80

	California	Maryland	Massachusetts	New York	Pennsylvania
1918	—	—	0.19	—	0.77
1919	0.32	0.41	0.19	0.22	0.54
1920	—	—	0.16	—	0.56
1921	0.32	0.66	0.20	0.18	0.41
1922	—	—	0.17	—	0.42
1923	—	0.09	0.19	0.22	0.52
1924	—	—	—	—	0.45
1925	0.40	0.21	0.16	0.21	0.44
1926	—	—	0.19	—	0.42
1927	0.30	0.33	0.22	0.20	0.36
1928	—	—	0.23	—	0.33
1929	0.40	0.24	0.20	0.22	0.34
1930	—	—	0.16	—	0.33
1931	0.24	0.28	0.18	0.19	0.26
1932	—	—	0.12	—	0.26
1933	0.29	0.23	0.10	0.13	0.23
1934	—	—	0.14	—	0.25
1935	0.25	0.23	0.14	0.14	0.24
1936	—	—	0.09	—	0.24
1937	0.26	0.21	0.14	0.16	0.26
1938	—	—	0.12	—	0.16
1939	0.17	0.18	0.09	0.12	—

Source: Fatalities are from California, *Report of the Industrial Accident Commission;* Maryland, *Report of the Industrial Accident Commission;* Massachusetts, *Report of the Industrial Accident Board;* New York Department of Labor and Industries *Bulletins;* Pennsylvania Department of Labor and Industries *Special Bulletin* 47 (1939). Employment data for all states except Pennsylvania and Massachusetts are from the *U.S. Census of Manufactures.* For years in which only wage earners were reported, employment was estimated using the previous ratio of employment to wage earners. A similar approach was applied to Massachusetts wage-earner data from that state's Department of Labor and Industries *Statistics of Manufactures in Massachusetts.* Pennsylvania data are for employees and are in Department of Internal Affairs, Bureau of Statistics, "Comparable Statistics for Manufacturing Industries in Pennsylvania, 1916–1962," series S-14 (June 1964).

Note: Massachusetts employment is on a calendar-year basis and injuries on a fiscal-year basis. New York fatalities are closed workmen's compensation cases.

TABLE A3.5. Determinants of Manufacturing Injury Rates, 1925 and 1927

Independent Variables	(1)	(2)
Temp cost	−0.004	−0.002
	(1.99)	(0.96)
Productivity (× 1,000)	−0.083	0.041
	(1.88)	(2.29)
Plant size (× 1,000)	−0.063	0.056
	(2.28)	(2.29)
Supervision	−1.868	−2.07
	(4.39)	(4.67)
Horsepower	0.013	0.031
	(1.23)	(2.82)
State dummies	yes	no
Industry dummies	yes	yes
R^2	0.74	0.70
N	369	369

Source: Injury frequency rates by state and industry are from "Statistics of Industrial Accidents in the United States to the End of 1927," BLS *Bulletin* 490 (Washington, D.C., 1929). Data on horsepower, plant size, supervision, and productivity by state and industry are from U.S. Census, *Biennial Census of Manufactures, 1925* and *1927*. Workmen's compensation costs by state are from various BLS publications.

Note: The dependent variable is the natural log of the frequency rate. Horsepower is per wage earner. Plant size is wage earners per establishment. Supervision and productivity are, respectively, salaried employees and value added per wage earner. Temp cost is average length of a covered temporary injury times proportion of all injuries covered times the percentage of the wage covered. Figures in parentheses are *t*-ratios. Both equations are employment-weighted and contain controls for year and differing state reporting requirements.

Labor Force Composition

The data in table A3.6 estimate the impact of sectoral shifts in labor force composition. The manhour data, taken from John W. Kendrick, *Productivity Trends in the United States*, NBER General Series 71 (Princeton: Princeton Univ. Press, 1961), need no discussion. The information on injury rates, however, was pieced together from a large number of sources. Injury and fatality rates for government are for 1935, from "Accident Experience of Federal Civilian Employees, 1933-1935," *MLR* 43 (Aug. 1936): 356-63. The injury data have been divided by 1.3 to adjust for medical cases not resulting in lost workdays. Transportation rates are from ICC *Accident Bulletin* 108 (1939), adjusted to include less-than-four-day injuries, which are 39.1 percent of the total. The agricultural fatality rate was computed by dividing fatalities to agricultural workers (from Max Kossoris and Swen Kjaer, "Industrial Injuries in the United States

TABLE A3.6. The Impact of Changes in Employment among Industry
Groups on Injury and Fatality Rates, 1869–1948

	Manhour Share					Injury Rate	Fatality Rate
	1869 (%)	1899 (%)	1929 (%)	1937 (%)	1948 (%)		
Government	1.78	2.29	4.08	8.13	6.45	16.65	0.200
Private	98.21	97.71	95.92	91.87	93.55	—	—
Farm	41.13	31.14	21.26	21.92	14.66	17.36	0.185
Nonfarm	57.09	66.57	74.66	69.95	74.66	—	—
Agricultural services	0.30	0.51	0.51	0.54	0.50	17.36	0.185
Mining	1.10	1.96	1.93	1.52	1.60	70.78	1.490
Construction	5.05	4.71	4.43	3.05	5.37	61.84	0.909
Manufacturing	18.41	19.78	20.27	19.36	25.14	15.43	0.088
Trade	10.19	13.99	19.66	19.49	21.29	9.33	0.027
FIRE[a]	0.41	1.15	3.14	3.17	3.20	3.90	0.036
Transportation	5.53	8.48	6.63	5.16	5.83	11.61	0.210
C&PU[b]	0.36	0.68	2.10	1.70	2.11	9.24	0.115
Service	15.42	14.92	15.19	15.13	12.78	9.53	0.050
Government enterprise	0.31	0.80	0.80	0.82	1.09	14.58	0.070
Average injury rate	14.27	15.59	16.17	15.46	10.93	—	—
Average fatality rate	0.182	0.182	0.165	0.133	0.162	—	—

Source: Sectoral shares of manhours are computed from John W. Kendrick, *Productivity Trends in the United States*, NBER General Series 71 (Princeton: Princeton Univ. Press, 1961), table A-XI. For the sources of injury and fatality rates, see text.

[a] Finance, insurance, and real estate.
[b] Communications and public utilities.

during 1937," *MLR* 48 [Mar. 1939]: 597–611, table 1) by total agricultural manhours (from Kendrick, table A-XI). For agricultural injuries I used (injuries divided by fatalities) for the entire economy times agricultural fatalities to adjust for likely undercounting. Mining is a manhour-weighted average for 1940 computed from data in W. W. Adams and M. F. Kolhas, "Metal and Nonmetal Mining Accidents in the United States," BM *Bulletin* 450 (Washington, D.C., 1941), table 36. All other data are for 1939 and are from Max Kossoris and Swen Kjaer, "Industrial Injuries in the United States during 1939," *MLR* 51 (July 1940): 86–108.

Table A3.7 presents estimates of the effects that changes in the composition of manufacturing employment (manhours) had on the average safety of work. Again, the manhour data are from Kendrick. The injury and severity rates are derived from Kossoris and Kjaer, "Industrial Injuries in the United States during 1939." Where industry matches were inexact, the following substitutions were used: for beverages, the rate for food; for apparel, the rate for men's and women's clothing; for lumbering, the rate for lumber and products minus furniture; for primary metals, the rate for iron and steel; for fabricated metals, the rate for iron and steel and products, minus iron and steel; for nonelectrical machinery, the rate for all machinery minus electrical machinery; for miscellaneous, the average for all industries.

Table A3.8 presents the effects of changing occupations on the economy-wide injury rate. The manhour shares are assumed to equal employment shares

TABLE A3.7. The Impact of Changes in Employment among Manufacturing Industries on Injury and Severity Rates, 1899–1948

| | Manhour Share | | | | | |
	1899 (%)	1929 (%)	1937 (%)	1948 (%)	Injury Rate	Severity Rate
Food	8.34	9.09	10.20	8.66	18.9	1.39
Beverages	1.37	0.44	1.19	1.33	18.9	1.39
Textiles	15.35	12.81	11.41	8.89	9.0	0.68
Apparel	7.42	6.42	6.56	6.88	5.5	0.27
Lumber	13.74	7.54	6.65	4.76	51.4	6.64
Furniture	2.04	2.40	2.09	2.17	19.7	1.91
Paper	2.32	3.22	3.22	3.27	20.5	1.95
Printing	5.16	6.06	5.79	5.29	7.0	0.72
Chemicals	2.76	3.60	4.07	4.50	10.0	1.83
Petroleum	0.81	1.44	1.22	1.43	8.7	1.71
Rubber	0.78	1.75	1.40	1.62	9.8	0.79
Leather	5.71	3.57	3.48	2.49	19.2	0.60
Stone, clay, glass	5.24	3.84	3.88	4.03	21.2	2.24
Primary metals	6.58	7.27	8.10	7.47	8.7	1.83
Fabricated metals	6.15	6.63	6.90	7.61	23.4	2.03
Nonelectrical machinery	8.45	10.37	10.37	13.15	15.2	1.12
Electrical machinery	0.99	4.54	3.92	5.55	5.6	0.83
Transportation equipment	4.45	6.35	6.79	7.74	13.1	1.54
Miscellaneous	2.35	2.65	2.75	3.15	15.4	1.64
Average injury rate	18.24	15.76	15.64	15.01	—	—
Average severity rate	2.04	1.76	1.73	1.56	—	—

Source: Manhour shares are computed from data in Kendrick, Productivity Trends in the United States, table D-IV. Injury and severity rates derived from Max Kossoris and Swen Kjaer, "Industrial Injuries in the United States during 1939," MLR 51 (July 1940): 86–108; for details, see text.

TABLE A3.8. The Impact of Changes in Employment among Nonfarm
Occupations on Injury and Fatality Rates, 1870–1940

| | Employment Share | | | | | | | |
| | 1870 | | 1900 | | 1940 | | | |
	All (%)	Women (%)	All (%)	Women (%)	All (%)	Women (%)	Injury Rate	Fatality Rate
Professional, technical managerial	16.28	6.95	16.10	11.71	17.89	16.76	1.10	0.034
Clerical and sales	7.18	0.93	12.04	10.21	19.73	30.04	6.12	0.053
Manual	54.30	25.27	57.33	34.26	48.18	22.54	30.22	0.284
Service	22.24	66.86	14.47	43.75	14.20	30.66	6.40	0.034
Average injury rate	18.11	12.01	18.60	13.43	15.95	9.39	—	—
Average fatality rate	0.171	0.097	0.168	0.122	0.158	0.096	—	—

Source: Employment shares for 1870 are computed from Janet Hooks, "Women's Occupations through Seven Decades," Women's Bureau *Bulletin* 218 (Washington, D.C, 1947); other years are from *Historical Statistics of the United States.* For a discussion of the sources of injury and fatality rates, see text.

derived from BLS publications. The injury and fatality rates for each occupational group were estimated as follows:

Professional, technical, and managerial workers: The railroad injury rate for this group for 1940 was 0.67 (ICC *Accident Bulletin* 109 [1940]). Adjustment of this figure for the absence of less-than-four-day injuries (which were 60.9 percent of all injuries) yields the result of 1.10 (0.67/0.609). The fatality rate is from the same source.

Clerical and sales workers: A weighted average of the two with weights of 0.591 and 0.409 computed from *Historical Statistics of the United States,* series D-182. The railroad injury rate for clerical workers in 1940 was 0.87; adjusting for the absence of less-than-four-day injuries yields the result of 1.43; the fatality rate was 0.02. The injury rate for sales workers is 12.9, from Max Kossoris and Swen Kjaer, "Industrial Injuries in the United States during 1940," *MLR* 53 (Aug. 1941): 327–54; the fatality rate is 0.10, which was estimated as the ratio of fatalities to total injuries times the frequency rate, both also from the same source.

Manual workers: The injury and fatality rates for manual workers are employment-weighted averages of those in manufacturing, mining, and construction, with weights taken from the 1940 Census:

Manual = 0.758(ManualMfg) + 0.076(ManualMining) + 0.166(ManualConst)

It was assumed that all workers in the latter two industries are manual workers. Injury and fatality rates for mining are manhour-weighted averages of all mining industries, taken from BM *Bulletin* 450, table 36. The construction injury and fatality rates are averages of 1939 and 1940 data, from Kossoris and Kjaer,

"Industrial Injuries in the United States during 1940." The rate for manual workers in manufacturing (Mfgm) was computed as follows. The average rate for all manufacturing workers (Mfgt) is from Kossoris and Kjaer, "Industrial Injuries in the United States during 1940." The rate for nonmanual workers (Mfgnm) was taken to be equal to the clerical sales rate above. Shares (s_i) of each group in manufacturing employment are from the 1940 Census. Thus,

$$Mfgt = s_1(Mfgm) + s_2(Mfgnm)$$

The estimated numbers are $15.43 = 0.629(Mfgm) + 0.371(1.43)$; hence, the estimated rate for Mfgm is 30.27.

Service: The injury rate is for personal services, from Kossoris and Kjaer, "Industrial Injuries in the United States during 1940." The fatality rate is the ratio of fatalities to all injuries for all services from the same source times the injury rate.

NOTES

ABBREVIATIONS

AIME   American Institute of Mining Engineers
AMC   American Mining Congress
ARA   American Railway Association
AREA   American Railway Engineering Association
ASCE   American Society of Civil Engineers
ASME   American Society of Mechanical Engineers
BLS   United States Bureau of Labor Statistics
BM   United States Bureau of Mines
BP   Bancroft Papers, Hagley Museum and Library
CAS   Casualty Actuarial Society
DP   DuPont Papers, Hagley Museum and Library
EMJ   *Engineering and Mining Journal*
EN   *Engineering News*
FD 512 Formal Docket 512, Interstate Commerce Commission, Record Group
        134, National Archives
GC   General Correspondence, Department of Mines, Record Group 45,
        Pennsylvania Archives
GCB   General Correspondence, Bituminous, Department of Mines, Record
        Group 45, Pennsylvania Archives
GCF   General Classified Files, Bureau of Mines, Record Group 70, National
        Archives
HCP   Hudson Coal Company Papers, Record Group 2, Historical Collections
        and Labor Archives, Pennsylvania State University
HML   Hagley Museum and Library
IAIABC International Association of Industrial Accident Boards and Commissions
ICC   Interstate Commerce Commission
ILO   International Labor Office
MLR   *Monthly Labor Review*
NAM   National Association of Manufacturers
NCAB   *National Cyclopedia of American Biography*
NSC   National Safety Council
NSN   *National Safety News*
PRRC   Pennsylvania Railroad Collection, Hagley Museum and Library

RA   *Railway Age*
RG   *Railroad Gazette*
RR   *Railway Review*
RRC   Records of the Railroad Commission, Record Group 41, Connecticut
          State Archives
SCCC   Stonega Coke and Coal Papers, Hagley Museum and Library
SE   *Safety Engineering*
USGS   United States Geological Survey

INTRODUCTION

1. Bert Wright Diary, Luther Collection, Eastern Regional Coal Archives, Blue-field, West Virginia. I am grateful to the archivist, Dr. Stuart McGehee, for bringing the diary to my attention.

2. Steve Pfarrer, "Machine Severs City Man's Arm," *Daily Hampshire Gazette*, Mar. 29, 1995, 1.

3. For a brief discussion of secondary materials on the history of work safety, see the Note on Sources.

4. On the importance of managerial changes, see Alfred D. Chandler, *The Visible Hand: The Managerial Revolution in American Business* (Cambridge: Harvard Univ. Press, 1977). On systematic management, see Daniel Nelson and Stuart Campbell, "Taylorism vs. Welfare Work in American Industry: H. L. Gantt and the Bancrofts," *Business History Review* 46 (Spring 1972): 1-16, and Daniel Nelson, "Scientific Management, Systematic Management, and Labor, 1880-1915," *Business History Review* 48 (Winter 1974): 479-500. William Lazonick, *Competitive Advantage on the Shop Floor* (Cambridge: Harvard Univ. Press, 1990), stresses managerial efforts to control the shop floor.

5. Of course, not all changes worsened safety. Larry Lankton, *Cradle to Grave: Life, Work, and Death in Michigan Copper Mines* (New York: Oxford Univ. Press, 1991), argues that the safety of Michigan copper mining did not deteriorate in the late nineteenth century. David Noble, *America by Design: Science, Technology, and the Rise of Corporate Capitalism* (New York: Alfred A. Knopf, 1977), stresses that technological change is not the result of "disembodied historical forces." For an argument that judges fashioned employers' liability law so as to encourage economic development, see Lawrence Friedman and Jack Ladinsky, "Social Change and the Law of Industrial Accidents," *Columbia Law Review* 67 (Jan. 1967): 50-83, and Morton Horwitz, *Transformation of American Law* (Cambridge: Harvard Univ. Press, 1977). See also Christopher Tomlins, "A Mysterious Power: Industrial Accidents and the Legal Construction of Employment Relations in Massachusetts, 1800-1850," *Law and History Review* 6 (Fall 1988): 375-438, and Jonathan Simon, "For the Government of Its Servants: Law and Disciplinary Power in the Workplace, 1870-1906," *Studies in Law, Politics, and Society* 1993:105-36.

6. Earl Ubell, "Is Your Job Killing You?" *Parade Magazine*, Jan. 8, 1989, 4-7. These jobs are not strictly comparable, because of differences in exposure (hours worked), but the conclusion in the text remains.

7. Daniel Nelson, *Managers and Workers: Origins of the New Factory System in the United States, 1880-1920* (Madison: Univ. of Wisconsin Press, 1975), is the source of "empire of the foreman." On the importance of the foreman in nineteenth-century railroading, see Walter Licht, *Working for the Railroad* (Princeton: Princeton Univ. Press, 1983), who also stresses the role of labor in forcing modifications in the old ways of hiring, firing, and promotion. On management, see Sanford Jacoby, *Employing Bureaucracy* (New York: Columbia Univ. Press, 1985). For a general discussion of

"welfare capitalism" that says very little about safety, see Stuart Brandes, *American Welfare Capitalism* (Chicago: Univ. of Chicago Press, 1976).

8. Compare David Rosner and Gerald Markowitz, eds., *Dying for Work* (Bloomington: Indiana Univ. Press, 1987), xv, who miss the evolution of Safety First ideas.

9. On the loss of workers' control, see especially Richard Edwards, *Contested Terrain* (New York: Basic Books, 1979); David Brody, *Steelworkers in America: The Nonunion Era* (New York: Harper and Row, 1960) and *Workers in Industrial America*, 2d ed. (New York: Oxford Univ. Press, 1993); David Montgomery, *Workers' Control in America* (New York: Cambridge Univ. Press, 1979) and *The Fall of the House of Labor* (New York: Cambridge Univ. Press, 1987); Licht, *Working for the Railroad;* and Lazonick, *Competitive Advantage.* For an argument that employers used safety improvements as a means to gain control over work, see Harold Aurand, "Mine Safety and Social Control in the Anthracite Industry," *Pennsylvania History* 52 (Fall 1985): 227–41.

CHAPTER ONE. PERILOUS BUSINESS

Epigraphs: Charles Francis Adams, Jr., *Notes on Railroad Accidents* (New York: Putnam's, 1879), 2; Joseph Nimmo, *First Annual Report on the Internal Commerce of the United States* (Washington, D.C., 1877), 170.

1. "The Saving of Lives and Limbs by Automatic Car Couplers," *EN* 41 (Jan. 19, 1899): 41.

2. "Report of Alexander Black, Commissioner, to the Stockholders of the South Carolina Canal and Railroad Company," *American Railroad Journal* 2 (May 25, 1833): 323. "Blew poor Sambo" is from Robert B. Shaw, *Down Brakes: A History of Railroad Accidents, Safety Precautions, and Operating Practices in the United States of America* (London: P. R. Macmillan, 1961), 26–27.

3. "Report of the Committee Appointed to Examine and Report the Causes of Railroad Accidents, the Means of Preventing Their Occurrence, etc.," New York State Senate Document 13 (Albany, 1853); Railroad Commissioners to New York and New Haven Railroad, Sept. 15, 1859, and to New Haven, New London, and Stonington Railroad, Apr. 16, 1862, vol. 2, RRC.

4. On Ashtabula, see Ohio Legislature, *Report of the Joint Committee Concerning the Ashtabula Bridge Disaster* (Columbus, 1877), and Stephen Peet, *The Ashtabula Disaster* (Chicago, 1877), who quotes the coroner's jury. Theodore Cooper, "American Railroad Bridges," ASCE *Transactions* 21 (July 1889): 1–59; New York Board of Railroad Commissioners, *Report on Strains on Railroad Bridges* (Albany, 1891).

5. "Smoke orders" and similar practices are from Gilbert Lathrop, *Little Engines and Big Men* (Caldwell, Ohio, 1954), 235.

6. Wrecks on the Nashville and Chattanooga are from Jesse Burt, "The Savor of Old-Time Southern Railroading," Railway and Locomotive Historical Society *Bulletin* 84 (1951): 36–45. "Holocaust" is from Adams, *Railroad Accidents*, 62; for the stationmaster, see 161.

7. U.S. Commissioner of Railroads, *Report* (Washington, D.C., 1881), 427. A list of locomotive whistle signals is contained in ARA *Proceedings* 1 (1886–93). Labor turnover is from U.S. Commissioner of Labor, *Fifth Annual Report, Railroad Labor, 1889* (Washington, D.C., 1890). H. Roger Grant, ed., *Brownie the Boomer* (DeKalb: Northern Illinois Univ. Press, 1991).

8. Kentucky Railroad Commission, *Fourth Annual Report* (Frankfort, 1884), 41. For evidence of sharp variation in the safety of rail yards, see Grant, *Brownie the Boomer.*

9. New York *Herald Tribune*, "A Railway Horror," Feb. 8, 1871, 1, and "Railroad Horrors," Dec. 26, 1872, 1.

10. Simmons's death is from P. Dennis to John Gould, Apr. 31, 1859, vol. 1, RRC.

11. Grover and Herenden are from P. M. Andrews to Railroad Commission, July 10, 1872, and Oct. 13, 1873, vol. 10, RRC.

12. The old-timer's recollection is from Burt, "Savor of Old-Time Southern Railroading." The accident on the Erie is from New York State Board of Railroad Commissioners, *Annual Report* (Albany, 1852), 76–80.

13. Fatalities for the Brotherhood of Railroad Brakemen are contained in ICC, *Third Annual Report, 1889* (Washington, D.C., 1890), 85. Accident and mortality rates for firemen and enginemen are from *Eastern Concerted Wage Movement, 1912–1913, Supplemental Report of the International Brotherhood of Locomotive Firemen and Enginemen* (1913), 326. If the annual mortality rate is x, then the cumulative probability of death over k years is $1 - (1 - x)k$.

14. E. M. Reed to John Hutchinson, July 26, 1872, vol. 10, RRC.

15. Charles B. George, *Forty Years on the Rail* (Chicago: R. R. Donnelley, 1887), 78; Chauncey Del French, *Railroadman* (New York: Macmillan, 1938).

16. The equations are:

$$\text{Worker fatality rate} = 2.10 + 0.017(\text{Time})$$
$$(1.03)$$
$$R^2 = 0.08; \text{D.W.} = 1.81; N = 115$$

$$\text{Passenger fatality rate} = 43.62 - 0.79(\text{Time})$$
$$(3.27)$$
$$R^2 = 0.09; \text{D.W.} = 1.95; N = 130$$

Figures in parentheses are t-ratios. Both equations were estimated using a Cochran-Orcutt correction for serial correlation. They are, respectively, weighted by employment and passenger-miles to correct for heteroscedasticity using a time series processor (TSP) routine. The states included in the regressions are Connecticut, Illinois, Iowa, Massachusetts, Michigan, Minnesota, Ohio, Wisconsin, and New York, but not all states collected data for all years. Other states either collected no data or began so late that they provide little information on long-term trends.

17. "Accidents on British Railways in 1888," *EN* 22 (Sept. 21, 1889): 281; H. Raynar Wilson, *The Safety of British Railways* (London: P. S. King, 1909), chap. 18.

18. "British Board of Trade Returns," *RG* 26 (Aug. 10, 1894), 552.

19. The facts in this and the following paragraph are from Zerah Colburn and Alexander Holley, *The Permanent Way and Coal-Burning Boilers of European Railways* (New York: Holley and Colburn, 1858).

20. Edward Bates Dorsey, "English and American Railroads Compared," ASCE *Transactions* 15 (Jan. 1886): 1–79 and (Nov. 1886): 733–90; the quotation is from 2 and the discussion of Parliament and the Board of Trade is from 4–5.

21. Saving scarce engineering talent is from W. Howard White, "European Railways—As They Appear to an American Engineer," ASCE *Transactions* 3 (May 1874): 61–66. Gordon's paper is "On the Economical Construction and Operation of Railways in Countries Where Small Returns Are Expected as Exemplified by American Practice," Institution of Civil Engineers *Proceedings* (London) 85 (1886): 54–85. See also Arthur Mellen Wellington, *The Economic Theory of the Location of Railways*, rev. ed. (New York: John Wiley, 1887). H. J. Habakkuk, *American and British Technology in the Nineteenth Century* (New York: Cambridge Univ. Press, 1962), briefly notes the role of capital and labor scarcity in shaping American railroad construction practices. Alexander J. Field stresses the importance of high American interest rates in the decision to construct a relatively flimsy permanent way, but he ignores traffic density;

see "Land Abundance, Interest/Profit Rates, and Nineteenth Century American and British Technology," *Journal of Economic History* 43 (June 1983): 405-32.

22. Gordon, "On the Economical Construction," 72 (quoting Whittemore), 66, 77.

23. This paragraph is based on ibid. (quotations from 77 and 66), and Dorsey, "English and American Railroads Compared." Wellington, *Economic Theory*, 124, also remarks on the American propensity to use lots of ties, which were cheap, in place of heavy rail, which was not. This was one of many ways in which natural resource endowments shaped railroad technology. See also J. Elfreth Watkins, "Development of American Rail and Track," ASCE *Transactions* 22 (Apr. 1890): 209-33. For English views, see "American and British Permanent Way," *The Engineer* 82 (July 10, 1896): 37, and Great Britain, Board of Trade, *Report of Visit to America by Lt.-Colonel H. A. Yorke, September 19th to October 31st 1902* (London, 1903).

24. Gordon, "On the Economical Construction," 55.

25. Untitled article, *EN* 31 (Apr. 19, 1894): 324. An English view is William Acworth, "English and American Railways," *Engineering Magazine* 5 (May 1893): 197-205, who claimed that in Britain, heavy trains employed two engines while American carriers were likely to use one locomotive and overfire it, thereby reducing fuel economy but saving labor and capital. He attributed the difference to the cheapness of men and engines in Britain and of coal in America. American engineers agreed; see David Barnes, "Distinctive Features and Advantages of American Locomotive Practice," ASCE *Transactions* 29 (Aug. 1893): 384-425. John White, *A History of the American Locomotive: Its Development, 1830-1880* (Baltimore: Johns Hopkins Press, 1968), 9, claims that American locomotives used thinner iron and carried higher steam pressure.

26. "British Board of Trade and Accidents," *RG* 24 (Aug. 5, 1892): 573. For general discussions of block signals in Britain and the United States, see ICC, *Report on Block Signal Systems* (Washington, D.C., 1907), which stresses the importance of traffic density on 7. See also U.S. Block Signal and Train Control Board, *First Annual Report* (Washington, D.C., 1909), appendix A and p. 33. The early development of cab signals in Britain resulted from the inability to see wayside signals in fog.

27. Adams, *Railroad Accidents*, 258 and 267. H. Raynar Wilson "British Railway Methods and Management with Special Reference to Safety in Operations," *EN* 56 (Aug. 30, 1906): 218-22, and H. D. Emerson, "The Train Order System and the Block System on American Railways," *EN* 53 (Jan. 5, 1905): 11-13, provide a general comparison of safety on British and American roads. The Block Signal and Train Control Board's *First Annual Report* and *Second Annual Report* (Washington, D.C., 1909) both review British signaling practice as it affected railroad safety.

28. The effects of differences in rolling stock on worker risks is stressed in "Car Couplers for English Railways," *EN* 37 (June 10, 1897): 361, and Wilson, "British Railway Methods."

29. See "Car Couplers on English Railways" and W. D. Phillips, "The Progressive Development of English Coupling," *RG* 31 (Oct. 20, 1899): 31-32. The three-link coupler was far less dangerous than the American link and pin, but it was not entirely benign, and after the automatic coupler was installed on American roads, Europeans evidenced considerable interest in applying it but found that it would not work well with existing buffers. In addition, its weight was a much greater disadvantage on the considerably smaller European rolling stock. See Royal Commission on Accidents to Railway Servants, *Report on the Causes of the Accidents, Fatal and Non-fatal, to Servants of Railway Companies and of Truck Owners* (London, 1900); William F. Pettigrew, "Report on Automatic Couplers," and G. Noltein, "Report on Automatic Couplers," in International Railway Congress *Proceedings* (Washington, D.C.), 2, 7th sess., sec. 8 (1905):

2–28 and 29–64; and Great Britain Board of Trade, *Third Report of the Committee Appointed to Examine and, Where Necessary, to Test, Appliances Designed to Diminish the Danger to Men Employed in Railway Service* (London, 1908). The three-link chain was used in the United States until the 1850s according to George, *Forty Years on the Rail*, 32.

30. *RG* 29 (Mar. 20, 1894): 232.

31. Adams's remarks are from *Railroad Accidents*, 164–5. The importance of labor costs is also stressed in ICC, *Report on Block Signal Systems*, 9–10. The quotation on the lack of training of telegraphers is from "Dangerous Retrenchment," *RG* 22 (Feb. 7, 1890): 94. Block Signal and Train Control Board, *Third Annual Report* (Washington, D.C., 1911), appendix E, reports the results of inspections of many signaling systems, which show wide variance in the quality of telegraphers. The comparison of British and American signalmen is in its *First Annual Report* and *Second Annual Report*.

32. Wilson, "British Railway Methods," 220. In an effort to reduce labor turnover, American carriers increasingly developed pension plans and other personnel policies. For details, see M. Riebenack, *Railway Provident Institutions in English Speaking Countries* (Philadelphia, 1905), and Bryce Stewart and Murray Latimer, *Pensions for Industrial and Business Employees*, vol. 3, *Railroad Pensions in the United States and Canada* (New York: Industrial Relations Counselors, 1929).

33. Wilson, "British Railway Methods," 219; William Acworth, "English and American Railways," *Engineering Magazine* 5 (Apr. 1893): 23–32.

34. The story of the Boston and Albany is from Stephen Salsbury, *The State, the Investor, and the Railway; Boston and Albany, 1825–1867* (Cambridge: Harvard Univ. Press, 1967), chap. 9. On the introduction of the telegraph, see Edward Hungerford, *Men of Erie* (New York: Random House, 1946), chap. 9. The origin and functions of early state railroad commissions are discussed in Frederick Clark, "State Railroad Commissions and How They May Be Made Effective," American Economic Association *Publications* 6 (1891): 473–583.

35. The Massachusetts commission's response to the Revere accident is in its *Third Annual Report* (Boston, 1872). The historian is Thomas McCraw, *Prophets of Regulation* (Cambridge: Belknap Press, 1984), 25–31, quotation on 29. Charles Francis Adams, "The Revere Catastrophe," *Atlantic Monthly* 37 (Jan. 1876): 92–103; Adams, *Railroad Accidents*, 244.

36. New York State Board of Railroad Commissioners, *Annual Report* (Albany, 1886), xviii. The railroads' failure to follow the board's urging is noted in the *Annual Report* (Albany, 1887), xiii.

37. Massachusetts Board of Railroad Commissioners, *Second Annual Report* (Boston, 1871), 25. A list of state regulations governing railroad safety is contained in "Report of the Committee on Safety Appliances," ARA *Proceedings* 1 (1886–93): 37–38.

38. This section is based heavily on Charles Clark, "The Railroad Safety Movement in the United States: Origins and Development, 1869 to 1893" (Ph.D. diss., Univ. of Illinois, 1966). For an excellent discussion of the technology, see John H. White, Jr., *The American Railroad Freight Car* (Baltimore: Johns Hopkins Univ. Press, 1993), chap. 7. See also Steven Usselman, "Air Brakes for Freight Trains: Technological Innovation in the American Railroad Industry, 1869–1900," *Business History Review* 58 (Spring 1984): 30–50.

39. Adams, *Railroad Accidents*, chap. 5, discusses telescoping. See also Shaw, *Down Brakes*, chap. 10.

40. Clark, "Railroad Safety Movement," 123–24. See also Charles Clark, "The Development of the Semiautomatic Freight-Car Coupler," *Technology and Culture* 13 (Apr. 1972): 170–208. The Pennsylvania decisions are from Theodore Ely to F. Sheppard, Dec. 7, 1888, and July 8, 1890, box 469, PRRC.

41. The need for interchangeability implied that there were systemwide externalities in coupler use. That is, one carrier benefited if another adopted a compatible coupler, while the benefits to the adopting carrier would be higher the more other carriers used compatible couplers. Hence, coupler adoption was "path-dependent," in that any coupler, if used by a few large carriers, could become the standard. The QWERTY example is from Paul David, "Clio and the Economics of QWERTY," *American Economic Review* 75 (May 1985): 332-37. The railroad press that opposed safety legislation also stressed that it might lock the industry into incompatible and incorrect couplers; see, for example, "Objections to National Legislation on Car Couplers," *RG* 23 (Nov. 20, 1891): 823. "In a fog" is from "Legislation for the Prevention of Accidents," *RG* 14 (Apr. 7, 1882): 211.

42. William F. Merrill to Henry B. Stone, June 19, 1884; Stone to T. J. Potter, June 19, 1884; and Potter to Stone, June 28, 1884; all in Automatic Brakes on Freight Trains File, box 33, 1880, Burlington Archives, Newberry Library.

43. The Westinghouse quotation and the 64 percent figure are from ICC, *Third Annual Report, 1889* (Washington, D.C., 1890), 335. For the New Haven, see "Proceedings of the Apr. 13, 1892 Meeting: Replies to Circular 81," in ARA *Proceedings* 1 (1886-93).

44. Wellington, *Economic Theory*, 488-89; Wisconsin Board of Railroad Commissioners, *Third Biennial Report* (Madison, 1889), xxiv-xxvii. For other early complaints about the MCB coupler, see "Derailments Caused by MCB Couplers Pulling Out," *RG* 24 (Nov. 25, 1892): 885.

45. The Westinghouse assessment is from ICC, *Third Annual Report, 1889*, 337. "Accidents to Railroad Employees," *RG* 13 (Sept. 28, 1881): 525; Kentucky Railroad Commission, *Report of the Railroad Commission* (Frankfurt, 1884), 82.

46. New Jersey Bureau of Statistics of Labor and Industries, *Eleventh Annual Report, 1888* (Trenton, 1889), 79; ICC, *Fifteenth Annual Report, 1901* (Washington, D.C., 1902), 275. Seung-Wook Kim and Price Fishback, "Institutional Change, Compensating Differentials, and Accident Risk in American Railroading, 1892-1945," *Journal of Economic History* 53 (Dec. 1993): 796-23, employ ICC data and find (table 2) that an increase in the fatality rate of 1 per million employee-hours raised wages by 0.028 (2.8 percent). My findings confirm the existence but not the size of the wage premium. For the years 1908-10 the *Message of the President of the United States Transmitting the Report of the Employers' Liability and Workmen's Compensation Committee*, 62d Cong., 2d sess., S.D. 338 (Washington, D.C., 1912), contains much more detailed occupational risk data but less detailed wage data than the ICC reports. The following equation includes the fatality rate per thousand employees (*FR*) and the permanent total, permanent partial, and temporary total injury rates (*PT, PP, TT*), as well as controls for thirty-two occupations and five regions. Figures in parentheses are *t*-ratios.

$$\ln(\text{Wage}) = 0.0016(FR) + 0.092(PT) + 0.003(PP) + 0.0006(TT)$$
$$\quad\quad (2.05) \quad\quad\quad (1.41) \quad\quad (0.86) \quad\quad\quad (2.31)$$
$$R^2 = 0.005; N = 720$$

This implies a considerably smaller premium than the Kim-Fishback figures: an increased fatality rate of 1 per thousand workers is (about) 1 per 2.8 million hours, which implies a wage premium of 0.0016/2.8 = 0.0006 per million manhours (vs. their 0.028). Thus, there is evidence of wage premiums, but inadequate data and controls make their magnitude open to question.

47. Wellington's assessment is in "The Money Value of Good Freight Brakes and Couplers," *EN* 22 (Dec. 21, 1889): 590-92. British observers also thought liability costs

in that country were too low to stimulate interest in employee safety; see Royal Commission on Railway Accidents, *Report* (London, 1877), 55.

48. Kentucky Railroad Commission, *Report of the Railroad Commission*, 82.

49. *Farwell v. Boston and Worcester Railroad*, 45 Mass. 49 (1842). A good assessment of the common law of employer's liability is E. H. Downey, *History of Work Accident Indemnity in Iowa* (Iowa City: State Historical Society, 1912). Its application on the railroads at this time is discussed in Clark, "Railroad Safety Movement," chap. 7. On law and economic development, see Willard Hurst, *Law and the Conditions of Freedom in the Nineteenth-Century United States* (Madison: Univ. of Wisconsin Press, 1956); Lawrence Friedman and Jack Ladinsky, "Social Change and the Law of Industrial Accidents," *Columbia Law Review* 6 (Jan. 1967): 50–82; Christopher Tomlins, "A Mysterious Power: Industrial Accidents and the Legal Construction of Employment Relations in Massachusetts, 1800–1850," *Law and History Review* 6 (Fall 1988): 375–438; and Morton Horwitz, *Transformation of American Law* (Cambridge: Harvard Univ. Press, 1977), chap. 3.

50. The railroad relief funds and contracts are described in Emory Johnson, "Railway Relief Departments," BLS *Bulletin* 8 (Washington, D.C., 1897), 39–57; U.S. Industrial Commission, *Report on Transportation* (Washington, D.C., 1901), 9:43; Senate Committee on Interstate and Foreign Commerce, *Hearings on Liability of Employers*, 59th Cong., 1st sess. (Washington, D.C., 1906); House Committee on the Judiciary, *Hearings on Employers' Liability*, H.R. 17036 (Washington, D.C., 1908); and U.S. Commissioner of Labor, *Twenty-third Annual Report: Workmen's Insurance and Benefit Funds in the United States, 1908* (Washington, D.C., 1909). The ICC survey is in its *Tenth Annual Report, 1896* (Washington, D.C., 1897), 108–11. Richard Posner, "A Theory of Negligence," *Journal of Legal Studies* 1 (Jan. 1972): 29–96, finds that court settlements in the period 1875–95 cost $5,600 for fatalities and over $15,000 for permanent disabilities, but these data are based on samples of only eight and four observations, respectively.

51. Paul Black, "The Development of Management Personnel Policies on the Burlington Railroad, 1860–1900" (Ph.D. diss., Univ. of Wisconsin, 1972); David Lightner, *Labor on the Illinois Central Railroad* (New York: Arno, 1977); Grant, *Brownie the Boomer*, 6. See also Walter Licht, *Working for the Railroad* (Princeton: Princeton Univ. Press, 1983). The statistical analysis is:

$$\text{Total compensation} = 41{,}500 + 38.38(\text{Injuries}) + 43.13(\text{Fatalities})$$
$$(1.16) \qquad\qquad (2.09)$$
$$R^2 = 0.17; \text{ D.W.} = 1.84; N = 15$$

The data are from Ohio Railroad Commission, *Annual Report* (Columbus, 1888). It was estimated using a Cochran-Orcutt correction for serial correlation. Figures in parentheses are *t*-ratios. No other state collected data that segregated the costs of injuries to workers from those to passengers and others.

52. "Much enthusiasm" is from Albert Fishlow, "Productivity and Technological Change in the Railroad Sector, 1840–1910," in National Bureau of Economic Research, *Output, Employment, and Productivity in the United States after 1800*, Studies in Income and Wealth 30 (New York: NBER, 1966), 583–646, at 634; this is also the source of the information on steel rails. "Comparatively sluggish" is from Usselman, "Air Brakes for Freight Trains," 31.

53. Clark, "Railroad Safety Movement," chap. 8, describes the state efforts to require automatic couplers. The quotation from the New York Commissioners is from *Annual Report* (Albany, 1890), xvi.

54. Garfield's bill and the *Gazette*'s comments are in "Government Inspection of

Railroad Accidents," *RG* 9 (Feb. 16, 1877): 74–75. See also "A Bill to Prevent Railroad Accidents," *RG* 11 (Dec. 12, 1879): 662.

55. For descriptions of Coffin's career, see Clark, "Railroad Safety Movement," chap. 9, and Stewart Holbrook, *The Story of American Railroads* (New York: Crown, 1948), chap. 24. The quotation is from Lorenzo S. Coffin, "Safety Appliances on the Railroads," *Annals of Iowa* 5 (Jan. 1903): 561–82.

56. The role of the ICC is described in Clark, "Railroad Safety Movement," chap. 9. Henry Cabot Lodge, "A Perilous Business and the Remedy," *North American Review* 154 (Feb. 1892): 189–95.

57. "Needed Railroad Legislation," *EN* 18 (Dec. 31, 1887): 477. See also "The Massachusetts Railroad Report," *EN* 21 (Mar. 23, 1889): 263–64, and the untitled editorial, *EN* 22 (Oct. 19, 1889): 373. Wellington's assessment of costs and benefits is in "Money Value of Good Freight Brakes and Couplers." The *Gazette*'s reluctant conversion is revealed in "Some of the Limits of a Law for Safety Appliances," *RG* 22 (Jan. 3, 1890): 8–9.

58. The comments by Adams, Ely, and Wall are all from appendix 10 of ICC, *Third Annual Report, 1889.*

59. For Haines's remarks, see House Committee on Interstate and Foreign Commerce, *Hearings on Automatic Couplers and Power Brakes* (Washington, D.C., 1892), 4. Coffin's comments are on 47–48; railroad support for legislation is documented on 108–9.

60. "Uniformity in Freight Car Draft Gear," *EN* 29 (Mar. 9, 1893): 228–29; "The Saving of Lives and Limbs by Automatic Car Couplers," *EN* 41 (Jan. 19, 1899): 41. "Period of resistance" is from Kurt Wetzel, "Railroad Management's Response to Operating Employees Accidents," *Labor History* (Summer 1980): 351–68. Experience under the act revealed it to be flawed in a number of ways, and Congress amended it on March 2, 1903—ten years to the day after its original passage. The most important amendment modified the requirement that trains have a "sufficient" number of air-braked cars, requiring instead that 50 percent of the cars on each train be so equipped, and giving the ICC power to increase the proportion if it so desired. The amendment also made it clear that the law required automatic couplers on locomotives and tenders as well as freight cars.

61. "The Enforcement of the Federal Coupler Law," *RG* 29 (Oct. 15, 1897): 727. A brief description of the hearings is presented in "The Hearings Regarding the Safety Appliance Law before the ICC," *EN* 38 (Dec. 9, 1897): 378–79.

62. The Alton is in "Testimony and Arguments," 158–60, box 84, FD 512. "Car famine" is from an untitled editorial, *EN* 38 (Sept. 30, 1897): 216.

63. Coffin's conversion, after a moving denunciation of railroad greed, is in "Testimony and Arguments," 310, box 84, FD 512; Coffin's prior willingness to settle for a two-year extension is in Lorenzo S. Coffin to B. B. Henderson, Jan. 15, 1897, book 8, box 86, FD 512.

64. "Coupler Extension Granted," *Railroad Trainman* 17 (Feb. 1900): 169–74.

65. Equations in which density and profits per car were omitted, or in which these variables and the regulation dummy were not interacted with time, also produced a negative coefficient for regulation.

66. "Why the Equipment of Freight Cars with Automatic Couplers Should Be Hastened," *EN* 25 (Apr. 25, 1891): 401–2. The *News* argument is as follows: Let S be the fraction of cars with automatic couplers and N the fraction with link and pin. AA is the fraction of all couplings that are automatic, LL the fraction that are link and pin, and AL the fraction that are joined. Then $AA = S^2$; $LL = N^2$; and $AL = 2SN$. If the injury rate associated with AA is a and the injury rates associated with LL and AL

are b and c respectively, and since $N = 1 - S$, the coupling injury rate I is $c + (2b - 2c)S + (a - 2b + c)S^2$. And if $b > c > a > 0$, then the coefficient of S will be positive and that of S^2 negative, and the injury rate from coupling will indeed rise for a time as the proportion of cars equipped with automatic couplers goes up.

67. See "Equipping Freight Cars with Air-Brakes and Automatic Couplers," *EN* 33 (June 6, 1895): 369, and "Progress toward Safer Railway Operation," *EN* 47 (June 19, 1902): 502-3. The ICC repeatedly commented on the poor maintenance of safety appliances in its annual reports from 1901 through 1910. The commission's crowing is in its *Fifteenth Annual Report, 1901*, 68.

68. Moseley's discussion of repair fees and the difficulties of maintaining brakes are in House Committee on Interstate and Foreign Commerce, *Hearings on H.R. 11059, the Automatic Coupler Bill* (Washington, D.C., 1902), 35. Moseley also noted that 4.5 percent more foreign than home cars were defective, in "Address of Mr. Moseley," *Daily Railway Age* (June 23, 1904), 1200-1202. Cullinane's remarks are in ICC, *Sixteenth Annual Report, 1902* (Washington, D.C., 1903), 290.

69. Sullivan's comments are in *Hearings on H.R. 11059*, 2-3. For inspectors' complaints, see ICC, *Fifteenth Annual Report, 1901*. Martin is in *Sixteenth Annual Report, 1902*, 281-83. West's observations are in his "Report on Brakes and Couplings," Sixth International Railway Congress *Proceedings* (Paris) 4, sec. 17 (1900): 1-28. See also "Break in Two's," *Railroad Car Journal* 6 (Aug. 1896): 193-94; "Communications," *Railroad Car Journal* 7 (Aug. 1897): 223; untitled articles in *Railroad Car Journal* 9 (June 1899): 137-99; and "Assault on the M. C. B. Coupler," *Locomotive Engineering* 12 (Mar. 1899): 126-27. A survey taken in 1901 and reported in "Replies to Circular 366," ARA *Proceedings* 3 (1899-1902), showed general satisfaction with the coupler but also lots of problems of breakage and failure to conform with MCB specifications. As late as 1904, ICC inspectors found coupler defects at the rate of 201 per thousand freight cars; see ICC, *Eighteenth Annual Report, 1904* (Washington, D.C., 1905), 348-51. For continuing complaints about the MCB coupler, see the testimony of Frank Cassady of the Switchmen's Union, in House Committee on Interstate and Foreign Commerce, *Hearings on the Bills Relating to Safety Appliances and Accidents*, Mar. 19, 1908 (Washington, D.C., 1908), 18-20.

70. ICC, *Nineteenth Annual Report, 1905* (Washington, D.C., 1906), 71-72; Association of Railroad Air-Brake Men, *Standard Form of Progressive Answers on the Air-Brake* (Boston, 1896).

71. Simple observation of the data reinforces the argument that it was the quality and manner of use, rather than the quantity of safety appliances, that mattered most. Fatalities from coupling cars fell from about 0.49 per thousand in 1890 (table A1.5) to 0.28 in 1900, or about 43 percent, while the proportion of rolling stock with automatic couplers rose from 10 percent to 94 percent. From 1900 to 1910, equipment using automatic couplers rose only 6 points to 100 percent, yet fatality rates fell another 57 percent, to 0.12 per thousand. The years after 1910 are even more telling. Use of automatic couplers remained unchanged, yet coupler fatalities declined another 52 percent, to 0.058 per thousand, by 1939.

72. The best source on the risks resulting from air brakes and couplers are the reports of the ICC inspectors published in the commission's annual reports between 1901 and 1910. Technical journals also contained similar material. See "Defective Freight-Car Brakes," *Locomotive Engineering* 9 (Jan. 1896): 36, and "Break-in-Two's," *Railroad Car Journal* 6 (Aug. 1896): 193-94. See also the testimony of Edwin Moseley in *Hearings on H.R. 11059*, 44-45, and the comments of Representative Esch in House Committee on Interstate and Foreign Commerce, *Hearings on the Bills Relating to Safety Appliances and Accidents*, Mar. 19, 1908, 22. Problems of clearances are discussed in Senate

Committee on Interstate and Foreign Commerce, *Hearings on S3194, Railway Clearances*, 54th Cong., 2d sess., Apr. 24-25 and May 3, 1916. The impact of air brakes on train speed is in ICC, *Fifteenth Annual Report, 1901*, 271-77. These changes in operating technique were entirely predictable. As early as 1889, Arthur Mellen Wellington had predicted that the new equipment would increase train speed and weight; see "Money Value of Good Freight Brakes and Couplers."

73. ICC, *Fifteenth Annual Report, 1901*, 68.

CHAPTER TWO. NEEDLESS PERILS

Epigraphs: Roy's remarks are in Ohio Inspector of Mines, *Annual Report, 1874* (Columbus, 1874), 7. The last words of Beach are from Andrew Roy, *A History of Coal Miners*, 3d ed. (Columbus, 1907). Jones's remarks are in Wyoming Inspector of Coal Mines, *Annual Report, 1911* (Cheyenne, 1911), 20.

1. The Bureau of Mines definition of a disaster is an event in which five or more lives are lost. In the following where there is some dispute on the number of lives lost I have relied on bureau estimates. For a description and analysis of the explosions, see H. B. Humphrey, "Historical Summary of Coal Mine Explosions in the United States—1810-1958," BM *Bulletin 586* (Washington, D.C., 1960); *New York Times*, Dec. 6, 1907, 1; and "The Needless Peril of the Coal Mine," *Harper's Weekly 52* (Jan. 11, 1908): 14.

2. American coal deposits are described in Heinrich Ries, *Economic Geology*, 6th ed. (New York: John Wiley, 1930), chap. 1, and H. F. Bulman, *The Working of Coal and Other Stratified Minerals* (New York: John Wiley, 1927), chap. 13. European/American comparisons are in George Rice and Irving Hartmann, "Coal Mining in Europe," BM *Bulletin 414* (Washington, D.C., 1939).

3. Descriptions of longwall and room-and-pillar methods of mining are contained in Bulman, *Working of Coal;* Rice and Hartmann, "Coal Mining in Europe"; and Hugh Archbald, *The Four Hour Day in Coal* (New York: H. W. Wilson, 1922), chap. 2. A good modern survey is Keith Dix, *Work Relations in the Coal Industry: The Hand Loading Era* (Morgantown: Univ. of West Virginia Press, 1977), chaps. 1-2.

4. For an argument that the cost of capital was higher in America than in Europe, see Alexander J. Field, "Land Abundance, Interest/Profit Rates, and Nineteenth Century American and British Technology," *Journal of Economic History* 43 (June 1983): 405-32. Coal prices and British wage data are from U.S. Commissioner of Labor, *Twelfth Special Report: Coal Mine Labor in Europe, 1904* (Washington, D.C., 1905); the wages for British miners cited in the text are from 433. American miners' earnings are from "History of Wages in the United States from Colonial Times to 1928," BLS *Bulletin 499* (Washington, D.C., 1929), table J-5. Examples of critics' enthusiasm for longwall methods are Oklahoma Inspector of Mines, *Annual Report, 1908* (Norman, 1908), 7-9; Lucas Mayer, "Longwall Methods of Mining a Coal Seam," *EMJ 86* (July 4, 1908): 19-23; Henry Payne, "American Longwall Methods," *EMJ 90* (Nov. 19, 1910): 1020-23; and Sim Reynolds, "Longwall and Conservation," *Coal Age* 1 (Jan. 20, 1912): 475-76. George Rice and James W. Paul, "Amount and Nature of Losses," in U.S. Coal Commission, *Report* (Washington, D.C., 1925), 3:1841-76, stress the importance of labor costs and coal prices in determining the extent of "waste," and are the source of the 65 percent figure.

5. Archbald, *Four Hour Day*, 33.

6. Salaried mineworkers in 1909 from *Thirteenth Census of the United States, 1909*, vol. 11, *Mines and Quarries: General Report and Analysis* (Washington, D.C., 1913), table 62. See also Pennsylvania Bureau of Mines, *Annual Report, 1901* (Harrisburg, 1901), and Archbald, *Four Hour Day*, chap. 2.

7. Good descriptions of mine work in the 1920s are in Carter Goodrich, *The Miner's*

Freedom (Boston: Marshall Jones, 1925), which also contains the quotations from the operator and the black miner on 16 and 43, and notes the article in *Industrial Management* on 17-18. See also Archbald, *Four Hour Day*, chaps. 1-2.

8. Ohio Inspector of Mines, *Annual Report, 1874* (Columbus, 1874), 7.

9. Ohio Inspector of Mines, *Annual Report, 1877*, 11; David Griffiths, "Needed Education in Coal Mining," Rocky Mountain Coal Mining Institute *Proceedings* 1 (1912): 15-20.

10. The coroner's verdicts are from Colorado Inspector of Coal Mines, *Biennial Report, 1897-1898* (Denver, 1898). For a long list of Huerfano County coroners' verdicts that absolve the mine operator from responsibility, see U.S. Commission on Industrial Relations, *Final Report and Testimony* (Washington, D.C., 1916), 8:7265-95. "Colorado Company Blamed for Miner's Death," United Mine Workers *Journal* 28 (June 14, 1917): 6-7; "The Lick Branch Disaster," *Mines and Minerals* 29 (Mar. 1909): 356-57. The liability payments by Stonega Coke and Coal for 1916-18 are from Price Fishback, "Liability Rules and Accident Prevention in the Workplace: Empirical Evidence from the Early Twentieth Century," *Journal of Legal Studies* 15 (June 1987): 305-28. (Out of forty-four fatalities, twenty-eight families were compensated about $560 each. Thus, the average cost of a fatality to Stonega at that time was about $356.) The Alabama song is from Marlene Rikard, "An Experiment in Welfare Capitalism: The Health Care Services of the Tennessee Coal, Iron, and Railroad Company" (Ph.D. diss., Univ. of Alabama, 1983), 49.

11. Roy's remarks are in Ohio Mining Commission, *Report* (Columbus, 1872), 60. Perry Gilpin is from Carl Oblinger, *Divided Kingdom: Work, Community, and the Mining Wars in the Central Illinois Coal Fields during the Depression* (Springfield: Illinois Historical Society, 1991), 141. The recollections of Crawford and Tuffs are from interviews in the Appalachian Oral History Project, Alice Lloyd College.

12. Aubrey Rose to Bureau of Mines, June 28, 1937, box 2645, GCF; Campbell interview in Appalachian Oral History Project, Alice Lloyd College.

13. The quotation on Mid-Lothian is from Howard Eavenson, *The First Century and a Quarter of American Coal Industry* (Privately printed: Pittsburgh, 1942), 96. Colorado Inspector of Coal Mines, *Biennial Report, 1909-1910*, 6, and *Biennial Report, 1911-1912*, 6-7.

14. Pennsylvania Inspectors of Mines, *Annual Report, 1876*, 165; Ohio Inspector of Mines, *Annual Report, 1877*, 11.

15. Charles Keenan, "Historical Documentation of Major Coal-Mine Disasters in the United States Not Classified as Explosions of Gas or Dust: 1846-1962," BM *Bulletin* 616 (Washington, D.C., 1963); Pennsylvania Inspectors of Mines, *Annual Report, 1883*, 137.

16. Pennsylvania Bureau of Mines, *Annual Report, 1900*, 313. Lack of brakes is discussed in Carl Allen to G. S. Rice, Oct. 6, 1920, box 469, GCF, and Albert Dickinson [Union Pacific Coal], "Our Aspect on Safety," NSC *Proceedings* 18 (1929): 181-84. On mule haulage and harnesses, see Frederick Whiteside, "Advantages of Trolley Locomotives for Underground Haulage from a Safety Standpoint," and E. L. Solomon, "Animal Haulage at Anthracite Mines," NSC *Proceedings* 10 (1921): 404-6 and 410-14. On coupling, see L. C. Ilsley and E. J. Gleim, "Some Information on Automatic Coupling of Mine Cars," BM *Information Circular* 7245 (Washington, D.C., 1943). The mule fatality is from E. H. Denny to Dan Harrington, Nov. 30, 1929, box 988, GCF.

17. The quotation is from Rice and Paul, "Amount and Nature of Losses," 1867. See also the discussion of a roof fall at Carbondale, Pennsylvania, in Keenan, "Historical Documentation of Major Coal-Mine Disasters." Hudson Coal Company, *The Story of Anthracite* (New York, 1932), 172-74.

18. Pennsylvania Inspectors of Mines, *Annual Report, 1883*, 32–33 (emphasis supplied).

19. Pennsylvania Inspectors of Mines, *Annual Report, 1895*, 535; John Brophy, *A Miner's Life* (Madison: Univ. of Wisconsin Press, 1964), 41. While piece rates created greater incentives to take chances than hourly rates would have, Price Fishback, "Workplace Safety during the Progressive Era: Fatal Accidents in Bituminous Coal Mining, 1912–1923," *Explorations in Economic History* 23 (1986): 269–98, has argued that miners did not increase risk taking when piece rates fell.

20. "Accident Report to G. W. Dale," Oct. 27, 1923, box 482, SCCC; West Virginia Mining Commission, *Report* (Charleston, 1907), 49; N. P. Reinhart [West Virginia's inspector], "Discipline and Its Relation to Safety," NSC *Proceedings* 25 (1935): 303–5.

21. Wyoming Inspector of Coal Mines, *Annual Report, 1915*, 4–5; Pennsylvania Inspectors of Mines, *Annual Report, 1882*, 101 and 105.

22. The observation on West Virginia is from a Travelers representative, quoted in BM, "Report of the Conference on State and Government Officials Regarding the Standardization of Mining Statistics and Mine Regulations," Feb. 24 and 25, 1916 (Washington, D.C., 1916), 31. New Mexico Inspector of Mines, *Annual Report, 1907* (Albuquerque, 1907), 45–48. For similar views, see Brophy, *Miner's Life*, 41.

23. The death of John Greenage is described in Pennsylvania Inspectors of Mines, *Annual Report, 1883*, 135–36.

24. For a history of the safety lamp, see J. W. Paul et al., "Flame Safety Lamps," BM *Bulletin* 224 (Washington, D.C., 1924). The British report cited is Royal Commission on Mines, *Second Report* (London, 1909), 47. Her Majesty's Commissioners Appointed to Inquire into Accidents in Mines, *Final Report* (London, 1886), 65–97, pointed out that the increased velocity of air in mines had made safety lamps no longer safe. "Hourly changing" is from Mammoth Mine Commission, "Report," *Pennsylvania Official Documents, 1891*, vol. 6, doc. 24 (Harrisburg, 1892), 18. That mines with safety lamps sometimes skimped on ventilation is asserted in Ohio Inspector of Mines, *Annual Report, 1875*, 32, and Pennsylvania Department of Mines, *Annual Report, Anthracite, 1905*, xi. Lighting the pipe is from Pennsylvania Inspectors of Mines, *Annual Report, 1890*, 208.

25. For the early history of coal mine accidents, see Eavenson, *First Century and a Quarter*; the quotation is from 96. See also Humphrey, "Historical Summary."

26. The data are from Albert Fay, "Coal Mine Fatalities in the United States, 1870–1914," BM *Bulletin* 115 (Washington, D.C., 1916), table 40. Fay calculated fatality rates per thousand 2,000-hour workers, which is per 2 million hours. Thus, the figures in the text are one-half of those Fay presented.

27. A. L. Murray and Daniel Harrington, "Accident Experience of the Coal Mines of Utah for the Period 1918 to 1929," BM *Information Circular* 6530 (Washington, D.C., 1931); S. H. Ash, "Accident Experience and Cost of Accidents at Washington Coal Mines," BM *Information Circular* 6529 (Washington, D.C., 1931).

28. Some intrastate shifts in mining may have raised fatality rates as well. According to C. S. Herbert, "Explosions in Illinois Coal Mines, 1883–1932," BM *Information Circular* 6764 (Washington, D.C., 1934), the opening up of deeper, more gassy seams in the southern part of that state after 1901 raised risks. Such shifts could also have raised fatality rates by increasing the variation in mining conditions and reducing the value of experience.

29. The technological changes in anthracite mining are described in R. V. Norris, "Labor Saving Devices in Coal Mining," *Engineering Magazine* 28 (Jan. 1905): 553–69, and Dever C. Ashmead, "Advances in the Preparation of Anthracite," AIME *Transactions* 66 (1920): 422–508. The 62 percent figure was derived as follows. From 1881–90

to 1900–1910, average mine risks rose from 3.22 to 3.49 per thousand workers, or by 0.27 point. If employment shares had remained unchanged at their average level for the 1880s, risks would have risen only to 3.32 per thousand, or by 0.10 point. Thus, 0.17 of the total rise of 0.27 point, or about 62 percent, was due to the shift of employment toward the more dangerous inside work.

30. Pennsylvania Inspectors of Mines, *Annual Report, 1892*, 413, and *Annual Report, 1883*, 136; Colorado Inspector of Coal Mines, *Biennial Report, 1907–1908*, 7. The belief that new immigrants were responsible for the rising fatality rate in mining was widespread. See, for example, U.S. Immigration Commission, *Report on Immigrants in Industries* (Washington, D.C., 1911), vol. 6, chap. 8, and Albert Fay, "Mine Accidents, English Speaking vs. Non–English Speaking Employees," NSC *Proceedings* 8 (1919): 807–21. Fay admitted that immigrants tended to be employed in the high-risk jobs.

31. Two other pieces of evidence also suggest the modest importance of declining worker quality in raising fatality rates. First, both anthracite and bituminous mining experienced roughly the same influx of new immigrants, yet anthracite fatality rates rose far less sharply—even when compared with bituminous mining in Pennsylvania alone. Second, immigration virtually stopped with World War I, and since immigrants' facility with English increased rapidly with their length of residence, most new immigrants would have understood the language by the mid-1920s. In addition, with employment stagnant or falling by that time, worker experience should no longer have been held down by a continuing influx of new workers. Thus, safety should have improved sharply in the 1920s, but it did not. Either the lack of experience and English was of modest importance in the early period, or the remediation of this lack in the 1920s was swamped by other forces.

32. "Will Coal Dust Explode?" *Colliery Engineer* 15 (Jan. 1895): 132; Pennsylvania Bureau of Mines, *Annual Report, 1899*, xiii. The progress of mechanization may be followed in the state inspectors' reports. A good summary is in Dix, *Work Relations*, chap. 1.

33. The number of splices is from G. S. McCaa, "A Gas Explosion in a Rock-Dusted Mine," BM *Information Circular* 6144 (Washington, D.C., 1929). The death of Martinocki is from Ohio Inspector of Mines, *Annual Report, 1908*, 162.

34. The experience with steam is recounted in Ohio Inspector of Mines, *Annual Report, 1877*, 35. The mule is from Edward Parker, "Coal Cutting Machinery," AIME *Transactions* 27 (1899): 405–59. Most mines generated their own direct current at this time. With the growth of utility-generated power they increasingly switched to alternating current, which precipitated a lively debate on which form of current was the more dangerous. See, for example, Daniel Harrington et al., "Some Suggestions on the Prevention of Electrical Accidents in Coal Mines," BM *Information Circular* 6919 (Washington, D.C., 1936), and W. B. Kouwenhoven et al., "Injuries Produced by Contact with Electric Currents," *Journal of the Franklin Institute* 215 (Jan. 1933): 1–26. Verba's death is recounted in Ohio Inspector of Mines, *Annual Report, 1908*, 158.

35. George S. Rice, "American Coal Dust Precautions," *Mines and Minerals* 34 (July 1914): 739–40, stresses the effects of trolley haulage on dust and ventilation, as does Ohio Inspector of Mines, *Annual Report, 1905*, 30–33, which also reports speeds of ten miles per hour.

36. Pennsylvania Inspectors of Mines, *Annual Report, 1879*, 82. Explosion risks from Fay, "Coal Mine Fatalities," table 4. For the importance of temperature and humidity, see George Rice et al., "The Explosibility of Coal Dust," BM *Bulletin* 20 (Washington, D.C., 1911), 54–69. See also "More Disastrous Coal Mine Explosions," *Mines and Minerals* 30 (Mar. 1910): 482–83. A regression (not shown) based on Pennsylvania data from 1902–18 with controls for supervision, inspection, explosives, trolleys, time, the

war years, and districts, demonstrates that larger mines (measured in terms of output) had higher fatality rates. By contrast, modern findings reveal larger mines to be safer; see National Academy of Sciences, *Toward Safer Underground Coal Mines* (Washington, D.C.: National Academy Press, 1982). On the relation of humidity to roof falls, see C. A. Sine, "Accident Report," Oct. 21, 1931, box 340, SCCC.

37. West Virginia Inspector of Mines, *Annual Report, 1900*, 313. The statistical analysis is:

$$\ln(\text{Gas}) = -11.27 + 1.67[\ln(\text{Depth})] + 0.826[\ln(\text{Coal})]$$
$$(9.50) \qquad\qquad (6.54)$$
$$R^2 = 0.70; N = 56$$

The data are from N. H. Darton, "Occurrence of Explosive Gases in Coal Mines," BM *Bulletin* 72 (Washington, D.C., 1915), 224.

38. The Rolling Mill mine is from Pennsylvania Bureau of Mines, *Annual Report, 1902*, 52–72. R. D. Hall, "Remarks," Coal Mining Institute of America *Proceedings* 28 (1912): 45, claimed that the risk of explosion rose with the square of the number of men employed. Paul's remarks are in West Virginia Department of Mines, *Annual Report, 1907*, x.

39. Harrison's remarks on the increase in solid shooting are in Ohio Inspector of Mines, *Annual Report, 1904*, 18–20, where he also stressed the importance of a market for fine coal. His description of the effects of solid shooting is from his "Shot Firers and Evils of Solid Shooting," *EMJ* 84 (July 27, 1907): 167. The Arkansas geologist's report is from Albert A. Steel, *Coal Mining in Arkansas* (Little Rock, 1910), 273. Harrison also emphasized the change in the coal market in his *Annual Report, 1909*, 53. Ohio Inspector of Mines, *Annual Report, 1888*, 64–65, reports solid shooting in that state. See also Pennsylvania Department of Mines, *Annual Report, Bituminous, 1907*, xi–xiii.

40. Ohio Coal Mining Commission, *Report* (Columbus, 1914), provides a balanced discussion of solid shooting and the mine-run vs. screened-coal controversy. Rice, "Explosibility of Coal Dust," 27–32, emphasizes the legal changes. For operators' views, see J. E. Fenney, "The 'Mine Run System' of Mining Coal," American Mining Congress *Proceedings* 14 (1911): 233–40. The miner is quoted in Steel, *Coal Mining in Arkansas*, 273. Kansas Inspector of Coal Mines, *Biennial Report, 1906–1908*, 110–11. The dangers of combining black powder and dynamite are from E. B. Wilson, "The New British Explosives Order," *Colliery Engineer* 27 (Dec. 1907): 224–25. See also S. P. Howell and M. W. Bernewitz, "The Hazards of Non-permissible Explosives," BM *Report of Investigation* 2583 (Washington, D.C., 1924).

41. "Peabody Coal Mine Explosion," *Mines and Minerals* 25 (Apr. 1905): 440–41. Illinois Coal Operators Association, *Powder Accidents in the Coal Mines of Illinois* (Chicago, 1919), describes the growth of powder use. See also Illinois Bureau of Labor Statistics, *Annual Coal Report, 1906*, and Earl Beckner, *A History of Labor Legislation in Illinois* (Chicago: Univ. of Chicago Press, 1929), 353–67.

42. Illinois Bureau of Labor Statistics, *Annual Coal Report, 1908* (Springfield, 1908), 3; Harrison, "Shot Firers and the Evils," 167. Quillen is from Appalachian Oral History Project, Alice Lloyd College.

43. Wyoming Inspector of Coal Mines, *Annual Report, 1911*, 20. For Roy, see Ohio Inspector of Mines, *Annual Report, 1874*, 7. Similar remarks are in Pennsylvania Inspectors of Mines, *Annual Report, 1875*, 109–10, and Colorado Inspector of Coal Mines, *Biennial Report, 1885–1886*, 3–4. For the Sunshine mine, see Colorado Inspector of Coal Mines, *Biennial Report, 1897–1898*.

44. "American Exposition of Safety Devices," *Mines and Minerals* 27 (Oct. 1906): 114–15; "The Safety of American Mines," *Colliery Guardian* 95 (Jan. 24, 1908): 174.

45. "Colliery Accidents in the United States," *Colliery Guardian* 96 (Nov. 20, 1908): 1011; "High Accident Death Rates in American Mines," *Mines and Minerals* 26 (Oct. 1905): 114–15; Thomas Morrison, "Comparison of the Dangers of Mining in This and Foreign Countries," Mine Inspectors' Institute *Proceedings* 2 (1910): 115–18. See also Frederick Horton, "Coal Mine Accidents in the United States and Foreign Countries," BM *Bulletin* 69 (Washington, D.C., 1913), 87–91.

46. Select Committee on Accidents in Coal Mines, *First Report* (London, 1853), 3; *Fourth Report* (London, 1854), 5; Royal Commission on Accidents in Mines, *Preliminary Report* (London, 1881), 422. The shift to longwall is also briefly described in B. R. Mitchell, *Economic Development of the British Coal Industry, 1800–1914* (New York: Cambridge Univ. Press, 1984), 70–73, and Roy Church, *Victorian Pre-eminence: 1830–1913*, vol. 3 of *The History of the British Coal Industry* (Oxford: Clarendon Press, 1986), 328–46.

47. Thomas Mather, "Remarks," Mine Inspectors' Institute *Proceedings* 7 (1914): 64. On "discipline," see Royal Commission on Accidents in Mines, *Preliminary Report*, 100.

48. Royal Commission on Accidents in Mines, *Preliminary Report*, 56, 100–101.

49. Ibid., 47, 206, 215–26, 285; Pennsylvania Inspectors of Mines, *Annual Report, 1894*, 86–88; "Accidents in Coal Mining," *Black Diamond* 15 (July 27, 1895): 110.

50. Royal Commission on Accidents in Mines, *Report of a Committee Appointed by the Royal Commission on Mines to Inquire into the Causes of and Means of Preventing Accidents from Falls of Ground, Underground Haulage, and in Shafts* (London, 1909), 85–86. The height of coal seams is stressed in "Accidents in Coal Mining," 110. See also A. L. Murray and D. Harrington, "Accident Experience of the Coal Mines of Utah for the Period 1918 to 1929," BM *Information Circular* 6530 (Washington, D.C., 1931).

51. Labor productivity from Mitchell, *Economic Development of the British Coal Industry*, table 10.1. The effect of British employment shares on American fatality rates is for the half-decade 1911–15. British data are from H.M. Chief Inspector of Mines, *Mines and Quarries: General Report and Statistics*, pt. 2, *Labor* (London, various years). American figures are from W. W. Adams et al., "Coal Mine Accidents: 1939," BM *Bulletin* 414 (Washington, D.C., 1940), table 70. On the comparative size of mine cars, see George S. Rice and R. V. Wheeler, "Stone Dust as a Preventive of Coal Dust Explosions: Comparative Tests," [Great Britain] Safety in Mines Research Board Paper 13 (London, 1925), and Erskine Ramsey, "European Mine Practice Compared with American," *Mining and Engineering World* 37 (Aug. 24, 1912): 349–51. Floyd Parsons, "Practice of Coal Mining in Great Britain," *EMJ* 87 (Oct. 23, 1909): 809–13, notes that longwall methods concentrated the work and reduced haulage for a given output.

52. The fatality rates for longwall mining are for the three counties in Illinois in which that method predominated. Similar conclusions based on a survey of all Illinois longwall mines (not just those in three counties) but for 1912 only are in S. O. Andros, "Mining Practice in District I (Longwall)," Illinois Cooperative Mining Investigations *Bulletin* 1 (1914): table 2. Texas mines too were comparatively safe, and the most important company in that state, the Texas and Pacific Coal Company, also mined using longwall methods. See Marilyn Reinhart, *A Way of Work and a Way of Life: Coal Mining in Thurber, Texas, 1888–1926* (College Station: Texas A&M Univ. Press, 1992).

53. For a survey of British mine safety legislation, see Andrew Bryan, *The Evolution of Health and Safety in Mines* (London: Ashire Publishers, 1975). For the early years, see O. O. G. M. MacDonagh, "Coal Mines Regulation: The First Decade, 1842-1852," in *Ideas and Institutions of Victorian Britain*, ed. Robert Robson (New York: Barnes and Noble, 1967), 58–86. A brief review of earlier legislation is also contained in Royal Commission on Mines, *Second Report* (London, 1909), 2–11; the quotation on man-

agers' duties is from 32. British fatality data are not available on a manhour basis until the 1920s; the data in the text on rates per worker are from H.M. Chief Inspector of Mines, *Mines and Quarries: General Report and Statistics for 1909*, pt. 2, *Labor* (London, 1910), appendix 1.

54. Sir Richard Redmayne, who was chair of the committee that drew up the electricity regulations, admitted that they were "very stringent" and had been applied to non-gassy mines in order to protect the market for mines that generated gas; see Royal Commission on the Coal Industry, *Report, 1925* (London, 1926), vol. 2, pt. A, p. 134.

55. The following discussion of the development of safety regulation in Pennsylvania is based on Alexander Trachtenberg, *The History of Legislation for the Protection of Coal Miners in Pennsylvania, 1824–1915* (New York: International Publishers, 1942). Early safety legislation is also discussed in Roy, *History of the Coal Miners of the United States*. Both authors stress the role of Britain as a model. On this issue generally, see Clifton Yearley, *Britons in American Labor* (Baltimore: Johns Hopkins Press, 1957).

56. Avondale is described in Trachtenberg, *History of Legislation*, chap. 3, who reports 179 fatalities. I have followed Keenan, "Historical Documentation of Major Coal-Mine Disasters," who places the death toll at 110.

57. The development of mine safety legislation in Illinois is based on Beckner, *History of Labor Legislation in Illinois*, chap. 12. On Ohio, see Ohio Mining Commission, *Report* (Columbus, 1872); Roy, *History of the Coal Miners of the United States;* and K. Austin Kerr, "The Movement for Coal Mine Safety in Nineteenth Century Ohio," *Ohio History* 86 (Winter 1977): 1–18.

58. Ohio Inspector of Mines, *Annual Report, 1874,* 7; *Annual Report, 1882,* 44; *Annual Report, 1877,* 11.

59. Mine safety regulation in West Virginia is discussed in Glenn Massay, "Legislators, Lobbyists, and Loopholes: Coal Mining Legislation in West Virginia, 1875–1901," *West Virginia History* 32 (Apr. 1971): 135–70. Some provisions of the new law are in West Virginia Inspector of Mines, *Annual Report, 1907,* xii–xvii. The ignorance of the foreman at the Red Ash mine is in *Annual Report, 1900,* 313.

60. Colorado Inspector of Coal Mines, *Biennial Report, 1903–1904,* 6, and *Biennial Report, 1907–1908,* 4. That the state did not in fact have a law is claimed by chief inspector James Dalrymple in House Committee on Mines and Mining, *Hearings on Conditions in the Coal Mines of Colorado Pursuant to H.R. 387,* 63d Cong., 2d. sess. (Washington, D.C., 1914), 18, which also contains testimony on 42 summarizing the influence of the operators in writing the law of 1913. Legislation in Colorado and other Rocky Mountain states is described in Brian Whiteside, *Regulating Danger: The Struggle for Mine Safety in the Rocky Mountain Coal Industry* (Lincoln: Univ. of Nebraska Press, 1990). On the Winter Quarters disaster, see Utah Inspector of Mines, *Annual Report, 1900,* 56–62, and Allan Kent Powell, "Tragedy at Scofield," *Utah Historical Quarterly* (Spring 1973): 183–94.

61. "The Benefits of Mine Legislation and Inspection," *Colliery Engineer* 10 (July 1890): 276–77; Kentucky Inspector of Mines, *Annual Report, 1895,* 21. For similar claims, see Ohio Inspector of Mines, *Annual Report, 1886,* 9, and Illinois Bureau of Labor Statistics, *Annual Coal Report, 1899,* ix.

62. Roderick's remarks are from Pennsylvania Department of Mines, *Annual Report, Anthracite, 1903,* xvii. Colorado Inspector of Coal Mines, *Biennial Report, 1911–12,* 7.

63. Data on inspections per mine in various states from annual reports. British data are reported in Royal Commission on Safety in Coal Mines, *Appendix* (London, 1938), table 1. The following equation with controls for bituminous vs. anthracite mining is based on data for 1884–1918 reported in Pennsylvania Department of Mines,

Annual Report, Bituminous, 1918. Fatalities are expressed per worker; the equation is employment-weighted using a TSP routine and was estimated using the Cochran-Orcutt correction.

$$\ln(FR) = -0.281[\ln(\text{Inspectors/Workers})] + 0.016(\text{Trend})$$
$$(5.94) \qquad\qquad\qquad (3.87)$$
$$R^2 = 0.47; \text{ D.W.} = 2.01; N = 70$$

Since the decline in the ratio of inspectors per worker from a peak in 1884 to a trough in 1904 was about 36 percent, it could have raised fatalities only about 10 percent (-0.36×-0.281).

64. For a scathing assessment of state codes governing electricity, see L. C. Ilsley, "State Mining Laws on the Use of Electricity in and about Coal Mines," BM *Technical Paper* 271 (Washington, D.C., 1920).

65. F. W. Cunningham et al. to James Roderick, Aug. 27, 1909, box 2, GCB.

66. The "storm of censure" is from Pennsylvania Department of Mines, *Annual Report, Bituminous, 1905,* xv. The effort to ban black powder is from Pennsylvania Department of Mines, *Annual Report, Bituminous, 1909,* vii-x (emphasis supplied). For earlier efforts to stretch the law that also apparently met with difficulty, see Pennsylvania Inspectors of Mines, *Annual Report, 1881,* 278, and *Annual Report, 1902,* 11.

67. West Virginia Department of Mines, *Annual Report, 1907,* xxi; Kansas Inspector of Coal Mines, *Biennial Report, 1906–1908,* 111. Paul's observation is in West Virginia Inspector of Mines, *Annual Report, 1897,* 13. British inspection data are routinely reported in H.M. Inspectors of Mines, *Annual Report* (London, various years). Pennsylvania's reports are especially candid about the difficulties of enforcement. For a comparison of Pennsylvania and Britain, see Pennsylvania Bureau of Mines, *Annual Report, 1897,* x-xiii. The efforts to close one Pennsylvania mine are documented in James McCanch to James Roderick, Sept. 9, 1909, and Roderick to McCanch, Oct. 19, 1909, both in box 1, GCB.

68. Francis Feehan to Henry Louttit, Nov. 9, 1906; Louttit to John Underwood, Nov. 10 and Nov. 13, 1906; Louttit to Naomi Coal, Apr. 29, 1907; "Statement of Regular Inspections of the Naomi Mine from Nov. 12, 1906 to Nov. 12, 1907"; all in box 1, GCB. The Nov. 18 letter and response are missing but are cited in Pennsylvania Department of Mines, *Annual Report, Bituminous, 1907,* 38-39. For the explosion itself, see Humphrey, "Historical Summary of Coal Mine Explosions in the United States."

69. Humphrey, "Historical Summary of Coal Mine Explosions in the United States"; "Monongah Disaster," *Mines and Minerals* 28 (Feb. 1908): 327-32; Floyd Parsons, "Disaster at Monongah," *EMJ* 84 (Dec. 14, 1907): 1121-23; "Report on the Disaster at the Yolande Mine," *EMJ* 88 (Dec. 17, 1910): 1218.

70. John Bell to Superintendent and Mine Foreman of Darr Mine, May 22, 1906; Archibald Black to Bell, May 23, 1906; Bell to Black, Feb. 22, 1907; Black to Bell, Feb. 25, 1907; William Neilson to Black, June 17, 1907; Black to Neilson, June 20, 1907; Neilson to Black, Sept. 14, 1907; Black to Neilson, Sept. 16, 1907; all in box 2, GCB. See also "Darr Mine Disaster," *Mines and Minerals* 28 (Mar. 1908): 377-82, and New Mexico Mine Inspector, *Annual Report, 1908,* 45-48.

71. Roderick is quoted in James T. Beard, "A Decade in the History of Mine Inspection," Mine Inspectors' Institute *Proceedings* 11 (1920): 13-21. "The Safety of American Mines," *Colliery Guardian* 95 (Jan. 24, 1908): 174-75; "Will Coal Dust Explode?" *Colliery Engineer* 15 (Jan. 1895): 132. The confusion over the explosibility of coal dust is revealed in a symposium entitled "Views Respecting Coal Mine Explosions" and in Audley H. Stow, "Is Coal Dust, as Such, Explosive?" both in *EMJ* 87 (Jan. 2, 1909): 17-19 and 12-16.

72. House Committee on Mines and Mining, *Hearings to Consider the Establishment of a Bureau of Mines*, Mar. 9–30, 1908, 16–24, 84; Parsons, "Disaster at Monongah." See also *Proceedings of Meeting of Coal Operators of West Virginia and Other States* (Washington, D.C., Jan. 8, 1908), 42.

73. Holmes's remarks are in Clarence Hall and Walter Snelling, "Coal Mine Accidents: Their Causes and Prevention," USGS *Bulletin* 323 (Washington, D.C., 1907), 4.

74. The quotation on the purpose of the bureau is from *Congressional Record*, 61st Cong., 2d sess., May 9, 1910, 45, pt. 6:5955. The appropriation is noted in *Congressional Record*, May 31, 1910, 45, pt. 7:7099. The campaign for a department or bureau may be followed in the pages of such journals as *Colliery Engineer* and *EMJ*, and in the *Proceedings* of the American Mining Congress. The best history is William Graebner, *Coal-Mining Safety in the Progressive Period* (Lexington: University Press of Kentucky, 1976), chaps. 1–2. For the Illinois operators' views, see House Committee on Mines and Mining, *Hearings to Consider the Establishment of a Bureau of Mines*, 16 and 55.

75. "Electrical Accidents in American Mines," *Colliery Guardian* 85 (Jan. 16, 1903): 150.

CHAPTER THREE. MANUFACTURING DANGERS

Epigraphs: John Jay, *Federalist Papers*, no. 3 (New York: New American Library, 1961); National Association of Manufacturers, *American Industries* 18 (Aug. 1917): 23; Royal Meeker, "International Aspects of the Safety Problem," NSC *Proceedings* 12 (1923): 50–57.

1. Frederick Hoffman, "Industrial Accident Statistics," BLS *Bulletin* 157 (Washington, D.C., 1915), 6. This figure was later estimated to be about 50 percent too high by statisticians from Metropolitan Life Insurance Company; see "The Occupational Factor in Accident Mortality," *Metropolitan Life Statistical Bulletin* 3 (May 1922): 6–8. Crystal Eastman, *Work Accidents and the Law* (New York: Charities Publication, 1910), 3–4; William Hard, "Making Steel and Killing Men," *Everybody's* 17 (Nov. 1907): 597–91; William Hard, "The Law of the Killed and the Wounded," *Everybody's* 17 (Sept. 1907): 361–71.

2. On the American system of manufacturing, see the Note on Sources. On the coming of the large firm, see Alfred D. Chandler, *The Visible Hand: The Managerial Revolution in American Business* (Cambridge: Harvard Univ. Press, 1977). An excellent brief discussion is Daniel Nelson, *Managers and Workers: Origins of the New Factory System in the United States, 1880–1920* (Madison: Univ. of Wisconsin Press, 1975). Daniel Nelson, "The American System and the American Worker," in *Yankee Enterprise*, ed. Otto Mayer and Robert Post (Washington, D.C.: Smithsonian Press, 1981), 171–88, defines the American system as the achievement of interchangeable parts and argues that plants that employed it improved working conditions. The argument in the text employs a broader definition of the American system — power- and machine-intensive methods — and argues that it worsened risks of serious injuries.

3. Pennsylvania shops are from *Railway Engineering and Maintenance of Way* 8 (Mar. 1912): 131. *Report to the Legislature of the State of New York by the Commission Appointed under Chapter 518 of the Laws of 1909 to Enquire into the Question of Employers' Liability and Other Matters, Mar. 19, 1910* (Albany, 1910), 5; David Van Schaack, *Safeguards for the Prevention of Industrial Accidents* (Hartford: Aetna, 1910), 1; "Some Woolen-Mill Safeguards," *Travelers Standard* 9 (July 1920): 137–42; Leslie Robertson, "Remarks," in NAM *Annual Meeting* 18 (1913): 121.

4. Eastman, *Work Accidents*, chap. 8; Ohio Inspector of Factories and Workshops, *Sixth Annual Report for 1889* (Columbus, 1890), 13. On employer's liability at common law, see the Note on Sources. Voluntary compensation is discussed by Robert Asher,

"The Limits to Big Business Paternalism," in *Dying for Work*, ed. David Rosner and Gerald Markowitz (Bloomington: Indiana Univ. Press, 1987), 19-33. On the diffusion of machinery including the universal miller, see Nathan Rosenberg, "Technological Change in the Machine Tool Industry, 1840-1910," *Journal of Economic History* 23 (Dec. 1963): 414-43. On the development of machine tools generally, see Robert Woodbury, *Studies in the History of Machine Tools* (Cambridge: MIT Press, 1972).

5. Charles P. Neill, "Remarks," NSC *Proceedings* 1 (1912): 74-75; John Calder, "The Mechanical Engineer and the Prevention of Accidents," *Machinery* 17 (Mar. 1911): 550-52; Meeker, "International Aspects of the Safety Problem." British statistics are from Great Britain, Home Department, *Statistics of Compensation and of Proceedings under the Workmen's Compensation Act, 1906, and the Employers' Liability Act, 1880* (London, 1908-). French figures are derived from U.S. Commissioner of Labor, *Twenty-fourth Annual Report: Workmen's Insurance and Compensation Systems in Europe, 1909* (Washington, D.C., 1911), vol. 1.

6. Harlan Halsey, "The Choice between High-Pressure and Low-Pressure Steam Power in America in the Early Nineteenth Century," *Journal of Economic History* 41 (Dec. 1981): 723-44. For the early history of boiler explosions and examples in the text, see Louis Hunter, *Steamboats on Western Rivers* (Cambridge: Harvard Univ. Press, 1949), chap. 6, and his *History of Industrial Power in the United States, 1780-1930*, vol. 2, *Steam Power* (Charlottesville: Univ. of Virginia Press, 1985), chap. 6. The Hartford's work is described in Glenn Weaver, *The Hartford Steam Boiler Inspection and Insurance Company* (Hartford, 1966).

7. "Explosion idiot" is from "Still Another 'Prolific Source of Boiler Explosions,'" *Locomotive* 3 (Feb. 1882): 27-28. Gilbert Lathrop, *Little Engines and Big Men* (Caldwell, Idaho, 1954), 26; "The Gaffney and Co. Boiler Explosion," *Locomotive* 2 (July 1881): 110.

8. "Indictment" is from "Boiler Explosions in England, Germany, and the United States," *Locomotive* 27 (Apr. 1909): 173-78. David Denault, "An Economic Analysis of Steam Boiler Explosions in the Nineteenth Century United States" (Ph.D. diss., Univ. of Connecticut, 1993), notes that many contemporaries believed that a boiler with sufficient water in it could not explode. The data suggest a long-term decline in the number of casualties per explosion, but the company attributed this to more complete reporting of minor explosions; see "Ten Thousand Boiler Explosions," *Locomotive* 27 (Jan. 1909): 131-32. In 1920 the company concluded that explosions had become less serious during the previous decade; see "Forty Years of Boiler Explosions," *Locomotive* 33 (Oct. 1920): 101-8.

9. Louis Ernst's death is from Ohio Inspector of Workshops and Factories, *Fifth Annual Report, 1888* (Columbus, 1889), 178. On flywheels, see William Christie, "Safety Appliances in the Engine Room," *Cassier's Magazine* 32 (July 1907): 333-49, and "The Danger in the Flywheel," *Aetna Accident and Liability Series* 43 (Feb. 1910): 57-60.

10. On machine and plant design, see A. W. Allen, "Safety and Health in Hydrometallurgical Plants," *EMJ* 106 (Sept. 14, 1918): 480-81. On wooden shafting, see "Notes on Mill Shafting," *Locomotive* 4 (Oct. 1883): 169-71. The stories of Andrew Jubreed and Walter Calhoun are recounted in Eastman, *Work Accidents*, 100. The Allen screw is described in *Textile World* 45 (Apr. 1913): 176.

11. Fred Colvin, *60 Years with Men and Machines* (New York: McGraw-Hill, 1947), 19-20. Michael Schlarth is from Ohio Inspector of Factories, *Fifth Annual Report*, 178.

12. Nathan Rosenberg, ed., *The American System of Manufactures* (Edinburgh: Edinburgh Univ. Press, 1969); F. R. Hutton, "Report on Machine Tools and Wood-working Machinery," in *Tenth Census of the United States, 1880*, vol. 22, *Report on Power and Machinery Used in Manufactures* (Washington, D.C., 1888). Accidental starting of ma-

chines is noted in "Industrial Motor Drive of Machines," *Travelers Standard* 1 (Dec. 1912): 41–47, and William Newall, "What Could Manufacturers of Woodworking Machines Do to Make Their Machines More Safe?" NSC *Proceedings* 6 (1917): 1141–43. Sarah Knisley is from Hard, "The Law," 363–64.

13. Buick is from Forrest Boswell, "Supervision and Its Relation to Accident Prevention," NSC *Proceedings* 11 (1922): 174–78. The stamping plant is described in August Kaems, "Die Construction—The Real Safety of Punch Press Work," NSC *Proceedings* 8 (1919): 316–27.

14. Ripsaws are from Minnesota Bureau of Labor Statistics, *Third Biennial Report* (Minneapolis, 1892), 65. The injury to Freer is from Ohio Inspector of Factories, *Fifth Annual Report*, 179; the Ohio inspector is quoted on 68. Maine Bureau of Industrial and Labor Statistics, *Eighth Annual Report, 1894* (Augusta, 1895), 183 and 190; George Orris, "Guarding Woodworking Machines from the Viewpoint of the Operator," NSC *Proceedings* 10 (1921): 888–89.

15. The edger is described by Henry Burr, "Safeguarding the Most Hazardous Machines in Woodworking Plants," NSC *Proceedings* 6 (1916): 429–44. The treatise is by John Richards, *On the Arrangement, Care, and Operation of Wood-working Factories and Machinery* (New York: E. and F. N. Spon, 1873), 73. The death of Gaskill is from Ohio Inspector of Factories, *Fifth Annual Report*, 182. The steam skidder is described in R. G. Buchman, "Remarks," NSC *Proceedings* 16 (1927): 192–93. See also Andrew Prouty, *More Deadly Than War: Pacific Coast Logging, 1827–1981* (New York: Garland, 1988), chap. 3.

16. Hashers are from A. E. Holstedt, "New Safety Kinks in the Meat-packing Industry," NSC *Proceedings* 24 (1935): 274–76. Early hazards in packing are also described by Charles Barth, "Preventing Accidents in the Meat Packing Industry," NSC *Proceedings* 23 (1934): 248–50. Maine Bureau of Industrial and Labor Statistics, *Eighth Annual Report, 1894*, 183. The quotation on mechanization of papermaking is from Judith McGaw, *Most Wonderful Machine* (Princeton: Princeton Univ. Press, 1987), 311. Charles Walker, "The Safe Finishing Room," *Paper* 4 (Oct. 1922): 911–12. On rubber, see Ernest Beck, "Engineering Revision and Mechanical Safeguarding," NSC *Proceedings* 14 (1925): 136–43.

17. On textile safety, see "Accident Prevention in the Weave Room," *Travelers Standard* 2 (Nov. 1914): 227–34, which compares America and Europe. The importance of machinery in textile injuries is described in John Calder, "The Prevention of Accidents in Cotton Mills," National Association of Cotton Manufacturers *Transactions* 99 (1915): 261–77, and David Beyer, "Accident Prevention in the Textile Industry," ASME *Transactions* (1917): 1049–71. J. M. Sandel, "Preventing Accidents from Flying Shuttles," NSC *Proceedings* 15 (1926): 973, claimed that shuttle speed had increased sufficiently to throw one thirty feet. Carmelia Teoli is from U.S. House Committee on Rules, *Hearings on the Strike at Lawrence Mass.*, 62d Cong., 2d sess., 1912, H.D. 671, 170–71 and 428–29.

18. Construction dangers are from *Minutes of Evidence Accompanying the First Report to the Legislature of the State of New York by the Commission Appointed under Chapter 518 of the Laws of 1909 to Enquire into the Question of Employers' Liability and Other Matters, Mar. 16, 1910* (Albany, 1910), 424–38.

19. *Electrical Worker* 10 (Sept. 1900): 6–30; Charles F. Marsh, *Trade Unionism in the Electric Light and Power Industry*, University of Illinois Studies in Social Science 16 (Urbana, 1928).

20. Changes in woodworking technology are described by Nathan Rosenberg, "America's Rise to Woodworking Leadership," in *America's Wooden Age*, ed. Brooke Hindle (Tarrytown, N.Y.: Sleepy Hollow Restorations, 1975), 37–62. For a study that

links severe accidents to machinery in a number of industries, see Arthur Carruthers, "An Analysis of 350,000 Industrial Accidents," *SE* 47 (Mar. 1924): 118–20.

21. The literature on the struggles of managers and workers to control the work process during this period is vast, but none of it addresses safety directly; for overviews, see works cited in the Note on Sources.

22. David Beyer, "The Need for Safety Standards for New Textile Machinery," NSC *Proceedings* 4 (1915): 380, notes the role of piece rates. The story of the pusher is recounted in M. S. Humphreys, "Eliminating the Screw Conveyer Accident," NSC *Proceedings* 18 (1929): 481–90. Reformers also claimed that fatigue was a major source of accidents. Josephine Goldmark et al., "Comparison of an Eight Hour Plant and a Ten Hour Plant," U.S. Public Health Service *Bulletin* 106 (Washington, D.C., 1920), discovered that while hourly output declined at the end of the shift, accidents increased at this time—seemingly the result of fatigue. Yet the Labor Department studies of the steel industry found no relation between hours worked and accident rates. Federated American Engineering Societies, *The Twelve Hour Shift in Industry* (New York: E. P. Dutton, 1922), also concluded that "there is little evidence to show that personal injuries to workmen have been [reduced by the shift to a shorter workday]." For some mixed statistical findings, see chap. 4 below.

23. Excellent contemporary descriptions of steelmaking technology are contained in U.S. Commissioner of Labor, *Working Conditions and Relations of Employers and Employees*, vol. 3 of *Report on Conditions of Employment in the Iron and Steel Industry* (Washington, D.C., 1913), and in a series of articles by Robert Streeter in *Engineering Magazine* 41 (June 1911) through 44 (Jan. 1913). American data from Lucian Chaney, "Causes and Prevention of Accidents in the Iron and Steel Industry, 1910–1919," BLS *Bulletin* 298 (Washington, D.C., 1922), table 65. German experience is derived from Hoffman, "Industrial Accident Statistics," table 97. Chaney's assessment is in his "Outstanding Safety Features in the Iron and Steel Industry," NSC *Proceedings* 11 (1922): 447–53. Royal Meeker claimed that foreigners were employed in relatively dangerous jobs in the steel industry; see his "Remarks" in New York State Department of Labor Industrial Safety Congress *Proceedings* 2 (1917): 53.

24. The evolution of blast furnace technology is described in William T. Hogan, *Economic History of the Iron and Steel Industry in the United States* (Lexington, Mass.: D. C. Heath, 1971), vol. 1, chaps. 4 and 12. J. H. Ayres, "Remarks," Pennsylvania Department of Labor and Industry Monthly *Bulletin* 2 (Sept. 1915): 63.

25. The slip and breakout are described in Frederick H. Willcox, "Blast Furnace Breakouts, Explosions and Slips, and Methods of Prevention," BM *Bulletin* 130 (Washington, D.C., 1917), 52 and 255. The hazards of newer furnaces are from Frederick H. Willcox, "Occupational Hazards at Blast Furnace Plants and Accident Prevention," BM *Bulletin* 140 (Washington, D.C., 1917), 4–5. The fatality rate is from Chaney, "Causes and Prevention," appendix.

26. J. H. Ayres, "Safety in Bessemer Operations," NSC *Proceedings* 5 (1916): 480–84. For statistics on puddling, see U.S. Commissioner of Labor, *Report on Conditions of Employment in the Iron and Steel Industry*, vol. 4, *Accidents and Accident Prevention* (Washington, D.C., 1913), 32–33.

27. For hand- and mechanical rolling, see U.S. Commissioner of Labor, *Accidents and Accident Prevention*, 33–35, and for occupational shifts, 108–10.

28. Arthur H. Young, "Industrial Personnel Relations," ASME *Journal* 41 (July, 1919): 581–86. Young's career is from *NCAB* (New York: James T. White), 51:136–37.

29. Hard, "Making Steel," 586, notes the size of the rail yard. As late as 1923, half the cars at Carnegie Steel still did not have automatic couplers; see J. W. Benner, "Remarks," NSC *Proceedings* 12 (1923): 571.

30. Hard, "Making Steel," 586. The changing nature of steel work is described in Montgomery, *The Fall*, and David Brody, *Steelworkers in America: The Nonunion Era* (New York: Harper and Row, 1960), chaps. 2–3.

31. The equation is:

$$\ln(\text{Freq}) = 0.227[\ln(\text{Size})] - 0.377(\text{Safety Organization})$$
$$(5.80) \qquad\qquad (4.13)$$
$$R^2 = 0.14; N = 430$$

Data for the regression equation are from U.S. Commissioner of Labor, *Accidents and Accident Prevention*, appendix A. Units of observation are the department. The variable "size" is the number of positions in the plant of which the department is a part. The presence or absence of a safety organization was determined from information in the text. The data are manhour-weighted using a TSP routine. Figures in parentheses are *t*-ratios. Other functional forms of the equation and estimation without safety organization all yield the same positive relationship between plant size and injury frequency.

32. New Jersey Bureau of Statistics of Labor and Industry, *Sixth Annual Report, 1883* (Trenton, 1884), 113–25.

33. The strikes are summarized in U.S. Commissioner of Labor, *Sixteenth Annual Report: Strikes and Lockouts, 1900* (Washington, D.C., 1901), table 10.

34. The Bridge and Structural Iron Workers Local 1 was a rare example of a union that pushed for safety among its members; see its "Industrial Accident Report, 1916–1917" (N.p.; copies in U.S. Labor Department library). For an argument that job risks were an important source of worker militancy, see Robert Asher, "Industrial Safety and Labor Relations in the United States, 1865–1917," in *Life and Labor: Dimensions of American Working Class History*, ed. Charles Stephenson and Robert Asher (Albany: SUNY Press, 1986), 115–30.

35. Eastman, *Work Accidents*, appendix 1.

36. The DuPont rules are in Safety File S1-1, Photographic Division, HML. William Nisbet to Mary Bush, May 7, 1974, National Safety Council Files, Chicago, refers to the use of the term *Safety First* by the H. C. Frick company in 1890. For claims that Illinois Steel inaugurated its safety department in the early 1890s, see "Milestones," *NSN* 87 (May 1963): 78–82, and R. W. Campbell, "Safety in the Iron and Steel Industry," NSC *Proceedings* 1 (1912): 279–91.

37. The chronology of events at U.S. Steel is from its Bureau of Safety, Relief, Sanitation, and Welfare *Bulletin* 1 (Oct. 1910) (which contains the quotation from Gary), 2 (July 1911), and 3 (Aug. 1912). See also Gerald Eggert, *Steelmasters and Labor Reform, 1886–1923* (Pittsburgh: Univ. of Pittsburgh Press, 1981), 44–46. Lucian Chaney, "Outstanding Safety Features in the Iron and Steel Industry," NSC *Proceedings* 11 (1922): 447–53, claimed that the first committees were organized at the Illinois Steel South Chicago works in March 1908. This seems to be the accepted date; see Carmen Fish, "A Century of Steel Making," *NSN* 76 (1957): 116–19, 231–36.

38. The *Tribune* story is noted in Eggert, *Steelmasters and Labor Reform*.

39. L. H. Burnett, "The Economic Value of Accident Prevention," Pennsylvania Safety Congress *Proceedings*, in Pennsylvania Department of Labor and Industry *Special Bulletin* 19 (Harrisburg, 1928), 16–18. Gary's pronouncements were brought together in U.S. Steel Bureau of Safety *Bulletin* 9 (Dec. 1922): 1–3.

40. Raynal Bolling, "Rendering Labor Safe in Mine and Mill," American Iron and Steel Institute, *Yearbook* 2 (1912): 106–9.

41. "Far exceeded" is from U.S. Steel Bureau of Safety, Sanitation and Welfare *Bulletin* 11 (1926): 3. The NAM quotation is from *American Industries* 16, suppl. (Apr. 1916): 2.

42. A brief chronology of the development of workmen's compensation is in Clarence Hobbs, *Workmen's Compensation Insurance* (New York: McGraw-Hill, 1939), chap. 4. See also Friedman and Ladinsky, "Social Change and the Law of Industrial Accidents."

43. The views of the New York commission are in *Report to the Legislature of the State of New York;* the comment on trade risks is from 7. The Illinois survey is in *Report of the Employers' Liability Commission of the State of Illinois* (Chicago, 1910), 12–13.

44. Gompers's views are in *Minutes of Evidence Accompanying the First Report to the Legislature of the State of New York,* 92–97; he gave the same testimony to the Illinois commission (*Report of the Employers' Liability Commission of the State of Illinois,* 234). See also "President Gompers' Report," American Federation of Labor *Proceedings* 32 (1912): 50. Studies of accident causation are reviewed in *Report of the Employers' Liability Commission of the State of Illinois,* 249.

45. Hard, "Making Steel," 585. For a review of the politics of workmen's compensation, see Roy Lubove, "Workmen's Compensation and the Prerogatives of Voluntarism," *Labor History* 8 (Fall 1967): 254–79.

46. The New York system is described in *Report to the Legislature of the State of New York,* 31; the Illinois commission estimated that only about 25 percent of all premiums went to beneficiaries; see *Report of the Employers' Liability Commission of the State of Illinois,* 11. Complaints about lawyers are from John Trix, "The Michigan Employers' Factory Inspection Plan," and J. C. Adderly, "Means and Methods for the Prevention of Accidents in Flour Mills," NSC *Proceedings* 1 (1912): 199–204 and 244–52. The NAM guidelines are from "Workmen's Compensation for Injury," NAM *Annual Meeting* 16 (1911): 152–53.

47. The Schwedtman quotation is from "Co-operation or—What?" *American Industries* 13 (Oct. 1912): 30–32. Alexander's speech is in NAM *Annual Meeting* 16 (1912): 152. For George Gillette's role, see Robert Asher, "Origins of Workmen's Compensation in Minnesota," *Minnesota History* 44 (Winter 1974): 142–53. See also Ferdinand Schwedtman and James Emory, *Accident Prevention and Relief* (New York: NAM, 1911).

48. The NAM's views are from Schwedtman and Emory, *Accident Prevention,* xii–xiv. E. G. Trimble, "Accident Prevention in the Laundry Industry, NSC *Proceedings* 1 (1912): 261–65. The material on GE is from *Minutes of Evidence Accompanying the First Report to the Legislature of the State of New York,* 288–92. Eastman, *Work Accidents,* 194.

49. Dawson's testimony is in *Minutes of Evidence Accompanying the First Report to the Legislature of the State of New York,* 391–92. Isaac Rubinow, *Social Insurance* (New York: Henry Holt, 1913), chaps. 10–12, provides an early statement that the rise in employers' liability cost drove companies to embrace workmen's compensation. James Weinstein, *The Corporate Ideal in the Liberal State* (Boston: Beacon, 1968), 45, suggests that fears over rising costs helped motivate important businessmen to support compensation. Anthony Bale, "Compensation Crisis: The Value and Meaning of Work-Related Injuries and Illnesses in the United States, 1842–1932" (Ph.D. diss., Brandeis Univ., 1986), argues that costs were rising under employers' liability, and the switch to compensation was an effort to hold them down. As the text makes clear, the evidence on such motives is mixed at best. Costs of the Federal Employers' Liability Act are reported in *Message of the President of the United States Transmitting the Report of the Employers' Liability and Workmen's Compensation Commission,* 62d Cong., 2d sess., S.D. 338 (Washington, D.C., 1912).

50. Miles Dawson, "Cost of Employers' Liability and Workmen's Compensation Insurance," BLS *Bulletin* 90 (Washington, D.C., 1910), 749–831; Schwedtman and Emory, *Accident Prevention,* 131; G. L. Avery, "Avery Company's Plan under the Illinois Workmen's Compensation and Employers' Liability Act," NSC *Proceedings* 1 (1912):

265–76. For Massachusetts's rates, see David Beyer, "The Organization of the Massachusetts Employees Insurance Association," NSC *Proceedings* 2 (1913): 98–100. The impact of the Michigan law is described in L. B. Robertson, "Remarks," NSC *Proceedings* 3 (1914): 293–96. Gillette's views are described in Asher, "Origins of Workmen's Compensation."

51. For the origins of workmen's compensation in various states, see, in addition to the works cited above, others contained in the Note on Sources.

52. Harvey Kelly, "The Safety Movement in the State of Washington," IAIABC *Proceedings* 7 (1920), in BLS *Bulletin* 281 (Washington, D.C., 1921), 40–44.

53. The Standard Accident Insurance example is from Cincinnati Chamber of Commerce, *Study of Workmen's Compensation* (Cincinnati, 1923), 759–60; the quotation on the value of schedule rating is from 466. For the introduction of experience and schedule rating, see Emile Watson, "Merit Rating in Workmen's Compensation Insurance," IAIABC *Proceedings* 3 (1916), in BLS *Bulletin* 210 (Washington, D.C., 1917), 58–75. Technical reviews of the development of experience rating are in G. F. Michelbacher, "The Practice of Experience Rating," CAS *Proceedings* 4 (May 1918): 293–324, from which the equations in the text are drawn, and Mark Kormes, "The Experience Rating Plan as Applied to Workmen's Compensation Risks," CAS *Proceedings* 21 (Nov. 1934): 81–132. A modern assessment of safety incentives for small business is Louise Russell, *Pricing Industrial Accidents*, National Commission on State Workmen's Compensation Laws, Supplemental Studies 3 (Washington, D.C., 1973), 27–38.

54. Minnesota Bureau of Labor Statistics, *Third Biennial Report*, 34–35; Iowa Bureau of Labor Statistics, *Tenth Annual Report, 1901–1902* (Des Moines, 1903), 18–19. Martin Lloyd, "Safety Legislation," *SE* 46 (July 1923): 14–19, provides a brief review of the development of state legislation. An early and critical assessment of its operation is "Efficient Enforcement of Labor Laws," *American Labor Legislation Review* 2 (Dec. 1912): 595–603.

55. The complaints about New York building laws are from *Minutes of Evidence Accompanying the First Report to the Legislature of the State of New York*, 133 and 144.

56. The origins and workings of the Wisconsin commission are described in Donald Rogers, "The Rise of Administrative Process: Industrial Safety Regulation in Wisconsin 1880–1940" (Ph.D. diss., Univ. of Wisconsin at Madison, 1983). See also John W. Hallock, "The Development of Industrial Safety Standards in Pennsylvania" (Ph.D. diss., Univ. of Pittsburgh, 1936).

57. Lloyd, "Safety Legislation."

58. C. W. Price, "The Wisconsin Industrial Commission Plan of Promoting Safety," NSC *Proceedings* 1 (1912): 61–66; Massachusetts State Board of Labor and Industries, *Annual Report* (Mass. Public Document 104), various years; E. G. Sheibley, "Annual Report of the Department of Safety," *California Safety News* 11 (Dec. 1927): 4; Industrial Commission of Wisconsin, *Wisconsin Labor Statistics* 4 (Mar. 1926): 5.

59. John Rennie to John Macadam, Dec. 27, 1919, BP; Louis DeBlois to F. L. Connable, May 4, 1914, series 2, pt. 2, box 1002, DP.

60. The quotation is from *American Industries* 14, suppl. (Oct. 1913): 3; the advertisement by the Conference Board is in *American Industries* 15 (Dec. 1914).

61. David Beyer, "Recent Application of Safety Devices to Textile Machinery as Seen from the Machine Builder's Viewpoint," NSC *Proceedings* 6 (1917): 479–82. On Norton's efforts, see Earl Morgan, "Remarks," NSC *Proceedings* 6 (1917): 1182. Good reviews of the development and adoption of standardized safety codes are in David Van Schaack, "Development of Standard Safety Codes," *SE* 56 (Sept. 1928): 83–86, and Leslie Peat, "The Place of Safety Codes in the Industries," *SE* 70 (Nov. 1935): 173–74.

62. Cyril Ainsworth, "Safety Code for Power Presses — How It Came About," NSC *Proceedings* 25 (1936): 401–4; Rogers, "Rise of Administrative Process"; and Hallock, "Development of Industrial Safety Standards."

63. For a review of the status of the ASA codes as of the mid-1930s, see "States Curb Loss of Life by Using American Standard Safety Codes," *Industrial Standardization* 6 (Oct. 1935): 266–70. On the development of the rubber code, see Ernest Beck, "Engineering Revision and Mechanical Safeguarding," NSC *Proceedings* 14 (1925): 136–42; E. A. Hoener, "Safety Needs Engineering," *NSN* 24 (July 1931): 19–20, 77; and C. W. Drake, "Will It Stop Quickly?" *NSN* 34 (Dec. 1936): 17–18.

64. Compensation costs are for Pennsylvania for 1916 and are from "Annual Report, Bureau of Workmen's Compensation, Department of Labor and Industry, of Pennsylvania, 1924," *SE* 49 (May 1925): 209–12. C. W. Crownhart, "The Relation of Compensation to Safety," NSC *Proceedings* 1 (1912): 57–61.

65. Magnus W. Alexander, "The Economic Value of Industrial Safety," and Hart Palmer, "Safety as It Is Practiced by the Western Lumber Industry," NSC *Proceedings* 1 (1912): 204–11 and 235–40; L. B. Robertson, "Remarks," NSC *Proceedings* 3 (1914): 293–96.

66. The steelman's comment is reported in Lucian Chaney, "Outstanding Safety Features," 449.

67. The purpose of the study of safety in the steel industry is revealed in the typescript of a talk by Ethelbert Stewart, "Cooperation with the States by the United States Bureau of Labor Statistics in the Matter of Accident Statistics," box 41, BLS General Correspondence, Record Group 257, National Archives. Lucian Chaney, "Safety as Promoted by Federal Bureaus," NSC *Proceedings* 2 (1913): 101–7, describes his development of injury statistics.

68. The story of Mansfield is in Samuel Davy, "Cutting Lost Time Accidents 69 Percent," *Manufacturing Industries* 14 (Oct. 1927): 255–58. Lucian Chaney stressed the value of statistics in revealing causes in "Analysis of Accident Experience," NSC *Proceedings* 6 (1917): 1153–63. Royal Meeker's assertion is in "The Why and How of Uniform Industrial Accident Statistics for the United States," IAIABC *Proceedings* 3 (1916), in BLS *Bulletin* 210 (Washington, D.C., 1917), 91–100. In the same volume W. H. Burhop, "Use of Accident Statistics for Accident Prevention," 101–5, argues that statistics are needed to convince small producers of dangers.

69. Royal Meeker, "Report of Committee on Accident Statistics," NSC *Proceedings* 3 (1914): 22. In 1918 the committee still reported "wide variation in methods followed" among its members; see "Report of Committee on Uniform Industrial Accident Statistics," NSC *Proceedings* 7 (1918): 30–37.

70. Massachusetts's activities are detailed in Massachusetts Industrial Accident Board, *Annual Report* (Mass. Public Document 105), various years.

71. California's safety work is revealed in *California Safety News* and in its Industrial Accident Commission's annual reports. For Wisconsin, see Rogers, "Rise of Administrative Process."

72. The quotation on 600 volts is from W. J. Pefferly, "Electrical Hazards Are More Dangerous than Mechanical Ones," *SE* 42 (Nov. 1921): 265–68; S. C. Coey, "Remarks," NSC *Proceedings* 5 (1916): 579. An electrical engineer at AT&T asserted that "voltages of 250 or less are not dangerous"; see H. S. Warren, "Danger of Low Tension Shocks," NSC *Proceedings* 4 (1915): 330–34. In 1926 S. E. Whiting, "Low Voltage Electrical Hazards," NSC *Proceedings* 15 (1926): 268–73, claimed that the average electrical engineer still believed that 750 volts or less could not prove fatal.

73. Walter Greenwood, "The Association of Iron and Steel Electrical Engineers and Safety," *Iron and Steel Engineer* 5 (Jan. 1928): 18–19. Palmer's career is chronicled

in "Lew R. Palmer Dies," *NSN* 51 (Apr. 1945): 30. "Missionary tour" is from Chaney, "Outstanding Safety Features," 449.

74. The council's creed is from president R. W. Campbell, "Remarks," NSC *Proceedings* 2 (1913): 68-74.

75. On the origins of the slogan Safety First, see Dianne Bennett and William Graebner, "Safety First: Slogan and Symbol of the Industrial Safety Movement," *Journal of the Illinois State Historical Society* 68 (June 1975): 243-56. The biographical sketch of DeBlois is from "Louis A. DeBlois," *NSN* 95 (Apr. 1967): 102. The quotation is from Louis DeBlois to F. L. Connable, May 4, 1914, box 1002, series 2, pt. 2, DP. The primacy of safety is stressed in "Safety and Efficiency in the Plant," *Travelers Standard* 14 (May 1926): 103-12, which commented, "Down at the bottom we are all family. We are morally responsible for one another and to one another."

76. Melville Mix, "The Business of Safety," *American Industries* 15 (Dec. 1914): 24-25; Ethelbert Stewart, "The Small Plant and Workmen's Compensation Coverage," IAIABC *Proceedings* 15 (1928), in BLS *Bulletin* 485 (Washington, D.C., 1929), 214-24, at 217; David Van Schaack, "President's Address," NSC *Proceedings* 7 (1918): 13-21.

77. William H. Doolittle [National Metal Trades Association], "Condition of Factories of Our Members," NSC *Proceedings* 1 (1912): 276; John Rennie to John Bird, Sept. 28, 1917, box 103, BP. The value of exhibits was told to David Van Schaack, "Organization of a Co-operative Safety Society," NSC *Proceedings* 1 (1912): 252-53. The author of the comment on punch presses was unidentified; see "Remarks," NSC *Proceedings* 9 (1920): 446.

78. The quotation on the value of professionalism is from "Report of the Special Committee on the Formation of an Engineering Section in the National Safety Council," NSC *Proceedings* 8 (1919): 36-37.

79. NAM safety work may be followed in *American Industries*. Work of the National Metal Trades Association is briefly noted in William Doolittle, "Accident Prevention Work and Results," *Iron Age* 93 (Jan. 15, 1914): 197. Other associations are listed in Ferdinand Schwedtman, "Co-operation in Safety Work among Manufacturers and Trade Associations," NSC *Proceedings* 3 (1914): 276-81.

80. An early textbook is David Beyer, *Industrial Accident Prevention* (Boston: Houghton Mifflin, 1916). A brief history of the American Society of Safety Engineers is contained in J. C. Stennett and A. D. Caddell, "The ASSE: Safety's Professional Fraternity," *NSN* 51 (Apr. 1945): 18-19, 44.

81. On the origins of trade mutuals, see John Bainbridge, *Biography of an Idea* (New York: Doubleday, 1952), chap. 17. For Lumberman's and Integrity Mutual, see Cincinnati Chamber of Commerce, *Study of Workmen's Compensation*, 962-66, 929-32. On the laundrymen, see E. G. Trimble, "Accident Prevention in the Laundry Industry," NSC *Proceedings* 1 (1912): 261-65.

82. For Aetna's report, see Massachusetts Industrial Accident Board, *Second Annual Report* (Boston, 1915), 264-69. The Travelers report is in *Third Annual Report* (Boston, 1916), 254-58; the work of the Massachusetts Employees' Insurance Association is on 259-60. The construction company is cited in Cincinnati Chamber of Commerce, *Study of Workmen's Compensation*, 856-57; the entry of Maryland Casualty into Georgia is on 741-42.

83. On Lumberman's activities, see Cincinnati Chamber of Commerce, *Study of Workmen's Compensation*, 962-66. Contractors Mutual is in Massachusetts Industrial Accident Board, *Second Annual Report*, 298-305. Safety-related spending is from Reed, *Adequacy*, table 58.

84. The discussion of insurance clinics is derived from Cincinnati Chamber of Commerce, *Study of Workmen's Compensation*; the quotation is from 713.

85. Ibid., 758–59.

86. Michigan and Integrity Mutual are from ibid., 898 and 932. The Travelers patents on safety devices are noted in "An Efficient Guard for the Platen Press," *NSN* 20 (July 1929): 36, and "Taming the Embossing Press," *NSN* 35 (Feb. 1937): 27.

87. The beginnings of safety at Slater mills are noted by William Ide, "Safety Education in the Textile Industry," NSC *Proceedings* 8 (1919): 1361–62. John Rennie to John Macadam, Feb. 25, 1920, and June 16, 1922, box 103, BP; "naked as a new-born babe" from Cincinnati Chamber of Commerce, *Study of Workmen's Compensation*, 980; Hart Palmer, "Safety as It Is Practiced in the Western Lumber Industry," NSC *Proceedings* 1 (1912): 235–39.

88. The injury reports are from Accident Records, Lancaster Collection, Baker Library, Harvard University.

89. B. F. Affleck, "Safety from the Executive's Point of View," NSC *Proceedings* 13 (1924): 184; Louis DeBlois, "Safety and the Individual," NSC *Proceedings* 17 (1928): 132–35. For more on Heinrich, see chap. 4 below.

90. Eastman, *Work Accidents*, chap. 6; Hard, "Making Steel," 587; Chaney, "Outstanding Safety Features," 449; Arthur Young, "Practical Aspects of the Safety Movement," *Industrial Management* 54 (Oct. 1917): 30–35; Fred Lange, "Safety and Accident Prevention," *Industrial Management* 61 (Apr. 1921): 257–59.

91. Edward Walsh, "Safeguarding Machines for Making Paper," NSC *Proceedings* 4 (1915): 297–301.

92. J. S. Herbert, "Analysis of Accident Causes and Prevention," NSC *Proceedings* 6 (1917): 163–64.

93. The "applied Christianity" quotation is from Lucian Chaney's "Remarks," NSC *Proceedings* 1 (1912): 8. The comments on human nature and elimination of fatalities are from his "Some Showings from Accident Records," IAIABC *Proceedings* 4 (1917), in BLS *Bulletin* 248 (Washington, D.C., 1918), 30–37. The theme of engineering revision dominated Chaney's writing. This discussion is also based on "Analysis of Accident Experience," NSC *Proceedings* 6 (1917): 1153–63 (which describes his development of severity rates), and "Three Periods of Engineering Revision," *SE* 39 (Jan. 1920): 1–3. See also Lucian Chaney and Hugh Hanna, "Can Serious Industrial Accidents Be Eliminated?" *MLR* 6 (Aug. 1917): 205–15; U.S. Commissioner of Labor, *Accidents and Accident Prevention* (which Chaney wrote); Lucian Chaney, "'Engineering Revision' as Seen by Safety Committees," *MLR* 7 (Dec. 1918): 1483–99; and Chaney, "Causes and Prevention." Biographical information on Chaney is from *NCAB*, 27:304; Elizabeth Chaney Ferguson, "Lucian West Chaney Jr. A Biography" (N.p., 1968), a copy of which was kindly lent by the author; and "Biographical Notes on Dr. Lucian W. Chaney," Chaney Papers, Carleton College.

94. "Widest possible application" is from Lucian Chaney, "Causes and Prevention," 192. "A notable" and "without exception" are from Chaney, "Is Industrial Death Necessary?" *SE* 38 (Oct. 1919): 196–98.

95. Calder, "Mechanical Engineer," 550–52; W. P. Barba, "Industrial Safety and Principles of Management," ASME *Transactions* 37 (1915): 909–19. The Hoover Commission report is the common name for American Engineering Council, *Waste in Industry* (New York: McGraw-Hill, 1921). Others who emphasized engineering over education included Walter Greenwood, who was an electrical engineer and became a safety engineer at Carnegie Steel. See his "Safeguarding Comes First," NSC *Proceedings* 5 (1916): 584–85; "Carelessness or Lack of Concern?" *SE* 33 (May 1917): 257–60; and "Accident Prevention," *Iron and Steel Engineer* 2 (Apr. 1925): 184–86. David Van Schaack stressed the importance of engineering revision in textiles in "Accident Prevention in Textile Industries," *SE* 35 (Feb. 1918): 137–44. See also C. P. Tolman, "Engi-

neering Revision—The Engineer's Part in Safety," *SE* 41 (June 1921): 279-80, and Arthur Carruthers, "Safeguarding First Gets Safety First," *SE* 58 (Dec. 1929): 289-90.

96. Biographical material on Beyer from *NCAB*, 27:55-56.

97. David Beyer, "Remarks," ASME *Transactions* 37 (1915): 891, and "Mechanical Safeguards," IAIABC *Proceedings* 4 (1917), in BLS *Bulletin* 248 (Washington, D.C., 1918), 16-26.

98. "Report of Committee on Code of Ethics," ASME *Transactions* 36 (1914): 23-27. "We have constantly" is from Frank Law, "Remarks," ASME *Transactions* (1915): 885.

99. Louis DeBlois, "The Safety Engineer," ASME *Journal* 40 (July 1918): 543-44.

100. Chester Rausch, "The Safety Engineer—His Qualifications and Duties," *SE* 38 (Nov. 1919): 261-302. "Using all your ingenuity" is from Sidney Williams, "Guards —Their Use and Abuse," *SE* 47 (June 1924): 47.

101. Membership is from "One Year's Progress," *SE* 41 (Feb. 1921): 68, and "Brief History of ASSE" (ASSE, n.d.). Qualifications and lobbying are from "Official Proceedings, ASSE," *SE* 42 (Sept. 1921): 134-35 and 44 (July 1922): 39. "The better your education" is from American Society of Safety Engineers, *The Organizational Position of the Industrial Safety Engineer* (Chicago, n.d.), 13. "Black sheep" is from "More Safety—Less Engineering," *SE* 92 (Oct. 1946): 33, 36. For evidence of modern concerns with professionalization, see, for example, Dan Petersen, "The Role of Safety in the 1990s: Our Choice," *Professional Safety* 40 (June 1995): 30-33.

102. For the introduction of safety into the engineering curriculum, see George Fallows, "Safety and Welfare Work in the Engineer's Education," ASME *Journal* 40 (July 1918): 545-47; "Safety Instruction in the Engineering College Curriculum," *NSN* 11 (July 1925): 21-22; John Hallock, "Safety Engineering and the Student," and R. McKeown, "Report of the Committee on Accident Prevention in Engineering Colleges," NSC *Proceedings* 20 (1931): 51-56 and 343; E. A. Holbrook, "Training Future Safety Engineers," *NSN* 36 (Dec. 1937): 13, 64; and W. Rupert MacLaurin and Paul Cohen, "Teaching Safety at M.I.T.," *NSN* 37 (Apr. 1938): 14-16. John Woltz's remarks are in "The Dividends of 'Safety First,'" *SE* 39 (June 1920): 312-16.

CHAPTER FOUR. A MANAGEMENT RESPONSIBILITY

Epigraphs: William Shakespeare, *The First Part of King Henry the Fourth*, 2.3.11; Ethelbert Stewart, "The Newer Industrial Accident Prevention and Workmen's Compensation Problem," New York State Department of Labor Industrial Safety Congress *Proceedings* 11 (1927): 23-28.

1. The Illinois survey is in Max Kossoris, "How Effective Are Safety Organizations?" *Illinois Labor Bulletin* 9 (Mar. 1929): 136-38. The national survey is in "A Preliminary Survey of the Industrial Hygiene Survey in the United States," Public Health Service *Bulletin* 259 (Washington, D.C., 1939).

2. "Stop the operation" is from W. J. Todhunter, "Remarks," NSC *Proceedings* 3 (1914): 15.

3. The description of the structure of the safety organization at U.S. Steel and its subsidiaries is taken from U.S. Steel Bureau of Safety, Relief, Sanitation, and Welfare *Bulletin* 2 (July 1911) and 4 (Nov. 1913); *Bulletin* 1 (Oct. 1910) and 4 reveal the number of recommendations accepted and the number of men on the committees. Illinois Steel Company *Safety Bulletin* 6 (Aug. 1912) reveals occupations of departmental safety committees at several plants.

4. The booklet was Ocean Accident and Guarantee Corporation Safety Service, "Accident Prevention Safety Committee Plan" (N.p., n.d.). This discussion is based largely on "Round Table Discussions," NSC *Proceedings* 2 (1913): 141-87; Price's remarks are on 145.

5. "Round Table Discussions," NSC *Proceedings* 2 (1913); Young's remarks are on 148 and Brading's on 150.

6. Robert and Arthur Young's remarks are in ibid., 163 and 179. For Commonwealth Steel, see "Chainmen's Conference," *Commonwealther* 10 (Jan.-Feb. 1924): 18. There is a picture of an integrated safety committee at the Rockeville (Connecticut) plant of the White, Corbin and Co. Division of U.S. Envelope in "Noteworthy Achievements in Safety," *SE* 66 (Nov. 1933): 155-56.

7. Nellie Schwartz, "Work Accidents among Women," New York State Department of Labor Industrial Safety Congress *Proceedings* 5 (1920): 80-84. For International Harvester, see A. E. Conrath, "Remarks," NSC *Proceedings* 7 (1918): 583. American Woolen's actions are described by I. McNulty, "Organizing the Human Element for Safety in the Textile Industry," NSC *Proceedings* 12 (1923): 1119-22, and [?] Dundee, "Remarks," NSC *Proceedings* 15 (1926): 97.

8. Price's comments are from "Round Table Discussions," NSC *Proceedings* 2 (1913): 186. Frank McKee, "Accident Prevention in Foundry and Machine Shop," NSC *Proceedings* 1 (1912): 227-35.

9. Robert Young, "Fundamental Principles of Safeguarding," NSC *Proceedings* 6 (1917): 98-107; C. B. Hayward, "Safety Engineering at the Winchester Repeating Arms Company," *American Machinist* 47 (Oct. 4, 1917): 577-81; W. E. Worth, "Does the Attitude of the Foreman Determine the Success of the Safety Engineer?" and J. J. Heelan, "Modern Methods of Safeguarding," NSC *Proceedings* 7 (1918): 95-99 and 99-104; M. H. Fellmer, "Safety Organization in the Woodworking and Logging Industry," NSC *Proceedings* 6 (1917): 1119-24.

10. The idea that companies make a "gift" to their employees to induce desirable behavior is from George Akerlof, "Labor Contracts as a Partial Gift Exchange," *Quarterly Journal of Economics* 97 (Nov. 1982): 543-69. The need for organizations to produce trust is discussed by Lynn Zucker, "Production of Trust: Institutional Sources of Economic Structure, 1840-1920," in *Research in Organizational Behavior*, ed. Barry Staw and L. L. Commings, vol. 8 (New York: JAI Press, 1986), 53-111. See also David Kreps, "Corporate Culture and Economic Theory," in *Perspectives on Positive Political Economy*, ed. James Alt and Kenneth Shepsle (New York: Cambridge Univ. Press, 1990), 90-143.

11. Robert Young, "Accident Prevention in Steel Plants," *Iron Age* 89 (Jan. 4, 1912): 30-40; "Editorial," Portland Cement Association *Accident Prevention Bulletin* 1 (May 1915): 4; Arthur Young, "Remarks," NSC *Proceedings* 2 (1913): 149. The Liberty inspector is from David Beyer, "Mechanical Safeguards," IAIABC *Proceedings* 4, in BLS *Bulletin* 248 (Washington, D.C., 1919), 16-26. Arthur Young, "Remarks," NSC *Proceedings* 2 (1913): 149.

12. Descriptions of the changes at U.S. Steel are from Young, "Accident Prevention"; David Beyer, "Safety Provisions in the United States Steel Corporation," *Survey* 24 (May 7, 1910): 205-36; and A. Russell Bond, "Safety in Steel Works," *Scientific American* 110 (Feb. 7, 1914): 121-22, 130. For the industry as a whole, see U.S. Commissioner of Labor, *Accidents and Accident Prevention*, vol. 4 of *Report on Conditions of Labor in the Iron and Steel Industry* (Washington, D.C., 1913), and the following works by Lucian Chaney: "The Safety Movement in the Iron and Steel Industry, 1907-1917," BLS *Bulletin* 234 (Washington, D.C., 1918); "Causes and Prevention of Accidents in the Iron and Steel Industry, 1910-1919," BLS *Bulletin* 298 (Washington, D.C., 1922); "Three Periods of Engineering Revision," *SE* 39 (Jan. 1920): 1-3; and "Is Industrial Death Necessary?" NSC *Proceedings* 8 (1919): 128-32. See also A. L. Touzalin, "Safe Practices in Blast Furnace Operations," NSC *Proceedings* 9 (1920): 720-25, and Lawrence Underwood, "Accident Prevention at Blast Furnaces," NSC *Proceedings* 16 (1927): 132-38.

13. Chaney, "Causes and Prevention."

14. For Kodak, see "Three Years of Accident Prevention," *Iron Age* 91 (May 1, 1913): 1058-60. For John Deere, see Illinois Chief Factory Inspector, *Twenty-first Annual Report, 1915* (Springfield, 1916), 118. Henry Owen, "Standard Guards for Textile Machinery," NSC *Proceedings* 8 (1919): 1351-61; "Reports of Safety Committees," box 103, BP. Burroughs is from "Workmen's Cooperation Reduces Accidents," *Iron Age* 95 (May 13, 1915): 1051-54.

15. Ford is quoted in "How Henry Ford Saves Men and Money," *NSN* 2 (Sept. 13, 1920): 3-8. See also Fay L. Faurote, "Ford Methods and Ford Shops—Methods Employed for Safeguarding the Workmen," *Engineering Magazine* 49 (June 1915): 372-93. Louis Resnick, "Saving Men and Money at the DuPont Plants," *NSN* 3 (Feb. 21, 1921): 3-8; General Manager to William Coyne, Sept. 10, 1913, box 1002, series 2, pt. 2, DP; A. O. Smith, *Shop Safety Bulletin* 1 (June 1915).

16. Comments on the machine-to-worker ratio in textiles are from G. W. Cook, "What Causes Textile Accidents?" NSC *Proceedings* 13 (1924): 1158-61. "Special Meeting of the Safety Committee," May 19, 1931, box 103, BP; J. D. James, "Remarks," NSC *Proceedings* 3 (1914): 150. "The question will come up" is from Benjamin Griffith, "The Keystone of Textile Safety," NSC *Proceedings* 15 (1926): 926.

17. The cost of calender rolls is noted in E. E. Jones, "Closeups on Paper Mill Guarding," NSC *Proceedings* 14 (1925): 716-23. The square sheer example is from W. S. Gundeck, "Safeguarding Machinery at Its Source," NSC *Proceedings* 23 (1934): 174-76.

18. United Shoe is discussed in John Calder, "Safety Provisions in the Textile Industry," NSC *Proceedings* 4 (1915): 355-68, and J. W. Lake, "Why the Lack of Accidents in the Boot and Shoe Industry?" NSC *Proceedings* 22 (1933): 305-6. On Fairbanks-Morse, see McKee, "Accident Prevention in Foundry."

19. Laundry machinery from E. G. Trimble, "Accident Prevention in the Laundry Industry," NSC *Proceedings* 1 (1912): 261-65. The head splitter and its diffusion are from A. E. Holstedt, "New Safety Kinks in the Meat Packing Industry," NSC *Proceedings* 24 (1935): 274-76. Blaming the manufacturer is from William Newell, "What Could Manufacturers of Woodworking Machines Do to Make Their Machines More Safe?" NSC *Proceedings* 6 (1917): 1131-33. Owen, "Standard Guards"; H. L. Robinson [Crompton and Knowles], "Remarks," NSC *Proceedings* 10 (1921): 824; David Beyer, "Fundamentals of Safeguarding," NSC *Proceedings* 9 (1920): 81-84. For a discussion of the interaction between producers and users in spreading machine tool innovations, see Nathan Rosenberg, "Technological Change in the Machine Tool Industry, 1860-1919," *Journal of Economic History* 23 (Dec. 1963): 414-43.

20. G. William Ellis, "Educating the Workers in Industrial Safety," *Industrial Management* 63 (Aug. 1922): 105-8, claimed that guarding encouraged workers to take chances. M. S. Humphreys, "Eliminating the Screw Conveyor Accident," NSC *Proceedings* 18 (1929): 481-91. The Burroughs example is from "Workmen's Cooperation." Robert Young, "Principles of Safeguarding," *SE* 32 (Sept. 1916): 164-66.

21. Frederick Ritzmann, "Remarks," NSC *Proceedings* 14 (1925): 248-49. See also "Safety Education in Industry," ILO *Industrial Safety Survey* 1 (Mar.-Apr. 1925): 1-14 and (May-June 1925): 29-42; and Frederick Ritzmann, "The International Labor Organization and the Prevention of Accidents," ILO *Industrial Safety Survey* 10 (July-Aug. 1934): 93-100.

22. For Illinois Steel rules, see Robert Young, "Remarks," NSC *Proceedings* 2 (1913): 158-59. See also J. R. Davis, "How Are We Able to Operate with So Few Lost Time Accidents?" NSC *Proceedings* 14 (1925): 936-39, and Harry Schreiber, "Essentials for Safety in a Woodworking Plant," NSC *Proceedings* 9 (1920): 1327-31.

23. Davis, "How Are We Able"; "Round Table Sessions," NSC *Proceedings* 2 (1913):

158-63; W. F. McClellan, "Value of Foreman's Instructions to New Employees," NSC *Proceedings* 9 (1920): 741-44.

24. On safety shoes, see "A. A. Williams, Shoe Inventor, Dies," *NSN* 74 (Aug. 1956): 92, and "Good Customers for the Shoe Business," *NSN* 66 (Oct. 1952): 122-23. Henry Guilbert, "Why a Mandatory Rule for Wearing Goggles?" *American Machinist* 73 (Aug. 1930): 279-80, claimed that he handed out safety glasses at U.S. Steel in 1907. For more on safety glasses, see W. H. Cameron, "Accidents to the Eye and How to Prevent Them," NSC *Proceedings* 1 (1912): 298-300, and "Safety Equipment," *NSN* 87 (May 1963): 48-49. On hard hats, see "Head Protection in the Twentieth Century," *NSN* 75 (May 1957): 24-25, and "How the Hard Hat Evolved," *NSN* 87 (May 1963): 66-68.

25. The experience of Lukens is from Russell Scheid, "Safety Shoes Come Back," *SE* 74 (Oct. 1937): 14-16. Improvements in goggles and shoes are noted in G. E. Sanford, "How We Get Employees to Wear Goggles," and J. B. Gibson, "How We Get Our Employees to Wear Safety Shoes," NSC *Proceedings* 19 (1930): 51-53 and 60-62. See also Raymond Stefan, "The Goggle Problem in a Paper Mill," NSC *Proceedings* 11 (1922): 626-29. The survey is in E. G. Tangerman, "Bill Smith Whistles While He Works," *American Machinist* 82 (Oct. 19, 1938): 931-33.

26. On GE, see "What Price Eye Injuries," *SE* 68 (Nov. 1934): 185-86. Buick is from Forrest Boswell, "Supervision and Its Relation to Accident Prevention," NSC *Proceedings* 11 (1922): 174-78. Pullman is from Guilbert, "Why a Mandatory Rule?" and Pullman Company, *Employee Accident Record, 1927-1941* (Chicago, n.d.). The NSC survey is reported in "Industry Saves Eyes," *NSN* 21 (Apr. 1930): 12-14, 80. The prevalence of occupationally induced blindness is from Louis Resnick, *Eye Hazards in Industry* (New York: Columbia Univ. Press, 1941), table 6.

27. Peter O'Shea, "Additional Safeguards Required for Women Employees," *Industrial Management* 57 (Apr. 1919): 301-2. See also Tracy Cupp, "The Physical Condition of Workshops Where Women Are Employed," NSC *Proceedings* 7 (1918): 434-38, and Schwartz, "Work Accidents among Women." Armour's ban on jewelry is noted in C. F. Scheer, "Packed with Safety," *NSN* 37 (June 1938): 10-12, 74-75. For "Sweet-Orr Womanalls," see *American Industries* 19 (Dec. 1918): 4. The style show is noted in Alice Jonsberg, "Women Invade Men's Industrial Meetings," *NSN* 20 (Oct. 1929): 89-90.

28. Zeke's fate is recounted by Fred Colvin, *60 Years with Men and Machines* (New York: McGraw-Hill, 1947), 29-30.

29. On women's protective equipment, see Fred Colvin, "Women in the Machine Shops," *American Machinist* 47 (Sept. 20, 1917): 507-12, and "Round Table Discussions," NSC *Proceedings* 2 (1913): 181-82 (in which GE's problems are recounted). Bancroft's difficulties are reported in John Rennie to John Bird, May 18, 1917, box 103, BP. See also B. C. Christy, "Shoes," NSC *Proceedings* 7 (1918): 751-56. On women's safety shoes, see "Good Customers for the Shoe Business" and the advertisement by Lehigh Safety Shoe Co. in *NSN* 45 (Apr. 1942): 7. Ruth Stone, "How Safety Looks to the Worker," NSC *Proceedings* 17 (1928): 152, claims that caps had become unnecessary in some mills. Women's hard hats are from "New Safety Equipment for Industry," *NSN* 47 (May 1943): 107. The Saf-T-Bra is from "Safety Museum Exhibits a Century of Protective Devices," *NSN* (Mar. 1980): 122-23. For continuing problems with women's safety clothing, see Charlotte Punski, "Do Blue Collars Protect Working Women?" *NSN* 128 (Oct. 1983): 34-38.

30. C. L. York, "Remarks," NSC *Proceedings* 2 (1913): 182. The woman butcher is described in Holstedt, "New Safety Kinks in the Meat Packing Industry."

31. L. F. Knickerbocker, "Safety from the Superintendent's Viewpoint," NSC *Proceedings* 11 (1922): 646-49, describes the problems at Kimberly-Clark. William Sellers

is from "Prevention of Accidents in the Foundry," *Iron Age* 92 (Oct. 9, 1913): 772–74. The ninety-nine-cuts rule is from A. E. Sinclair, "Our Outstanding Contributory Causes for Safe Plant Operation," NSC *Proceedings* 24 (1935): 271–72. Charles Hook is quoted from his "Industrial Safety—Its Relation to the Business of Today," NSC *Proceedings* 26 (1938): 18–22. Worker resistance to the new guards and work practices is also noted in Frank Small, "Machine Operations, Employment, and Supervision," Ohio Safety Congress *Proceedings*, 1936, 38–41; Val Klammer, "The Machinist and the Guard," *American Machinist* 53 (Aug. 19, 1920): 348; and J. M. McCann, "Personal Protective Equipment in Meat Packing Plants," NSC *Proceedings* 26 (1937): 372–73, who claimed that "we had considerable difficulty in converting one of our old time butchers to our safety program."

32. F. E. Morris, "How to Organize for Safety," NSC *Proceedings* 7 (1918): 84–95; R. T. Solensten, "The Bulletin Board—An Indispensable Safety Advertiser," NSC *Proceedings* 12 (1923): 134–40; "Safety Education in Industry," ILO *Industrial Safety Survey* 2 (May–June 1925): 37–38.

33. The use of glass eyes is from W. R. Rasmussen, "Methods of Promoting Safety Education in a Plant," NSC *Proceedings* 8 (1919): 293–95.

34. The banquet is described in "Round Table Sessions," NSC *Proceedings* 2 (1913): 163–64, 175–76. G. A. Orth, "Getting the Colored Employee Interested," NSC *Proceedings* 15 (1926): 1005–6.

35. C. L. Harrison, "Are Sawmill Industries Keeping Pace with Accident Prevention Progress?" and F. E. Morris, "How to Organize for Safety," NSC *Proceedings* 7 (1918): 84–95 and 604–5.

36. On Murray, see "This New Plant Reversed Its Safety Program," *NSN* 22 (Oct. 1930): 65–67, 134. See also R. F. Caldwell, "They're Eager to Help," *NSN* 37 (May 1938): 19–20, 53.

37. Safety Section to P. S. DuPont and others, July 30, 1920, box 70, accession 1662, DP; "Report of Safety Committee," May 18, 1926, box 103, BP; Edna Coyle, "Different Ways of Getting There—A Study of Eight Representative Publications," NSC *Proceedings* 11 (1922): 720–29; Marathon Paper Company *Safety Bulletin* 1–6 (1914–19); Milwaukee Western Fuel Company *Transfer* 4 (June 20, 1914). For the *Atlantic Seal*, see Carl B. Coxe, "Putting Safety across with a Punch—Selling Safety to the Folks at Home by Means of the Plant Paper," NSC *Proceedings* 14 (1925): 836–40.

38. Robert Young, "Remarks," NSC *Proceedings* 2 (1913): 154–71. On DuPont, see Harold Miner and George Miller, "Millions of Man-hours Made Safe," *NSN* 24 (Oct. 1931): 57–60; Harold Miner, "How Can We Correct Accident Causes?" NSC *Proceedings* 24 (1935): 203–8; and Harold Miner, "Attacking Personal Injury," *SE* 77 (May 1939): 15–16, 18.

39. Paper industry safety contests are reviewed in W. J. Peacock, "Report of the Chairman [of the Pulp and Paper Section]," NSC *Proceedings* 17 (1928): 343–50. The Portland Cement Association contests were regularly reported in its *Accident Bulletin*.

40. "Report of Safety Committee," Mar. 14, 1924, box 103, BP. F. H. Rader, "Remarks," NSC *Proceedings* 15 (1926): 484–85, described the effects of a bonus. That men often kept the money is noted by F. W. Johnson, "Remarks," NSC *Proceedings* 13 (1924): 687–89. The trophy is described in J. R. Curtis, "Analysis of Accidents in the Cement Industry," NSC *Proceedings* 26 (1937): 250–52.

41. "Report of Safety Committee," Mar. 14, 1924, box 103, BP. For a clear statement that the difficulties of supervision and discipline made contests and bonuses especially attractive to street railways, see Robert Clair, "Discipline, Cash Bonuses, or Instruction," *NSN* 22 (July 1930): 17–18, 90. The surveys of bonus programs are contained in "Report of Committee on Award Systems," NSC *Proceedings* 13 (1924): 380–85; G. T.

Hellmuth, "What Are the Results of the Bonus and Award System?" NSC *Proceedings* 14 (1925): 376–89; and G. T. Hellmuth, "Bonus System—Its Value in Claims Work," American Electric Railway Claims Association *Proceedings*, 1926, 37–45, which also reports on effectiveness. Other examples of effectiveness are in A. L. Hodges, "Accident Prevention Bonus—A Means to an End," *Electric Railway Journal* 69 (Jan. 29, 1927): 215–16. Philip Stremmel, "Should Prizes Be Given for Safety Work?" NSC *Proceedings* 9 (1920): 741–44, thought they cheapened safety. Morris's remarks are in "How to Organize for Safety," 84–95.

42. G. L. Avery, "Avery Company's Plan under the Illinois Workmen's Compensation and Employers' Liability Act," NSC *Proceedings* 1 (1912): 265–76.

43. Colvin, *60 Years*, 24–26; "Safety Bulletin 393," box 113, series 2, pt. 3, DP.

44. F. E. Morris, "Safe Practices in Sheet Mills," NSC *Proceedings* 6 (1917): 1199–1206. The comments of DuPont's physician are reported in "Safety Bulletin," July 17, 1925, box 71, accession 1662, DP. "Thin and wiry types" is from W. F. McAnally, "The Advisability of a Physical Examination of All Applicants for Employment," *Industrial Management* 67 (May 1924): 308–9.

45. Mary Baker, "The Employment Secretary," NSC *Proceedings* 9 (1920): 993–98. National Cash Register is from F. G. Barr, "Physical Examinations and the Placement of Workers," NSC *Proceedings* 23 (1934): 73–75. National Industrial Conference Board, *Medical Supervision and Service in Industry* (New York, 1931), table 3.

46. The reorganization at DuPont is noted in Resnick, "Saving Men and Money." Its importance is stressed by Willis Harrington, "Talk," May 2, 1933, box 15, Harrington Papers, HML. For Inland, see Fred Geyer, "Safety in Blast Furnace Maintenance," NSC *Proceedings* 27 (1938): 481–48. The experience of electric companies is from K. R. MacKinnon, "Report of Accident Prevention Committee," National Electric Light Association, *Proceedings of the Fiftieth Convention*, 1927, 507–8.

47. "High councils" is from C. S. Cing, "The Place and Qualifications of the Safety Engineer," *SE* 70 (July 1935): 18. "No need" is from "The Needs of the Safety Engineer," *SE* 64 (Oct. 1932): 165–66. David Beyer, "Day of the Safety Engineer," *SE* 42 (Nov. 1921): 227.

48. Robert Young, "Accident Prevention in Steel Plants"; Arthur Young, "Remarks," NSC *Proceedings* 2 (1913): 171; Milwaukee Western Fuel Company *Safety Bulletin* 1 (Mar. 20, 1914) and 4 (June 20, 1914).

49. The equations are:

$$\ln(\text{Freq}) = -0.156(\text{Bonus}) - 0.100(\text{Trend}) - 0.109(\text{Bonus} * \text{Trend})$$
$$(0.43) \qquad (1.23) \qquad (1.18)$$
$$R^2 = 0.14; \text{D.W.} = 2.01; N = 60$$

$$\ln(\text{Sev}) = -0.828(\text{Bonus}) - 0.008(\text{Trend}) + 0.076(\text{Bonus} * \text{Trend})$$
$$(1.11) \qquad (0.11) \qquad (0.44)$$
$$R^2 = 0.24; \text{D.W.} = 1.80; N = 60$$

Data are from Lucian Chaney, "The Foremen's Bonus," *MLR* 9 (Sept. 1919): 272–81. Figures in parentheses are *t*-ratios. Both equations also contain departmental dummies and were estimated using a Cochran-Orcutt correction.

50. Thomas H. McKenney, "Remarks," NSC *Proceedings* 6 (1917): 127–35; the quotation is from 128. For Consolidated Water Power and Paper, see Frank Drumb, "Safety in the Woodroom," NSC *Proceedings* 11 (1922):631. Youngstown Sheet and Tube, "Boost for Safety: Rules and Regulations for the Government of Employees," 2d ed., Jan. 1, 1912 (U.S. Interior Department library). That promotions depended on safety is from McKenney, "Remarks."

51. C. W. Price, "How to Organize for Safety," NSC *Proceedings* 6 (1917): 92-98; Fred Johnson, "Safe Practices in Rolling Mills," NSC *Proceedings* 10 (1921): 386-93. The Kimberly-Clark vice president is from J. T. Doerfler, "Remarks," NSC *Proceedings* 13 (1924): 685-86.

52. Louis DeBlois, "Supervision as a Factor in Accident Prevention," NSC *Proceedings* 8 (1919): 132-36; Arthur Young, "Remarks," NSC *Proceedings* 8 (1919): 138; Arthur Young, "Safety at the Quarter Century Mark," *NSN* 28 (July 1933): 19-20, 50-51. DeBlois later elaborated on these ideas in his *Industrial Safety Organization for Executive and Engineer* (New York: McGraw-Hill, 1926). For modern thinking on the role of management, see Thomas Planek and Kevin Fearn, "Reevaluating Occupational Safety Priorities, 1967-1992," *Professional Safety* 38 (Oct. 1993): 16-21.

53. "Plenty of [which] are serious" is from William Hudson to H. F. Brown, May 31, 1911, box 1002, series 2, pt. 2, DP. Activities of the safety committees are reviewed in "Annual Report," Feb. 20, 1914, box 1002, series 2, pt. 2, DP. The early organization of DuPont safety work is discussed in "Savings Due to Safety Work in the Dupont Company," n.d. (about 1922), box 70, accession 1662, DP. The study of U.S. Steel's procedures is in H. M. Barksdale to T. C. DuPont, Nov. 29, 1913, box 1002, series 2, pt. 2, DP. Membership of the safety commissions is revealed by "Black Powder Safety Commission Recommendations," box 93, series 2, pt. 2, DP. DeBlois's request is in Louis DeBlois to Irénée DuPont, Oct. 8, 1913; the response is in DuPont to DeBlois, Oct. 13, 1913; DeBlois's cave-in is in DeBlois to DuPont, Oct. 14, 1913; DuPont finally gave in and agreed to join—see DuPont to DeBlois, Dec. 6, 1913; all in box 1002, series 2, pt. 2, DP. On the DuPont management generally, see Alfred Chandler, *Strategy and Structure* (New York: Doubleday, 1962). Donald Stabile, "The DuPont Experiments in Scientific Management: Efficiency and Safety, 1911-1919," *Business History Review* 61 (Aug. 1987): 365-86, argues that the company ultimately rejected Taylorism because of the potential conflict with safety.

54. The vice president referred to is W. F. Harrington, "Talk," May 2, 1933, box 13, Harrington Papers, HML.

55. The decision to join the Delaware Safety Council can be followed in Louis DeBlois to Irénée DuPont, Aug. 4, 1921; DuPont to W. C. Spruace, Aug. 17, 1921; Spruace to DuPont, Aug. 17, 1921; and DuPont to DeBlois, Aug. 18, 1921; all in box 70, accession 1662, DP. Concern with the engineering department is indicated in DuPont to DeBlois, Aug. 14, 1925, box 71, accession 1662, DP. DeBlois to DuPont, Dec. 31, 1923, encloses a "Study of Savings by Accident Prevention Work . . . for which you asked." The 60 percent return is mentioned in "Safety Bulletin 395," Apr. 13, 1926, series 2, pt. 3, DP.

56. Higher rates in the acquisitions are shown in F. L. Evans to W. F. Harrington, "Frequency and Severity Rates—Special Conference Group," Oct. 14, 1932, box 12, Harrington Papers, HML. "The next year" is from S. E. Whiting, "Remarks," NSC *Proceedings* 20 (1931): 804.

57. "Every precaution" is from Irénée DuPont to Louis DeBlois, July 20, 1925, accession 1662, box 71, DP. In fact, DuPont may not always have taken "every precaution." For a critique of the company's response to evidence of the carcinogenicity of products used in its dye manufacture, see David Michaels, "Waiting for the Body Count: Corporate Decision Making and Bladder Cancer in the U.S. Dye Industry," *Medical Anthropology Quarterly*, n.s., 2 (Sept. 1988): 215-32.

58. "Practically all accidents" is in Irénée DuPont to Louis DeBlois, Oct. 28, 1923, box 70, accession 1662, DP. "We will never be satisfied" is from Harrington, "Talk." Lammot DuPont to All General Managers and Presidents, "Accidents are Increasing," Aug. 4, 1933, box 72, accession 1662, DP.

59. Louis DeBlois to Irénée DuPont, Jan. 31, 1924, box 71, accession 1662, DP. In his 1926 text *Industrial Safety Organization*, 100, DeBlois also emphasized that the safety engineer "should be paid on an equal footing with production and service executives with whom he must cooperate."

60. Leonard Hatch, "What the Accident Record Shows," and Ethelbert Stewart, "Are Accidents Increasing?" *American Labor Legislation Review* 16 (June 1926): 167–77 and 161–66; W. G. Voogt and A. H. Mowbray, "Industrial Accident Rates in the Business Cycle," and Leslie Hall, "On the Tendency of Labor Saving to Increase Compensation Costs," CAS *Proceedings* 12 (Nov. 1925): 10–26 and 62–73; "Are Industrial Fatalities Increasing?" *SE* 51 (Mar. 1926): 168. Louis DeBlois thought that injury rates were falling but that the result was obscured by better reporting; see his "Has the Industrial Accident Rate Declined?" CAS *Proceedings* 14 (Nov. 1927): 84–96. Verne Burnett, "Rise and Decline of the Safety Crusade," *Industrial Management* 63 (May 1922): 302–3, 312, claims that the post–World War I depression led to the cessation of much safety work.

61. F. P. Sinn of New Jersey Zinc, "Remarks," NSC *Proceedings* 5 (1916): 107–9, asserted that better safety would reduce labor turnover. The nut in the gears is from G. A. Kuechenmeuster, "Smashing Traditions in the Safety Program," NSC *Proceedings* 19 (1930): 44–51. Charles Hook, "Remarks," NSC *Proceedings* 7 (1918): 113–14. See also W. B. Hall, "The Conservation of the Human Element," *SE* 46 (Dec. 1923): 301, and "The True Cost of Accidents," Portland Cement Association *Accident Prevention Bulletin* 4 (Nov. 1918): 3–5.

62. L. A. Alford, "Real Safety Movement to Come," *Management and Administration* 10 (Aug. 1925): 61–62. Louis DeBlois promptly sent a copy to Irénée DuPont informing him that the article "expresses the modern trend of opinion in safety work"; DeBlois to DuPont, Sept. 2, 1925, box 71, accession 1662, DP. The wire stop is from Stephen Tenner, "Safety as an Indispensable Part of an Efficient Manufacturing Organization," NSC *Proceedings* 4 (1915): 106–12. The crane bucket is from F. F. Marquand, "Safe Practices in Byproduct Coke Plants," NSC *Proceedings* 10 (1921): 378. The roundheaded planer is from P. G. Farrow, "Evolution of Safety in Woodworking Machinery," NSC *Proceedings* 14 (1925): 1116–19. For other examples, see Charles Hook, "The Dollar Side of Safety," NSC *Proceedings* 11 (1922): 157–60 (who claims that Armco redesigned the mud gun for plugging tap holes in blast furnaces, thereby improving both its safety and its efficiency), and John Oartel, "Safety and Production from a Practical Viewpoint," NSC *Proceedings* 10 (1921): 58–60.

63. Saw guards are from G. E. Sanford, "How Can Woodworking Guards Be Kept in Place?" NSC *Proceedings* 10 (1921): 879–81. In the same volume G. R. Keene, "The Mechanical Side of Accident Prevention in the Packing Industry," 503, describes a cutter guard that raised productivity in meat packing. August Kaems reported his findings in "Die Construction—The Real Safety of Punch Press Work," NSC *Proceedings* 8 (1919): 316–27. That he paid his own way is claimed in August Kaems, "Why a Power Press Section?" NSC *Proceedings* 15 (1926): 422–24. In the same volume David Beyer, "Building Safety into Power Press Tools," 424, notes Kaems's impact on the Liberty engineer. The reprint is August Kaems, "Increasing Productivity by Safeguarding Powerpress Operation," *American Machinist* 53 (Aug. 26, 1920): 398–99.

64. Walter Greenwood, "Accident Prevention," Association of Iron and Steel Electrical Engineers *Proceedings* 19 (1925): 46–49.

65. American Engineering Council, *Safety and Production* (New York: Harper Brothers, 1928); the quotations revealing the purpose of the study are from 7 and 13; the "finding" of a moral responsibility is on 35. The review, which was more critical than most, was by Frederick Ritzmann, "The Relationship between Accident Pre-

vention and Productive Capacity in Industrial Undertakings," ILO *Industrial Safety Survey* 4 (Nov.-Dec. 1928): 151-60.

66. Biographical information on Heinrich is from David Gibson, "Herbert Heinrich," *Professional Safety* 25 (Apr. 1980): 20-24, who lists Heinrich's birth date as 1881; other sources put it in 1886. H. W. Heinrich, "The Incidental Costs of Accidents, *Travelers Standard* 14 (Dec. 1926): 244-57. The article was reprinted nine times in 1927 and 1928 in sources listed in Public Affairs Information Service. Associated General Contractors of America, *Manual of Accident Prevention* (1928), claimed that the hidden costs were even higher. As a measure of the returns to safety work, Heinrich's accounting is flawed. It includes overhead and is thus an average, not a marginal concept, and it double-counts lost wages and lost output.

67. See Herbert Heinrich, "The Origin of Accidents," *NSN* 18 (July 1928): 9-12, and "The Foundation of a Major Injury," *NSN* 19 (Jan. 1929): 9-12. Heinrich's importance in the development of a new cause code is briefly noted in Max Kossoris, "Statistics of Industrial Accidents in the United States," ILO *Industrial Safety Survey* 14 (Nov.-Dec. 1938): 165-75. See also Max Kossoris, "Accident Statistics and the World of Tomorrow," and R. L. Forney, "Industry's Experience with Accident Cause Codes," NSC *Proceedings* 28 (1939): 83-88 and 78-82.

68. That Heinrich's text was still the standard as late as 1980 is claimed by Gibson, "Herbert W. Heinrich." His 88:10:2 division was still being debated in 1978; see J. W. Jeffries, "Unsafe Acts vs. Unsafe Conditions," *Professional Safety* 23 (Mar. 1978): 47-48. For examples of fault-tree analysis, see David Brown, "Cost-Benefit of Safety Investments Using Fault Tree Analysis," *Journal of Safety Research* 5 (June 1973): 73-82, and V. E. Denny et al., "Risk Assessment Methodologies: An Application to Underground Mine Systems," *Journal of Safety Research* 10 (Spring 1978): 24-34.

69. The Massachusetts data are cited in Cincinnati Chamber of Commerce, *Study of Workmen's Compensation Laws and Service: Monopoly or Competition* (Cincinnati, 1923), 462. The Illinois survey is in Kossoris, "How Effective Are Safety Organizations?"

70. Ethelbert Stewart, "The Newer Industrial Accident Prevention and Workmen's Compensation Problem," New York State Department of Labor Industrial Safety Congress *Proceedings* 11 (1927): 23-28. Firm size data are from "Industrial Accidents and Hygiene," *MLR* 23 (Nov. 1926): 50-51. The council's survey is in G. G. Grieve, "Small Plants Need Safety," *NSN* 23 (Jan. 1931): 21-22. See also S. W. Homan, "What Size of Plant Is the Most Hazardous?" *Pennsylvania Labor and Industry* 17 (July 1930): 4-7. These and similar studies are flawed because they fail to control for industry; yet even with such controls, small plants had relatively high injury rates. For some modern findings, see "Workers at Risk: Chance of Getting Hurt Is Generally Far Higher at Smaller Companies," *Wall Street Journal*, Feb. 3, 1994, 1.

71. U.S. Department of Commerce, *Biennial Census of Manufactures, 1927* (Washington, D.C., 1929); Stewart, "The Newer Industrial Accident Prevention and Workmen's Compensation Problem."

72. Perceptive analyses of safety problems in small plants are James Hamilton, "The Need for Safety in the Small Plant," NSC *Proceedings* 15 (1926): 74-79; Louis DeBlois, "The Small Plant—Our Unsolved Problem," *NSN* 18 (July 1928): 13-14; and Harry Immel, "Small Plant Safety Committee Problems as Applied to Woodworking Shops," NSC *Proceedings* 19 (1930): 776-80. See also Joseph Faust, "Carrying the Safety Message to the 92 Percent," NSC *Proceedings* 28 (1939): 87-90. Difficulties in safeguarding general-purpose machines are noted in C. B. Auel, "Circular Saws and Shapers," NSC *Proceedings* 12 (1923): 1126-27. Economies of scale in guard production are noted in Harry Guilbert, "Construction of and Cost of Making Safeguards in Shops," NSC *Proceedings* 4 (1915): 598-602.

73. Louis DeBlois to G. d'A. Belin, Aug. 26, 1925, box 113, series 2, pt. 3, DP.

74. DeBlois, "Small Plant," and Louis DeBlois, "What about Your Accident Rate?" *NSN* 15 (Mar. 1927): 21–23, discuss the misperception of risk that is likely in small plants.

75. The textile survey is reported in R. C. Stratton, "Safety Organization Work in the Textile Industry," NSC *Proceedings* 14 (1925): 1083–87. G. W. Cook, "Organized Accident Prevention in Cotton Mills," NSC *Proceedings* 15 (1926): 938–42.

76. G. M. Gadsby, "By-products of Accident Prevention," *NSN* 16 (Dec. 1927): 30–31. Colax is from James W. Burnison, "Industry Is More Humane Now and More Efficient," *NSN* 32 (Dec. 1935): 12–14, 48. W. V. DeCamp, "Management's Responsibility Is Clearcut," *NSN* 22 (Nov. 1930): 34–36.

77. The NSC budget is reported by Joseph Banash, "Presidential Address," NSC *Proceedings* 22 (1933): 11–15. California and Hawaiian Sugar is from William Swain, "Depression Dividends," *NSN* 30 (Dec. 1934): 9–10. The encouraging article is R. P. Priest, "Our Safety Department Earns a Profit," *NSN* 26 (Oct. 1932): 26–28, 74–75. The BLS claim is in "Industrial Accidents," *MLR* 37 (Dec. 1933): 1888–94. J. D. Williams, "Why Minnesota Changed from an Elective to a Compulsory Compensation Act," IAIABC *Proceedings* 25, in Division of Labor Standards *Bulletin* 24 (1938): 152–55. Massachusetts dropouts are noted in Samuel Horovitz and Josephine Klein, "The Constitutionality of Workmen's Compensation Acts," IAIABC *Proceedings* 24, in Division of Labor Standards *Bulletin* 24 (1938): 155–81. On Colorado and Pennsylvania, see Arthur Reede, *Adequacy of Workmen's Compensation* (Cambridge: Harvard Univ. Press, 1947), 23.

78. Carmen Fish, "The Biggest Industrial Safety Job Ever Attempted," *NSN* 29 (Feb. 1934): 19–20; Sidney Williams, "Four Million Green Men," NSC *Proceedings* 23 (1934): 76–78; Arthur C. Carruthers, "Putting Four Million Men to Work Safely under C.W.A.," *SE* 67 (Feb. 1934): 43–46.

79. Cyril Ainsworth, "New A.S.A. Standards Required in PWA Contracts," *SE* 67 (Mar. 1934): 100; Cyril Ainsworth, "ASA Safety Codes Play Important Role in NRA," *SE* 67 (May 1934): 197–98; "Safety Is Stressed on WPA Projects," *NSN* 32 (Oct. 1935): 82–83; "Uncle Sam Sees to Workers' Safety," *SE* 72 (Oct. 1936): 141–42; W. O. Wheary, "Safety Serves on Public Works," *NSN* 35 (Jan. 1937): 49–50, 80.

80. The injury frequencies are from Wheary, "Safety Serves."

81. DeBlois, *Industrial Safety Organization*, 44, 103; DeBlois, "The Organization of Safety Services in Industrial Undertakings in the U.S.A.," ILO *Industrial Safety Survey* 14 (Sept.–Oct. 1938): 133–42. Ford's safety regulations are related in Hartley W. Barclay, *Ford Production Methods* (New York: Harper Brothers, 1936), 44–54. "Control of environment" is from J. C. Stennett, "The Double 'C' of Industrial Safety," *NSN* 40 (Dec. 1939): 24–25, 75–78. For a discussion of systematic management, see Sanford Jacoby, *Employing Bureaucracy* (New York: Columbia Univ. Press, 1985), and his "The Development of Internal Labor Markets in American Manufacturing Firms," in *Internal Labor Markets*, ed. Paul Osterman (Cambridge: MIT Press, 1984), 23–70.

82. Robert Shaw, "Is Your Plant a Safe Place to Work?" NSC *Proceedings* 25 (1935): 201–4. The editorial is "Are We Forgetting Fundamentals?" *NSN* 28 (Aug. 1933): 7.

83. The twenty-two forms are in Youngstown Sheet and Tube, "Boost for Safety." Youngstown's later procedures are described by Herman Spoerer, "How Accidents Are Investigated in Our Company," NSC *Proceedings* 37 (1938): 116–20. For procedures at GE and Western Electric, see the articles with the same title by M. A. Gimbel and A. G. Bungenstock in the same volume, 120–21 and 122–24. Armco is from C. H. Murray, "The Training of Employees to Work Safely," Ohio Safety Congress *Proceed-*

ings 4 (1931): 349–53. On U.S. Leather, see Glenn Bonser, "Investigate It!" *NSN* 36 (July 1937): 23–24, 66.

84. Van Hunter, "Developing Safe Workers in Metal Working Industries through the Regular Supervisory Force," NSC *Proceedings* 26 (1937): 232–34. The textile company is from Sydney Ingham, "Plant Hazards Taken Apart," *NSN* 23 (Jan. 1931): 34–36. J. F. Kolb [National Metal Trades Association], "What Makes a Safety Program Effective?" NSC *Proceedings* 25 (1936): 198–200; McClellan, "Value of Foreman's Instructions to New Employees"; R. R. Howard, "Training—Not Band-Playing—Makes Safe Plants," *Factory and Industrial Management* 82 (July 1931): 349.

85. C. H. Murray, "Employee Training: The Most Scientific Kind of Safety Work," *NSN* 33 (Apr. 1936): 10–11, 50–53; W. Dean Keefer, "The Foremen as Teachers," *NSN* 29 (Feb. 1934): 9. "Hard boiled foreman" is from George Hodge, "Accident Prevention Is an Essential Part of Good Management," *Manufacturers News* 35 (Mar. 1929): 25–26, 52.

86. Boyd Fisher, *The Mental Causes of Accidents* (Boston: Houghton Mifflin, 1922). The British literature from this period is considerable; for summaries, see Eric Farmer, *The Causes of Accidents* (London: Sir Isaac Pitman, 1932), and H. M. Vernon, *Accidents and Their Prevention* (New York: Macmillan, 1936). W. V. Bingham of the Personnel Research Foundation, who studied accident-prone workers on the Boston El, described his own and the British findings in "Safety and the Individual: Results of a Psychological Approach to the Accident Problem," NSC *Proceedings* 18 (1929): 89–93. See also A. E. Sinclair, a safety director at a packing house, who notes the accident-prone literature in "Our Accident Record—What and How?" NSC *Proceedings* 25 (1936): 288–90. A more modern review of the literature on accident-proneness that includes some of the important early work is William Haddon and others, *Accident Research* (New York: Harper and Row, 1964).

87. Training and job design are stressed in W. Graham Cole, "The Accident Prone Employee," *NSN* 23 (May 1931): 17–18, 70–71. Miner's remarks are in "Attacking Personal Injury," 15–16. For Bancroft, see "Report of Safety Committee," Sept. 10, 1934, box 103, BP. For GE, see George Sanford, "Study the Accident Repeaters," *NSN* 32 (Jan. 1931): 32, 86–87. Carl Auel, "What Do We Mean by Accident Prone?" *NSN* 26 (Sept. 1932): 19–20, 83. For companies that did use the accident-prone literature, see Cleveland Railway, *The Accident Prone Employee* (New York, 1929), and Boston Elevated Railway, *Safety on the El* (Boston, 1929).

88. For the paper industry, see Allan Hyer, "Safety on the Paper Machine," NSC *Proceedings* 20 (1931): 238–46. On the guillotine, see Holstedt, "New Safety Kinks." Betty Piontkowsky's remarks and the unguarded crane are from Ann Banks, ed., *First Person America* (New York: Norton, 1991). Textile print machines are from [?] Stowell, "Remarks," NSC *Proceedings* 10 (1921): 824. F. A. Wiley, "Safety Organization—General Safety Rules," American Iron and Steel Electrical Engineers *Proceedings* 16 (1922): 682–90.

89. Robert Young, "Accident Prevention in Steel Plants," claimed that safety was being designed into new construction at U.S. Steel in 1913. DuPont is discussed in Louis DeBlois, "Annual Report of Safety Commissions" to H. G. Haskell and others, Feb. 20, 1914, box 1002, series 2, pt. 2, DP, and in Resnick, "Saving Men and Money." The automobile plant is from Burnett, "Rise and Decline of the Safety Crusade." For Anheuser Busch, see George Eads, "The Safety Story of Bevo and Budweiser," *NSN* 6 (Aug. 1922): 9–11. For Lever Brothers, see Carmen Fish, "A Soap Plant Sets an Example in Cleanliness," *NSN* 32 (1935): 14–16. The Jones and Laughlin mill is described in "Safety Started with the Blueprints," *NSN* 38 (July 1938): 14–15, 38. Daniel Nelson,

Managers and Workers: Origins of the New Factory System in the United States, 1880–1920 (Madison: Univ. of Wisconsin Press, 1975), chap. 2, discusses the impact on safety of evolving factory design. The following equation supports the claim in the text that larger steel plants had become relatively safe:

$$\ln(\text{Freq}) = -0.229(\ln[\text{Size}])$$
$$(6.56)$$
$$R^2 = 0.25; N = 494$$

It is manhour-weighted using a TSP routine and also contains controls for departments. The figure in parentheses is a t-ratio. Size is measured by employees per plant. The data are for 1929 from NSC, *Industrial Accident Statistics, 1930 Edition* (Chicago, 1930). Although differences in controls and variable definitions imply that the 1910 and 1929 equations are not entirely comparable, the positive relation between size and injury frequency for 1910 holds up even if safety programs are not controlled.

90. On die design, see George Koch, "Safety in Tool Design," NSC *Proceedings* 24 (1935): 382–84; C. E. Ralston, "Purchasing for Safety," *NSN* 37 (Mar. 1935): 9; and George Price, "Purchasing for Safety," *NSN* 40 (Aug. 1939): 12–13, 75.

91. Everett King, "Safety Engineering in the Textile Plant," NSC *Proceedings*, 10 (1921): 819–23; Hyer, "Safety on the Paper Machine." For rubber machinery, see C. W. Drake, "Will It Stop Quickly?" *NSN* 34 (Dec. 1936): 17–19.

92. G. M. Briggs, "Safety's Third Fundamental," *NSN* 26 (Aug. 1932): 25–27, 62; G. M. Briggs, "Building Safety into the Machine," *NSN* 26 (Sept. 1932): 24–27; G. M. Briggs, "Safety Influences in Machine Design," *NSN* 26 (Oct. 1932): 36–38.

93. Briggs, "Safety's Third Fundamental," contains the quotation.

94. See Briggs, "Building Safety into the Machine" and "Safety Influences in Machine Design." Lucian Chaney asserted that electrification reduced steel mill dangers in "Three Periods of Engineering Revision." Elimination of flywheels is noted in David Beyer, "Standards of Safety in Relation to Machinery," *Iron Age* 88 (July 13, 1911): 88–89. Many other safety workers stressed the importance of electric direct drive; see, for example, "Individual Motor Drive of Machines," *Travelers Standard* 1 (Dec. 1912): 41–47, and "Electric Motors for Machine Operation," *Travelers Standard* 12 (Nov. 1924): 223–26. For an overview of electrification that ignores safety, see Warren Devine, "From Shafts to Wires: Historical Perspective on Electrification," *Journal of Economic History* 43 (June 1983): 347–72.

95. R. E. Simpson, "Illumination and One Year's Accidents," *Travelers Standard* 3 (Oct. 1914): 206–15.D. W. Blakeslee, "Illumination in Relation to Safety," *Iron and Steel Engineer* 5 (Jan. 1928): 8–9, stresses the impact of declining costs. The lighting surveys are described in National Electric Light Association, *Proceedings of the Fifty-first Convention*, 1928, 561–81.

96. R. E. Simpson, "The High Cost of Poor Lighting," *Travelers Standard* 8 (Oct. 1920): 205; see also R. E. Simpson, "Accidental Lighting Costs," Illuminating Engineering Society *Transactions* 23 (July 1928): 633–38. Two of the many other articles claiming that better lighting reduced injuries are O. E. Tichnor, "Reducing Accidents through Efficient Industrial Lighting," *SE* 44 (Oct.–Nov. 1922): 175, and W. H. Rademacher, "Improved Lighting as a Factor in Accident Prevention," *SE* 52 (July 1926): 78–82.

97. Louis Resnick, *Eye Hazards in Industry* (New York: McGraw-Hill, 1941), chap. 7. The quotation is from "Safety—And Mechanical Handling," *Factory and Industrial Management* 70 (Aug. 1925): 103–8. David Beyer, "Safety in Materials Handling," ASME *Journal* 47 (Jan. 1925): 475–80, claims that machine loading in cement quarries had a lower severity rate than did hand methods. Nelson Kyser, "The Correction of

Unsafe Practices in Foundries," *Iron and Steel Engineer* 5 (Oct. 1928): 453–55, thought that mechanization had reduced risks to foundrymen. See also "Mechanical Muscles Don't Ache," *NSN* 17 (June 1928): 13–14, and R. F. Thalner, "Hazards of Interdepartmental Trucking," NSC *Proceedings* 19 (1930): 433, both of whom argue that mechanization reduced risks only with proper safeguarding.

98. G. M. Briggs, "How Industry Is Keeping the Oiler out of the Machinery," *NSN* 20 (July 1929): 19–20; W. F. Schaphorst, "Lubricating Modern Machinery," *NSN* 33 (May 1936): 23–24, 53–54, and "Lubricating Modern Machinery," *NSN* 35 (May 1937): 19–20.

99. For brief discussions of the BLS data, see "Industrial Accidents," *MLR* 37 (Dec. 1933): 1388–94, and Max Kossoris, "Industrial Injuries in the United States during 1939," *MLR* 51 (July 1940): 86–108.

100. Separations are from Sanford Jacoby, "Industrial Labor Mobility in Historical Perspective," *Industrial Relations* 22 (Spring 1983): 261–82. The equation is:

$$\ln(F) = -0.075(\text{NSC}) - 0.037(\text{Trend}) + 0.516[\ln(NH)]$$
$$(0.97) \qquad\quad (5.33) \qquad\qquad (4.28)$$
$$+ 0.960[\ln(H)] - 0.007(\text{NSC} * \text{Trend})$$
$$(4.24) \qquad\quad (1.12)$$
$$R^2 = 0.77; \text{D.W.} = 2.17; N = 38$$

Frequency rates per million hours worked (F) are from NSC, *Accident Facts*, and "Handbook of Labor Statistics for 1950," BLS *Bulletin* 1016 (Washington, D.C., 1951); weekly hours (H) and accession rates (NH) are from *Historical Statistics of the United States*, series D-803 and D-1022. Absence of data prevents estimation of equations for fatality and severity rates. NSC is a dummy that is 0 for the BLS injury rates and 1 for the NSC injury rates; NSC * Trend is a dummy that is 0 for the BLS injury rates and 1 * Trend for the NSC injury rates. The equation also contains a constant term and was estimated using a Cochran-Orcutt correction. Figures in parentheses are t-ratios. The impact of reduced hours may be capturing the effect of some other unmeasured variable, since equations for the steel industry (not shown) reveal no effect of declines in hours on either frequency or severity rates. The 50 percent decline is [(exp $-0.037 \times 20) - 1 = -0.50$].

CHAPTER FIVE. COMBATING COLLISIONS AND OTHER HORRORS

Epigraphs: A. H. Rudd, "Automatic Train Control," *Engineers and Engineering* 43 (Jan. 1926): 20–29. The poet is quoted in Walter Greenwood, "Remarks," NSC *Proceedings* 4 (1915): 538–39.

1. ICC, *Twenty-first Annual Report, 1907* (Washington, D.C., 1908), 127.

2. For "Railway Massacres," see *Outlook* 85 (Jan. 12, 1907): 59–60. Such was the public fascination with train disasters that a number of carriers actually staged wrecks. The fashion began in Texas, in 1896, where the Missouri, Kansas, and Texas engineered a head-on collision for the entertainment—the papers reported—of thirty thousand spectators. At the moment of collision both boilers exploded, adding perhaps more realism than many had bargained for, as a number of sightseers were killed or maimed by the blast. See Stewart Holbrook, *The Story of American Railroads* (New York: Crown, 1948), 219–21. F. A. Schmidt, "The Great Locomotive Crash," *National Railway Bulletin* 44 (May 1979): 12–15, describes another staged crash on the Big Four on July 4, 1900, and claims that they were a common form of entertainment.

3. John J. Esch, "Should the Safety of Employees and Travelers on Railroads Be Protected by Legislation?" *North American Review* 179 (Nov. 1904): 671–84; Carl

Vrooman, "Can Americans Afford Safety in Railroad Travel?" *McClure's* 29 (Aug. 1907): 421-27. See also Frank Haigh Dixon, "Railroad Accidents," *Atlantic Monthly* 99 (May 1907): 577-90, and Carroll Doten, "Recent Railway Accidents in the United States," *Quarterly Publications of the American Statistical Association* 9 (Mar. 1905): 155-81.

4. Complaints about the popular press are vented in "Perversion of Truth about Railway Accidents," *RA* 38 (Oct. 14, 1904): 539, and Samuel Dunn, "The Truth about Railway Accidents," *RA* 51 (Dec. 8, 1911): 3-8. An untitled editorial, *EN* 46 (Sept. 26, 1901): 216, calls for an accident investigation. The demand for automatic stops is in "Automatic Stop Adjuncts to the Block Signal System," *EN* 49 (Feb. 19, 1903): 174-75; another call for federal accident investigations is in "More Concerning Government Investigation of Railway Accidents," *EN* 56 (Nov. 22, 1906): 547-48. The call for ICC supervision of safety is in *EN* 62 (Dec. 30, 1909): 951. See also "Automatic Control of Trains," *RR* 46 (Oct. 6, 1906): 776-77; "Automatic Train Stops," *RR* 49 (Oct. 16, 1909): 922-23; and "The Responsibility for Accidents," *RA* 32 (Nov. 8, 1900): 523. The collisions formula is from "The Relations between Traffic and Disaster," *RA* 40 (Dec. 15, 1905): 746-47.

5. The claim that obeying the rules could lead to punishment is in "Safety vs. Delayed Trains," *RA* 41 (Feb. 23, 1906): 275. "Discipline and Signal Systems," *RA* 43 (Jan. 11, 1907): 32-33, claims that automatic signals would reduce "human agency . . . to a minimum" and notes that train control would work "in spite of the engineman." "Preached this doctrine" is from "Prevention of Collisions," *RG* 37 (Dec. 16, 1904): 633. "Bring the laggard" is from "Compulsory Block Signals," *RG* 37 (Dec. 23, 1904): 653.

6. See ICC, *Annual Report*, various years. This ambitious legislative agenda was argued to a wider audience by Edwin Moseley, the commission's longtime spokesman on safety; see his "Railroad Accidents in the United States," *American Monthly Review of Reviews* 30 (Nov. 1904): 592-96.

7. The fireman is quoted in Kansas Bureau of Labor and Industry, *Sixteenth Annual Report for 1900* (Topeka, 1901). I owe the discovery of this to Professor Susan Carter, of the University of California at Riverside. William Z. Ripley, "Railway Wage Schedules and Agreements," in *Report of the Eight Hour Commission* (Washington, D.C., 1918), appendix 6, 288-303, relates the Hours of Service Act to the growth of train weight. John H. White, *American Locomotives* (Baltimore: Johns Hopkins Press, 1968), and Alfred Bruce, *The Steam Locomotive in America* (New York: Norton, 1952), describe the development of locomotive size and performance.

8. Some conductors protested the law; see "Protest against Limiting Hours of Labor," *RA* 42 (Dec. 21, 1906): 788. The position of the railroad press is from an editorial in *RG* 42 (Mar. 8, 1907): 291-92. See also "Hours of Labor in Train Operation," *RA* 41 (Mar. 23, 1906): 398. The quotation by Mudge is from House Committee on Interstate and Foreign Commerce, *Hearings to Limit the Hours of Service of Railroad Employees*, 59th Cong., 2d sess., Jan. 21 and 25, 1907, 37.

9. The testimony by Moseley and Borland is in House Committee on Interstate and Foreign Commerce, *Hearings to Limit the Hours of Service of Railroad Employees* (Washington, D.C., 1906), 30, 35, 72.

10. The survey is in "Effects of the 16 Hour Law on Trainmen," *RG* 44 (May 1, 1908): 609-10.

11. Murphy's role is described "A Great Victory," *Railroad Telegrapher* 24 (Mar. 1907): 337-41. Gray's claims are in House Committee on Interstate and Foreign Commerce, *Hearings to Amend the Act Limiting the Hours of Service of Railway Employees*,

Feb. 5, 1908. See also "The Hours of Service Law and Telegraph Operators," *RA* 45 (Jan. 17, 1908): 69 and (Mar. 6, 1908): 297-98.

12. "Exceedingly large number" is from "New Item," *RG* 44 (Mar. 6, 1908): 324. The signal engineer was James B. Latimer, "The Block Signal Question," *EN* 63 (June 30, 1910): 746. The behavior of the Burlington and the Illinois Central and the lack of experience are noted in U.S. Block Signal and Train Control Board, *Second Annual Report* (Washington, D.C., 1909), 10-17.

13. The carriers' views on full-crew and train-limit legislation are presented in Bureau of Railway Economics, "The Arguments for and against Train Crew Legislation," *Bulletin* 77 (Washington, D.C., 1915), and "Arguments for and against Limitation of Length of Freight Trains," *Bulletin* 92 (Washington, D.C., 1916). The cost of the state laws is from Special Committee on the Relations of Railway Operation to Legislation, "Minimum (Full) Crews," *Bulletin* 61 (Chicago, 1914). See also Charles G. Dow, "Safety and Short Trains," in *The Railway Library and Statistics, 1914*, ed. Slason Thompson (Chicago: Bureau of Railway News and Statistics, 1915), 162-74.

14. The best description of the timetable system is in Robert B. Shaw, *Down Brakes: A History of Railroad Accidents, Safety Precautions, and Operating Practices in the United States of America* (London: P. R. Macmillan, 1961). This history of block signaling is based on Railroad Gazette, *American Practice in Block Signaling* (New York, 1891); Braman B. Adams, *The Block System of Signalling on American Railroads* (New York, 1901); ICC, *Report on Block Signals and Appliances for the Automatic Control of Trains* (Washington, D.C., 1907); Association of American Railroads, *American Railway Signaling Principles and Practices* (New York, 1946); and "A Brief History of Railway Signaling," *Railway Signal Engineer* 26 (May 1933): 118-26. The role of William Robinson is described in ARA Signal Section, *The Invention of the Track Circuit* (New York, 1922).

15. ICC, *Report on Block Signals*, 20, 26.

16. Block Signal and Train Control Board, *First Annual Report* (Washington, D.C., 1909), 7, 10, appendix A, and *Second Annual Report* (Washington, D.C., 1909), 30-31.

17. Block Signal and Train Control Board, *Third Annual Report* (Washington, D.C., 1911); the quotation is from 25-26, and the inspections are described in appendix E. The *Fourth Annual Report* (Washington, D.C., 1912), appendix C, also reports some inspection results described in the text.

18. Block Signal and Train Control Board, *Final Report* (Washington, D.C., 1912), 22, and *Fourth Annual Report*, 14.

19. "By no means insures" is from ICC, *Twenty-sixth Annual Report, 1912* (Washington, D.C., 1913), 65. The ICC's conversion from block signals to train control is documented in its annual reports for the other years listed. The first of many lists of collisions that the ICC claimed could have been prevented by train control appears in ICC, *Thirty-first Annual Report, 1917* (Washington, D.C., 1918), 47.

20. These measured variables may also be picking up the impact of omitted variables such as Safety First activities that also improved safety.

21. Compare with Charles Clark, "The Railroad Safety Problem in the United States," *Transport History* 7 (Summer 1974): 97-123, who says that "the most serious danger to safety, however, was the problem of excessive working hours" (110). The ICC data appear in *Congressional Record*, 59th Cong., 1st sess., June 26, 1906, 40:9268, and 59th Cong., 2d sess., Jan. 9, 1907, 41:812-19. Note that if the act raised train speed, its net impact would have been even less.

22. "Danger of serious derailment" is from ICC, *Twenty-sixth Annual Report, 1912*, 62.

23. Early work by the American Society of Civil Engineers, the American Society

of Testing Materials, and the American Railway Engineering Association is discussed in W. C. Cushing, "The Question of the Improvement of Rail Design, and Specifications from 1893 to the Present Time," AREA *Bulletin* 144 (Feb. 1912): 853-62, and in Steven Usselman, "Running the Machine: The Management of Technological Innovation on American Railroads, 1860-1910" (Ph.D. diss., Univ. of Delaware, 1985), chap. 7. For the Pennsylvania's complaint, see A. C. Shand to W. H. Brown, May 9, 1904, accession 1810, unprocessed, PRRC. The New York survey is reported in "Defective Rails," *RG* 42 (May 17, 1907): 674-77. Popular concern is revealed in William Irwin, "Improvement in Steel Rails," *Scientific American* 85 (June 6, 1901): 4, and many subsequent articles in that journal. For other examples, see James Bayless, "Steel Rails," *Independent* 63 (July 11, 1907): 82-85, and Dexter Marshall, "The Problem of the Broken Rail," *McClure's* 29 (Aug. 1908): 428-33. Regulation was threatened in National Association of Railway Commissioners *Proceedings* 24 (1912). For the joint funding, see M. H. Wickhorst, "American Research Work on Rails," *Iron Age* 90 (Sept. 12, 1912): 614-16.

24. The quotations are from "Broken Rails and Railroad Accidents," *Scientific American* 96 (Apr. 20, 1907): 326, and "A New Method of Testing Rails," *Scientific American Supplement* 72 (Dec. 23, 1911): 403-4. Overviews of the debate on the causes of rail failures are contained in Harold Coes, "Steel-Rail Breakages: Questions of Design and Specifications," *Engineering Magazine* 35 (June 1908): 417-26; Charles B. Dudley, "Some Features of the Present Steel Rail Question," American Society of Testing Materials *Proceedings* 8 (1908): 198-220; and "A Speedy Solution to the Broken Rail Problem" and "The Peril of the Broken Rail—Cause and Cure," *Scientific American* 96 (May 18, 1907): 406 and 409-10. The ICC also called attention to poorly manufactured rails. See, for example, ICC, *Report of the Chief Inspector of Safety Appliances Covering His Investigation of an Accident Which Occurred on the Great Northern Railway Near Sharon, North Dakota, December 30, 1911* (Washington, D.C., 1912). An English view is "Heavy Rail Sections in America," *Engineering* 84 (Nov. 15, 1907): 688-89. For the lot with 22 percent defective rails, see J. R. Onderdonk, "Remarks," American Society of Testing Materials *Proceedings* 8 (1908): 121-22.

25. The steel companies' position is reported in numerous articles in *Iron Age;* see especially H. V. Wille, "Greater Loads on Rails," *Iron Age* 80 (Oct. 3, 1907): 922-23. This became the official industry position when James Farrell, president of U.S. Steel, included it in testimony to Congress; see House Committee on Investigation of United States Steel Corporation, *Hearings* (Washington, D.C., 1912), 4:2680-83. Before Farrell spoke, a word-for-word identical claim had been made to the Pennsylvania by president E. A. Clarke of Lackawanna Steel; see E. A. Clarke to A. W. Gibbs, Jan. 17, 1912, box 5, accession 1807, PRRC.

26. Cushing, "Question of the Improvement of Rail Design." The ARA activities may be followed in Committee on Standard Rail and Wheel Sections, "Report," ARA *Proceedings*, 1903-8. For the Pennsylvania, see "The Pennsylvania Railroad and the Steel Rail Problem," *Scientific American* 98 (Feb. 22, 1908): 122, and "New Pennsylvania Railroad Specifications for Rails," *Iron Age* 81 (Feb. 13, 1908): 526. For the New York Central, see "Improvements in Steel Rails," *Engineering Magazine* 37 (June 1909): 427-29. For work of the AREA, see its Rail Committee's "Report" in AREA *Proceedings*, various years. Comparative failure rates for Bessemer and open-hearth steel are in M. H. Wickhorst, "Rail Failure Statistics for 1915," AREA *Bulletin* 188 (Aug. 1916): 201-4.

27. The story of the Pittsburgh and Lake Erie is in "Axle Loads, the Track Structure, and Rail Failure," *Railway Engineering and Maintenance* 24 (June 1927): 293-94.

On locomotive and track design, see also "Catching up with the Locomotive," *Railway Engineering and Maintenance* 23 (July 1928): 328–34, and Michael Duffy, "Rail Stresses, Impact Loading, and Steam Locomotive Design," *History of Technology* 9 (1984): 43–101.

28. For the ICC's discovery and analysis of transverse fissures, see its *Report of Accident on the Line of the Lehigh Valley Railroad Near Manchester, New York, August 25, 1911* (Washington, D.C., 1912), and *Report on the Formation of Transverse Fissures in Steel Rails and Their Prevalence on Certain Railroads* (Washington, D.C., 1923).

29. A review of the problem of transverse fissures is in "Progress in the Rail Problem Marked by Sharp Differences in View," *EN* 78 (May 31, 1917): 455–59. My discussion of the railroads' efforts to detect transverse fissures is based on "Joint Investigation of Transverse Fissures," AREA *Proceedings* 25 (1924): 432–37; W. C. Barnes, "Detection of Transverse Fissures in Track," AREA *Bulletin* 315 (Mar. 1929); and W. C. Barnes, "Operation of the A.R.A. Rail Fissure Detector Car," AREA *Bulletin* 333 (Jan. 1931): 355–56.

30. The breakthrough was reported in C. P. Sandberg et al., "Effect of Controlled Cooling and Temperature Equalization on Internal Fissures in Rails," *Metals and Alloys* 3 (Apr. 1932): 89–92. The earlier American work was by F. M. Waring and K. E. Hofamann, "Deep Etching of Rails and Forgings," American Society for Testing Materials *Proceedings* 19 (1919): 183–97. For Moore's work, see H. F. Moore, "Progress Report of the Joint Investigation of Fissures in Railroad Rails," AREA *Bulletin* 376 (June 1935). See also J. F. Woschitz, "No Shatter Cracks in Rail—No Transverse Fissures," *RA* 108 (Apr. 13, 1940): 668–70.

31. The story of ash-pan legislation is based on Senate Committee on Interstate and Foreign Commerce, *Hearings on Safety Appliances, Automatic Ashpans*, Apr. 9, 1909, and House Committee on Interstate and Foreign Commerce, *Hearings on H.R. 19795, Ash Pan Bill* (Washington, D.C., 1908), which contains the quotations in the text.

32. Alfred Bruce, *The Steam Locomotive in America* (New York: Norton, 1952), 137. The data on deaths and injuries were presented by H. E. Wills representing the Brotherhood of Locomotive Engineers to the Senate Committee on Interstate and Foreign Commerce, *Hearings on S236 and S6702 to Promote the Safety of Employees . . . by Compelling Common Carriers . . . to Equip Their Locomotives with Safe and Suitable Boilers and Appurtenances Thereon*, 61st Cong., 2d sess., Mar. 22, 1910, S.D. 446. Somewhat lower estimates of fatalities and much lower figures for injuries (also from the ICC) are in *Railroad Accidents, 1903–1908*, 60th Cong, 2d sess., S.D. 682. I cannot reconcile these data, and so I have chosen the larger figures. For more details on locomotive boiler inspection, see my "Safe and Suitable Boilers: The Railroads, the Interstate Commerce Commission, and Locomotive Safety, 1900–1945," *Railroad History* 171 (Autumn 1994): 23–44.

33. The role of A. A. Row is from "Boiler Explosions—Bill to Provide for Locomotive Boiler Inspection," *Locomotive Firemen and Enginemen's Magazine* 48 (Feb. 1910): 231. The claim that the push for federal regulation began with the brotherhood is from Angus Sinclair, "Boiler Inspection," *Railway and Locomotive Engineering* 25 (Nov. 1912): 406.

34. The positions of the carriers and their critics are presented in *Hearings on S236 and S6702*; the exchange between Paulding and Burkett is on 20. The railroad survey of boiler explosions is summarized in the hearings. It is from Special Committee on Relations of Railway Operations to Legislation *Bulletin* 4 (Chicago, 1910). A useful history of the legislation is contained in *Locomotive Boiler Inspection*, 61st Cong., 3d sess., Jan. 23, 1904, H.R. 1974.

35. "Vindictive" is from "Federal Boiler Inspection," *RA* 48 (June 17, 1910): 1533–34. See also "The Locomotive Boiler Inspection Legislation," *RA* 50 (Jan. 10, 1911): 266–67, and "Federal Boiler Inspection," *RA* 50 (Feb. 17, 1911): 308–9.

36. Inspection costs are reported in "The Arguments for and against Train Crew Legislation," Bureau of Railway Economics *Bulletin* 73 (Washington, D.C. 1915), 20. The ICC proclaimed victory in *Annual Report of the Chief Inspector of Locomotive Boilers* 4 (1914), 12. "Deteriorated condition" is from *Annual Report of the Chief Inspector of Locomotive Boilers* 12 (1923), 6.

37. The claim is in *Annual Report of the Chief Inspector of Locomotive Boilers* 18 (1929), 8. For statistics on accidents by cause, see my "Safe and Suitable Boilers."

38. For more detail on the decline in boiler explosions, see my "Safe and Suitable Boilers."

39. Biographical data are from "Ralph C. Richards, Past President, N.S.C. Dies," *NSN* 14 (Feb. 1925): 19, and Edward L. Tinker, "Ralph C. Richards," *American Magazine* 76 (Dec. 1913): 44–45. Origins of Safety First are from Ralph Richards, "The Safety First Movement on American Railways," in Second Pan American Scientific Congress *Proceedings* (Washington, D.C.) 11 (1917): 326–35, and Ralph Richards, "Origin of the Safety First Movement," Association of Railway Claim Agents *Bulletin* 5 (Sept. 1920): 72–73. For more detail on railroad Safety First work, see my "Safety First Comes to the Railroads, 1910–1939," *Railroad History* 166 (Spring 1992): 6–33.

40. ICC, *Twenty-sixth Annual Report, 1912*, 66. The claim of the Chicago and North Western is in its *Report of the Central Safety Committee, 1911–1912* (Chicago, 1913), 20.

41. On employers' relief systems, see ICC, *Tenth Annual Report, 1896* (Washington, D.C., 1897), 108–11; Emory Johnson, "Railway Relief Departments," BLS *Bulletin* 8 (Washington, D.C., 1897), 39–57; U.S. Commissioner of Labor, *Twenty-third Annual Report: Workmen's Insurance and Benefit Funds in the United States, 1908* (Washington, D.C., 1909), chap. 3; and the testimony of H. R. Fuller in U.S. Industrial Commission, *Report on Transportation* (Washington, D.C., 1901), 9:43. Fuller told the commission that major railroad relief systems were still compulsory and were financed largely by employees' contributions; see 298–303. On the importance of workman's compensation, see Frank Whiting, "Workman's Compensation," in *The Railway Library and Statistics, 1913*, ed. Slason Thompson (Chicago: Bureau of Railway News and Statistics, 1914), 176–83. The role of job risks in wage arbitration is discussed in Association of Railway Executives, Conference of Managers, "Statements before the United States Railroad Labor Board," *Railroad Wage Hearings, 1920* (Chicago, 1920), 1:13.

42. Seung Wook Kim and Price Fishback, "Institutional Change, Compensating Differentials, and Accident Risk in American Railroading, 1892–1945," *Journal of Economic History* 53 (Dec. 1993): 796–823, also argue that the increase in liability compensation contributed to safety.

43. Richards, "Origin of the Safety First Movement," 79; R. H. Newbern, "The Pennsylvania's System for Preventing Personal Injuries," in Pennsylvania Railroad, *Information for Employees and the Public* (Jan. 1914); Charles J. Hill, "Organized Safety on the New York Central System," ARA Safety Section *Proceedings* 20 (1940): 89–105. The importance of rising claim costs in motivating the safety movement on electric railroads is stressed in "The 'Safety First' Movement," *Electric Railway Journal* 45 (Jan. 2, 1915): 34–46, and "Safety First in Seattle," *Electric Railway Journal* 46 (Jan. 8, 1916): 70–74.

44. W. L. Park, "Publicity for Railroad Accidents," Western Railroad Club *Proceedings* 21 (Mar. 12, 1909): 189–225. The Rice quotation is from ARA *Proceedings*, May 1912, 819–21.

45. The subcommittee report is in ARA *Proceedings*, May 1913, 16–17.

46. *Railroad Trainman* 28 (Sept. 1911): 710; "Safety vs. Delayed Trains," *RA* 41 (Feb. 23, 1906): 275; "Killing Trackmen—The Cheapest Way to Lessen It," *RG* 41 (Aug. 17, 1906): 30.

47. See Ralph Richards, *What the Safety Committees of the Chicago and North Western Railroad Have Done for the Conservation of Men* (Chicago and North Western, 1912), 40. "What Are We Going to Do about Railroad Accidents?" *RG* 44 (Jan. 31, 1908): 144-45, (Feb. 28, 1908): 270-71, and (Mar. 13, 1908): 336.

48. Charles Dow, "Safety and Short Trains," in *Railway Library and Statistics, 1914,* ed. Thompson, 162-74; Ralph Richards, "Enthusiasm for Safety, How We Can Get It," in Proceedings of Minnesota Industrial Safety Conference Dec. 1911, Minnesota Bureau of Labor, Industries, and Commerce, *Accident Bulletin* 5 (Apr. 1912): 12-19. For Tyler, see "Union 'Safety First' Rally at Kansas City," *RA* 53 (Oct. 25, 1912): 796. The interest of the Pennsylvania in favorable publicity is revealed in "An Achievement of the Highest Public Service," in Pennsylvania Railroad, *Information for Employees and the Public* (Feb. 6, 1914), and in Samuel Rea to James McCrea, June 10, 1909, Executive Department, box 120, PRRC, who praised the favorable publicity the Pennsylvania's accident record had received and noted that it "must also have affected a substantial saving in our expenses."

49. See Richards, "Prevention of Accidents on Railroads," 9. Homemade guards are from Richards, "Enthusiasm for Safety," 13. Efficiency is stressed in "Meeting of the Regional Safety Committee," Sept. 2, 1927, Safety Department Files, PRRC. A broad spectrum of safety benefits are claimed in Richards, "Prevention of Accidents on Railroads." See also Herman H. Larson, "Remarks," ARA Safety Section *Proceedings* 8 (1928): 84-93, and George Bradshaw, "The Personal Injury Problem," in *Railway Library and Statistics, 1914,* ed. Thompson, 151-61.

50. "Not inevitable" is from Richards, *What the Safety Committees of the Chicago and North Western,* 9. "If you want to change" is from Richards, *Address to the Operating Men of the Chicago and North Western Railway on the Prevention of Accidents* (Chicago, 1910), 13. Richards, "Remarks," NSC *Proceedings* 1 (1912): 129, claimed that he learned of Illinois Steel's safety work after he had set up the North Western system. C. I. Leiper, "Safety from a General Manager's Standpoint," ARA Safety Section *Proceedings* 7 (1927): 70-79.

51. W. L. Park, "Discipline vs. Accidents," *RG* 44 (Jan. 10, 1908): 48-49; Walter Greenwood, "Remarks," NSC *Proceedings* 4 (1915): 538-39.

52. Richards was quoted in "The Campaign against Accidents on the Chicago and North Western," *RA* 49 (Sept. 2, 1911): 391-92; Richards, "Safety First Movement on American Railways," 332.

53. W. J. Wallace, "The Safety Movement," *Locomotive Engineer's Journal* 47 (Nov. 1913): 967-68; "Safety Last," *Locomotive Engineer's Journal* 54 (Mar. 1920): 271. See also "Safety First," *Journal of the Switchmen's Union* 15 (June 1913): 379-80; A. A. Graham to Editor, "Safety First Affecting the Legal Rights of the Employee," *Journal of the Switchmen's Union* 17 (Aug. 1915): 564-65; and "Why Safety First?" *Railway Conductor* 30 (Sept. 1913): 677.

54. "The time has come" is from "For the Prevention of Accidents," *Railroad Trainman* 28 (Oct. 1911): 785-88. The editor's disillusion with the early safety movement is shown in "An Object Lesson in Safety First," *Railroad Trainman* 32 (Oct. 1915): 985-86. See also "Safety Committees," *Railroad Trainman* 29 (Feb. 1912): 158-59, and "The Safety First Movement," *Railroad Trainman* 30 (Apr. 1913): 356-58.

55. "There was no uniform" is from H. W. Belknap, "What the U.S. Railroad Administration Expects of the Different Safety Organizations," NSC *Proceedings* 7 (1918): 860-64. Cease's comment is in "Safety First under National Direction," *Railroad*

Trainman 35 (July 1918): 531–32. See also H. W. Belknap, "The Importance of Organized Safety Work," *Railroad Trainman* 35 (July 1918): 483–87, and W. J. Patterson, "Remarks," ARA Safety Section *Proceedings* 5 (1925): 101–3. U.S. Railroad Administration, Division of Operation, Safety Section, "Report on the Accident Drive," *Bulletin* 9 (Washington, D.C., 1919); U.S. Railroad Administration, "Suggestions and Recommendations Relative to Uniform Methods of Organizing and Conducting Safety Work," *Bulletin* 3 (Washington, D.C., 1918), describes the safety organization. See also U.S. Railroad Administration, *Annual Report of Walker D. Hines, Director General of Railroads, Division of Operations, 1919* (Washington, D.C., 1920), 85–87.

56. Cease described the Chicago meeting in "Safety First," *Railroad Trainman* 37 (Nov. 1920): 674–75. See also "Safety First," *Railroad Trainman* 39 (May 1922): 290. W. G. Lee, "Benefits Accruing to the Railroad Trainmen Due to Organized Safety upon the American Railroads," and Isaiah Hale, "Discussion," NSC *Proceedings* 14 (1925): 1017–23. For the other journals' response, see "Safety Department," *Railway Conductor* 37 (Nov. 1920): 631–34, and "Our Safety First Corner," *Journal of the Switchmen's Union* 22 (Nov. 1921): 678–79. *Locomotive Firemen and Enginemen's Magazine* also began a Safety First section in January 1922.

57. The response of the men is contained in "Safety First," *Railroad Trainman* 39 (Jan. 1922): 13–19. "Would it not be better" is from "Safety First Preaching and Practice," *Locomotive Engineer's Journal* 55 (Apr. 1921): 360–61.

58. "No safety appliance" is from George Bradshaw, *Prevention of Railroad Accidents, or Safety in Railroading: A Heart to Heart Talk with Employees* (New York, 1912), 28. For the rules cited in the text and others, see C. H. Boltzell, "Prevention of Accidents Due to Employees Getting on and off Cars," NSC *Proceedings* 6 (1917): 1043–47; "Safety First," *Railroad Trainman* 39 (Jan. 1922): 13–19; H. H. Larson, "Remarks," ARA Safety Section *Proceedings* 8 (1928): 85–93; and Chicago and North Western Railway, *Report of the Central Safety Committee* (Chicago, 1913). The Pennsylvania's rules are briefly described in "Pennsylvania Puts Force behind Its Safety Rules," *Railway Engineering and Maintenance* 27 (July 1931): 646–48.

59. "An old dog" and the employees' views from D. L. Cease, "Safety First," *Railroad Trainman* 39 (Jan. 1922): 13–19.

60. F. W. Mitchell, "The Foreman and His Relation to Safety," NSC *Proceedings* 14 (1925): 1006–9. Information on the Pennsylvania is from "Meeting of the Regional Safety Committee," Sept. 2, 1927, PRRC; W. R. Davis to W.R.P., Sept. 25, 1930, Safety Department, PRRC; and C. W. Van Nort to All Employees, M[aintenance] of W[ay] Department, Oct. 23, 1930, box 635, PRRC.

61. The ICC comment is in its *Twenty-eighth Annual Report, 1914* (Washington, D.C., 1915), 55. "Chicago Great Western Reduces Casualties 88 Percent in 11 Years," *RA* 85 (Nov. 10, 1928): 929–32.

62. The trainmen's stories are from "Safety First," *Railroad Trainman* 39 (Jan. 1922): 13–19.

63. Cease reprinted his talk in ibid.

64. W. G. Lee, "Organized Labor's Interest in Safety Work," NSC *Proceedings* 8 (1919): 1241–44. Lake's claim is from "Some Pro's and Con's on Railroad Safety Methods," ARA Safety Section *Proceedings* 10 (1930): 101–17. "Safety First," *Railroad Trainman* 39 (Jan. 1922): 13–19 and (Aug. 1922): 491–92.

65. "Discipline and Signal Systems," *RA* 43 (Jan. 11. 1907): 32–33; W. L. Park, "Causes and Remedies for Railway Accidents," *RA* 53 (Aug. 2, 1912): 192–93. The situation on the Rock Island is described by A. G. Shaver, "The Effect of Block Signals and Automatic Stops on Accidents," *RA* 54 (Mar. 7, 1913): 442. "The Struggle to Make This Railroad Safe," in Pennsylvania Railroad, *Information for Employees and the Pub-*

lic (1913); "What the Pennsylvania Railroad Does for Safety—The Result in 1913," in Pennsylvania Railroad, *Information for Employees and the Public* (Feb. 1914).

66. Thomas Carrow, "Employment of New Men and Their Liability to Injury," NSC *Proceedings* 6 (1917): 991-1002. On the use of medical examinations, see ARA, *The American Railroad in Laboratory* (Washington, D.C., 1934), 2:95-96. Efforts to reduce seasonality are described in "Extent to Which It Is Practicable to Stabilize Employment in the Maintenance of Way Department," AREA *Proceedings* 28 (1927): 285-88. See also H. G. Hassler, "Accident Prevention in a Steel Car Repair Shop," ARA Safety Section *Proceedings* 6 (1926): 224-31, and H. H. Larson, "Remarks," ARA Safety Section *Proceedings* 8 (1928): 84-93.

67. See "Modern Equipment Promotes Safety in Maintenance Work," *Railway Engineering and Maintenance* 29 (Mar. 1933): 144-45; A. H. Peterson, "Does Work Equipment Promote Safety?" *Railway Engineering and Maintenance* 32 (Mar. 1936): 169-71; and "Work Equipment—A Valuable Adjunct to Safety," *Railway Engineering and Maintenance* 35 (July 1939): 405. Also see "Effects of Recent Developments in Maintenance of Way Practices on Gang Organization," AREA *Proceedings* 33 (1932): 385-90.

68. Dow, "Safety and Short Trains," 166; Hassler, "Accident Prevention in a Steel Car Repair Shop," 229.

69. The survey is from George Warfel, "Report of Committee on Safety Contest Methods," NSC *Proceedings* 19 (1930): 649-54.

70. The banner is described in T. H. Carrow to S. E. Eby, Mar. 2, 1928, Safety Department, PRRC. Elisha Lee to C. S. Krick, May 26, 1927, Safety Department PRRC. The motto is reported in Hassler, "Accident Prevention in a Steel Car Repair Shop," 230. T. H. Carrow, "Safety on the Pennsylvania Railroad in 1929," box 635, PRRC.

71. The quotation is from ICC *Accident Bulletin* 99 (1930): 1. The carriers' injury reports are in "Report to the Interstate Commerce Commission on Reliability of Railroad Employee Accident Statistics" (N.p., 1942). The commission's views on underreporting are in *Accident Bulletin* 97 (1928): 3, and *Accident Bulletin* 98 (1929): 1-2; the ratio of reportable to nonreportable injuries is in *Accident Bulletin* 108 (1939): 5.

72. W. N. Doak, "Safe and Efficient Hand Brakes," *Railroad Trainman* 47 (Jan. 1930): 6-9.

73. The story of the Wolverine is reported in Interstate Commerce Commission, *Report of the Chief of the Bureau of Safety Regarding Investigation of an Accident on the New York Central Railroad Near South Byron New York on January 12, 1919* (Washington, D.C., 1920). Fred McArdle, *Everything behind the Engine for Conductors and Brakemen* (Chicago, 1910), 65, describes the operation of home and distant signals. Harry Forman, *Rights of Trains*, rev. ed. (New York, 1929), describes the proper procedures for flagging in block-signal territory.

74. For more detail on automatic train control, see my "Combating the Collision Horror: The Interstate Commerce Commission and Automatic Train Control, 1900-1939," *Technology and Culture* 34 (Jan. 1993): 49-77.

75. This history and description are based on ARA Committee on Automatic Train Control, "Automatic Train Control," *Bulletin* 1 (Nov. 1930); ICC, *Report on Block-Signal Systems;* "History of Automatic Train Control," *Railway Signaling* 17 (Mar. 1924): 105-7; "The Fundamentals of Automatic Train Control," *RR* 76 (Jan. 31, 1925): 237-41, (Feb. 7, 1925): 282-84, (Feb. 14, 1925): 310-11, and (Feb. 21, 1925): 357-58; and U.S. Railroad Administration, *Annual Report of Walker D. Hines, Director General of Railroads, 1919, Automatic Train Control Committee* (Washington, D.C., 1920), 15.

76. The Signal Section of the ARA had a committee devoted to the economics of railway signaling. During the 1920s and 1930s it published numerous studies demon-

strating the profitability of block signals, interlocking, car retarders, crossing protection, and centralized traffic control. For example, see "Estimated Savings to Be Effected on Five Divisions of a Railway System by Replacing Manual Block System with Automatic Block System" and "Economics of Car Retarders at Hump and Gravity Yards," both in ARA Signal Section *Proceedings* 23 (Mar. 1926): 495-503. See also "Economics of Modern Signaling," *Railway Signaling* 26 (May 1933): 111-18.

77. For evidence that the railroads did as little as possible, see "Automatic Train Stops," *RR* 49 (Oct. 16, 1909): 922-23; "Automatic Train Control," *RR* 50 (Jan. 17, 1911): 540-41; and "Automatic Train Stops—III," *RA* 57 (July 24, 1914): 151-52. Private installations are reviewed in "In the Matter of Automatic Train Control Devices, Docket 13413," 69 ICC *Report* (1922), 258-79. *Railway Review*'s conclusion is in "One Way in Which Railroads Have Not Progressed," *RR* 69 (Dec. 24, 1921): 877-78.

78. "Wise step" is from "The Call for Automatic Train Stops," *RA* 72 (Jan. 21, 1922): 211. "Selected with regard" is from "The Automatic Train Control Order," *RA* 72 (Feb. 4, 1922): 308. Interest in cab signals is revealed in C. E. Chatford, "Cost of ATC," *RR* 59 (Oct. 21, 1916): 559-60, and "Three Hundred and Fifteen Passengers Killed," *RA* 65 (Oct. 11, 1916): 652. "What could be more" is from "Progress in Automatic Train Control," *RA* 72 (Apr. 29, 1922): 1001-2.

79. The commission quotations are from 69 ICC *Report* (1922), 258-79. The hearings are reported in *RA* 72 (Mar. 25, 1922): 766, (Apr. 15, 1922): 927-28, and (Apr. 22, 1922): 971-72; and in "The Hearing on Train Control," *RR* 70 (Apr. 1, 1922): 464-65.

80. Cab signals controlled by a track circuit can increase track capacity. The activities of the Pennsylvania and the consequences of forbidding the automatic stop are described by A. H. Rudd, "Continuous Train Control, Pennsylvania Railroad," *RR* 75 (Nov. 1, 1924): 654-57, and "Results of Train Control Tests on the Pennsylvania," *Railway Signaling* (Oct. 1924): 391-93. Problems with track capacity had been noted by the ICC in its 1907 *Report on Block Signals*, 56-57.

81. The second order is 91 ICC *Report* (1924), 426-51. "42 Roads Object to Train Control Order," *RA* 76 (May 17, 1924): 1209-14.

82. Campbell and Aicheson are quoted in "Hearing on Automatic Train Control Order," *RA* 76 (May 10, 1924): 1145-48. The hearings are also reported in "The ICC Train Control Hearing" and "ICC Train Control Hearing Concluded," *Railway Signaling* 17 (May 24, 1924): 195-97 and (June 24, 1924): 234-42.

83. The unsatisfactory results of the Pennsylvania's experiment with continuous train control are reported in A. H. Rudd to C. B. Heiserman, June 5, 1925, box 633, PRRC. The switch to simpler devices is described in "Train Stop or Train Control?" *RA* 78 (Aug. 29, 1925): 385; "Mo Pacific Authorized to Install Block Signals Instead of Train Control," *RA* 78 (May 29, 1926): 1452; and "Train Control Order Suspended as to KCS," *RA* 78 (Aug. 7, 1926): 249-50.

84. 148 ICC *Report* (1928), 188-210. Esch's objections are revealed in ICC Commissioners' Minutes, July 11, 1927 (copy in ICC library). Voluntary installations are listed in ARA Committee on Automatic Train Control, *Automatic Train Control*, table 2.

85. Borland's remarks are in "Address by W. P. Borland," ARA Signal Section *Proceedings* 23 (Mar. 1929): 891-92. The hearings are reported in "ICC Train Control Hearing," *Railway Signaling* 21 (Apr. 1928): 140-43 and (May 1928): 177-79; "Signal and Train Control Hearing Ends," *Railway Signaling* 21 (June 1928): 223-25; "Hearings on ATC," *RA* 84 (Mar. 3, 1928): 535-37; "Further Hearings on ATC," *RA* 84 (Apr. 28, 1928): 971-77; and "Block Signal and Train Control Hearing Ended," *RA* 84 (May 5, 1928): 1049-52. The decision is in 148 ICC *Report* (1928), 188-210.

86. "Economics of Changing from Automatic Train Control to Cab Signals," ARA Signal Section *Proceedings* 32 (Mar. 1935): 35-41; 186 ICC *Report* (1932), 131-36; 190

ICC *Report* (1932), 162–70, 182–90. The changes allowed up to 1934 are noted in John Dunn, "Signaling Construction Limited in 1934," *RA* 98 (Jan. 26, 1935): 150–54.

87. The following equation was fitted to data on individual carriers for 1929 from ICC *Accident Bulletin* 98 (1929) to estimate the impact of automatic train control on collision frequency:

$$CR = 0.255(CR'22) + 0.476(MS'29) - 2.71(AS'29) + 0.207(D'29) + 1.99(ATC'29)$$
$$\quad (7.43) \qquad (0.67) \qquad (3.20) \qquad (3.78) \qquad (0.935)$$
$$R^2 = 0.33; N = 152$$

The equations also include a constant term. CR and $CR'22$ are number of collisions per million locomotive-miles in 1929 and 1922. $MS'29$ and $AS'29$ are the proportion of track with manual and automatic block signals in 1929. $D'29$ is locomotive-miles per mile of track in 1929. $ATC'29$ is the proportion of track with automatic train control in 1929. Figures in parentheses are t-ratios. The equation contains a constant term and is weighted by locomotive-miles using a TSP routine.

88. Rudd's assessment is in "Automatic Train Control," *Engineers and Engineering* 43 (Jan. 1926): 20–29.

89. "The Senate Passes the Train Limit Bill," *RA* 103 (Aug. 7, 1937): 155–57. For federal efforts, see Senate Committee on Interstate and Foreign Commerce, *Hearings on S1288*, 74th Cong., 1st sess., July 9 and 10, 1935; *Hearings on Railroad Track and Bridge Inspection, S1888*, 75th Cong., 1st sess., Mar. 26, 29, and 30, 1937; and *Hearings on S2625, Limiting the Car Length of Trains*, 73d Cong., 2d sess., Apr. 24–25 and May 4–5, 1934.

90. Chauncey Del French, *Railroadman* (New York: Macmillan, 1938), 20; "Some Current Lessons from the Railway Safety Record," *RA* 99 (July 26, 1935): 65–67.

91. The findings in table A1.10 suggest that federal employers' liability law (Fela '08) resulted in a sharp improvement in safety. But if the date of the law is taken to be 1906 (when the first law was passed), it is statistically insignificant in all the equations. Similarly, the effect on fatality rates of the 1901 change in reporting requirements is unclear, for it is conditional on the date chosen for the employers' liability law. As can be seen, legal changes probably did increase reported injury rates after 1910, however.

92. French, *Railroadman*, 20.

CHAPTER SIX. LESS BLOOD ON THE COAL, MORE DESPAIR IN THE HOMES OF THE MINERS

Epigraphs: Howard Eavenson, "Safety Methods of United States Coal and Coke," AIME *Transactions* 55 (1915): 331; Edward O'Toole to All Superintendents, Jan. 7, 1911, in West Virginia Department of Mines, *Annual Report, 1911*, 263.

1. Herbert M. Wilson, "The United States Bureau of Mines," Coal Mining Institute of America *Proceedings*, 1910, 231–33.

2. Harry Gandy to Scott Turner, June 7, 1927, box 208, GCF. Dan Harrington to O. P Hood, June 20, 1927, box 208, GCF, claims that officials of the National Coal Association thought about a "break" with the bureau over this matter.

3. Dan Harrington to Arthur Murray, Mar. 29, 1930, box 1185, GCF. "Involuntary manslaughter" is from H. Tomlinson to Dan Harrington, Mar. 12, 1930, box 1183, GCF. Francis Feehan to Scott Turner [n.d., ca. Feb. 28, 1929], box 969, GCF; United Mine Workers *Journal* 51 (Mar. 15, 1940): 3. On Harrington's background, see *Who Was Who in America* (Chicago: Marquis Who's Who, 1976), 6:182. For similar difficulties in the bureau's relationship with the oil industry in the 1920s, see Joe Pratt, "Letting the Grandchildren Do It: Environmental Planning during the Ascent of Oil as a Major Energy Source," *Public Historian* 2 (Summer 1980): 28–61.

4. "Editorial," *Coal Age* 1 (Dec. 23, 1911): 3. David Ross, "Workmen's Compensa-

tion," AMC *Proceedings* 15 (1912): 237, notes that the congress officially went on record in favor of compensation in 1910. For Stonega, see *Annual Report, 1918*, box 211, and General Manager to C. G. Duffy and others, Oct. 4, 1918, box 490, SCCC.

5. Rice explained his motives in a letter to O. P. Hood, June 6, 1929, box 969, GCF. George Rice to Van Manning, Feb. 14 and 19, 1915, box 169, GCF. For Rice's career, see *NCAB* (New York: James T. White), 38:52, and *Dictionary of American Biography*, suppl. 4, pp. 690-91.

6. Dan Harrington to F. C. Hill, Jan. 9, 1932, box 1590, GCF.

7. Herbert Wilson, "Coal Mine Inspection in Kentucky," *Coal Age* 17 (June 17, 1920): 1259-61; C. A. Herbert to Dan Harrington, Nov. 11, 1932, box 1593, GCF; R. E. Howe [Southern Appalachian Coal Operators Association], "Mine Safety," Mine Inspectors' Institute *Proceedings* 20 (1929): 83-86. The experience modifier can be found in Pennsylvania Compensation Rating and Inspection Bureau, Coal Mine Section, *Pennsylvania Bituminous Coal Mine Compensation Rating Schedule, 1926* (Harrisburg, 1925). See also Hugh Wolfin, "The Effects of Compensation Laws and Differential Compensation Insurance Rates on Coal Mine Safety Conditions," in U.S. Coal Commission, *Report* (Washington, D.C., 1925), 3:1727-88.

8. For more detail on mine explosions, see my "Preventing the 'Needless Peril of the Coal Mine': The Bureau of Mines and the Campaign against Coal Mine Explosions, 1910-1940," *Technology and Culture* 36 (July 1995): 483-518.

9. For the history of ideas about the explosibility of coal dust by an expert, see George Rice, "The Explosibility of Coal Dust," BM *Bulletin* 20 (Washington, D.C., 1911); the quotation on the Wallsend colliery is from 11. Michael Faraday and Charles Lyell, "Report on the Subject of the Explosion at the Haswell Collieries, and on the Means of Preventing Similar Accidents," *Philosophical Magazine*, n.s., 26 (1845): 16-34; quotation from 27. See also Henry Hall, "The Coal Dust Question in Great Britain," *EMJ* 87 (May 29, 1909): 1084-89, and *First Report of the Royal Commission on Explosions from Coal Dust in Mines* (London, 1891). For American understanding of the problem, see "Influence of Coal Dust on the Explosiveness of Fire Damp," *EMJ* 21 (Feb. 23, 1876): 199, and "Dust as an Explosive," *Scientific American Supplement* 5 (May 25, 1898): 1985.

10. The establishment of European facilities is from Rice, "Explosibility of Coal Dust," 19-21, 31-33.

11. Rice's tour of Europe is mentioned in his "Review of Coal Dust Investigations," AIME *Transactions* 71 (1925): 1130-63. The stress on prevention is made clear in George Rice, "Investigations of Coal Dust Explosions," AIME *Transactions* 50 (1914): 552-85.

12. George Rice, "Coal Dust Explosion at Experimental Mine," in Herbert Wilson and Albert Fay, "First National Mine Safety Demonstration," BM *Bulletin* 44 (Washington, D.C., 1912), 35-36; Joseph A. Holmes, "Statement," n.d., box 32, GCF. Hall's remarks are in "Minutes of Meeting of Mine Accident Committee," Nov. 6, 1911, box 12, GCF. The Alabama mining men are reported in Dan Harrington to J. J. Forbes, May 25, 1927, box 593, GCF.

13. For a brief history of the idea that rock dust would stop an explosion, see George Rice, "Stone Dusting or Rock Dusting to Prevent Coal-Dust Explosions, as Practiced in Great Britain and France," BM *Bulletin* 225 (Washington, D.C., 1924). Garforth provided some early history and stated his claim in W. E. Garforth, "A Record of the Origin of the Principle of Stone-Dusting for the Prevention of Explosions," Institution of Mining Engineers *Transactions* 45 (1913): 562-75. The bureau's findings are from George Rice and H. P. Greenwald, "Coal Dust Explosibility Factors Indicated by Experimental Mine Investigations, 1911-1929," BM *Technical Paper* 464 (Washington, D.C., 1929).

14. George Rice, "American Coal Dust Investigations," Institution of Mining Engineers *Transactions* 49 (1915): 1–50, and the response of his audience, 51–77.

15. R. V. Wheeler and G. S. Rice, "Cooperative Research between the United States Bureau of Mines and the Safety in Mines Research Board, Annual Report for 1929," BM *Report of Investigation* 3010 (Washington, D.C., 1930); H. P. Greenwald, "Notes on Large Scale Tests of the Explosibility of Coal Dusts Made in the United States and Britain," BM *Report of Investigation* 3462 (Washington, D.C., 1939).

16. F. Kenneth Cochran to Bureau of Mines, Apr. 27, May 9, and May 21, 1925, box 199, GCF.

17. For some early history on the development of low-flame explosives, see *Minutes of Evidence Taken before the Royal Commission on Explosions from Coal Dust in Mines* (London, 1894), vol. 2, and Hall, "Coal Dust Question." Permissible explosives are described in S. P. Howell and M. W. von Bernewitz, "The Hazards of Nonpermissible Explosives," BM *Report of Investigation* 2583 (Washington, D.C., 1924), and Dan Harrington and S. P. Howell, "Preventing Accidents by the Proper Use of Permissible Explosives," BM *Technical Paper* 567 (Washington, D.C., 1936). Early use of permissible explosives is described in Pennsylvania Department of Mines, *Annual Report, Bituminous, 1913*, 9. See also George Otis Smith, "Circular Letter to Explosives Manufacturers," Jan. 9, 1909, box 19, GC.

18. The history of the safety lamp is summarized in James W. Paul et al., "Flame Safety Lamps," BM *Bulletin* 224 (Washington, D.C., 1924). The prohibition of the methane detector is from W. H. Glasgow to F. W. Willhofft, Apr. 11, 1928, box 12, GC.

19. For a brief history of electric cap lamps, see L. C. Ilsley and A. B. Hooker, "Permissible Electric Cap Lamps," BM *Bulletin* 332 (Washington, D.C., 1930), which notes the Colorado law. Their development at the Reading is from J. T. Jennings, "Historical Development of the Miners' Electric Safety Cap Lamp," Coal Mining Institute of America *Proceedings*, 1916, 229–39. See also Pennsylvania Department of Mines, *Annual Report, Anthracite, 1912*, 8. That electric cap lamps did not qualify as safety lamps in Pennsylvania mines is from James Roderick to Frank Dyer, Dec. 1, 1911, and the reversal is noted in Roderick to H. H. Hirsch, June 13, 1913, both in box 21, GC.

20. The deaths from using the Draeger equipment are noted in New Mexico Inspector of Coal Mines, *Annual Report, 1913*, 6. The Gibbs rescue equipment is described by Van Manning, "Mine Safety Devices Developed by the U.S. Bureau of Mines," in Smithsonian Institution, *Annual Report, 1916* (Washington, D.C., 1917), and D. J. Parker, "The Desirability for Standardizing Mine Rescue Training and Plan for Standardization," NSC *Proceedings* 8 (1919): 854–57. For the self-rescuer, see S. H. Katz et al., "Use of the Miners' Self Rescuer," BM *Miners' Circular* 30 (Washington, D.C., 1928). McCaa's contribution is noted in J. J. Forbes, "Advanced Mine-Rescue Training Course of the United States Bureau of Mines," in AMC, *1937 Yearbook of Coal Mine Mechanization* (Washington, D.C., 1937), 326–33.

21. On early British practice, see *Historical Review of Coal Mining* (London, 1942), chap. 16. For early American rescue work, see Forbes, "Advanced Mine-Rescue Training Course," and "Coal Companies Establish Rescue Stations," *EMJ* 87 (May 8, 1909): 951, which lists four private stations and several more in the works, and claims that "this is a direct outcome of the demonstration in rescue work being made by the United States Geological Survey."

22. The importance of Haldane's work is stressed in George Rice, "Mine Rescue Work in the United States," Institution of Mining Engineers *Transactions* 75 (1927–28): 1–21. The establishment of the rescue stations and cars is from BM, *Annual Report, 1911* (Washington, D.C., 1912), 20–21. Berton Braley, "The Boys of the Rescue Crew," *Coal Age* 4 (Nov. 13, 1913): 685.

23. Matthew Shields, "First Aid to the Injured in Coal Mines," *EMJ* 85, coal mining supplement (1908): 42–43. His work at Tennessee Coal, Iron, and Railroad is from "Alabama Coal Operators Discuss Mining Problems," *EMJ* 88 (July 31, 1909): 215. First-aid competitions are noted in Pennsylvania Department of Mines, *Annual Report, Anthracite, 1906* (Harrisburg, 1907), 6–10. Holmes's activities are in Wilson and Fay, "First National Mine Safety Demonstration," 8–10. The Reading's assistance is from H. M. Wilson to W. J. Richards [general manager of the Reading], Oct. 7, 1908, box 5, GC.

24. That the bureau's efforts were designed to encourage private demand is stated in BM, *Annual Report of the Director, 1911* (Washington, D.C., 1911), 20–21, and *1913* (Washington, D.C., 1913), 13–14. For early private work, see Rice, "International Conference of Mine Rescue Stations," 64. The 1937 estimate is from Forbes, "Advanced Mine-Rescue Training Course," 328. A general survey of these stations is J. J. Forbes et al., "Central Mine Rescue Stations," BM *Miners' Circular* 39 (Washington, D.C., 1938).

25. The annual contests are reported in W. D. Ryan, "Safety in Mines as Affected by First Aid and Mine Rescue Contests," BM *Information Circular* 6153 (Washington, D.C., 1929). That the losers hated the bureau is from J. J. Forbes to Dan Harrington, Nov. 17, 1930, box 1195, GCF.

26. C. A. Sine to Superintendents, July 21, 1922, box 489, SCCC, notes first-aid contests among black workers. On the Interracial League, see R. E. Clay to C. B. Bowers, July 24, 1923, box 494, SCCC. Bureau policy toward training black miners is from D. J. Parker to Mr. Chisholm, Feb. 8, 1921, box 717, GCF. In an intracompany first-aid contest at Woodward Iron Company, the winning white team scored 99.3 points while the winning black team scored 98. At an intercompany contest held in Birmingham in 1930, the winning white team received 99.4 points and the winning black team 97.6 points. See "Report of First Aid Contest Woodward Iron Company," July 4, 1940, and "Twelfth Alabama First Aid Contest," July 12, 1930, both in box 1196, GCF.

27. Schedule-rating credits and the quotation from Parker are from D. J. Parker to Acting Chief Engineer, Apr. 8, 1919, box 442, GCF.

28. Alexander McCanch to James Roderick, Jan. 18, 1917, and John Pratt to Roderick, Jan. 19, 1917, both in box 21, GC. Anaconda stopped paying for first-aid training because of labor turnover; see John Boardman to R. R. Sayers, Feb. 17, 1927, box 614, GCF.

29. For a description of the first-aid course, see J. J. Forbes, "Some Results of First Aid Training of All the Employees of a Mine or Plant," BM *Information Circular* 6957 (Sept. 1937); "conservatively estimated" is from 4. See also H. Foster Bain, "Ten Years of Mine Rescue and First Aid Training," BM *Report of Investigation* 2234 (Washington, D.C., 1921). The numbers trained are from Ryan, "Safety in Mines," 10, and Forbes, "Some Results of First-Aid Training," 3. In its early annual reports the bureau published figures on the number of men trained but later found that it could not verify them; see J. J. Forbes to Dan Harrington, Oct. 8, 1928, box 787, GCF. The reports of men saved in mine disasters are from BM, *Annual Report, 1917*, 34.

30. W. H. Glasgow to [?] Ross, Oct. 16, 1928, box 1, GCB. The survey is in E. J. Gleim and H. B. Freeman, "Maintenance of Electrical Mine Equipment from the Viewpoint of the Safety Inspector," BM *Technical Paper* 537 (Washington, D.C., 1932); the quotation is from 20–21. The 40 percent figure is from BM, *Minerals Yearbook 1940* (Washington, D.C., 1940).

31. The Owl Creek Coal dispute is reported in Wyoming Inspector of Coal Mines, *Annual Report, District 2, 1913*, 33–34. The Oklahoma strikes are reported in "Conference, Oklahoma Permissible Powder and Explosion Hazard Tests," Mar. 4, 1926, box

969, GCF. See also E. J. Gleim, "State Regulations Pertaining to Blasting on Shift," BM *Information Circular* 7165 (Washington, D.C., 1941), and L. C. Ilsley, "Who May Set off Blasts in Coal Mines?" BM *Report of Investigation* 2488 (Washington, D.C., 1923).

32. See *Proceedings of Joint Conference of Coal Operators and Coal Miners of Western Pennsylvania, Ohio, and Indiana* [Cincinnati, Ohio, Mar. 8–29, 1910] (Columbus: Stoneman Press, 1910).

33. The Alabama inspector is from Edward Flynn, "Remarks," Mine Inspectors' Institute *Proceedings* 9 (1916): 82. George Rice to Dan Harrington, May 12, 1920, and Harrington to Rice, July 12 and Sept. 24, 1920, box 559, GCF.

34. The miners' complaints are revealed in John Walker [president of the Illinois State Federation of Labor] to Dan Harrington, Apr. 29, 1929, box 969, GCF, who claimed (incorrectly) that the battery for the electric cap lamp weighed fifteen to seventeen pounds and that men had been killed from acid burns when the battery leaked. For an early assessment of miners' lamps, see Edwin Chance, "Portable Miners' Lamps," *Coal Age* 11 (Apr. 28, 1917): 744–48. H. M. Chance, "Acetylene and Electric Cap Lamps from a Safety Standpoint," *SE* 36 (Oct. 1918): 297–300, argues that the poor light from electric cap lamps made them more dangerous than acetylene. The technical development of the lamp through the mid-1930s is traced in Graham Bright, "Value of Better Underground Illumination," Coal Mining Institute of America *Proceedings* 49 (1935): 80–89, and also in his "Trend in Underground Lighting," AIME *Transactions*, 119 (1936): 113–36.

35. Van Manning to [?] Garfield, Apr. 20, 1918, box 366, GCF. George Deike, "Advantages in Use of Permissible Electric Lamps in Non Gaseous Mines," NSC *Proceedings* 6 (1917): 1440–54, discusses schedule rating discounts, as does Chance, "Portable Miners' Lamps."

36. Colorado Inspector of Coal Mines, *Annual Report, 1919*, 11; Percey Tetlow to D. A. Lyon, May 15, 1923, and Lyon to Philip Murray, May 9, 1923, box 1075, GCF.

37. See Elias Phillips to James Roderick, May 24, 1911 (who reports that the Buffalo and Susquehanna Coal Company requested a shift to open lights), and Ed Suppitt [general superintendent of Jamison Coal] to [?] Ross, July 6, 1912 (notifying him of a return to open lights), both in box 1, GCB. For similar behavior, see "Staff Meeting, Apr. 8, 1930," microfilm reel 57, Office Files, HCP. J. J. Forbes and C. W. Owings, "Coal Mine Explosions in West Virginia," BM *Information Circular* 6802 (Washington, D.C., 1934), 35.

38. Rice's remarks are in George Rice, "Memo Regarding Mine Explosions," Jan. 2, 1926, box 461. The strike is noted in W. W. Fleming to M. von Sichlen, Mar. 2, 1923, box 888. The order is in W. G. Roberts [assistant state mine inspector] to William Jones [Rock Island Coal], Dec. 22, 1923, box 1224. All in GCF.

39. C. A. Herbert to W. W. Fleming, Feb. 29, 1924, reports Boyle's stance. It and the "Synopsis" are in box 1224, GCF.

40. H. Foster Bain to Tom Bost, Mar. 27, 1924, and Bost to Bain, Mar. 31, 1924. The bureau's appeal to the UMW is in Bain to D. A. Franton, Mar. 27, 1924. The decision to intervene is in Franton to Andrew McGarry, Apr. 1, 1924, and Bain to H. L. Kerwin, Apr. 10, 1924. All in box 1224, GCF.

41. Boyle's order, the injunction, and the bond are in two letters from W. W. Fleming to H. Foster Bain, May 19, 1924. Boyle's escape from the injunction is in Fleming to Bain, May 23, 1924. Edward Boyle to Bain, June 23 and 26, 1924, informs him that the bureau's Francis Feehan is attempting to get the mines to disobey his (Boyle's) orders and requests Feehan's recall. George Rice to Fleming, June 25, 1924, acknowledges receipt of Boyle's draft mining law. E. Comfort to Director, Bureau of Mines,

July 3, 1924, mentions the injunction. Francis Feehan to J. B. Hynal, Nov. 18, 1925, announces that the state supreme court upheld Boyle. All in box 1224, GCF.

42. [Illegible] of Peabody Coal to O. P. Hood, Sept. 22, 1926, refers to the rock-dusting as an effort to show the men that the company would spend money to improve safety. C. A. Herbert to Dan Harrington, Sept. 5, 1926, notes that the mine employed permissible explosives and had been closed for thirty days for cleaning. Boyle's actions are in C. A. Herbert, "Report of Explosion, No. 29 Mine Superior Smokeless Coal and Mining Company," Sept. 26, 1926. These and the miners' handbill are all in box 465, GCF.

43. Dan Harrington, "Memo Concerning Mr. Herbert's Final Report on Explosion in No. 29 Mine Tahona, Oklahoma," Oct. 23, 1926, and Herbert, "Report of Explosion, No. 29 Mine Superior Smokeless Coal and Mining Company," Sept. 26, 1926, both in box 465, GCF. Boyle was not reelected in 1929, and in that year a new Oklahoma mining law required closed lights.

44. Princeton Mining Company's efforts are in R. J. Smith [president] to Mine Safety Appliance Company, Apr. 28, 1924. That the Sullivan explosion was due to open lights is in C. A. Herbert to T. T. Read, Mar. 9, 1925. The history of efforts to introduce electric cap lamps in Indiana is in J. T. Ryan to Read, Mar. 2, 1925. All, along with the miners' petition, in box 202, GCF.

45. The later explosion and the fine for use of electric cap lamps are from C. A. Herbert, "Report of Explosion, King Station Mine, Princeton Mining Company, Princeton, Indiana," Nov. 12, 1937, box 2643, GCF. The press release, a draft of which is dated Feb. 21, the day after the explosion, suggests that the bureau was waiting for a good time to make its case. Ryan's meeting with Wilson is in W. D. Ryan to T. T. Read, Mar. 20, 1925; Read to Ryan, Apr. 11, 1925; and Ryan to Read, Apr. 13, 1925; all in box 202, GCF. The use of electric cap lamps is in "Number of Approved Electric Cap Lamps Installed in Mines by States, with Total for United States, up to June 1, 1926," box 440, GCF.

46. Lamp use is from "Number of Approved Electric Cap Lamps," box 440, GCF. Zook's appeals are revealed in Joseph Zook to Scott Turner, May 27, 1929, and R. P. Lamont to Zook, May 27, 1929. The bureau's interest is revealed in "Memorandum Concerning Pending Legislation in Illinois," May 15, 1929." George Rice, "Memo to Acting Director," June 6, 1929, describes a meeting with the governor of Illinois. All in box 969, GCF.

47. The quotation that the miners were justified is from Dan Harrington to A. U. Miller, Nov. 15, 1929. "Sooner or later" is from Joseph Zook to All Members Illinois Coal Operators' Labor Association, June 14, 1929. Both in box 969, GCF. For further developments, see "Federal Bureau Answers Denny's Buglight Idea," *Illinois Miner* 9 (Nov. 30, 1929): 8.

48. Colorado Inspector of Coal Mines, *Biennial Report, 1911–1912* (Denver, 1912), 7, notes that Delagua had begun rock-dusting. Rice's role is from his "Review of Coal Dust Investigations," AIME *Transactions* 71 (1925): 1130–63. J. J. Forbes, "Methods of Rock-Dusting American Coal Mines," BM *Report of Investigation* 3465 (Washington, D.C., 1939), also lists Delagua as the first mine to use rock-dusting. The bureau's recommendation of rock-dusting is in Rice, "Explosibility of Coal Dust," 84–97. R. Dawson Hall, "Stone-Dust in Mine Explosions," *Coal Age* 1 (Nov. 25, 1911): 206–7; George Rice et al., "Methods of Preventing and Limiting Explosions in Coal Mines," BM *Technical Paper* 84 (Washington, D.C., 1915). The conversion of Old Ben is noted by its safety engineer, J. E. Jones, "Coal Dust Explosions: How They Can Be Prevented—Simple Remedy in Practical Operation," *Coal Mine Management* 3 (May 1924): 25–32.

49. For a typical letter to a manufacturer, see Van Manning to Connersville Blower

Co., Feb. 29, 1916. See also "List of Crusher Manufacturers." Both in box 215, GCF. "General Specifications for Rock Dusting Machine," *Coal Age* 9 (Apr. 15, 1916): 672–73. The figure of fewer than a dozen is from "Status of Rockdusting in the United States," BM *Report of Investigation* 2856 (Washington, D.C., 1928), 1. That a campaign was being planned is from R. R. Sayers to R. C. Williams, Feb. 7, 1924, box 1224, GCF.

50. On the explosion in Old Ben, see H. Foster Bain to D. W. Buchanan, Feb. 3, 1922, box 716, GCF. Dan Harrington to Chief Mining Engineer, Feb. 28, 1923, box 1061, GCF. The second effort to create a supply of rock-dust machines is revealed in Bain to Sullivan Machinery Company, Dec. 6, 1923, box 1061, GCF, which notes that similar letters were sent to other manufacturers. Enthusiastic responses by the manufacturers are in the same box. Oliver Bowles, "Sources of Limestone, Gypsum, and Anhydrite for Dusting Coal Mines to Prevent Explosions," BM *Bulletin* 224 (Washington, D.C., 1925). Standards for fineness and silica content are discussed in A. C. Fielder to George Rice, Apr. 28, 1824, box 1061, GCF. The possibility of using the state penitentiary as a supply is from L. D. Tracey to Charles Zahniser, Nov. 22, 1924, box 1211, GCF.

51. H. P. Greenwald, "Explosibility of Coal Dust from Four Mines in Utah," BM *Technical Paper* 306 (Washington, D.C., 1927). On the Benwood mine, see Jones, "Coal Dust Explosions."

52. Harrington's remarks are in Dan Harrington to B. W. Dyer, Mar. 24, 1924, box 1224, GCF. The visit is noted in C. Lorimer Colburn, "American and British Engineers Confer on Coal Mine Safety," *NSN* 8 (Apr. 1924): 27–31, and "Our English Visitors," *Coal Mine Management* 3 (Apr. 1924): 40. Rice's assessment of the reading skills of mine operators is in George Rice to C. W. Owings, May 25, 1927, box 593, GCF.

53. R. Dawson Hall to George Rice, Dec. 8, 1924, box 1211, GCF. There is an extended correspondence with Andrews for 1924-25 in box 1223, GCF.

54. State laws as of 1939 are in Forbes, "Methods of Rock-Dusting." The cost of Castle Gate is from Dan Harrington to James Paul, Apr. 1, 1924, box 1221, GCF. Schedule-rating discounts in 1924 are from Edward Steindle, "How Rock Dusting Cures the Epidemic of Mine Explosions," *Coal Age* 26 (Dec. 1924): 825-29. The views of Rice and McAuliffe are in George Rice to H. W. Heinrich, June 21, 1934, box 1961, and Eugene McAuliffe to Rice, July 16, 1934, box 1964, GCF.

55. The data are from "Status of Rockdusting in the United States"; W. W. Adams, "Use of Rockdust in Bituminous Coal Mines, 1930-1938 (A Statistical Survey)," BM *Report of Investigation* 3543 (Washington, D.C., 1940); and H. P. Greenwald, "Use of Rock Dust to Prevent Dust Explosions in Coal Mines, 1938-1943," AIME *Transactions* 157 (1944): 116-20.

56. That rockdusting was no panacea is stressed in Dan Harrington to T. T. Read, Dec. 8, 1924, box 1211, and Harrington to Engineers of Safety Division, Aug. 30, 1928, box 462, GCF. G. S. McCaa, "A Gas Explosion in a Rock-Dusted Mine," BM *Information Circular* 6144 (Washington, D.C., 1929); W. J. Fene to Harrington, Sept. 10, 1928, box 969, GCF; Eugene McAuliffe, "Remarks," AIME *Transactions* 157 (1944): 122-23. The survey is in Greenwald, "Use of Rock-Dust to Prevent Dust Explosions."

57. Because black powder and open lights were alternative sources of ignition, safety depended upon the joint use of permissibles and electric cap lamps. If their use were uncorrelated, joint use would rise more slowly for a time than use of either. That is, if 20 percent of mines used each, joint use would be 4 percent. That rock dust saved two hundred lives a year is claimed in Dan Harrington, "Safety Work of the Bureau of Mines and Some of Its Results," BM *Information Circular* 7070 (Washington, D.C., 1939). Bureau data by state and year from "Status of Rockdusting" and Adams, "Use of Rock Dust in Bituminous Coal Mines," yield the following equation, which is

manhour-weighted using a TSP routine and estimated with the Cochran-Orcutt correction:

$$\ln(EFR) = -0.007[\ln(PEXP)] - 1.36[\ln(PRD)]$$
$$(0.57) \qquad\qquad (3.39)$$
$$R^2 = 0.16;\ \text{D.W.} = 1.66;\ N = 174$$

EFR is the explosion fatality rate per million manhours, *PEXP* is the percentage of explosives that are permissible, and *PRD* is the percentage of manhours in rock-dusted mines. The equation also contains controls for productivity and a trend. Figures in parentheses are *t*-ratios. In the late 1930s rock-dusted mines accounted for about 40 percent of all manhours and yielded a 54 percent (1.36 × 40) reduction in the fatality rate compared with what it otherwise would have been.

58. J. H. Dague and S. J. Phillips, *Mine Accidents and Their Prevention* (New York: Delaware, Lackawanna, and Western Coal Co., 1912). H. C. Frick was another producer that demonstrated an early interest in safety; see "Rules of the H. C. Frick Coke Co.," *Mines and Minerals* 29 (Aug. 1908): 15, and Stephen Goodale, "Safety the First Consideration," *Mines and Minerals* 32 (Aug. 1911): 5–8.

59. On Phelps Dodge, see H. C. Henrie, "Employees' Representation at the Copper Queen Branch of the Phelps Dodge Corporation and the Relation of Industrial Representation to the Safety Movement," NSC *Proceedings* 15 (1926): 242–53, and Cleveland Dodge, "Educating the Miner in Safety," NSC *Proceedings* 17 (1928): 250–53 and subsequent discussion. Koppers made a similar discovery; see L. C. Campbell, "Accident Prevention: Whose Responsibility?" National Coal Association *Proceedings* 22 (1939): 51–53.

60. Thomas Fear, "Producing Coal Safely," Rocky Mountain Coal Mining Institute *Proceedings* 30 (1931): 29–35; Illinois Mining Institute *Proceedings* 41 (1932): 127–30; E. H. Shriver, "Accident Prevention in Mining," West Virginia Coal Mining Institute *Proceedings* 22 (1929): 56–64.

61. Howard Eavenson, "Safety Methods of United States Coal and Coke Co.," AIME *Transactions* 55 (1915): 319–64; John Walker, "Coal Mining Methods at Gary, West Virginia," *EMJ* 88 (July 3, 1909): 6–10; W. Z. Price, "The Steel Company Mines at Gary," *Mines and Minerals* 34 (Mar. 1914): 463–72; Frank H. Kneeland, "Safety in West Virginia," *Coal Age* 5 (Feb. 7, 1914): 243–46 and (Feb. 14, 1914): 314–18; J. R. Booth, "How Mining Engineering Eliminates Accidents," *Mines and Minerals* 35 (Nov. 1914): 206–7. See also the annual reports of the West Virginia Department of Mines for 1911 and 1912, which describe inspections of the Gary mines and reprint many of the company's safety materials. U.S. Steel's mines retain an excellent safety record to this day; see John Braithwaite, *To Punish or Persuade* (Albany: SUNY Press, 1985), chap. 3.

62. Kentucky Inspector of Mines, *Annual Report, 1902,* 40–43; W. H. Forbes to E. H. Denny, "Report on Roof Fall in Hayden Mine No. 3, Haybro Colorado," Nov. 9, 1937, box 2649, GCF. Harrington's comment is penciled in the margin.

63. The quotation is from Eavenson, "Safety Methods," 331. On U.S. Coal and Coke, see the citations in n. 61 above.

64. The comment on Frick is in Herbert Wilson to Director, May 24, 1912, box 41, GCF. On the Frick mines, see Goodale, "Safety the First Consideration." On Tennessee Coal, Iron, and Railroad, see R. D. Currie, "Coal Mine Safety Organizations in Alabama," BM *Technical Paper* 489 (Washington, D.C., 1931). "Model mine" is from F. E. Cash, "Safety Report on Columbia Mine, Columbia Steel Co., Columbia, Utah," Apr. 1928, box 772, GCF. D. J. Parker, "Safety Practices and Achievements at the Columbia Mine of the Columbia Steel Co.," BM *Information Circular* 6745 (Washing-

ton, D.C., 1933); H. B. Humphrey, "Report of Safety Inspection of Mine No. 1, Wisconsin Steel Co., Benham, Kentucky." [1936], box 2427, GCF; Donald Baker, "Ford Collieries Co. Reduced Its Accident Insurance Cost," *Coal Age* 17 (Apr. 15, 1920): 743-48; C. Lorimer Colburn, "Mine Safety Methods of the Ford Collieries Company," *NSN* 10 (July 1924): 31-33; C. W. Jeffers, "Safety at the Mines of the Ford Collieries Co.," BM *Information Circular* 6339 (Washington, D.C., 1930).

65. Eugene McAuliffe, "Remarks," Rocky Mountain Coal Mining Institute *Proceedings* 30 (1931): 38. Biographical material on McAuliffe is from *NCAB* 48:45. On the company's safety program, see J. A. Smith, "Safety Department," AMC *Journal* 16 (Feb. 1930): 138-40, 143, which is part of a whole issue devoted to Union Pacific Coal. See also A. W. Dickson, "Make It Safe," *Coal Industry* 7 (Mar. 1924): 108-11; Eugene McAuliffe, "Safety Practices in the Wyoming Mines of the Union Pacific Coal Company," Mine Inspectors' Institute *Proceedings* 29 (1938): 49-54, and his "Fifteen Years of Safety Work in Bituminous Coal Mines," AIME *Transactions* 138 (1938): 468-76.

66. George Pryde, "Corrected Goggles for Mine Workers," *Mechanization* 1 (Dec. 1937): 10-12. The transfer of hiring is from R. R. Knill, "Training Personnel in the Problems of Mechanical Mining in Bituminous Coal Mining," NSC *Proceedings* 30 (1941): 492-94. See also Union Pacific Coal Company, *History of the Union Pacific Coal Mines, 1868-1940* (Omaha, 1940), chap. 26; Montgomery Budd, "Union Pacific Coal Company: The Safety Program," *Explosives Engineer* 30 (May-June 1952): 90-97; and George Pryde, "The Union Pacific Coal Company, 1868 to August 1952," *Annals of Wyoming* 25 (July 1953): 191-205.

67. Elsworth Shriver, "Factory Methods Bring Attendance at Nellis Mine under Control of Management," *Coal Age* 38 (Sept. 1933): 297-98. See also G. N. McLellan, "Saving Lives and Limbs by Systematic Planning," *Coal Age* 36 (May 1931): 243-46.

68. Frank Fugate, Appalachian Oral History Project, Alice Lloyd College; Nicholas Evans to James Roderick, May 8, 1917, GC; C. A. Sine to F. E. Taggart, Feb. 20, 1923, box 489, SCCC.

69. Consolidation's safety courts are noted in F. E. Bedale, "Haulage Accidents and How They May Be Avoided," Coal Mining Institute of America *Proceedings* 45 (1931): 77-86.

70. Dan Harrington, "Bonuses to Encourage Safe Work and for Work Safely Done," BM *Information Circular* 6625 (Washington, D.C., 1932); B. Grady [Carrs Fork Coal] to the Women Folk of Our Men, Jan. 1940, box 3082, GCF.

71. Scott Turner to E. F. Stevens [Union Colliery], Feb. 17, 1932, box 1388, GCF. For two of the large number of bureau publications on these topics, see A. U. Miller, "Safety as Affected by Supervision and Discipline," BM *Information Circular* 6194 (Washington, D.C., 1929), and Dan Harrington, "Accident Costs and Safety Dividends," BM *Information Circular* 6855 (Washington, D.C., 1935), which employs Heinrich's rule of four. Beginnings of the inspection service are in BM, *Annual Report, 1924* (Washington, D.C., 1924), 12-13.

72. The safety course is briefly described in J. J. Forbes to Dan Harrington, July 14, 1930, box 611, GCF. Dan Harrington et al., "The Joseph A. Holmes Safety Association and Its Awards," BM *Bulletin* 421 (Washington, D.C., 1940); E. B. Swanson to N. S. Greensfelder [editor of *Explosives Engineer*], Apr. 1, 1924, box 1225, GCF; "Enter the National Safety Competition," *Explosives Engineer* 3 (Jan. 1925): 16-21.

73. Alabama's efforts to crack down are described in W. B. Hillhouse [chief mine inspector of Alabama], "Prevention of Fatalities from Roof Falls," NSC *Proceedings* 20 (1931): 218-20. Bureau praise is in Dan Harrington to W. B. Hillhouse, Apr. 5 and 12, 1932, box 1591, GCF. The publication was Arthur Murray and Dan Harrington, "Accident Experience of the Coal Industry of Utah for the Period 1918 to 1929,"

BM *Information Circular* 6530 (Washington, D.C., 1931). See also O. F. McShane to Harrington, Jan. 7, 1932; McShane to Harrington, Jan. 28, 1932; McShane, Circular Letter to Operators, Jan. 6, 1932; and McShane, Circular Letter to Inspectors, Jan. 6, 1932; all in box 1184, GCF.

74. Dan Harrington to John B. Andrews, June 20, 1930, box 1190, GCF; George Rice, Memo Regarding Mine Explosions, Jan. 2, 1926, box 461, GCF.

75. Walter Glasgow to Sidney Hale [editor of *Coal Age*], Oct. 23, 1929; William Jennings to Glasgow, Nov. 22, 1928; Glasgow to Jennings, Nov. 28, 1928; all in box 20, GC. See also Glasgow to Vesta Coal, Dec. 28, 1927, and Glasgow to L. E. Young [vice president, Pittsburgh Coal], June 28, 1928, box 9, GC.

76. The 1912 circular and responses are in file 442, box 1, Selected General Correspondence, BM, Record Group 70, National Archives.

77. The special appropriation is reported in "Bureau Studies Falls of Roof and Coal," *Coal Age* 30 (Aug. 19, 1926): 248. See also J. W. Paul to Scott Turner, Feb. 16, 1927, box 213, GCF, who makes it clear that the initiative came from Congress. The claim that the bureau did not know how to study roof falls is in Rice to D. A. Lyon, Oct. 18, 1925, box 213, GCF. A brief history of roof bolting is in Edward Thomas, "Roof Bolting in the United States," BM *Information Circular* 7583 (Washington, D.C., 1950).

78. On the results of World War I, see Dan Harrington and W. J. Fene, "Are New Hazards Being Introduced in Coal Mines Faster Than Existing Hazards Are Eliminated?" BM *Information Circular* 7140 (Washington, D.C., 1940).

79. Margaret Schoenfeld, *Physical Conditions in American Bituminous Coal Mines* (N.p., 1930; copy in Department of Labor library), suggests that pillar extraction was widespread in the late 1920s. "Report of Fatal Accident to E. S. Pennington," box 482, SCCC. The increasingly dangerous character of anthracite mining is noted in "Anthracite Mine Finds That Safety Lies in Safety-Minded Men," *Coal Age* 40 (Jan. 1935): 13–15. The increased dangers from pillar extraction and mining in caved ground at Hudson Collieries are noted in Carl Peterson to Cadwallader Evans, Sept. 24, 1925, box 1, file 1, and Cadwallader Evans to All Superintendents, Feb. 25, 1933, box 1, file 5, Carl Peterson Papers, Historical Collections and Labor Archives, Penn State University.

80. C. G. Brehm et al., "Safety at the M. A. Hanna Properties," AMC *Journal* 18 (Apr. 1932): 13–16, 31–32; E. L. Berger, "Constructive Safety Work," Illinois Mining Institute *Proceedings* 43 (1934): 109–12; Washington State, *Annual Report of Coal Mines* (Olympia, 1927), 7. A more positive assessment of Washington's safety committees is in Simon Ash, "Safety Committees in the Coal Mines of the State of Washington," BM *Information Circular* 6283 (Washington, D.C., 1930).

81. Joseph Davies, "Report of Explosion, Stonega Coke and Coal," Sept. 10, 1934, box 1967, GCF. Charlie Campbell is from Appalachian Oral History Project, Alice Lloyd College.

82. Cadwallader Evans, "Safety Problems Faced in Anthracite Coal Mining," NSC *Proceedings* 28 (1939): 455–57; Simon Ash to J. J. Forbes, Aug. 29, 1939, box 3082, GCF. For Evans's efforts, which consisted mostly of denying the need to spend money on safety and blaming his superintendents, see Minutes of Staff Meeting, May 4, 1929, and Feb. 14, Apr. 8, and May 29, 1930, microfilm reel 57, Office Files, HCP; and Cadwallader Evans to All Colliery Superintendents, Nov. 23, 1927, and Evans to Walter Glasgow, Jan. 5, 1928, box 9, GC. See also Carl Peterson, "Safety Key Men," NSC *Proceedings* 28 (1939): 457–59.

83. Dan Harrington to F. E. Cash, Oct. 21, 1930, box 779, GCF. The costs are from

testimony of E. A. Holbrook in House Committee on Mines and Mining, *Hearings to Provide Additional Mine Rescue Stations Etc., Looking to Greater Safety in the Mining Industry*, 68th Cong., 2d sess., 1924, 39. Mine net income was 36 cents per ton in 1922, according to U.S. Coal Commission, *Report* (Washington, D.C., 1924), 4:2226.

84. For claims that excessive competition worsened the dangers of mining, see Joseph A. Holmes, "Prevention of Coal Mine Accidents," *Mines and Minerals* 30 (Jan. 1910): 329; "Federal Mining Law," United Mine Workers *Journal* 26 (Nov. 4, 1915): 4; "Organization and Uniform Laws for Safety," United Mine Workers *Journal* 26 (Dec. 30, 1915): 4; and William Graebner, *Coal-Mining Safety in the Progressive Period* (Lexington: University Press of Kentucky, 1976), chap. 5. On market power in the anthracite industry, see Eliot Jones, *The Anthracite Coal Combination in the United States* (Cambridge: Harvard Univ. Press, 1914), who claims that while the industry was characterized by price cutting before 1898, collusion had become effective by the twentieth century, and in 1907 twelve major producers controlled about 90 percent of output. A variant of the argument connected excessive competition to lax mine laws. Yet the failure of Pennsylvania to press for hard hats and the periodic efforts of some states to tighten enforcement suggest that much more could have been done.

85. Annual Report of Operating Department, 1921, box 211, SCCC; Dan Harrington to H. I. Smith, Apr. 9, 1924, box 1222, GCF. F. G. Tryon et al., "Drastic Liquidation of Excess Mine Capacity Brightens Prospects for Future," *Coal Age* 36 (Feb. 1931): 79–81, notes excess capacity and describes the decline in the number of mines. In a letter to Dan Harrington, Sept. 28, 1928, box 779, GCF, West Virginia's mine superintendent, Robert Lambie, claimed that the low price of coal discouraged the hiring of supervisors. See also Circular Letter, Aug. 22, 1928, which contains the quotation from Glasgow, and Richard Maize to Walter Glasgow, Aug. 27, 1928, both in box 5, GC.

86. Joseph Davies, "Report on Robert Gage Coal," Nov. 28, 1928, and Charles Coryell [Robert Gage Coal], to Scott Turner, Nov. 30, 1928, box 772, GCF.

87. "Mine Accidents," AMC *Journal* 15 (Oct. 1929): 722; J. C. Bryden to Walter Glasgow, Feb. 16, 1929, box 9, GC.

88. Attendance statistics are from NSC *Proceedings* 11 (1922): 478–49. Francis Feehan, "Remarks," NSC *Proceedings* 18 (1929): 219; Harry Gandy, "Keeping Everlastingly at It," NSC *Proceedings* 16 (1927): 208–13.

89. Eugene McAuliffe, "Accident Prevention in Its Broader Phases," NSC *Proceedings* 16 (1927): 231–42.

90. Robert Lambie, "Remarks," and C. F. Richardson, "Remarks," National Coal Association *Proceedings* 13 (1930): 37–42 and 42–43; Milton Fies, "The Safety Plan of the National Coal Association," NSC *Proceedings* 20 (1931): 196–202.

91. For discussions of hard-rock mining, see the Note on Sources. On technological change, see Y. S. Leong et al., *Technology, Employment, and Output per Man in Copper Mining*, U.S. Works Projects Administration National Research Project Report E-12 (Philadelphia, 1940); N. Yaworski et al., *Technology, Employment, and Output per Man in Iron Mining*, U.S. Works Projects Administration National Research Project Report E-13 (Philadelphia, 1940); and Vivian Spenser, *Production, Employment, and Productivity in the Mineral Extractive Industries, 1880–1938*, U.S. Works Projects Administration National Research Project Report S-2 (Philadelphia, 1940).

92. On the number of mines and companies, see *Sixteenth Census of the United States, 1940: Mineral Industries, 1939*, vol. 1, *General Summary and Industry Statistics* (Washington, D.C., 1944), 321 and 384. For concentration in copper, iron, and soft coal, see U.S. Federal Trade Commission, *Report on the Copper Industry* (Washington, D.C., 1947), table 39; U.S. Temporary National Economic Committee, *Iron and Steel Indus-*

try, Iron Ore, pt. 18 of *Investigation of Concentration of Economic Power*, 76th Cong., 2d sess. (Washington, D.C., 1940), exhibits 1352 and 1353; and Morton Baratz, *The Union and the Coal Industry* (New Haven: Yale Univ. Press, 1955), xv.

93. This discussion of metal mine safety work relies on William Conibear, "System of Safety Inspection of the Cleveland-Cliffs Iron Co.," Lake Superior Mining Institute *Proceedings* 17 (1912): 94-111; Dwight Woodbridge, "Mine Accident Prevention at Lake Superior Iron Mines," BM *Technical Paper* 30 (Washington, D.C., 1913); Lake Superior Metal Mine Prevention of Accidents Conference, June 19 and 20, 1919, *Report* (Washington, D.C., 1919); Dan Harrington, "Accident Prevention in the Mines of Butte, Montana," BM *Technical Paper* 229 (Washington, D.C., 1920); Richard Ageton, "Safety Work at Ironwood, Michigan," BM *Report of Investigation* 2251 (Washington, D.C., 1921); and F. S. Crawford, "Safety Organizations at Lake Superior Iron Mines," BM *Technical Paper* 515 (Washington, D.C., 1932). See also C. W. Goodale and John L. Boardman, "Bureau of Safety of Anaconda Copper Mining Company," AIME *Transactions* 68 (1922): 8-32; William Conibear, "An Appraisal of Safety Activities: The Cleveland-Cliffs Iron Company," and A. A. Bawden [Pickands, Mather], "Discussion," NSC-Lake Superior Mine Safety Association *Proceedings* 16 (1939): 29-36 and 36-39; E. D. Gardner and D. J. Parker, "Safety Organizations in Arizona Copper Mines," BM *Technical Paper* 452 (Washington, D.C., 1929); R. I. C. Manning and Thomas Soule, "Safety at the Morenci Branch of the Phelps Dodge Corporation, Morenci, Arizona," BM *Information Circular* 6351 (Washington, D.C., 1930); R. I. C. Manning and Albert Tallon, "Safety at the Old Dominion Copper Mine, Globe, Arizona," BM *Information Circular* 6546 (Washington, D.C., 1931); and Benjamin F. Tillson, "Accident Prevention by the New Jersey Zinc Co.," *EMJ* 98 (Dec. 12, 1914): 1034-39, and "Recording of Accidents and Safety Measures Employed by the New Jersey Zinc Co.," *EMJ* 103 (Apr. 7, 1917): 627-34. The best modern discussions of metal mine safety work are Alan Derickson, *Workers' Health, Workers' Democracy* (Ithaca, N.Y.: Cornell Univ. Press, 1988), chap. 8, and Larry Lankton, *Cradle to Grave: Life, Work, and Death in Michigan Copper Mines* (New York: Oxford Univ. Press, 1991), chap. 8.

94. A. A. Bawden [Pickands, Mather], "Safety Accomplishments during the Past 25 Years by an Old Timer," NSC *Proceedings* 29 (1940): 522-27.

95. Manning and Soule, "Safety at the Morenci Branch"; Manning and Tallon, "Safety at the Old Dominion Copper Mine," 14.

96. Hiring at Phelps Dodge is discussed in Gardner and Parker, "Safety Organizations in Arizona Copper Mines."

97. The Quincy supervisor is quoted in Lankton, *Cradle to Grave*, 141. Benjamin Tillson, "Accident Prevention"; Dan Harrington, "Accident Prevention in the Mines of Butte, Montana"; Gardner and Parker, "Safety Organizations in Arizona Copper Mines"; F. S. Crawford, "Safety Posters at the Calumet and Hecla Mines," BM *Information Circular* 6827 (Washington, D.C., 1935).

98. Accident figures for Phelps Dodge are from Manning and Tallon, "Safety at the Old Dominion Copper Mine." The original data are per thousand manshifts; in the text the data are multiplied by 300 to convert them to 300-day workers. The employment share is from Federal Trade Commission, *Report on the Copper Industry*, table 25.

99. M. D. Kirk to Scott Turner, Nov. 7, 1932, box 1582, GCF. On Alabama, see Dan Harrington to F. E. Cash, Apr. 13, 1931, box 1400, GCF. For deteriorating safety at Stonega, see A. R. Gordon to J. D. Rogers, Dec. 1, 1933; Gordon to N. H. Ingles, Nov. 30, 1933; and Rogers to A. H. Reeder, Dec. 1, 1933, all in box 469, SCCC. "Preliminary Report of the Explosion, Duvin Mine, Duvin Coal Co.," July 14, 1939, box 3078, GCF.

100. Ivan Given, "Wide Safety Gains Reflect Cooperation of Management and Men at Knox Consolidated Mines," *Coal Age* 40 (May 1935): 183-87.

101. On Phelps Dodge, see "Mine Experience Shows Value of Safety Shoes," *NSN* 28 (Aug. 1933): 36. The price of toes is from D. W. Jones, "Safety without Decreasing Production or Increasing Production Cost," AMC *Journal* 22 (Sept. 1936): 72-76.

102. C. Lorimer Colburn, "Stiff Hats for the Protection of Miners against Falling Rock," BM *Report of Investigation* 2124 (Washington, D.C., 1920); "Safety Work a Paying Proposition at Madeira, Hill Collieries," *Coal Age* 38 (June 1933): 177-79. Early safety glasses are referred to in "Eye Accidents to Coal Miners," *SE* 36 (Sept. 1918): 208. George Pryde, "Corrected Goggles for Mine Workers," *Mechanization* 1 (Dec. 1937): 10-12, 32; V. O. Murray, "Benefits Accruing from the Wearing of Goggles by Underground and Surface Employees at Properties of the Union Pacific Coal Company," Rocky Mountain Coal Mining Institute *Proceedings* 34 (1935): 87-89; "You Can't Sell Coal at a Profit If You Buy Eyes on the Side," *Coal Age* 43 (Feb. 1938): 89.

103. For evidence that use of personal protective equipment was voluntary, see E. L. Berger [Bell and Zoller], "Constructive Safety Work," Illinois Mining Institute *Proceedings*, 1934, 109-12; Jeffers, "Safety in the Mines of the Ford Collieries Co.", BM *Information Circular* 6339 (Washington, D.C., 1930); "Safety at Hanna Coal," *Coal Age* 39 (Dec. 1935): 480-83; "Staff Meeting, Edy Creek Colliery," Mar. 29 and Aug. 13, 1937, microfilm reel 40, Office Files, HCP; and F. G. Wilcox [Price-Pancost Coal] to Walter Glasgow, Jan. 4, 1930, box 20, GC. For the survey, see C. E. Berner, "Standards for Safety Clothing and Their Relation to Accident Reduction," AIME *Transactions* 157 (1944): 124-37. See also R. D. Currie and W. J. Fene, "Protective Clothing in the Mining Industry," BM *Information Circular* 6724 (Washington, D.C., 1933); West Virginia Department of Mines, *Annual Report, 1936-1938*; and Alabama Department of Mines, *Annual Report, 1938*, 54.

104. A good brief survey of unionism in coal is David Brody, *In Labor's Cause* (New York: Oxford Univ. Press, 1993), chap. 4. For union views on the safety of nonunion mines, see, for example, "Needless Slaughter," UMW *Journal* 35 (July 15, 1924): 6, and "Two More," UMW *Journal* 37 (Feb. 1, 1926): 6. On Washington's safety committees, see Simon Ash to Dan Harrington, Dec. 22, 1929, box 988, GCF. Eugene McAuliffe's remarks are in a letter to George Rice, Mar. 31, 1927, box 593, GCF. See also Ash, "Safety Committees in the Coal Mines of the State of Washington." The conference is noted in "Mine Safety Conference to Be Called," UMW *Journal* 50 (Jan. 1, 1939): 9.

105. Dan Harrington to Simon Ash, Jan. 3, 1930, box 988, GCF. Section 8 of the code is in "Bituminous Coal Flies the Blue Eagle," *Coal Age* 38 (Oct. 1933): 327-28, 350-53. Feehan is quoted in "Miners' Safety and Health," *Coal Age* 39 (Nov. 1934): 424-26. For a modern discussion that also emphasizes problems of trust, see Thomas Kochan et al., *The Effectiveness of Union-Management Safety and Health Committees* (Kalamazoo, Mich.: Upjohn Institute for Employment Research, 1977).

106. For operators' worries, see "Is Safety Imperiled by New Deal?" *Coal Age* 39 (June 1934): 227, 233. "Miners' Safety and Health," *Coal Age* 39 (Nov. 1934): 424-26.

107. The Arkansas experience is from "Double Entry System in Arkansas," *Coal Age* 6 (Sept. 5, 1914): 372-73, and Francis Feehan to J. J Forbes, Jan. 3, 1934, Dan Harrington to Feehan, Feb. 5, 1934, and Feehan to Harrington, Feb. 5, 1934, box 1968, GCF.

108. Yablonski's remarks are in "Report of Joint Commission on Complaint RE: Wearing of Safety Caps and Goggles, Crescent Local Union vs. Pittsburgh Coal Co.," Mar. 14, 1934, box 1969, GCF. United Mine Workers, *Wage Agreements, Bituminous Coal Industry, 1935-1937, Together with the Guffey-Snyder Coal Stabilization Act and the Appalachian Agreement* (N.p., n.d.).

109. Dan Harrington, "Effect of Mechanization of the Coal-Mining Industry upon the Frequency and Severity of Accidents," BLS *Bulletin* 536 (Washington, D.C., 1931), 183-91; Dan Harrington, "Growth of Mechanization Means New Problems in Safety,"

Coal Age 34 (May 1929): 282–85; Dan Harrington, "Safety Record of Coal Industry Shows Improvement Despite Increasing Hazards," *Coal Age* 40 (July 1935): 295–97. That electricity should be banned is from Dan Harrington to C. W. Jeffers, Mar. 10, 1930, box 1189, GCF.

110. "Mechanization and Safety," AMC *Journal* 14 (Oct. 1928): 745. For a few of the many similar articles stressing the connection between mechanized loading, concentration of work, and better supervision, see Patrick Mullen, "New Mining Method in the Connelsville Region," *Coal Age* 10 (Oct. 28, 1916): 700–703; Alphonse Brodsky, "Machine Loading Advances by Bounds during Past Year," *Coal Age* 27 (Jan. 15, 1925): 67–70; Lyman Fearn, "Has Mechanized Mining Brought Safer Coal Mining?" AMC *Journal* 20 (Feb. 1934): 31–32; L. E. Young et al., "Reducing Accidents in Mechanized Loading," AMC *Journal* 15 (July 1929): 540–45; and "Safety Makes Gains with Increased Mechanization in Rocky Mountain States," *Coal Age* 39 (Apr. 1934): 132–34.

111. The quotation is from Paul Weir, "Mechanized Mines vs. Non-mechanized Mines—Their Relation to Safety," NSC *Proceedings* 27 (1938): 550–52. Jerome White, "Mechanization Necessitates Management Changes," *Coal Age* 31 (Apr. 14, 1927): 529–31, stressed the need for mass production in coal mining. Calculations by the author; the Bureau of Mines changed its method of calculating underground manhours in 1942. To make the figures comparable, I have recalculated the later data using the bureau's earlier methods.

112. Robert Schultz [Utah deputy coal mine inspector] to Dan Harrington, Dec. 28, 1931, box 1184, GCF; "Preliminary Report of the Explosion, Duvin Mine, Duvin Coal Company," July 14, 1939, box 3078, GCF. The number of explosions is from Humphrey, "Historical Summary of Coal Mine Explosions," 41. Dan Harrington to W. W. Adams, May 9, 1927, box 606, GCF; Dan Harrington, "Hazards in Connection with Concentrated Coal Mining," BM *Information Circular* 6070 (Washington, D.C., 1928); Harrington and Fene, "Are New Hazards Being Introduced in Coal Mines Faster Than Existing Hazards Are Eliminated?" On West Virginia, see "Crossbars at Face Cut Accidents," *Mechanization* 6 (Sept. 1942): 76–77.

113. Data in A. U. Miller, "Coal Mine Mechanization and Accident Frequency Rate of Hand and Mechanical Loading in Illinois," BM *Information Circular* 7063 (Washington, D.C., 1939), allow estimation of the following relationship:

$$\ln(FR) = 0.0008(\text{Pct. Mech. Loaded})$$
$$(0.43)$$
$$R^2 = 0.09; \text{D.W.} = 1.97; N = 177$$

FR is the fatality rate per million manhours. The equation also contains a set of company dummy variables as well as controls for days worked and mine size and a trend. It is manhour-weighted using a TSP routine and estimated using the Cochran-Orcutt correction. The figure in parentheses is a *t*-ratio.

114. Dan Harrington, "What's Wrong with Mine Safety Programs?" AMC *Journal* 23 (Apr. 1937): 18–31, reprinted as BM *Information Circular* 6958 (Washington, D.C., 1937); Harrington and Fene, "Are New Hazards Being Introduced in Coal Mines Faster Than Existing Hazards Are Eliminated?"

115. The information on Pond Creek is mostly from M. J. Ankeny et al., "Final Report on Gas and Dust Explosion, Jan. 10, 1940, in Mine No. 1 of the Pond Creek Pocahontas Company, Bartley, McDowell County, West Virginia" [1940], box 3301, GCF. That the mine was one of the most gassy in the country is from Dan Harrington to Philip Drinker, Feb. 3, 1940, box 3301, GCF.

116. The information on Willow Grove is from J. J. Forbes et al., "Final Report,

Explosion Willow Grove No. 10 Mine, Hanna Coal Company of Ohio, Neffs, Ohio, Mar. 16, 1940" [1940], box 3301, GCF.

CHAPTER SEVEN. CONCLUSION

Epigraphs: Adam Smith, *An Inquiry into the Nature and Causes of the Wealth of Nations* (New York: Modern Library, 1937), 164; T. T. Read to George Rice, Aug. 12, 1925, box 213, GCB.

1. On the effects of economic development on the composition of output and employment, see William Baumol, "The Macroeconomics of Unbalanced Growth," *American Economic Review* 57 (June 1967): 415-26. See also Victor Fuchs, *The Service Economy* (New York: NBER, 1968), chap. 4, and Robert Costrell, "The Effects of Technical Progress on Productivity, Wages, and the Distribution of Employment," in *The Impact of Technological Change on Employment and Economic Growth*, ed. Richard Cyret and David Mowery (Washington, D.C.: National Academy of Sciences, 1988), 73-130.

2. For budget studies of turn-of-the-century urban households, see Louise More, *Wage Earners' Budgets* (New York: Henry Holt, 1907). Jeffrey Williamson, "Consumer Behavior in the Nineteenth Century: Carroll D. Wright's Massachusetts Workers in 1875," *Explorations in Entrepreneurial History* 4 (Winter 1967): 98-135, analyzes early consumer behavior. For other budget studies and a general discussion of the impact of productivity growth on the quality of life, see William Baumol et al., *Productivity and American Leadership: The Long View* (Cambridge: MIT Press, 1989), chap. 3. Hendrick Houthakker and Lester Taylor, *Consumer Demand in the United States* (Cambridge: Harvard Univ. Press, 1970), provide econometric estimates of the income and price elasticity of demand for food.

3. On agricultural productivity, see Harold Barger and Hans Lansberg, *American Agriculture, 1899-1939: A Study of Output, Employment, and Productivity* (New York: NBER, 1942). Willis Peterson and Yoav Kislev, "The Cotton Harvester in Retrospect: Labor Displacement or Replacement," *Journal of Economic History* 47 (Mar. 1986): 199-216, argue that rising manufacturing wages reduced the labor supply in cotton production, thereby inducing mechanization.

4. Floyd Clymer, *Album of Historical Steam Traction Engines and Threshing Equipment* (New York: Bonanza Books, 1949), 3. Kansas data are from Kansas State Board of Health, "Agricultural Accidental Death Report" (Topeka, 1958); "Kansas Accidental Deaths" (Topeka, 1939); and "Report of Agricultural Accident Mortality in Kansas, 1950" (Topeka, 1950). See also National Safety Council, *Accident Facts, 1940* (Chicago, 1940); C. L. Hamilton, "Agriculture's Safety Challenge," *Agricultural Engineering* 26 (Apr. 1945): 145-48; and Merlin Hansen, "Reducing Tractor Fatalities," *Agricultural Engineering* 47 (Sept. 1966): 472-74.

5. On productivity growth in trade and services, see Harold Barger, *Distribution's Place in the American Economy since 1869* (Princeton: NBER, 1955), chap. 1, and Fuchs, *Service Economy*. On the role of technological change and wage/price-induced substitution in manufacturing, see, for example, Louis Cain and Donald Paterson, "Biased Technological Change, Scale, and Factor Substitution in American Industry, 1850-1919," *Journal of Economic History* 46 (Mar. 1986): 153-64.

6. Productivity and market changes in copper mining are discussed in Y. S. Leong et al., *Technology, Employment, and Output per Man in Copper Mining*, U.S. Works Projects Administration National Research Project Report E-12 (Philadelphia, 1940), and Larry Lankton, *Cradle to Grave* (New York: Oxford Univ. Press, 1991).

7. On iron mining, see N. Yaworski et al., *Technology, Employment, and Output per*

Man in Iron Mining, U.S. Works Projects Administration National Research Project Report E-13 (Philadelphia, 1940).

8. BM, *Mineral Resources of the United States, 1927*, pt. 2 (Washington, D.C., 1928), 404–25; Arthur Little and R. V. Kleinschmidt, "Coal Consumption as Affected by Increased Efficiency and Other Factors," Second International Conference on Bituminous Coal *Proceedings* (Pittsburgh) 1 (1928): 110–71; F. G. Tryon and H. O. Rogers, "Statistical Studies of Progress in Fuel Efficiency," Second World Power Conference *Transactions* (Berlin), 1930:343–64.

9. Tryon's remarks are in BM, *Mineral Resources of the United States, 1926*, pt. 2 (Washington, D.C., 1927), 447.

10. These data are from BM, *Mineral Resources of the United States, 1930* (Washington, D.C., 1933), tables 64–67; BM, *Minerals Yearbook, 1940* (Washington, D.C., 1940), table 17; and Little and Kleinschmidt, "Coal Consumption as Affected by Increased Efficiency." L. P. Alford, "Technical Changes in Manufacturing Industries," in Committee on Recent Economic Changes of the President's Conference on Unemployment, *Recent Economic Changes* (New York: NBER, 1929), 1:96–166, discusses reasons for efficiency gains in electric power. On fuel use in cement production, see Nicholas Yaworski, *Fuel Efficiency in Cement Manufacture, 1909–1935*, U.S. Works Projects Administration National Research Project Report E-5 (Philadelphia, 1938).

11. The productivity data are from Vivian Spenser, *Production, Employment, and Productivity in the Mineral Extractive Industries, 1880–1938*, U.S. Works Projects Administration National Research Project Report S-2 (Philadelphia, 1940), tables A1 and A2. T. T. Read to George Rice, Aug. 12, 1925, box 213, GCB.

12. Andrew Prouty, *More Deadly Than War: Pacific Coast Logging, 1827–1981* (New York: Garland, 1988).

13. "Decline in demand" is from Alfred J. Van Tassel, *Mechanization in the Lumber Industry*, U.S. Works Projects Administration National Research Project Report M-5 (Philadelphia, 1940), 111. The rise in wood prices is from Robert Manthy, *Natural Resource Commodities: A Century of Statistics* (Washington, D.C.: Resources for the Future, 1978).

14. On wood use, see Brooke Hindle, ed., *America's Wooden Age* (Tarrytown, N.Y.: Sleepy Hollow Restorations, 1975), and also his *Material Culture of the Wooden Age* (Tarrytown, N.Y.: Sleepy Hollow Restorations, 1981). On conservation, see Van Tassel, *Mechanization in the Lumber Industry*, and Sherry Olson, *The Depletion Myth* (Cambridge: Harvard Univ. Press, 1971).

15. Income elasticities for various products including automobiles may be found in Houthakker and Taylor, *Consumer Demand in the United States*.

16. On the decline of domestic service, see David Katzman, *Seven Days a Week: Women and Domestic Service in Industrializing America* (New York: Oxford Univ. Press, 1978), who claims that domestics were paid more than factory workers but fails to adjust adequately for differences in hours of work. See also Ruth Cowan, "The Industrial Revolution in the Home: Household Technology and Social Change in the Twentieth Century," *Technology and Culture* 17 (Jan. 1976): 1–42, who notes the role of higher wages in attracting women from service to manufacturing.

17. On the role of large firms generally, see Alfred D. Chandler, *The Visible Hand: The Managerial Revolution in American Business* (Cambridge: Harvard Univ. Press, 1977). JoAnne Yates, *Control through Communication: The Rise of System in American Management* (Baltimore: Johns Hopkins Univ. Press, 1989), stresses the importance of new office technologies. Dan Clawson, *Bureaucracy and the Labor Process: The Transformation of U.S. Industry* (New York: Monthly Review Press, 1980), provides a Marxist interpretation of the growth of white-collar work.

18. For discussions of individual companies, see Chandler, *Visible Hand*, and the sources cited therein. On the growth of scientific and technical employment in industry, see David Noble, *America by Design: Science, Technology, and the Rise of Corporate Capitalism* (New York: Alfred A. Knopf, 1977), and Leonard Reich, *The Making of American Industrial Research: Science and Business at GE and Bell, 1876–1926* (New York: Cambridge Univ. Press, 1988). On Dudley's career at the Pennsylvania, see George Fowler, "Origin and Development of the Pennsylvania Railroad Testing Laboratory," *Railway and Locomotive Engineering* 36 (Mar. 1923): 72–74, and "Charles Benjamin Dudley," *Dictionary of American Biography* (New York: Charles Scribner's Sons, 1930), 5:479–80.

19. The growth in salaried employment is from *Sixteenth Census of the United States, 1940: Manufacturers, 1939*, vol. 1 (Washington, D.C., 1942), table 4.

20. The equation is:

$$\ln(\text{Irate}) = 5.06 - 1.92(\text{Female}) - 4.59(\text{Salaried}) - 0.017(\text{Trend})$$
$$(25.9) \qquad\qquad (1.74) \qquad\qquad (1.77)$$
$$R^2 = 0.97; \text{D.W.} = 2.02; N = 28$$

Data are from Pennsylvania Department of Internal Affairs, Bureau of Statistics, *Report on Productive Industries* (Harrisburg, various years), which contains employment by sex, occupational group, and industry, and William McGuire, "Accidents to Working Women in Pennsylvania," *Pennsylvania Labor and Industry* 18 (June 1931): 6–9, which presents accident data by sex and industry. Occupational segregation may have worsened women's health, however; see my "Determinants of Mortality among New England Cotton Mill Workers during the Progressive Era," *Journal of Economic History* 42 (Dec. 1982): 847–64.

21. These safety statistics are from ICC *Accident Bulletin* 114 (1946); Eugene McAuliffe, *A Study of Twenty-three Years' Effort toward Reduction of Accidents in the Mines of the Union Pacific Coal Company* (N.p., n.d.; copy in U.S. Interior Department library); Forrest Moyer et al., "Injury Experience in Coal Mining, 1948," BM *Bulletin* 509 (Washington, D.C., 1949); and "Handbook of Labor Statistics, 1950," BLS *Bulletin* 1016 (Washington, D.C., 1951).

22. "Shipyard Injuries, 1944," BLS *Bulletin* 834 (Washington, D.C., 1946). On the role of the National Committee for the Conservation of Manpower in War Industries, see Division of Labor Standards, "Safeguarding Production in the Arsenal of Democracy" (Washington, D.C., 1942), and Division of Labor Standards, "Men, Minutes, and Victory" (Washington, D.C., 1944). On the role of the NSC, see Ned Dearborn, "The Attack on Accidents," NSC *Proceedings* 32 (1943): 8–15. The fatalities in manufacturing are from "Handbook of Labor Statistics."

23. Recall that there has been some disagreement on the defining characteristics of the "American system" (see chap. 3, n. 2) and that I am using it as a label for American methods that, whatever their defining characteristics, were typically more dangerous than techniques used in Europe.

24. For a discussion of learning by using and its application to the aircraft industry, see Nathan Rosenberg, *Inside the Black Box* (New York: Cambridge Univ. Press, 1982).

25. For several studies that find compensation laws to have had little impact, see John Worrall, ed., *Safety and the Work Force* (Ithaca, N.Y.: ILR Press, 1983).

26. For an analysis of "efficiency jobs" at Ford, see Daniel Raff, "Ford Welfare Capitalism in Its Economic Context," in *Masters to Managers*, ed. Sanford Jacoby (New York: Columbia Univ. Press, 1991), 90–110.

27. "Manager's brains" is from David Montgomery, *The Fall of the House of Labor*

(New York: Cambridge Univ. Press, 1987), 45, who was quoting William Haywood and Frank Bohn.

28. Richard Wokutch, *Worker Protection Japanese Style* (Ithaca, N.Y.: Cornell Univ. Press, 1992), contrasts the engineering orientation of modern American firms with the more behavioral approach of the Japanese.

29. An implication of the analysis is that the modern move to enrich jobs, if not done carefully, could worsen worker safety. For some confirming evidence, see J. T. Saari and J. Lahtela, "Job Enrichment: Cause of Increased Accidents?" *Professional Safety* 24 (Dec. 1979): 28-32.

30. Chauncey Del French, *Railroadman* (New York: Macmillan, 1938), 20. Frank Fugate is from Appalachian Oral History Project, Alice Lloyd College. "Mighty good thing" is from "Safety First," *Railroad Trainman* 39 (Jan. 1922): 13-19. "All bluff" is quoted in David Beyer, "Mechanical Safeguards," IAIABC *Proceedings* 4, in BLS *Bulletin* 248 (Washington, D.C., 1919), 16-26. Cease's remarks are in "An Object Lesson in Safety First," *Railroad Trainman* 32 (Oct. 1915): 985-86.

31. Small firms remain a thorn in the side of the safety movement. See Barbara Marsh, "Workers at Risk: Chance of Getting Hurt Is Generally Far Higher at Smaller Companies," *Wall Street Journal*, Feb. 3, 1994, A1. Old and dangerous equipment can be very long-lived. A junkyard near where I live still uses an ancient, and completely unguarded, metal shear.

32. Max Kossoris, "The War-time Trend in Work Injuries," NSC *Proceedings* 32 (1943): 67-71, at 71.

33. The debate over automatic train control (sometimes termed positive train control) has recently been revived. See Don Phillips, "Rail Crash Lends Urgency to Safety Task," *Washington Post*, Nov. 25, 1993, A3, and Gus Welty, "Is PTC Worth $859 Million?" *RA* 195 (Aug. 1994): 45-46.

34. The difficulties of mandating safer working conditions were rediscovered by the Occupational Safety and Health Administration (OSHA). See, for example, John Mendeloff, *Regulating Safety* (Cambridge: MIT Press, 1979); Lawrence Bacow, *Bargaining for Job Safety and Health* (Cambridge: MIT Press, 1980); and W. Kip Viscusi, *Risk by Choice: Regulating Health and Safety in the Workplace* (Cambridge: Harvard Univ. Press, 1983).

35. Charles Noble, *Liberalism at Work: The Rise and Fall of OSHA* (Philadelphia: Temple Univ. Press, 1986), claims that OSHA's failings result from its political weakness, a claim that is similar to my argument on the efficacy of regulatory threats. For a modern discussion of persuasion, see John Braithwaite, *To Punish or Persuade* (Albany: SUNY Press, 1985).

36. For a similar argument, see Braithwaite, *To Punish or Persuade*.

37. That richer is safer is a claim made by Aaron Wildavsky, *Searching for Safety* (New Brunswick, N.J.: Transaction, 1988). See also Viscusi, *Risk by Choice*, chap. 6. "Nature knows best" was claimed by Barry Commoner, *The Closing Circle* (New York: Alfred A. Knopf, 1972), 43.

APPENDIX ONE. STEAM RAILROAD INJURY AND FATALITY RATES

1. Harold Barger, *The Transportation Industries, 1889-1946: A Study of Output, Employment, and Productivity*, NBER 51 (New York: Columbia Univ. Press, 1951), table B-1.

2. The best discussion of the ICC's accident data is in its *Accident Bulletin* 74 (1919): 66-69, which manages to leave many questions unanswered; the quotation in the text is from 67. Moseley's views are in "Address of Mr. Moseley," *Daily Railway Age*, June 30, 1903, 1237-40.

3. A brief discussion of the effects of the new reporting rules is contained in *Accident Bulletin* 40 (1911). The ICC's concern with safety contests is voiced in *Accident Bulletin* 99 (1930).

4. The discussion of suicides is in *Accident Bulletin* 103 (1934): 1. Subsequent fatalities are reported and discussed in *Accident Bulletin* 99 (1930): 2 and again in *Accident Bulletin* 108 (1939): 5. The BLS treatment of subsequent fatalities is from Max Kossoris, "Manual on Industrial-Injury Statistics," BLS *Bulletin* 667 (Washington, D.C., 1940), 68–69. The treatment of such fatalities in coal mining is from Albert Fay, *Suggested Standard Forms for Mine Statistics* (Washington, D.C.: U.S. Bureau of Mines, 1916).

5. These data were computed by multiplying Kendrick's index of railroad manhours (1929 = 100) for each year by the 1929 figures; see his *Productivity Trends in the United States*, NBER General Series 71 (Princeton: Princeton Univ. Press, 1961), table G-III. The results of these calculations, while unverifiable, are at least plausible. They yield an estimated 2,176 million manhours worked in 1889, which implies 2,945 annual hours per employee. As with the data on injury and fatality rates per worker, the years 1908–10 are treated slightly differently. Here Kendrick's index is multiplied by 1929 manhours on line-haul Class I railroads to make the data more comparable with the accident statistics.

6. Use of accident rates per manhour rather than per worker has virtually no effect on the coefficients of the reporting variables. For trainmen, identical equations (not shown) revealed no statistically significant impact of reporting on fatality rates. Similarly, equations employing traffic density, a time trend, and two reporting dummies to predict passenger fatality rates per billion passenger-miles and "other" fatalities suggest no underreporting of either type of accident.

7. ICC *Accident Bulletin* 106 (1937): 6. The 1939 investigation is in ICC, "Report on Reliability of Railroad Employee Accident Statistics" (N.p., 1942; copy in ICC library), 8.

APPENDIX TWO. COAL AND METAL MINE INJURY AND FATALITY RATES

1. For discussions of the early data, see Frederick Horton, "Coal Mine Accidents in the United States, 1896–1912," BM *Technical Paper* 48 (Washington, D.C., 1913), and Albert Fay, "Coal Mine Fatalities in the United States, 1870–1914," BM *Bulletin* 115 (Washington, D.C., 1916).

2. Horton, "Coal Mine Accidents," 10–12.

3. Albert Fay, *Suggested Standard Forms for Mine Statistics* (Washington, D.C.: U.S. Bureau of Mines, 1916), table 3.

4. Albert Fay, "Report of the Committee on Standardization of Mining Statistics," BM *Technical Paper* 194 (Washington, D.C., 1918).

5. W. W. Adams, "Coal Mine Fatalities in the United States, 1926," BM *Bulletin* 283 (Washington, D.C., 1927).

6. W. W. Adams, "Coal Mine Fatalities in the United States, 1931," BM *Bulletin* 373 (Washington, D.C., 1933).

7. Daniel Harrington, "Safety in the Mining Industry," BM *Bulletin* 481 (Washington, D.C., 1950), 15–16.

8. The bureau publication is *Bulletin* 115. The WPA study is Vivian Spenser, *Production, Employment, and Productivity in the Mineral Extractive Industries, 1880–1938*, U.S. Works Projects Administration National Research Project Report S-2 (Philadelphia, 1940), table B-2.

9. Again the bureau source is *Bulletin* 115. The WPA study is Willard Hotchkiss

et al., *Bituminous-Coal Mining*, U.S. Works Projects Administration National Research Project Report E-9, vol. 2 (Philadelphia, 1939), table B-1.

10. The values for the shares over this period are as follows: fatality costs, 0.0100; labor costs, 0.8434; energy costs, 0.0588; and salaries, 0.0874. These are unweighted state-year averages. Use of weighted data to estimate elasticities of substitution yields very similar figures.

11. Most of these data are from *Fifteenth Census of the United States: Mines and Quarries, 1929, General Report and Report for States and Industries* (Washington, D.C., 1933), or *Sixteenth Census of the United States, 1940: Mineral Industries, 1939*, vol. 1, *General Summary and Industry Statistics* (Washington, D.C., 1944). Wages were computed by dividing the Census total wage bill by manhour data from the Bureau of Mines; salaries are the salary bill divided by the number of salaried workers. The above censuses contain the price of purchased power for 1929 and 1939 only; for 1919 the figures are the average rates charged for commercial power in 1917, from U.S. Bureau of the Census, *Census of Electrical Industries, 1917* (Washington, D.C., 1920), table 87. Total energy costs were taken to be the cost of fuel plus purchased power.

12. The formula is from Hans Binswanger, "The Measurement of Technical Change Biases with Many Factors of Production," *American Economic Review* 64 (Dec. 1974): 964-76. There have been a number of historical studies that have tried to estimate elasticities of substitution and the bias in technological change for American manufacturing. For example, see Louis Cain and Donald Paterson, "Factor Biases and Technical Change in Manufacturing: The American System, 1850-1919," *Journal of Economic History* 41 (June 1981): 341-60; John James, "Structural Change in American Manufacturing," *Journal of Economic History* 43 (June 1983): 433-60; and Louis Cain and Donald Paterson, "Biased Technical Change, Scale, and Factor Substitution in American Industry," *Journal of Economic History* 46 (Mar. 1986): 153-64.

13. The elasticity of substitution between accidents and labor can also be estimated using the following equation derived from a constant elasticity of substitution production function: $\ln(A/L) = a + b * \ln(W/WC)$, plus controls for states and time. Here b, the estimated elasticity of substitution, is 0.28, which is quite close to that presented in the text.

14. Frederick L. Hoffman, "Fatal Accidents in American Metal Mines," *EMJ* 89 (May 5, 1910): 511-13. Hoffman claimed that these figures underestimated true fatality rates because they probably contained some manhours but not fatalities at ore-processing plants. The absence of data from dangerous states is noted in an editorial, "Accidents in Metalliferous Mines," *EMJ* 89 (May 5, 1910): 496. The days worked used to compute 300-day workers for 1894 and 1902 are a weighted average for days worked in copper and iron mining, from Y. S. Leong et al., *Technology, Employment, and Output per Man in Copper Mining*, U.S. Works Projects Administration National Research Project Report E-12 (Philadelphia, 1940), table A-1, and N. Yaworski et al., *Technology, Employment, and Output per Man in Iron Mining*, U.S. Works Projects Administration National Research Project Report E-13 (Philadelphia, 1940), table A-4. The 1894 figure is interpolated.

15. More complete reporting of injuries is noted in Harrington, "Safety in the Mining Industry," 68.

16. Leong, *Technology, Employment, and Output per Man in Copper Mining*, table A-1.

17. Yaworski, *Technology, Employment, and Output per Man in Iron Mining*, table A-4.

NOTE ON SOURCES

In writing this book I have relied mostly on primary printed and archival materials. Many of the journals cited changed names, some more than once. I have not tried to follow all these twists and turns but rather have cited the name that was employed at the time. There is also a modest secondary literature that bears on the history of work safety in the United States, most of it part of studies whose primary focus is business, technology, or some other aspect of labor history. Finally, there is a large literature on modern work safety that must be consulted to discover current professional thinking on many of the issues raised in this book. This note describes the archives and primary printed materials I consulted. I also note the most valuable secondary sources and contemporary literature.

Archives

The collections housed at the Hagley Museum and Library in Wilmington, Delaware, are an exceedingly valuable resource. These included the records of the DuPont Company and the closely associated papers of Willis Harrington, as well as the Pennsylvania Railroad archives and the Stonega Coke and Coal materials. All contain rich documentation of company accidents and safety work. Also at Hagley, the records of the Joseph Bancroft and Sons textile mills provide glimpses of that company's activities; I found only scattered safety-related materials in other collections there. The Hagley library also contains an extensive collection of early photographs depicting railroad and industrial work safety.

At the National Archives, the records of the Bureau of Mines (Record Group 70) are enormous and invaluable. The general records of the Department of Labor (RG 174) and the records of the Bureau of Labor Statistics (RG 257) are disappointing in that they contain little on safety work. In the records of the Interstate Commerce Commission (RG 134) Formal Docket 568 yields insights on the carriers' maneuvering to postpone introduction of air brakes and automatic couplers. Minutes of the commissioners' meetings yield little, however, while most of the records of the Bureau of Safety, except for its un-published accident reports, were apparently destroyed. The records of the Bureau of Locomotive Inspection include materials on individual carriers, but the general correspondence was destroyed. The records of the U.S. Railroad Administration (RG 14) contain a small amount of material on automatic train control and its other safety activities, but most of the records of its Safety Section were also destroyed.

The records of Pennsylvania's Department of Mines (RG 45) in the state archives at Harrisburg are extremely valuable for documenting that state's regulatory efforts. The Historical Collections and Labor Archives at Pennsylvania State University contain the records of the Hudson Coal Company and the papers of Carl Peterson (who worked for Hudson), which together provide a rich source on Hudson's safety work. Also at Penn State, the T. R. Johns papers and the records of the Clearfield Bituminous Coal Company contain small amounts of safety material.

The records of the Chicago, Burlington, and Quincy Railroad at the Newberry Library contain useful evidence on that company's decision to purchase air brakes. Railroad accidents and state safety concerns from the 1850s on are documented in the Records of the Railroad Commission (RG 41), Connecticut State Archives. At Harvard's Baker Library, the records of Lancaster Mills contain detailed injury data beginning in the 1890s but little on company policy; similar material may be found in the Lyman Mills collection. The National Safety Council files in Chicago were disappointingly thin. Similarly, the Charles P. Neill papers at Catholic University contain very little pertaining to Neill's work in the safety movement. Aetna's corporate archives contain glimpses of that company's involvement in safety and worker rehabilitation. The Lucian Chaney papers at Carleton College relate largely to Chaney's early career as a teacher at that institution. The Eastern Regional Coal Archives contain an excellent collection of mining photographs as well as a small amount of archival material. The Denver and Rio Grande materials at Fort Lewis College contain a small cache of detailed documentation of that company's accident investigation procedures.

Primary Printed Material

MANUFACTURING AND GENERAL

Before the twentieth century, sources on work safety in manufacturing are exceedingly thin. State labor bureau reports contain occasional materials, and these are indexed in U.S. Bureau of Labor, *Index of Reports Issued by Bureaus of Labor Statistics in the United States Prior to March 1, 1902* (Washington, D.C., 1902). I found valuable surveys and discussions of safety-related issues from the 1880s on in reports from Iowa, Maine, Michigan, Minnesota, New Jersey, and Ohio. The *Report on Power and Machinery Employed in Manufactures*, vol. 22 of *Tenth Census of the United States, 1880* (Washington, D.C., 1888), contains much detail that is illuminating for what it reveals about machine manufacturers' lack of concern with workers' safety. Similar materials may be found in *Scientific American* from the 1850s on. John Richards, *On the Arrangement, Care, and Operation of Wood-working Factories and Machinery* (New York: E. and F. N. Spon, 1873), yields brief insights into early woodworking safety. Hartford Steam Boiler Inspection and Insurance Company, *The Locomotive*, provides much valuable detail on boiler and (occasionally) power transmission safety.

Beginning about 1910, several states set up employers' liability or workmen's compensation commissions that contain information on working conditions. I found the following most helpful: Employers' Liability Commission of the State of Illinois, *Report* (Springfield, 1910); Massachusetts Commission on Compensation for Industrial Accidents, *Report* (Boston, 1912); Michigan Employers' Liability and Workmen's Compensation Commission, *Report* (Lansing, 1911); and *Report to the Legislature of the State of New York by the Commission Appointed under Chapter 518 of the Laws of 1909 to Enquire into the Question of Employers' Liability and Other Matters, March 19, 1910* (Albany, 1910).

In the twentieth century, most state departments of labor and industrial accident boards discuss safety work or the result of workmen's compensation from time to time in their annual reports and various other publications. The reports of the California Industrial Accident Commission and the Massachusetts Industrial Accident Board often contain extremely useful information on state, company, and insurance company activities. Massachusetts safety orders and inspections may be followed in the annual reports of its State Board of Labor and Industries. Many states also published bulletins containing material on their own and company safety work and on workmen's compensation injuries and payments. These include the New York Department of Labor *Industrial Bulletin*; *California Safety News*; *Illinois Labor Bulletin*; the Pennsylvania Department of Labor *Special Bulletin* and *Pennsylvania Labor and Industry*; and *Wisconsin Labor Statistics* and *Wisconsin Safety Review*. From time to time useful articles are contained in the *Proceedings* of the New York State Industrial Safety Conference and of the Ohio Industrial Commission Safety Congress. The *Proceedings* of the International Association of Industrial Accident Boards and Commissions contain much useful material, especially in the early volumes.

Around 1900 the engineering and trade literature also begins to address safety issues. From 1884 on many of these journals may be accessed in *Engineering Index* or (after 1913) *Industrial Arts Index*. The most valuable sources are the industrial section meetings of the National Safety Council's *Proceedings* and its *National Safety News*. Considerable useful material also exists in the American Iron and Steel Institute *Yearbook*; *American Industries*; *American Machinist*; the American Society of Mechanical Engineers *Journal* and *Transactions*; the Association of Iron and Steel Electrical Engineers *Proceedings*; *Engineering Magazine*; Casualty Actuarial Society *Proceedings*; the International Labor Office *Industrial Safety Survey*; *Iron Age*; *Iron and Steel Engineer*; the National Association of Manufacturers *Proceedings*; the Portland Cement Association *Accident*

Prevention Bulletin; Safety Engineering; Scientific American; and *Travelers Standard.* Modern ideas and concerns can be followed in *Professional Safety* and the *Journal of Safety Research.*

Safety-related materials appear less frequently in *Electrical Worker; Electrical World; Factory: The Magazine of Management; General Electric Review; Industrial Standardization;* the Illuminating Engineering Society *Transactions; Light; Management Engineering;* the National Electric Light Association *Bulletin* and *Proceedings;* and *Paper Industry.*

Journals dealing with health and personnel matters are generally disappointing. There is little in *Industrial Psychology, Journal of Industrial Hygiene, Journal of Industrial Welfare, Personnel Journal,* or *Personnel and Public Health Journal.*

The most valuable federal government sources come from the Department of Labor. U.S. Commissioner of Labor, *Sixteenth Annual Report: Strikes and Lockouts* (Washington, D.C., 1901), provides glimpses of the role of safety issues in labor disturbances. The *Twenty-third Annual Report: Workmen's Insurance and Benefit Funds in the United States* (Washington, D.C., 1909), provides the first comprehensive review of that subject, while the *Twenty-fourth Annual Report: Workmen's Insurance and Compensation Systems in Europe,* 2 vols. (Washington, D.C., 1911), contains accident statistics as well as a detailed review of policy. The multivolume *Report on Conditions of Labor in the Iron and Steel Industry* (Washington, D.C., 1913), is a mine of valuable information on all aspects of labor and contains the first accurate American injury and fatality rates. The Bureau of Labor Statistics *Bulletins* continue to report injury statistics on that industry and contain much other information on workmen's compensation, accidents, and safety work. They are indexed in "BLS Publications 1886–1971," BLS *Bulletin* 1749 (Washington, D.C., 1972). The *Monthly Labor Review* contains similar materials and is indexed in Hugh Hanna, "Subject Index to the *Monthly Labor Review,*" BLS *Bulletin* 695 and 696 (Washington, D.C., 1941 and 1942). Safety is occasionally discussed in the Public Health Service *Bulletins* as well. The most useful is "A Preliminary Survey of the Industrial Hygiene Problem in the United States," *Bulletin* 259 (Washington, D.C., 1939).

Safety work for Great Britain can be found in the *Annual Report of the Chief Inspector of Factories,* while accident statistics are presented in Home Department, *Statistics of Compensation and of Proceedings under the Workmen's Compensation Act, 1906 and the Employers' Liability Act, 1880.* A number of early investigations into working conditions are contained in British Parliamentary Papers, *Industrial Revolution: Factories,* vol. 31 (Shannon: Irish Univ. Press, 1968).

Among the many early discussions of employers' liability, work safety, and compensation, the following are the most important. Crystal Eastman, *Work Accidents and the Law* (New York: Charities, 1910), provides an early and perceptive analysis of the effect of accidents on workers' lives under the regime of employers' liability. An influential assessment of employers' liability and workmen's compensation is Ferdinand Schwedtman and James Emory, *Accident Prevention and Relief* (New York: NAM, 1911). David Beyer, *Industrial Accident Prevention* (Boston: Houghton Mifflin, 1916), and David Van Schaack, *Safeguards for the Prevention of Industrial Accidents* (Hartford: Aetna, 1910), are among the first textbooks on safety engineering. Louis DeBlois, *Industrial Safety Organization for Executive and Engineer* (New York: McGraw-Hill, 1926), emphasizes management responsibility. American Engineering Council, *Safety in Production* (New York, 1928), provides many useful examples of early safety work and is also aimed at managers. Herbert Heinrich, *Industrial Accident Prevention* (New York: McGraw-Hill, 1931), summarizes much early work and was the most influential of the early writers. Hartley Barclay, *Ford Production Methods* (New York, 1936), supplements earlier articles on safety at Ford, and Fred Colvin, *60 Years with Men and Machines* (New York: McGraw-Hill, 1947), provides a rare glimpse of the dangers of early shop practice. Louis Resnick, *Eye Hazards in Industry* (New York: Columbia Univ. Press, 1941), provides perspective on the role of work accidents in causing blindness.

On accident-proneness and related issues, see Eric Farmer, *The Causes of Accidents* (London: Sir Isaac Pitman, 1932); H. M. Vernon, *Accidents and Their Prevention* (New York: Macmillan, 1936); and Boyd Fisher, *The Mental Causes of Accidents* (Boston: Houghton Mifflin, 1922). A more modern review of the literature on accident-proneness that includes some of the important early work is William Haddon et al., eds., *Accident Research* (New York: Harper and Row, 1964). On the role of fatigue and safety, see Josephine Goldmark et al., "Comparison of an Eight Hour Plant and a Twelve Hour Plant," Public Health Service *Bulletin* 106 (Washington, D.C., 1920); Federated American Engineering Societies, *The Twelve Hour Shift in Industry* (New York, 1922); and P. Sargent Florence, *Economics of Fatigue and Unrest* (New York: Henry Holt, 1924).

There is an ephemeral company literature that contains details of individual safety programs. Collections of it may be found at the Library of Congress and at the U.S. Department of Labor library. The U.S. Steel Bureau of Safety, Sanitation, and Welfare *Bulletin* is full of detail, as is the Illinois Steel *Safety Bulletin*. I also used American Car and Foundry, *Safety Work*; Commonwealth Steel, *The Commonwealther*; A. O. Smith, *Shop Safety Bulletin*; the Milwaukee Western Fuel Company *Safety Bulletin*; and the Marathon Paper Company *Safety Bulletin*.

RAILROAD SAFETY

For railroads the best sources of material on early work safety are the reports of the various state commissions. Most are post–Civil War, but Connecticut's and New York's date back to the 1850s. An early overview is provided by "Report of the Committee Appointed to Examine and Report the Causes of Railroad Accidents, the Means of Preventing Their Occurrence, etc.," New York Senate document 13 (Albany, 1853), and a later one in Board of Railroad Commissioners, *Report on Strains on Railroad Bridges of the State* (Albany, 1891). In addition to Connecticut and New York, the most consistently informative reports are those of Colorado, Illinois, Indiana, Iowa, Kansas, Massachusetts, and Ohio, but there are scattered materials in many other state reports as well, which are unfortunately rarely indexed. Valuable insights into the dangers of early railroading are also contained in Ohio Legislature, *Report of the Joint Committee Concerning the Ashtabula Bridge Disaster* (Columbus, 1877). Railroad labor matters are also contained in state labor bureau reports, which as noted above are indexed in U.S. Bureau of Labor, *Index of Reports.*

The railroad technical press becomes increasingly rich throughout the nineteenth century. Fortunately, after 1884 much of it is indexed in *Engineering Index.* The *Engineering News, Railroad Gazette, Railway Review,* and *Railway Age* provide general coverage of all aspects of domestic and foreign railroading including accidents, labor, management, safety, and technology. These need to be supplemented by the large number of more specialized technical journals and society proceedings. The most valuable include the American Railway Association (ARA) *Proceedings;* ARA, Committee on Automatic Train Control, "Automatic Train Control," *Bulletin* 1 (Nov. 1930); ARA, *The American Railroad in Laboratory,* 2 vols. (Washington, D.C., 1934); ARA Safety Section *Proceedings;* ARA Signal Section *Proceedings* and its *The Invention of the Track Circuit* (New York, 1922); and *American Railway Signaling Principles and Practices* (New York, 1934). Specialized aspects of safety and technology are also contained in *Locomotive Engineering, Railroad Car Journal, Railway and Locomotive Engineering, Railway Engineering and Maintenance, Railway Mechanical Engineer,* and *Railway Signal Engineer.*

The *Proceedings* and *Bulletins* of the American Railway Engineering Association and the *Proceedings* of the American Society of Testing Materials are especially valuable for following the attempts to improve steel rails. Early work on rails, locomotives, and bridges is also contained in American Society of Civil Engineers *Transactions;* American Institution of Mining Engineers *Transactions;* and the *Journal of the Franklin Institute.* The *Proceedings* of the Master Car Builders and Master Mechanics Association contain background on the development of air brakes and automatic couplers. I also found some material in the Western Railway Club *Proceedings.*

Beginning in the 1890s, both the U.S. Senate and House Committees on Interstate and Foreign Commerce held hearings on safety appliances, limitations on trainmen's hours, locomotive safety, block signals, full-crew laws, and many other aspects of work safety. These can be accessed using the Congressional Information Service *Congressional Committee Hearings Index* (Washington, D.C., 1981–). Occasional safety-related material is also in the *Reports* of the U.S. Commissioner of Railroads. The most useful executive branch sources on railroad safety are the various ICC publications. Its early *Annual Report* and *Statistics of Railways* contain both accident statistics and general discussions of railroad safety-related matters, as does (in the twentieth century) its *Accident Bulletin.* See also the Bureau of Safety *Accident Report* and *Annual Report,* and the Bureau of Locomotive Inspection *Annual Report.* The commission also issued detailed reports from time to time such as its *Report on Block Signal Systems* (Washington, D.C., 1907); *Report on the Formation of Transverse Fissures in Steel Rails and Their Prevalence on Certain Railroads* (Washington, D.C., 1923);

and *Report on Reliability of Railroad Accident Statistics* (N.p., 1942; copy in ICC library). On signaling, consult also the Block Signal and Train Control Board *Report* (various years). The U.S. Railroad Administration also issued a number of pamphlets detailing its brief safety campaign.

Railroad accident relief, pensions, and labor turnover are discussed in early BLS *Bulletins*. See also U.S. Commissioner of Labor, *Fifth Annual Report, Railroad Labor* (Washington, D.C., 1890); U.S. Industrial Commission, *Report on Transportation* (Washington, D.C., 1901); *Employers' Liability and Workmen's Compensation Commission Report*, 62d Cong., 2d sess., S.D. 338 (Washington, D.C., 1912); M. Riebenack, *Railway Provident Institutions in English Speaking Countries* (Philadelphia, 1905); and U.S. Federal Coordinator of Transportation, *Cost of Railroad Employee Accidents, 1932*, 74th Cong., 1st sess., S.D. 68 (1935).

A good review of all aspects of railroading is *The American Railway: Its Construction, Development, Management, and Appliances* (Secaucus, N.J.: Castle, 1988). Early discussions of accidents and safety are in Charles Francis Adams, *Notes on Railroad Accidents* (New York: Putnam's, 1879), and S. A. Howland, *Steamboat Disasters and Railroad Accidents* (Worcester, 1840). On construction practices, see especially Zerah Colburn and Alexander Holley, *The Permanent Way and Coal-Burning Boilers of European Railways* (New York, 1858), and Arthur Mellen Wellington, *The Economic Theory of the Location of Railways* (New York, 1887). Valuable information on the railroad response to safety legislation is contained in the hard-to-find *Bulletins* of the Special Committee on Relations of Railway Operation to Legislation, which I used at the Library of Congress and the University of Virginia. The Bureau of Railway Economics *Bulletins* discuss safety issues, and its *Automatic Train Control in the United States: A Bibliography* is invaluable. On signaling, see Bramen B. Adams, *The Block System of Signaling on American Railroads* (New York, 1901). Harry Forman, *Rights of Trains* (New York, 1925), provides details on train control.

For British railway safety, a basic source is Great Britain Board of Trade, *General Report on Accidents*. Early safety investigations are contained in British Parliamentary Papers, *Transport and Communications*, vols. 14–15 (Shannon: Irish Univ. Press, 1968). Also important is Royal Commission on Accidents to Railway Servants, *Report into the Causes of Accidents, Fatal and Non-fatal, to Servants of Railway Companies, and of Truck Owners* (London: HMSO, 1900). See also Board of Trade, *Report on a Visit to America, September 19th to October 31st, 1902, by Lieut. Colonel H. A. Yorke* (London, 1903), and Board of Trade, *Third Report of the Committee Appointed to Examine and, Where Necessary, to Test, Appliances Designed to Diminish the Danger to Men Employed in Railway Service*, appendix (London, 1908). Good discussions of British railway safety may also be found in H. Raynar Wilson, *Safety of British Railways* (London: P. S. King, 1909); in *Engineering* (London); and in many of the American railroad journals cited above. International Labor Office, *Automatic Couplers and the Safety of Railway Workers*, Studies and Reports, series F, second section (Safety), no. 1

(Geneva, 1924), provides international comparisons of the use and effects of safety appliances. Both foreign and domestic issues are also discussed in the International Railway Congress Association *Proceedings* and *Bulletin*.

I found a number of reminiscences written by railroad men that discussed early safety and operating procedures, including Chauncey Del French, *Railroadman* (New York: Macmillan, 1938); Charles B. George, *Forty Years on the Rail* (Chicago: R. R. Donnelley, 1887); H. Roger Grant, ed., *Brownie the Boomer* (DeKalb: Northern Illinois Univ. Press, 1991); Ollie H. Kirkpatrick, *Working on the Railroad* (Philadelphia: Dorrance, 1949); Gilbert Lathrop, *Little Engines and Big Men* (Caldwell, Ohio, 1954); and J. Harvey Reed, *Forty Years a Locomotive Engineer* (Prescott, Wash., 1913).

Safety-related materials are also scattered throughout company publications and employee magazines published by the Baltimore and Ohio, the Chicago and Northwestern, the New York Central, the Pennsylvania, and the Union Pacific. Railroad labor journals rarely contain much on safety but from time to time provide the unions' point of view. The most valuable is *Railroad Trainman*, but see also *Railroad Telegrapher*, *Locomotive Engineer*, *Locomotive Firemen and Enginemen's Magazine*, *Railway Conductor*, and *Journal of the Switchmen's Union*.

MINE SAFETY

As with railroads, the best sources on early mine safety are the reports of state mining departments. Pennsylvania's are the most valuable as well as the earliest, but I found virtually all of them to be useful. Some states also investigated mining conditions. I found the following valuable: Ohio Mining Commission, *Report* (Columbus, 1872); Mammoth Mine Commission, "Report," *Pennsylvania Official Documents, 1891*, vol. 6, doc. 24 (Harrisburg, 1892); and West Virginia Mine Investigating Committee, *Report of Hearings* (Charleston, 1909). See also Albert A. Steel, *Coal Mining in Arkansas* (Little Rock, 1910).

Beginning in 1910 the U.S. Bureau of Mines published an immense amount of material on mine employment, safety, and technology, all of which is indexed in Hazel Stratton, "List of Publications Issued by the Bureau of Mines from July 1, 1910, to January 1, 1960," BM *Special Publication* (Washington, D.C., 1960). The House Committee on Mines and Mining held hearings on safety-related issues from time to time, while the Senate Committee on Interstate Commerce investigated labor conditions in the coal fields. See also U.S. Industrial Commission, *Report on Capital and Labor Employed in the Mining Industry* (Washington, D.C., 1901), and U.S. Commission on Industrial Relations, *Final Report and Testimony*, vols. 7–8 (Washington, D.C., 1915). U.S. Coal Commission, *Report*, pt. 3 (Washington, D.C., 1925), discusses accidents and their compensation, inefficiency and waste in mining, and labor unrest and turnover.

Mine safety is also discussed in general engineering publications such as those referenced above. I found especially valuable the following trade publications and society proceedings and transactions (which are usually cited in *Engineering Index*): American Institution of Mining Engineers *Transactions*; American Mining Congress *Journal*, *Proceedings*, and *Yearbook of Coal Mine*

Mechanization; Coal Industry; Coal Mine Management; Colliery Engineer (which becomes *Mines and Minerals*); *Coal Age;* Coal Mining Institute of America *Proceedings; Engineering and Mining Journal; Explosives Engineer;* Illinois Mining Institute *Proceedings;* Lake Superior Mining Institute *Transactions;* Mine Inspectors Institute *Proceedings;* National Coal Association *Proceedings;* and Rocky Mountain Coal Mining Institute *Proceedings.*

For contemporary discussions of mining methods and mine labor, see Hugh Archbald, *The Four Hour Day in Coal* (New York, 1922); Carter Goodrich, *The Miner's Freedom* (Boston: Marshall Jones, 1925); and Andrew Roy, *A History of Coal Miners in the United States* (Columbus, 1902). The United Mine Workers *Journal* (1890–) becomes increasingly interested in safety in the twentieth century, while *Illinois Miner* also contains glimpses of labor's views of safety. The impact of immigrants on mine safety is discussed in U.S. Immigration Commission, *Report on Immigrants in Industries*, vol. 6 (Washington, D.C., 1911). Miners' own voices are contained in the Appalachian Oral History Project, Alice Lloyd College; Carl Oblinger, *Divided Kingdom: Work, Community, and the Mining Wars in the Central Illinois Coal Fields during the Depression* (Springfield: Illinois Historical Society, 1991); and John Brophy, *A Miner's Life* (Madison: Univ. of Wisconsin Press, 1964). The library of the U.S. Department of Labor contains a number of contracts and conferences between mine operators and unions, including *Proceedings of Joint Conference of Coal Operators and Coal Miners of Western Pennsylvania, Ohio, and Indiana* [Cincinnati, Ohio, Mar. 8–29, 1910] (Columbus: Stoneman Press, 1910). A good company history is Union Pacific Coal Company, *History of the Union Pacific Coal Mines, 1868–1940* (Omaha, 1940).

Mine safety in the United Kingdom was the subject of various royal or parliamentary investigations that have been reprinted in British Parliamentary Papers, *Mining Accidents*, vols. 1–10 (Shannon: Irish Univ. Press, 1968). On British practice, see also Great Britain, Mines Department, H.M. Chief Inspector of Mines, *Mines and Quarries: General Report and Statistics* (London, various years), and Great Britain, Home Office, Mines Department, Safety in Mines Research Board, *Papers.* See also the Institution of Mining Engineers *Transactions; Iron and Coal Trades Review;* and *Colliery Guardian.* Especially useful is F. G. Tryon and Margaret Schoenfeld, "Comparison of Physical Conditions in British and American Coal Mines," *Coal and Coal Trade Journal* 35 (Sept. 1 and 8, Oct. 7, and Nov. 4, 1926): 934, 965–67, 1087–89, 1202–6. Mining-related material also appeared in the Institution of Civil Engineers *Proceedings* and U.S. Commissioner of Labor, *Twelfth Special Report: Coal Mine Labor in Europe* (Washington, D.C., 1905).

Secondary Works

MANUFACTURING AND GENERAL

On American and British factory technology, the literature is immense and growing. The best single history is David Hounshell, *From the American Sys-*

tem to Mass Production, 1800–1932: The Development of Manufacturing Technology in the United States (Baltimore: Johns Hopkins Univ. Press, 1984). I also found valuable the analysis and evidence in Alexander J. Field, "Land Abundance, Interest/Profit Rates, and Nineteenth Century American and British Technology," *Journal of Economic History* 43 (June 1983): 405–32, and the many works by Nathan Rosenberg, especially *Technology and American Economic Growth* (New York: Harper and Row, 1972); *The American System of Manufactures* (Edinburgh: Edinburgh Univ. Press, 1969); "Technological Change in the Machine Tool Industry, 1840-1910," *Journal of Economic History* 23 (Dec. 1963): 414-43; and Edward Ames and Nathan Rosenberg, "The Enfield Arsenal in Theory and History," *Economic Journal* 78 (Dec. 1968): 827-42. Paul David provides a sophisticated discussion of many of the issues in *Technical Choice, Innovation, and Economic Growth: Essays on the American and British Experience in the Nineteenth Century* (London: Cambridge Univ. Press, 1975).

On the development of machine tools generally, see Robert Woodbury, *Studies in the History of Machine Tools* (Cambridge: MIT Press, 1972). British and American choice of steam techniques is analyzed in Harlan Halsey, "The Choice between High-Pressure and Low-Pressure Steam Power in America in the Early Nineteenth Century," *Journal of Economic History* 41 (Dec. 1981): 723-44. American woodworking technology is discussed in Brooke Hindle, ed., *America's Wooden Age* (Tarrytown, N.Y.: Sleepy Hollow Restorations, 1975).

There is a small literature that emphasizes safety and its regulation, much of it concerned with boiler explosions. See Louis Hunter, *Steamboats on Western Rivers* (Cambridge: Harvard Univ. Press, 1949), and his *History of Industrial Power in the United States, 1780–1930*, vol. 2, *Steam Power* (Charlottesville: Univ. of Virginia Press, 1985). See also Glenn Weaver, *The Hartford Steam Boiler Inspection and Insurance Company* (Hartford, 1966), and David Denault, "An Economic Analysis of Steam Boiler Explosions in the Nineteenth Century United States" (Ph.D. diss., Univ. of Connecticut, 1993). U.S. Steel's early safety and welfare work gets a skeptical assessment in Charles Gulick, *Labor Policy of the U.S. Steel Co.* (New York: Columbia, 1925). Carl Gersuny, *Work Hazards and Industrial Conflict* (Hanover, N.H.: University Press of New England), ranges widely but not deeply. Andrew Prouty, *More Deadly Than War* (New York: Garland, 1988), discusses the dangers of logging and lumbering but is not very analytic. John W. Hallock, "The Development of Industrial Safety Standards in Pennsylvania" (Ph.D. diss., Univ. of Pittsburgh, 1936), provides a useful guide to one state's activities, as does Donald Rogers, "The Rise of Administrative Process: Industrial Safety Regulation in Wisconsin, 1880-1940" (Ph.D. diss., Univ. of Wisconsin at Madison, 1983).

On the coming of the large firm, see especially Alfred Chandler, *Strategy and Structure* (New York: Doubleday, 1962), and also his *The Visible Hand: The Managerial Revolution in American Business* (Cambridge: Harvard Univ. Press, 1977). Also important is Daniel Nelson, *Managers and Workers: Origins of the New Factory System in the United States, 1880–1920* (Madison: Univ. of Wisconsin Press, 1975), which is one of the very few works to discuss factories' physical layout. Company personnel matters are treated in Sanford Jacoby, *Employing Bureaucracy* (New York: Columbia Univ. Press, 1985). Donald Stabile, "The DuPont Experiments in Scientific Management: Efficiency and Safety, 1911–1919," *Business History Review* 61 (Aug. 1987): 365–86, is one of the few writers to discuss the relation between the safety and efficiency movements.

In the immense literature on labor developments, I found the following the most helpful: David Brody, *Steelworkers in America: The Nonunion Era* (New York: Harper and Row, 1960); Richard Edwards, *Contested Terrain* (New York: Basic Books, 1979); William Lazonick, *Competitive Advantage on the Shop Floor* (Cambridge: Harvard Univ. Press, 1990); and David Montgomery, *The Fall of the House of Labor* (New York: Cambridge Univ. Press, 1987) and *Workers' Control in America* (New York: Cambridge Univ. Press, 1979). For an argument that job risks were an important source of worker militancy, see Robert Asher, "Industrial Safety and Labor Relations in the United States, 1865–1917," in *Life and Labor: Dimensions of American Working Class History*, ed. Charles Stephenson and Robert Asher (Albany: SUNY Press, 1986), 115–30. Gerald Eggert, *Steelmasters and Labor Reform, 1886–1923* (Pittsburgh: Univ. of Pittsburgh Press, 1981), briefly discusses the beginnings of safety in that industry.

Among the vast writings on employers' liability and workmen's compensation, one of the most useful is Lindsey Clark, "The Legal Liability of Employers for Injuries to Their Employees, in the United States," BLS *Bulletin* 74 (Washington, D.C., 1908). Studies of the costs of accidents include Richard Posner, "A Theory of Negligence," *Journal of Legal Studies* 1 (Jan. 1972): 29–96, and Price Fishback, "Liability Rules and Accident Prevention in the Workplace: Empirical Evidence from the Early Twentieth Century," *Journal of Legal Studies* 15 (June 1987): 305–28. Voluntary compensation is discussed by Robert Asher, "The Limits to Big Business Paternalism," in *Dying for Work*, ed. David Rosner and Gerald Markowitz (Bloomington: Indiana Univ. Press, 1987), 19–33.

Good early overviews of workmen's compensation include Ralph Blanchard, *Liability and Compensation Insurance* (New York: Appleton, 1917), and his *Industrial Accidents and Workmen's Compensation* (New York: Appleton, 1917); Walter Dodd, *Administration of Workmen's Compensation* (New York: Commonwealth Fund, 1936); Clarence Hobbs, *Workmen's Compensation Insurance* (New York: McGraw-Hill, 1939); and Arthur Reede, *Adequacy of Workmen's Compensation* (Cambridge: Harvard Univ. Press, 1947). The origins of compensation laws are described in the many articles by Robert Asher, including "The 1911 Wisconsin Workmen's Compensation Law: A Study in Conservative Labor Reform," *Wisconsin Magazine of History* 56 (Winter 1973): 123–40; "Origins of Workmen's Compensation in Minnesota," *Minnesota History* 44 (Winter 1974): 142–53; "Business and Workers' Welfare in the Progressive Era: Workmen's Compensation Reform in Massachusetts, 1880–1911," *Business History Review* 43 (Winter 1969): 452–75; and "Failure and Fulfillment: Agitation for Employers' Liability Legislation and the Origins of Workmen's Compensation in New York State, 1876–1910," *Labor History* 24 (Spring 1983): 199–222. See also Roy Lubove, "Workmen's Compensation and the Prerogatives of Voluntarism," *Labor His-*

tory 8 (Fall 1967): 254-79; Patrick Reagan, "The Ideology of Social Harmony and Efficiency: Workmen's Compensation in Ohio, 1904-1919," *Ohio History* 90 (Winter 1981): 316-31; and Robert Wesser, "Conflict and Compromise: The Workmen's Compensation Movement in New York, 1890-1913," *Labor History* 12 (Summer 1971): 344-72. For Illinois, see Alfred H. Kelly, "A History of the Illinois Manufacturers Association" (Ph.D. diss., Univ. of Chicago, 1938).

Valuable although controversial overviews of work accident law are provided by Lawrence Friedman and Jack Ladinsky, "Social Change and the Law of Industrial Accidents," *Columbia Law Review* 6 (Jan. 1967): 50-82, and Morton Horwitz, *Transformation of American Law* (Cambridge: Harvard Univ. Press, 1977). The functionalist approach is criticized in Christopher Tomlins, "A Mysterious Power: Industrial Accidents and the Legal Construction of Employment Relations in Massachusetts, 1800-1850," *Law and History Review* 6 (Fall 1988): 375-438. See also Jonathan Simon, "For the Government of Its Servants: Law and Disciplinary Power in the Workplace, 1870-1906," *Studies in Law, Politics, and Society* 1993:105-36.

Modern thinking on safety can be accessed through the journals noted above. I also found useful John Grimaldi and R. V. Simonds, *Safety Management* (Homewood, Ill.: Irwin, 1956), and Roland Blake, ed., *Industrial Safety* (Englewood Cliffs, N.J.: Prentice-Hall, 1963). There is also a considerable economic literature. Useful overviews of many of the issues are provided by Lawrence Bacow, *Bargaining for Job Safety and Health* (Cambridge: MIT Press, 1980); John Mendeloff, *Regulating Safety* (Cambridge: MIT Press, 1979); Michael Moore and W. Kip Viscusi, *Compensation Mechanisms for Job Risks* (Princeton: Princeton Univ. Press, 1990); Robert Smith, *The Occupational Safety and Health Act* (Washington: AEI, 1976); W. Kip Viscusi, *Risk by Choice: Regulating Health and Safety in the Workplace* (Cambridge: Harvard Univ. Press, 1983); and John Worrall, ed., *Safety and the Work Force* (Ithaca, N.Y.: ILR Press, 1983).

RAILROADS

Few general histories of railroads or railroading say much about accidents and safety. An important exception is Edward Kirkland, *Men, Cities, and Transportation* (Cambridge: Harvard Univ. Press, 1948), who provides a good discussion of early New England railroad technology, safety, and experience with employers' liability. Stephen Salsbury, *The State, the Investor, and the Railway: Boston and Albany, 1825-1867* (Cambridge: Harvard Univ. Press, 1967), discusses how that carrier modified its management structure in response to accidents. Thomas McCraw, *Prophets of Regulation* (Cambridge: Belknap, 1984), contains the best discussion of Charles Francis Adams as a regulator.

On railroad technology the literature is vast. I found most valuable John H. White, *American Locomotives* (Baltimore: Johns Hopkins Press, 1968), and his *The American Railroad Freight Car* (Baltimore: Johns Hopkins Univ. Press, 1993), as well as Alfred Bruce, *The Steam Locomotive in America* (New York: Norton, 1952). Signaling is discussed in Mary Brignano and Hax McCullough, *The Search for Safety* (New York: Union Switch and Signal, 1981), which also contains a good bibliography. Rail developments are discussed in William H. Sellew, *Steel Rails: Their History, Properties, Strength, and Manufacture* (New York: D. Van Nostrand, 1913). The impact of these changes is evaluated in Albert Fishlow, "Productivity and Technological Change in the Railroad Sector, 1840-1910," in National Bureau of Economic Research, *Output, Employment, and Productivity in the United States after 1800*, Studies in Income and Wealth 30 (New York: NBER, 1966), 583-646.

The best story of the development of automatic couplers and air brakes is Charles Clark, "The Railroad Safety Movement in the United States: Origins and Development, 1869 to 1893" (Ph.D. diss., Univ. of Illinois, 1966). Also valuable is Steven Usselman, "Air Brakes for Freight Trains: Technological Innovation in the American Railroad Industry, 1869-1900," *Business History Review 58* (Spring 1984): 30-50. Train accidents and their causes are expertly discussed in Robert B. Shaw, *Down Brakes: A History of Railroad Accidents, Safety Precautions, and Operating Practices in the United States of America* (London: P. R. Macmillan, 1961).

A fine general discussion of railroad labor is Walter Licht, *Working for the Railroad* (Princeton: Princeton Univ. Press, 1983). Good case studies include Paul Black, "The Development of Management Personnel Policies on the Burlington Railroad, 1860-1900" (Ph.D. diss., Univ. of Wisconsin, 1972); James Ducker, *Men of the Steel Rails: Workers on the Atchison, Topeka, and Santa Fe Railroad, 1869-1900* (Lincoln: Univ. of Nebraska Press, 1983); and David Lightner, *Labor on the Illinois Central Railroad* (New York: Arno, 1977). Kurt Wetzel, "Railroad Management's Response to Operating Employees Accidents," *Labor History* (Summer 1980): 351-68, discusses the origins of railroad safety work. Efforts to stabilize labor are described in Bryce Stewart and Murray Latimer, *Pensions for Industrial and Business Employees*, vol. 3, *Railroad Pensions in the United States and Canada* (New York: Industrial Relations Counselors, 1929).

MINING

The best overview of coal mining is Keith Dix, *Work Relations in the Coal Industry: The Hand Loading Era* (Morgantown: Univ. of West Virginia Press, 1977), and his *What's a Coal Miner to Do?* (Pittsburgh: Univ. of Pittsburgh Press, 1988). Valuable detail on mining and mining methods as well as descriptions of early accidents can be found in Howard Eavenson, *The First Century and a Quarter of American Coal Industry* (Privately printed: Pittsburgh, 1942). Anthony Wallace, *Saint Clair* (New York: Alfred A. Knopf, 1987), is a superb discussion of early anthracite mining and safety. Priscilla Long, *Where the Sun Never Shines* (New York: Paragon, 1989), contains a valuable discussion of western coal mine safety around the turn of the century. Carlton Jackson, *The Dreadful Month* (Bowling Green: Bowling Green Univ. Popular Press 1983), contains much useful information but is marred by the absence of adequate references. Robert Ward and William Rogers, *Convicts, Coal, and the Banner Mine Tragedy* (Tuscaloosa: Univ. of Alabama Press, 1987), is a history of that tragedy. Price Fishback, *Soft Coal, Hard Choices* (New York: Oxford Univ. Press, 1992), supplies an economist's perspective on the coal labor market. Marlene Rikard, "An Experiment in Welfare Capitalism: The Health Care Services of the Tennessee Coal, Iron, and Railroad Company" (Ph.D. diss., Univ. of Alabama, 1983), is a valuable case study of that company's health and safety work.

Good discussions of coal geology, mining methods, and technology are contained in Willard Hotchkiss et al., *Bituminous-Coal Mining*, U.S. Works Projects Administration National Research Project Report E-9 (Philadelphia, 1939); Heinrich Ries, *Economic Geology*, 6th ed. (New York: John Wiley, 1930); and A. T. Shurick, *The Coal Industry* (Boston: Little, Brown, 1924).

Studies that focus on miners' lives and work provide context but rarely say much about safety. I consulted Kathleen Harvey, *The Best-Dressed Miners* (Ithaca, N.Y.: Cornell Univ. Press, 1969); David Corbin, *Life, Work, and Rebellion in the Coal Fields: The Southern West Virginia Miners, 1880–1922* (Champaign: Univ. of Illinois Press, 1981); Dorothy Schweider et al., *Buxton: Work and Racial Equality in a Coal Mining Community* (Ames: Iowa State Univ. Press, 1987); and Ronald Lewis, *Black Coal Miners in America* (Lexington: University Press of Kentucky, 1987). Curtis Seltzer, *Fire in the Hole: Miners and Managers in the American Coal Industry* (Lexington: University Press of Kentucky, 1985), ranges over politics, industry, and work.

British coal-mining practices and safety are discussed in B. R. Mitchell, *Economic Development of the British Coal Industry, 1800–1914* (New York: Cambridge Univ. Press, 1984), and Roy Church, *Victorian Pre-eminence: 1830–1913*, vol. 3 of *The History of the British Coal Industry* (Oxford: Clarendon Press, 1986). For a survey of British mine safety legislation, see Andrew Bryan, *The Evolution of Health and Safety in Mines* (London: Ashire Publishers, 1975). On early British practice, see *Historical Review of Coal Mining* (London, 1942). Harrison Bulman, *The Working of Coal and Other Stratified Minerals* (New York: John Wiley, 1927), provides insight into British mining methods.

The beginnings of American coal mine safety regulation are told by Alexander Trachenberg, *The History of Legislation for the Protection of Coal Miners in Pennsylvania, 1824–1915* (New York: International Publishers, 1942); Earl Beckner, *A History of Labor Legislation in Illinois* (Chicago: Univ. of Chicago Press, 1929); and Glenn Massay, "Legislators, Lobbyists, and Loop-holes: Coal Mining Legislation in West Virginia, 1875-1901," *West Virginia History* 32 (Apr. 1971): 135-70. For western developments, see Brian Whiteside, *Regulating Danger: The Struggle for Mine Safety in the Rocky Mountain Coal Industry* (Lincoln: Univ. of Nebraska Press, 1990). The best study of the origins and early work of the U.S. Bureau of Mines is still William Graebner, *Coal-Mining Safety in the Progressive Period* (Lexington: University Press of Kentucky, 1976). More recent but less persuasive is David Curran, *Dead Laws for Dead Men* (Pittsburgh: Univ. of Pittsburgh Press, 1993).

There are a number of good discussions of the methods and dangers of hard-rock mining. Charles Mitke, *Mining Methods* (New York: McGraw-Hill, 1930), provides an introduction to metal-mining techniques. For broader and more modern discussions, see Larry Lankton, *Cradle to Grave: Life, Work, and Death* in *Michigan Copper Mines* (New York: Oxford Univ. Press, 1991); Mark Wyman, *Hard Rock Epic: Western Miners and the Industrial Revolution, 1860–1910* (Berkeley: Univ. of California Press, 1979); and Ronald Brown, *Hard Rock Miners: The Intermountain West, 1860–1920* (College Station: Texas A&M Press, 1979). Alan Derickson, *Workers' Health, Workers' Democracy* (Ithaca, N.Y.: Cornell Univ. Press, 1988), contains an excellent discussion of safety work in the metal mines. Also insightful is Lilian Tretton, "Traprock Workers: The Culture of Work and Risk at an Underground Copper Mine" (Ph.D. diss., Univ. of Michigan, 1987).

There are many studies that discuss modern mine safety. They are useful in educating one on current issues and for grasping the links between past and present. John Braithwaite, *To Punish or Persuade* (Albany: SUNY Press, 1985), is a perceptive comparative assessment that confirms the dominant role of mine management in safety, as does National Academy of Sciences, *Towards Safer Underground Coal Mines* (Washington, D.C.: NAS, 1982). A useful overview that discusses the impact of modern safety regulations is General Accounting Office, *Low Productivity in American Coal Mining: Causes and Cures* (Washington, D.C., 1981).

There is also a considerable econometric literature, most of which focuses on regulation. For a sampling, see W. H. Andrews and C. L. Christenson, "Some Economic Factors Affecting Safety in Underground Bituminous Coal Mines," *Southern Economic Journal* 40 (Jan. 1974): 364-76; Michael Lewis-Beck and John Alford, "Can Government Regulate Safety? The Coal Mine Example," *American Political Science Review* 74 (Sept. 1980): 745-56; Hal Sider, "Safety and Productivity in Underground Coal Mining," *Review of Economics and Statistics* 65 (May 1983): 225-33; and Scott Feuss and Mari Loewenstein, "Further Analysis of the Theory of Economic Regulation: The Case of the 1969 Coal Mine Health and Safety Act," *Economic Inquiry* 28 (Apr. 1990): 354-83.

INDEX

interstate shifts and, 55–56, 75, 240; mine characteristics and, 50–51, 55, 59–60, 233–34, 236–37, 241, 334n; new immigrants and, 56–57, 75, 334n; operator incentives, 48–51, 62, 74–75, 212–15, 279–80; operator safety work, 69, 217, 221–24, 226, 229–31, 233–39, 241–44, 250–51, 253, 256–58, 384n; popular concern, 41, 67, 212–13, 231–32; roof falls, 42, 50–53, 55–61, 64–66, 71, 223, 234, 239–41, 255–56; rules and discipline, 47–48, 52, 62, 64, 234–39, 255; shooting off the solid, 60–62; statistics and statistical analysis, 3, 55–56, 65–66, 210, 216, 233, 236–37, 240–41, 251, 256–57, 272, 298–305, 378n, 390n; surveys, 222–23, 232, 251; ventilation and gas, 41, 47–55, 60, 64, 66–69, 71–73, 90, 215–19, 225, 228–29, 231, 235, 255–57, 335n
Coal mining methods: British and American, 42–44, 63–66, 75, 217–18; longwall, 43–44, 63–65, 273; room-and-pillar, 44–46, 234, 241, 255, 273
Coffin, Lorenzo, 33–36
Colburn, Zerah, 17–20
Colliery Engineer, 57, 63, 69, 74
Colliery Guardian, 63, 74–75
Collisions, railroad, 11, 13–14, 21, 25, 38, 168–69, 171, 174, 176–79, 202–8, 285
Colorado Fuel and Iron, 69
Colvin, Fred, 81, 134, 142
Commonwealth Steel Company, 125, 129
Competition. *See* Market structure
Consolidation Coal Company, 233, 238, 250
Construction risks, 83–84
Copper mining. *See* Metal mine safety
Courrieres, France, mine explosion, 216

Darr, Pennsylvania, mine explosion, 73–74, 257
Dead work, 43–45
DeBlois, Louis, 102, 109, 111, 114, 118, 147–50, 154, 157–58; management responsibility and, 145–46
Delagua, Colorado, mine explosion, 230
Delaware and Hudson Coal Company, 221, 241–42
Depression, the, and safety work, 209; in manufacturing, 156–57; in mining, 242, 250
Derailments, 11, 21, 178–84, 192, 285
Dorsey, Edward Bates, 18, 25
DuPont, Irénée, 146–49
DuPont, Lammot, 146–48

DuPont Company, 102, 109, 115, 119, 122, 129, 137, 139–40, 142–43, 152, 154, 158–60, 197, 250, 275, 282; early interest in safety, 91; injuries and fatalities at, 77, 309; management responsibility, 143–48
Dynamite, 61, 219, 245

Eastern Railroad, 25–26, 30
Eastman, Crystal, 76–77, 79, 86, 90–91, 93, 95–96, 115
Eastman, Joseph, 207–8
Eavenson, Howard, 211, 236
Economic development, 3–4, 77, 259–60, 271, 280
Economic structure. *See* Labor force composition
Education and training. *See safety work under specific industries*
Efficiency: movement, 4, 86; safety and, 38, 117–18, 124, 126, 140, 148–52
Electrical Worker, 84
Electrical workers, risks of, 84, 86
Electric cap lamps. *See* Personal protective equipment: in mining
Electricity, and job risk: in manufacturing, 162–63, 166; in mining, 55, 57–59, 71–72, 233, 235–37, 240–41, 255, 257
Employers' liability, 5–6, 76, 214, 233; business and, 94–97; compensation under, 49, 93–94, 259, 273; in mining, 49, 233–34, 247–48; on railroads, 29–30, 39, 96, 168, 189–92, 194, 371n; state commissions on, 84, 93–94, 99–101; technological change and, 78–79, 273–74
Engel's law, 262–63
Engineering News, 18, 20, 25, 30, 34–38; on accident investigation, 170; on safety appliances, 9, 34–38
Engineering revision, 3, 115–20, 123, 126, 127–32, 145, 152, 160–61, 277; evolution of, 157–59
Engineers: 103, 108–11, 112–13, 124, 126, 132, 144, 148–50, 152, 157–163, 166; safety, as professional responsibility, 109, 117–20; safety education, 120
Erie Railroad, 11, 15, 25, 174
Esch, John J., 169, 171–72, 179, 206–7
Evans, Cadwallader, 241–42
Experience, firm-specific, 86; in mining, 52, 54–55; on railroads, 13–15, 30
Experience rating (*see also* Workmen's compensation), 99–100, 153, 214–15, 241–42, 281

LIBRARY OF CONGRESS CATALOGING-IN-PUBLICATION DATA
Aldrich, Mark.
    Safety first : technology, labor, and business in the building of
American work safety, 1870-1939 / Mark Aldrich.
        p.   cm. — (Studies in industry and society ; 13)
    Includes bibliographical references and index.
    ISBN 0-8018-5405-9 (alk. paper)
    1. Industrial safety—United States—History—19th century.
2. Industrial safety—United States—History—20th century.
I. Title.   II. Series.
T55.A38   1997
363.11'5'097309041—dc20   96-28998